WOOD

MATERIALS · TECHNOLOGY

MICHAEL CROSS

Edco

CONTENTS

GETTING STARTED

1 Introduction 1
2 Health and safety 3

MATERIALS WOOD

3 Wood; what is it? 8
4 Types of tree 13
5 Hardwoods and softwoods 26
6 Timber and the environment 32
7 Conversion of timber 36
8 Timber seasoning 40
9 Diseases and defects 46
10 Preserving timber 53
11 Manufactured boards 58

OTHER MATERIALS

12 Properties of materials 64
13 Metals 67
14 Plastics 77
15 Other materials 87

TOOLS AND MACHINES

16 Hand tools 91
17 Sharpening tools 115
18 Power tools 119
19 Machines 129

PROJECTS 136

COMMUNICATION AND DESIGN

20 Design 152
21 Report writing and presentation 162
22 Computer aided design (CAD) 179

WORKING WITH WOOD

23 Joining methods 187
24 Shaping and carving 202
25 Veneering, inlay and marquetry 213
26 Woodturning 224
27 Bending and laminating wood 237

ASSEMBLY AND FINISH

28 Adhesives 242
29 Finishes 250
30 Fastenings and Fixtures 264

MECHANISMS

31 Structures, forces and mechanisms 278

ELECTRONICS

Simple electronic circuits 287

Foreword

This newly revised book fully covers the Junior Certificate course in Materials Technology Wood and will appeal to students and teachers of the subject. As a further aid to understanding, clear and detailed diagrams support text explanations. The book generously addresses the requirements of the exam in both the project and written papers.

Students are guided through the design process with clear and simple project examples [suited to both Higher and Ordinary Levels]. The projects will assist the student in understanding the stages of the design process, and the area of report writing and folio presentation.

Health and safety while using tools, power tools and machines is highlighted throughout the book. New technology areas are also explored: CAD, structures, forces and mechanisms.

Finally, thanks are due to Denis O'Connor for his advice and assistance; Roger Geagan for manuscript proofing; Anthony Murray, Senior Editor at EdCo and Aengus Carroll who edited the book. Thanks also to my wife and family for their help and patience throughout.

Michael Cross

CHAPTER ONE

GETTING STARTED

INTRODUCTION

The study of Materials Technology (wood) is about solving problems, mostly design problems. You will discover a great deal about many materials, particularly wood, how they are formed and how best to work these materials into various items. You will learn by doing and by actually making useful projects.

You will develop different skills while making projects and you will learn how to develop an idea using the design process; from plan through to a completed piece of work. You will also be able to bring the results home.

At all times you must be conscious of your own safety and that of others. Throughout this book safety will be highlighted.

The Materials Technology Room

As you have probably seen by now, the Materials Technology Room is different from other classrooms. It is specially equipped with the tools and machines which you use while doing your projectwork. This equipment is exactly the same as that used by craftspeople in industry – so safety should always be put first.

The layout of the Materials Technology Room varies in different schools, but the work that you will do in it will be like that done by students all over the country: designing and making projects from a variety of different materials.

The Materials Technology Room

Tools are usually kept in lockers or cupboards, with machines and other equipment in different positions around the room. It is important that you treat the equipment that you use with care and replace tools neatly in their correct locker positions after use. This will help to keep your work area both neat and safe.

Remember the rule:- **a place for everything and everything in its place.**

There are also storerooms available for the storage of materials and projectwork. These areas should also be kept neat and tidy.

You will work at a bench which is not like a normal desk, it is heavier and has equipment attached to it to aid you in your work. The bench is well made and has to be sturdy to provide the craftsperson with a stable platform to work at. It is usually made from pine. It has a vice and a bench-stop on each side and often there is a shallow central portion called a well on the top of the bench.

The vice is made from metal and usually has cheeks made from a hardwood, such as oak. The cheeks, or sides of the vice, protect the material while it is being gripped tightly in the vice. The vice holds the material allowing you to use both hands for processing. The bench-stop prevents timber slipping along the bench when it is being planed or sanded, and is usually made from beech or another hardwood.

There may be other work areas in the room such as sanding tables, pillar drills, etc. These are designed for specific tasks.

You must take care of your bench as it can be damaged. Damaged surfaces may affect the quality of your own work. Keep the bench clean and protect it from scratches while sawing or from damage from hammers, nails, etc. The surface can be protected by using a waste piece of wood under the work-piece, particularly when applying adhesives and finishes. The vice too should be maintained properly, with the cheeks kept free and clear of anything which might cause damage to work being held in the vice.

At the end of class put away all of the equipment, sweep off your bench and the equipment that you have used. Leave the room as you would like to find it – clean and tidy.

Exercises

1. Draw a simple plan of your Materials Technology Room and identify on the plan the important items of equipment. Show also the escape route from the room, in the event of a fire.
2. Make a list of the tools in your locker.
3. List the items of machinery in the room.
4. Draw a diagram of a Materials Technology bench and name the parts.
5. Why is it important to keep your bench and the room tidy?
6. Design a poster which shows the result of an untidy Materials Technology Room and carries the message that it is important to keep the room tidy.

CHAPTER TWO

HEALTH AND SAFETY

Safety is of primary importance in the Materials Technology Room, particularly in view of the type of work you will do here. Keep your own safety and the safety of others in mind at all times. Accidents can be avoided so – **think safety and stay healthy**.

Potentially, there are many things which can be hazardous in the Materials Technology Room:

- equipment
- processes
- materials
- adhesives
- finishes.

The risks or danger may be to your health or to the wider environment.

Safety

If your tools and equipment are damaged, or used incorrectly, they can be dangerous. Your teacher will show you the correct and safest way to use the tools. Keep equipment tidily in your work area, as a tidy working environment is a safe one. Report all damaged equipment immediately. It is important when you are using any cutting tool that you keep your hands and fingers **behind** or **away from** the tool's cutting edge. When carrying tools always hold the tool by your side, pointing it to the floor.

Some jobs are more hazardous than others and may require the use of special safety clothing and equipment. Follow your teacher's instructions in relation to safety equipment carefully; for example, always wear full face protection when using equipment like the woodworking lathe. Safety equipment is there for your protection – **wear it**.

Some materials, such as fine wood dust or hot metal and plastic, can be dangerous, so it is important to be aware of the dangers associated with various materials and be sure to take appropriate precautions. When using adhesives and finishes which are solvent-based, it is important to take care to follow all the manufacturer's instructions and be guided by their warnings.

Note:
Always read and follow all instructions given by manufacturers on products and equipment.

Tidiness

Tidiness is important in the work-shop. Your hands should be clean, so as not to dirty the material you are working with. You should dress to avoid accidents. As well as the necessary safety equipment, keep loose clothing (ties, ribbons, etc.) tidy, as they can get caught in machinery. Long hair also needs to be tied up as it might get caught, resulting in serious injury.

Work in a tidy manner, keeping your bench and work areas clean and free from debris and unnecessary tools. This will avoid work being damaged and tools from falling off a crowded bench onto someone's foot. If something does fall on the floor pick it up and store it properly, as someone might easily trip on it. Tools and work pieces which are not in use should be stored away in their appropriate place.

Spillages of adhesive, oil, varnish or other liquids should be immediately reported and cleaned up.

Untidy bench

Tidy bench

Safety Rules

- Always follow the teacher's instructions
- Do not move around the room without good reason and **never run** in the room
- Safety equipment should be worn appropriately but particularly when using any machines or as instructed by your teacher
- Always read and follow the manufacturer's instructions and warnings carefully
- Never interfere with others when they are working, especially when they are using power tools or machines
- Report all damaged equipment immediately. Do not try to fix it yourself, and do not use it until it has been repaired

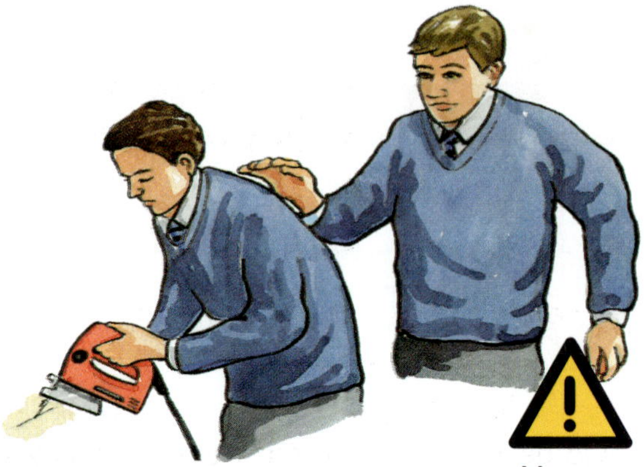

Never

- Always turn power tools off and disconnect them from the mains when they are not in use
- Report all accidents, no matter how small, to your teacher

- Always keep your hands and fingers **behind** the cutting edge of tools
- Electricity is dangerous – do not tamper with electrical fittings and use electrical equipment only as instructed.

Never

BEWARE! **Remember: accidents don't just happen – they are caused.**

Safety equipment

Safety equipment should be provided for your use. The first aid kit is a most essential part of the Materials Technology Room's safety equipment and should be kept well stocked. There are many types of safety equipment which can be placed into a number of categories:

- Eye protection
- Ear protection
- Respiratory (breathing) protection
- Hand protection.

Face visor provides full face protection

Protecting your face and eyes is important, especially while operating power tools and machinery, as eyes can be easily damaged even by very small particles. Safety glasses and goggles can and should be worn to prevent this. When operating the lathe a full face visor should be worn.

Even when not working with machines you could damage your eyes by blowing dust off a work surface. Use a brush to do this; there should be one at every bench.

Protecting your hearing is extremely important. The human ear is very sensitive and can be damaged gradually by loud noises such as music, machinery, and other loud environmental noise, eventually leading to hearing damage or loss, which often cannot be reversed. Much can be done to protect yourself like the ear protection shown below. These should be worn if you are exposed to loud noise, or noise for long periods of time.

Ear plugs & ear muffs

Use dust masks or respirators when doing any work which generates a lot of dust, such as sanding, particularly with some hardwoods whose dust can be injurious to your health. They prevent dust being breathed into your lungs. Respirators give added protection against dust and gas vapours. They are fitted with disposable filters or cartridges. These differ depending on the type and level of protection you require.

Dust masks & respirators

Gloves or hand protection should be worn when handling sharp or hot items or for protection against some chemicals, such as white spirit, wood preservatives, paint or varnish stripper.

Fire safety

In the event of a fire in the room you should know the fire drill and where the exit is.
There should be a fire extinguisher in every room, find it and read the instructions on it. Never tamper with fire safety equipment.

Safety with power tools and machines

Because they are powered and move faster than hand tools, these tools pose more of a risk and, therefore, you have to be more careful using them. There are two types of tool powered usually by electricity:

- Machines – morticers, circular saw, planer, sanders, etc. These are usually fixed in position
- Hand-power tools – drills, saws, planes, router, etc. These are usually portable.

The electricity that powers these tools is dangerous. There should be circuit breakers and cut-off buttons around the room and on all machines for safety. These can cut power off when necessary. Transformers can also be used to reduce the power of electric tools and improve safety. It is important to note that powered tools remain in motion for a short time even when the power supply has been cut off.

Tools should be properly wired and should include an earth wire which directs current away from the user in the event of an electrical accident. They should have no faulty parts or wiring before you should use them. Tell your teacher of any faulty equipment immediately.

Hand power tools

Only use power tools as shown by your teacher and after being instructed on their safe use.
Follow these guidelines for your added safety;

- Always use the tools as instructed
- Before changing bits, belts or glasspaper for sanders, or making other adjustments to any tool, switch off the tool and disconnect it from the socket
- Always keep the cutter or moving parts of the tool pointing **away** from yourself and others
- Ensure that the electric flex of the tool does not come into contact with the moving parts of the power tool
- Do not let others interfere with you while you are working, and do not disturb others while they are operating equipment
- Always ensure that you are wearing the appropriate protective safety equipment for the job
- If in doubt seek, the assistance of your teacher
- Never leave a power tool running unattended
- Always wait for the power tool to come to a complete stop before walking away from it
- Guards are there for your safety; do not tamper with or tie them back, and if they are damaged report it immediately.

Woodworking machinery

Most of the machinery in the room is for the use of the teacher only, however, the morticer, the woodturning lathe, pillar drills and some sanders are used by students. Most of the guidelines above apply to machinery also.

Before using any machine:

- Ensure that the machine is in good working order
- Before making adjustments turn off the power to the machine and let it stop fully
- Machinery should only be used as instructed and only under teacher supervision
- Always wear the correct protection, glasses, goggles, dust masks are essential
- Keep your hands away from the cutters or moving parts of machinery
- When you have finished using the machine, switch it off and let it come to a full stop before leaving it
- Never leave a machine running unattended
- Always leave machinery clean and in good working order.

Design

Safety can and should be accounted for in your project design. It is important that items are designed and made in a way that is safe. It is also important that when you are designing items you are mindful of how they are to be used; for example, when designing items for young children you should ensure that they have no sharp corners and that any finish which you might apply would be non-toxic, as young children tend to put things into their mouths. Similarly, if you were asked to design a foot stool for a living room you should assume that the stool is going to be used for standing on occasionally, and make sure that it has adequate strength.

Exercises

1. List two safety rules that apply when using the electric drill.
2. List three safety rules to be observed when working on the lathe.
3. List three safety rules that should be followed when using power tools.
4. Why is a transformer used when using hand powered electric tools that are connected to the mains?
5. Give two advantages and two disadvantages of using a rechargeable electric drill.
6. Give two safety precautions to be taken when using adhesives.
7. Why should you never run in the MT Room?
8. Why should you never touch the edge of a chisel with your finger?
9. Why should you always use a brush to sweep sawdust off a bench?
10. Explain the meaning of these safety signs:

11. Find and sketch some other safety symbols.
12. What safety considerations would you need to observe when designing a child's toy?

CHAPTER THREE

WOOD; WHAT IS IT?

Trees and wood have fulfilled many different roles for mankind down through the centuries. Trees, and the products derived from trees, will continue to be an essential and renewable resource for all of us to use and enjoy.

Trees

- Give us woodland and forestry for leisure activities
- Give us a renewable source of fuel energy
- Sustain the balance of the earth's oxygen and carbon-dioxide levels
- Provide habitats for vast numbers of species of animal and plant life
- Enhance the beauty of our environment
- Provide fruit and many other products
- Provide the material for man-made woods and paper.

Wood is

- Used for many household items and utensils
- Used extensively in the construction industry
- Used in furniture-making
- Used in boat building.

Trees are the largest plants on the planet and some have been living for 5000 years, such as the Bristlecone pine of California. We depend on trees and the things they provide us with for our daily life. Put simply, life without trees and wood would be inconceivable.

Some of the many uses of trees and timber

Historically wood was a primary manufacturing material. It has been used in furniture for centuries and this is still one of its main uses.

Famous designers of furniture who lived and worked during what is known as the *golden age of furniture making* (1770-1800) were Thomas

Chippendale, Robert Adam, George Hepplewhite and Thomas Sheraton. These designers developed the skill and art of working with wood to an outstanding degree, and their furniture and designs are highly valued and emulated to this very day.

A chair from the 1780s

Trees

Trees are plants which can (and are being) grown as a crop rather like wheat. An industry has developed around the planting, managing, harvesting and processing this crop from seed to finished product. This industry employs a large number of people in its various sectors all around the world.

There are two types of forest; natural forest which has evolved over many centuries and planted forestry which is just like a crop. Ireland has few natural forests left despite being largely covered in forest some centuries ago. The largest areas of natural forest are located in Co. Wicklow and Co. Kerry.

However, most of our natural oak forests were felled, exported and used in construction, making wine barrels and for boat building long ago, and as a result they are very depleted today.

Natural forests

Planted forests

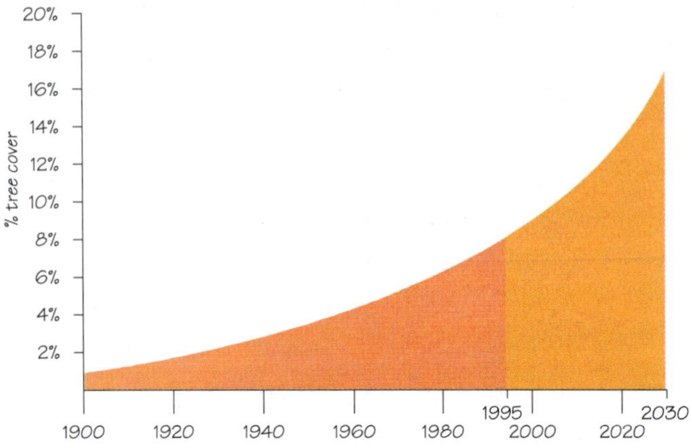

The development of Irish forest cover

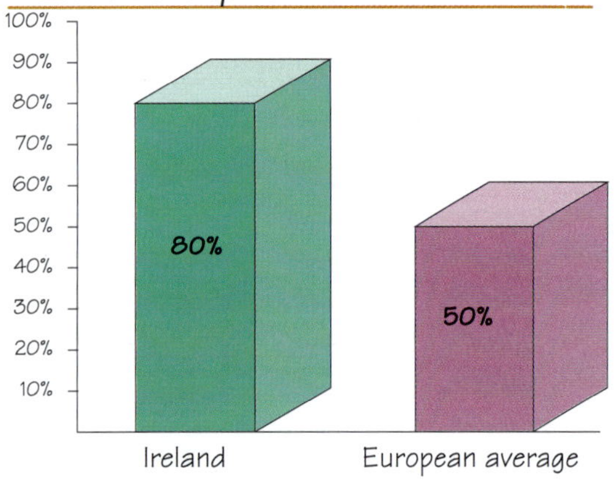

Timber requirements imported

Forestry in Ireland

Over the centuries the natural forests in Ireland have been felled almost completely.

Half of Ireland's forests are under 25 years old. **Ireland has fewer trees than any other country in Europe**. Only 8 per cent of the country is forested compared with 24 per cent in most European countries.

Because of the global demand for wood and wood products, research is constantly being done to develop varieties of tree that will be of a high quality and grow quickly in many climatic conditions. The species which are planted in greatest numbers are **Sitka Spruce** and **Lodgepole Pine**. These conifers grow quickly and to a high quality in Irish conditions, which are commonly in poor and wet bog lands in the more remote areas of the country.

Young trees are planted and grown in nurseries before being transplanted by foresters into the forest plantations. There they will be tended to by foresters until maturity. The trees are thinned at intervals as the trees grow larger, and are eventually felled after 30–50 years.

Ireland is one of the least forested countries in Europe, but that is quickly changing, due to the incentives available for farmers and other individuals to plant and grow trees. The grant

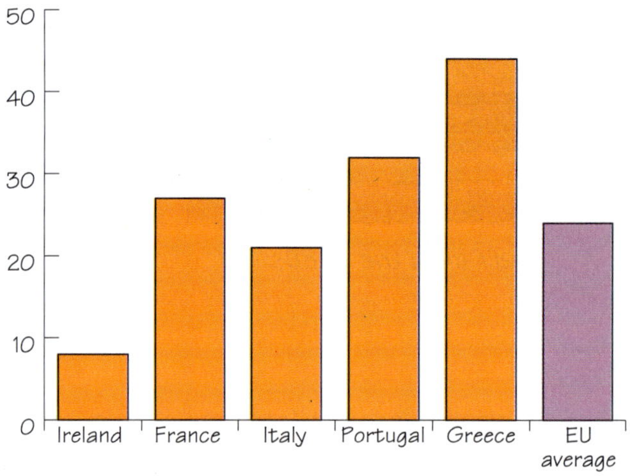

Forest cover in Ireland compared with other EU countries and the European average

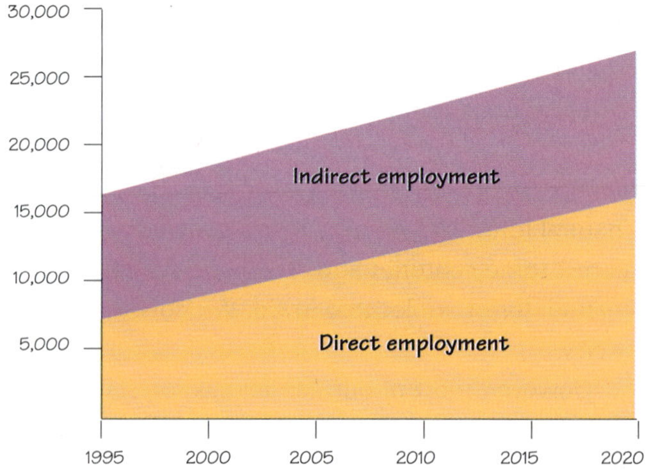

Economic impact of forestry. Employment in forestry

schemes encourage the planting of smaller farm areas which give an added income to farmers, who use land which otherwise might lie dormant. This helps to keep people living in rural areas. These smaller plantations are less damaging to the environment compared to the problems associated with large areas of coniferous forest.

Coillte is the company which is charged with the development of Irish forests. The Department of Agriculture, Food and Forestry is the government agency responsible for the control and regulation of forestry in Ireland. Coillte, in conjunction with this department, has invested considerable sums of money in the research and development of forestry. It has nurseries where young trees are grown, forest sites, twelve forest parks, sawmills, and has interests in some of the plants making manufactured boards. All of these employ a large number of people.

Tree nursery (Coillte)

Trees are planted in managed forests after the soil has been drained and areas fenced. After a number of years, depending on the species, the trees are then thinned and are thinned at regular intervals thereafter. These thinnings can be used in the making of chipboard and fibreboards or for use as Christmas trees. (There are special plantations of Christmas trees in Wicklow, Roscommon and Tipperary, which even export Christmas trees to Europe.) When mature, the trees are felled, their branches are stripped and they are transported to sawmills and factories to be processed into timber or boards or other timber products.

Timber and employment

The timber industry, in all its forms, provides employment for thousands of people. Coillte employs 1900 permanent staff. Transportation, sawmilling, board production and furniture manufacture also employ large numbers of people, as does the manufacture of doors, windows and other wooden items used in the construction industry.

Joinery workshop

Imported timber

Ireland currently imports much of its timber from Scandinavia, North America and countries in the tropics such as Brazil, Argentina, Indonesia and Burma. As timber is depleted from the tropical sources it will become very expensive and we will have to rely more and more on our own resources for our timber needs. It is important that we plan for this eventuality and plant trees, especially hardwood species, which will fulfil this demand in the future.

Timber by-products

Trees provide many things other than wood and man-made boards. They provide fruit, rubber, drugs, cellulose for plastic manufacture and a wide range (

Exercises

1. How do natural and planted forests differ?
2. List four of the organisations which are associated with the forestry and wood-related industries.
3. What are the principle types of wood that are grown in Ireland and where are these woods used?
4. List as many items in your home that you can, which are made from wood and which you depend on daily?
5 Wood is back in fashion. Discuss.
6 Make a poster or collage which shows the present day uses of wood?

Timber by-products

CHAPTER FOUR

TYPES OF TREE

There are two main categories of trees: broad-leaved trees (usually hardwoods) and conifers (usually softwoods). You will use both hardwood and softwood timbers in your project work. Hardwoods and softwoods grow in Ireland - many are native here, but some were introduced from other areas of the world. In past centuries wealthy landowners with large estates imported various species into this country.

Hardwood timbers like iroko, mahogany, sapele, purpleheart and rosewood are native to tropical climates. These woods are used in furniture, veneering, woodturning and marquetry (making pictures from veneers). These timbers, however, are rare, and therefore expensive, and by using them we participate in the destruction of important tropical rainforests (we will learn more of this later).

Most of the wood you will work with will be hardwood or softwood timber which grow in Ireland. These are listed below.

Location of forested areas in Ireland

Hardwoods

Oak

The oak is native to Ireland and grows very slowly. At one time oak was the principal tree in Irish forests, and was found in abundance over most of the country. There are still forests of oak growing in Abbeyleix, Glengarriff, Killarney and Coolattin, Co. Wicklow. Oaks can live for 600 to 800 years. In open areas they develop a large trunk and a broad crown. They can grow to a height of 40 metres. There are many members of the oak family, including the common oak, sessile oak, durmast oak, red oak and holm oak (evergreen).

'Great oaks from little acorns grow'

Most of the oak from trees in Irish forests was used in buildings and ships in Ireland and Britain and exported for use in making wine barrels. The great demand for oak and the clearance of forests for agricultural land, depleted most of the great oak forests. These forests were not replanted and the Irish landscape eventually became one of the least forested in Europe.

The seeds of the oak are called acorns and are held in sockets called lobes

The wood

Oak is very durable, tough and relatively easy to work. It is light in colour and has an attractive grain pattern. The grain is coarse and open. When the oak is cut radially, the ray cells show up in an attractive pattern known as **silver grain**. Most of the oak used in Ireland is imported from North America. You should note that **tannin** in the wood is corrosive to steel, so use brass screws and fittings when using oak.

Uses

Oak is perhaps the most important and widely used hardwood in Europe and North America. The wood lasts for many hundreds of years if it is treated properly. Much of the oak wood in Henry VIII's ship, the Mary Rose, was almost perfectly preserved after it had been under water for a few hundred years. It has been used in construction in the form of large oak beams, and in churches for roofs and doors for centuries. It is used in boatbuilding and outdoor woodwork as well as furniture making.

Elm

The elm

The Wych elm is a native Irish tree. The elm tree usually grows to a height of 40 metres. The trunk is long and straight and has a rounded crown. It grows in highland and lowland areas. It is the tallest of our native trees.

Most of the elm trees in Ireland, and indeed Europe, have been killed in the last thirty years by Dutch elm disease. This fungal disease is carried from tree to tree by a beetle cutting off the food supply under the bark of the tree. In recent years a cross-bred elm tree, which is disease-resistant, has been developed.

Leaves & buds of the elm tree

Birch tree – note the white bark

The wood

Elm is a very beautiful timber. It is a coarse-grained wood with a reddish-brown colour and attractive grain. The grain can be irregular. The heartwood is as durable as the sapwood. Elm is a very strong timber.

Uses

The wood is resistant to moisture and in some countries, has been used in piles for foundations (Venice is built on elm piles). It is also used in the production of coffins, weather boards and garden furniture. It is a popular wood for turning because of its irregular grain. It has elastic properties and does not split easily. Unfortunately, however, elm does tend to warp.

Birch

Birch is another native hardwood which was plentiful in Ireland in the past. It still grows wild in all parts of the country, gardens and public places. The tree is very beautiful and is much sought after for its speed of growth and beauty. The birch tree is plentiful in Russia and is the only tree that grows in Greenland. The tree can often be recognised because it branches cluster very closely together, looking like a bird's nest. This cluster is the result of a parasitic disease in the tree.

Birch leaves & seed

The wood

Birch wood is dense and tough. The straight grain makes it suitable for use as **plywood**. The wood is light in colour with very little grain pattern. It has a tendency to warp.

Uses

Used in plywood manufacture and turning. As the birch tree, when fully grown, has quite a small diameter, boards of usable sizes are unavailable.

Ash

The ash tree was associated closely with the oak in the forests of ancient Ireland and has always been held in great regard. The ash grows in most soils, but prefers fertile soils. The tree grows quickly, often to a height of 30 metres. The black buds make the tree easily identifiable in winter. Ash trees are being planted as forestry as they reach maturity in 50–60 years.

Ash tree

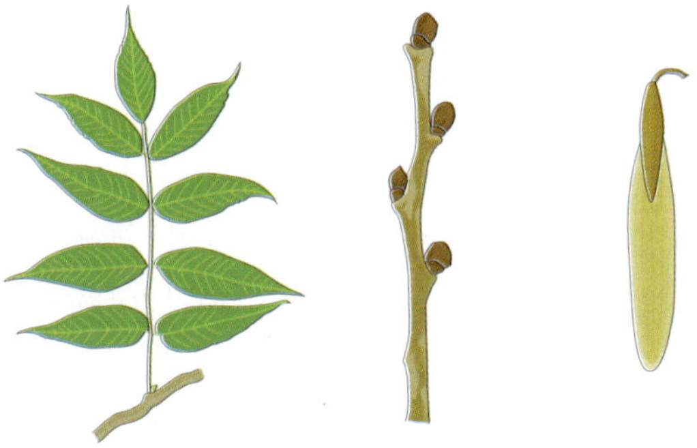

Leaves & buds of the ash tree

The wood

The wood is light yellow in colour. It is very hard and durable with good elastic properties. The grain is very distinct and attractive. The annual rings can be seen clearly. Its density and hardness can make it difficult to work but it finishes well.

Uses

Ash is used in furniture, veneers and in the manufacture of hurleys (20,000 ash trees are used each year to make hurleys). It is used also in the handles of tools because of its toughness and elasticity. It can be easily bent into different shapes.

Bent ash laminates supports this model plane

Beech

The beech tree was introduced from England in the 17th century and is now very common all over Ireland. It grows best in limestone soils. The tree is easily identified by its smooth grey bark. The trees do not bear seeds until they are at least 40 years old. The seed is contained in a triangular shell called **mast**. The leaves are broad, and in autumn they turn a lovely golden bronze. The leaves remain on the tree for most of the winter. It is a slow growing tree. Beech is planted as a hedge. Copper beech is a decorative variety of beech grown in parks and gardens.

Beech tree

Leaves & masts

The wood

The wood is reddish-yellow or light brown. Its grain is very close which makes the timber very durable. The close grain can easily be recognised as beech. A special fleck grain can also be seen in the wood but it is not as attractive as oak because the ray cells are much smaller. It is an easily obtainable, strong wood which finishes well. Acids in the beech timber react with all metals.

Uses

Beech is used in furniture making, tools (mallets, planes, bench hooks and gauges) and floors (wood blocks). It is widely used in scandinavian countries. It is used for steam bending. Many kitchen and household items are made from beech.

Horse chestnut

The horse chestnut was introduced into Ireland from western Asia and south eastern Europe. It thrives best on moist rich soil. The tree has very distinct leaves which grow in groups. They are known as **digitate** – this means that they resemble spread out fingers. The seeds (conkers) are contained in a spine-protected nut. The crown of the tree is tall and wide. Horse chestnut trees are easily grown from seed. The tree is very beautiful when in flower and is often grown in parks.

Horse chestnut

Horse chestnut leaf, buds and seed

The wood

The wood is light and not very durable. It is of little value, but is sometimes used as wood pulp and in packing cases.

Lime

Limes are planted in large parks and estates and also along roadsides. The tree is planted in cities as it absorbs harmful city air pollution. The tree is fast growing and reaches a height of 30 metres. The flowers are yellowish-white and have an attractive fragrance. The leaves are easily recognised because they are heart-shaped.

Lime tree

Lime leaf and seed

The wood

The wood is not very hard, even though it comes from a broad-leafed tree. It is a pale light colour with distinct annual rings. It is not a very decorative wood, but it is quite durable. The wood is cheap and easy to work, but it is prone to shrinkage during seasoning and swells when it soaks up moisture in damp conditions.

Lime is used in musical instruments, for carving and for making pencils.

Cherry

This tree is planted in parks and gardens all over the country. It has a beautiful wood, with orange to brown colour and distinctive grain pattern. The wood finishes very well.

The wood is used in high quality furniture, veneers and for panelling.

Cherry tree

Sycamore

A tree widely seen around the country. It has distinctive leaves and winged seeds. It grows quickly with a deep root system. The wood is light in colour with an attractive grain pattern. It is a durable and hard wood. Its uses include turning, carving, kitchen utensils, furniture, violin-making and veneers.

Sycamore trees

Sycamore leaves & seeds

Softwoods

Scots pine (Northern pine/Scots fir)

This tree is widespread throughout Europe from Greece to the Polar regions. In the open landscape it is a very beautiful tree. The Scots pine is unlike other conifers in shape. It stands tall, has few branches which are quite large, and often grows to a height of 40 metres. The crown is perched very high up on the trunk, the bark is a reddish-orange colour, and the needles grow in pairs. It grows in almost any climate and in poorer and drier soils. It is a slow growing tree and therefore, is not planted as forestry nowadays.

Scots pine tree

Pine cone, needles and seed of the Scots pine

The wood

The wood is light cream in colour with distinct red grain lines. The wood is known as **red deal**. It is fairly strong and durable and is relatively inexpensive. The wood is easy to work and finishes well. It also takes preservatives well.

Uses

Red deal is used in the construction industry. It is a popular wood for furniture and for doors of kitchen and bedroom units. The wood darkens with age to a rich golden brown colour. It is the wood mostly used in the Materials Technology Room and your work benches are usually made of red deal. It is also used for telegraph poles.

Douglas fir

This softwood is a native of North America and was introduced to Ireland around 1850. It is sometimes called the Oregon pine or Colombian pine. The tree grows quickly to 50 metres or more. It does not bear cones until it has reached 25 years of age. The tree grows best in deep moist soil with good drainage and shelter as high winds can cause it damage. The Douglas fir is cultivated today in forests around Europe because of its rapid growth rate and the high quality of its wood.

The reddish-brown buds, flattened needles growing out from all around the twig, and the oval-shaped pine cones make it easy to identify.

Douglas fir

Douglas fir cone & needles

The wood

The wood is reddish-brown in colour. The grain and colour is unusual and decorative, and the annual rings are clearly visible. The wood is tough, durable and strong and when properly seasoned, will withstand heavy continuous wear. The Douglas fir is highly resistant to decay and acid attack. The wood is easily worked but it will blunt tools easily.

Uses

Used for high-class joinery and structural work, plywood, for furniture making and veneers. Its straight trunk is used for railway sleepers and telephone poles when properly treated.

Norway spruce (common spruce)

This tree is native to central Europe and grows on high altitudes and mountainous regions. About 4% of Irish forestry is planted with Norway spruce. The crown will reach a height of 40 metres. Like all spruces, the needles are borne on peg-like projections which would give the twig a rough texture if the leaves were to fall off. The root system is shallow, and the tree is prone to being blown down

Norway spruce tree

during storms. It requires fertile soil and moist air, but is resistant to frost.

Norway spruce needles, seed and cone

The wood

The wood, called **white deal**, is flexible and soft. It is light in colour, with a lighter grain pattern than red deal. The knots in red deal are darker than in white deal. The wood is easily worked, although it is not as durable as red deal.

Uses

It is used for Christmas trees, flooring, plywood, internal woodwork and fibreboard manufacture.

Sitka spruce

Sitka spruce

The needles are sharp and blue-green in colour, making the Sitka spruce easily recognisable. The needles are borne on peg-like projections from the twig. Originally the Sitka spruce came from the western coast of America. It is sometimes called the silver spruce because of the colour of its needles. It was introduced to Ireland in 1834. In 1990, 76 per cent of all forestry in Ireland was planted with Sitka spruce. The tree is ideally suited to boggy types of soils and it needs high rainfall. It can grow to a height of 45 metres.

Sitka spruce pine cone and needles

The wood

It is a strong, straight-grained wood and is light in colour.

Uses

The timber is used in the construction industry for joists and other structural timbers, for paper making, floorboards, and for chipboard, fibreboard and hardboard manufacture.

Larch

The Japanese larch is the variety most commonly grown in Ireland. It is the only conifer in the country which loses its leaves in autumn. The pine needles are light green in colour. The tree is tall, growing to a height of 40 metres. It produces seeds early: at the age of fifteen years. The larch is a fast growing, attractive and sun-loving tree. It requires good light and clean air. It is resistant to frost and heat, and has a very strong root system to secure it to the soil.

Larch in summer

Larch needles & cone

The wood

The wood is of a very good quality. The heartwood of which there is a high proportion, is reddish-brown or pink in colour with lighter coloured sapwood. The wood has good elastic properties and high durability. It also resists water well, but does tend to warp.

Uses

Larch is used in boat-building and for light furniture, and wall nameplates. It is also used for timber fence posts.

Lodgepole pine

The lodgepole pine is the second-most planted tree in Irish forestry. A native of the west coast of America, it was introduced here as it grows well on poor, wet soils and in conditions that most other trees will not tolerate. Its trunk can be distorted and long straight lengths are difficult to find. The needles come in pairs and are grouped densely on the branches.

The wood

The dense wood is attractive if the tree is grown in good soils, but the wood suffers if grown on poor soils. It has a rich, reddish-brown appearance with prominent grain. Without care the tree develops many branches and this gives the wood an abundance of knots making it unsuitable for use.

Uses

Can be used for internal woodwork but is more often used in the manufacture of chipboard, hardboard and medium density fibreboard (MDF).

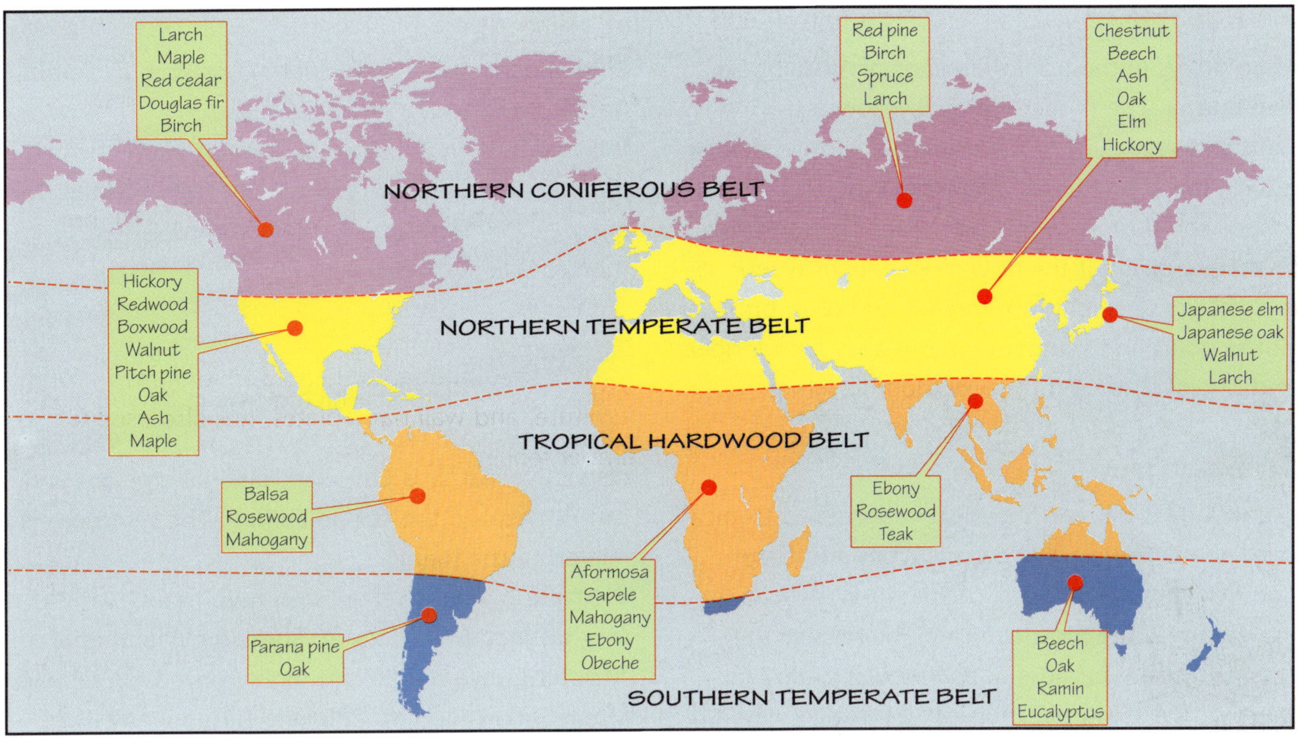

Locations indicating tree belts of the world

Other Important Timbers

There are other timbers which are used by students in projectwork. Most of these trees are imported from tropical rainforests. We should only use timber from the tropics if we are sure that they are grown in sustained forests. The tropical rainforests are being destroyed at an alarming rate and we should do our best to save them. The map above shows the four timber regions of the world – it also shows where different species of tree are commonly found.

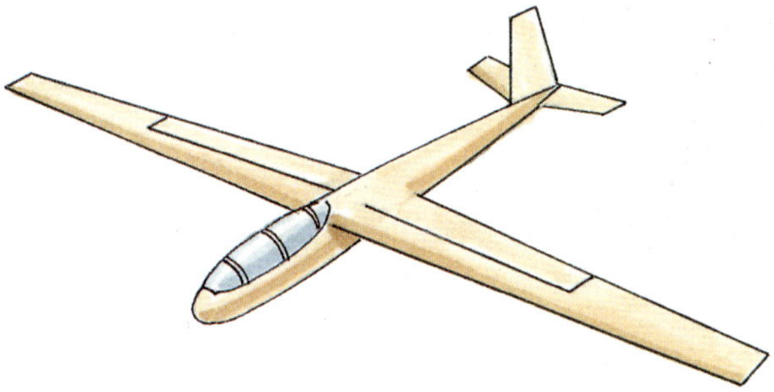

Model aircraft made from balsa

Balsa

This hardwood tree grows in the topical rainforests of South America.
The wood is light cream in colour and is one of the lightest timbers known. It is used in model-making, particularly for light model aircraft like gliders, which must be light to be able to fly.

Ebony

Ebony is grown in the African topical belt and in the tropical rainforests of south-east Asia. It is a dark wood, almost black, very hard and dense, making it extremely heavy. Ebony is rare and very expensive. It is used for exclusive furniture, instrument making, carving and inlaying. Its density and hardness make this a difficult timber to work.

Iroko (teak)

Iroko grows in the tropical regions of Africa, India and Burma. The timber is a dark yellow-brown. It is hard and very durable, particularly against chemical attack; this is due to the presence of oils in the wood. The dust from the cut timber causes people to cough, giving it the nickname 'pepper wood'. It is similar to teak in its appearance and uses, but is not as good. In Ireland it is used mainly for windows and doors, gates and other outdoor furniture.

Mahogany

Mahogany is perhaps the most widely used tropical hardwood. There are two basic types and they come from different parts of the world. African mahogany is the most common, but it is of the poorest quality because of its irregular grain pattern. The grain direction can be in two ways on one surface, making it very difficulty to plane and finish. Mahogany from central America is perhaps the best quality and is known as Cuban or Honduras mahogany. The grain is clear and straight, making it very easy to work.

Honduras mahogany shows a fiddle-backed, speckled, grain pattern. The colour of mahogany varies from light reddish-brown to a deep reddish-brown or chestnut.

Mahogany has been popular with furniture-makers since it was first used in the early 18th century. Nowadays the name mahogany is used for a wide variety of woods of a reddish-brown colour, such as Sepele and Utile, even though they may not be true mahogany. As with every other tropical hardwood, good quality mahogany is becoming more and more scarce due to the destruction of the rainforests.

Mahogany is used for furniture, veneers for manufactured boards, veneering, turning, carving and ship-building. It is durable, resistant to fungal and insect attack, and stable (it does not warp easily).

Rosewood

Rosewood grows in tropical regions such as South America and south-east Asia.

It is dark brown in colour and is very hard and durable. It is used for high quality knife handles, for good quality furniture, veneers and tools (e.g. mortise gauge).

Maple

Maple is a hardwood which grows in Ireland and other temperate regions. The maple has a very distinctive leaf. It is Canada's national emblem and can be seen on the Canadian flag. The sycamore is related to the maple.

Maple is a light yellowish-brown timber with a very distinct grain pattern. Some types of maple (e.g. Bird's-eye maple) are highly prized for veneers. Maple is hard and durable and is frequently used for hardwood flooring. It is also used for turning and furniture, but it is not an easy timber to work with.

Walnut

The walnut is a native of south-eastern Europe, especially Turkey. It grows in Britain and Ireland, but most walnut timber is now imported from North America.

Walnut is a dark brown, almost coffee coloured, wood with black lines of grain. It displays a beautiful grain pattern. It is durable, easily worked and it finishes very well. It is used in high class furniture-making, carving, marquetry and turning.

Boxwood

Boxwood grows in the North American temperate belt and in the southern, warmer parts of Europe. But there is also a British variety. It is a very slow growing tree.

The wood is bright yellow, very hard and heavier than water. The timber is very durable but is expensive. It is used mainly for inlaying, but once was used for chisel handles, rules and in musical instruments.

Hickory

This tree grows in North America. It is a light brown hardwood, durable, and has certain elastic properties which enable it to resist severe shocks. For this reason hickory is used in the manufacture of hammer-handles, tennis rackets and skis.

Yew

Yew tree

The yew tree is a conifer which can be found in many graveyards around this country. It couldn't be planted widely as it is poisonous to livestock if eaten. The tree is slow growing. The wood is unusual as the sapwood is a light creamy–white colour and the heartwood (of which there is a large proportion) is a beautiful orange brown colour with distinctive grain. The wood is hard which makes it seem like a hardwood. It is much sought after for furniture, turning and carving.

Exercises

1. Where does mahogany come from?
2. What are the four regions of tree growth in the world and explain the differences between each?
3. Name two hardwood and two softwood trees which are native to Ireland.
4. Collect the leaves of some trees in your area, sketch the leaves and seeds and identify each tree.
5. Why is iroko a suitable timber for making windows and doors?
6. Suggest suitable woods from which to make the following items, giving reasons for your choice;
   - (a) A yachts mast
   - (b) A salad bowl
   - (c) A turned lamp in hardwood
   - (d) Turned softwood candlesticks
   - (e) A lawn bench
   - (f) A dining chair
   - (g) A hardwood coffee table.
7. Why are hardwoods so popular for making furniture?
8. What woods are most suitable for (a) carving and (b) turning?
9. What types of softwood are grown in Ireland and for what are they mostly used?
10. Describe the Oregon pine and what are its main identifying features?
11. Give another name for the Scots pine.
12. How does the larch differ from other softwood trees?

CHAPTER FIVE

HARDWOODS & SOFTWOODS

Trees can be divided into two main categories: **broad-leaved** *hardwoods*, which lose their leaves in winter (deciduous) and **coniferous** *softwoods*, which are evergreen.

Conifers

- Give us **softwood** timber
- Evergreen (except larch)
- Have straight vertical trunk
- Smaller branches radiate from trunk
- Have needle-like leaves
- Seeds are borne in pine cones
- Symmetrical in shape generally
- Generally grow more quickly than broad-leaved trees
- Wood generally of lesser value than broad-leaved trees
- Wood generally less durable
- Grow well in colder areas and in high altitudes.

Broadleaves (deciduous)

- Give us **hardwood** timber
- Loose their leaves in autumn - deciduous (except holly)
- Trunk divides to develop the large branches
- Branches generally larger and more irregular than conifers
- Leaves are large and broad
- Seeds are borne in ovaries
- Trees usually develop large crowns
- Generally grow more slowly than conifers
- Wood generally more valuable than conifers
- Wood generally more durable.

Conifers

The shape of the tree allows it to bend in strong winds. Because many coniferous trees grow in areas of high snowfall, their shape enables snow to fall off the tree easily without breaking branches. In hot weather the needle-like leaves help to reduce moisture loss keeping the tree alive until rain falls again. The larch tree loses its needles in autumn and in winter you can easily see where larch trees have been planted in softwood forests; only under larch can sunlight reach the ground.

The timber of the conifer is known as softwood, but not all softwood timber is soft. Many softwoods are hard and durable.

Broadleaves

The wood from these trees is usually more expensive than conifers. This is because hardwood trees grow more slowly and trees that are cut down take longer to replace. An oak tree, for instance, takes 100 years before it will teach maturity, while elm takes 60 years or more. Some softwoods are ready for harvesting within 30 or 40 years.

The wood is usually harder than softwoods. Balsa wood is an exception to this rule. Balsa is a soft, light hardwood which is used in model-making, particularly the making of model aircraft.

The structure of hardwoods and softwoods

A knowledge of the structure of timber is important. It helps us understand more about how the woods can be worked. By understanding its properties we can understand how best to apply adhesives and finishes.

Softwoods

Softwoods are made up of millions of tiny cells. The main cells are called **tracheids**. They are similar to scaled tubes and have tiny holes in the sides called **pits**. The cells form together in the direction of the grain or growth. (The grain of the timber is the direction of the cells as they lie together.) **Ray** cells radiate out from the centre of the tree and are not very prominent in softwoods.

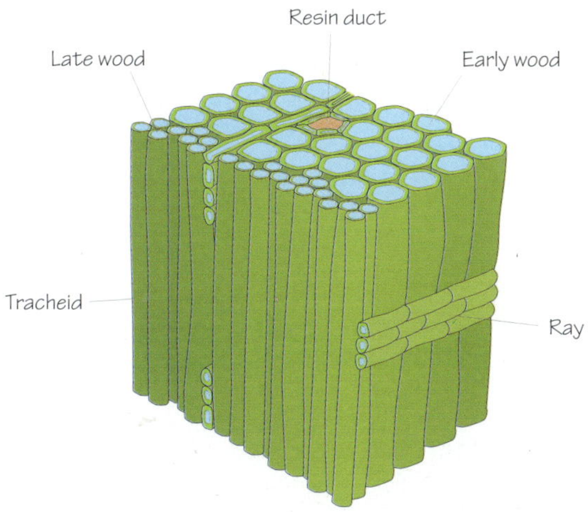

Structure of softwood

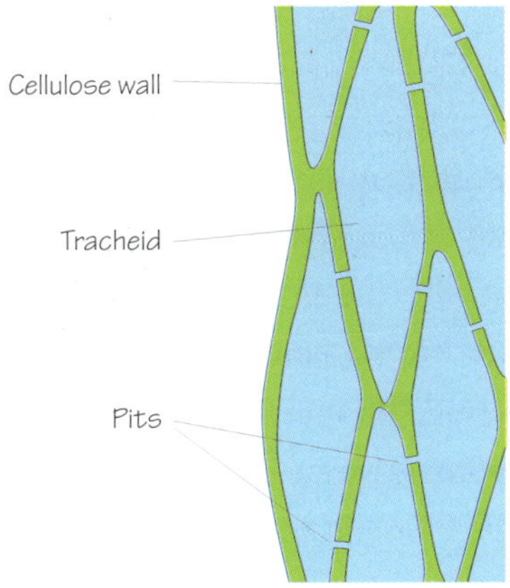

Cells in softwood

Hardwoods

Hardwoods are very different in structure to softwoods. They're made up of two main types of cell, fibres and pores. **Fibres** are small, long and narrow cells. They provide strength and hardness because of their very thick cell walls. They do not carry food or sap. **Pores** (vessels) are like pipes or channels which carry the food and moisture around the tree. They act rather like the veins and arteries in our bodies. Ray cells in hardwoods are similar to those in softwoods but are often more visible. In oak they are clearly seen and give the **silver grain** pattern when cut.

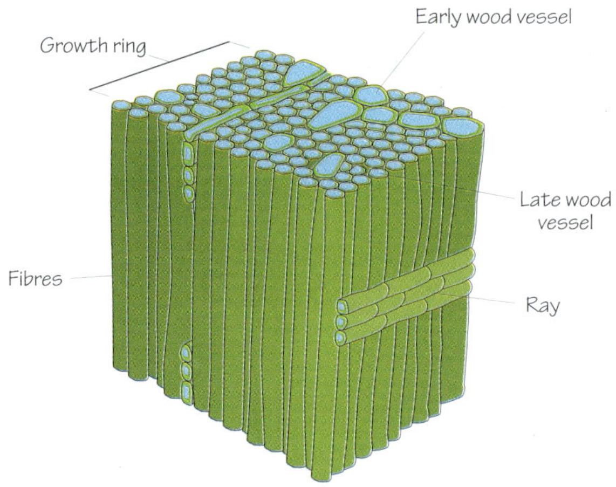

Structure of hardwood

Both the following diagrams show wood which grows in temperate climates and these have annual rings as they grow with the seasons, they are called **ring porous**. In the tropics where the growth rate is steady and constant the wood does not exhibit the usual annual rings and is called **diffuse porous** wood, mahogany is an example.

Ring porous – Oak, Ash, Sycamore, Cherry

Diffuse porous-Mahogany, Teak, Iroko, Rosewood

Growth of Trees

We know that there are many different types of trees and we have examined some of them; now let's examine how trees grow to become the largest living plants on earth.

All plants have a life cycle, trees are no different. They start life as a seed and some will live for thousands of years before they finally die. Many trees grow to a great size; some Redwood trees in the United States of America have archways through their trunks large enough to drive through.

How trees grow

Like other seeds, tree seeds are planted, fall from the tree or are dispersed naturally to the ground. After time the seed sprouts and the **plumule** which will form the stem, makes its way to the surface of the ground. The **radicle** or root grows down into the ground to provide the anchorage and support for the plant – it will also begin to absorb nutrients from the soil.

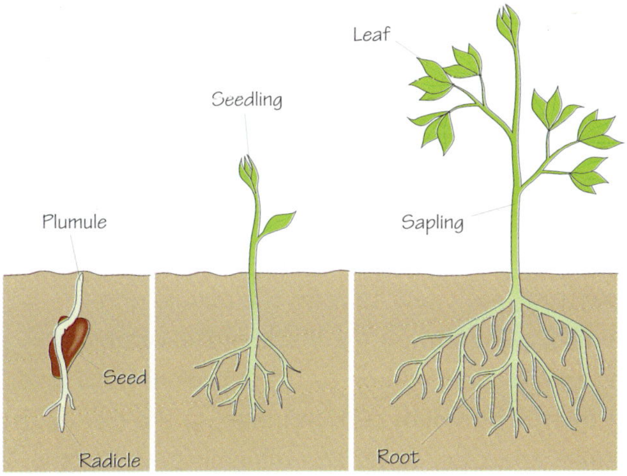

Stages of growth in the young tree

As the young plant breaks through the soil surface, **leaves** start to form and the process of growth begins by means of the energy from the sun. Each year as the tree grows it produces a new layer of cells which form as rings in the wood. These are called **annual rings**. With the addition of each new ring the trunk and branches become thicker. If a tree is felled, it is possible to tell its age by counting the number of annual rings.

There are a number of complex processes going on in the tree, these are shown in the drawing opposite. The nutrients from the soil are brought as sap through the root hairs, root and the trunk up to the leaves. The upward movement of the sap is made possible by the evaporation of moisture from the leaves (**transpiration**) which tends to draw moisture up from the roots to replace this lost moisture. The process is aided by **capillary action** which makes liquids stick to the sides of thin containers (cells).

In the leaves the **sap** is converted into glucose which provides the tree with nourishment. It does this using a substance in the leaves called **chlorophyll**. Sunlight reacts with the chlorophyll in a process called **photosynthesis**. It is a complex chemical reaction during which oxygen is released into the air and carbon dioxide is absorbed into the leaves through millions of tiny holes called **stomata**. The food (glucose) is then transported in the sap through the tree.

Processes within the tree

Parts of the tree

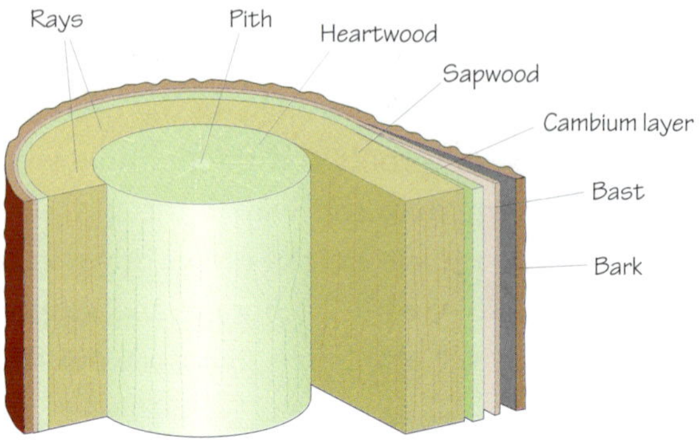

Exploring the parts of the inner trunk

Bark (cortex)

The bark of the tree is a layer of tough fibres surrounding the tree like a skin. It has two main functions. Firstly, it protects the tree from damage from animals, insects, fungi and the weather. Secondly, it helps to retain the moisture and minerals inside the trunk. The colour and texture of the bark can help us to identify particular trees.

Sapwood

The sapwood is the living part of the tree. The cell walls contain **lignin** and **cellulose**.
Cellulose is used in the manufacture of cellulose acetate, which in turn is used in the manufacture of artificial silk and some plastics.

Sapwood is softer, less durable and more likely to be attacked by fungi and insects than the heartwood of the tree. The sapwood is usually a lighter colour than the heartwood. The sapwood of timber can be made more durable by proper treatment with preservatives or finishes.

Heartwood

The heartwood is located in the centre of the trunk under the sapwood and is usually darker in colour. It provides the tree with support and may be regarded as the backbone of the tree. The cells of the heartwood are more blocked with waste substances and are deprived of oxygen by the more vigorous sapwood. The heartwood provides the best timber because of its durability and natural resistance to fungal and insect attack.

Bast (phloem)

Often called the inner bark the bast (or phloem) is a layer of important cells just inside the bark. Its function is to carry food in the form of sap down from the leaves to nourish the tree. The sap is taken by the ray cells into the interior of the tree.

Cambium layer

The cambium layer lies under the bark. This is the most important layer of the trunk, as this is where the growth of the tree occurs. Cells are added on to the trunk each year to form the annual rings. **Xylem** cells form on the inside of the cambium layer and these add on to the annual rings to give growth. The xylem cells continue up the tree to the leaves and carry water and minerals from the soil, up the tree, to the leaves.

Ray cells

These cells radiate out from the centre of the trunk and branch at right-angles to the other cells present. They carry sap to and from the bast. In trees such as oak, ray cells can display an attractive grain pattern known as silver grain.

Pith (medulla)

This is the very centre of the trunk. It is made up of dead cells, soft and dark in colour. This is what remains of the young tree.

Annual rings

The temperate climate in Ireland, with its growing seasons, cause annual rings to form. Trees grow very little if at all over the winter, but in spring vigorous growth takes place and a new ring begins.

The cells grow quickly and are large and have thin walls giving them a light colour. As the growing season comes to an end the cells are smaller with thicker cell walls due to the slower growth rate and consequently they are darker in colour.

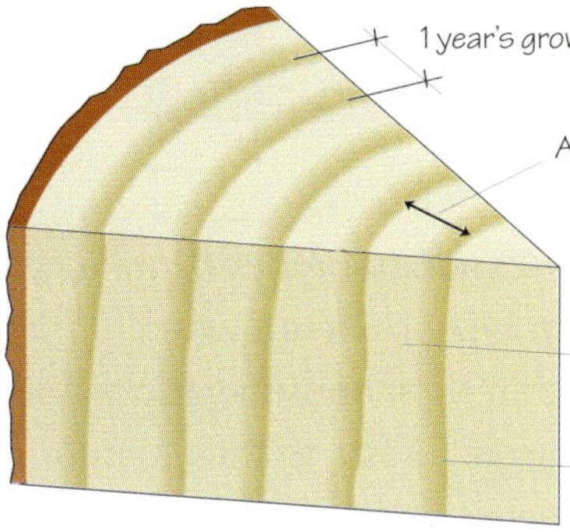

What is an annual ring?

It is possible to tell from a tree's rings whether the weather for a given year was good as the growth would be greater than that of a bad year.

Exercises

1. Fill in the blanks. Coniferous trees ___________ their leaves in winter and deciduous trees __________ their leaves. The seeds of coniferous trees are contained in ________.
2. From the list of trees, say whether each is coniferous or deciduous:

Ash	Beech	Sitka
Spruce	Walnut	Holly
Yew	Sycamore	Oak
Lodgepole pine.		

3. State the features of both coniferous trees and broad-leaved trees.
4. Why are hardwoods more expensive, in general, than softwoods? Give two reasons.
5. Collect some leaves from different local trees and identify each tree type using a reference book. Write a note on each.
6. Give exceptions to the rule that broad-leaved trees lose their leaves in winter and coniferous trees are evergreen.
7. Complete the following sentence: Trees absorb water and __________ through their roots. The water is combined with __________ absorbed from the air and sunlight energy trapped by the pigment __________ in the leaves to produce __________.
8. Forests and woodlands are valuable resources, not simply as a source of sawn timber. Discuss this statement.
9. Sketch the different stages of growth in the early part of a tree's life. Label each part of the plant.
10. Find a small log and take it into the classroom. Examine the end of the log and identify the following:

Pith	Ray cells	Softwood
The bark	Cambium layer	Heartwood
The bast	Annual rings.	

11. Explain the function of ray cells in the feeding of the tree.
12. What is the function of xylem and phloem?
13. Explain the terms photosynthesis, chlorophyl and transpiration.
14. What is silver grain?
15. Explain how annual rings are formed and sketch an annual ring.
16. Explain the difference between ring-porous hardwoods and diffuse porous hardwood trees.
17. In what way do the cells of softwoods differ from the cells of hardwood trees?

CHAPTER SIX

TIMBER & THE ENVIRONMENT

People have inhabited the earth for a relatively short time compared to trees, yet we have a tremendous impact on the earth, and on trees in particular. Trees are the largest and most highly developed form of plant life on earth. They have been used by us since the earliest times, but in recent years their over-use has led to a serious and worrying **deforestation** problem. As research and science advance, we discover more and more that the natural world in which we live is very much affected by everything that we do. All these effects are interrelated, so that cutting down the rainforests affects the atmospheric temperature, the ocean currents, the oxygen levels in the atmosphere, etc. Therefore, we all have a responsibility to ourselves and to future generations to leave our world, not as we find it, but better than we find it.

At home

Forestry is planted and managed here in Ireland by individuals and State bodies who follow guidelines to ensure that forests are not going to interfere with the balance of nature. Forestry should not, for example, be planted too close to rivers and streams as falling leaves would clog the water with rotting vegetation killing fish. The forests provide a rich natural habitat for bird, animal and plant life, which should be taken into account when trees are felled. Human life has also to be considered when planning forestry so that rural households are not left isolated by large scale forests as they mature, this is why it is now necessary to get planning permission before planting forests over certain sizes.

Trees are important for aesthetic (visual appearance) reasons too. Trees enhance the appearance of cities, towns and built up areas greatly and are referred to as the urban forest. You can make a difference to the appearance of a field, garden or even a small area of ground by planting a tree. This will also help the environment, if everyone did a little we could make a great difference.

The urban forest

Tropical rainforests

- Are the richest source of life on earth
- Hold half of the animal and plant species in the world
- Have been called *the lungs of the world.*

Destruction of the rainforests

The greatest advantage of timber is that it is a **renewable resource**. However, this is only of benefit if we replant trees as we use them. In the tropical regions of the world, for many different and complex reasons, trees are being cut down at an alarming rate. In the time it takes you to have a shower, a medium-sized farm of trees (100 acres) is cut down. Disgracefully, most of this timber is simply burned.

Causes of the destruction

There are a variety of factors which have contributed to the destruction of rainforests. People in developed and developing western countries want tropical timbers for furniture, doors, etc. There is a great demand for wood for pulping to be used in making paper and fibreboard and for use in plywood manufacture.

Governments in these less developed tropical countries do not exert enough control over the destruction of their vast resources. They have often encouraged policies which forced people from good farmland to areas of tropical forestry, where they would have to fell the trees to grow crops to survive. They fell the trees to grow crops and to graze livestock, but the land will only sustain one or two poor crops so the farmer is forced to fell more trees.

There is a lack of commitment and realisation on the part of many countries to face up to and tackle this growing problem. The absence of a clear workable and agreed plan is also contributing to the problem.

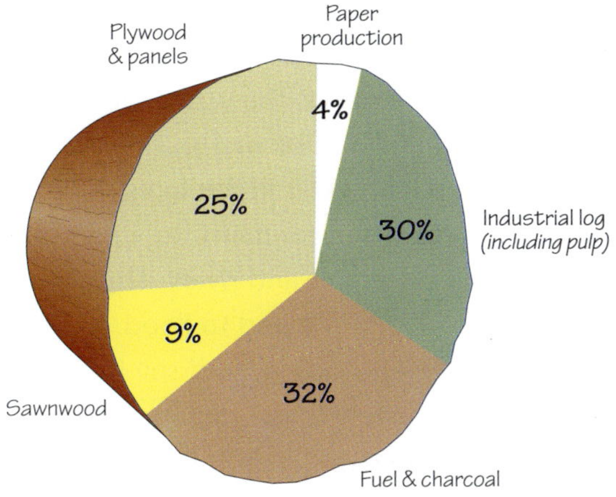

How we use the timber of the world

Effects

The many effects of deforestation are not completely understood but are becoming clearer. As trees give off oxygen and regulate water vapour through transpiration, the felling of large areas of tropical rainforests affects the world's atmosphere and weather, contributing to global warming and the greenhouse effect.

The burning of the felled trees in South America causes huge smoke clouds which contribute to air pollution and cause health problems with the local population.

We are all familiar with the water cycle. In tropical forests like those in Asia and South America evaporation occurs from the trees inland to continue the cycle into the centre of the continent, as is illustrated below.

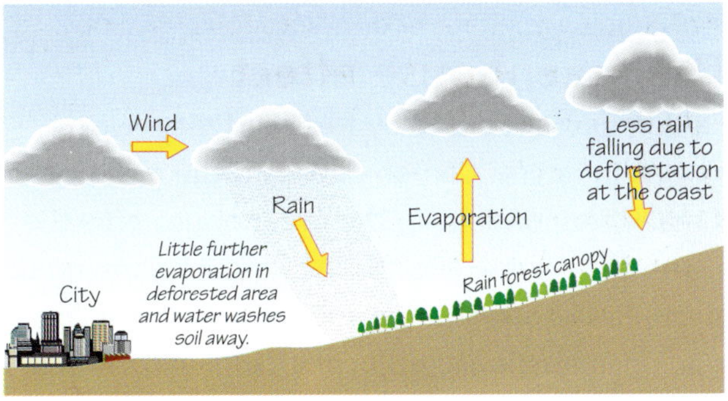

How the rainforest operates

The development of cities and, therefore, felling of trees, is initially concentrated near the coast and moves inland. This upsets the water cycle and reduces the water being picked up to travel inland. This causes a lack of water in the forests inland.

With the trees removed, rainwater flows off the land rapidly into streams and rivers. This volume of water causes rivers to rise and to flood. Flooding also erodes the best (top) layer of soil from the land and this causes people to cut down more trees to make a living from farming. This flooding and erosion was thought to be natural, but studies show they are linked to deforestation. The destruction of the rainforest in Nepal was considered to be have caused the flooding in Bangladesh.

Solutions

- Encourage the growth of native hardwoods and softwoods in Ireland
- Do not use or waste tropical hardwoods like mahogany and iroko unless they have come from carefully managed forests, where replanting is being carried out
- Spread the word that the destruction of the rainforests is a very serious problem
- Use veneers rather than the solid wood
- Encourage the use of manufactured boards for shopfronts and other painted items
- Try to buy items made from temperate woods (ash, oak, softwoods, etc.) instead of tropical woods.

The greenhouse effect

Carbon dioxide is used by trees and they release oxygen in return. Carbon dioxide is the gas which is mainly responsible for the **greenhouse effect**.

The greenhouse effect is the gradual warming up of the earth's atmosphere and surface. This increase in temperature is caused by the build-up of gases such as carbon dioxide and methane in the atmosphere. These gases come from the burning of oil and coal and also from the large numbers of cattle in the world. The gases act like the glass in a greenhouse by trapping heat which has reflected off the surface of the earth from escaping into space. The heat is reflected back down to the earth again to further warm the planet surface. Carbon dioxide is used by all living plants in photosynthesis. The more trees and other plants there are, the less of a problem the greenhouse effect will be. Put another way the more trees we cut down, the worse the greenhouse effect will become.

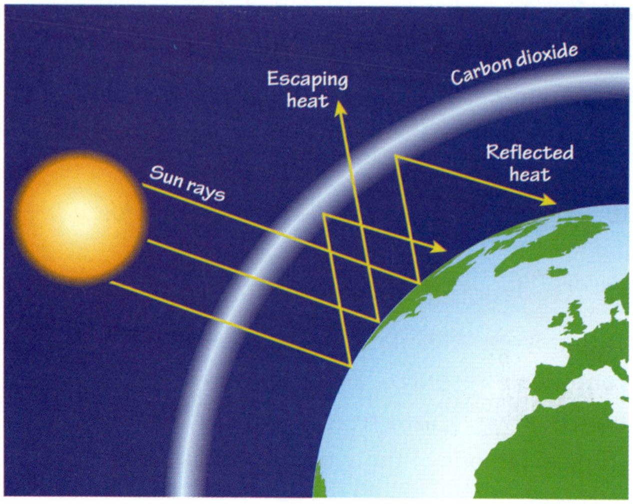

The greenhouse effect

Acid rain

Acid rain is caused by two main chemical pollutants, sulphur dioxide (SO_2) and nitrogen oxides (NOX). These gases are released into the atmosphere when oil and coal products are burned. We all contribute to the build up of acid rain by burning coal and other fossil fuels (oil, coal, etc.). These gases rise into the atmosphere when they are released. They dissolve into the water in clouds and increase the acidity of the rain. The gases can be carried by winds for hundreds of miles. Acid rain effects northern Europe and Scandinavia more than Ireland, as the main winds carrying the rain come from the west.

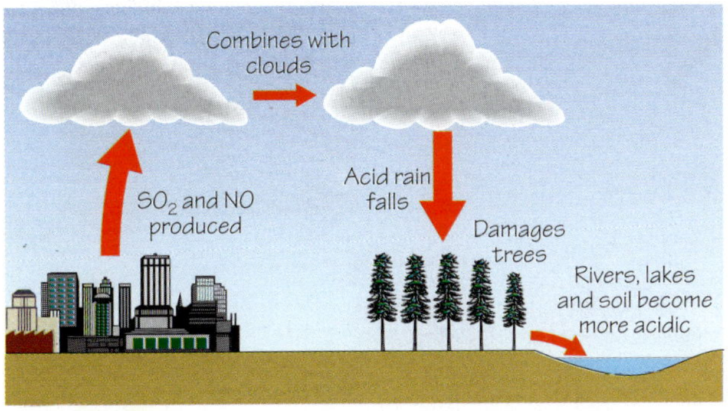

Acid rain

Acid rain falls on forests, cities and farmland. It gets into rivers, lakes and streams polluting them, causing the death of fish and wildlife. It falls on the stonework of buildings, eroding the stone. The sulphuric and nitrous acids damage forests by attacking the leaves of trees and by changing the chemical composition of the soil in which the trees are growing. All of these effects cause the tree tops and the leaves to die and fall off. Conifers are particularly at risk, as they are evergreen, and so are always under attack.

The problem is a large one affecting up to 50% of trees in countries like Britain, Sweden, Greece, Belgium, Holland and Norway. Some pollution is likely to blow from Ireland and Britain to the rest of Europe, so we may well be helping to kill forests in other countries.

Acid rain can be reduced by:

- Using unleaded fuels
- Burning low sulphur fuels (smokeless) or using hydroelectric-power
- reducing all waste of energy
- reducing air pollution generally.

We must all become more aware of how we damage our environment and try to take measures to change things for the better.

Exercises

1. What does deforestation mean?
2. List some ways in which deforestation affects the environment.
3. Find out, from libraries, timber companies and environmental agencies, more information about felling of tropical rainforests.
4. Discuss a plan to grow some trees from seed to plant in your school which will improve the appearance of the grounds.
5. Explain what the greenhouse effect is and how it will effect the earth in the future.
6. How does acid rain effect trees of the world particularly in countries like Britain, Norway, Sweden and Germany?
7. How can the use of manufactured boards and timber preservatives contribute towards a reduction in the deforestation of the tropical rainforests?
8. The destruction of tropical rainforests has caused major ecological problems. How do we in Europe contribute to these problems and how can we help lessen this destruction?
9. Trees are a very important part of the environment. Discuss.

CHAPTER SEVEN

CONVERSION OF TIMBER

Felling

Felling is the harvesting or cutting down of timber. The first step is choosing the right tree. For example, in a forest of oak not all trees will be of the same quality. A trained forester must choose the best for a particular purpose, e.g. oak furniture. In many forests, however, the trees are clear felled and are usually replanted afterwards. This is more economical.

Trees are usually cut down in the autumn and winter. Although they can be cut down in summer, there are two advantages to winter felling:

- There is less sap in the tree because most trees do not grow during winter
- There is less risk of too rapid seasoning (drying out) which could cause the logs to split.

Tropical timbers can be felled at any time since these trees have no fixed periods of growth.

Trees being felled

Conversion

After the tree is felled, the branches are stripped off. The logs are transported to a sawmill by road, rail or river. The branches are not wasted because they are used in the paper or wood fibre industries or for garden mulch.

Once at the sawmill the log is cut into boards. Over the centuries many techniques have been developed for cutting logs into boards. Nowadays a large **bandsaw** is used for cutting the log. In the past, before the invention of the power saw, the logs were sawn by hand in a saw pit.

The way in which the logs are cut will affect the appearance and strength of the board. Logs are converted into boards:

- To get the timber into a more usable form or size to build houses, make furniture and a host of other applications

- To help assess the quality of the timber
- To assist the seasoning process.

Trees being transported

The three main methods of conversion are:

- **Through and through** sawing (also called flat, plain or slash sawing)
- **Quarter** sawing (also called radial or rift sawing)
- **Tangential** sawing.

Through and through

This is a very popular form of conversion. The logs are cut in parallel cuts in the direction of the grain. This form of conversion has certain advantages and disadvantages. It is also known as plain sawing or slash sawing.

Section of a log cut through and through

Grain pattern on a board cut using the through and through method

A saw pit

Advantages:

- It is usually the cheapest form of conversion
- The machining needed is straightforward, reducing labour costs
- There is very little waste and so the maximum amount of timber is obtained
- The method is used mostly for softwoods
- Low cost.

Disadvantages:

- The timber shows no particular grain pattern or decorative figure
- It is not particularly suitable for structural timber
- With this method **cupping** caused by tangential shrinkage is a problem (cupping is the warping of the plank away from the heart of the tree).

When the boards have been sawn the bark is sawn off to give a square edge.

Quarter sawing

This method of sawing leaves the annual rings of the converted timber meeting with the face of the board at 45° or more.

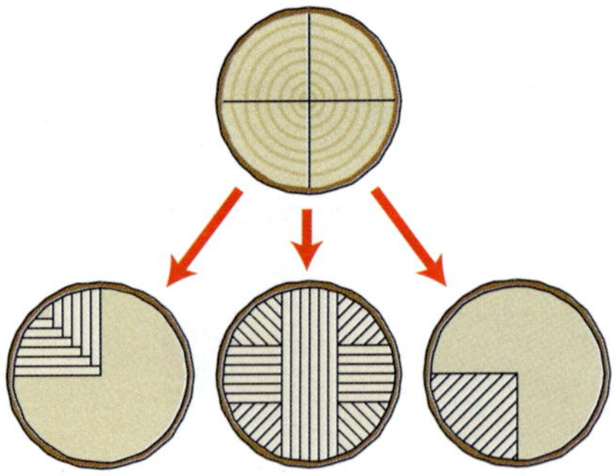

Quarter sawing or radial sawing

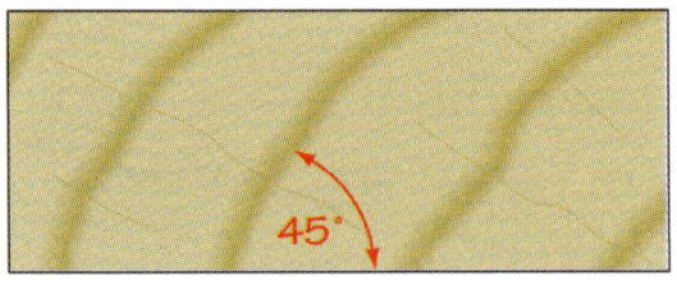

The angle that the annual ring makes with the face of the board is 45° or more in quarter sawn timber

The log must be rotated each time a cut is made. This makes the process time consuming and laborious. The method produces silver grain in woods which have clearly defined medullary rays. This attractive grain pattern is particularly found in oak and is much sought after.

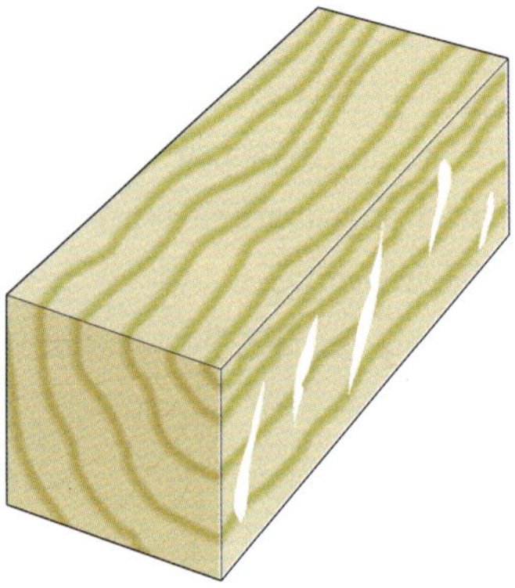

Quarter sawing reveals an attractive grain pattern called silver grain in oak

Advantages:

- An attractive grain pattern is obtained
- Boards sawn in this way are more stable and shrink less than those sawn by the through and through method
- The sawn timber wears more evenly. This is important in flooring, for example.

Disadvantages

- There is more work needed in the machining of the log as it has to be turned for each cut
- It is more expensive than plain-sawn timber.

Tangential sawing

With this method of conversion the cut taken is tangential to the annual rings as shown below.

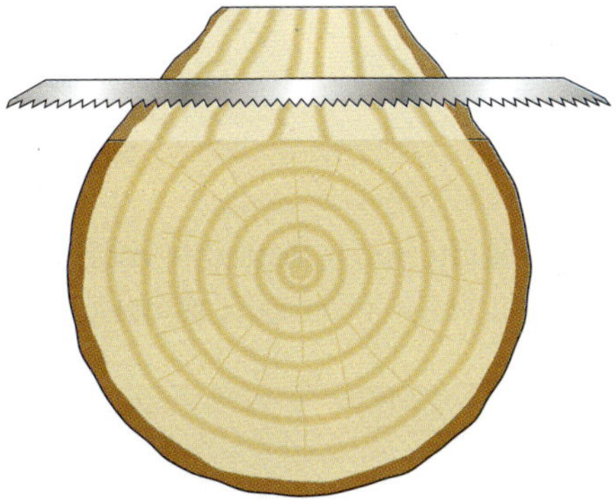

Sawcuts are tangents to the annual rings

Timber converted this way will show up **flame figure**, which occurs in woods which have very distinct annual rings. Pitch pine and Douglas fir show flame figure to great effect.

This method requires a lot of work, turning the log through 90° for each cut. This increases costs and the final selling price.

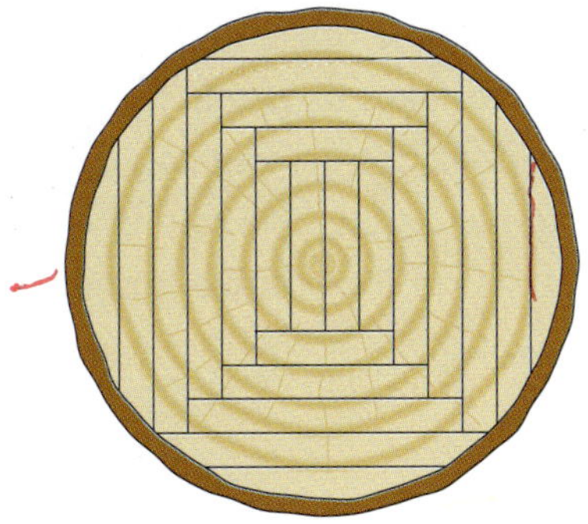

Tangential sawing

Advantages:

- These boards season quicker than those converted in other ways
- The boards are harder to split with nails than in other conversion methods
- The flame figure is seen
- The timber has good structural strength for building work.

Disadvantages:

- Boards converted this way shrink more in their width than other boards
- The timber is prone to warping
- Due to the extra processing the timber is more expensive.

Exercises

1. What time of year is best for felling trees in Ireland and why?
2. What does the term 'conversion' mean?
3. Why do we need to convert timber from log form into planks or boards?
4. Describe the three methods of conversion. Use sketches in your answer.
5. Describe the advantages and disadvantages of through and through sawing.
6. Give three advantages of tangential sawing.
7. Why are logs cut using the tangential sawing method?
8. What advantages does the quarter sawing method have?
9. Give two other names for through and through sawing.
10. Outline by schematic diagram the conversion process from felling to a piece of furniture for sale in a shop.

CHAPTER EIGHT

TIMBER SEASONING

When a tree is felled, it contains a large amount of water. This can amount to 50% or more of its total weight. Some of the moisture is contained in the cell cavities, called **free moisture** and some of it is contained in the cell walls, called **bound moisture.** This newly felled timber is called **green timber**.

When the log is converted this moisture starts to dry out quickly. This can cause many problems and can ruin good timber if the drying out process is not controlled. Defects caused by poor drying out limit the usefulness and value of the timber.

The controlled drying out of timber is called **seasoning**. The aim of seasoning is to dry out the wood to a suitable moisture content of 20% or less.

Reasons for seasoning are:

- Wood will dry naturally, seasoning allows us to control the process and keep the timber stable and more useful
- To avoid splitting the wood
- The drier the timber, the less likely it is to be attacked by insects or fungi
- When dry, wood is less likely to be affected by shrinkage or distortion
- It will be lighter, harder and also stronger
- It will be easier to work with.

This table gives the most desirable moisture content of timber in different situations or uses.

% Moisture Content	Situation
22%-20%	Limit of good air seasoned wood
20%	Limit of dry rot occurring
16%	Outdoor furniture
12%-14%	Occasional heated areas/bedroom furniture
11%-13%	Reasonable heating/livingroom furniture
9%-11%	High degree of central heating/office furniture

In order for controlled seasoning to take place, water must evaporate from the surface of the wood gradually. As the surface dries, moisture from the centre of the wood takes its place. It is important that the surface does not dry out too quickly or **case hardening** will result. The rate of drying of the wood depends on the relative humidity of the air around the wood.

Relative humidity

There is a certain amount of water vapour in the air at all times. The exact amount depends on the time of year. You cannot see this water vapour, but it effects things like the speed clothes dry on a line or the drying of wood.

Relative humidity
Is the amount of moisture in the air at a given temperature, compared with the maximum amount of moisture the air could hold at that same temperature.

As wood is a substance which is affected by moisture changes (hydroscopic), it will release or absorb moisture to reach an equilibrium with the surrounding air. Wood, even in its finished form, for example a door, will soak up or let out water in order to reach this balance. Have you ever noticed how some outside doors will swell in winter and shrink in summer? This is because the wood absorbs moisture from the surrounding air in winter and in summer it dries out.

There are two methods of seasoning timber:

- Natural or air seasoning
- Kiln seasoning.

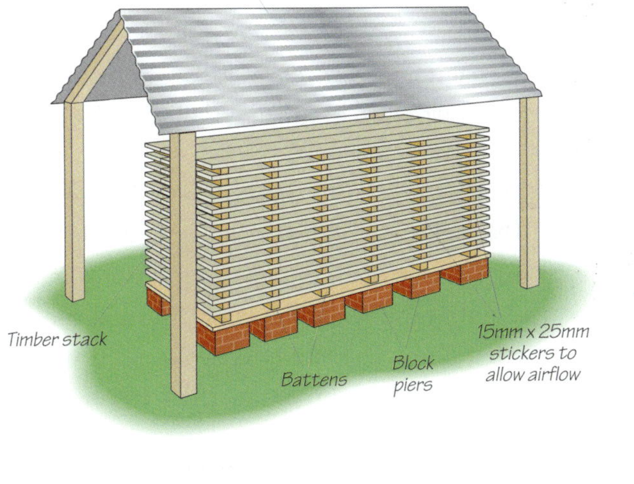

Natural seasoning

Natural seasoning

The planks or boards are laid down on large battens which are raised above the ground. The planks are laid parallel to each other but have a gap between them. This gap allows air to circulate up and down the stack. Stickers or skids are small pieces of wood about 15mm x 25mm in section. The stickers allow air to pass through the stack and should be spaced at intervals of 0.5m or more depending on both the type and the thickness of the wood. Boards of timbers that are less likely to warp can have stickers placed further apart.

The stack should be covered with a lean-to roof surface overhanging all round to allow rainwater to run off. The stack should be on a dry clean site. It should not be any more than 2 metres in thickness to allow a free flow of air and to ensure that the stack dries evenly.

Timbers of the same species should be kept in the one stack. Also boards of the same thickness and width should be kept together in the same stack to keep the drying rate uniform.

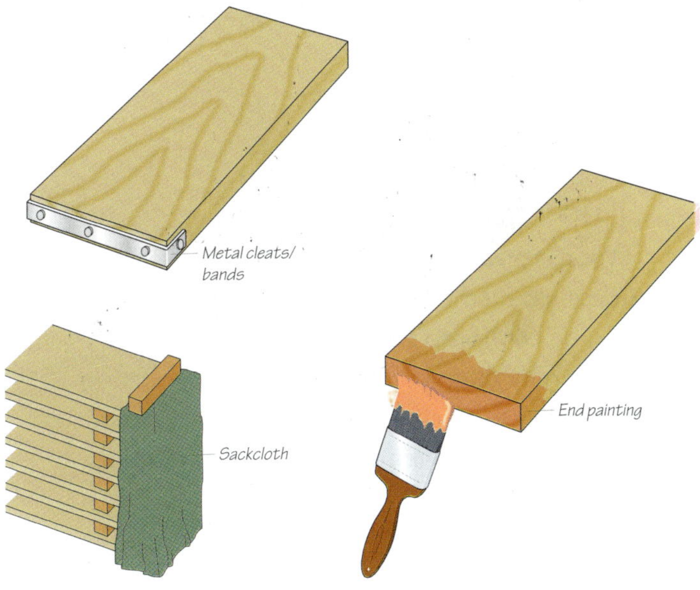

Methods to prevent ends of boards splitting

The ends of the boards should be protected from the sun, which may cause them to dry more quickly than the rest of the boards causing the ends to split. The ends can be painted or covered with sackcloth if the sun is too strong. Another method to prevent ends cracking is to protect them with metal hoops or cleats.

The air seasoning method can only reduce the moisture content of a board to between 18% and 22%. Timber with this moisture level is suitable for joinery to be used out of doors. If a further reduction in moisture level is needed the boards must be kiln dried.

Advantages of air seasoning:

- No expensive equipment needed
- Small labour cost once the stack is made
- Not wasteful of energy.

Disadvantages of air seasoning:

- Slow drying rate
- Large area of space required for a lot of timber
- Dependent on the weather conditions
- Rate of seasoning cannot be carefully controlled
- Only seasons to a content of 20%-22%.

Kiln seasoning

Wood is also seasoned in large kilns (ovens). In these kilns temperature, humidity and drying rates can be controlled by the operator to achieve uniformity of drying. The operator uses drying schedules for each type of timber and its particular thickness, as different thicknesses of wood dry at different rates.

There are two types of seasoning kiln (oven)

(a) Compartment kiln

(b) Progressive kiln.

Compartment kiln

The timber is stacked in a similar way to that used in the air seasoning methods, except it is put on a trolley which runs on rails. The trolley is rolled into the kiln.

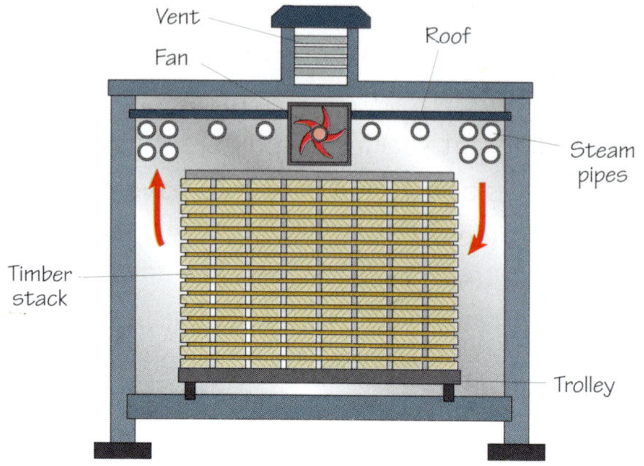

Section through a compartment kiln

Heated steam is piped into the kiln by steam jets which heats the wood through to the centre without any drying taking place. If drying were to take place at the start of the process the surface of the boards would dry out too quickly causing shrinkage and distortion of the wood.

Once the wood has been heated by the steam the relative humidity of the kiln is reduced while the heat is maintained. This allows the moisture in the wood to evaporate gradually until the required moisture content is reached.

The steam is introduced through pipes or jets in the kiln. The pipes are on the walls, floor and ceiling. The fans circulate the air around the kiln making sure that the air is circulated through the whole stack quickly. The air vents allow moist wet air out of the kiln and fresh air in. The fresh air absorbs moisture being evaporated from the wood. Removing the moisture laden air improves the efficiency of the kiln giving speedy and efficient seasoning.

The progressive kiln

The progressive kiln is similar to the compartment kiln except that the timber undergoes various stages and drying temperatures as it moves through the kiln on the trolley. As the dry timber emerges from one end, green timber is loaded at the other end ensuring the kiln is always full. One disadvantage to the progressive kiln is that it must be stacked with the same species and size of timber because different species and different sizes dry at different rates and would therefore have different drying schedules.

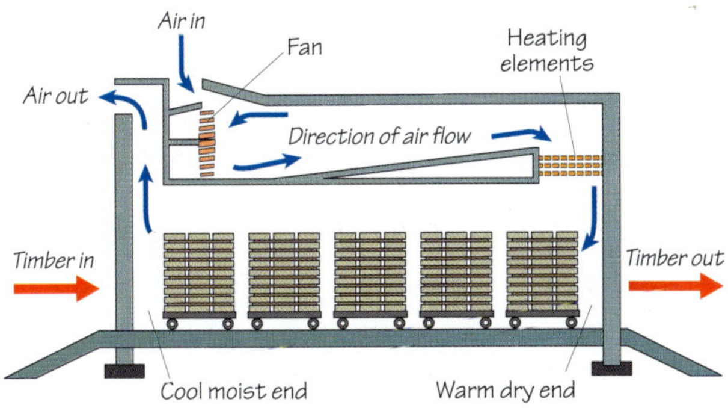

Section through a progressive kiln

The process of kiln seasoning may be helped by first air seasoning the timber, to dry it out slightly. This is necessary with some woods and is advisable with most, as it speeds up the kiln stage and will also help to cut down the final drying cost.

Kiln seasoning

Advantages:

- Quicker due to higher temperatures, ventilation and air circulation
- Achieves a lower moisture content
- Greater degree of control (drying schedules) in the drying process
- More precise rates of drying for various timber species and thickness of boards
- Uniform circulation through the stack
- Control over moisture content and rate of drying can be achieved
- Defects associated with drying can be controlled.

Disadvantages:

- It is expensive
- Requires supervision by a skilled operator
- Is dependant on energy.

Moisture content

The amount of moisture present in wood is shown as a percentage (%) of the weight of the wood when dry.

While seasoning is taking place boards must be checked for moisture content at intervals to make sure that the wood is being dried properly. The boards to be checked are taken from the middle of the stack. A loose board is withdrawn so samples can be taken at intervals.

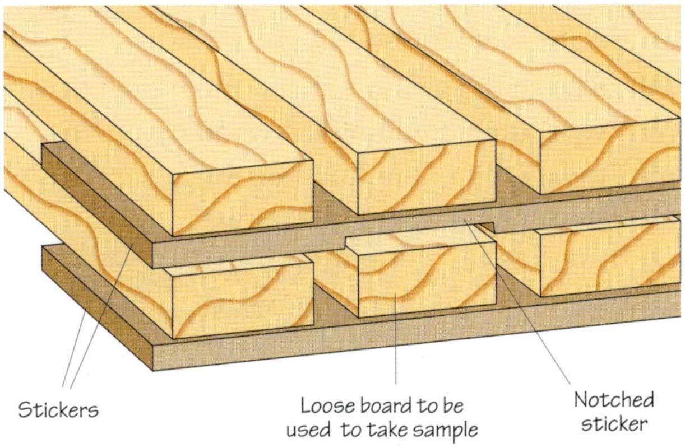

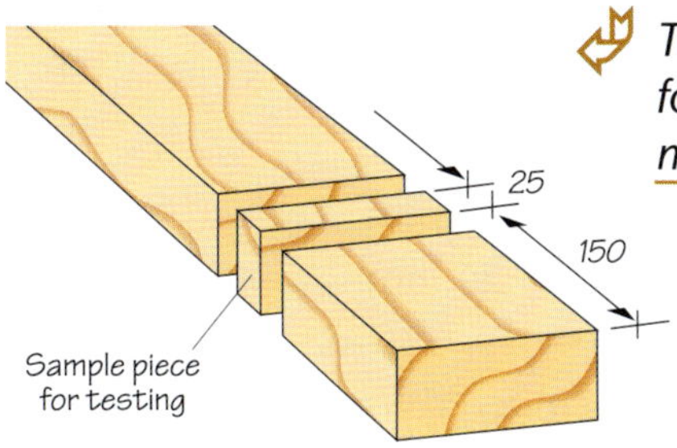

Taking a sample for testing moisture

This sample is then tested to find the moisture content as shown in the experiment described below.

However, electronic moisture metres, with their increased accuracy, are replacing this test. Moisture meters are electronic instruments which have a dial or digital read-out which indicates the percentage moisture content of the timber. The two electrodes of the meter are pushed into the timber.

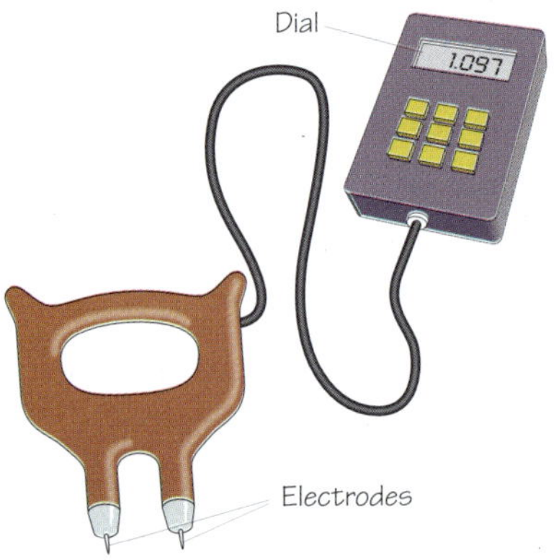

A moisture metre

A general rule of thumb is often used for kiln seasoning:

Softwoods	1 week per 25mm thickness up to 75mm
Hardwoods	2 weeks per 25mm thickness

Other seasoning methods

Radio frequency heating

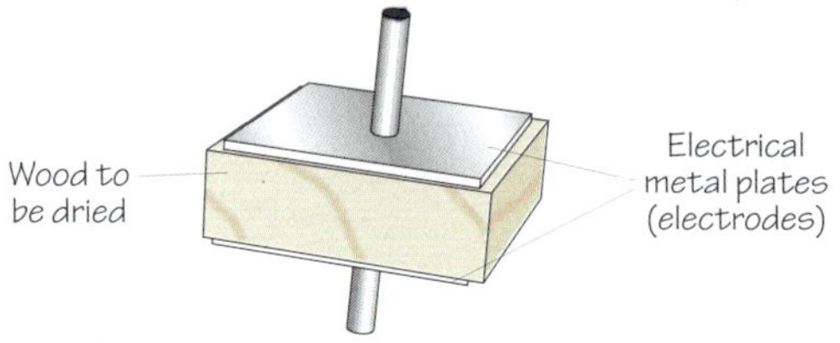

Radio frequency heating

With this method moisture in the wood is heated by high frequency radio waves. These waves go all the way through the wood giving an even drying out process. Eventually when the moisture reaches boiling point it will escape,

Experiment to find the moisture content of a piece of wood.

Take a piece of green wood and weight it. For unseasoned wood this is known as its **wet weight**. Then remove all the water from the wood by placing it into an oven or kiln at 100°C weighing periodically, until the weight of the wood does not decrease any further. This final weight is the **dry weight**. Use this formula to find the moisture content:

$$\text{\% Moisture} = \frac{\text{Wet weight} - \text{Dry weight}}{\text{Dry weight}} \times 100$$

Drying Times

Wood	Size	Air to 18–20%	Kiln Dried (10%)
Hardwood	50 mm	18–24 months approx.	1 – 12 weeks
	25 mm	6–8 months approx.	1 – 12 weeks
Softwood	50 mm	6 months approx.	7 – 14 days
	25 mm	3 months approx.	2 – 7 days

It must be remembered that these are only approximate figures and they will change depending on the sizes and the types of timbers, season of the year, initial moisture content, etc

provided the wood is porous enough. This means that the wood is dried very quickly and very evenly.

Temperature gradient method

The wood is again heated by radio frequency. This time only the inside of the piece is heated while the outside is cooled by moist air. This makes moisture move from the hotter inside to the colder outside surfaces. This method is very expensive and is rarely used.

Re-seasoning

Before undertaking a project the seasoned wood for the item should, if possible, be allowed to acclimatise with the room or surrounding heating conditions in which it will be placed. This will allow the wood to reach a balance with the surroundings and avoid distortion or cracking later on. The pieces should be left for about a month before starting work. This treatment helps to keep the wood stable in its final environment.

Exercises

1. What is green timber?
2. Name the two methods of drying out timber before it can be used by the woodworker.
3. Explain in detail how wood must be stacked to give even seasoning. Draw a sketch to illustrate your answer.
4. Why is it necessary to stack timber as in question 3 and what function do stickers serve?
5. What is meant by the natural method of seasoning?
6. Explain, with sketches, how the kiln method of seasoning works.
7. What function do the following play in kiln seasoning: steam jets, heating coils, trolley, circulating fans?
8. Describe what seasoning does to the wood.
9. How is the kiln seasoning different from air (natural) seasoning? Give three advantages.
10. What is % moisture content?
11. What is relative humidity?
12. Find the % moisture content of these samples of wood given the following information:
    (a) Wet weight 100g, dry weight 86g
    (b) Wet weight 250g, dry weight 200g.

CHAPTER NINE

DISEASES AND DEFECTS

Like any other living organism, trees can and do get diseases – they have imperfections just like other living things. Artificial defects are often caused by incorrect felling and seasoning. Diseases and defects affect the strength and the quality of wood. Sometimes defects in wood can look well and can increase its value, but more often a defect will decrease the value of the wood.

Burr veneers and burr wood can be valuable

Natural defects

Some of these can be very decorative and very pleasing to the eye, others create many problems. There is little that can be done with unwanted defects, apart from cutting them out of the wood during the conversion and processing stages.

Knots

Knots are formed when the branches of the trees are cut off or fall off from the trunk. Some knots in timber become loose and are called **dead knots** and they fall out eventually. Other knots remain part of the wood and are called **live knots**. Live knots show up in timber and they can be an attractive feature, particularly in softwoods.

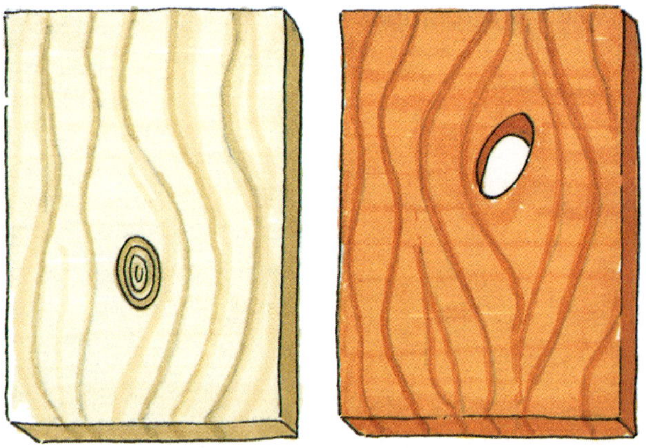

Live and dead knots

Knots are more numerous in softwoods than hardwoods because they have more smaller branches stemming from the central trunk. In hardwoods the branches are larger, further apart and there are fewer of them.

All knots reduce the strength of the timber. This is because all of the fibres of the wood change directions around the knot. This makes the wood around the knot difficult to work and causes blemishes. Therefore, knots are usually seen as defects.

Resin pockets

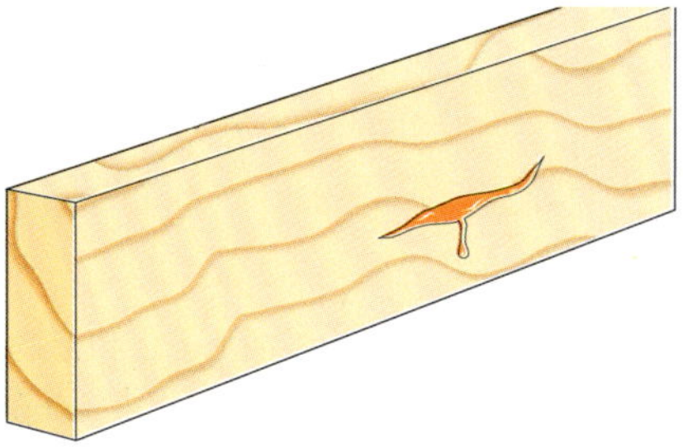

A resin pocket exposed, with resin oozing out

These are small cavities or thin vein-like hollows in the wood which are filled with resin. These pockets are often hidden from view and can cause weakening of the timber. When exposed they are unsightly and the sticky resin can be messy.

Shakes

Shakes are splits in the end grain of wood. They happen along the ray lines and also along the annual rings. These splits are caused by tension forces which build up in the wood while the tree is growing. When it is felled, or during seasoning, these forces may be released. The weaker points in the wood break, like the weak link in a chain, and the split occurs. Different types of split (shake) have different characteristics.

Radial shakes

These occur in the direction of the rays. They include heart shakes, frost shakes and star shakes.

Radial shakes

Tangential shakes

Tangential shakes occur in the direction of the annual rings. This occurs in old age in the tree, in seasoning or in strong wind. These include cup shakes where the split only runs along the annual ring. A ring shake is when the split runs right around the annual ring.

Tangential shakes

Cross (thunder) shakes

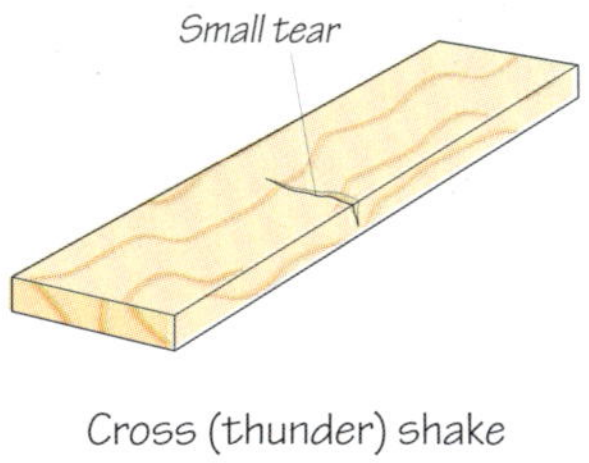

These are probably caused when the tree is subjected to a severe shock such as during felling or by a strain in the tree while it is living. The difference between these shakes and other kinds is the split or tear across the grain.

Artificial defects

These defects occur as a result of stresses caused by poor stacking or seasoning. All timber shrinks some amount, but some types shrink and distort more than others, therefore, it is necessary to take account of this when choosing timber for different uses.

Cupping

This form of shrinkage forms a curve if you view a plank from either end.

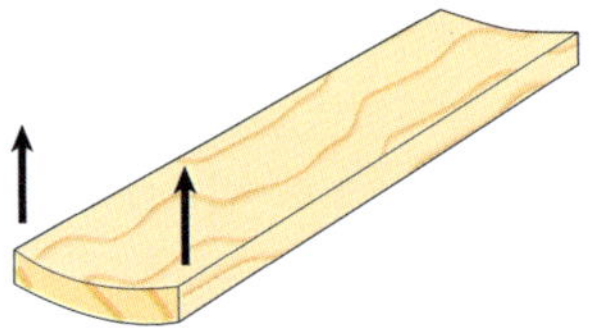

Cupping

Bowing

This takes the form of a bend along the length of the piece. Both cupping and bowing defects are often due to incorrect stacking of the boards during seasoning, where the stickers are too far apart or perhaps not directly above each other. It may also be as a result of poor stacking in a timber yard.

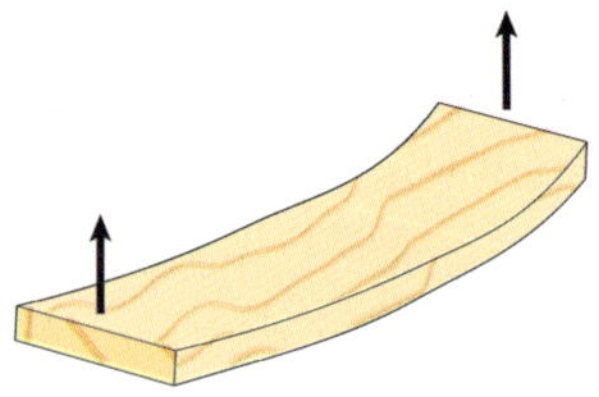

Bowing

Twisting or warping

The two edges of the piece remain straight but the faces are distorted as if the two ends were twisting in opposite directions.

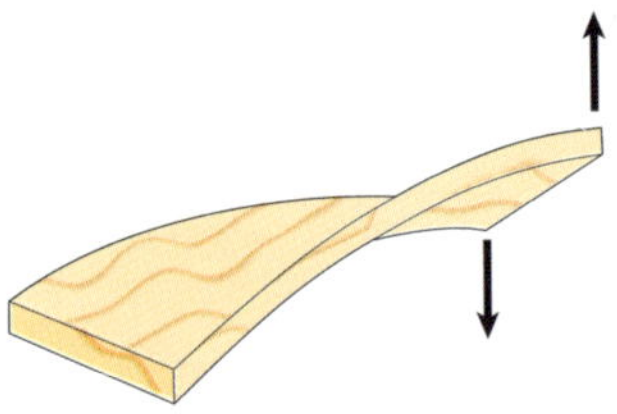

Twisting or warping

End splitting

This is caused if the ends of boards dry out too quickly, due to exposure to the sun or heat. It is very common in naturally seasoned timber. It can often be prevented by painting or treating the ends during seasoning.

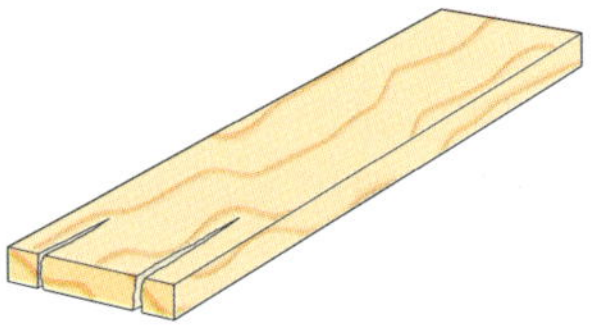

End splitting

Case hardening

This happens when boards are seasoned too quickly. The surface and the centre do not dry at the same rate. This creates stresses in the wood. There is compression on the inside of the pieces and tension on the surfaces.

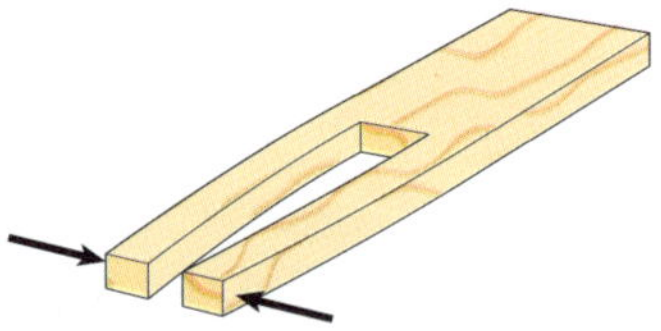

Case hardening

Honeycomb checks

The interior or inside of the wood splits. This happens when, due to case hardening, the outer surfaces are stiffened and rigid. When the board dries out, shrinkage occurs inside the wood causing splits.

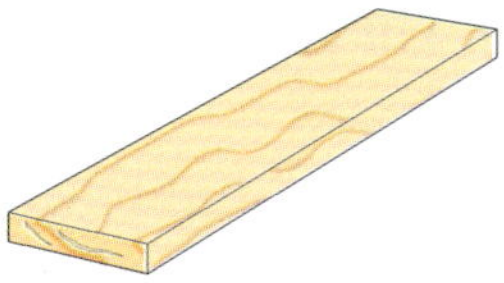

Honeycomb checks

Collapse

When the moisture in the wood is taken out too fast, and air does not have time to replace the water, the cells collapse. They collapse in the same way as when the air is sucked out of a drinking straw which is sealed at one end. It gives a wrinkly washboard effect. The spring

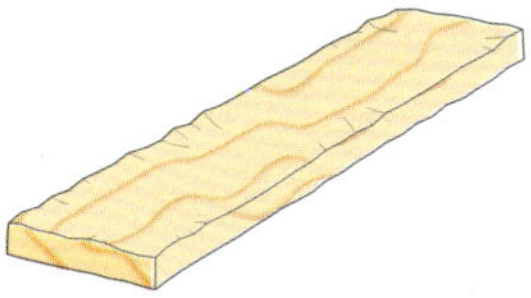

Collapse

wood is affected more than summer wood. The wood shrinks and warps substantially.

Stains and discoloration

Timber can be stained by chemicals (e.g. black-bog oak), weathering and fungi. Fungal staining is caused by fungi infecting the wood and feeding on the carbohydrates in the timber. The moulds stain the wood; blue, grey, black, pink and white. Sometimes they occur on the surface and can be sanded off, but often they grow deep into the wood (usually softwoods). These fungi do not affect the strength of the timber but the discoloration is often undesirable.

These stains occur due to poor seasoning. If the correct moisture content is achieved (20% or below) the fungi cannot survive.

Chemical stains

Nearly all timbers react to different acids or alkali, causing some staining of the woods. You could try different acids, soaps, detergents on different samples or woods to find out their reactions.

Weathering and wear

If wood is not treated or protected from the weather it will eventually deteriorate from attacks to its surfaces from heat, rain, frost, snow, etc. These affect both the strength and appearance of the wood and eventually the wood will begin to rot.

Fungal attack

Fungi attack and cause damage by feeding on the cellulose or lignin in the cells of the wood. They soften the wood and eventually it decays. Fungi need certain conditions before they can live on the wood. These conditions are:

- Moisture, – a moisture content above 20%
- Food supply – the wood
- Oxygen – particularly still air
- Warmth.

A fungus is made of cells called **hyphae**. When there are a large number of hyphae together this is called a **mycelium**. The hyphae penetrate the wood to feed and get moisture. Fruit bodies called **sporophores** are formed which produce tiny spores which are blown by the wind and carried to other wood. They germinate there to grow into more fungi (page 50).

There are many kinds of wood rotting fungi. They can be classified as:

- **Wet rot** (white rot)
- **Dry rot** (brown rot).

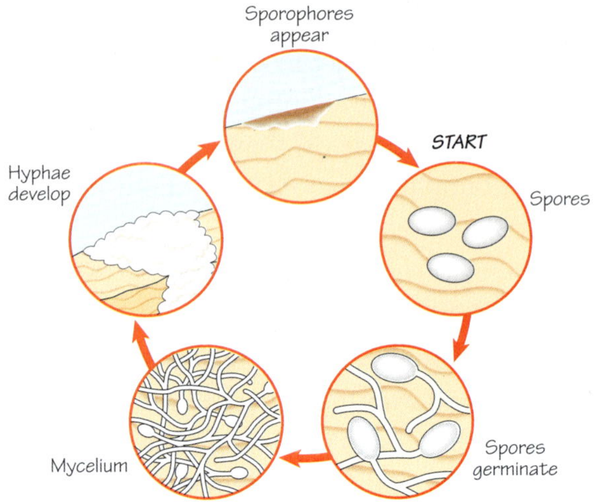

Life cycle of a fungus

Wet rot

This occurs outdoors. The fungus feeds on both the cellulose and the lignin in the wood. This fungus rots fence posts, window frames, logs, doors, etc. The affected wood is very moist and slimy and sometimes a white residue is present.

Dry rot

The fungi which cause brown rot are called *merulius lacrymans*. They can occur outdoors but are mostly found inside, for example underneath wooden floors. The fungi attacks timber, eating the cellulose in the wood. The wood appears dry and the surface cracks in rectangular shapes, like wood which has been charred by fire.

Conditions must be right for the spores to germinate and once they have started to grow the fungi can get water through the hyphae. These are seen as white silky threads. They spread out and can penetrate brick walls. Dry rot usually occurs in damp areas with poor ventilation. The attack can seriously damage large areas of woodwork, weakening infected wood. It is usually recognised by the cube-like cracking of the wood and its musty smell. Treatment of the affected areas must be drastic.

Treatment

- All infected wood and uninfected timber 500mm beyond the infected wood is cut away and burnt
- All surrounding brickwork and other materials must be scorched or treated with a fungicide to kill any further remaining infections
- All remaining timber and blockwork must be treated with preservative
- The cause of the outbreak must be identified and corrected, (improve ventilation, for example)
- Replacement timber must be treated with preservative.

Insect attack

Some insects will attack and feed on timber much like a fungal attack. Some insects spend most of their life living in and feeding on wood. The life cycle of many of these insects follows similar patterns.

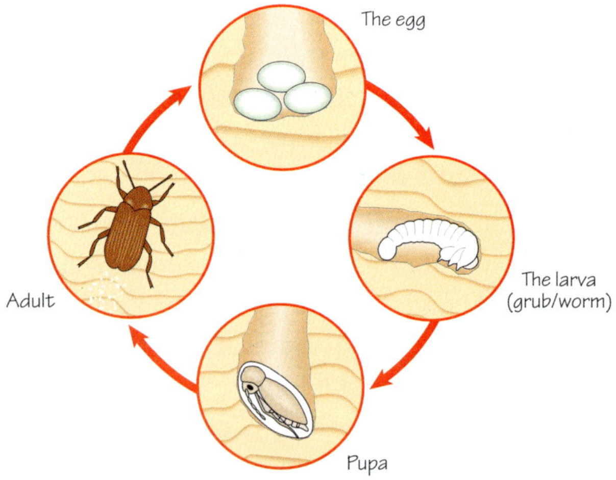

The life cycle of a typical wood boring insect

1. The adult lays the egg in an old insect hole, or crack in the wood.

2. The egg hatches and the larva or grub then proceeds to feed on the starch in the wood. Some beetles feed on moulds in the wood, e.g. the Ambrosia beetle. Usually only the sapwood is attacked because most beetles cannot digest cellulose, which is present in large amounts in the heartwood. This feeding leaves tunnels under the surface of the wood.
3. The larva eventually constructs a special chamber for itself. This is near the wood surface. The larvae makes a cocoon like shell around itself and then it pupates for a period of time. During this stage (**pupa**) it changes into the adult beetle.
4. The adult then emerges breaking out to the surface to continue the cycle leaving behind a flight hole and fine dust (waste) called **fras**.

Furniture beetle (woodworm)

The common furniture beetle, or woodworm as it is more widely known, is probably the most common pest in Irish household wood. Woodworm attacks both hardwoods and softwoods, such as mahogany, oak and pine. However, it usually only attacks the sapwood of these timbers. The adult beetles emerge in June and July. Some tropical hardwoods are somehow immune from attack, as are modern plywoods and chipboard, because the adhesives used in their manufacture are harmful to the beetle.

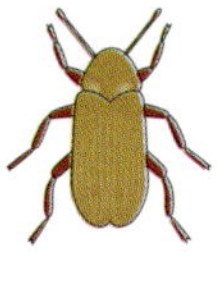

Furniture beetle (woodworm)

Deathwatch beetle

This beetle is not found in Ireland very often. However, it is found in southern England. It is bigger than the furniture beetle. It attacks damp timbers usually at the ends of decayed beams which are embedded into walls. The adults emerge during June, July and August. If timber is painted with all the cracks and holes properly filled, it greatly reduces the risk of attack.

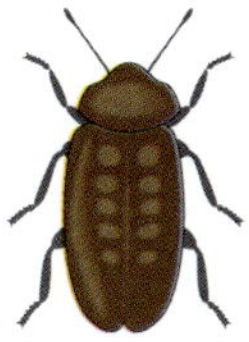

Deathwatch beetle

Powder post beetle

It is reddish brown in colour and generally attacks the sapwood or new hardwoods particularly during or after seasoning.

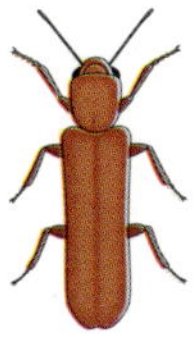

Powder post beetle

Marine borers

These attack timber which is in use in the sea or other salt water places such as wharves, jetties, piers, boats, etc. Two examples of marine borers are:

- **Shipworm** *(toreda navillis)* which is a mollusc
- **Gribble** *(limnoria lignorum)* which is a crustacean.

The shipworm tunnels deep into the timber and can destroy it in a very short time. The gribble attacks and tunnels just below the surface. Damage may not be as serious as that caused by the shipworm. There are, however, a number of timbers which are naturally durable against attack by these borers, i.e., Greenheart,

Lignum Vitae, Jarrah and Afrormosia. However, they are expensive and in short supply. It is important to treat all other woods with the proper preservatives.

Treatment

- Put a sheeting of wood or nylon around the timbers
- Coat the timber using *creosote* or similarly effective preservative.

Timbers in conditions treated with *creosote* have been found to be free from marine borer damage after 20 years.

Exercises

1. Explain the differences between natural and artificial defects in timber.
2. Sketch the following and explain how they are caused; (a) knot (b) star shake (c) resin pocket (d) warping.
3. What is a fungus?
4. Describe the stages of growth of a fungus
5. What is sap stain and how does it affect wood?
6. Why is it necessary to protect timber from the weather and wear?
7. What is the most common wood pest in Ireland and how would you recognise its presence?
8. What is the main cause of splits in timber?
9. Why is an attack of wood-boring insects so damaging to wood?
10. Describe the life cycle of the common furniture beetle.
11. *Merulius lacrymans* is a wood rotting fungus:
    (a) What is the more common name for it, and what are the characteristics of timber infected with it?
    (b) Describe in detail how areas affected with this fungus should be treated to remove attack and prevent its reoccurrence.
12. List the conditions necessary for the growth of a wood-rotting fungus.
13. List the steps necessary for preventing attack of wood-rotting fungus.
14. Describe the main differences between wet rot and dry rot.

CHAPTER TEN

PRESERVING TIMBER

Timber should be protected from wear and tear, the effects of weathering and from attack by insects and fungi. Timber is preserved to prolong the life of the wood and prevent its natural decay. Some timbers are more durable (resistant to decay) than others, and in general hardwoods are more durable than softwoods. Softwood timbers are widely used today, as hardwood timber is no longer in plentiful supply. Softwood timber generally contains a lot of sapwood which decays and is easily attacked unless it is preserved in some way. Most preservation methods are used on less durable timbers to make them more durable, thus avoiding the cost of using more expensive timbers. This also helps to conserve tropical timbers which tend to be naturally durable. It is wiser to use properly treated home-grown softwoods than costly imported hardwoods.

Preservation can be defined as anything which is done to extend the useful life of timber and timber products.

The preservation of wood includes painting and other applied finishes, but preservation principally refers to the many methods of treating exterior timber with various chemicals.

Some substances were being used as preservatives on wood as long ago as Roman times, but preservation has only become widespread in the last hundred years. Timber preservation became necessary because naturally durable timbers became scarce, so ways of improving the durability of cheaper timbers were developed.

Preservative types

The main forms of preservative are:

- Tar oil preservatives
- Water borne preservatives
- Solvent-based preservatives.

Different preservatives

These preservatives can protect the timber in two ways. Firstly, they give physical protection by stopping fungi and insects getting at the wood. Secondly, they give chemical protection, making the wood poisonous to insects and fungi. Paint, for example, gives excellent physical protection.

Tar oil preservative

Creosote is perhaps the most important of these preservatives and has been used since 1836. It is used for the pressure treatment of telegraph poles which will last almost indefinitely afterwards. It is made from a mixture of 160 different chemicals. It is distilled from coal tar. Tar oil preservatives can be applied by brushing, spraying, dipping or pressure treatment.

Advantages:

- Cheap and plentiful
- Highly toxic to insects and fungi and marine borers
- Penetrates the timber well, especially if heated
- Permanent, as they cannot be easily washed out of the wood (leaching).

Disadvantages:

- Strong smell
- Toxic to plants
- It may bleed into plasterwork
- Cannot be painted over unless well weathered
- Not suitable for indoor use
- Can have a poor effect on strength of timber.

Water-borne preservatives

These preservatives are made from different toxic salts which are carried by water into the wood. When the water dries out, the toxic salts remain. Chemicals such as copper chrome arsenates (CCA) and borates are used as preservative salts. These are particularly good for protecting softwoods in damp conditions. Water-borne preservatives are usually pressure impregnated, although they can be applied by other methods.

Advantages:

- Timber is clean after treatment
- No bleeding (such as occurs with oil in hot weather)
- Generally colourless
- Timber can be painted after treatment
- Transportation is easy as the preservatives come in highly concentrated form
- They do not pose a fire hazard and can be combined with fire retarding chemicals
- They do not cause staining of plaster
- They are usually odourless and so can be used indoors.

Disadvantages:

- Many types can be washed out of the wood
- Timber needs to be dried out by kiln or air seasoning after treatment
- Can cause distortion and swelling due to the water
- They do not protect against weathering effects.

Organic solvent preservatives

These are toxic substances which are dissolved in a solvent other than water. Usually this is an oil solvent, which is easily evaporated such as white spirit. After treatment the solvent evaporates leaving the preservative in the wood. This type of preservative penetrates the wood well because of the light oil solvent.

Advantages:

- Resistant to leaching and is suitable for indoor and outdoor use
- Can be painted over after the solvent has evaporated
- Usually do not stain or creep
- Not corrosive to metals
- Better penetration, so are more suitable for brush and spray application.

Disadvantages:

- There can be a fire hazard
- Can have a strong odour
- More expensive than other types.

Safety

All preservatives must be handled with care. Read any instructions on the container carefully. At all times ensure it is safe for use in the room or house and that it will not harm people, animals or the environment in any way. When working with any chemicals you should wear all the appropriate protective clothing. Remember that safety and care of the environment also applies to the disposal of cartons and containers which hold the preservatives.

A gate being brushed with preservative

Methods of application

There are a number of different methods of applying preservatives. They can be applied without pressure or with the aid of pressure. The type of method used will depend on the degree of preservation required, the amount of timber to be treated and the time and cost of that treatment.

Brushing & spraying

Preservatives can be applied using a brush or a spray gun. This method is the easiest to use and is not too costly. The preservative, however, doesn't penetrate deep into the wood and the treatment needs to be repeated regularly to keep the wood protected.

Immersion

The wood is placed into a container of preservative. The wood absorbs the preservative over a short time. The immersion can be done for a short time (dipping) or for a longer period (steeping). The immersion process penetrates better than brushing and can be even more effective if the preservative is heated. Often the ends of fence posts are treated in this way for a couple of days using creosote before they are placed into the ground.

Piece of timber being immersed

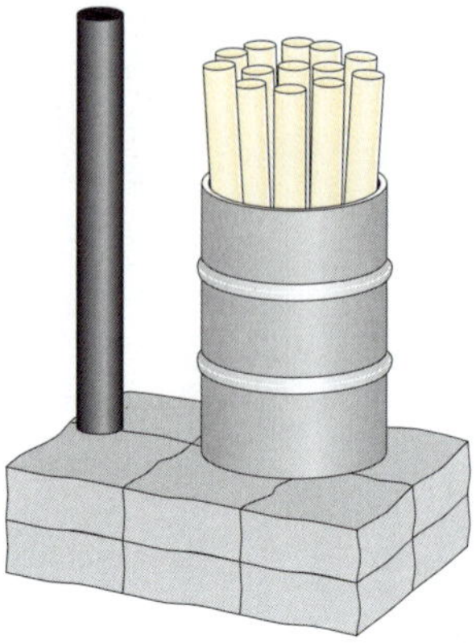

Treatment of the ends of fence posts

Pressure treatment

The most effective method of applying preservative is by forcing the preservative into the wood under pressure. This pressure can come from inside (vacuum) or outside (pressure).

The timber is put into a treating cylinder. The air is sucked out of the cylinder and held for a few minutes to let all the air come out of the wood. Woods which are less permeable to air are held for a longer time in the partial vacuum, to get the air out. The cylinder is then flooded with preservative while the vacuum is held. The vacuum is released allowing the preservative to take the place of the air in the wood. Then pressure is applied forcing the preservative into the wood. A final vacuum is applied for a short time to remove any excess preservative, this is done so that no preservative is wasted.

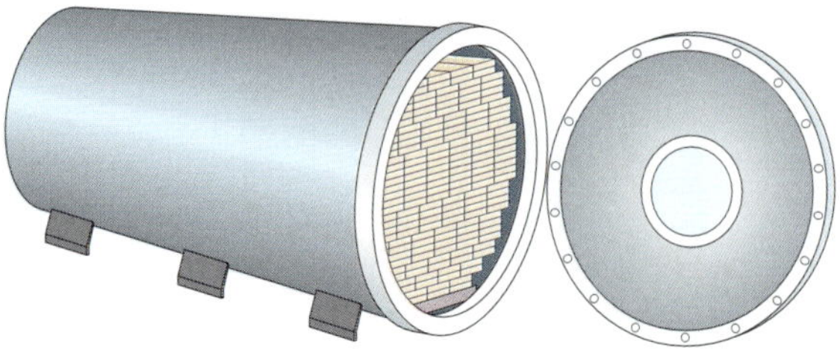

Pressure treatment chamber

Exercises

1. Make a list of all the types of different preservative treatments that can be found in your local hardware store.
2. List the different places in your garden and home where preservative could be used and suggest the type of preservative to be used.
3. List two classes of wood preservative.
4. List the advantages that organic solvent preservative has over tar oil preservative.
5. Describe how you would apply creosote to a small garden gate and suggest another suitable preservative for this purpose.
6. Describe a pressure impregnation process of preserving wood.
7. Describe the advantages of the pressure treatments over the non-pressure treatments.
8. How does timber preservation helps to conserve the world-wide tree population?
9. Suggest the most suitable preservative for the following items, saying why each is suitable:
   Fence posts
   Picnic table
   Garden shed
   Telegraph pole
   Window box.

Types of preservatives and their properties

Desirable properties of a preservative	Tar oils	Organic Solvent	Water-borne
Toxic to fungi and insects.	Yes	Yes	Yes
Permanent	Yes	Yes	Yes
Easily obtainable	Yes	Yes	Yes
Safe to handle	Yes	Manufacturer's instructions should be carefully followed	
Easy to apply	Yes	Yes	Yes
Non-corrosive to metals	Not normally corrosive	Not normally corrosive	Not normally corrosive
Capable of good penetration	Yes	Yes	Yes
No additional fire hazard	Freshly treated timber is more inflammable than untreated but after a few months the volatile fractions of the oil evaporate and the fire hazard is greatly reduced	Volatile solvents may be somewhat inflammable. Care is therefore necessary when used in confined spaces and in storage. After the solvent has evaporated the treated wood is not more inflammable	No additional fire hazard
Can be painted	No	Yes, if suitable solvent is used	Yes, after the treated wood has dried
Odourless	No	Some have strong odour, others are free from odour	Yes
Colourless where it is desired to retain natural appearance of timber	No	Some are colourless, others are not	No

CHAPTER ELEVEN

MANUFACTURED BOARDS

Man-made woods or manufactured boards have become very important as a substitute for solid woods over the last number of years. They have a number of important advantages over solid timber. They are an important substitute to solid wood, helping to conserve tropical forests through use of veneered boards. They are an economical alternative and have become important materials in their own right. They provide large, flat areas of stable wood of uniform thickness. They are mainly used for work tops, bedroom and kitchen units for which they are well suited.

Manufactured boards

Plywood

Plywood is made by gluing together thin veneers or sheets of wood like a sandwich to form the thickness of sheet required. Veneers are sheets of wood cut from the surface of a plank, or by rotary cutting, from a log.

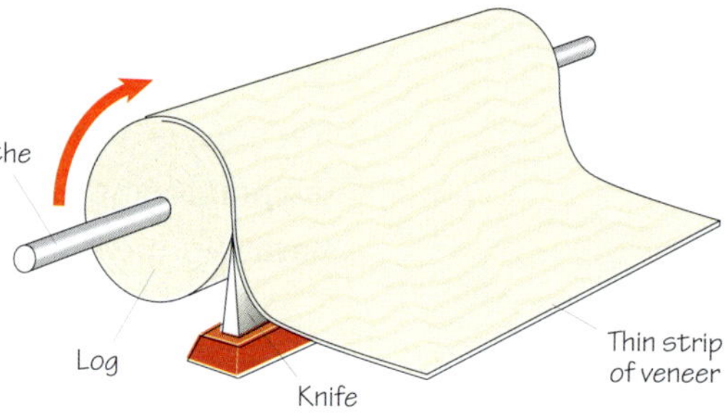

Rotary cutting of veneer

In plywood, each layer is positioned so that the grain is at 90° to the layer below it as shown overleaf. The veneers are glued together by *casein glues* or synthetic resin glue (urea formaldehyde). There are always an odd number of plies in plywood 3,5,7, etc., so that the grain of the two facing (outside) veneers are aligned in the same direction. If an even number of veneers were used the sheet would be inclined to warp or cup.

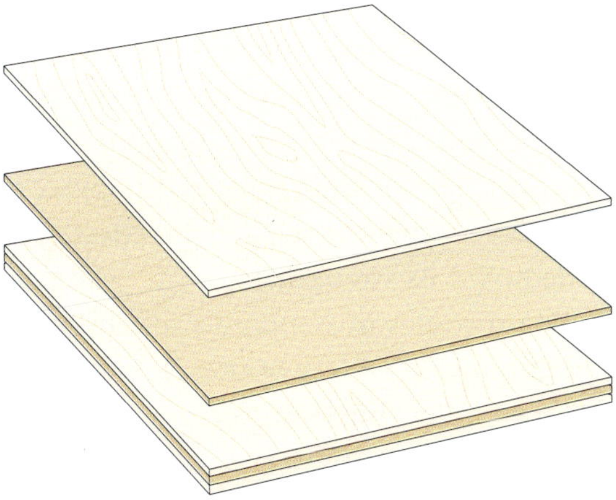

How plywood is put together – the grain direction of each ply is at 90° to the next

Plywood was first made for use in tea chests for bringing tea leaves around the world. Three ply, made of a central piece with two facing veneers, was used. This made the box very light.

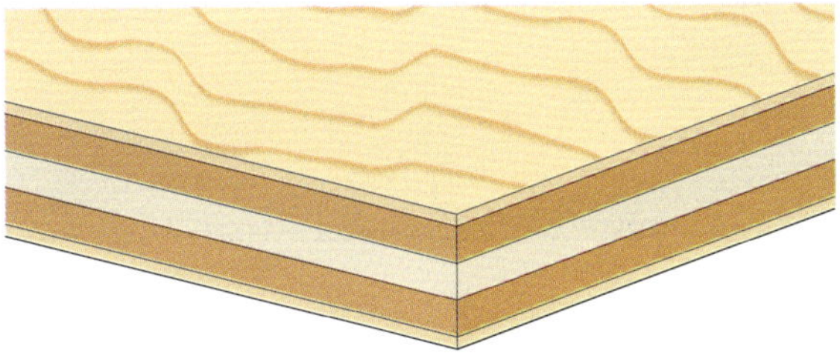

Stoutheart

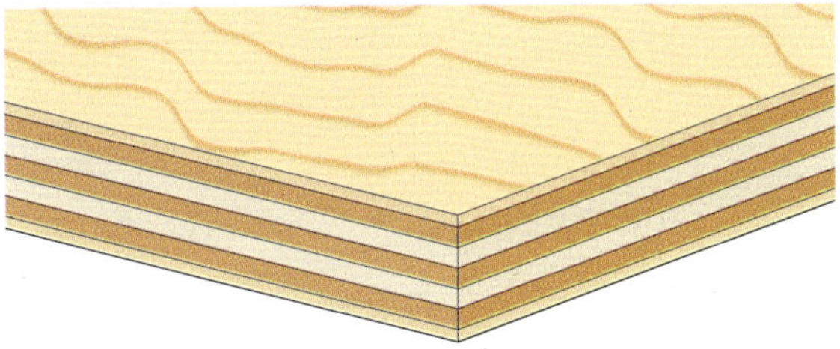

Multiply layers of the same thickness to make up one very strong board. Usually more expensive due to number of veneers/plies

Plywood can be obtained in two main grades for interior and exterior use:

The **interior** type contains veneers which would not withstand exterior conditions and the adhesive used in it is not moisture resistant.

The **exterior** type often referred to as **WBP (water and boil proof)** contains more durable veneer types and the adhesives used in their construction are very resistant to water, heat, chemical, fungal and insect attack.

Marine plywood contains high quality veneers of naturally durable timbers bonded together with WBP glue. It is used where the plywood will be exposed to water for long periods of time, for example, in boat building, etc.

Strip core boards

Strip-core boards are made of solid timber (gaboon, birch or softwood) in the centre or core. These pieces of strips are glued together and faced with a veneer on each side.

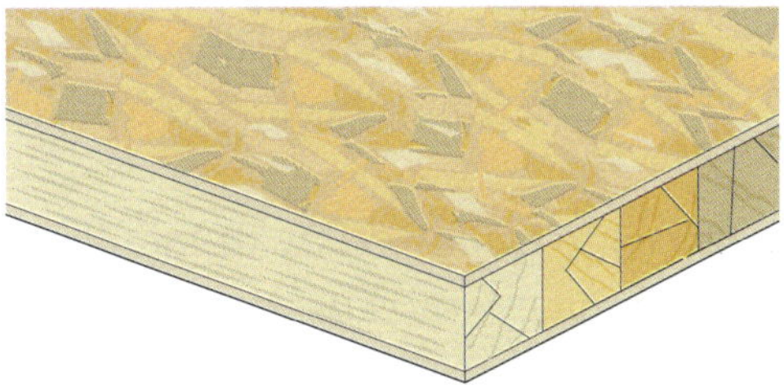

Strip core board

The boards are named according to the sizes of the core pieces. Strip core boards are usually 12mm thick or more, as thinner sheets would be difficult to make successfully. The main advantage that strip core boards have is that screws and nails are easily driven into the edges of them and they hold well. The battens or cores run the length of the board, so the facing veneer usually is placed with its grain going across the width of the sheet.

Plywood and stripcore

Advantages:

- Cover large areas easily with a uniformly thick sheet
- They are very stable and do not swell, shrink, warp or twist
- Will not split when nailed into their faces due to opposing layers or veneers
- Good strength due to different directions of veneers
- Available in large sheets making them more economical with less waste
- Smooth and uniform finish with standard thicknesses
- Little preparation required
- Light plywood can be bent and laminated to almost any required shape
- The edges of stripcore boards can be screwed and nailed into easily.

Disadvantages:

- Generally the surface veneer is plain due to the rotary cutting method. This can be improved by putting a decorative veneer on top
- Edges need to be covered with mouldings or iron-on laminates or veneers, etc
- Surface veneers are easily damaged and difficult to repair because they are so thick
- Cannot easily screw or nail into edge of plywood.

OSB – orientated strand board

Oriented strand board is a relatively new manufactured board. It is made in Ireland in Waterford by Louisiana Pacific. It is a material that looks similar to chipboard but has many of the characteristics of plywood.

Wooden strands or flakes are processed from the tree log and are then bonded together under heat and pressure, using a synthetic adhesive and wax. The strands are aligned in two outer layers and an inner core positioned at right angles to the outer layers creating a three ply effect. This gives the board its strength.

The board comes in standard sizes and is suitable for a wide variety of uses. It is used in packing cases, flooring, furniture manufacture and timber framed buildings. It has moderate moisture resistance and resistance to fungal attack.

OSB boards

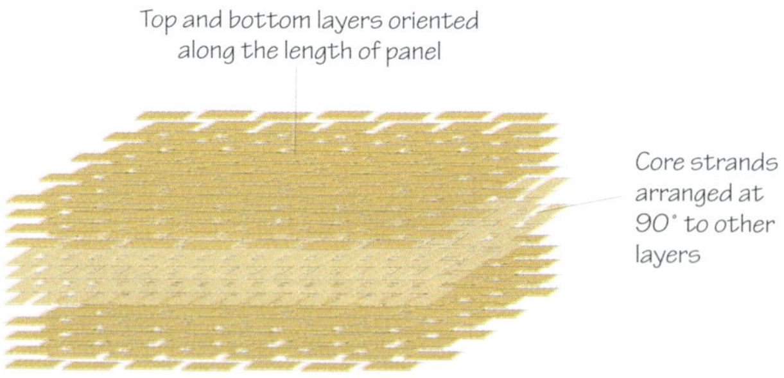

Structure of OSB

Particles boards (chipboards)

These boards are made by taking graded wood chips and mixing them with synthetic resin glue. Then the mixture is pressed or formed into rigid sheets of regular thicknesses. They are sanded down to give the finished product.

They are used for laminating with plastic laminates or decorative wood veneers such as oak, mahogany, ash and teak for furniture construction, worktops, bedrooms or kitchen units. There is also a floor grade used on the building industry.

Particle boards have become very popular. They help in the conservation of trees. The waste from timber felling and conversion can be included in this manufacture.

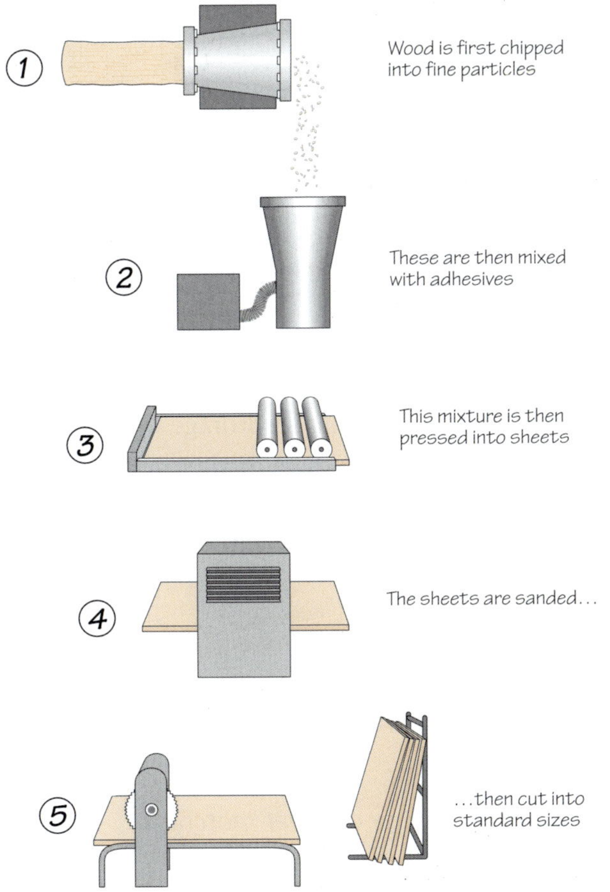

The manufacture of chipboard

OSB and chipboard

Advantages:

- Uniform thickness obtained
- Can be veneered with decorative veneers and laminates
- It is relatively cheap
- Can use timber which would otherwise be wasted.

Disadvantages:

- Surfaces and edges normally are too rough to be good finished surfaces so they require a veneer or laminate
- Chipboards are weak. They are easily broken if bent
- Water and moisture will make the sheet swell and eventually disintegrate
- Generally chipboards do not take screws or nails well, as the small particles are easily separated. However, special chipboard screws are available which help to reduce this problem

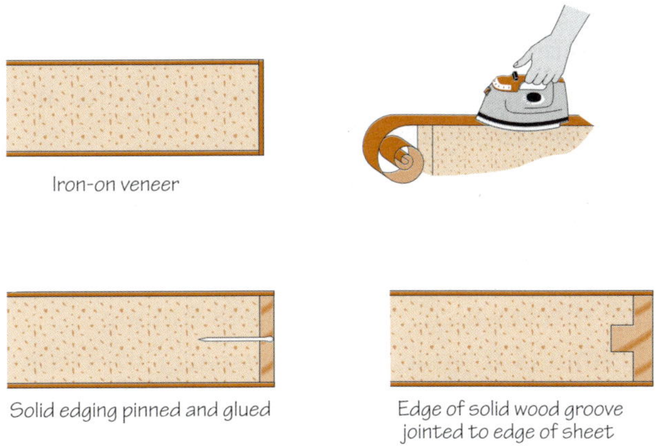

Treating/covering the edges of sheet material

Hardboard and Fibreboard

Hardboard

This is made from wood pulp with added water. The water is removed and the pulp is pressed under high pressure and temperature. Bonding of the fibres is assisted by resins in the wood and the addition of about 5% bitumen. The finished sheet is a uniform material with high density. The sheets are smooth on one side and have an uneven surface on the other side. They are usually obtained in thin sheets (between 3mm and 9mm). Hardboard is inexpensive and can be obtained with surface laminates. It is used in the bottoms of drawers, the back of cupboard carcasses and as a hard wearing underlay to floor coverings and in interior door construction.

Fibreboards

Another fibre board has become very popular. It is known as MDF (medium density fibreboard) and is made in Ireland by Medite. It comes in standard sheet sizes and thicknesses. The board is similar to hardboard in colour but it is considerably stronger. It is finished to a smooth surface on both sides. These surfaces do not need to be sanded before finishing. Other types of fibreboard are HDF (high density fibreboard) and LDF (low density fibreboard).

Sizes

Usually manufactured boards are obtained in large sheets which are 2438mm (8 ft) long 1219mm (4 ft) wide. However, smaller sizes can also be obtained in some outlets. Plastic laminated chipboard can be obtained in smaller standard widths in the full lengths. These have edge laminates which make them suitable for making shelves and units. Both come in a variety of standard thicknesses and finishes from 6mm to 25mm.

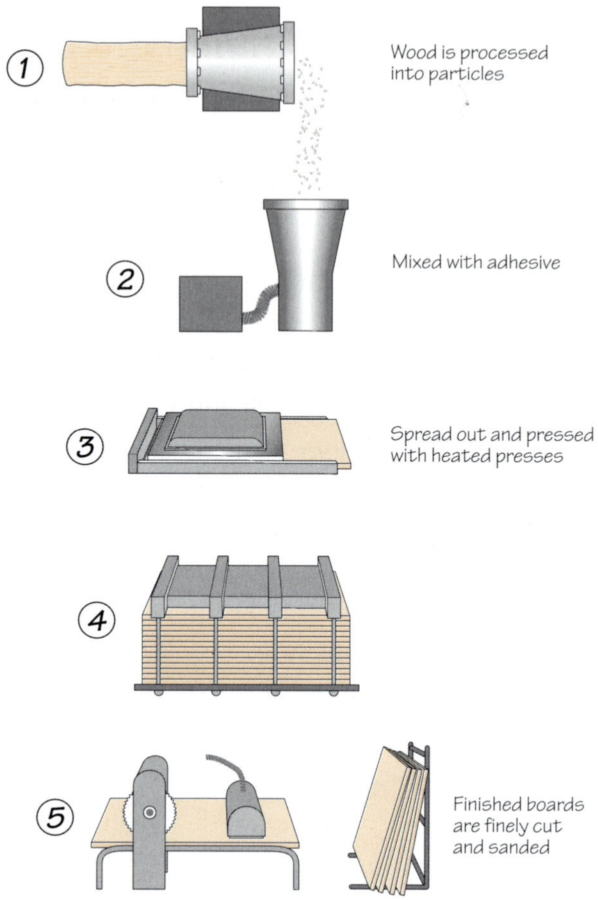

Manufacture of MDF

Care of sheets

Sheets of boards should be stacked for storage on the flat as shown. Incorrect storage can result in distortion or other damage to the sheets. They must be stored indoors or in dry sheltered areas to protect them from the weather or dampness.

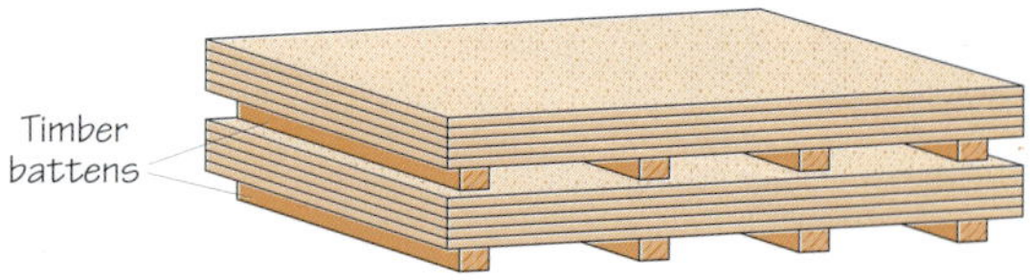

Correct storage of sheet materials

Exercises

1. Make a display of different types of man-made boards.
2. Draw a diagram showing how plywood is made.
3. Describe briefly the process of rotary cutting of veneer.
4. Make a small piece of block board for yourself using some strips of wood and 6mm plywood as facing veneers.
5. Test the glue used in plywood by putting a piece of ply into a container of water. Leave for a period of weeks to see what happens. You could record your results and compare different types of manufactured board also.
6. List three different manufactured boards and their uses.
7. Suggest the reasons why manufactured boards have become so popular as an alternative to solid wood.
8. How is chipboard made and give two of its disadvantages?
9. Describe the manufacturing process of MDF and blockboard.
10. MDF and chipboard are two of the most widely used manufactured boards – compare the two materials under the following headings:
    (a) Manufacture
    (b) Uses.
11. Describe the difference between blackboard and chipboard.
12. How does the use of man-made woods benefit natural forests?
13. Sketch the correct method for starting manufactured boards.
14. List four advantages of MDF.
15. What dust control methods should be used when working with MDF?

CHAPTER TWELVE

PROPERTIES OF MATERIALS

Wood is an attractive and functional material that we mostly use in the Materials Technology Room. Metals, plastics, rubber, textiles, glass and ceramics can be used also. Each of these materials have distinct properties which may make them more suitable for use in different situations. Knowing the properties of the materials that you commonly use will assist you in choosing the best one for your particular project.

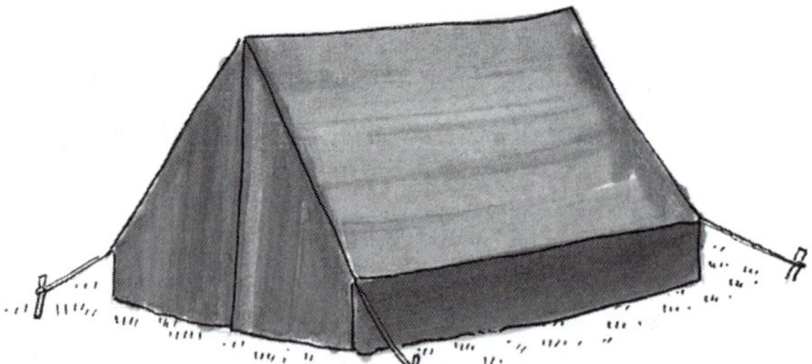

You wouldn't make a tent from sheet metal as it could not fold away easily, so a water resistant cloth material is more suitable because of its properties.

Strength

The strength of a material is its ability to resist force without bending or breaking.

As there are different types of force, there are also different types of strength:

- **Compressive strength** – the ability of a material to withstand compression
- **Tensile strength** – the ability of a material to withstand tension forces
- **Bending strength** – the ability to withstand bending forces
- **Shear strength** – the ability to withstand shear forces
- **Torsion strength** – the ability to withstand twisting forces

Hardness

The hardness of a material is its ability to resist denting and scratching. It is important for tool bits, chisels and hammer heads to be hard, so that they will keep their surface and shape for long periods of time. The blades of chisels are made of hardened steel so that they will hold their edge better. If they were made of softer steel they would go blunt rapidly.

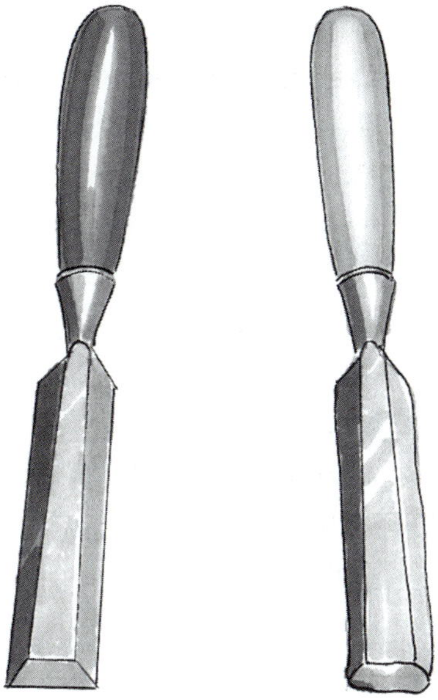

Density

The density of a material is the mass (kg) of a material per unit of volume (m^3). A block of steel and a block of wood of the same size will have different weights because of the different densities of each.

$$\text{Density} = \frac{\text{Mass}}{\text{Volume}} \ (\text{kg/m}^3)$$

Mass = The weight of an object, measured in kilograms (kg)

Volume = The amount of space an item takes up, measured in m^3

Water has a density of 1000 kg/m^3. Any substance with a density lower than 1000 will float on water. Can you suggest why most woods float on water?

Toughness

The toughness of a material reflects the ability of a material to absorb energy. Ash is an example of a tough wood which will not crack under a load. The opposite to toughness is brittleness. Glass is an example of a material which is not tough.

Elasticity

This is the ability of a material to return to its original shape after the forces which have changed it have been released. Ash is a wood which has good elastic properties.

Most materials have some elasticity, but if a material is deformed beyond a certain point it will not return to its original shape. This point is called a material's **elastic limit**.

Ductility

A ductile material is one that changes shape easily, under loading conditions, without breaking. Steel, wood and copper are ductile materials.

Plasticity/malleability

A material is malleable if it can be easily changed into different shapes without cracking. Lead is an example of a malleable metal.

Durability

This is a material's ability to resist the effects of weathering, corrosion and decay. Teak and oak are examples of durable woods.

Insulation

Electric wires are covered with rubber or plastic, because these materials do not allow the wire's electric current to pass through. Rubber and plastic are therefore electrical insulators. Other materials may insulate heat (fibreglass), light (dark curtains) or sound (polystyrene board on sound studio walls). Some materials provide a number of forms of insulation. You could do some tests to examine this property. In general, wood is a good heat and electrical insulator, while metals are poor insulators of heat and electricity.

Colour

Colour is a property that affects the design of objects. Different materials have different colours in their natural state, even though the colour may be changed or covered by painting or coating. In some materials, like wood, the material's natural colours can be enhanced by staining.

Exercises

1. Taking some samples of materials (wood and metal), which you may find in the Materials Room, write a sentence or two describing the texture and colour of each.
2. Using the samples from (1) above try to scratch and dent the surfaces of each piece and record the hardness of each piece.
3. Test each piece for strength and list the materials you have samples of, in order of compressive strength and tensile strength from the strongest to the weakest.
4. What is elasticity? Name three materials which have good elastic properties and three materials which have poor elastic properties.
5. Investigate various materials' resistance to water. Set up samples and leave them outdoors and check them regularly.
6. Below are a list of materials. State whether each is a good insulator or a poor insulator of: (a) sound (b) heat (c) electricity:

Oak	Foam rubber
Brass	Copper
Acrylic (perspex)	Pine
Steel	Ash
Fibreglass	Mahogany.

7. Explain why it is necessary for chisel blades to be made from hardened steel.

CHAPTER THIRTEEN

METALS

People have used metal as a material for thousands of years.

Stone age	300 000 – 1 900 BC
Bronze age	1900 – 500 BC
Iron age	500 – 51 BC

Metals are found naturally in the earth and on its surface in the form of metal ores.

Some metals, such as gold, copper and silver, have been found in an almost pure state. These were, therefore, among the first metals to be used by humans, who found that when they were hot they could be moulded by using stone hammers. Metals such as gold and silver were used for jewellery. Other metals – iron and copper, for instance – were used for tools and weapons.

Properties of metals:

- Most metals are solids
- Generally good conductors of heat
- Good conductors of electricity
- Are generally quite dense
- Most can be worked and shaped either cold or with heat
- They expand when heated.

Groups of Metals

Metals can be divided into three groups:

- **Ferrous metals**
- **Non-ferrous metals** (pure metal)
- **Alloys** (mixture of metals).

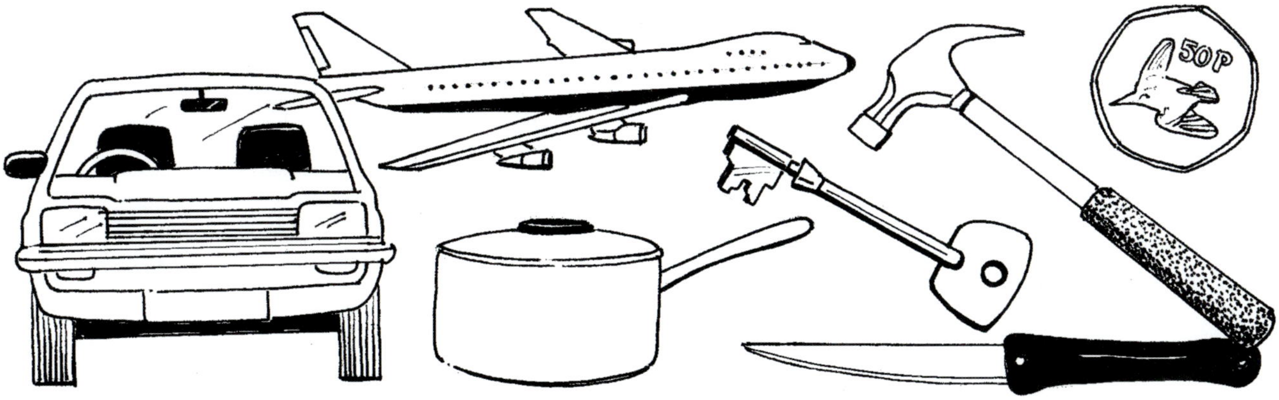

Examples of metals in everyday use

Ferrous metals

Ferrous metals are metals that contain a certain amount of iron. Iron is found naturally as a red-coloured ore. It is processed in a furnace at a smelting works. The iron is extracted in a **blast furnace.** Air is blown into the furnace through a pipe. The iron ore and limestone are placed into the furnace, which is fuelled with coke, a high carbon solid fuel. The iron is melted down and the impurities rise to the top. This **slag**, as it is called, is then drained off. The molten iron beneath the slag is drawn off and cast into moulds. These moulds are called pigs and the iron is known as **pig iron**.

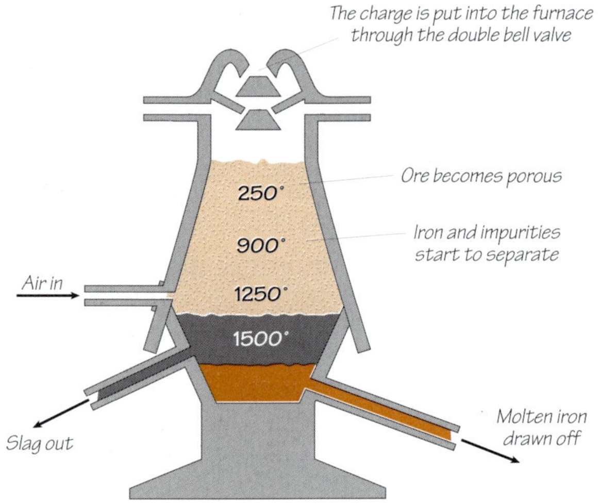

Blast furnace

Cast Iron

Pig iron can be cast into moulds to produce different items, such as gates, railings, etc.

The process is known as casting and is where the name **cast iron** comes from.

Steel

Steel is a mixture of iron and carbon. It is produced in a **basic oxygen furnace**.

In this type of furnace, scrap steel can be melted down and mixed with molten pig iron. A maximum of 30% of scrap can be used.

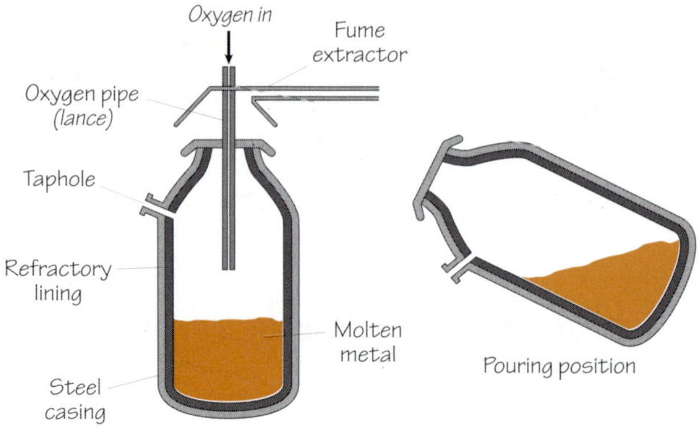

Basic oxygen furnace

Carbon is an element that can exist in many forms. Graphite is its most common form. This is a black, shiny substance which is used in the lead of pencils. It was known as **black lead** long ago and this is where pencil lead got its name. It is carbon which gives steel its strength.

There are other forms of steel, formed by mixing different amounts of carbon with iron, and also by mixing in other metals to form alloys of steel.

High carbon steel (**tool steel**) – used in blades of chisels, planes, etc.

High speed steel is an alloy of steel which is a combination of steel and tungsten (18%). This is a very hard steel.

Stainless steel is another alloy, combining steel with 8% chromium and 18% nickel.

Non-ferrous metals

Non-ferrous metals are metals that contain no iron. There are four main non-ferrous metals in use today. Together with their many alloys, they account for much of the metals used:

- Aluminium
- Copper
- Zinc
- Lead.

Metal	Composition	Properties	Uses
1. **Mild Steel**	Iron with 0.24% carbon	Malleable, ductile metal, rusts easily, has good strength	Used in nails, screws, bolts, nuts – engineering work – sheet, rod and tube form
2. **High carbon steel**	Iron with .7% – 1.5% carbon	Less malleable and ductile, can be hardened and strengthened	Tools, springs and gauges
3. **Cast Iron**	Iron with 3.5% carbon	Brittle, hard surface skin strong on pressure, rusts slowly	Vice and machine bodies, car engines
4. **High speed steel**	Carbon steel with 18% tungsten	Self-hardening and will retain hardness at red heat	Machine, drill lathe tools, cutters
5. **Stainless steel**	Carbon steel with 8% chromium and 18% nickel	Hard tough, highly resistant to wear and corrosion	Cutlery, furniture, frames, jewellery
6. **Aluminium**	Pure metal	Light, soft, ductile, resists corrosion well. Good for casting; good conductor	Cooking items, engine parts
7. **Copper**	Pure metal	Very malleable, ductile, good conductor of heat and electricity, resists corrosion	Water pipes, electrical work, decorative work
8. **Brass**	Copper with 35% zinc	Strong but ductile	Casting, plumbing, fittings, screws, decorative work
9. **Bronze**	Copper with 10% tin	Strong, resists corrosion well and has good wearing properties	Bearings, gears, machine parts, ship fittings
10. **Lead**	Pure metal	Heavy but soft, malleable, resists corrosion by water and acid	Plumbing work, roof covering, containers

Aluminium

Aluminium is the most plentiful metal on earth. It is mined in the form of **bauxite**, the aluminium ore. This is then refined to a white powder called **alumina**. Alumina is produced in Aughinish Island, on the Shannon Estuary in county Limerick.

The production of aluminium is done in two stages; the first is the production of alumina, the second is **electrolysis**. Here, the aluminium and oxygen are separated from the alumina by a powerful electric current. Much aluminium is used in this pure form, but more is alloyed with other metals such as copper, magnesium and manganese. There are more than seventy aluminium alloys in common use today. They are used in electric wires, pots, pans, windows, doors, cars, boats, aerials, drink cans and even spacecrafts.

Copper

Copper is reddish brown in colour and can be highly polished. It is a pure metal. Copper is a good conductor of heat and electricity and therefore is widely used in electrical cables. It is easily worked (cut and filed) which makes it highly suitable for a wide variety of uses, particularly in project work. It is resistant to corrosion, which is why it is used in water pipes and also on the roofs of some buildings.

Alloys of copper

Brass

Brass is an alloy of copper produced by mixing copper with zinc. It is a yellowish metal, but the precise colour depends on the amount of zinc. Brass is widely used for ornamental work – door handles and letter boxes, it is also used for making screws and other fittings that are used in damp conditions, since brass is resistant to corrosion. Brass can be highly polished and is very attractive.

Bronze

Bronze is another alloy of copper, produced when copper is mixed with tin. It is a strong metal which resists corrosion well. Bronze is used widely for casting statues, machine parts and ship fittings.

Zinc

Zinc is a dull silvery metal which is used in alloys with copper to produce brass. It is used also for coating steel to prevent rusting; this process is called **galvanising**.

Lead

Lead is a dull, grey metal. It is very heavy, soft and malleable. Lead is used in car batteries and in the construction industry (for gutters and around chimneys to keep out water). It does not corrode.

Working with metals

Metals cannot easily be marked out with a pencil because of their hard shiny surfaces, so other ways of drawing lines, curves and joints on the surfaces must be used. The processes for making these lines are very similar to those used for marking timber.

Some of the more common tools are:

Scriber

Used for scratching the surface of a metal, instead of a pencil.

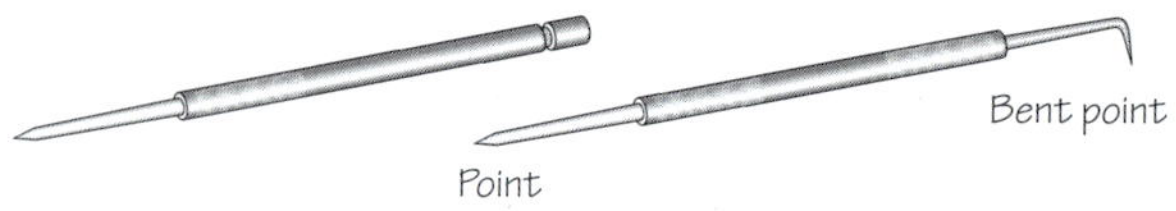

Dot punch

Used to punch small dots in the surface of metal through which lines can be drawn.

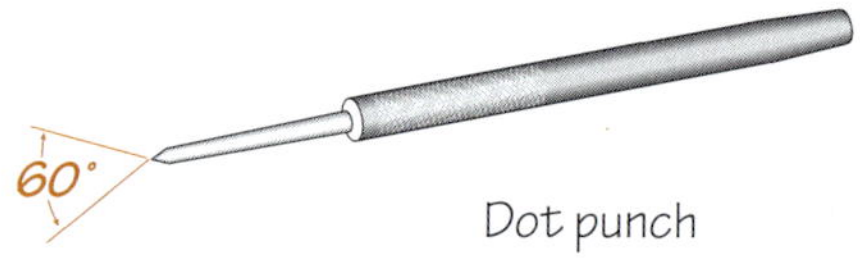

Centre punch

Used to make a small hole in the surface of the metal before drilling so that the drill bit will not slip. It ensures that the hole is accurately drilled.

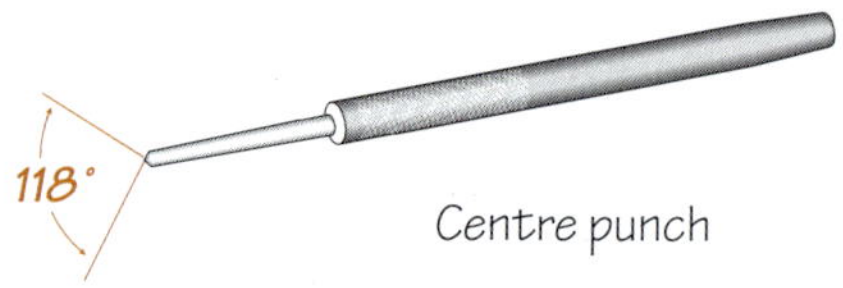

Hacksaws

Used to cut small sections of metal.

Hacksaw

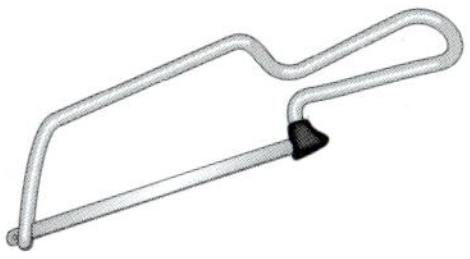
Junior hacksaw

Snips

Used for cutting sheet metal.

Files

Various types – used to shape edges of metal making them smooth and square. Also used for working with plastics.

Beaten metal work

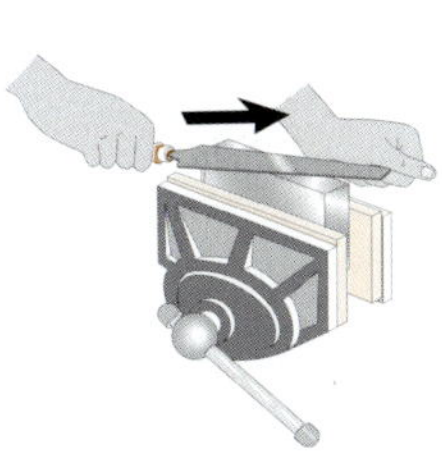
Cross-filing

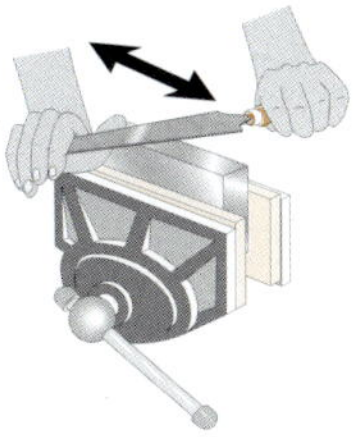
Draw-filing using a single cut file. This removes cross-filing marks.

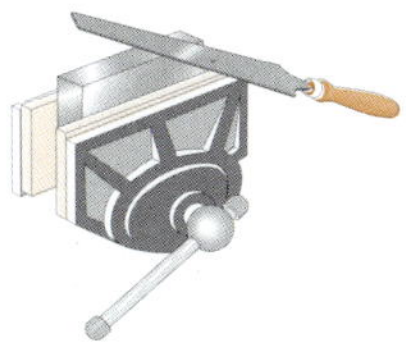
Deburring removes slight ragged edges at the edges of the piece

Decorative shapes can be formed in sheet metal such as gold, silver and copper brass sheet. A cold hammering process is used. Bowls and other decorative shapes can be formed in copper sheet and brass sheet by this process. However, these metals will begin to crack as they are being worked, unless they are heated from time to time to allow the grain of the metal to reform. This is called **annealing**. The metal is heated to a dull red and then is allowed to cool slowly. Copper can be quenched in water, but brass may fracture if it is quenched. Always use a **tongs** when handling hot metals.

> **BEWARE!** **All sheet metals should be handled with care. Protective gloves should be worn at all times because sheet metal often has sharp edges**

The heating process leaves a light scale of oxide on the surface of brass and copper. It can be removed with diluted sulphuric acid (**pickling**). Safety precautions should be taken when using acids in case they splash; always wear protective gloves and safety glasses.

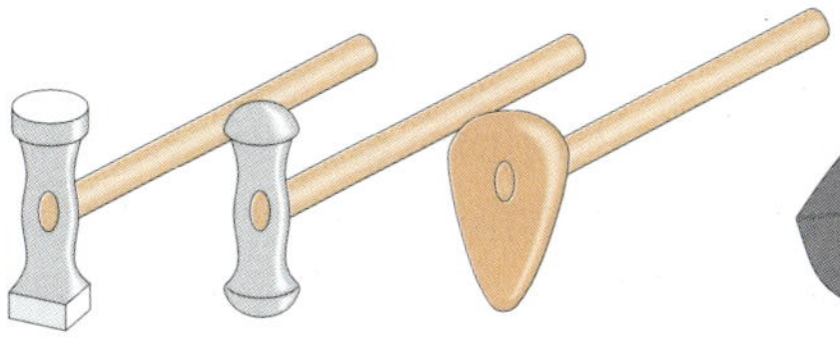
Hammer and mallets

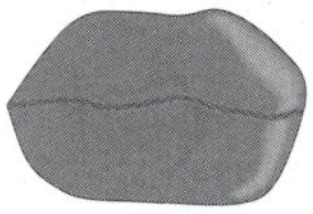
Leather sandbag

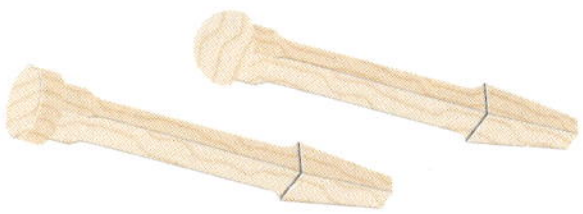
Stakes

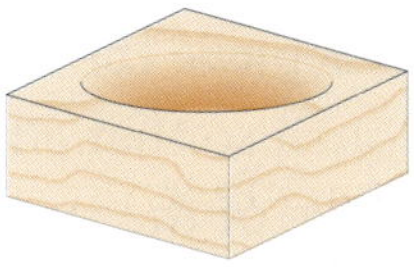
Wooden former block

Equipment for beaten metalwork

First, the metal sheet is hollowed or sunk to form the basic curved shape. This is done with a wooden block or a sandbag and a mallet. Once the basic shape has been formed, the metal bowl can be **planished**, to give a final finish.

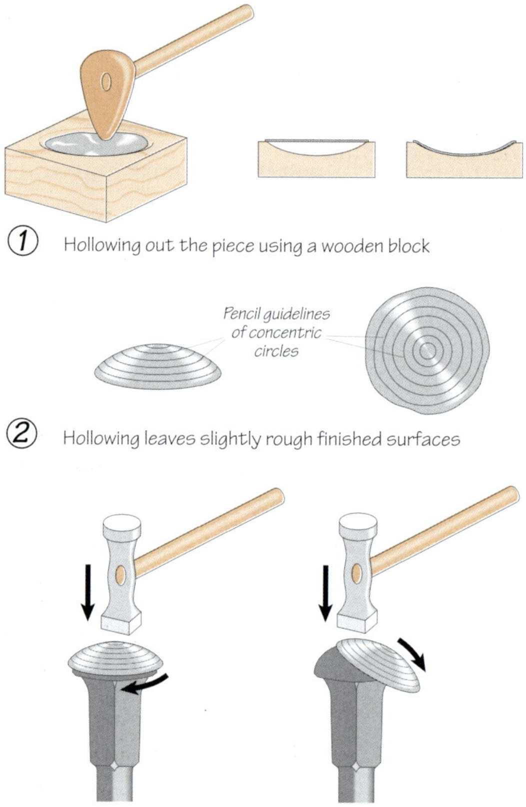

Hollowing and planishing process

Planishing

The rough shape is formed more accurately into a true curve. It is finely finished and hardened by using a planishing hammer over the metal. Gentle hammering from the centre outwards, using pre-masked pencil guidelines, will enable you to achieve the final shape. The workpiece is positioned so that all the hammering is done at the centre of the stake.

The job is finished by *truing-up* the rim or edges of the work by file first and finally with emery paper.

Joining metals

Metals may be joined in many ways. They can be joined with mechanical fasteners such as rivets, nuts, bolts and screws, or by bonding with adhesives. They can also be welded or soldered. Examples of how metals can be joined to each other and to other materials are shown below.

Ways in which metals are joined and fixed

Metal finishes

Metals, like other materials, will decay over time. They get dirty and scratched; some are corroded by rain and other elements. Many metals we use are not very attractive. Metals are often finished to give them a protective coating (from rust) and to give them a decorative finish. Metals can be finished in three different ways depending on the metal and its final use. These finishes are:

- Polishing – for quality metals in decorative situations
- Painting - general finishing of steel, etc
- Coating – protective coating of non-corroding metal (galvanising) or plastic.

Oxidation

Oxidation or **rust** is the process of corroding metal. Rust is formed when oxygen in the air combines with the surface of the metal. It is a chemical reaction. Rust is an oxide of iron which forms on the surfaces of steel and iron; it corrodes the metal and will gradually eat its way through the material. Most other metals, such as copper, aluminium, zinc, lead and brass are not as badly affected by oxidation because the oxide forms a protective coat. This is the green **patina** of copper, for example.

Surface finishes

The surfaces and edges of metals must be finished with a file and emery board to give a smooth, well-finished surface. These surfaces are cleaned of dirt and grease before a finish can be applied or ready for polishing.

Polishing

Polishing can be done by hand or machine, depending on how detailed the work is. Hand-polishing is used for fine detailed work. A cloth and polishing compound such as *Brasso* can be used.

> **Note:** When using different compounds always follow the directions and warnings on the label carefully.

Polishing by machine can be easily done with a mop or brush which can be attached to a spindle (on a lathe) or can be obtained as an attachment for an electric drill.

Various mops can be bought which are made from different fabrics – felt, calico or swansdown – each gives a high quality finish.

If a mop is attached to a drill, the piece of work must be firmly held in a vice. If the spindle mop is attached to the polishing machine, the piece of work is held firmly and pressed against the revolving mop.

Polished metal becomes hot with the machine's friction. Use gloves to pick-up the work. Do not use an apron or a piece of loose clothing because these could get caught in the machine.

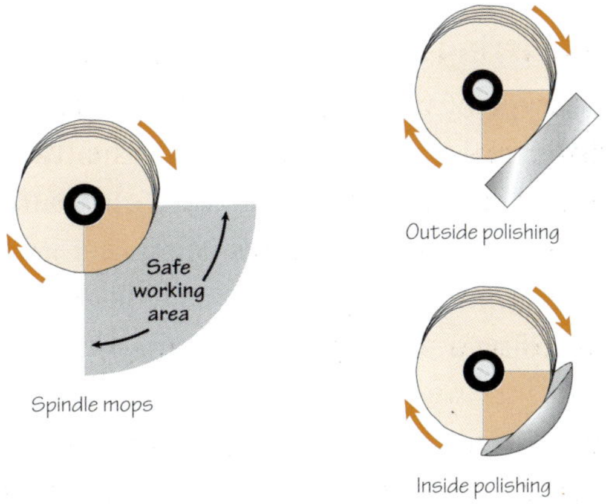

Polishing metals by machine

Painting

Metal is painted in a similar way to wood. Ferrous metals are often painted because they rust easily, and paint gives good protection against oxidation.

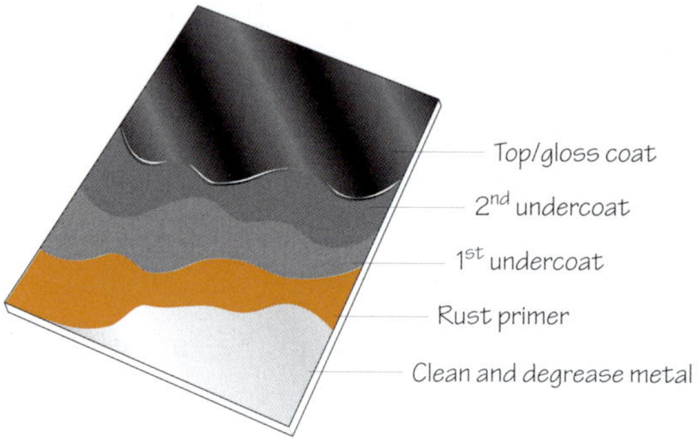

Painting metal

Dust, rust and grease are first cleaned off the metal surface. Then the first coat, a special rust priming coat, is applied. When this is dry, one or sometimes two undercoats are applied. The finishing coat is painted on when the undercoat is dry.

Although paint will eventually allow rust to develop, it has the advantage that colours can be used and they can be changed each time you have to paint.

Lacquering

This is a type of paint finish which is applied to polished metal. It is decorative and usually transparent. Lacquering allows the full beauty of the polished metal to shine through. Before the lacquer is applied, the metal surface is de-greased, using a white spirit, and then dried.

Plastic coating

Metals can also be treated with a coating of plastic. This often allows bright colours to be used.

The method uses a thermoplastic powder, such as polystyrene. The metal is heated in an oven to a temperature of about 180°C. The metal is then picked up with a tongs and dipped into a container of the powder, which melts onto the metal surface. The workpiece is briefly reheated to ensure that the powder has completely fused to the surface of the metal.

Metal coating

Metal objects can be coated with another metal by one of two processes, dipping or electroplating.

Dipping

The piece of metal is dipped into a bath of molten metal such as zinc. This is generally used as a means of weatherproofing a metal that corrodes easily. Galvanising is the process of dipping steel into zinc to protect it. It is used on nails, gates, dustbins and corrugated roofing.

Electroplating

This process gives a protective or decorative coat to a base metal. It is used to coat cheaper metals with thin layers of more expensive metals (gold). The process uses a direct electrical current. It is an expensive process and is used on very fine work. The work must be very well finished because the electroplating process will highlight scratches and other flaws in it.

Enamelling

Enamelling is a method of coating metal with a film of melted glass; the glass can be obtained in powder form. It is placed on the surface of the metal (different designs can be made using various colours of enamel). The metal is then very carefully put in a small kiln or oven and heated to a temperature of 750°C. The glass will melt and flow slightly on the metal. It is then taken out of the kiln and allowed to cool. This is a very effective finish and protects the metal.

After cleaning the adhesive is applied with a brush

The enamel is then applied through a sieve

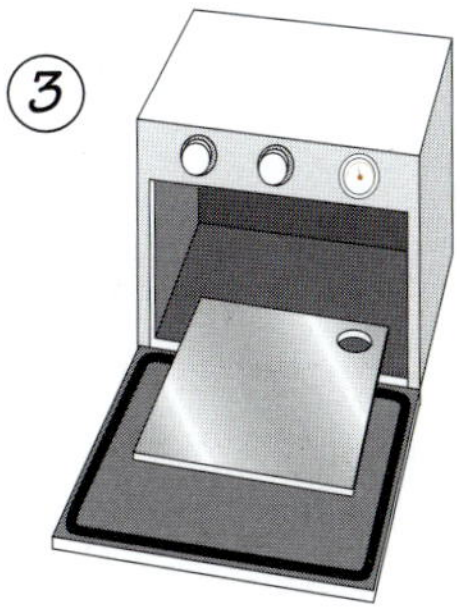

Heating enamel in a kiln to a temperature of 750°C

Enamelling

BEWARE! Always wear protective gloves when handling chemicals and hot metal

Preparation of the work is very important. The metal piece must be cleaned in an acid bath, and then scoured with a pumice. The surface must be kept clean, so take care not to touch it with your fingers. A thin layer of adhesive is spread over the surface, this helps to bond the metal and the enamel, but it is burned off during the heating process.

Different colours can be added by blanking out some parts with paper on a stencil and sieving on the colour after adhesive has been applied. The stencil is then removed and the work heated, allowing the enamel to melt and flow together.

Enamelling metal is very useful for making small items of jewellery or decorating a bowl or cup. It is also used to protect steel items such as lockers and washing machines.

BEWARE! Always wear protective clothing and eye protection when handling chemicals

Etching

Etching is a method of producing a textured design on a polished surface of metal by using different acids.

Acid will attack any metal exposed to it, gradually eating deeper and deeper into the surface. If parts of the surface are covered to separate the surface from the acid, many patterns can be designed. Wax may be used as a separating medium – varnish, candle wax or paraffin wax are all used.

When the acid has finished working, the piece is rinsed under running water. Then the wax or varnish is removed with a detergent or solvent and the piece is cleaned again. The piece can be repolished and finally lacquered.

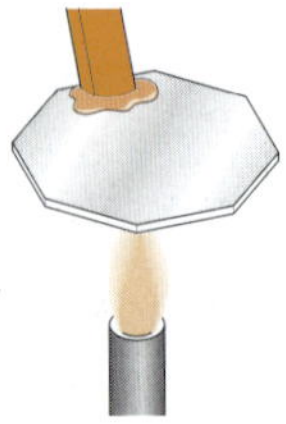

①
First the wax is melted onto the work surface. Both sides and edges must be covered.

②
Design is traced onto the hard wax surface using a pencil and carbon paper.

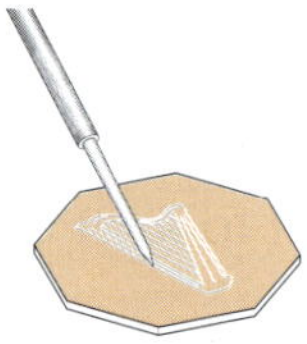

③
The wax is scratched through to the metal surface using a sharp pointed tool such as a scriber. This is used for lines but larger areas may be exposed by scraping off the wax.

④
Work placed into dish with acid. The acid corrodes the exposed metal surface.

The etching process

Exercises

1. Explain the difference between ferrous and non-ferrous metals.
2. List three ferrous and three non-ferrous metals and describe a use of each.
3. An 'alloy' is _____________. Finish this sentence.
4. Give three examples of an alloy and say where each might be used.
5. List five properties which are common to most metals.
6. Test various pieces of metal for corrosion by placing them in jars of damp cotton wool. After a couple of weeks, report on your findings. Nails, screws and metal offcuts can be used.
7. Describe briefly how steel is made.
8. What ferrous metal is used for the blades of woodworking tools and explain why.
9. Explain the following :

Enamelling	Soldering
Bronze	Etching
Lacquering	Galvanising.

10. The sketch of a design for a candle stand is shown below. It includes a piece of metal (A) which protects the wooden part (B) from hot wax. Name the process used to make the metal piece and suggest a suitable metal which could be used for this piece.

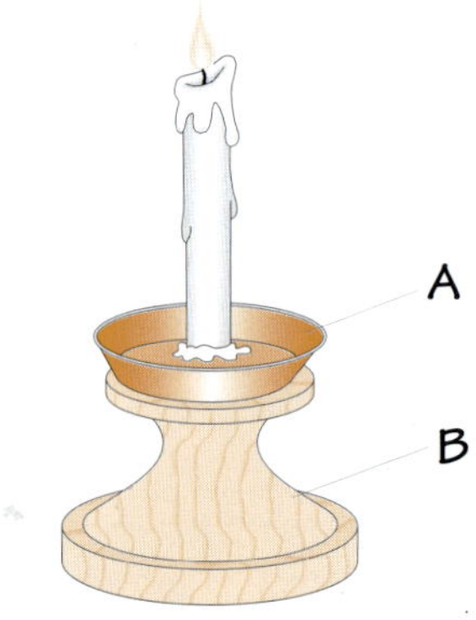

CHAPTER FOURTEEN

PLASTICS

Plastics are all around us in the western world. If there were no plastics, just think how different the world would be: certain bottles, handles, chairs, car dashboards, the casing on all kinds of electrical items, such as televisions, videos, computers and stereos, would vanish. Plastics are processed from their raw form by a variety of methods, which provide us with so many different items from each type of plastic. Plastics are useful, versatile and durable materials, but they also have the disadvantage that they do not readily decompose which makes the dumping of plastic products a major environmental problem.

Types of plastic

Plastics come in many forms but we can classify them easily into two groups:

- Thermosetting plastics
- Thermoplastics.

Thermosetting plastic

This type of plastic can be heated to form it into a shape but this can be done only once. When the plastic cools and sets, it cannot be resoftened again by re-heating; the chemical change that takes place when the plastic is heated cannot be

reversed. Thermosetting plastic is very useful where an item – an ashtray or a handle for a saucepan – may have to withstand high temperatures.

Thermoplastics

Unlike thermosetting plastics, thermoplastics can be softened and reshaped by re-heating. There are many different thermoplastics. Each type is softened at a different temperature. Some thermoplastics can withstand temperatures over 100°C, although most will become soft at temperatures lower than 100°C.

Properties of plastics

Plastics have advantages over many natural materials like wood, stone and metal. There are many different types of plastic, some are hard, some are soft, some are brittle while others are flexible. Some plastics are resistant to high temperatures and chemicals – most are good electrical insulators. They can be moulded quite easily into complex shapes. A jug kettle is made from plastic, which must resist high temperatures, be water resistant and also not conduct electricity. The following is a list of the most common plastics and their properties.

> People do not generally call plastics in everyday use by their scientific names. They are simply referred to as plastic. It is important for us to know some of the more common plastics and where they are used. See page 79.

Sources of plastics

Plastics come from two main sources:

- Natural sources – plastics such as cellophane and celluloid are obtained from natural sources, such as oil, plants and trees
- Synthetic plastics – man-made.

Natural plastic

Rubber is a natural plastic substance. Natural rubber comes from the latex of rubber trees. Latex is a milky fluid which is drained from the trees and then processed to form the rubber we know. The rubber tree is a native of the forests of the Amazon Basin in Brazil, but natural rubber trees are grown as a crop in south-east Asia (Malaysia, Indonesia). Rubber was named when it was first used to erase pencil marks in the eighteenth century.

Rubber coming from rubber tree

In 1823, Charles Macintosh used rubber to make clothes water-proof. This is when the *Macintosh*, a waterproof raincoat, was born. However, there were problems with rubber. It got hard when cold and became sticky in warm weather and so the material perished. These difficulties earned rubber a very bad name. Charles Goodyear found a way to make rubber far more durable using a process called **vulcanisation**. This process is still used today to make car tyres.

Rubber is different from other materials because of its elasticity. It will often stretch up to thirteen times its original length.

Plastic Thermoplastics	Trade Name	Properties	Uses
Polyvinyl Chloride	(PVC) Corvic, Welvic	Strong, good chemical resistance, abrasion resistance, does not absorb moisture	Rigid form: pipes, plumbing, corrugated roofing Flexible form: textiles, packaging, upholstery
Acrylic (Polymethyl Methacrylate)	Perspex, Diakon	Many colours are available, hard, rigid, transmits light well	Display signs, cases, jewellery, furniture
Nylon (polyamide)	Kapton, Maranyl	Resistant to high and low temperatures, tough and durable, chemical resistance is good	Washers, bearings, bristles, clothing, stockings and upholstery
Polystyrene	Lustnex, Styron	Light, buoyant, good insulator. Durable, resists breakage, resistant to low temperature	Insulation, model-making, packaging
Polythene or Polyethylene	Rigidex visqueen	Transparent, but takes colour well	Bags, bottles, buckets, food containers, toys
Thermosetting plastics			
Phenolic resin	Bakelite	Inexpensive, hard, rigid and strong, black and brown in colour	Handles, electric appliances, electric switch covers
Polyester resin	Various	Good surface hardness, can be formed without heat and pressure	Light switches, used in GRP products, such as boat hulls
Epoxy resin	Araldite	Good adhesive properties, high strength with reinforcement, low shrinkage	Bonding agent, laminating, surface coating
Polyurethane	Suprasec Daltolac	Weather resistant, resistant to tearing	Floats, insulation materials (rigid) upholstery, mattresses and paint, (flexible)
Urea – formaldehyde	Aerolite	Good adhesive, hard, stiff	Adhesives, electrical fittings, laminating timber

Synthetic rubbers were developed during World War II because it was difficult to obtain rubber from Malaysia. A number of synthetic rubbers are now in use.

Synthetic rubbers

Polychlorophrene or Noeprene

This is used in wet suits and buildings. It is foam-like and very resistant to flames and solvents because of the presence of chlorine in its structure.

Silicone rubber

This rubber is unique since it contains no carbon in its central chain. It is built around silicon and oxygen atoms. Silicone rubber is resistant to chemicals and is very useful in high temperatures up to 300°C, where other rubbers break down.

These synthetic rubbers are synthetic plastics, which are formed by a process of combining many chemical compounds into long chain molecules called **polymers** (polymer = having many units). These polymers can have between 200 and 2 000 units. The main raw material is carbon in the form of crude oil or coal. The process of making these molecules or polymers is called **polymerisation**. The polymers are obtained in raw form as resins or granules.

Plastic litter

Plastics and the environment

People all over the world are more environmentally conscious today. Plastics are continuing to have a major impact on our environment. Plastics litter our streets, parks, fields and beaches, causing danger to wildlife and nature. Plastics do not decay or break down as easily as other materials, and so we must be careful how we dispose of them. For example, burning plastics can cause a build up of poisonous chemicals in the air.

Plastics are being developed which will break down and decay after a time. We must dispose properly of all the plastics we use and recycle them, when possible.

Working with plastics

The plastics available in schools are generally in solid form. With a number of simple tools and processes they can be quite easily worked. They can be cut using saws; filed and planed, and their edges can be sanded smooth. Usually, only surfaces which are cut or worked in some way need filing and finishing, as most plastics already have a smooth surface finish.

Cutting plastic

Plastic is generally obtained in solid form as rods, sheets or rolls. It must then be cut to size. Thin sheets of plastic can easily be cut with a scissors or a sharp marking knife, and a rule is necessary to obtain a straight edge.

Sheets between 1mm and 10mm thick, such as acrylic, can be cut by a hand saw or a machine, such as the band saw and scroll saw. When sawing, the blade should be kept at a low angle to stop damage to the sheet of the materials.

Cutting acrylic with a hand saw

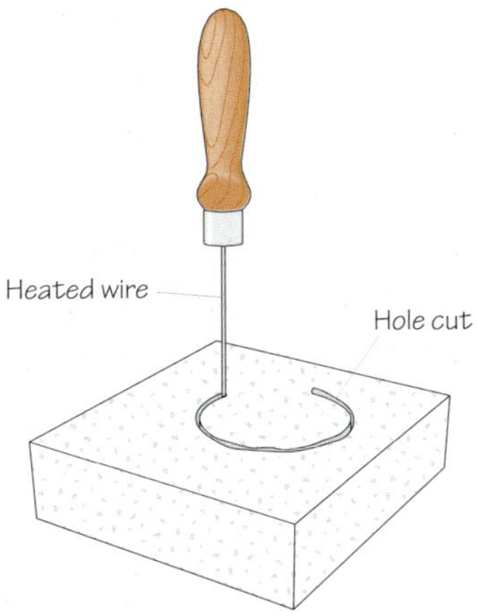

Polystyrene can be cut using a hot wire cutter

Polystyrene can be cut with a special heated wire cutter (rather like a scroll saw). The wire is heated electrically – when the polystyrene is pressed against it the heat melts the plastic – giving a clean cutting action. This is very useful for cutting shapes for model-making. Similarly, holes can be cut out with a hot wire rod. The rod is heated over a flame. When the piece of metal gets cool, it is simply re-heated.

While holding plastics in a vice, the surfaces of the piece can easily be scratched. These surfaces can be protected by placing smooth pieces of wood in the vice as shown below.

Piece being held in vice

Filing and planing

Once the workpiece has been cut or shaped with a saw, the edges of the plastic must be finished with a plane or file.

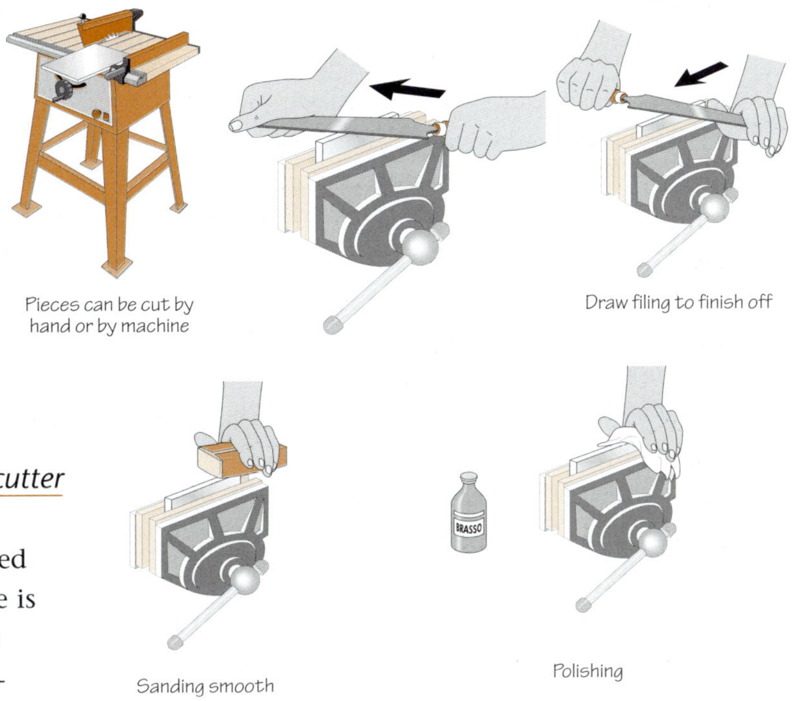

Stages of finishing a piece of acrylic

The work must be held low in the vice to secure the piece and to support it while it is being worked on. A block plane is most suitable because its blade is set at a very low angle; which allows for a slicing cut. The plane is held at an angle to the piece, as shown here.

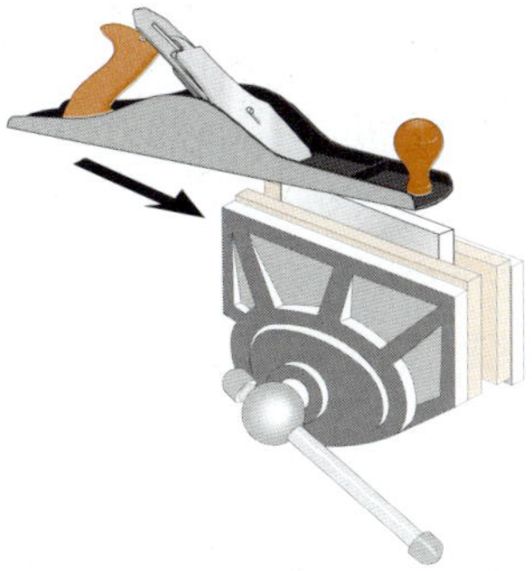

Plane at an angle to piece

A file can be used in much the same way to bring a piece down to a line. This is done in two stages, firstly, the piece is cross filled down to the line, then it is draw filed to remove file marks. The edge can then be sanded smooth and finally polished.

Drilling plastic

Plastics can be drilled to form holes to take joints, screws, nuts, bolts and other fittings. The ordinary twist drill bit can be used. This is the same type of bit used to drill holes in metal and wood. However, the twist drill bit must be modified slightly in order to cut plastic. The tip is re-ground to give a lower angle to the tip. This modification is necessary to prevent the tip breaking through the thin sheets of plastic, before the full cutting edge has made contact with the face.

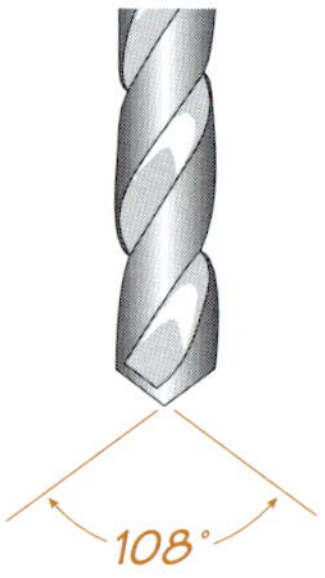

Drill bit modified

When drilling plastic the speed of the drill bit must be quite fast to prevent chipping. However, the piece should be drilled slowly (the feed rate) to allow the drill bit to cut properly. A waste piece should be placed underneath to prevent the bench or drill press being damaged, and to keep the piece firm while it is being drilled.

Bending

Thermoplastics, particularly acrylic, are very useful for projectwork. Because acrylic can be re-heated with no ill-effect, it can be shaped into straight-forward or complex patterns by simple but precise heating. When the acrylic cools, it hardened into the desired shape. It is necessary to clearly plan the shape required. Draw out a development of the shape on the plastic sheet. The basic stages of producing a small item from bent acrylic can be seen overleaf.

Strip heater

There are two ways of heating the acrylic sheet:

- Strip heating (localised, along the bend)
- Oven heating (heats the whole piece).

With the strip heater the plastic sheet is being heated along the bend line until soft, allowing the piece to be bent. When more complex forms need to be made, the piece can be ovenheated in an oven to soften the whole piece, so that no uneven stresses are built up in the piece.

Note: do not overheat the acrylic because the surface will bubble. Remember to allow for the bend in the length of the piece by adding the thickness of the sheet to the length. Remember to wear protective gloves and goggles when handling hot materials.

BEWARE!

When handling perspex care must be taken not be put too much pressure on the plastic, as it might crack or splinter

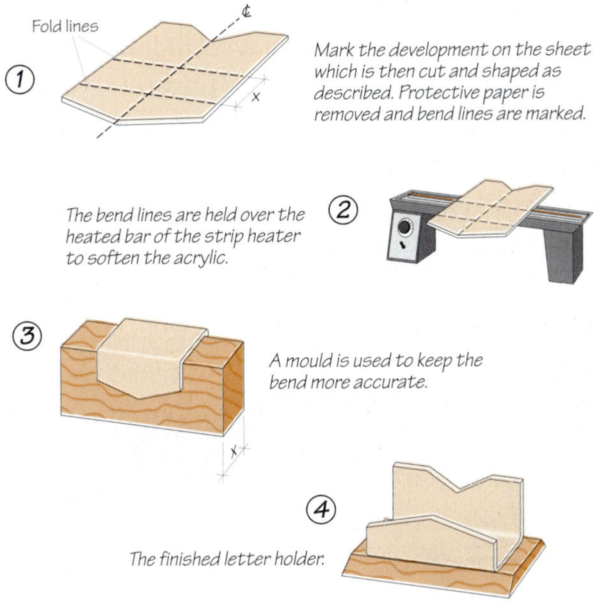

Making a simple bending project

- Mark the development on the sheet. This is then cut and shaped as described above. Remove the protective paper and mark the lines where the bends are to be done on the piece
- Hold the marked bend line over the heated bar of the strip heater until the piece can be bent
- A mould can be used to keep the bend more accurate.

Overheating of a piece in oven

Formers

A **former** is a shape around which the plastic is moulded. Wood is an excellent material for making formers. It does not cool the plastic before it has had a chance to be shaped, and wood is very easy to mould into shape. Formers and jigs ensure that shapes can be accurately copied many times. Allowances should be made when bending acrylic, as it tends to spring back slightly to its original shape on cooling.

Shaping plastic

Plastics can also be shaped in other ways:

- Casting
- Moulding
- Forming.

Casting

Casting is the term used for pouring plastics in liquid form into a prepared mould, where it sets to form a complicated shape, which is an exact copy of the mould. There are two forms of casting: **tray casting** and **cold casting**.

Tray casting

This is a simple form of casting, using thermoplastic powders such as polythene. A shallow metal tray serves as a mould in which panels or tiles of plastic are formed. The plastic powder is placed into the tray and heated in an oven, where it melts and forms the shape of the tray. With thermoplastic, other plastic shapes can be placed on top of the base tile and re-melted to give a design of different colours.

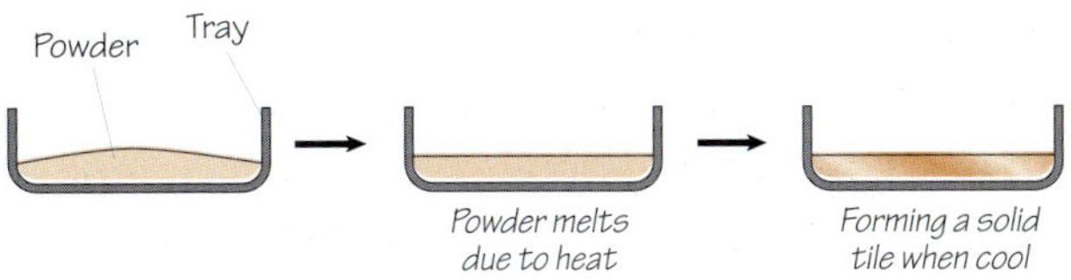

Cold casting

This method of casting uses thermosetting plastics in the form of liquid resins (usually polyester resin or epoxy resin). They are mixed and poured into the moulds, using hardeners. **Catalysts** are added to speed up the setting time. Once the plastic has hardened, it cannot be changed or worked by heat.

Moulds can be made from lots of different materials, such as wax or plaster. Other materials used include paraffin wax, aluminium foil, rubber and glass. Polystyrene is the only material that cannot be used since the resin dissolves it.

Moulding

There are many ways that plastics can be made or forced into moulds. In all cases, moulds must be very accurately made and then thousands of the same particular item can be produced accurately and easily.

Injection moulding

The liquid plastic is forced into the mould under pressure. A wide range of thermoplastics can be used; polythene, PVC., nylon, polystyrene. When the plastic cools it can be taken out of the mould. Buckets, bowls, toys and safety helmets are made in this way.

Blow moulding

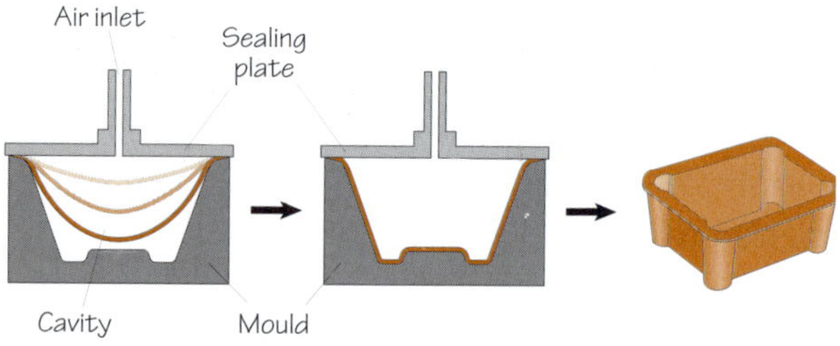

Blow moulding

Here compressed air is used to force the plastic sheet, softened by heat into a mould, rather like blowing up a balloon. Industry uses this type of moulding to make plastic bottles and containers.

Forming

Press forming

Here two formers are used. The softened plastic sheet is pressed between them to form the shape.

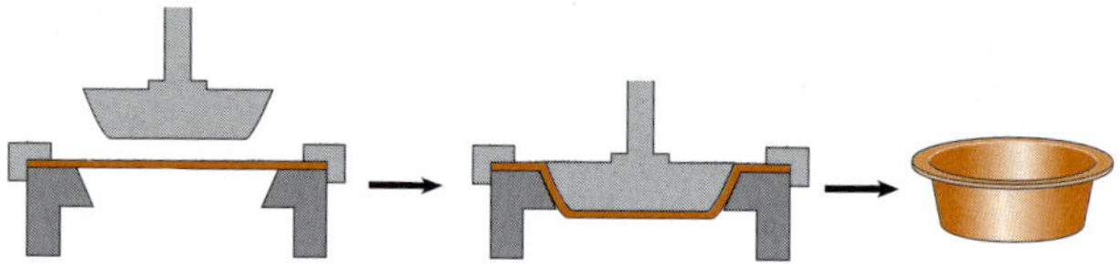

Press forming

Vacuum forming

Very complex shapes can be formed with this process. A thin sheet of thermoplastic is heated until it is soft. It is then drawn over or into a shaped mould, using a vacuum. Trays, dishes, masks and relief maps can be made in this way. This method usually uses thin sheets of thermoplastic.

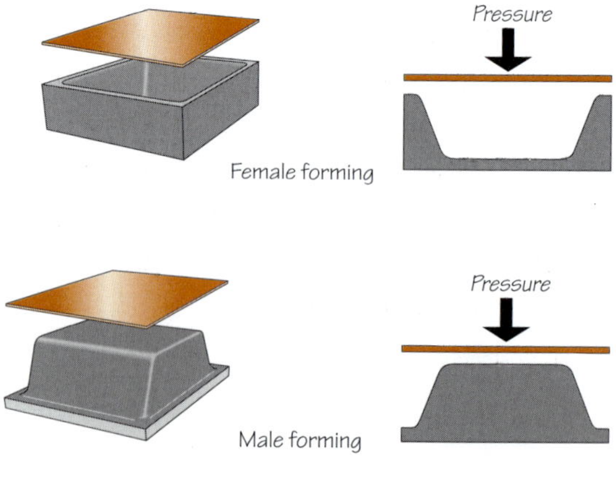

Vacuum forming

Vacuum former

Glass reinforced plastic (GRP)

Polyester resins can be strengthened with elastic strands of glassfibre. The material is formed into a laminate which can then be moulded. Carbon fibre can be used and is a much stronger form of reinforcement. However, it is more expensive.

Glass reinforced plastic is used widely for the hulls of boats and canoes, car and bus bodies, moulded seats, and even tennis and squash racquets. It is an extremely strong, tough, durable and hard wearing material.

Exercises

1. Make a list of all the items in the MTW room which are made from plastics.
2. Make a list of things that we use daily which are made from plastic. Then suggest what materials were used to make these items in the past. Can you suggest reasons why plastics are used today instead?
3. What are the two main groups of plastic and give the main difference between them?
4. Using sketches to illustrate your answer, describe two common methods of shaping plastic.
5. When a piece of plastic (acrylic) has been cut to size and shape, describe, using sketches, how you would get a good finish on the edges of the piece.
6. Using plastic and wood, design an item which will hold a regular sized photograph and display it in a decorative way.
7. Design a lamp with a lampshade and holder to be made from acrylic sheet, and which can be attached to a wall or clipped onto a shelf. It is to take a standard 60 watt bulb.
8. The drawing shows a bed tray with a perspex (acrylic) top and laminated bent wood legs. Describe with the aid of sketches how you would make the perspex top.

9. Identify which of these plastics are thermoplastic and thermosetting:

Acrylic	PVC	Nylon
Bakelite	Polyester	Polythene.

10. Shown in the sketch is a simple photograph holder made from acrylic:

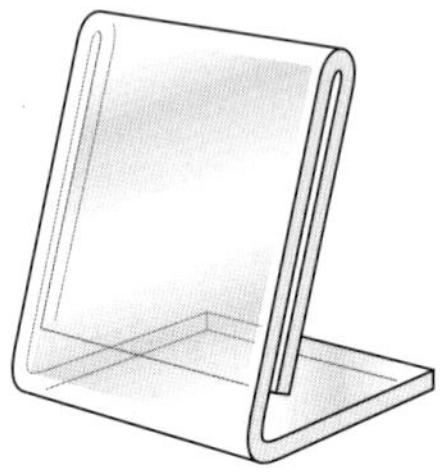

Pictorial

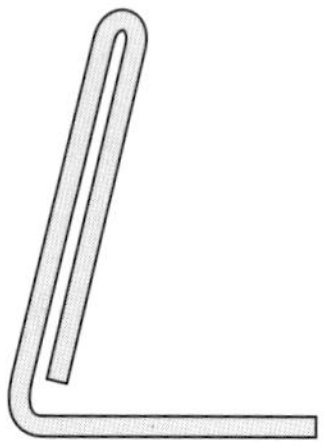

End view

(a) On square grid paper, draw the development or pattern that would need to be marked out on the acrylic sheet in order to produce this holder.

(b) With the aid of sketches, describe how you would cut out and form the photograph holder.

CHAPTER FIFTEEN

OTHER MATERIALS

There are many useful materials available which can be used in projectwork. When choosing a material for a particular part of a project you must choose a material which both looks well and functions well.

Textiles

Textiles or cloth materials are very useful when making projects. Cloth materials can be used to add colour and comfort to chairs, stools, jewellery, boxes and many other items. For example, cloth is used on a snooker table for colour and to give a uniformly smooth surface for the balls to travel on. Foam is used for the snooker table cushions, net for the pockets, and slate is put under the table's cloth surface to provide a steady level bed for the balls. The snooker table is a very good example of using many different materials to achieve an effective result.

There are a variety of different cloths and materials on the market. Information about them can be found by inquiring in your local fabric shop. It is worth a visit there to see the many different fabrics and other materials available.

Foam

There are different foams available; sizes and densities vary. They are used for padding on the seats of stools and chairs, and are easily cut with a scissors or knife, but be careful not to cut your fingers while using these tools.

BEWARE!

Make sure when you are buying foam that it has passed the fire safety regulations

Leather

Leather comes naturally from processing the hide (skin) of animals such as cattle, goats and pigs. Leather is used for clothing, shoes and bags, as well as for upholstery (furniture covering). Because leather is expensive, leatherette, a form of imitation leather, was developed. It consists of a cloth-backed plastic which has a natural leather-like pattern pressed into it (embossed). It can be obtained in a range of colours and grades. Leatherette can be glued to timber surfaces with a contact adhesive or PVA adhesive, or it can be fixed with staples or tacks.

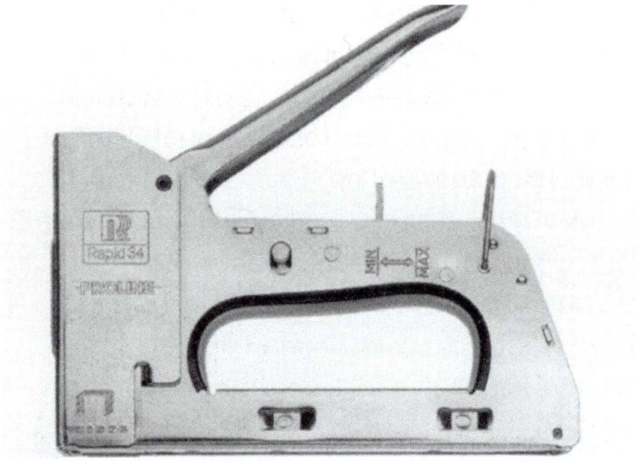

The staple gun can be used to fix textiles to wood

Cloth

There is a huge variety of different types of fabric, easily available in most fabric shops. They come in a wide range of patterns and colours. Some are light fabrics and others are meant for heavier use, such as the material for a seat covering.

Baize

Baize is a red or green cloth which is like felt. It is used to cover snooker tables and as lining for the inside of jewellery boxes. It is also used to cover the tops of card tables. It provides a soft, unglossy surface and gives protection to delicate items such as jewellery. It can easily be applied, using a thin layer of contact adhesive, such as bondex. It can also be bought on a roll with a self adhesive backing.

Cords, wools and rope

There is a large variety of decorative cords and rope on the market which can be put to good use in projectwork: handles for drawers, decorative edgings – your imagination is the only limit. Fishing line can be used in mobiles or for hanging up pictures. It is strong, light and almost colourless and so it can be hidden. Wool can be used to represent hair or an animal's tail. The strands of wool are clumped together, trimmed and attached to the timber by a staple or similar fixing.

When using adhesives on materials always test a little piece first on a spare piece of the material, to gauge the suitability of the adhesive.

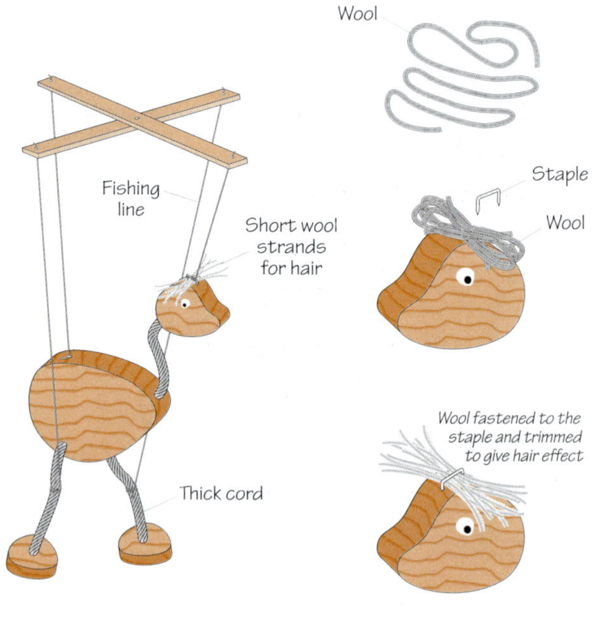

Use of cords & wool in projectwork

Glass

Glass is a ceramic material which is made by mixing sand, soda ash, limestone, feldspar cullet (broken glass) at high temperatures (1200°C – 1600°C). The liquid which is produced is then formed into sheets of various sizes. Glass of different qualities and properties can be obtained by treating these sheets using various processes.

Sheet glass

This glass is 'drawn' and is then cut into large sheets. The two surfaces of the sheet are not quite parallel or flat. This results in a slight distortion of vision, but is satisfactory for most uses.

Plate glass

The surfaces of this glass are ground and polished so that they are perfectly flat and parallel. Plate glass is used in high quality windows.

Stained glass lampshade

The surfaces of glass can be patterned which prevents you from seeing through it, this is called **obscured glass**. It is used for windows in bathrooms and door panels where privacy and decoration are important. Glass can be **reinforced** with wire which adds strength to the sheet. Glass can also be **toughened** so that if it breaks, it will shatter into very small fragments, which are less dangerous than shards. This glass is used in the windows of cars. **Stained glass** of different colours is also very popular being used in lamp shades and glass panel for doors, etc. It can be used to make beautiful patterns. It could easily be incorporated into projectwork.

Ceramics

Ceramics is the name given to a large range of compounds that lie between non-metals and metals. These include clays, glass, cement and gems. Ceramics are strong in compression but are weak in tension. They can be quite brittle and are prone to cracks.

Ceramic materials

Ceramics are divided into two groups: crystalline and non-crystalline. **Crystalline** ceramics include diamonds and other gems and semi-conductors which are used in electronics. **Non-crystalline** ceramics include clay and ceramic tiles used for pottery flooring, etc. Ceramic tiles are useful for projects and can be incorporated into items like table tops and pot stands as they resist heat well and can be easily cleaned.

Pot stand made with wood and ceramic tile

Exercises

1. Describe briefly how glass is made.
2. What are ceramics?
3. Collect some samples of different types of glass, textiles and ceramics and suggest where each might be used in projectwork.
4. Give three distinctive properties of glass.
5. Describe the difference between toughened glass and reinforced glass.
6. List some ceramic items in common use.
7. What type of material would you use on the inside of a jewelery box and why?
8. What type of glass would you use for:
   (a) the door of a bathroom cabinet
   (b) the top of a coffee table?
9. You are asked to make a coffee table from wood and to incorporate a material which is heat resistant, into the top of the table:
   (a) describe two suitable materials which you could use for this purpose
   (b) draw a sketch of a suitable design for your coffee table.
10. Describe two materials which would be suitable for covering the seat of a small stool which is to be used in a kitchen.

CHAPTER SIXTEEN

HAND TOOLS

In this chapter we will look at some of the tools you will use in the workshop. At all times you must use the tools safely. Your teacher will show you the correct and safest way to use the tools.

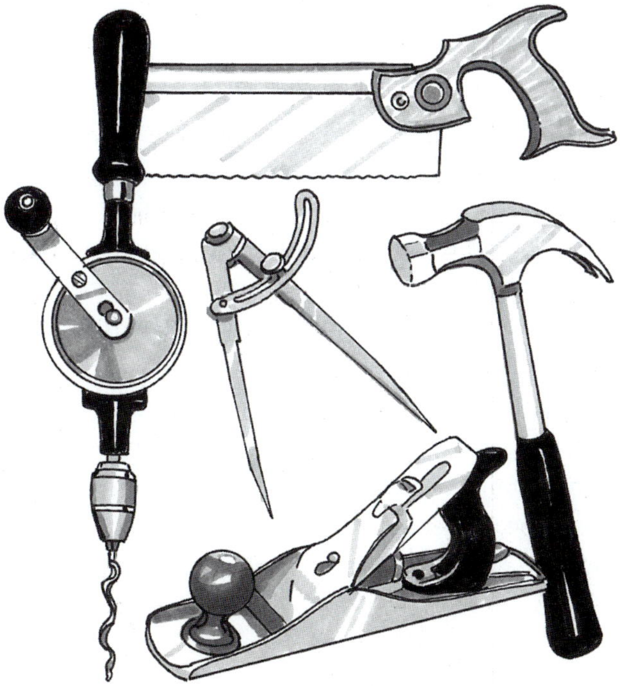

The basic tools which you will use can be divided into the following groups:

- Marking out tools
- Cutting tools
- Impelling/impact tools
- Shaping tools
- Boring tools
- Others.

Marking out tools

The rule

The rule can be made from stainless steel or boxwood. Stainless steel is stable and will not rust or distort at room temperature. Measurements are in millimetres (mm) and they are taken from the end of the rule. The most widely used rule is 300mm long but 1 metre steel rules and retractable tapes are also used.

The rule is used for measuring distances accurately. Inaccurate measurements could result in making joints the wrong size, either too loose or too tight. Be careful, the millimetre is a small unit of length and it is easy to make a mistake.

There is an old saying –
Measure twice – cut once

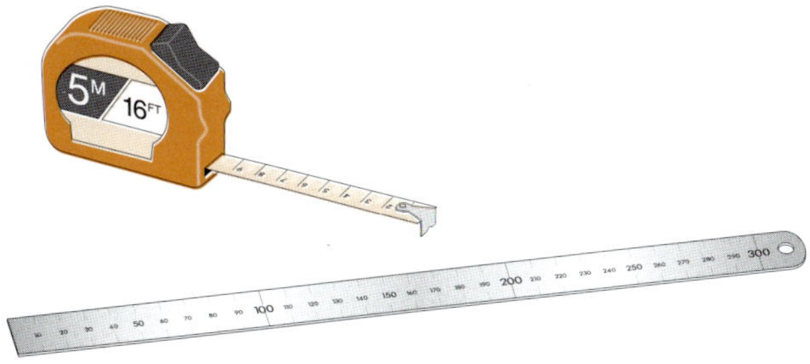

Rules & tape

Pencil and marking knife

These tools are used for marking out joints, etc. The pencil can be used for almost all jobs. A 2H pencil should be used for marking out timber. Pencils must be kept sharp at all times. Materials should be kept clean so avoid making any unnecessary markings on your pieces.

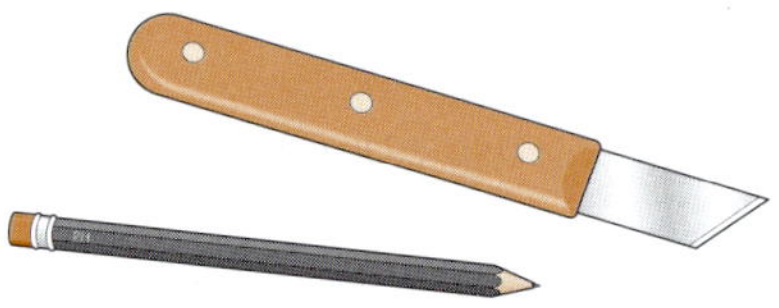

Pencil & marking knife

The marking knife, or craft knife, has a short blade made of steel which is held by a handle of wood or plastic. It is used for making a permanent cut in material, or for cutting veneers, card, leather, etc.

When using a pencil or marking knife along a rule or try-square, the knife or pencil must be inclined at about 60°

Try-Square

This is used for the following:

- Testing to ensure that surfaces are square to each other
- For drawing lines (squaring) at right angles to the face side and face edge of a piece of wood.

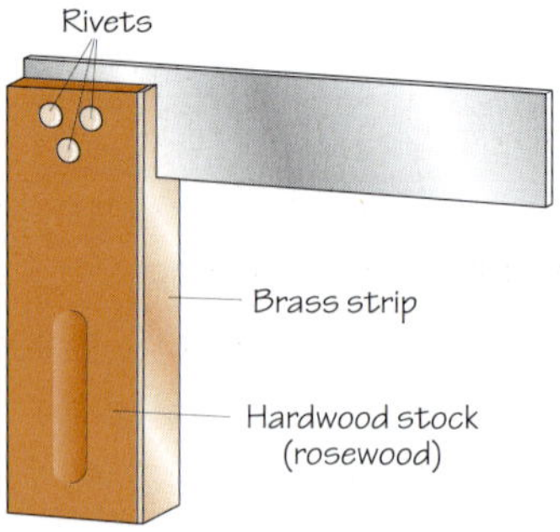

Parts of the try-square

Uses of the try-square

The stock is made of hardwood, usually **rosewood** or **mahogany** and the blade is of **high carbon steel**, hardened and tempered. There is a brass strip on the edge of the stock which prevents it from wearing down.

There are different sizes of try-squares according to the length of the blade. These vary from 100mm to 300mm in length. The square should be protected against knocks and falls and it should be tested for squareness regularly.

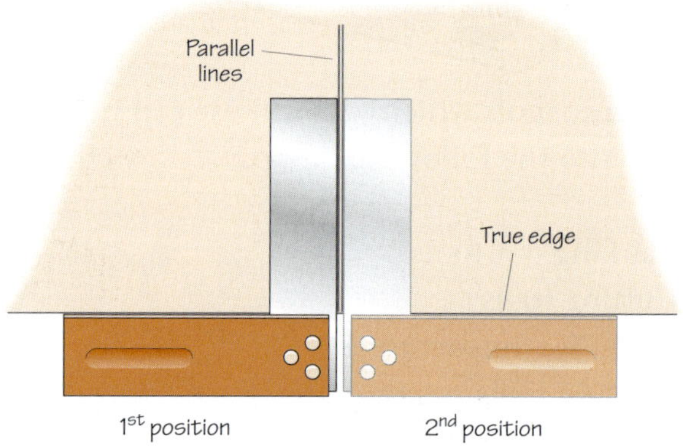

Testing the accuracy of the try-square

Marking gauge

The gauge is usually made of **beech** with a plastic or metal (brass) locking screw. There are often two brass strips set into the stock to reduce wear. The gauge is used to mark lines on timber or plastic which are parallel to an edge or surface. It is also used for marking out centre points for holes which need to be drilled.

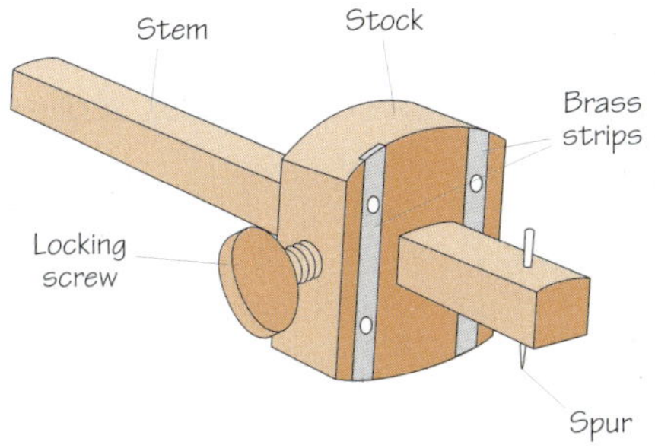

Parts of the marking gauge

The gauge is used by dragging the spur, not by pushing it. The stock must be held tightly against the side of the wood.

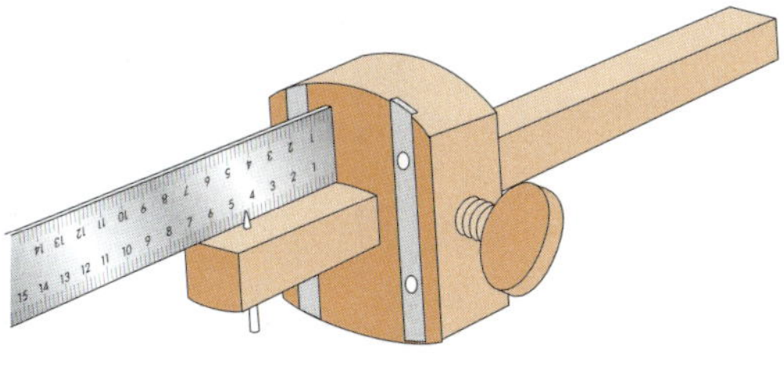

Setting the gauge

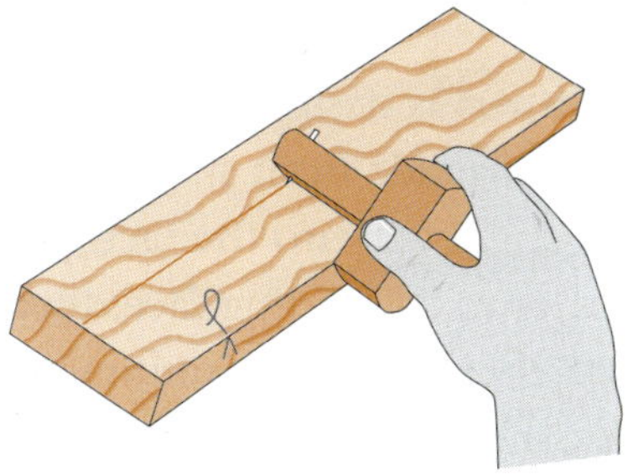

Using the gauge

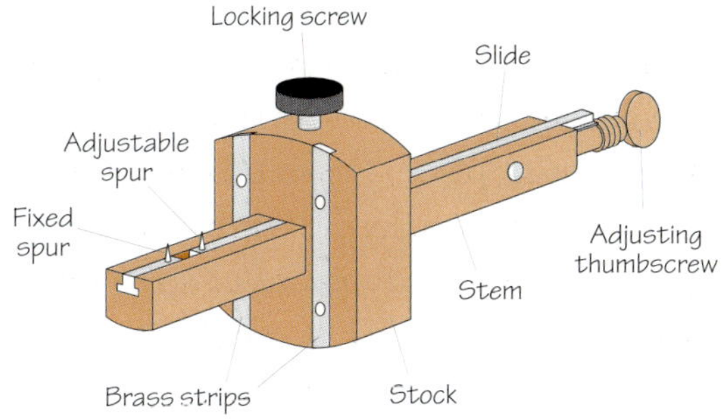

Parts of the mortise gauge

Mortise gauge

This is made from **mahogany**, **rosewood** or other hardwoods. It is used when two parallel gauge lines are required such as in a mortise and tenon joint. The distance between the two spurs is set first by adjusting the thumbscrew at the end of the stem. The distance between the adjustable spur and the stock is set then as for the marking gauge. The mortise gauge is used in the same way as the marking gauge.

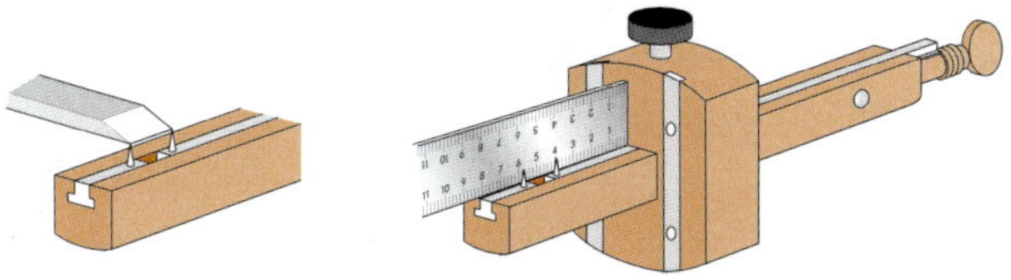

Using a mortise chisel to set the distance between the spurs

Using the rule to set the distance between the stock and the first spur

Setting the mortise gauge

Thumb gauge

This gauge is made from wood, usually hardwood. It is small and its function is to assist in marking lines for chamfers on timber. The gauge can be quickly made as required to the particular size of chamfer.

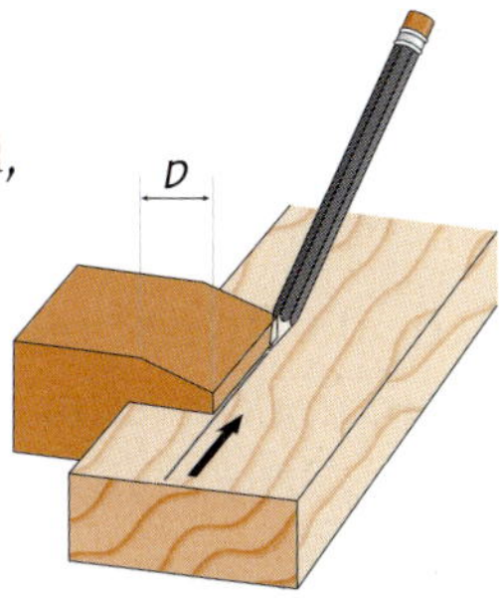

Thumb gauge

Cutting gauge

The cutting gauge is similar to the marking and mortise gauges. Instead of a spur, a wedge holds a small cutter in place. The depth of the cutter can be adjusted for a deeper cut and it also allows the blade to be replaced or sharpened. The cutting gauge is used to cut small rebates in wood or for cutting the fibres of the wood across the grain.

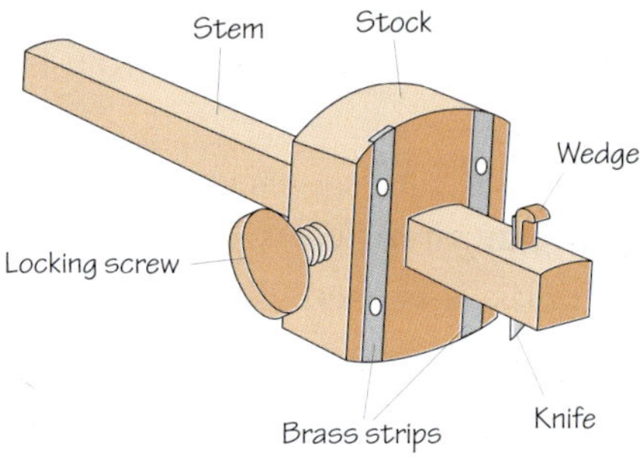

Cutting gauge

Sliding bevel

The sliding bevel is made from the same materials as the try-square. The sizes of the blades range from 150mm to 350mm. The bevel allows lines to be marked, which are at various angles to the edge of a piece.

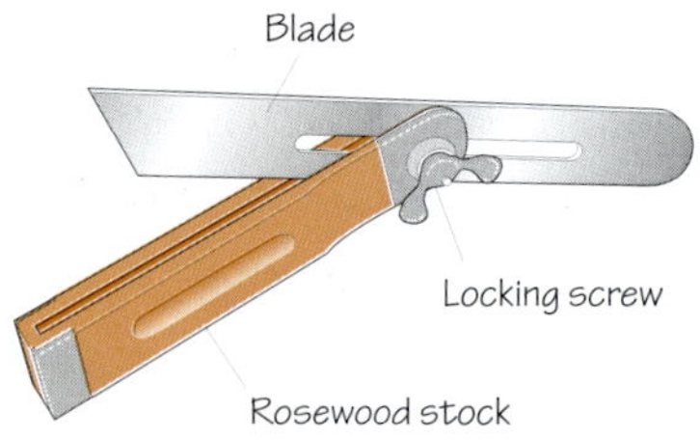

Sliding bevel

Compass/dividers

The dividers or ordinary compass, is used for marking curves or arcs on metals, plastics and wood. The dividers are also used for checking measurements and for transferring measurements from full scale plans to work in woodturning and in carving.

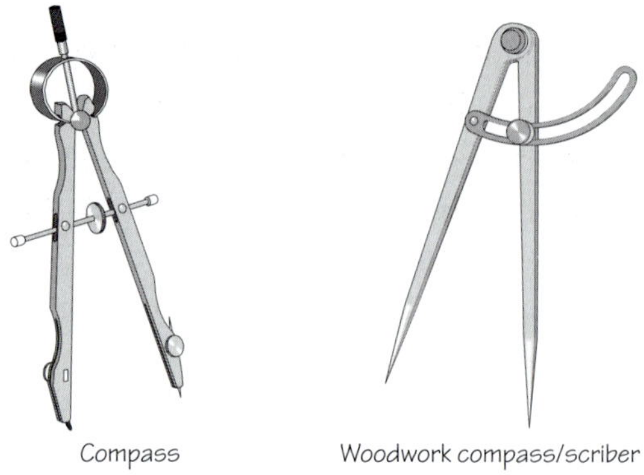

Compass & woodwork compass/scriber

Vernier callipers

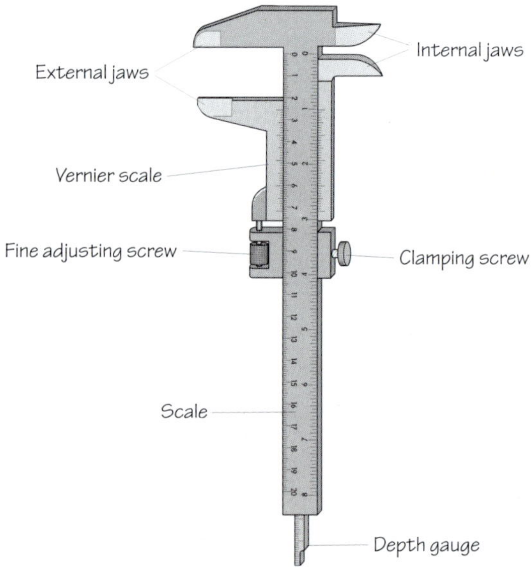

Vernier callipers

The Vernier callipers is designed for very accurate measurement. It is made from stainless steel. A vernier scale is engraved into the face of the main scale and onto the sliding face. It can measure accurately to 0.01 of a millimetre and is used for measuring thicknesses, depths and diameters of holes. It is often used in metal work and wood turning.

Inside and outside callipers

Both inside and outside callipers are made from steel and can be easily adjusted. They are used for measuring diameters of holes and inside cylinders. They are also used for metalwork and wood turning.

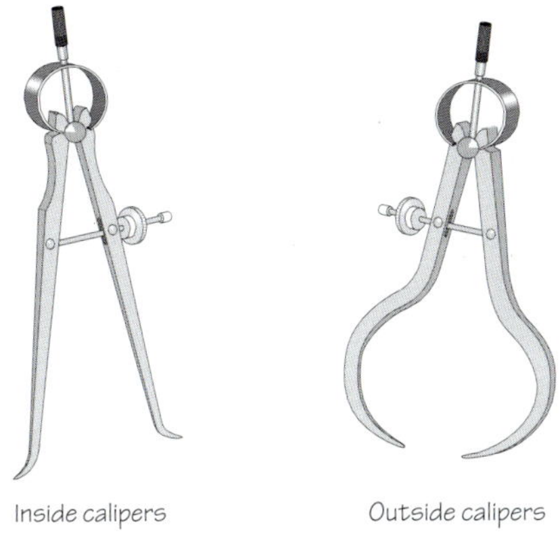

Inside callipers & outside callipers

Cutting Tools

Saws

There are many types of saw. Each type is designed to be used in a particular situation. Each job or process will dictate the type and size of saw, the size of the blade and the size and number of the teeth on the blade.

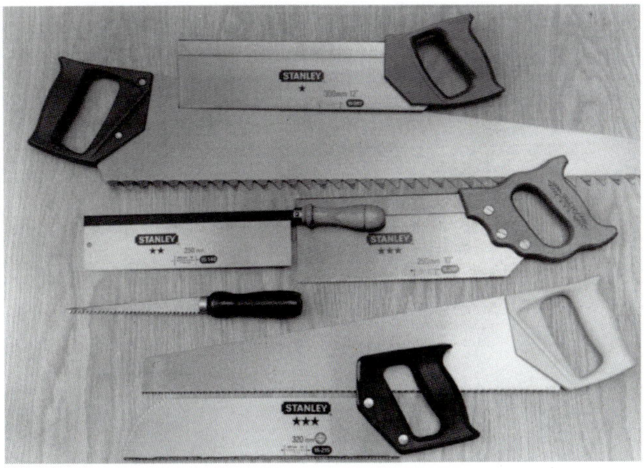

Different types of saws

As we will see later, machines and portable power tools are replacing some of the handsaws for doing repetitive work. Handsaws are still in use because they are safer and you can take more time to be careful and accurate with them.

Handsaws can be divided up into three groups according to use:

- Those used for cutting larger sections and sheet materials
- Those used for smaller sections to a fine finished cut
- Those used for cutting small curves finely and accurately.

The large handsaws are used mainly by the carpenter and joiner to cut large sheets or sections of wood. There are three different types. The difference between them is in the way the teeth cut the wood fibres.

Ripsaw

The ripsaw is used for cutting timber along the direction of the grain. The blade of the ripsaw varies in length between 500mm to 700mm.

The ripsaw has teeth which are shaped in such a way that the cutting action is similar to a chisel paring through a trench. The ripsaw should leave tiny shavings after sawing instead of dust, due to the chiselling action of the teeth.

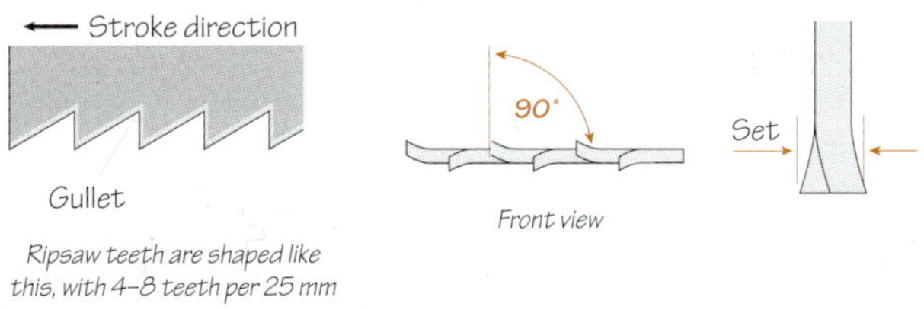

Shape of teeth of ripsaw

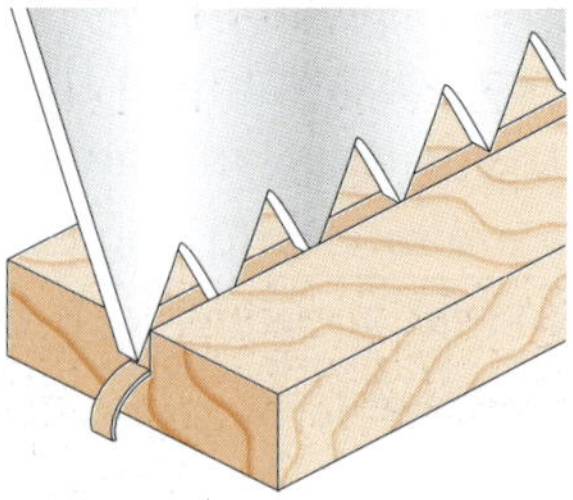

Teeth leave a flat-bottomed cut

Chiselling action of the teeth

The angle of the blade to the face of the work is 60° for rip-sawing

Angle of use of the ripsaw

Cross cut saw

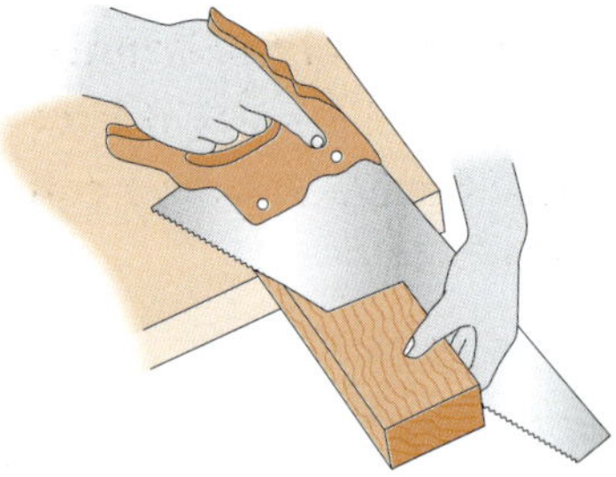

Cutting across the grain with a cross cut saw

This type of handsaw is used to cut across the fibres of the grain. The action of the teeth is similar to two knives cutting the fibres of the wood on each side of the saw set.

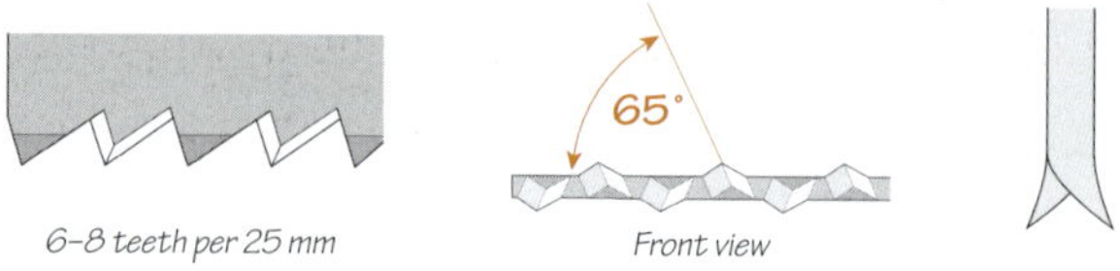

Shape of the teeth of the cross cut saw

The angle of the saw is 45° to the work surface when cross-cutting

Angle of use of the cross cut saw

The cross cut saw is used by the carpenter for cutting timber sections to length. The piece is supported on a saw horse or saw trestle.

BEWARE!

The end of the piece being cut should be supported as you saw through to prevent the piece splintering.

Universal saw

The rip saw and cross cut saw are special saws and they perform best when used as they were designed to cut either along the grain (rip) or across the grain (cross cut). Neither saw works well for any other purpose. However, the universal saw has teeth which will allow cutting successfully in the direction of the grain and across the grain.

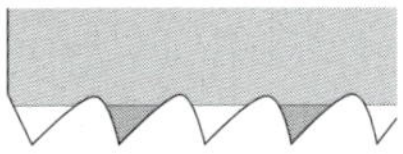

Teeth of the universal saw

Panel saw

This is a saw whose teeth are very like those of the cross cut saw. It is used for cutting thin sheet material such as plywood, chipboard and fibreboards. The difference between it and the cross cut saw is that there are more teeth per 25mm on the panel saw.

Tenon saw

The handle of the tenon saw is made of beech or plastic and is usually closed, giving more strength to the handle and preventing it from splitting. The handle is secured by screws.

The tenon saw

The blade is made of high carbon steel. The stiffening rib weights and strengthens the blade. It also stops the blade from buckling keeping it straight in the cut (**kerf**) but it does limit the depth of cut since it is wider than the blade. Tenon saws are available in different lengths from 200mm to 400mm.

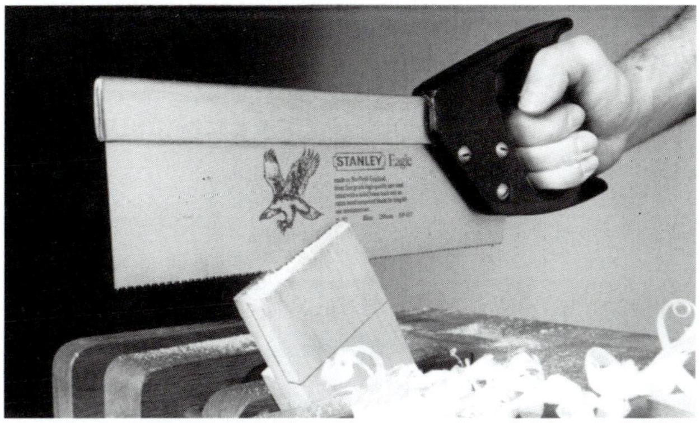

The tenon saw in use

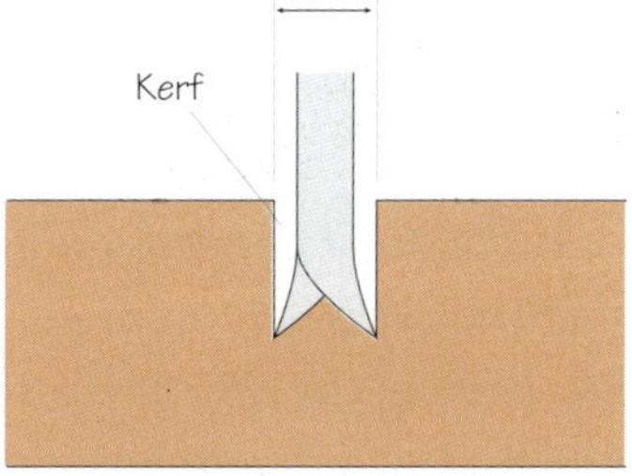

The saw kerf – how the set gives clearance to the blade

The tenon saw is used for general light work, particularly for cutting tenons, hence its name. When gripping the saw, it is held firmly with the first finger along the side of the handle. When starting a cut begin on the waste side of the line to be cut and draw the blade back a couple of times to start a kerf (cut).

Correct grip on the saw

Cutting a tenon

When cutting a tenon accuracy is important. The following process is always followed for best results.

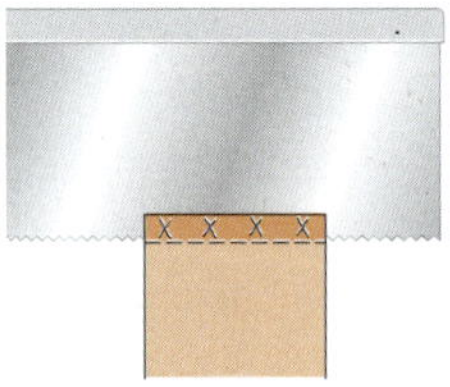

- *Firstly the piece is held vertically in the vice and a cut is made vertically down 5mm-6mm*

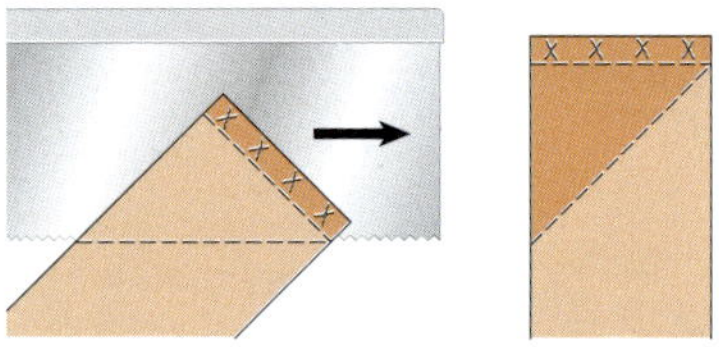

- *The piece is the tilted forward and fixed in the vice again. The cut is continued down along the gauge line, keeping the edge of the saw in the full kerf as the sawing continues*

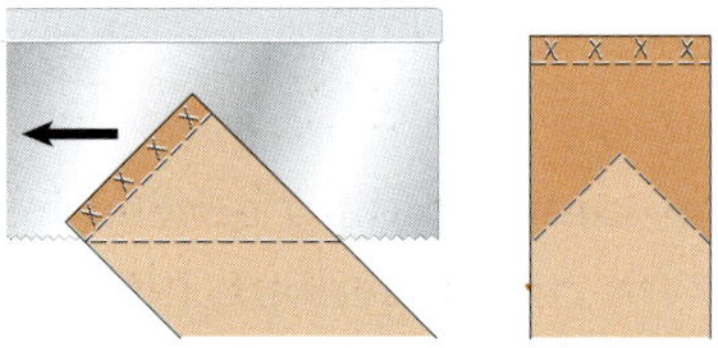

- *The piece is reversed at the same angle and the saw cut is repeated on the other side leaving a small triangular piece unsawn inside the tenon*

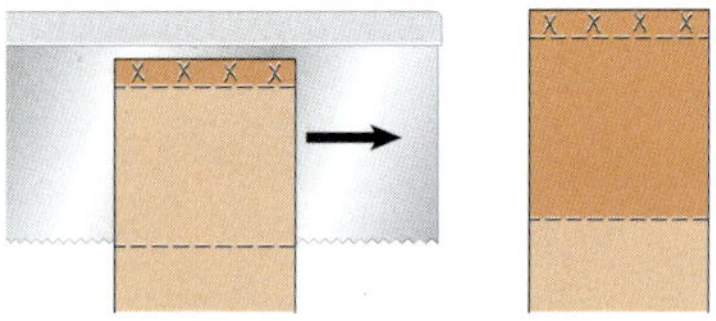

- *The piece is finally fixed in a vertical position once more for the last cut to be made which removes the triangular piece with a cut down to the line*

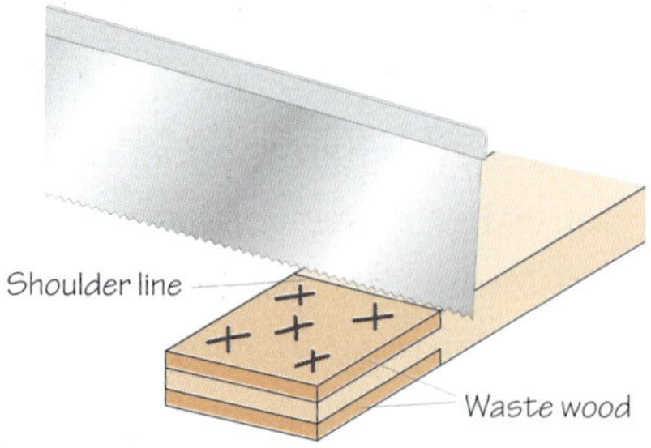

- *The shoulders can then be removed*

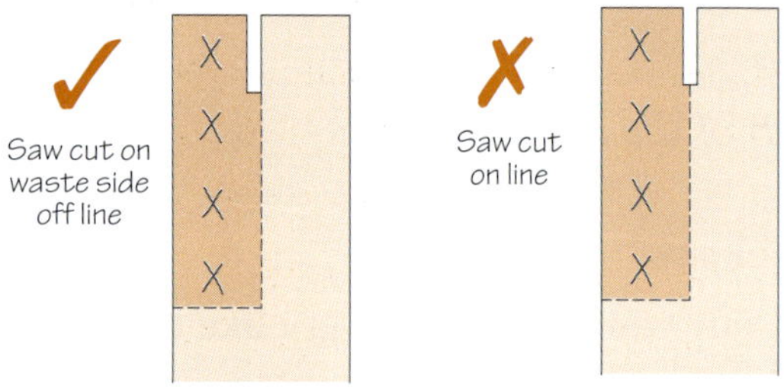

Dovetail saw

The dovetail saw is a smaller saw with finer teeth than the tenon saw and it is used for cutting dovetails and other very fine work.

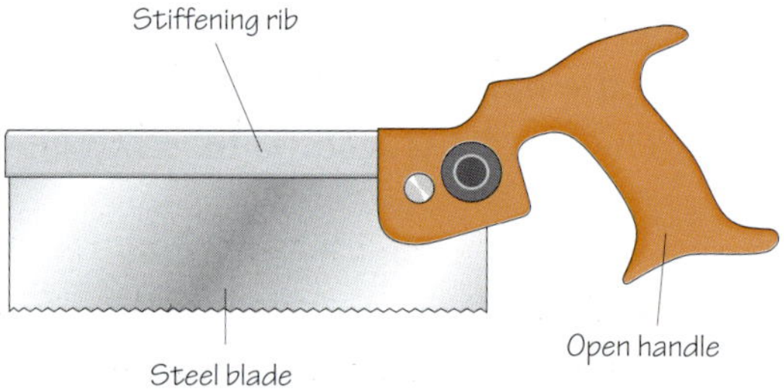

Dovetail saw

The table below shows the various saw types and the number of teeth each has in every 25mm of blade.

Saw Type	Use	Teeth per 25mm
Rip saw	Sawing large sections of timber and boards in the direction of the grain	4 – 8
Cross cut saw	Sawing across the grain, usually larger sections of timber	6 – 8
Universal saw	Can be used in the same way as the rip saw and the cross cut saw	5 – 7
Panel saw	Sawing sheet material up to 20mm thick	10 – 12
Tenon saw	General light work across and along the grain. Named from its main use, cutting tenons	10 – 15
Dovetail saw	Finer teeth meaning more accurate cutting than the tenon saw, used mainly for cutting fine dovetails	8 – 20
Bow saw	Used in curved work on thick pieces of wood up to 25mm	9 – 10
Compass saw	Mainly used on curved work	7 – 9
Coping saw	General light curved work, tighter curves can be cut	5 – 16
Pad saw	Small holes	9 – 14
Fret saw	Very fine metal and woodwork	Numerous and difficult to count

Teeth

The type and quality of cut is determined by the type, size and number of teeth on the blade of a saw. The number of teeth per 25mm (inch) is usually marked on the blade of the saw. A tenon saw usually has between 10 and 15 teeth per inch (TPI).

Saw teeth must be well maintained, sharpened regularly and protected against knocks and falls. Care should also be taken not to cut into nails hidden in old wood or to cut through concrete which has bonded to wood.

The following saws are specially designed for use in the cutting of curves.

Coping saw

This saw is used for cutting small curves in wood. The blade is stretched between two slotted pins on the frame. It can be loosened for replacement or when adjusting the blade. This is done by unscrewing the handle. The blade is slotted into the pins with the teeth pointing back towards the handle. The handle is retightened and the sighting pins are aligned. The saw is unusual in that it cuts on the return stroke when you pull it back towards you.

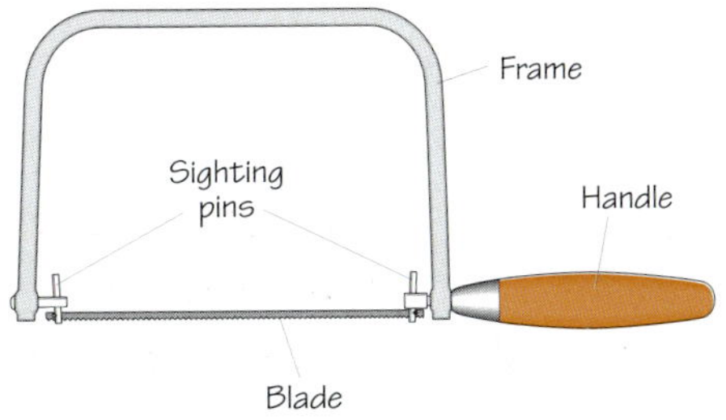

The coping saw

The bow saw

The bow saw is an old design of saw made from wood (beech). The key is turned which twists the string. The pull on the frame from the string puts tension on the blade. The blade can be twisted around to follow the curve being cut. The bow saw can be used when the coping saw cannot reach a cut, because of its smaller frame size.

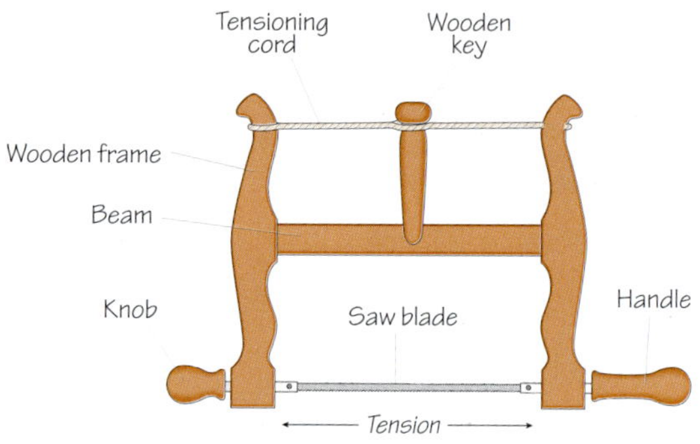

The bow saw

Fret saw

This saw is very like the coping saw but the frame is higher and the blade is finer. It is used to cut wood, metal and plastic, as in jigsaw puzzles, and other light work. It will also cut very sharp curves because of its narrow blade. The teeth of the blade point towards the handle like the coping saw.

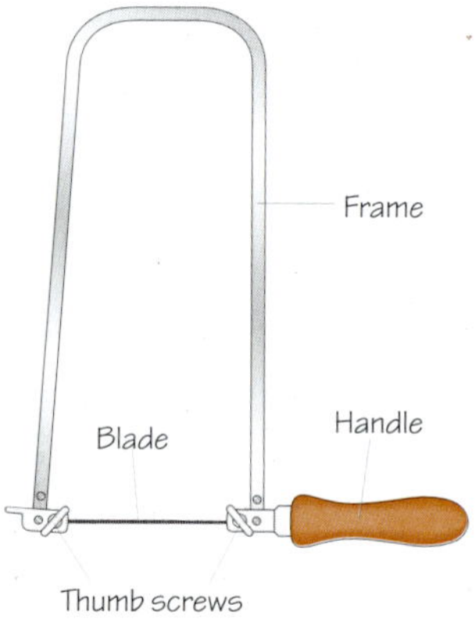

The fret saw

The compass saw

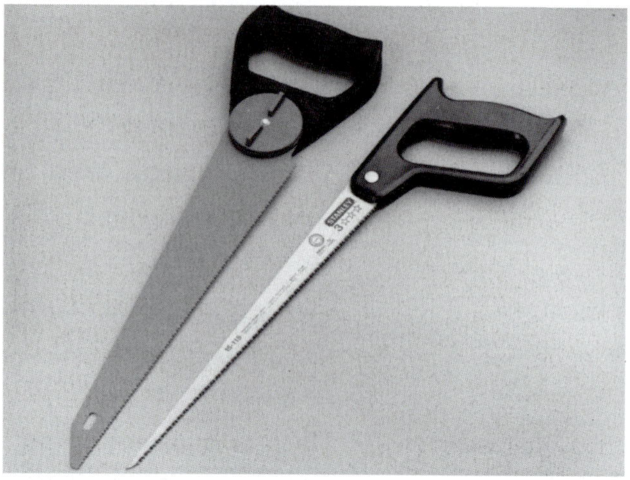

This saw is used for cutting curves which cannot be reached by the coping saw or bow saws because their frames would get in the way. Care should be taken with this saw when using it because the blade can be easily bent. Damage is difficult to repair and the blade needs to be replaced.

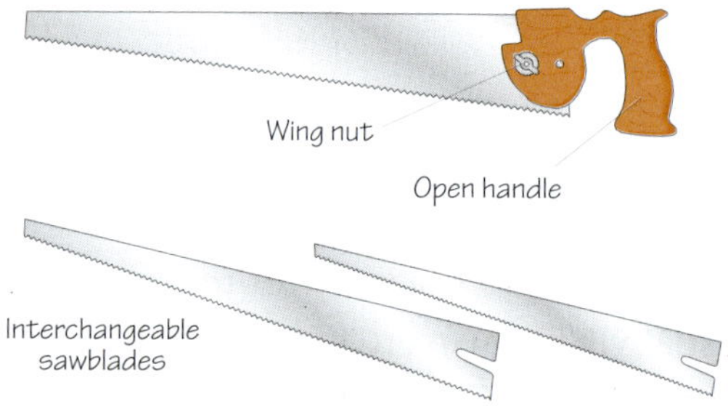

The compass saw

Pad saw

This saw is used for small holes which cannot be reached with other saws. Also known as a keyhole saw. The blade is easily bent and damaged. The blade can be adjusted by retracting it into the handle.

Jig saw

This is a modern hand held power tool. The motor drives the blade up and down to cut the material. The jig saw can cut tight corners and is very versatile. The Jig saw will be examined in greater detail in Chapter 18.

The jig saw

Scroll saw

This has a small blade which is attached to two arms of the saw. These move up and down allowing cutting to take place. It is used for cutting thin sections of wood, mainly plywood, MDF, veneer and plastic. It can turn into very tight curves and corners with ease because of its thin blade. The piece of work is held down onto the table and the line along which the cut is to be made is fed through the moving blade.

Band saw

This is a machine used for cutting larger pieces. It will be described further in Chapter 19.

Chisels

The chisel is a very important tool. It is used to cut out trenches and to pare wood down to a required line. The chisels in your locker are mainly for paring to straight lines such as in the sketches below, but there are special chisels available for carving work and also a special type for woodturning.

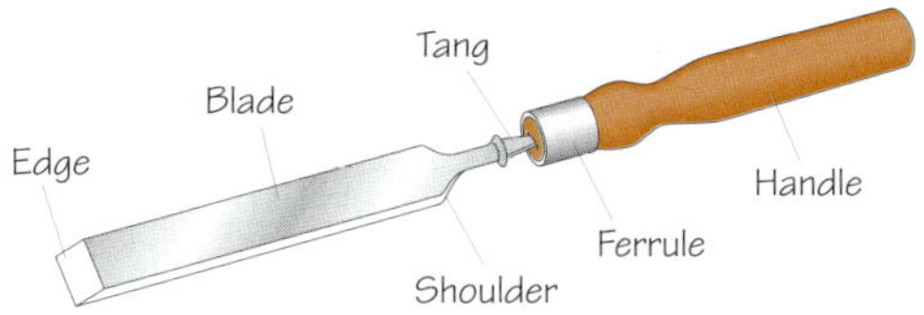

Parts of the chisel

Blade – high carbon steel, hardened & tempered
Shoulder – prevents the tang being driven into the handle
Tang – fits into the handle
Ferrule – a brass collar which prevents the handle from splitting
Handle – made from hardwood (ash, boxwood) or plastic

The edge of the chisel has two very different angles (bevels). The first between 20° and 25° is achieved by grinding on a grinding stone. The second bevel, about 30° is achieved by sharpening on an oilstone. This sharpening is sometimes called **honing**.

The sizes of bevel edge and firmer chisels range in widths from 3mm to 50mm. The bevelled edge chisel is not as strong as the firmer chisel but is useful for getting into tight corners.

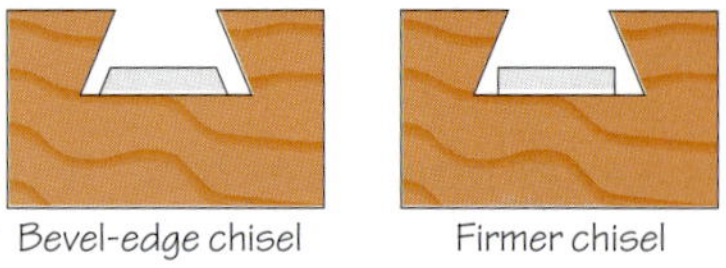

Bevelled edge chisel fits into the tight corners of dovetails

The bevelled edge and firmer chisel is used for paring trenches mostly, but if the length of the trench is too long, a paring chisel may be used. This has a longer blade than ordinary chisels and it usually has a bevelled edge.

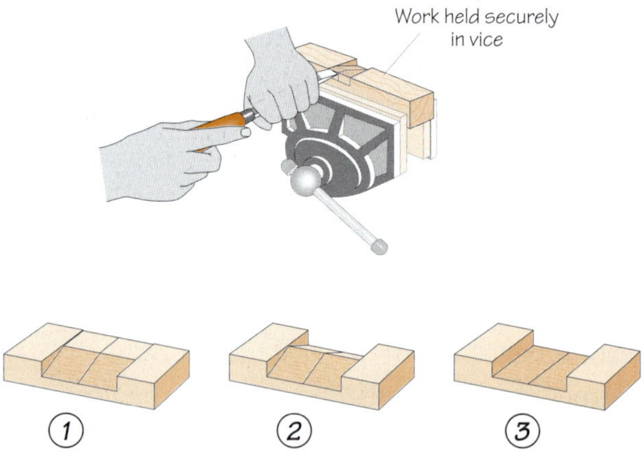

Paring a trench

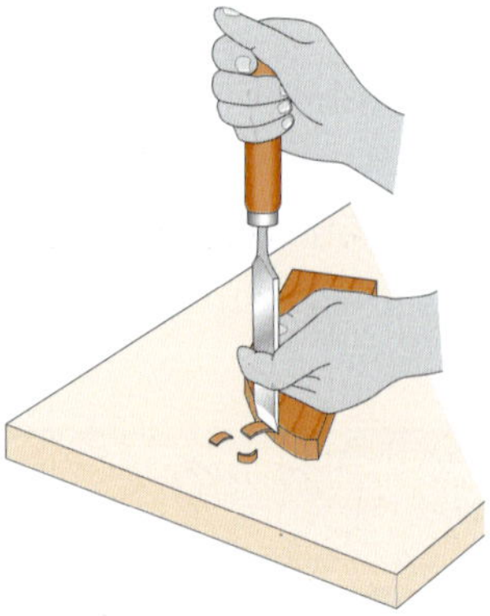

Vertical paring

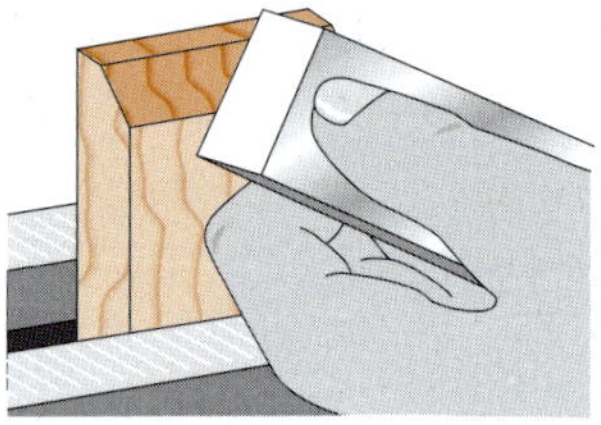

Chamfering with the chisel

Mortise chisel

The mortise chisels are used to cut holes in timber. Modern mortise chisels have plastic handles which are more durable than wooden ones, even though all wooden handles are strengthened with a metal ferrule. The plastic handles are socketed into the blade. This method is also used for the larger timber handled mortise chisels.

The blade of the mortise chisel is stronger and thicker than other chisels. It is used with the mallet – therefore its blade needs to be thicker and stronger to withstand the constant impacting of the mallet.

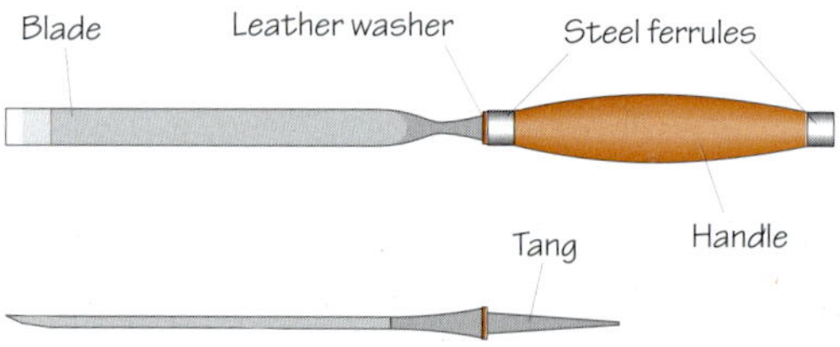

Mortise chisel

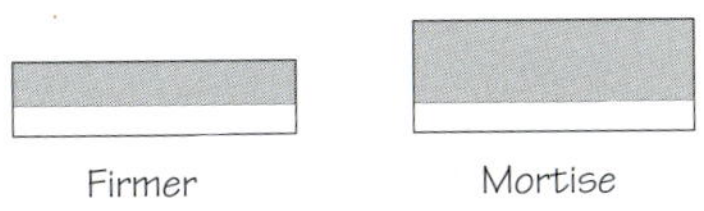

Section through the blades of firmer & mortise chisel

Hammer and mallet

Both the mallet and hammer are called percussion or impact tools.

The hammer is used to drive nails or panel pins into wood or other materials. There are a number of different kinds of hammer:

- Claw hammer
- Warrington hammer
- Ball-pein hammer
- Pin hammer or telephone hammer.

The hammer has two parts the handle and the head. The head is held on by wedges and these prevent it from becoming loose. Hammers can be chosen by weight (18oz, 21oz, etc).

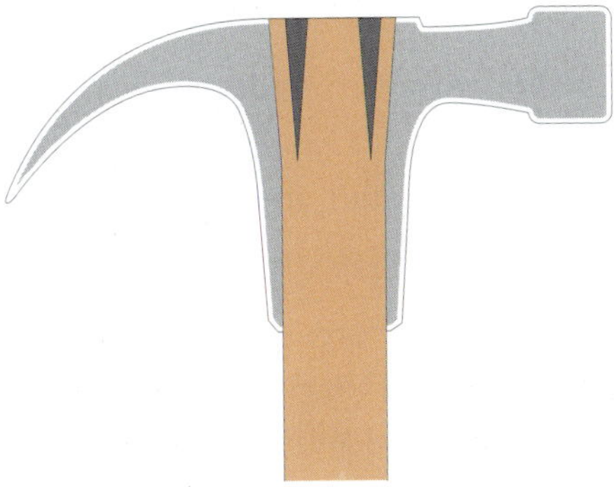

Head held on by wedges

Steel claw hammer

This is used for general purpose and heavy work. It can be used to lever nails out of timber.

Warrington hammer

This is used for lighter work, e.g. hammering panel pins and light nails.

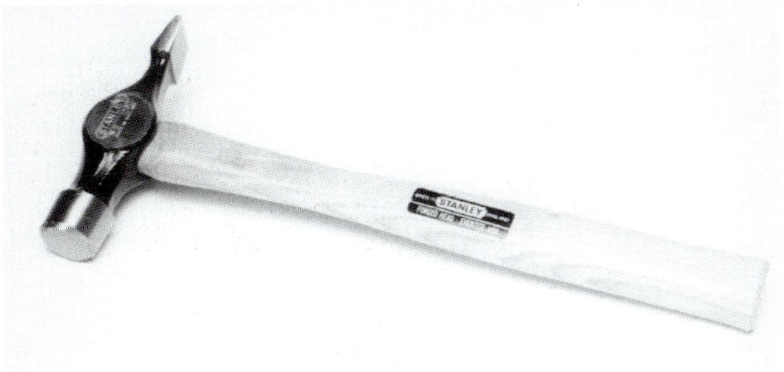

Warrington hammer

Ball-pein hammer

This is used mainly when working with metals. Various kinds are available in different sizes and shapes.

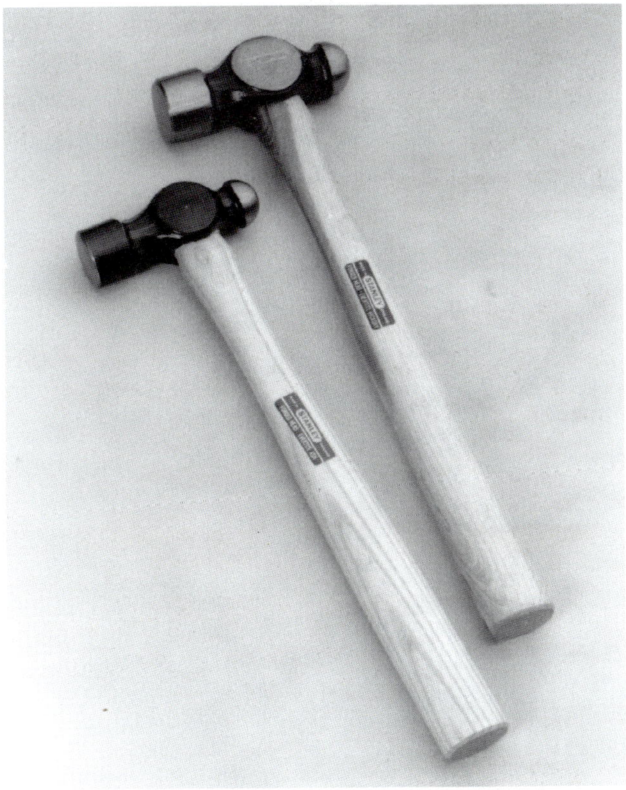

Ball-pein hammer

Pin hammer

Similar to a Warrington hammer in shape but it is a lot lighter. It is used mostly by upholsterers for driving light pins and tacks.

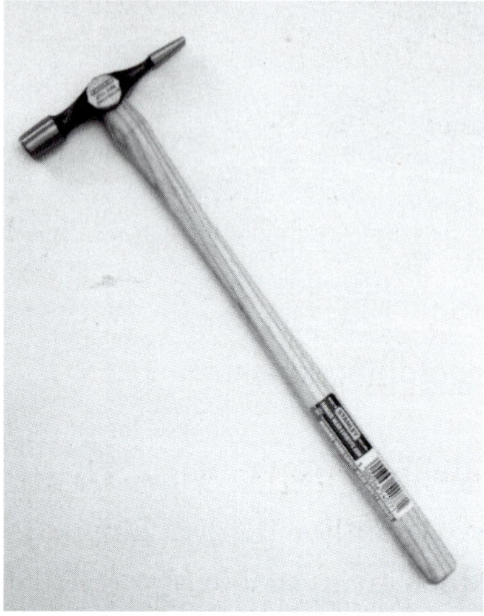

Pin hammer

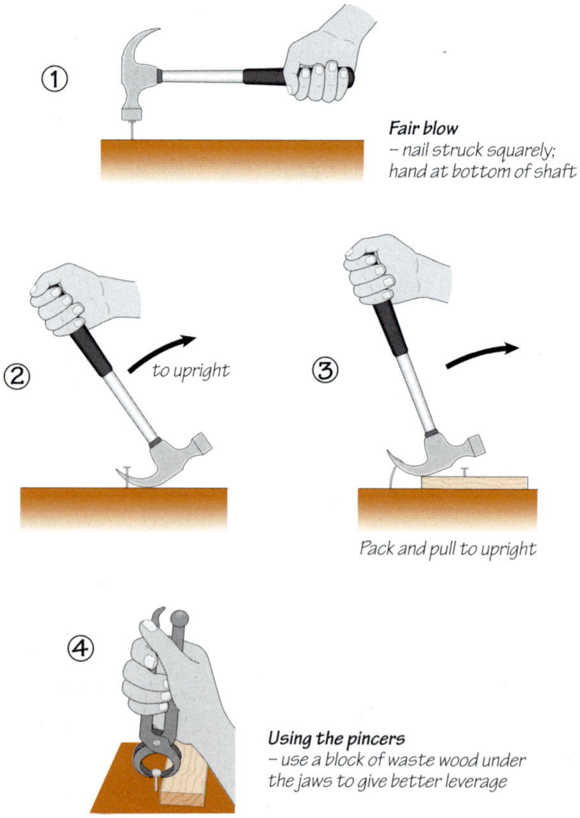

Driving & withdrawing nails

BEWARE!

Always check that the head of a hammer is not loose before you use it.

When using hammers or the mallet, great care should be taken:

- Hold the handle firmly at the end
- The face of the head should strike squarely on the head of the nail

Mallets

The mallet is made of beech. It is used to strike chisel handles when heavy cutting is required, when taking out a mortise or when carving.

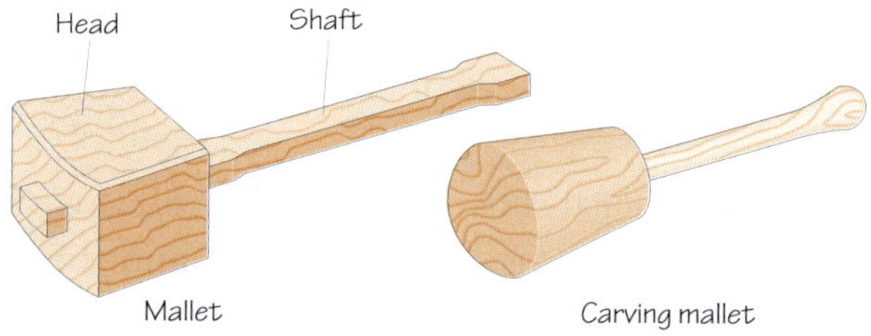

Mallet & carving mallet

The mallet comes in various sizes according to the size of the head. Usually 100mm – 150mm. The faces of the mallet are sloped so that the face strikes the handle of a chisel squarely on the top.

Pincers

Pincers are used for pulling nails, panel pins. etc., out of wood.

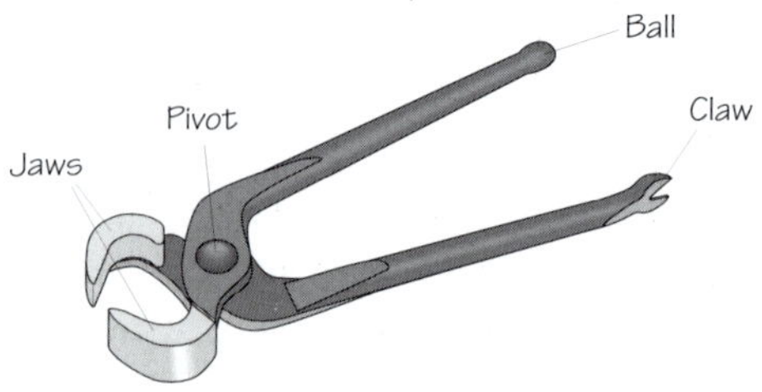

Pincers

Boring tools

- Brace and bit
- Wheel brace
- Pillar drill
- Electric drill
- Gimlet
- Bradawl.

Boring tools are used to cut/drill holes in wood or other materials. Boring tools normally have a **chuck** with jaws which hold the bit firmly. It is the bit which does the cutting. The chuck revolves and so turns the bit. Some boring tools are manually powered and some are electric.

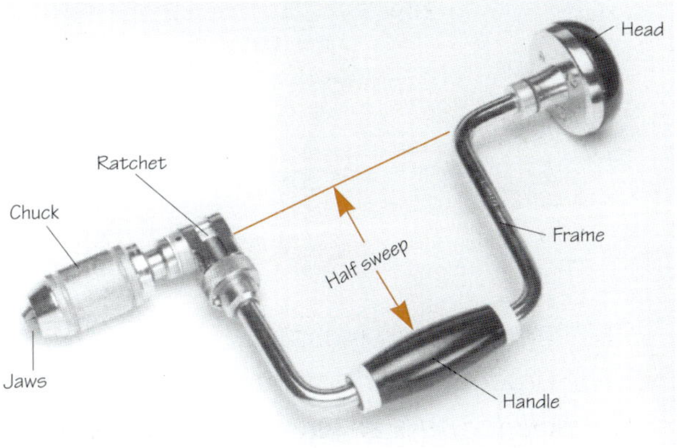

The carpenter's brace

Brace and bit

The carpenter's brace has been in existence since the early fifteenth century. The first braces had fixed bits but eventually these bits were detachable and fitted onto a simple holder.

Today, the brace is made of steel. It can be obtained in different sizes, determined by the **sweep** of the handle. The bit is held into the chuck by means of two jaws, which tighten onto the shank of the bit when they are tightened up. Most braces have a **ratchet** which allows the tool to be used in confined spaces where a full revolution of the handle could not be made. The ratchet allows the bit to bore in one direction only. Your teacher will demonstrate this.

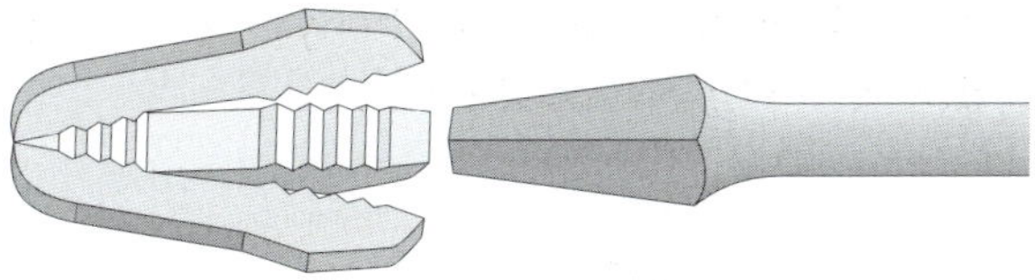

The jaws of the chuck

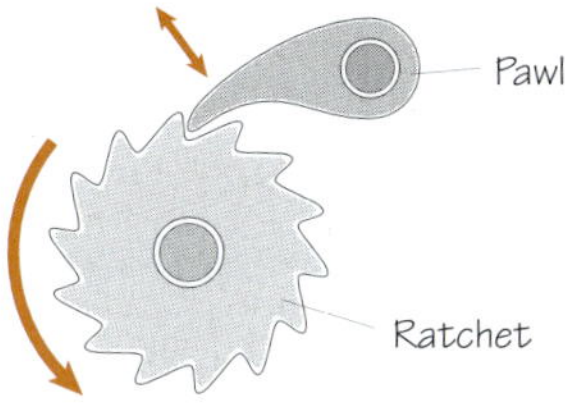

The ratchet mechanism – allows movement in one direction only

Bits for carpenter's brace

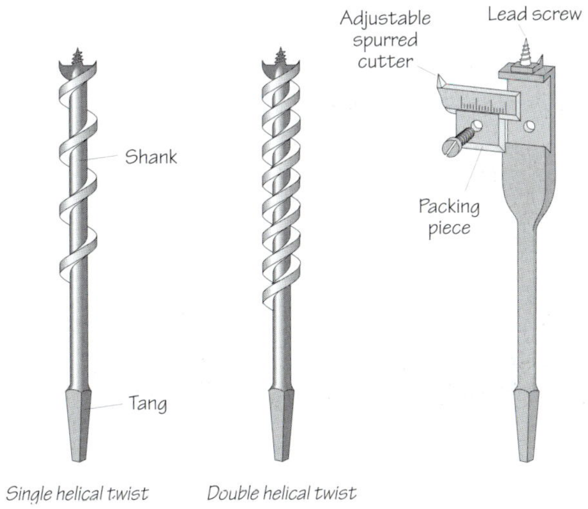

Bits for carpenter's brace

The carpenter's brace is used mostly for drilling larger holes in wood. The bits generally used in the brace are **Auger bits** which are made from steel. There are two types; the *Jennings pattern* which has double helical twist and the *Solid centre* or *Irwin pattern* which has a single helical twist. Both types have a lead screw which draws the bit into the wood once it has got a grip. These bits can be obtained in a range of sizes for various diameter of hole. Alternatively, an expansive bit is available which can be set to different cutting diameters.

Using the brace

Mark the centre point of the hole (on both sides of the work if the hole is going right through) and then mark with a bradawl. It is important that the brace should be at 90° to the surface of the wood to allow the hole to be bored correctly in line. Bore with slight pressure until the point of the lead screw breaks through to the opposite surface of the timber. Then reverse the work in the vice, position the lead screw in this hole and continue boring until the hole is complete. This method prevents the damage which would result on the reverse surface if the hole was bored straight through.

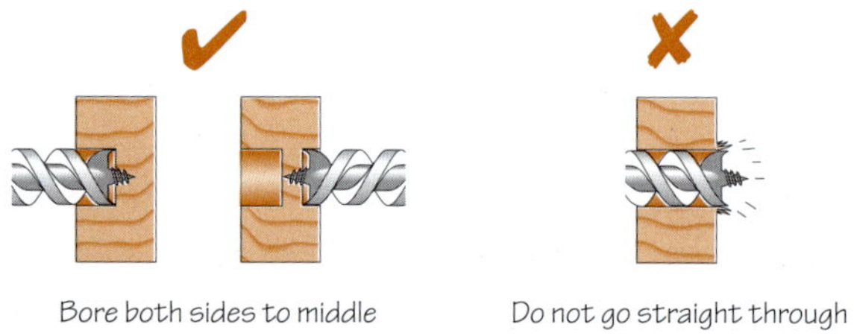

The stages of boring a hole through wood with a brace

Bradawl

The bradawl is used to make small shallow holes in timber, such as pilot holes for nails and screws. The steel blade is 2 – 5mm in diameter. The point works by splitting the fibres of the wood but care must be taken especially at the ends of timber to avoid splitting the ends of the piece. You make the hole by pushing the blade into the material and twisting clockwise and anti-clockwise.

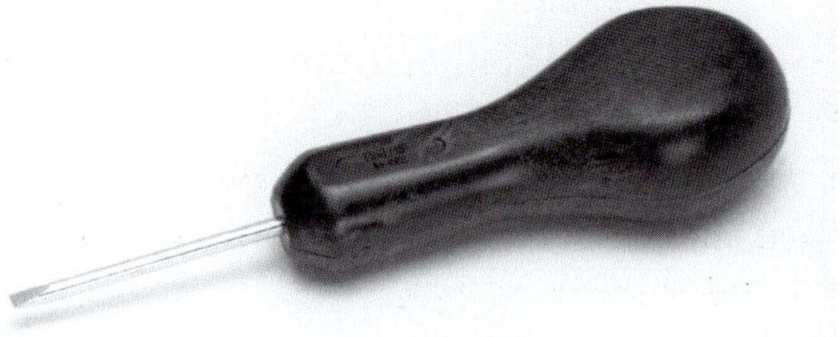

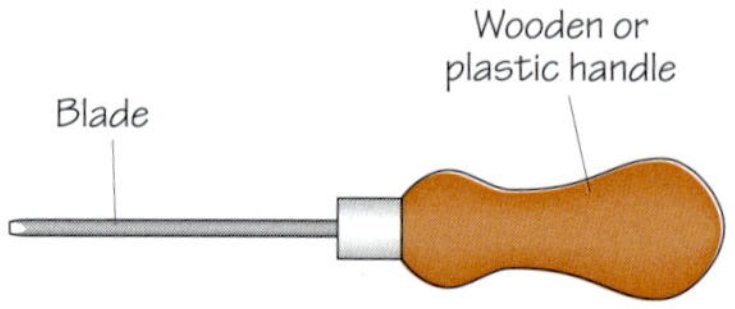

The bradawl

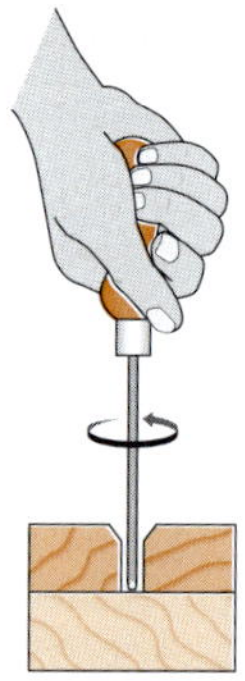

The bradawl is twisted into the piece to make a pilot hole for nails or screws

Gimlet

This is similar to the bradawl and it works in a similar way. It has a screw thread at the end of the blade. The blade is longer and stronger than the bradawl and the handle is arranged so that it can easily be twisted into the wood.

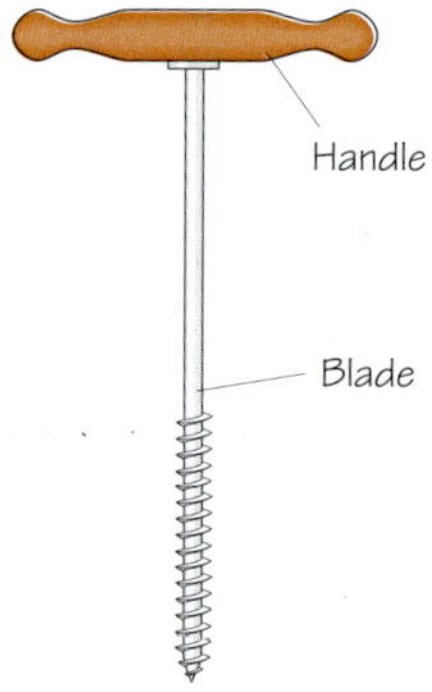

The gimlet

Wheel brace

This is sometimes called a hand drill. It is used to drill small holes from 1mm – 10mm in diameter. It is also used to drill small accurate holes in wood and plastic. The breast drill which is larger has three handles as shown.

The hand drill/wheelbrace

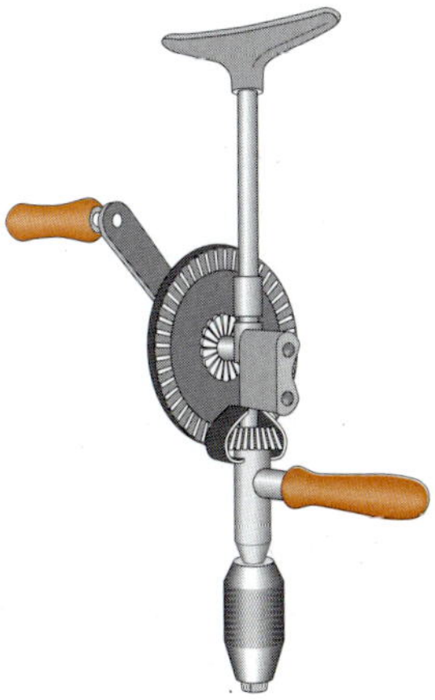

The breast drill

Drill bits

These are also known as bits or drills. They fit into the chuck of various boring tools. They are available in different types and sizes.

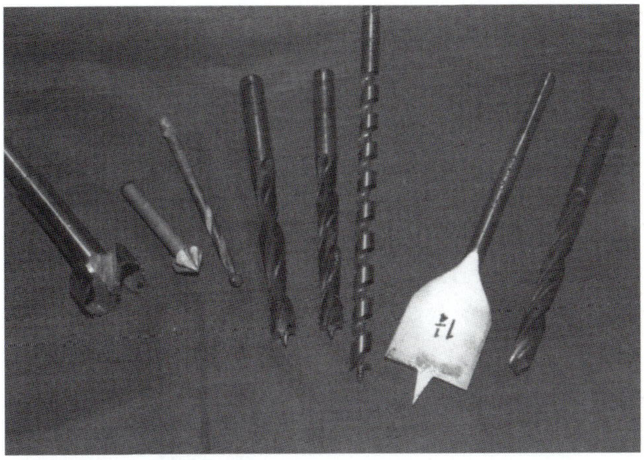

Drill bits – wood boring bit, masonry bit, metal boring bit, countersink bit

Planes, surforms, files, spokeshaves

These tools are used for either smoothing or shaping wood in various different ways.

Planes

There are numerous types of planes. In the past, this was due to the fact that many mouldings were made by special planes. These planes were often designed, and made by the craftsman, for one particular moulding and are now becoming collectors items. They were made of timber (beech) as were the first bench planes. Planes can be divided into two main groups:

- bench or general purpose planes
- special planes.

Never leave the cutting edge of a plane down on any hard surface, it will damage the blade

Jack plane

The name of this plane comes from the expression 'Jack of all trades'. It is a general purpose plane. The sole of the jack plane is about 300mm long and the width of the blade is 50mm or more. It is used to smooth the surfaces of timber even after it has been *squared up* by a surface planer. It can also be used to square up the edges of a piece of timber or to plane timber to size, etc.

Jack plane

Smoothing plane

This is used to make surfaces ready for glasspapering and also to smooth out any irregularities. The plane is about 230mm long and the blade is 50mm wide or more.

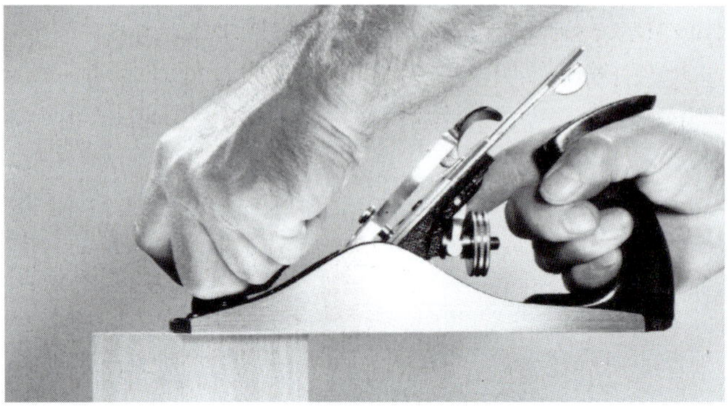

Smoothing plane

Blades of the smoothing plane

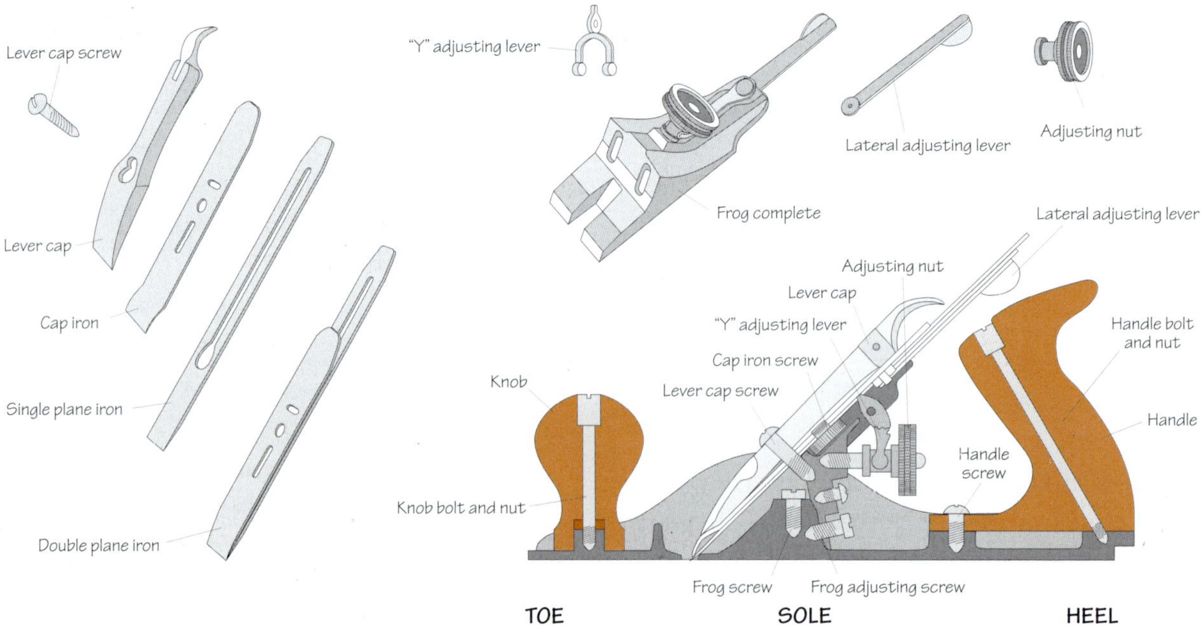

Parts of a plane

Try-plane

This is a long plane used to smooth very long boards and when preparing the edges of long boards for edge jointing. It planes the high parts and spans the hollows, smoothing out the whole surface. The lengths of the sole range from 450mm to 650mm and the blade is between 60mm and 70mm wide.

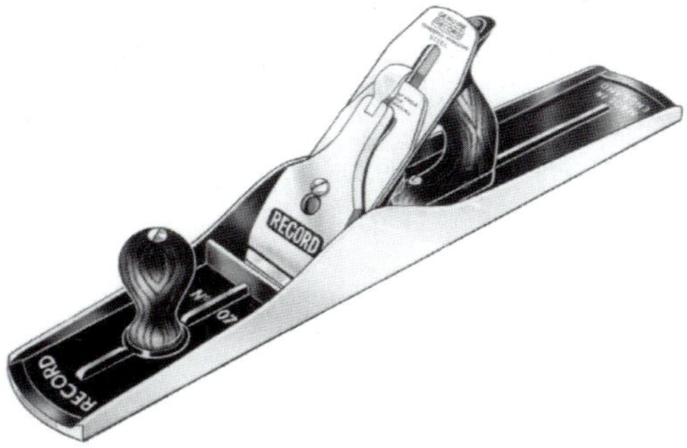

Try-plane

Rebate plane

The rebate plane is used to form rebates in timber. It has a depth stop to prevent you planing off more than you want to and a fence to stop you going too far in from the edge.

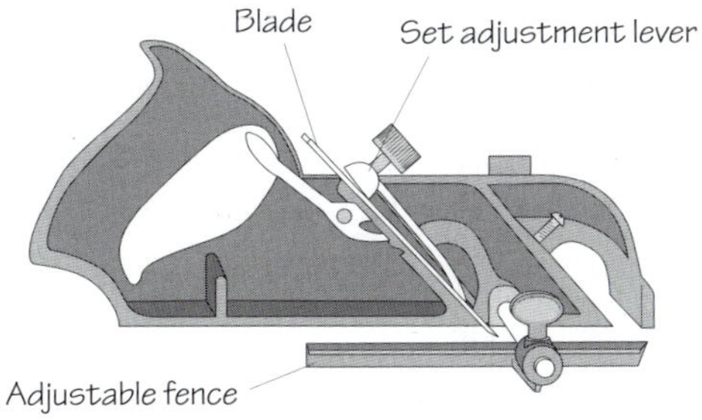

Rebate plane

The rebate plane has a spur which cuts the fibres of the wood like a knife as it goes forward. This is very useful when planing a rebate across the grain. The blade can be moved to the front of the plane to produce a stopped rebate. The blades range in widths from 12mm to 38mm.

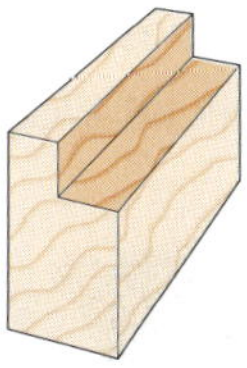

Rebate

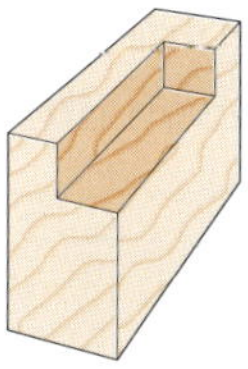

Stopped rebate

Plough plane

This plane cuts grooves in wood. It has a depth stop and a fence just like the rebate plane but the blades come in different widths to suit a number of sizes of grooves. These vary from 3mm – 15mm.

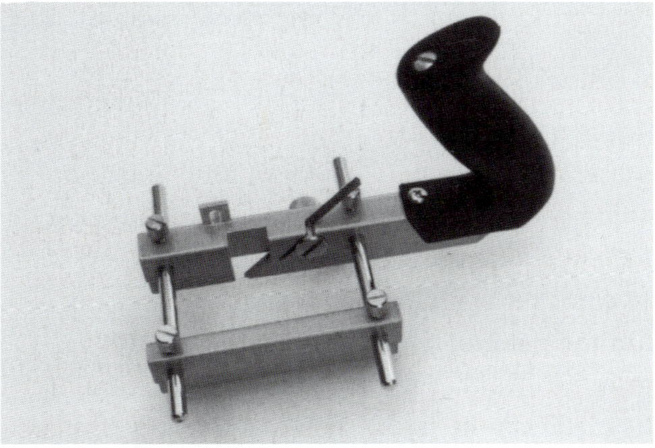

Plough plane

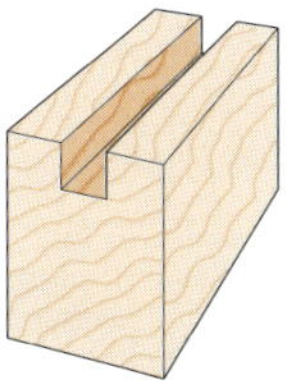

Plough groove

Combination plane

This can be used for different operations from rebates to grooves to beading. It works across the grain and along it. This plane is similar to a plough plane, but comes with many different blades, in various shapes and sizes, which form the various mouldings. Because of the many blades, the combination plane can do the same work as six or seven different special wooden moulding planes.

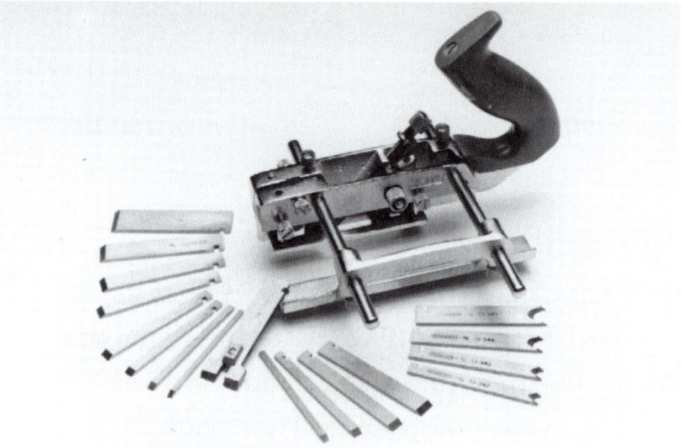

Combination plane with assorted cutters

Block plane

This is a very short plane and is extremely easy to use. It is about 150 – 200mm long and about 40mm wide. There is no cap iron which makes the blade different from other bench planes. It does not have a handle, but rests comfortably into the palm of your hand which you use to push it forward. The depth and the position of the blade can be set by screws and levers similar to the jack plane. The block plane is used for light planing, chamfers, and end grain.

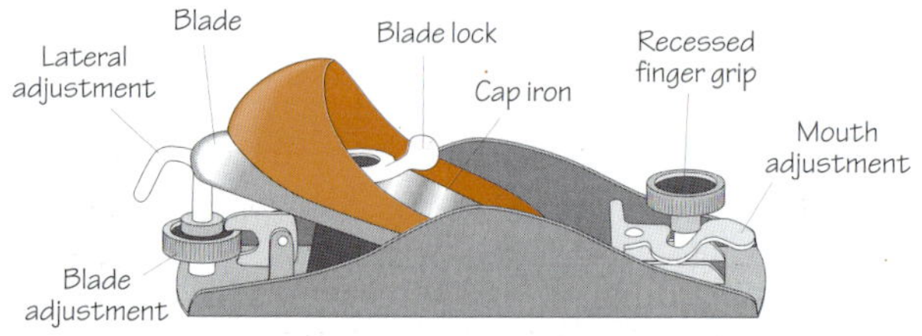

Planing end grain

When planing the end grain of wood care must be taken to ensure the fibres of the wood do not splinter or tear away from the piece at the edge. There are a number of ways that this can be achieved successfully. The smoothing plane is possibly the most suitable plane for the task but others can be used also. The blade must be very sharp when planing end grain.

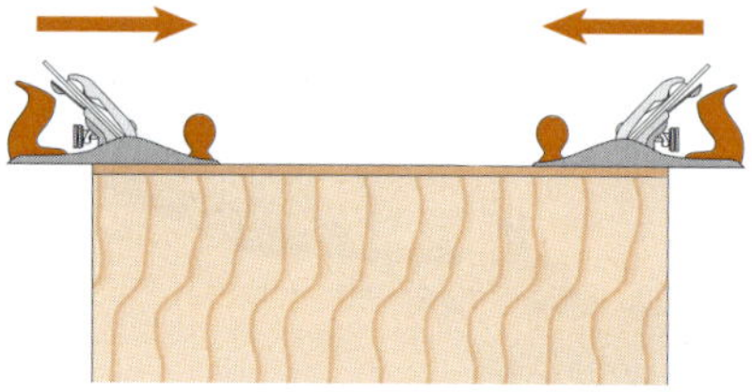

End grain is planed from each side working towards the centre. The high spot in the centre is finally finished off with care

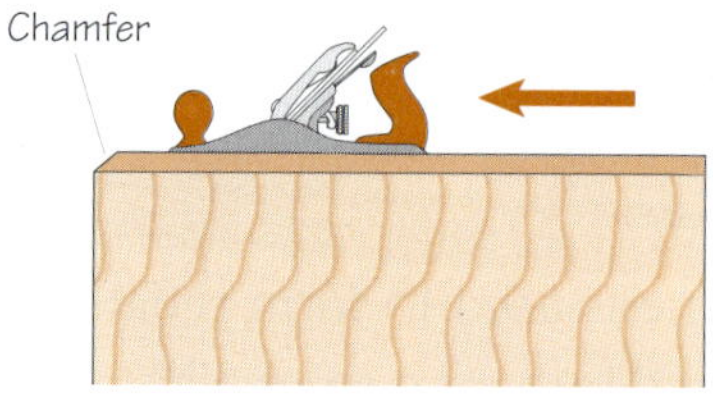

The end grain may be planed through if a chamfer is cut off before planing down to the line. Care must be taken in the last few cuts as they will remove the chamfer

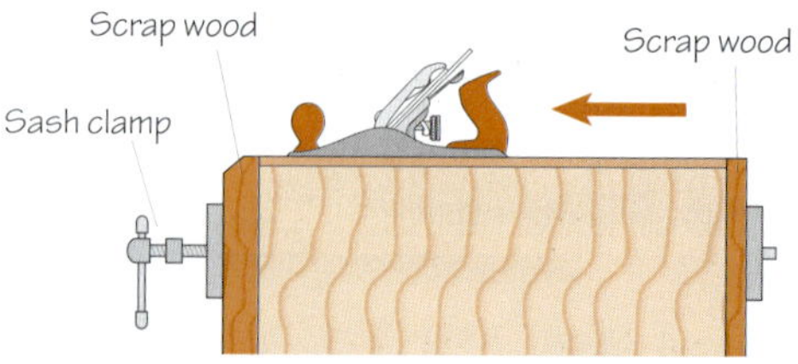

The end of the piece can be supported with a waste block cramped to the piece. This holds the fibres of the workpiece intact and sacrifices the waste piece

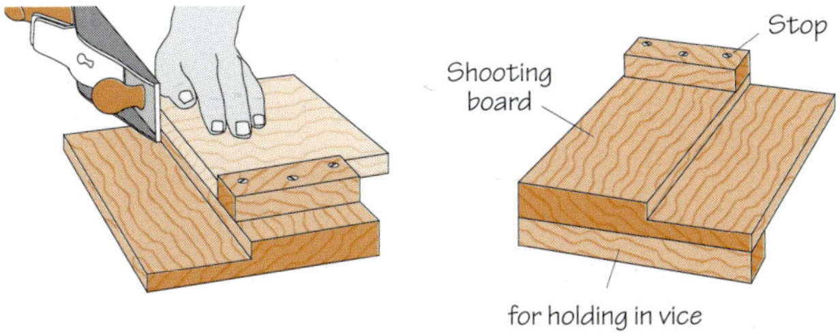

The ends of narrow pieces can be planed using a shooting board

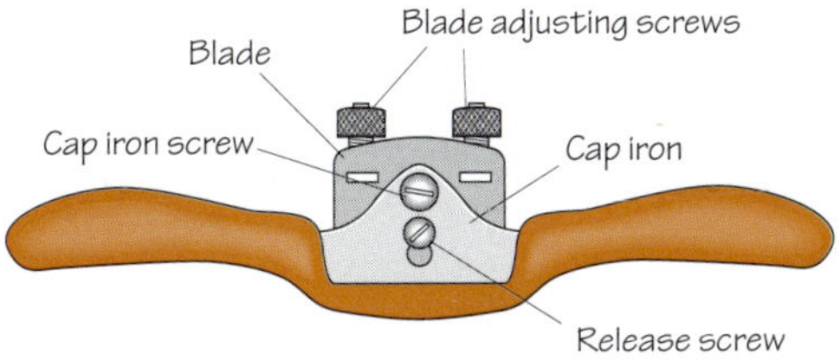

Spokeshave

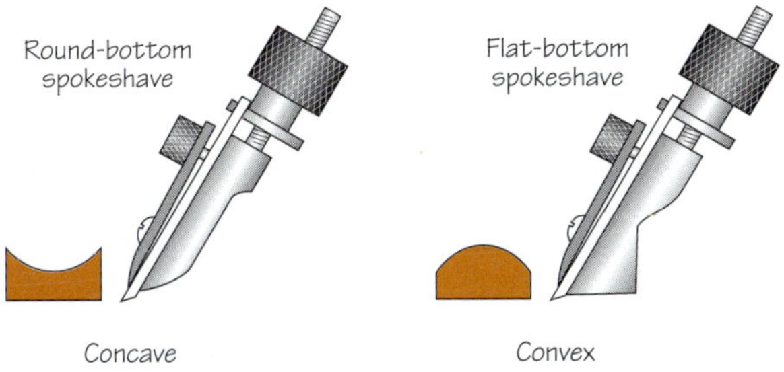

Two types of spokeshave – concave – convex

Spokeshaves

These are members of the plane family and are used to plane curves. The blade is fixed in place by a locking cap and locking screw. There are also two screws which adjust the depth of blade on both sides.

There are two types of spokeshave:

(i) Convex (flat)

(ii) Concave (rounded).

The sole of the convex spokeshave is flat and the sole of the concave is rounded to enable it to easily fit the concave curves.

The spokeshave can be difficult tool to use. It must always be used in the direction of the grain as shown, or the result will be a very rough finished surface.

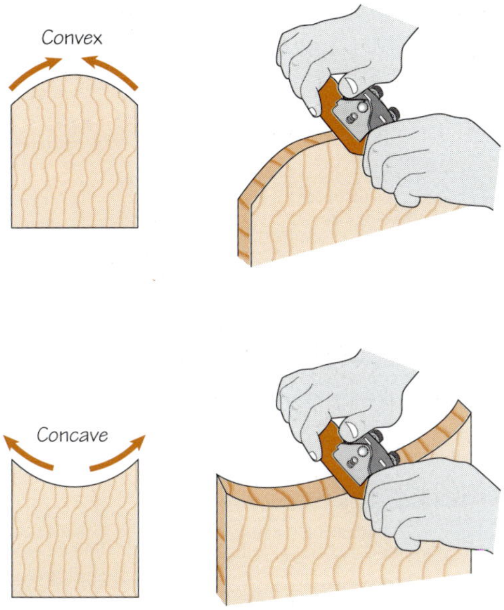

Using the spokeshave

Files and rasps, surform tools

These tools are very useful for shaping wood, metal and plastics. They are used to smooth out surfaces and to form various shapes. They are quite versatile and can get into most curves and corners. One drawback is that they leave surfaces quite rough, unlike the planes we have looked at so far. It is therefore necessary to smooth the surfaces afterwards with sandpaper. There are many different types of shaping tools available. Each does a certain type of cut or surface well.

Files

The file and the rasp are very alike. The shape of the teeth is the main difference between each type. The rasp has very rough and coarse teeth while the file's teeth are more regular and finer.

Files are mainly used for working on metals and plastics as their fine surfaces are suited to this task. There are various shapes of file blades, semi-circular, circular (rat-tail file), flat or triangular. The rat tail file is very suitable for smoothing out keyholes and enlarging them. The triangular file is also used for sharpening saw teeth.

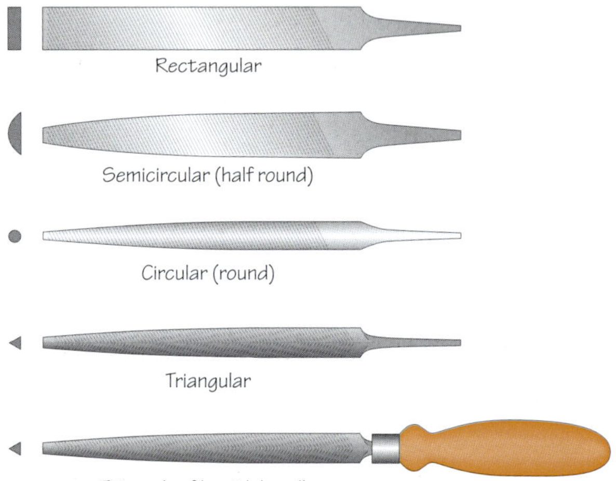

Types of file

When a file gets clogged with material it is cleaned using a very fine wire brush called a file card.

Rasp

The teeth on a rasp are larger than those of the file. They remove material quicker but the finished surface can be rough.

> **BEWARE!** The rasp and file can be bought without a handle. A handle should always be fitted before use as the point of the tang could puncture your hand

The rasp and file go blunt with use and they are difficult to sharpen. To get around this problem the surform was developed.

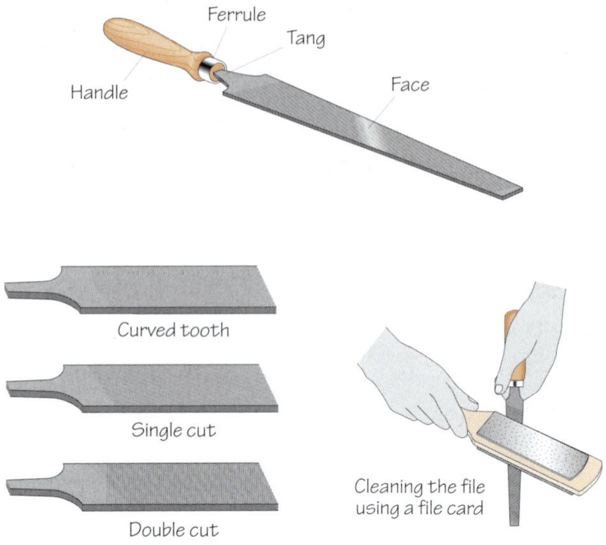

Parts of the rasp/file

Surform tools (shapers)

Surform tools are a cross between traditional planes and rasps. They come in different shapes and sizes of blade to suit almost every job.

Surform tools

The blades have open teeth which means that the tool does not clog up as easily as the rasp and file. When the blade breaks or gets worn it is easily replaced. The work is done very quickly with surform tools but the finished surface is not as smooth as that from a plane. Surfaces must be sanded down after using these shapers. The one problem that occurs with surform tools is that they cannot get into really tight corners. But nevertheless, they are a popular carving tool and are great for preliminary or secondary shaping.

Screwdrivers

There are a number of different screwdriver to suit different jobs and the different types and sizes of screws. The more common types are listed below.

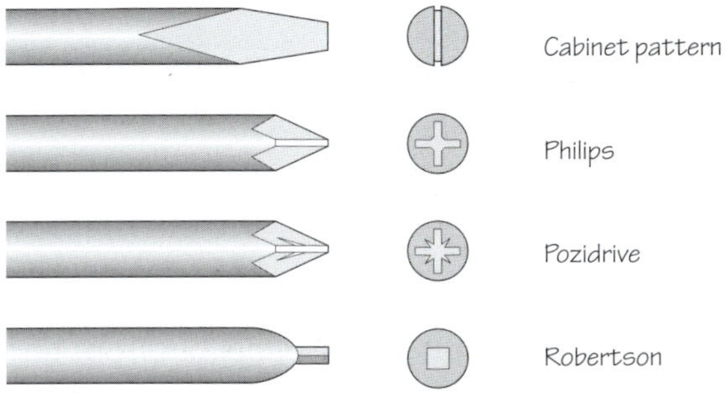

Types of screwdriver head

Cabinet pattern is the most common screwdriver and is used with a straight slotted screw. Usually it has a wooden or plastic handle. It can be obtained in different sizes.

Phillips screwdriver is used with screws which have self centering heads. The head of the screw is less easily damaged because of the shape of the screw driver head. The handle is usually plastic and it comes in various sizes.

Ratchet screwdrivers make driving screws easier. They are used where there are many screws to be driven or where you are working in a tight corner. With the ratchet you can turn the handle without turning the blade. So the blade turns when the handle is turned in one direction only.

The heads of screws can be damaged easily if they are over tightened or if the incorrect size of screwdriver is used; or if a pilot hole is not drilled. So care must be taken not to damage the heads of screws when driving them into the materials, as this gives a poor finish.

Pozidrive and **philips screws** are less easily damaged and are therefore, becoming more popular. Another reason for their popularity is the use of the screw gun or screw attachment for an electric drill.

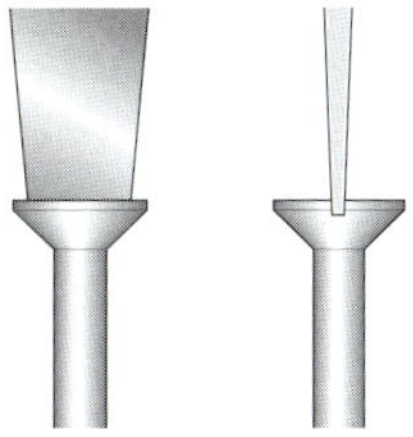

Ensure that the screwdriver head fits the screw properly

- *Too large – it will damage the screw and the material*
- *Too small – it will damage the screw*

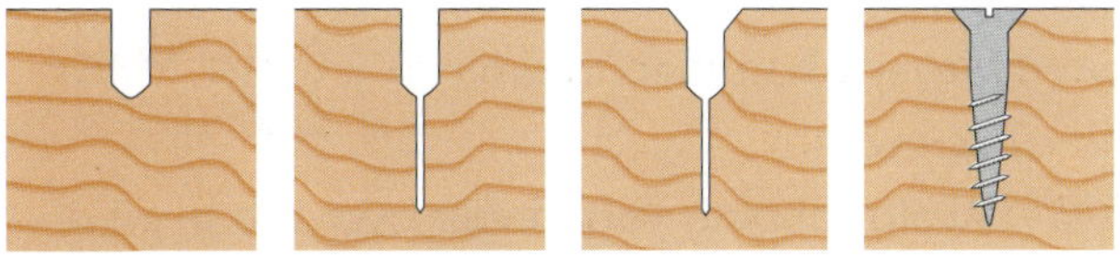

Drilling a pilot hole for a screw

- *Locate & bore a shank hole*
- *Bore a hole, smaller than the thread of the screw*
- *Countersink the hole if needed*
- *Insert the screw*

When driving screws you should always hold the screwdriver with both hands as shown below with the work gripped or supported in the vice.

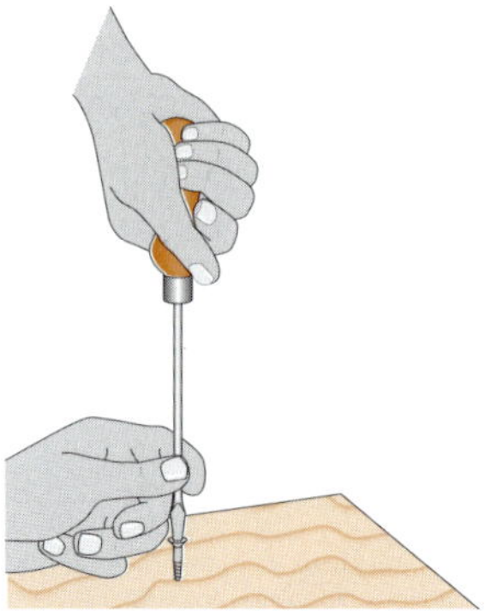

Always hold the screwdriver with both hands

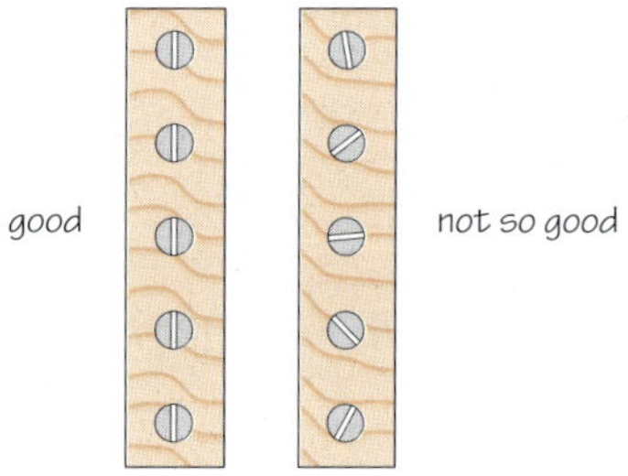

The work looks better if all the screw slots are lined up

- Always use a screwdriver, never a hammer, to drive a screw
- Avoid rubbing your finger over the head of a screw when it has been driven home as bits of metal splinters (swarf) may cut you

Exercises

1. Draw diagrams of the following tools and label all the parts of each on your diagram:
   (a) Try-square
   (b) Tenon saw
   (c) Bevel edged chisel
   (d) Marking gauge
   (e) Mallet
   (f) Coping saw.
2. Give the function of the tools listed in question 1.
3. Explain how you would test a try-square for accuracy.
4. Sketch a thumb gauge and describe its function.
5. Explain, using notes and sketches, how you would remove a nail or panel pin from timber using a pincers or claw hammer.
6. Sketch and describe the use of each of the following:
   (a) Pincers (c) Bradawl
   (b) Ratchet (d) Countersink bit.
7. (a) Describe the Jack plane and state its function
   (b) Name three parts of a Jack plane and explain the function of each.
   (c) What are the differences between the Jack plane and the block plane?
8. Describe in detail, with the aid of sketches, how you would plane the end grain of a piece of wood. Explain why you would need to plane the end grain.
9. Explain where each of the following is used:
   (a) Compass saw (c) Coping saw
   (b) Bow saw (d) Fret saw.
10. (a) Using sketches, describe four types of screwdrivers and give the uses of each.
    (b) Explain how you would join two pieces of wood using countersink screws.

CHAPTER SEVENTEEN

SHARPENING TOOLS

In order to perform correctly and safely, tools must be kept in proper working order. Cutting tools must be kept sharp by regular sharpening (**honing**). Some tools are designed so that their cutting edges or blades are simply replaced when they become worn. These include drill bits, coping saw blades and jig saw blades. However, most cutting tools such as chisels, planes, tenon saws, etc must be sharpened regularly.

Sharpening chisel/plane

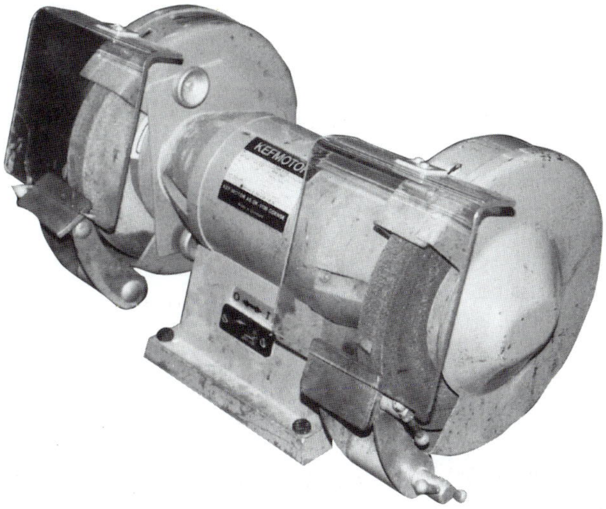

Grindstone

Sharpening stones

Tools such as chisels are sharpened using two processes; grinding and sharpening. Grinding is done from time to time as required to remove excessive wear or damage. Grinding is done on a **grindstone**, which can be an oil cooled horizontal type or a vertical type, where the tool must be regularly cooled in water to prevent the tool overheating.

Sharpening is performed on an oilstone. There are two types of oilstone, artificial and natural. Naturally occurring stones such as Arkansas and Washita are expensive and because of their natural origin, they may vary in quality. Artificial stones are made form abrasive grits and can be obtained in various grades of fineness. Some stones have a fine grit on one side and a coarser grit on the other; these are known as **combination stones**. Oilstones are usually made in a rectangular form, but can be obtained in other various shapes, as shown below, and these are called **slipstones**.

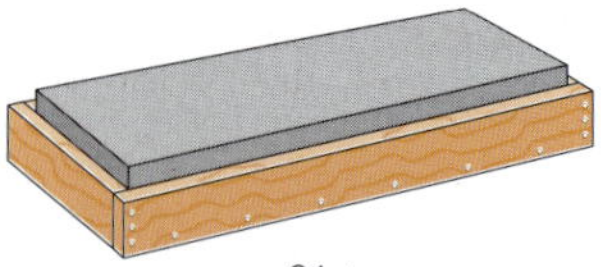

Oilstone

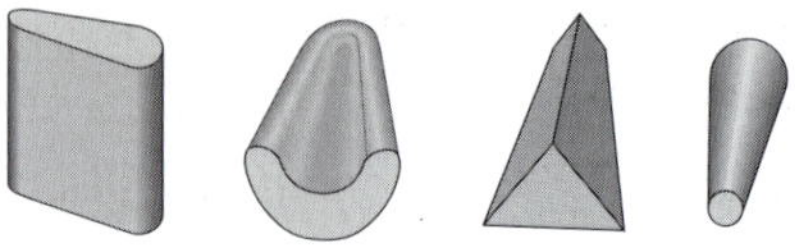

Slipstones

Oilstones and slipstones

Slipstones are specially shaped so that they can be used to sharpen gouges and carving chisels which have shaped blades which would be difficult to sharpen on an ordinary flat stone.

Grinding and sharpening

The edge of a tool is ground when:

- It has worn down
- It has been damaged by misuse
- It has been rounded over by incorrect sharpening.

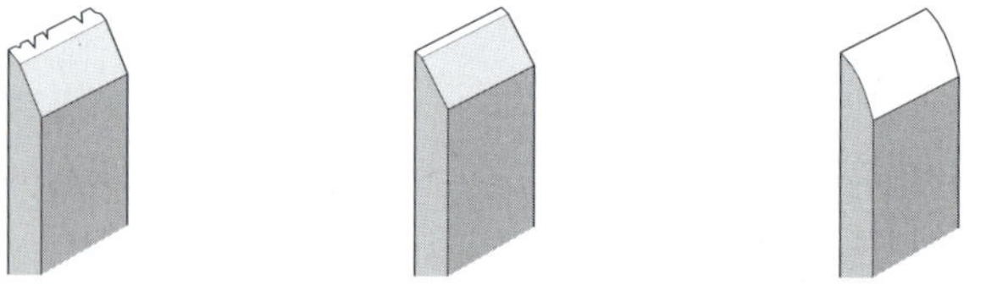

The edge is damaged

The edge wears down after repeated sharpening

The edge becomes rounded or curved from incorrect sharpening

Three situations where grinding is required

Grinding removes a lot of steel quite quickly, so it is best not to grind a blade too often. If tool edges are protected and used carefully they should only need to be ground occasionally.

Grinding is done on the grindstone to an angle of 25°. The horizontal grinder is perhaps the most appropriate one to use as the vertical grinder can overheat the edge, causing a loss of the temper on the blade and general weakening. The blades of chisels and planes are hardened and tempered by a process of heating and cooling.

Sharpening should be carried out regularly to keep the cutting edge of the tools very sharp. Firstly, oil is put on to the oilstone to keep the stone lubricated which helps the tool to move on the stone and it also reduces wear and clogging of the stone.

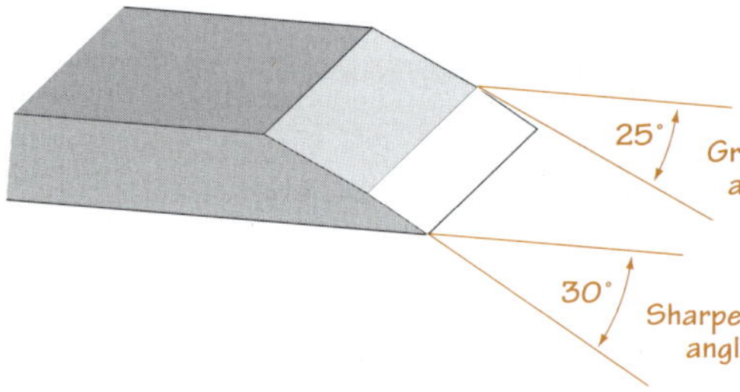

Grinding and sharpening angles

Sharpening is carried out to an angle of 30°. A sharpening guide can be used to keep the blade at the correct angle. It is important when sharpening to keep this angle constant so that the blade is not sharpened to a curved edge. The blade is sharpened by rubbing it back and forth along the stone at the correct angle 30°. Also the blade of the tool must be held so that the edge is kept at 90° to the sides of the blade.

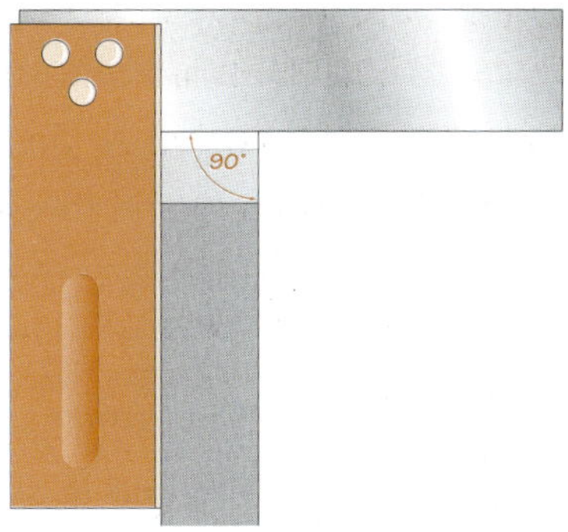

The edge should be 90° to the sides of the blade

When a sharp edge is achieved, the blade is placed, flat side down, on the stone and the **burr** is removed by rubbing the flat surface back and forth along the stone. This process is called **backing off**.

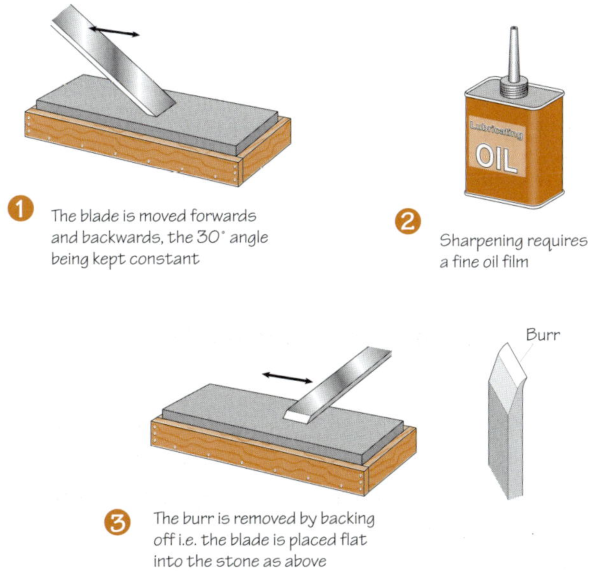

The sharpening process

Sharpening saws

Saws are sharpened by a skilled tradesman (often called a *saw doctor*). Usually a saw only needs sharpening occasionally if properly used. Many modern saws have teeth which are strengthened at the points or have points made from tungsten. These saws generally keep their edge for a long time but are never sharpened. The saw is simply replaced when the blade becomes blunt.

There are several stages to sharpening a saw. Firstly, the saw teeth are levelled to bring them all into the one line, using a file mounted in a piece of hardwood. The saw is held in a vice during this process. Following this the teeth are reshaped and sharpened with a triangular file. The teeth of the rip saw are sharpened in a slightly different way to the teeth of other saws, because they are different in shape.

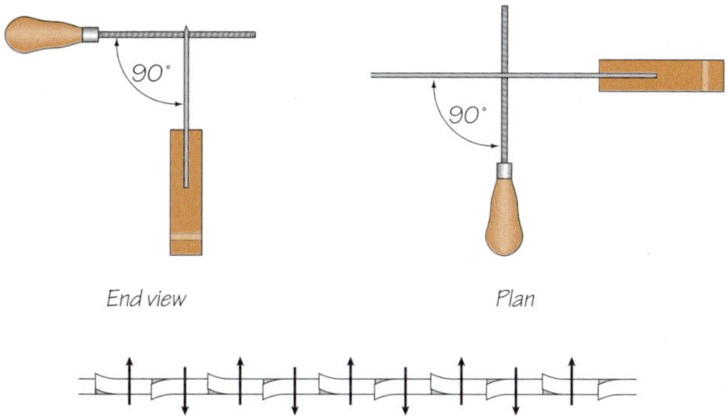

Filing the rip saw

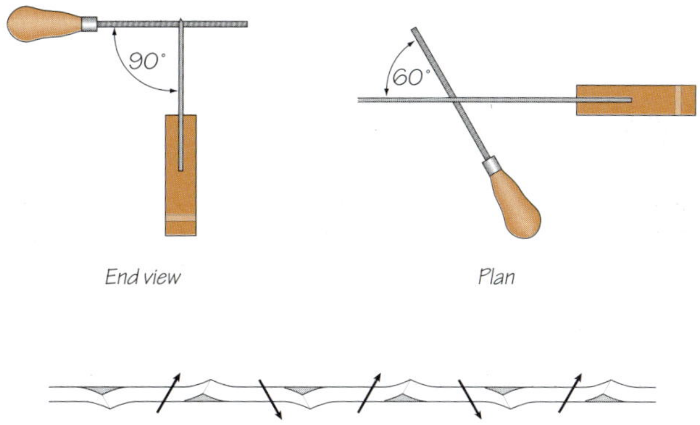

Filing the tenon saw, panel saw and cross cut saw

Once each tooth has been filed to a sharp point, they have to be 'set'. Alternative teeth are bent slightly to each side of the blade. This is done so that the cut made by the teeth of the saw will be wider than the blade, so that it will move through the cut freely. This is called the **set** of the saw and must be accurately done using a tool called a saw set. Operating like a pliers, the saw set pushes the tooth to the side of the blade.

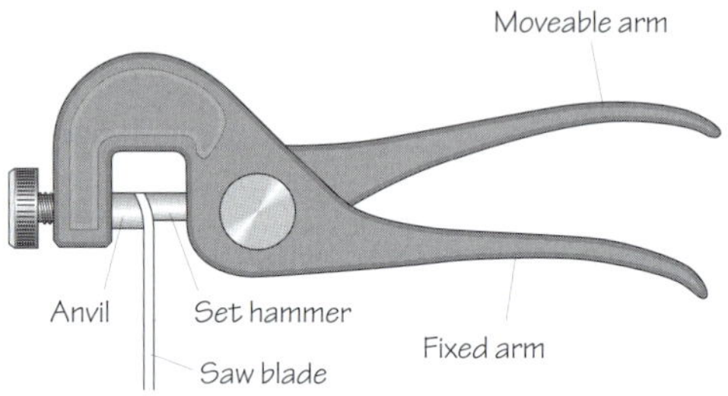

The saw set

Exercises

1. The cutting edges of tools are sharpened to two important angles. Name these angles.
2. The ______________ angle is ____°.
   The ______________ angle is ____°.
3. Name the tools used to sharpen saws.
4. Name the type of stone used to sharpen carving chisels.
5. It is necessary to keep tools sharp. Give two reasons why this so.
6. List the stages of sharpening a chisel.
7. Describe with the aid of sketches when it would be necessary to grind the blade of a chisel or plane.
8. Why is oil used on an oilstone?
9. It is important not to overheat the blade of a tool whilst grinding. Explain in detail why this is so.
10. Explain how a tenon saw blade is sharpened.
11. Explain what the 'set' of a saw is and how it is formed.

TOOLS AND MACHINES

CHAPTER EIGHTEEN

POWER TOOLS

Power tools have replaced many hand tools for doing work in the home and the workshop. They allow more work to be carried out in less time than hand tools, particularly if it is repetitive work where accuracy is required. Power tools are usually powered by electricity and have blades or cutters which travel at high speed. This obviously makes them dangerous and it is important that care is taken with them at all times. Many of the power tools described here are too dangerous to be used by students in the workshop. Power tools are not a substitute for quality hand work.

Power tools

Advantages:

- They allow work processes to be carried out quickly
- Repetitive work can be carried out accurately
- Complex work can be done easily
- They are portable.

Disadvantages:

- They are expensive
- They usually need a power source
- They are more dangerous than hand tools
- The need for a power cable can cause difficulties
- They take time to set up and use accurately.

With the growth of do-it-yourself market, many new power tools have been developed recently. Re-chargeable power tools are becoming popular – they do not have electric cords but run on battery power. The battery is simply re-charged from the mains power supply when they run down. They reduce the risk of electric shock, but are still dangerous. Their main advantage is that they can be used where an electric power supply is unavailable.

Using a cordless drill to fix the cabin door on a small yacht

BEWARE!

Many people have been very seriously injured while using power tools improperly. Even in the safest hands accidents can happen. The least distraction can lead to very serious injury. **Safety is vital. Only use the power tools as shown by your teacher and after being instructed in their safe use**

Some tools and machines are more dangerous than others, but danger is always present. Follow these guidelines for your added safety.

- Always use the tools as instructed
- Always ensure that you are wearing the appropriate protective safety equipment for the job
- Before changing bits, belts or glasspaper for sanders, or making other adjustments to any power tool, switch off the tool and disconnect it from the mains
- Always keep the cutter or moving part of the tool pointing away from yourself and others
- Ensure that the electric flex of the tool does not come into contact with the moving parts of the power tool
- Do not let others interfere with you while you are working and do not disturb others while they are operating equipment
- If in doubt seek the assistance of your teacher
- Never leave a power tool running
- Always wait for the power tool to come to a complete stop before walking away from it
- Guards are there for your safety; do not tamper with them or tie them back, and if they are damaged report it immediately
- Disconnect the power supply when the tool is not in use
- Have all power tools regularly serviced.

Types of power tools

Power tools:

- Sanders
- Drills & drill presses
- Screwdrivers
- Iron
- Saws
- Planes
- Router
- Biscuit jointers
- Pyrography tool.

Machines:

- Planers
- Circular saw
- Band saw
- Scroll saw
- Sanders
- Mortisers
- Spindle moulders
- Lathes.

Sanders

There are a few types of sanders available. The sander smooths down the surface of wood in preparation for a finish.

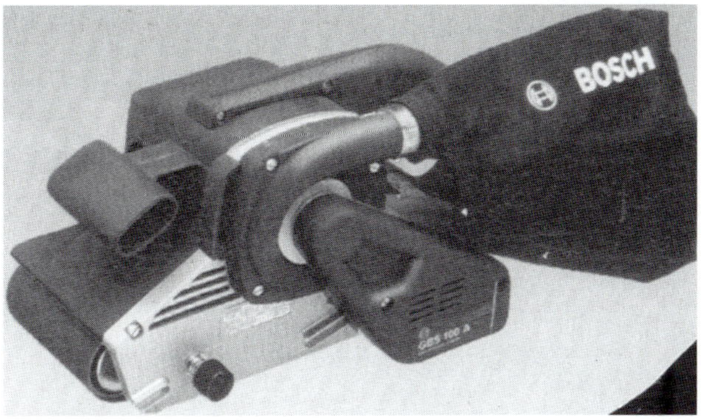

Belt sander

Belt sander

This is a large and robust sander. The abrasive belt is stretched over two rollers which drive it forward. The belt, which is a strong cloth type with abrasive grit on it, can be changed when required. Different grades of abrasive belt can be obtained, but the belt sander is usually used to give an initial levelling to rougher or damaged wood, often larger flat surfaces. The widths of the sander vary from 50mm to 100mm.

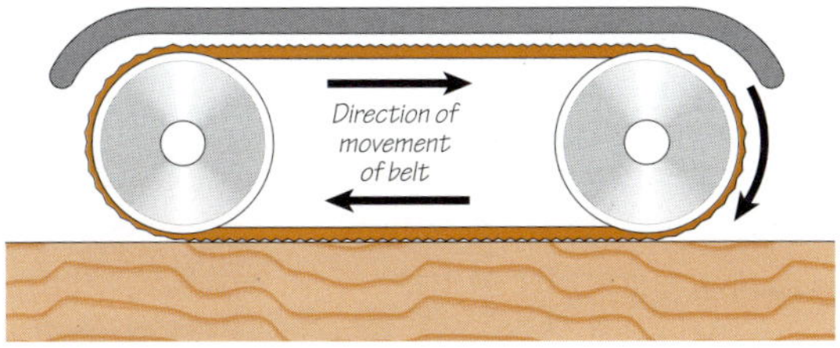

Sketch of the direction of belt

Orbital sander

The orbital sander has a flat pad which vibrates in tiny circular motions at speed. It is used to smooth flat surfaces and a high quality finish can be achieved. Specially made rolls of heavy quality abrasive paper are used with this sander, although ordinary sheet sandpaper can be cut to the size of the pad. The abrasive paper is held on to the pad by spring loaded clamps. Abrasive paper of different grades can be used and interchanged quickly and easily.

One disadvantage of this sander is that the small circular motions of the pad can leave tiny circular scratches on the surface of wood. These scratches will show up on the surface of the wood particularly if the wood is to be stained or polished. A final sanding should be done by hand to remove these scratches, to achieve the best results.

Orbital sander

Disc sander

This is used in a similar way to the orbital sander. The pad is circular and the special sanding discs have a self adhesive back. The pad spins and vibrates also like an orbital sander.

Disc sander

Sanding discs and attachments can be bought for the electric drill. These are used for sanding and light shaping of shaped surfaces which would be unsuitable for the orbital sander.

When using sanders or sanding attachments it is important to let the power of the machine and the abrasive paper do the work. Pressure should **not** be put on the machine/drill as this will damage them.

Drills

There are a great number of drills available; some have different power levels and other special functions such as variable speed, hammer action (for drilling into masonry) and forward and reverse action for driving screws. The bit of the drill is held in a chuck as with hand drills. Chucks are tightened using a chuck key, although modern drills have keyless chucks.

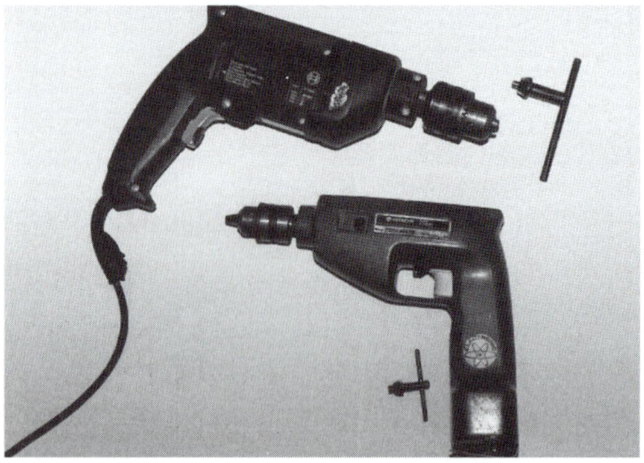

Electric power drill

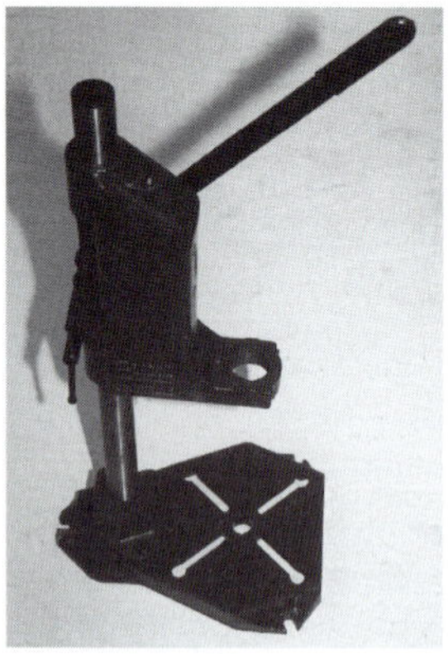

Drill stand

Pillar drill

Drills can be used in a drill stand for vertical and more precise drilling. Also used for drilling is the **pillar drill.**

BEWARE!

- Make sure that the drill is disconnected from the power supply before changing bits or making adjustments
- Always ensure that the bit is securely fastened in the chuck before use
- Always remove the chuck key from the chuck before using the drill

Drilling

The drilling machine (pillar drill), or the portable electric drill, can be used to bore holes in metal, plastic or wood. The pillar drill, with its fixed table and sensitive feed lever mechanism, is very accurate, although the electric drill can be used also with a drill press for accurate drilling.

When drilling any materials with a power drill, the workpiece must be held firmly against a solid background – whether it is a base of a drill press or a waste piece of timber held behind the workpiece in a vice. When drilling metal, the centre of the hole must first be punched with a centre punch. The hole is then aligned with the drill bit. The drill is turned on and the hole drilled at a uniform rate.

Always take care never to handle **swarf** (metal shavings) from the hole; splinters can get into your hands and they are very painful. Also metal becomes very hot when it is being worked. Always brush the swarf away with a hand brush.

Drill (bits)

Cutting tools that fit into power drills are called 'bits' or 'drill bits'.

The drill bits used to cut metal and plastic are called twist drills. They vary in length and diameter, have a parallel cylindrical shape, and fit into the jaws of the drill chuck. The sizes of twist drills range from less than 1mm upwards. The chucks of power drills vary in size, most taking a twist drill of 12mm diameter. Twist drills of larger diameter can be obtained with a tapered shank, which fits into the standard chuck.

Power screwdrivers

Powered screwdrivers can be obtained as screwguns and are used mostly in any industry where continuous use is needed, i.e. securing plasterboard to walls and ceilings. These screwguns can have magnetic heads/bits which pick up the screws easily for immediate use. Smaller powered screwdrivers and cordless screwdrivers are used for light general use.

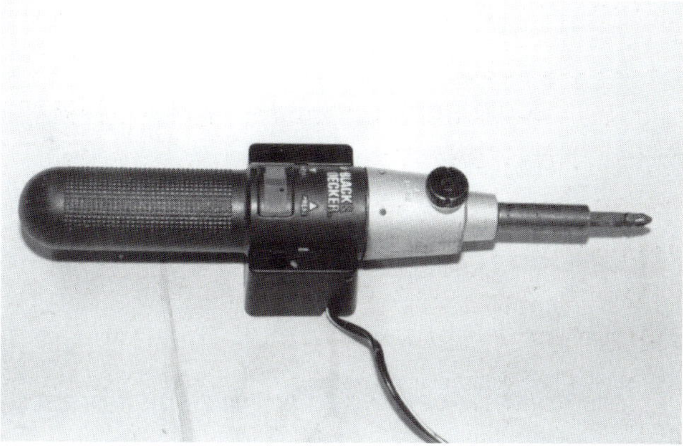

Cordless screwdriver and charger

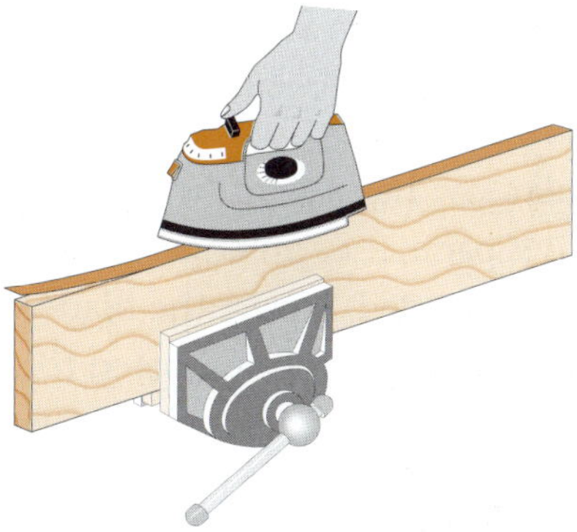

Iron on edging being applied

Iron

The ordinary clothes iron is a tool which is used in the Materials Technology Room. It is used for applying iron-on veneers. These veneers are used for finishing off the edges of sheet material. The iron can also be used for removing small bruises from the surface of wood.

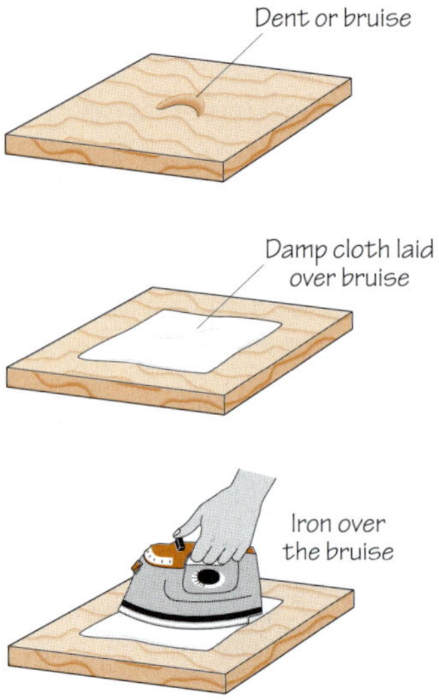

The iron can be used to remove small bruises from wood

Circular saw

This portable power tool is used for cutting sheet material and other work done by the larger table saw. It is often more convenient to bring the tool to the work.

The circular saw has a fence which keeps the blade running parallel to an edge. A guard, which is spring loaded, covers the blade when not in use. The blade can be adjusted to vary the cutting depth and the angle of cut can be adjusted.

Portable circular saw

Always disconnect the saw from the mains when not in use. Hands must always be kept away from the blade

Jigsaw

The jigsaw has a narrow blade which can be easily changed when broken. Various types and sizes of blade are available capable of cutting different materials. Blades are bought to suit the particular type and model of jigsaw you might have, but are quite cheap and easily obtained.

The jigsaw

The motor drives the blade up and down to cut the material. The jigsaw can cut tight corners and the saw is very versatile. The saw can be fitted with a fence for cutting straight lines but it is usually used to cut curves. One disadvantage of the jigsaw is that the depth of cut is limited.

The soleplate or baseplate of the saw can be set to different angles in a similar way to the circular saw.

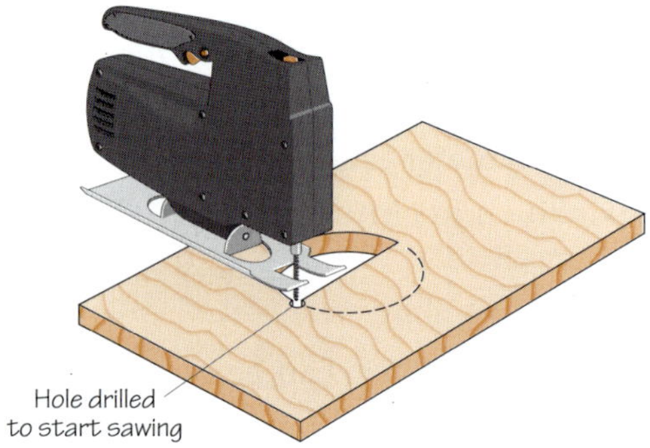

Using the jigsaw to cut out holes in material

- Use safety goggles when using the jigsaw
- The workpiece should be held firmly, in the vice or to the bench using a G-cramp
- Disconnect the tool before making adjustments
- Always keep the power cable away from the blade

The electric planer

Planes

Powered planes are similar to the hand plane. They are powered usually by an electric motor which drives a cylindrical block. The cutting is done by two knives which are slotted into this block and fixed in place using bolts.

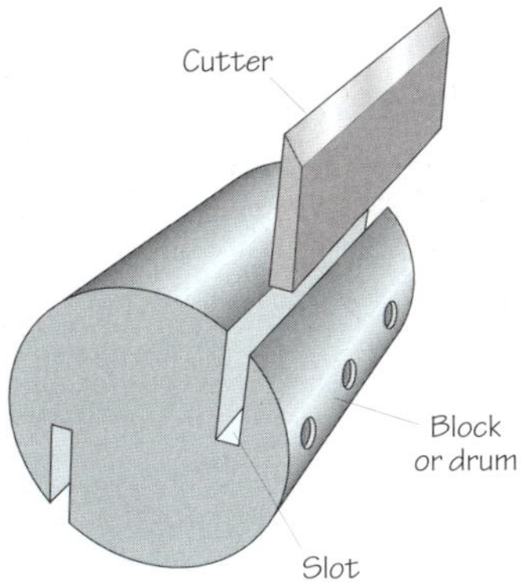

Cutter knives fixed into the block

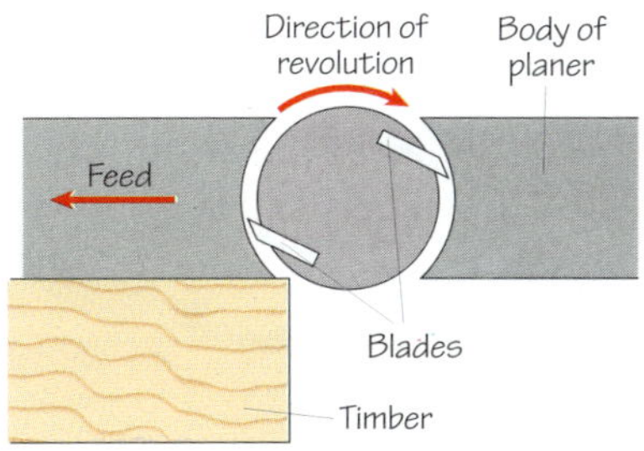

The cutting action of the planer

The planer is used for smoothing rough wooden surfaces and for removing wood to bring material to the required width and thickness. The planer does this more quickly than the ordinary hand plane. It is, however, more dangerous as the cutters have no guards. The planer can be fitted with a fence to assists in planing square edges, etc.

The cutter block can be adjusted to remove more or less material.

- Keep your hands and the power cable away from the blades at all times
- Disconnect from power supply and store on its side when not in use
- The tool should be fully stopped and disconnected before making any adjustments
- Always use the appropriate safety equipment for protection when operating the planer

Biscuit joiner

The biscuit joiner is a modern power tool which is used in the making of joints. The machine is like a small circular saw which cuts a small slot in both pieces of wood to be joined. A biscuit, which is usually made from pressed beech, is glued and inserted into the grooves and it acts like a loose tongue. This type of joint is very useful and strong, it also joins the edges of man-made boards very well.

The biscuit jointer

The router

Router

The router is a portable power tool which is used for cutting mouldings in timber. It is a very versatile tool and can be used with a number of specialised attachments which will cut joints such as mortises, rebates, housings and dovetails. Special templates can be used to produce carved effects. Routers can be obtained in different sizes according to how powerful they are. The router has a detachable fence.

The router uses multiple interchangable cutters which are varied in design and size. These cutters are fixed into a special chuck which is driven by an electric motor.

The cutter protrudes below the baseplate to do the cutting. The baseplate can be raised and lowered to allow the depth of cut to be adjusted; it also allows the cutter to be plunged into the material, cut the required amount and be lifted, by means of a spring action.

BEWARE!

- Always keep the cutter facing away from yourself and others
- Always keep the power cable away from the cutter
- Always disconnect from power supply before making adjustments and when not in use
- Always use proper safety protection when using the router
- Allow the cutter to stop before placing the router on the bench

Remember that working with any power tool is dangerous. Only use power tools as directed by your teacher with his or her permission.

The router is a particularly dangerous tool and should only be used with adult supervision

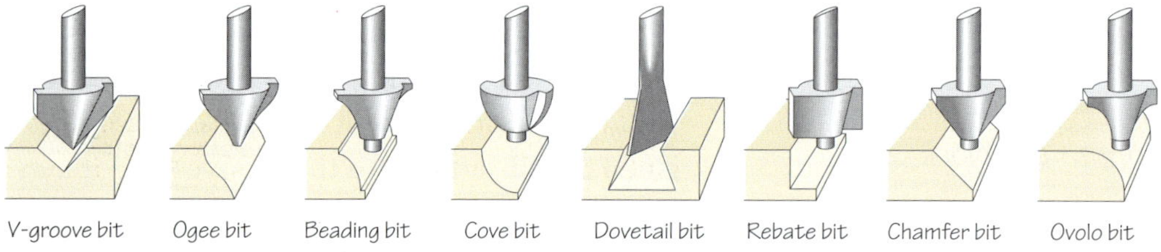

Some of the cutters and the mouldings they produce

Power supply

Power tools are usually electrically powered or run by battery which is charged by a mains supply. In this country the electricity in the mains supply has a voltage of 220 volts. The power tool is connected to the supply through the plug. Plugs must be wired correctly to ensure safe use.

The electrical cable may have two wires, a **live** which is brown in colour and a **neutral** which is blue. However cables have a third wire called the **earth** wire, coloured green and yellow. This earth wire is important for safety: in the event of an accident, the earth wire directs current safely to the ground through the electrical supply, possibly preventing serious injury.

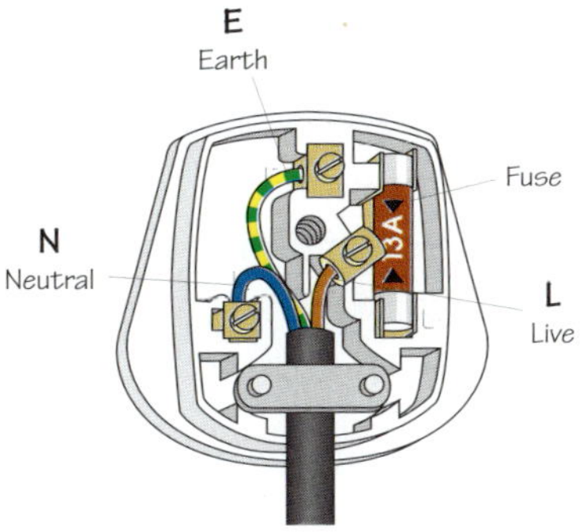

Correct wiring for electrical plug

Plugs are fitted with a **fuse**, which prevents too much current getting through to the appliance. Most plugs are supplied with a 13 amp fuse but this is generally unsuitable for most power tools. You should fit the correct fuse for the particular tool before it is used. The correct amps rating for the tool should be given in its instruction manual, but can be easily calculated.

The calculation is based on **Ohm's Law**

$$V = I \times R$$
$$W = V \times I$$

where:

W = power (watts)
V= voltage (volts)
I = current (amps)

Example

Calculate the correct fuse amps rating for a 600 watt power drill which will be connected to a 220 volt mains supply.

$$W = V \times I$$
$$\text{so} \quad I = \frac{W}{V}$$
$$I = \frac{600}{220}$$
$$I = 2.73 \text{ amps}$$

So a 3 amp fuse will be sufficient for the drill.

Plugs should be sturdy to be able to resist occasional knocks. To be sure the tool is safe to use at all times the wiring to a plug should be checked occasionally to ensure wires are not loose, etc.

Exercises

1. List four key safety rules which must be followed when using power tools.
2. Name each of these power tools and state their uses.

3. List situations where it would be important to use safety goggles, saying why they should be used.
4. Give two advantages and two disadvantages that power tools have compared to hand tools.
5. Name the mouldings shown here and name the power tool used to produce them.

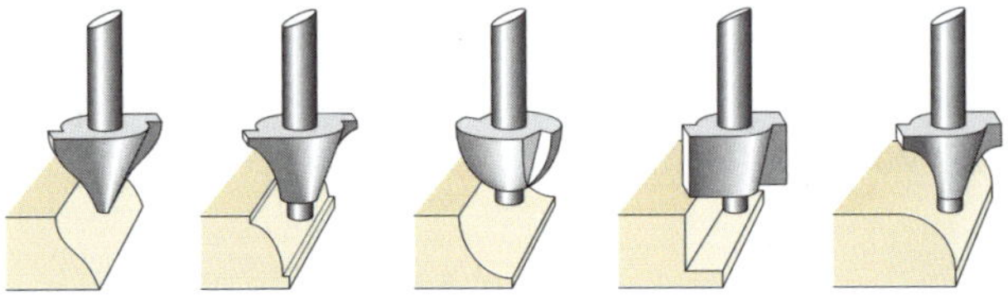

Ogee bit *Beading bit* *Cove bit* *Rebate bit* *Ovolo bit*

6. In what ways have power tools improved the way that work is done both in industry and at home?
7. Select two items of furniture and list the power tools that might have been used to help make them.
8. Describe how an electric iron can be used to remove bruising in timber.
9. An electric plug is shown in the diagram. Identify the live, neutral and earth wires and state the colour code of each. What is the function of D?

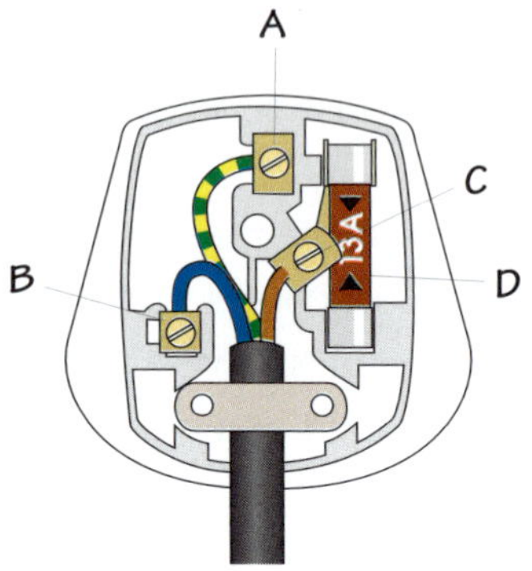

(1) ______________ colour ______________
(2) ______________ colour ______________
(3) ______________ colour ______________

10. A 500 watt electric router is connected to a 220 volt mains supply. Calculate a suitable size of fuse to be fitted in the plug.

TOOLS AND MACHINES

CHAPTER NINETEEN

MACHINES

Machines differ from power tools in two respects.

- Machines are usually larger and more powerful
- A machine is stationary and would be fixed to a bench or the floor. The work is usually fed to the machine.

Machines allow work of all types to be done in large amounts, with speed and ease. Machines can also cope with larger pieces of work than power tools. Your teacher uses the machines in the Materials Technology Room to prepare many of the materials that you use for your projectwork in class. Machines are dangerous because of the speed of the blades or cutters and also because of their power. There are, however, some smaller machines which you may use with the permission and supervision of your teacher.

BEWARE!

Always use protective safety equipment when using any machine

Saws

There are a number of different machine saws available, each suited to particular jobs. Some saws cut boards across the grain; some cut along the grain (ripping) and others are particularly suited for cutting panels or sheet material. All can be obtained in different sizes, according to their power.

Cross-cut saw

The cross-cut saw, or radial arm saw as it is sometimes called, is used for cutting boards to length. It cuts across the grain of the material. The saw is mounted on an arm and is pulled out across the piece, which is placed on the table. The depth of cut can be varied by adjusting the height of the saw blade above the table. The saw can also be set to cut angles up to 45°.

Chop saw

There is a small portable cross cut saw sometimes called a **chop saw** which is used on building sites for cutting boards to length and for cutting angles for mitres, etc.

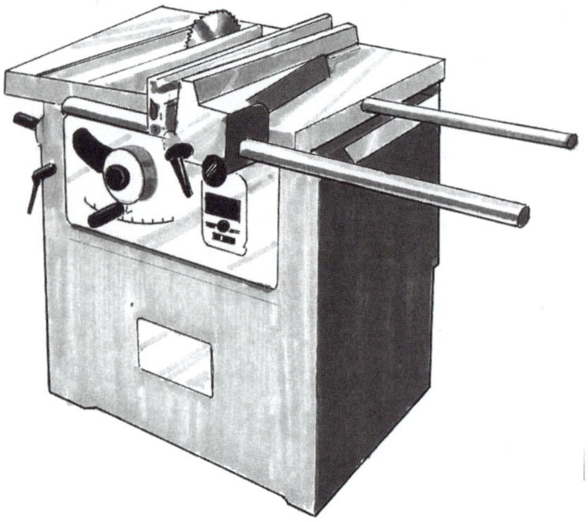

Circular saw

- Care should be exercised as the circular saw is very dangerous
- Never interrupt someone using the saw or any machine
- The guards and other safety equipment should always be used and kept in good order
- Always keep the area around the saw free and clear from any debris, etc

Circular saw

There is usually a circular saw in every workshop. Sometimes it is called a table saw and it is used for ripping boards, cross cutting material and other general cutting. There are special saws with larger sliding tables which are used for cutting sheet materials like MDF and plywood. These are called panel saws.

For safety, material is pushed through the saw using a push stick which ensures that the operator's hands are kept at a safe distance from the blade.

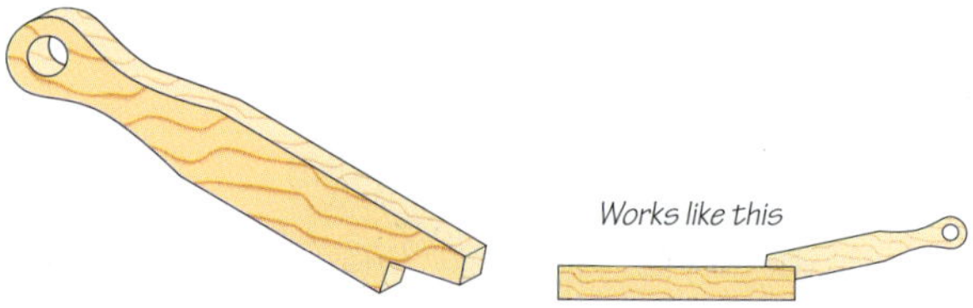

Push stick

Scroll saw

The scroll saw is present in most school workshops. It is a small saw which cuts using a thin blade fixed between two arms. These arms move up and down and cut the material which is held firmly down on the table of the saw. The scroll saw cuts material which is relatively thin (up to 30mm thick, depending on the material). It can cut very tight curves because of its thin blade.

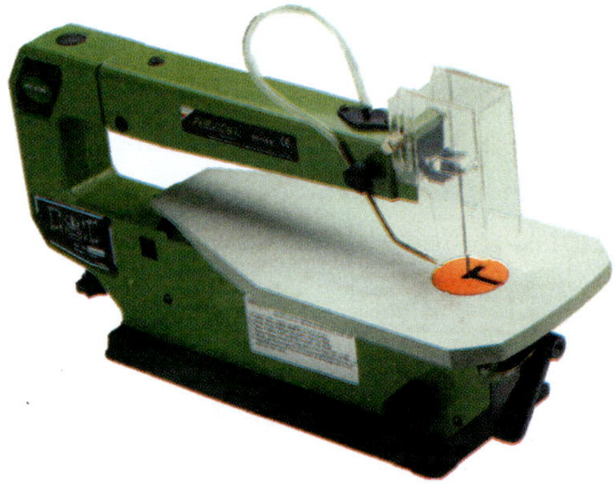

Scroll saw

- Always use safety goggles when operating the scroll saw
- Always use the guard
- Keep your hands and fingers away from the blade of the machine

Bandsaw

The bandsaw is used in many Materials Technology Rooms. Different sizes of bandsaw are available – larger sizes for heavier work. There is a horizontal type used in the conversion of logs to boards.

The blade of the bandsaw is thin and forms a continuous circle like a rubber band. The blade is mounted between two wheels which revolve, allowing the blade to cut. The blade and the wheels are concealed behind a metal case with only a small portion exposed to cut the material. The blade is kept steady by adjusting guides and rollers which are positioned on an arm above the table, which also supports the guard. The blade passes through a slot in the table of the saw. The piece is fed to the blade while being held firmly down on the table. Different thicknesses can be cut by raising or lowering the guard.

Bandsaw

The bandsaw is used to cut curves, or it can also be used with a fence to cut straight parallel cuts such as ripping. Blades of different widths can be put on allowing tighter curves to be cut.

The bandsaw is a dangerous machine, as the cutting edge of the blade is left unguarded to allow the piece to be fed into it:

- Always keep your hands on either side of the saw line – away from the blade
- Always use safety equipment – goggles, dust mask, etc. Ask your teacher for the equipment

Mortiser

The mortiser combines a chiselling action with a drilling action which removes a square hole in timber. This allows both through and stopped mortises to be removed quickly and accurately. It also allows for many similar mortises to be done in a short time.

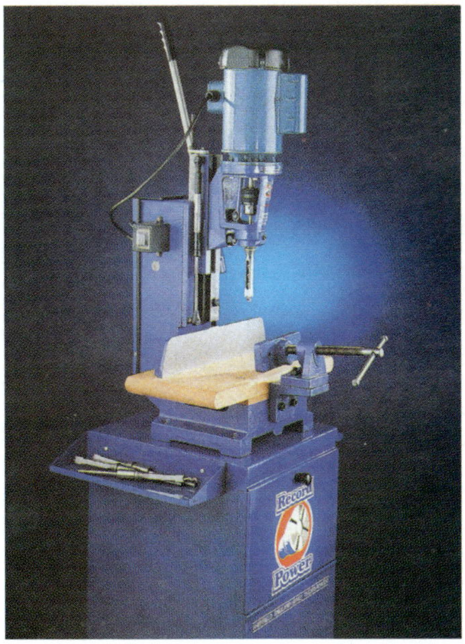

Mortising machine

The mortiser has a cutter which consists of a hollow chisel which is square, while inside there is a special auger drill bit which is fixed in a chuck. The workpiece is secured to the bed/table by a cramp. As the cutter is brought down to the wood, the drill bit cuts a hole through the wood, the sharp square chisel cleans off the cut as it follows. The cutter (chisel and bit) can be changed quite easily for a different size. Sizes range from 6mm to 25mm or more.

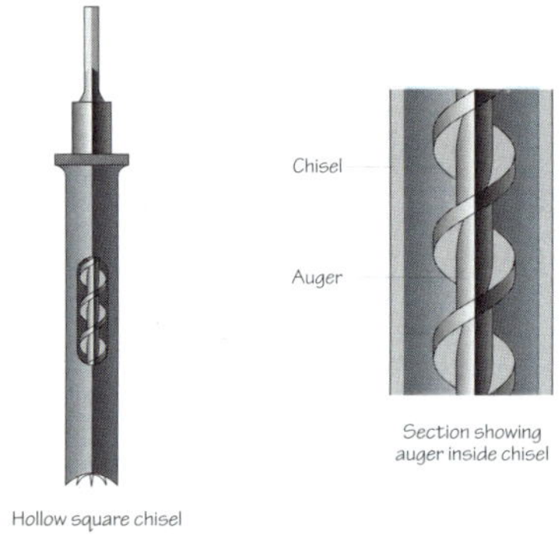

Hollow square chisel with auger inside

As with hand mortising, when using the machine, both sides of the wood are marked for a through mortise and the mortising is done from each side into the centre.

> **BEWARE!** In addition to the usual safety rules, the following should be observed when using the mortiser:
> - Make all adjustments when the machine is turned off and completely stopped
> - Always keep your hands away from the cutter

Planer

The planer/surfacer is designed to perform two functions. Firstly, it planes a smooth surface on timber and then planes a second edge square (90°) to the first. It also planes one surface parallel to another, which planes them to their required thickness.

The planer/thicknesser

The planer cuts with two, three or four cutting knives mounted in a cylindrical block of steel similar to a hand planer. The block spins at great speed in the machine.

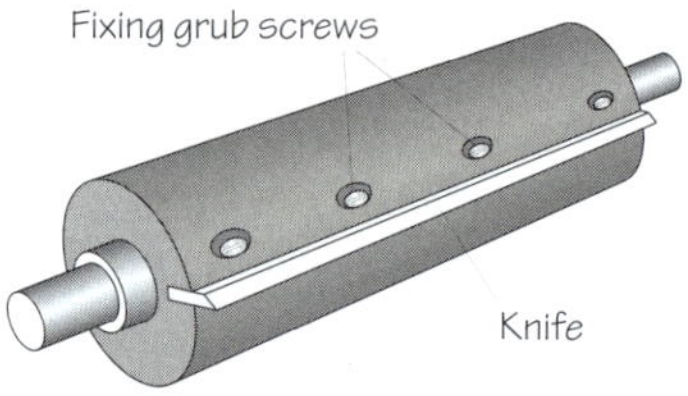

Cutter block

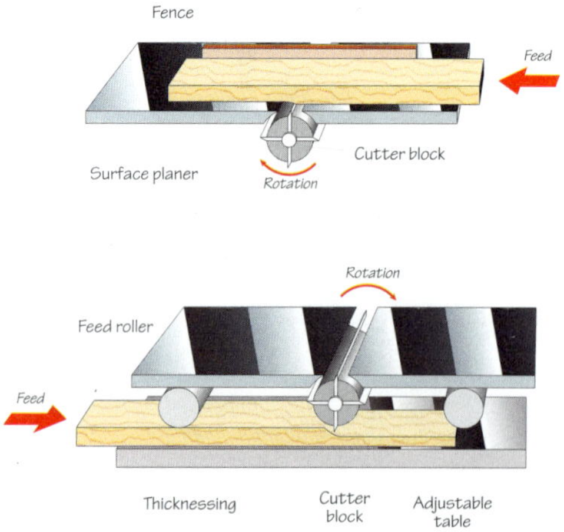

Section through the planer showing the direction of feed

As the cutters spin they touch the wood in one spot, taking a shaving. The effect of this is a *ripple effect*. By slowing down the rate at which the wood is fed into the machine, you can reduce the amount of rippling.

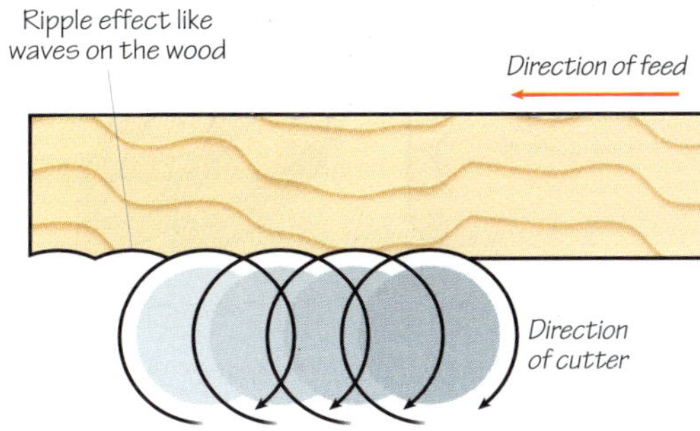

Ripple effect produced by the action of the cutters

The timber is fed into the machine against the rotation of the cutters. At all times when surfacing, the material must be held firmly down in contact with the tables, of the planer.

The thicknesser (underneath the table) planes the wood down to thickness by setting the distance between the cutters and the adjustable table below.

- Keep clear of the machine while it is being used
- Allow the operator to use the machine without interruption
- Do not make adjustments to the machine

Sanding machines

There are a number of different sanding machines available and each can be got in different sizes. The sanding machine is used for sanding curves, end-grain, etc.

Angles can be sanded with the aid of sliding fence. Some sanders combine a disk sander and a belt sander; some can be separate disk or belt sanders. There is also a type which has a small drum (bobbin) in a vertical position on a table which can be used to sand curved work.

Disk & belt sander can be found in many materials technology workshops

These machines use the abrasive paper to smooth down the material and to remove material to a line or curve. It is important not to put too much pressure on the machine while sanding, as this will damage the machine. The speed of the machine and the abrasive will do the work.

- As these machines create a lot of dust, always wear a dust mask and safety goggles when sanding
- Keep hands away from the sanding surface. The speed of the abrasive can cause a nasty gash if fingers make contact with the abrasive
- Always tie up loose clothing and long hair to keep them from getting caught in the machine

BEWARE!

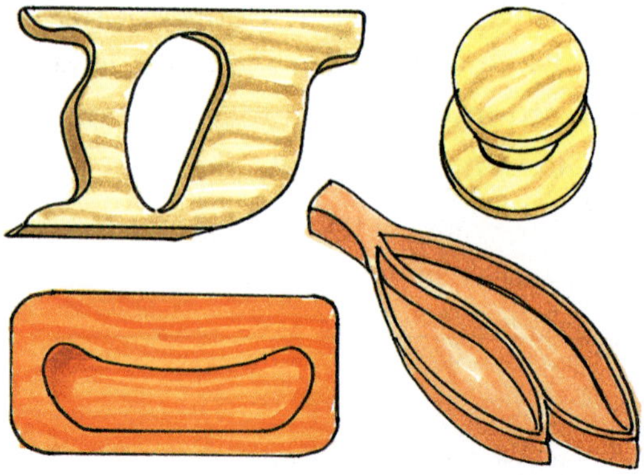

Examples of computerised router work

Woodturning lathe

The lathe can be found in most school workshops and it is a very useful machine. We will look more closely at the lathe later.

Computer Aided Manufacture (CAM)

Many machines used in industry are being improved by adding computer control. This computer aided manufacture (CAM) ensures that an operation, or series of operations, can be repeated many hundreds of times with complete accuracy and great speed. The computerised lathe and router are now quite common. Designs, in the form of commands or drawings, can be stored in the computer and these can be selected and produced at will.

Computerised router

Dust extractor

Modern machines and power tools are fitted with connections which allow them to be fitted to dust extractors. Dust extractors act like a vacuum cleaner, sucking away wood particles and fine dust, from the machine to a collection bag or bin. Fine dust and fumes created while working with machines, spraying equipment and so on can cause irritation and it is best that the air we breath be as clean as possible, dust extractors help to make this possible. Dust extractors can be of the moveable type as shown or larger fixed systems can be housed seperately and connected by ducting to all the machines.

Dust extractor

Exercises

1. Name these machines and state the function of each.

2. What is a push stick used for?
3. List three safety rules which must be observed when using machines.
4. Describe the cutting action of the mortiser.
5. Why does the planer produce a slightly uneven surface on timber?
6. What safety equipment should be worn when using a sander?
7. Give two advantages of computer aided manufacture.

Project 1

Design and make a decorative item for keeping keys tidy in a kitchen or hallway.

Analysis:

~ It must look well and be well made and well finished.

~ It should hold keys that are commonly used.

~ The keys must be secure and be easily seen and retrieved.

~ It must be capable of being secured to a wall.

Possible themes for the back plate

- Nature
- Sport
- Clouds
- Cartoons
- Football
- Music
- Animals

These theme words should assist in getting ideas for the back plate.

Investigation:

~ Keys – How many, what size – bunches or single keys?

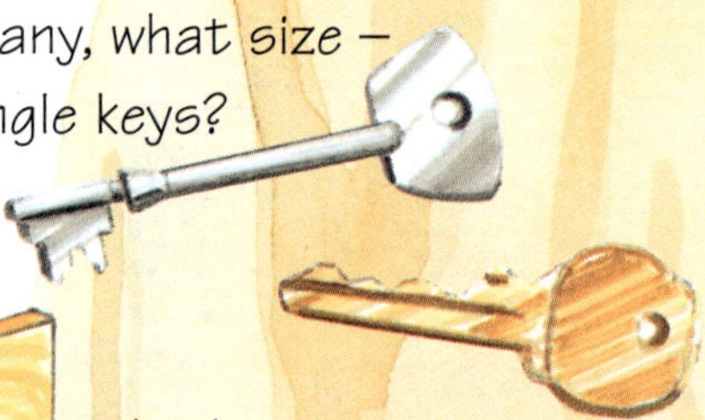

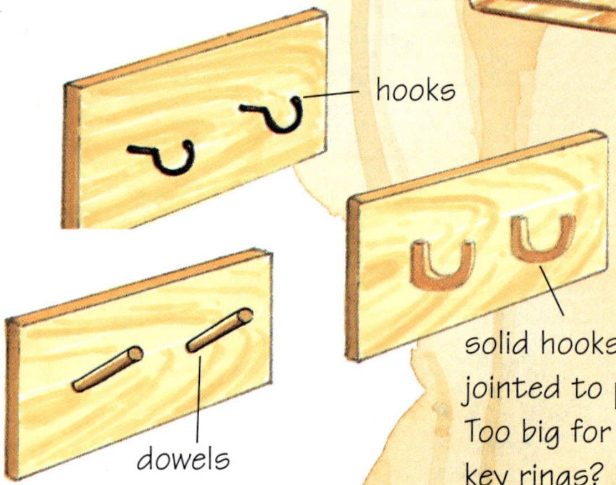

Ideas/Solutions:

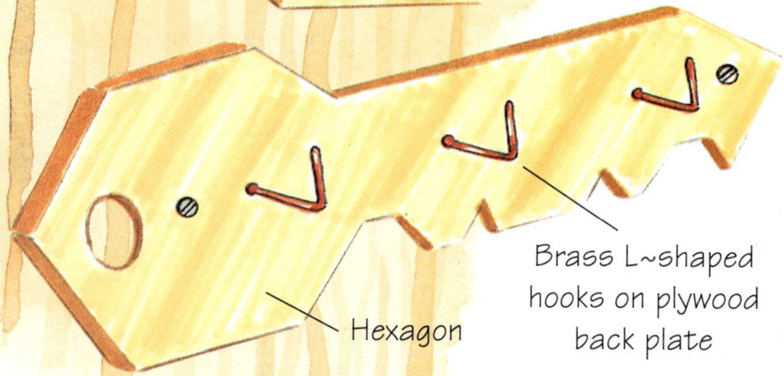

Key plate secured to the wall

How?

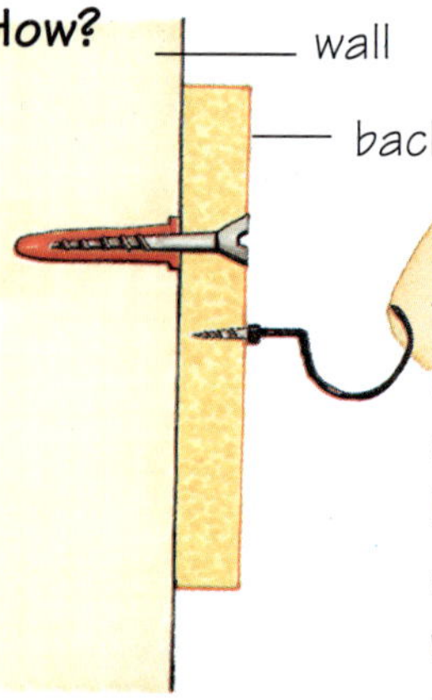

The finish could be clear such as danish oil or varnish, on a solid wood (ash) back. The back plate could be made from MDF or plywood finished with paint in various colours.

Working Drawing:

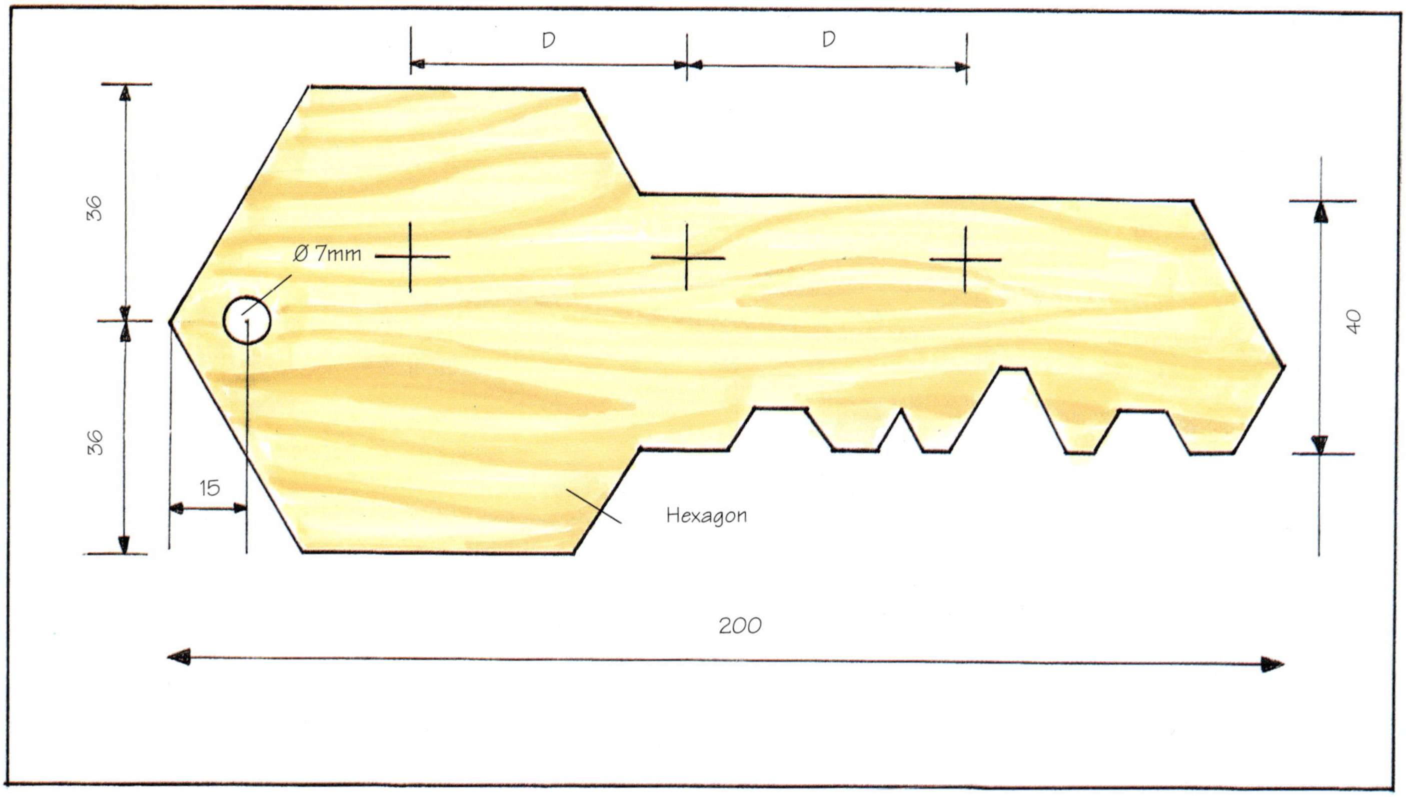

Evaluation:

Design:

The design is good as it is, based on a key, so its function is clear. Provided it is well finished it will look good.
The hooks are in a line so keys won't obstruct each other. The design is simple and uncomplicated and so time is not wasted when making it.

Manufacturing:

Some of the sawing was difficult to do accurately. It was important to mark the centre points for the hooks before any cutting is done.

Finished Item:

The piece looks well and was finished with an oak stain and varnish. The hooks were in brass which looks well with the dark colour. Possibly, another hook could have been included for added capacity.

Project 2 Design and make a model racing car which will travel along the ground.

Analysis:

~ It must be like a racing car in appearance
~ The wheels must move freely
~ It must be well proportioned
~ Should be safe in use

Investigation:

Wheels:
Wood
Plastic
Ready made ~ Where do I get them?

Size:
Should be small, made from
20mm or 30mm thick stock (wood)
The project should be simple to make

Materials:
Softwood/Hardwood

Finish:
The finish could be paint or varnish
Paint would be better as there is a wide choice of colours.

Ideas/Solutions:

Too wide

Old 1920's style car

Too "old style" in appearance

Doesn't look like a racing car, too rounded. Something more sleek and pointed is needed.

Wheels are too small

Better but it needs a spoiler

Wheels ~ solid wooden dowel
Dowel moves freely through the body of the car and is glued in place to the wheel.

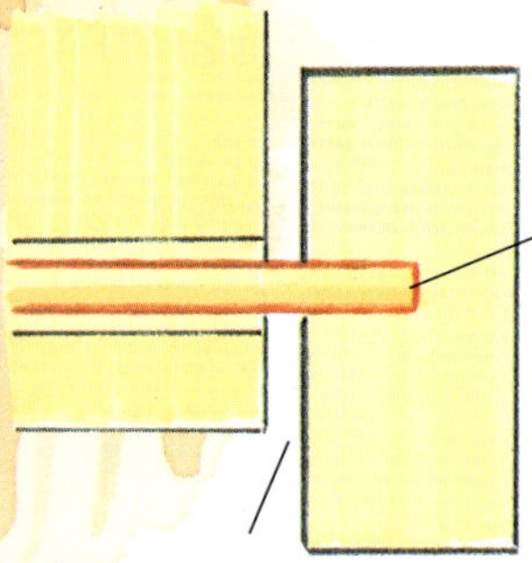

Final Solution:

Working Drawing:

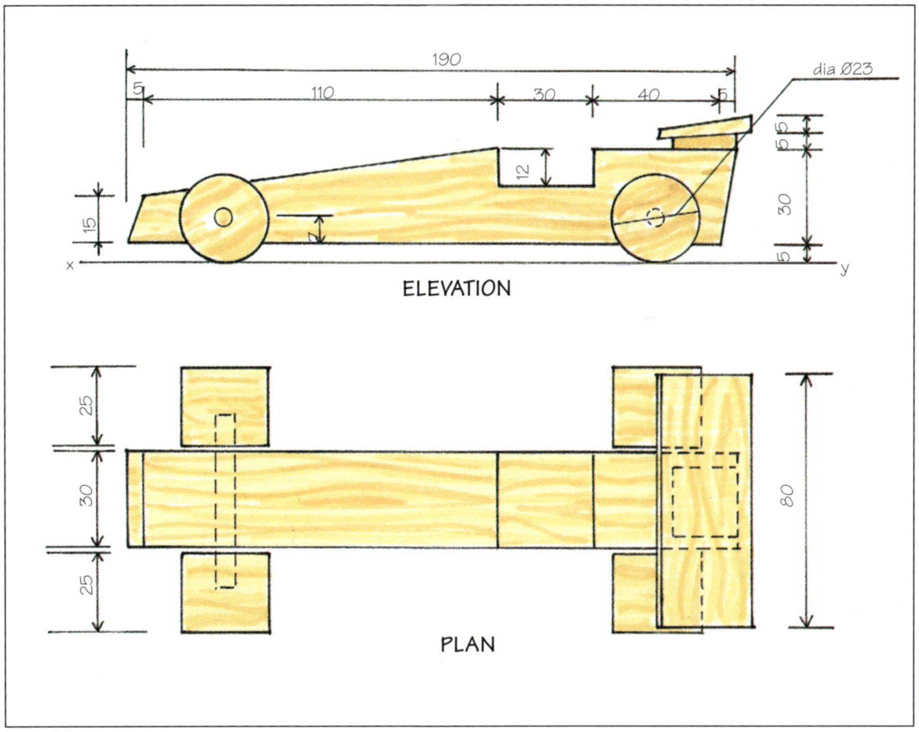

Evaluation:

Design:

The design was simple and quite easy to make. The shape is long and narrow with a pointed front. The spoiler at the back makes the car look well and similar to a racing car. It would have been better if I had used plastic wheels, bought in a shop.

Manufacture:

The making was quite easy ~ it was important to keep the bottom of the seat section flat. the holes for the wheels had to be drilled accurately. The spoiler was difficult to make and it had to be evenly centred on the body of the car at the back.

Finished Item:

I was happy with the finished car. This is a model car and not a toy. It would not be suitable for young children as small parts could be broken off or easily swallowed.

Project 3

Design and make an artefact on which to put hot dishes and pots.

Analysis:

~ Must be heat proof
~ Should be big enough to hold pots/dishes
~ Must be stable & safe in use
~ Must have nice appearance

Investigation:

How big are pots?

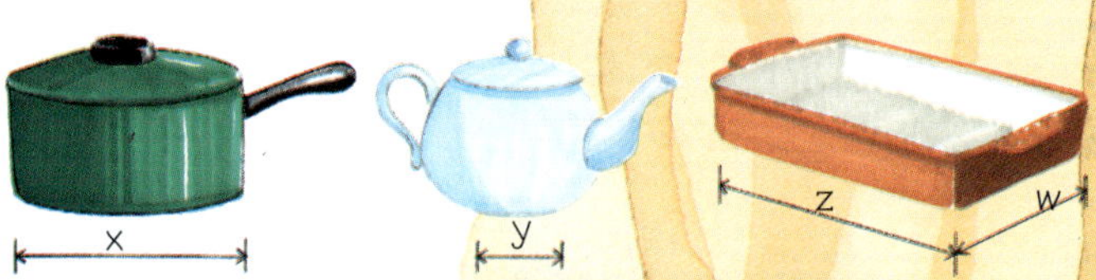

What materials will resist heat?

Wood ~ good insulator
ceramic ~ easily cleaned and retains heat

What finish?

Varnish
Danish oil
Wax ~ unsuitabke - it will melt and it can't be washed.

Find examples of hot plates in shops, magazines, etc.

Ideas/Solutions:

From the analysis and investigation You can develop some suitable solutions

flat plate

~ square shape too plain
~ octagon shape better

Triangle (equilateral) solid wood or MDF/plywood

flat plate with legs

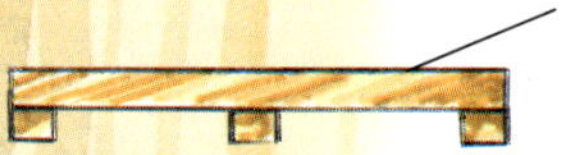

3 pins/dowels for stability

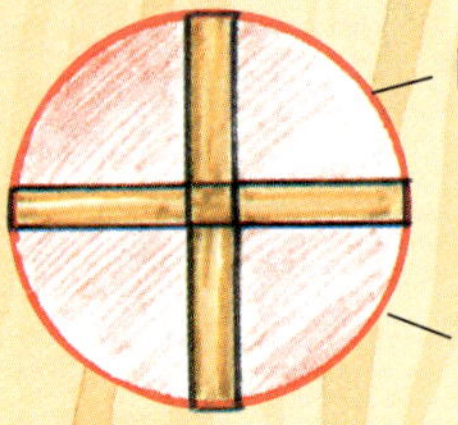

4 pieces jointed together

ceramic tile on MDF

Ceramic tile on MDF Base with moulding or frame of solid wood

Design based on an equilateral triangle

Same shape using 3 pieces of solid wood with corners mitred

Final solution:

Working Drawing:

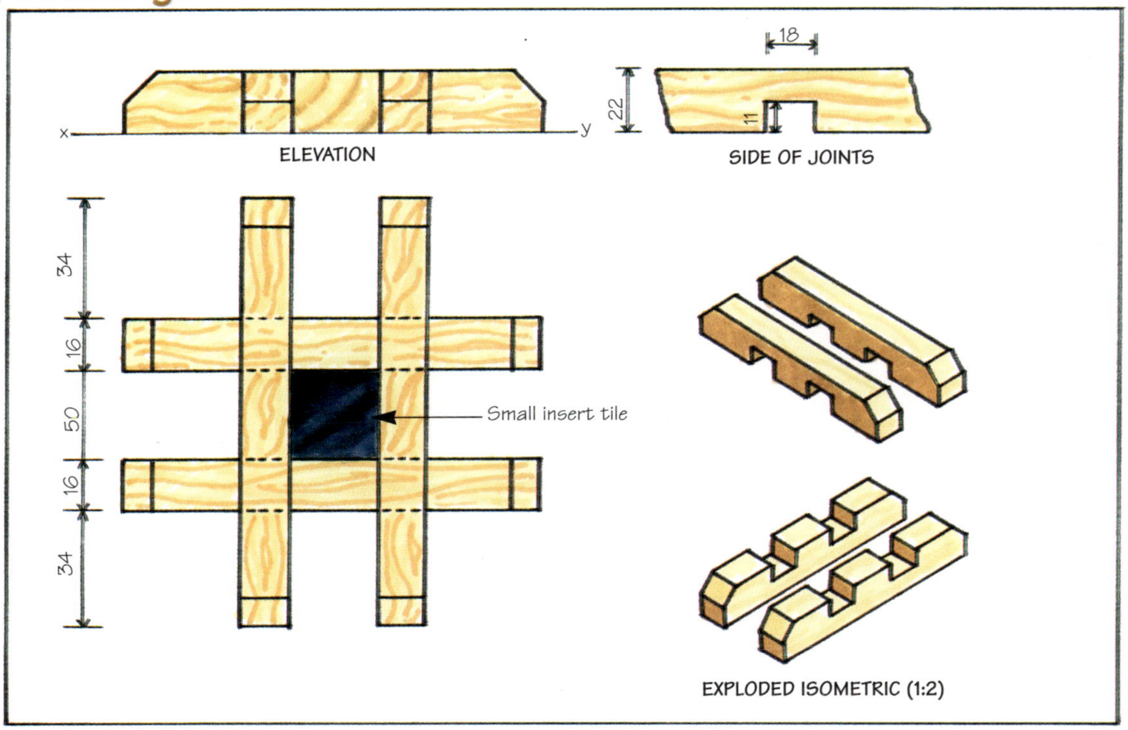

Evaluation:

Design:

Simple but looks good, I could have made it from a different wood, elm or ash perhaps. Design is small and the item could be made from offcuts of wood which would be discarded.

Manufacturing:

The distance for the tile has to be accurately marked to allow the tile to fit exactly. The trenches for the joints have to be carefully cut, and worked so that the tops are flush when the pieces are assembled. It was difficult to clean the tile adhesive from the piece, fully.

Finished Item:

The hot plate looks well and it is stable on the work surface. The overall size could be made bigger for accommodating larger pots or dishes.

Project 4

Design and make an artefact to hold pens, pencils and drawing equipment in your bag.

Analysis:

- Must store/contain all my pens, pencils, etc in my schoolbag.
- Must be strong as it will be knocked about in the bag
- Must look good
- The function of the box must be clear by its appearance
- Must be light, easily stored in the bag

Investigation:

- List the items to be stored
- Record the measurements of items to be stored

List:

4 pens
3 pencils
sharpener
eraser
compass

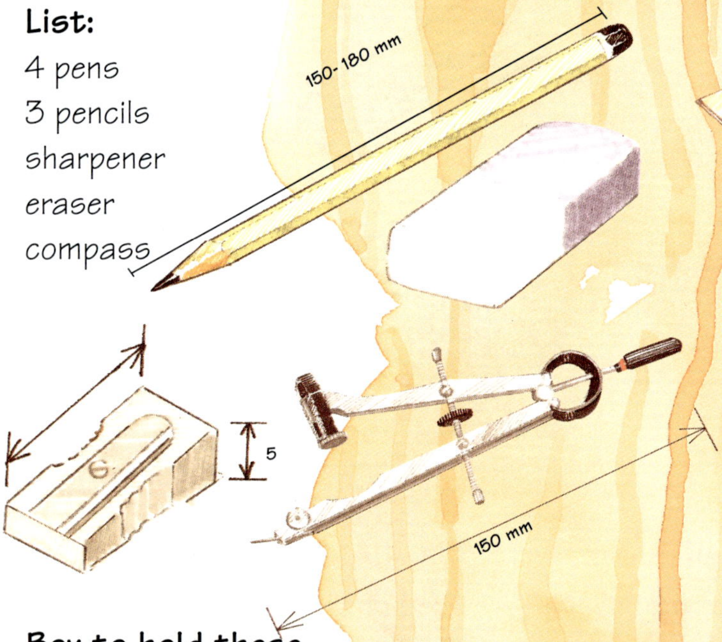

Box to hold these

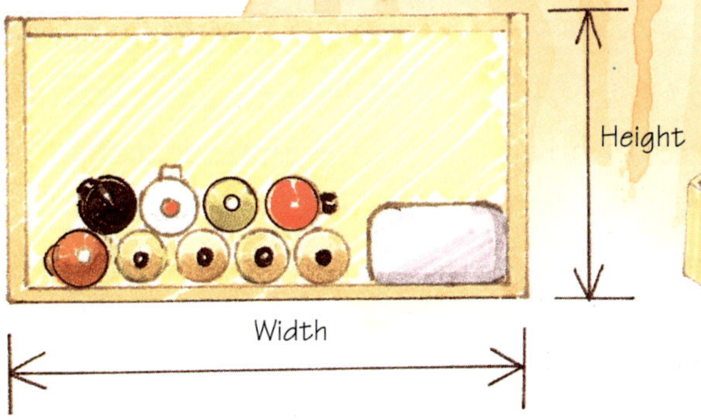

How will lid be put on?

The sliding top is probably most suitable as you can get what you want without emptying out contents

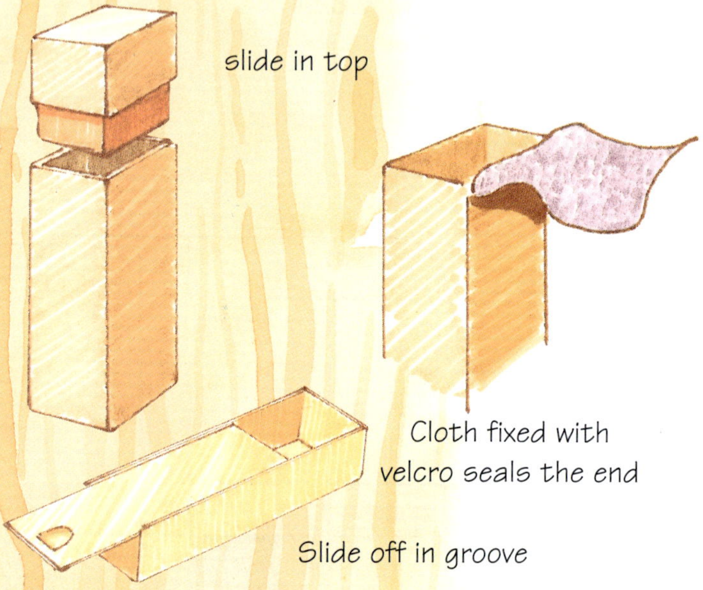

Ideas/Solutions:

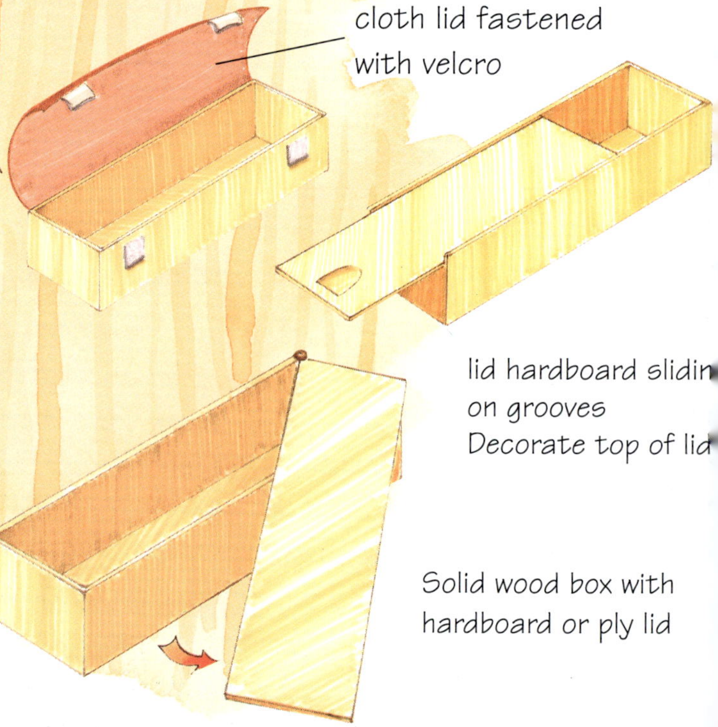

To make the function clear

~ Text ~ **"Pencils"** or **"Pens"** written on box lid or side or carved onto side.

~ Picture of pens or pencils draw onto th box and sealed with varnish.

~ Picture of pen/pencil made in veneers ~ marquetry.

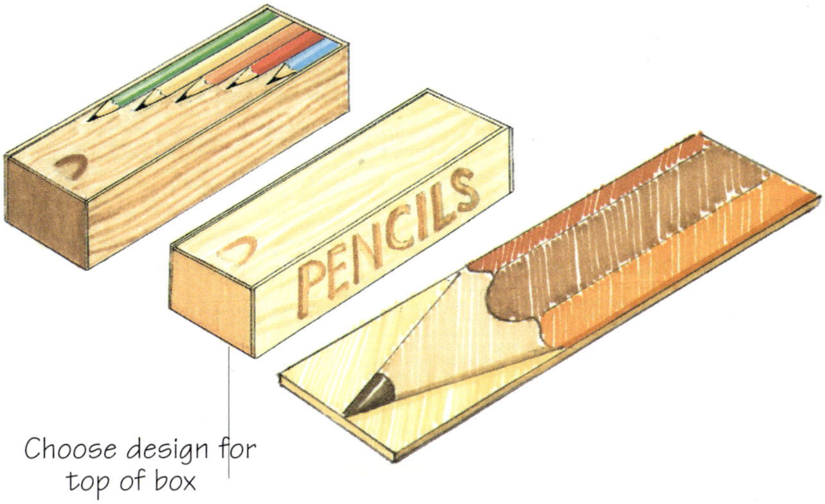

Working Drawing:

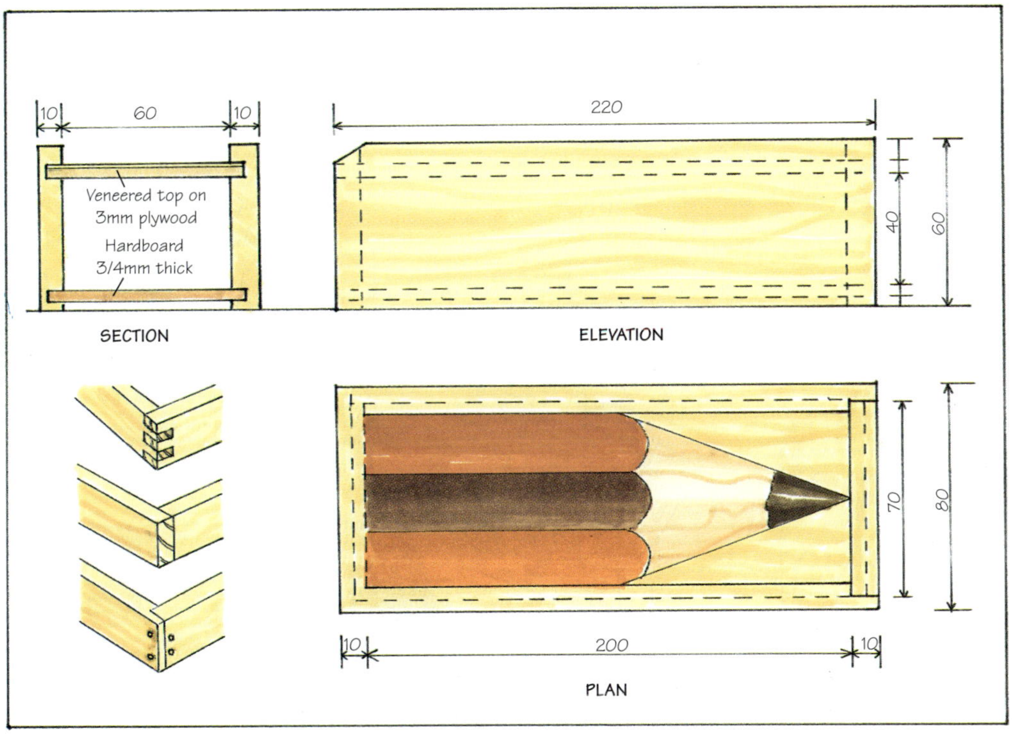

Evaluation:

Design:

The design was quite big to fit comfortably in a bag. It will accomodate more than enough pens and pencils and the depth of the box could be reduced in size, to make it more streamlined.

Manufacturing:

The making of the box was not easy and it was difficult to get it square. Joints have to be well made in a box or gaps in the joints will weaken it.

The veneered picture had to be carefully cut and assembled to ensure that it looked well.

Small gaps can be filled with wax later after sanding the surface smooth.

Finished Item:

The piece was attractive and useful in my school bag. The corners could be rounded over to make it more soft in appearance. The movement of the lid was a problem which was overcome by sanding the edges and underside of the lid so that it fitted better.

Project 5

Design and make a decorative artefact with the theme of "sport"

Analysis:

- ~ It should reflect a sport or sporting theme
- ~ It must look well and could be a simple design
- ~ It should be strong and stable
- ~ It could include some woodturning, carving etc.
- ~ It should be small and light
- ~ It should be well finished and easily cleaned

Investigation:

Sports: ~ Swimming, sailing, soccer, football, hurling, basketball, camogie, dance,

~ sport in general

~ **Olympic signs for the sports**

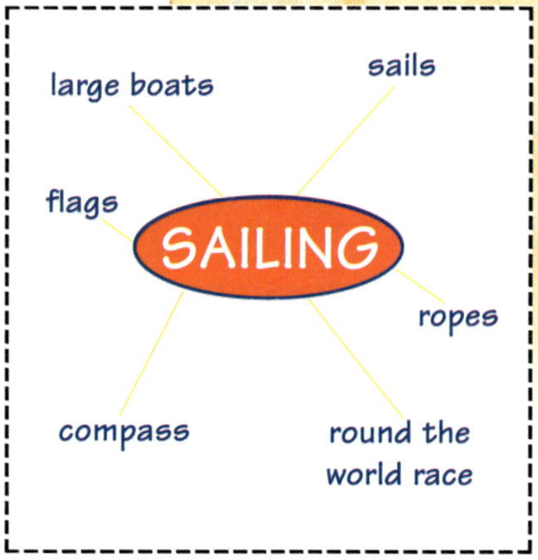

Ideas & Solutions:

Based on "sails"

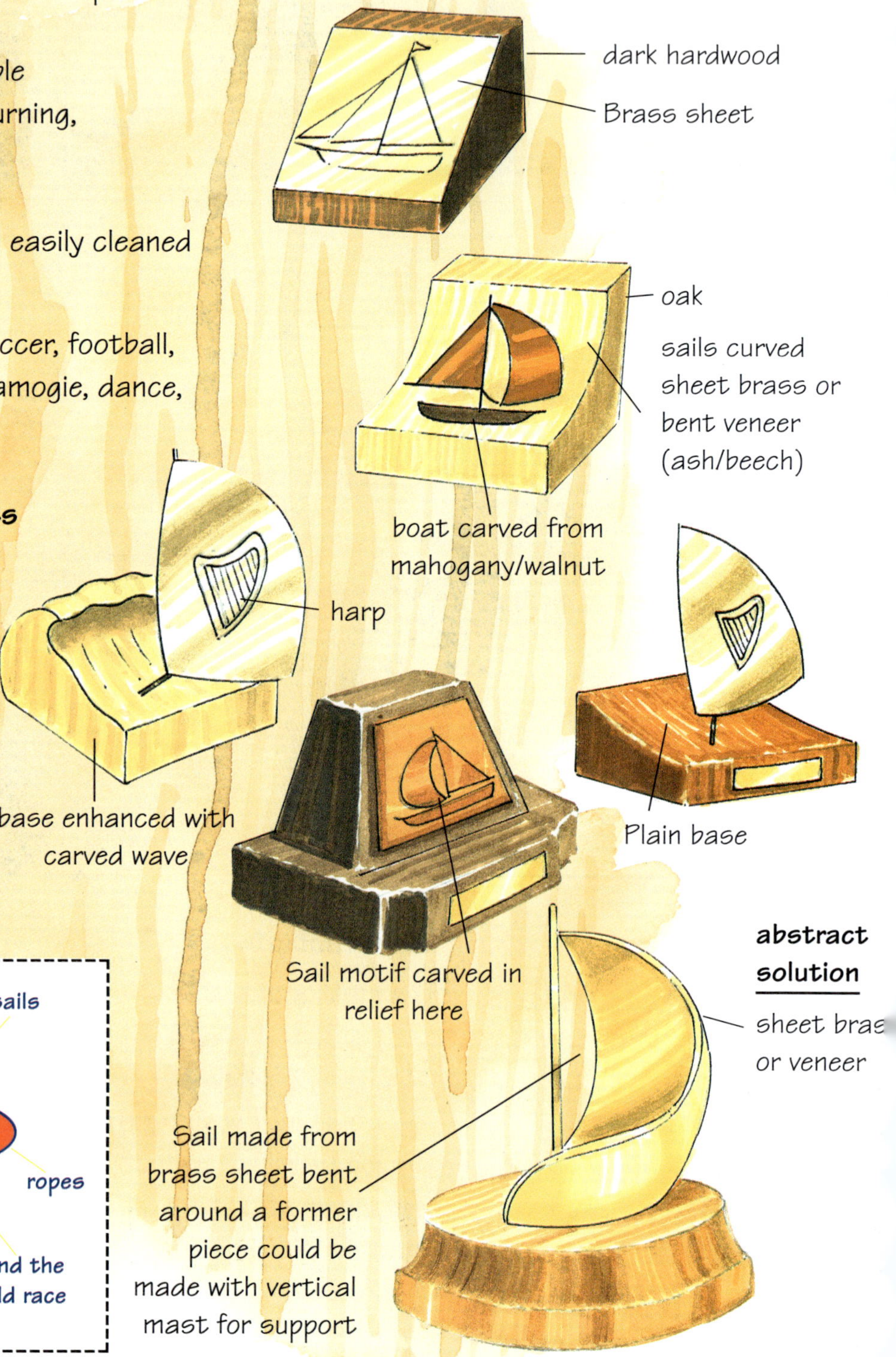

Final solution:

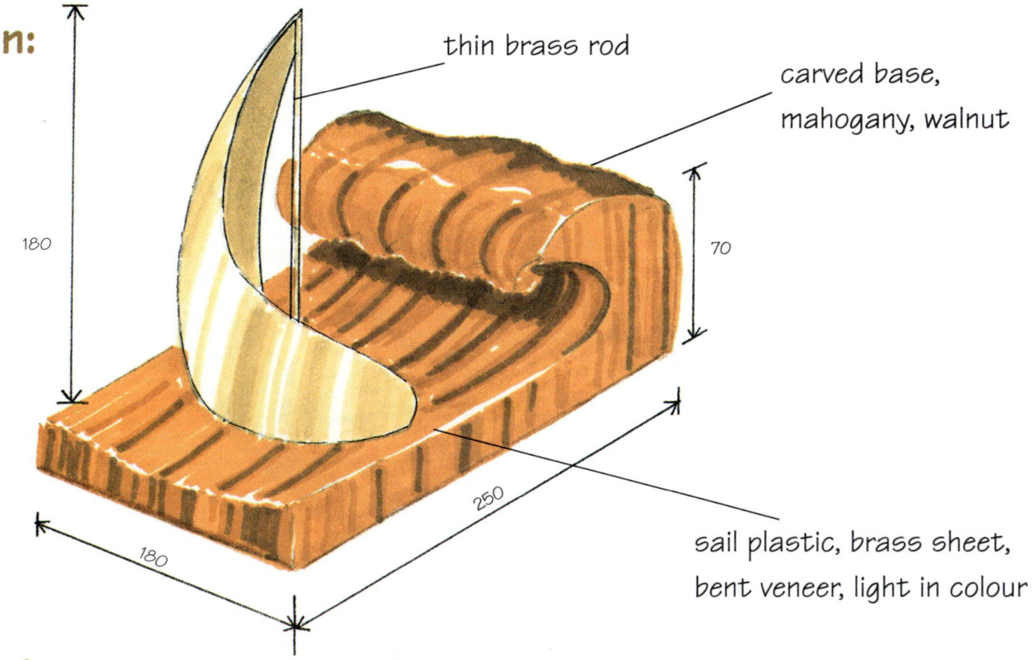

Working Drawing:

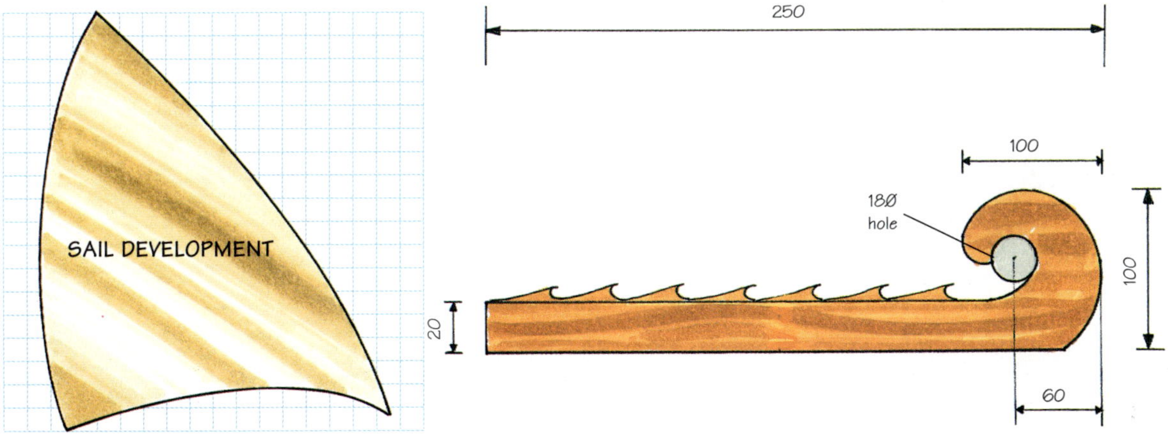

Evaluation:

Design:

The design is good based on the sail shape. The sail shape if used was poor and more investigation could have been done to see what shapes sails actually have by looking in sailing shops, or writing to sailing clubs.

Manufacture:

Getting the proportions correct on the carving wasn't easy and it was difficult to carve the wave shape easily. The piece should be as good as you can get it from the chisels and gouges because sandpaper tends to round off fine edges.

Finished Item:

The sail looks well in brass but it wasn't easy to finish, it would look good in a light coloured veneer, but a mould would be needed to form the 3D shape.
The item possibly looks plain but this simple design is very effective.

Project 6

Design and make an artefact which will hold at least 12 CD's in a safe and tidy way.

Analysis:

~ Could it be a box or a rack?
~ It should hold 12 CD's or more
~ It must look good, could have decorative features ~ mouldings etc.
~ Should it have a lid? Yes
~ Should the lid be secured?
~ How should the lid be hinged?
~ Are the disks to be seen through the lid?

Investigation:

Disk sizes

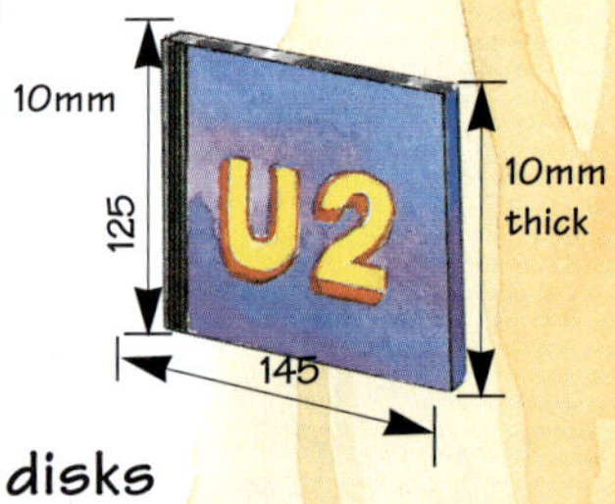

Layout of disks

How should the lid of the box be put on

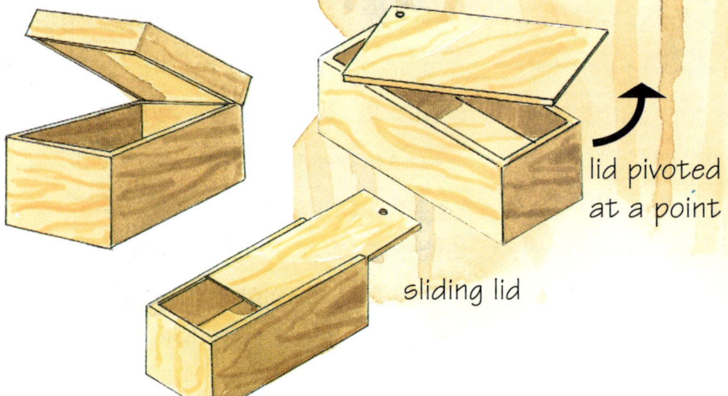

Ideas/Solutions:

Final Solution:

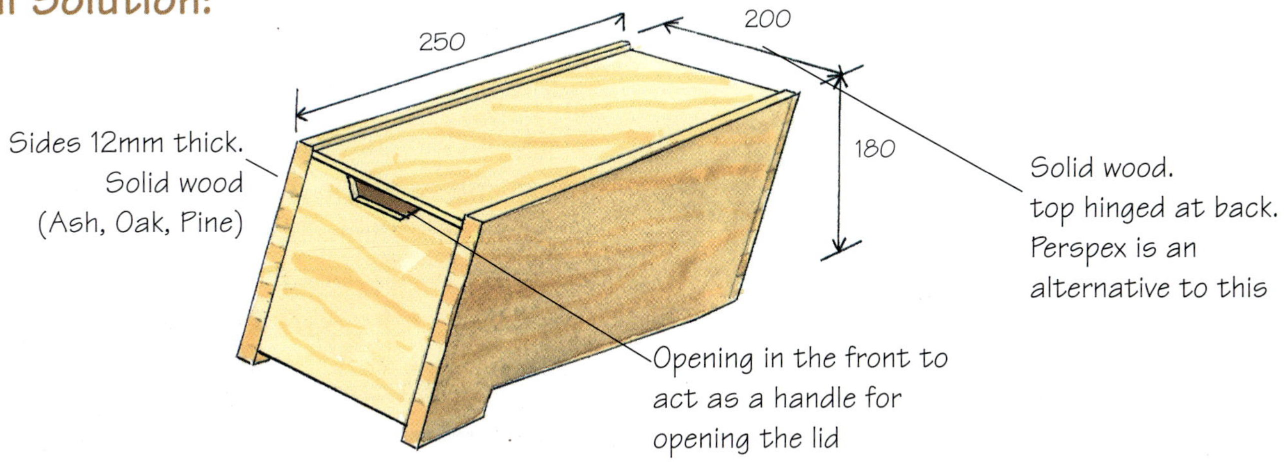

Working Drawing:

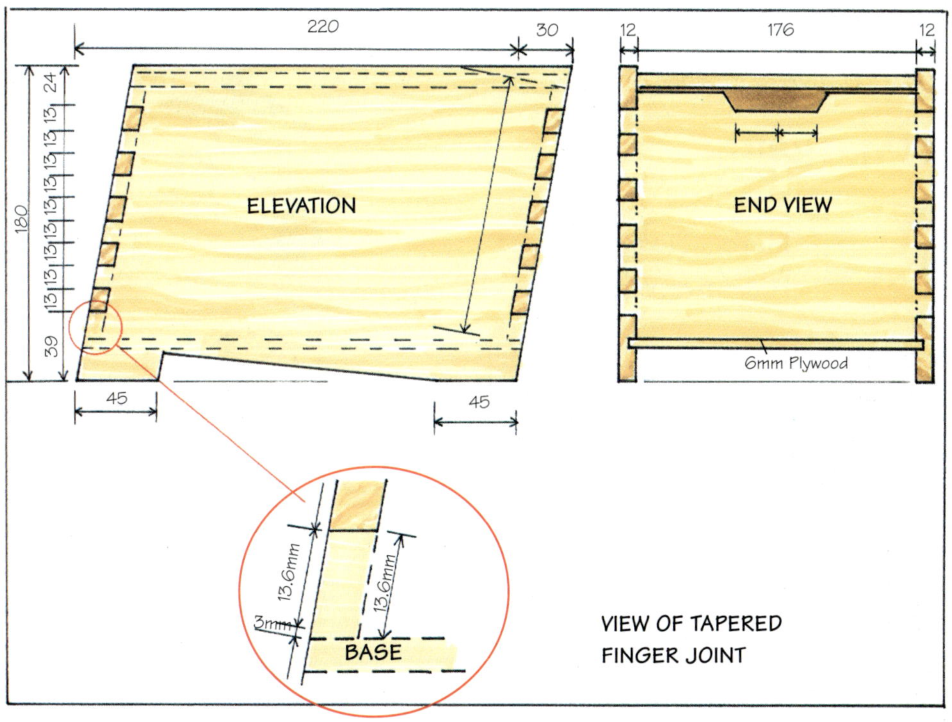

Evaluation:

Design:

The design was different but it was not easy to produce as the angles were difficult to achieve. An acrylic lid would be a good idea as it would allow you to see inside the box. The finger joints which were used look well and add to the overall appearance although they were difficult to mark out and cut.

Manufacture:

Making the box was hard due to the angles on the sides which made the joints complex and took time. The hinging of the lid wasn't easy to get right and although I used the smallest hinges I could find, they were still a little big.

Finished Item:

The CD box looks well and it is well made. The box I made was in ash, but it would look just as nice made from pine. The finished piece does wobble a little on a flat surface but other than that it was a successful and enjoyable project.

Project 7 Design and Make a Clock

Analysis:

- ~ Can be wall mounted or it could also sit on a mantlepiece - horizontal surface
- ~ Should be easily read even from a distance
- ~ Should be stable - have a hanger or rest on the surface, without falling over
- ~ Should be interesting to look at and well made. It should have a good appearance
- ~ I would use a combination of at least two woods to give contrast

Investigation:

Clock — Wall Clock ☐
Clock — Mantle Clock ☑

Clock face — bought or made?

Here the movement is inserted into a prepared hole - looks well but is quite expensive and is not easily read if quite small

Most clocks seem to have bought faces. I would like to make my own

I need clock movements. Where do I obtain these? Ask teacher for some contact addresses.

These movements have shafts for the hands which can be got in different lengths. 15mm, 17.5mm and 21mm. There are a selection of styles of hands to suit them.

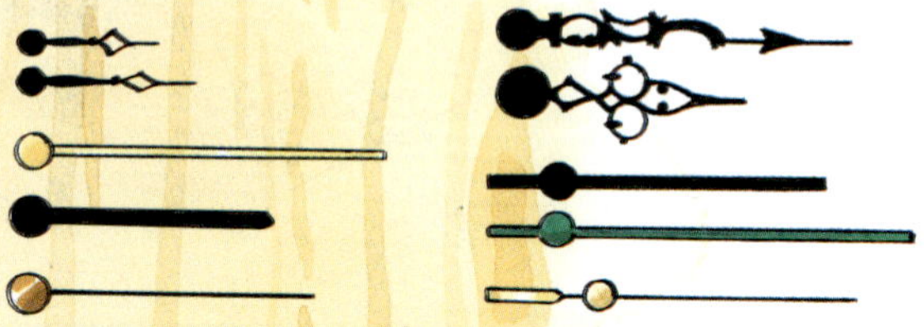

Ideas and Solutions

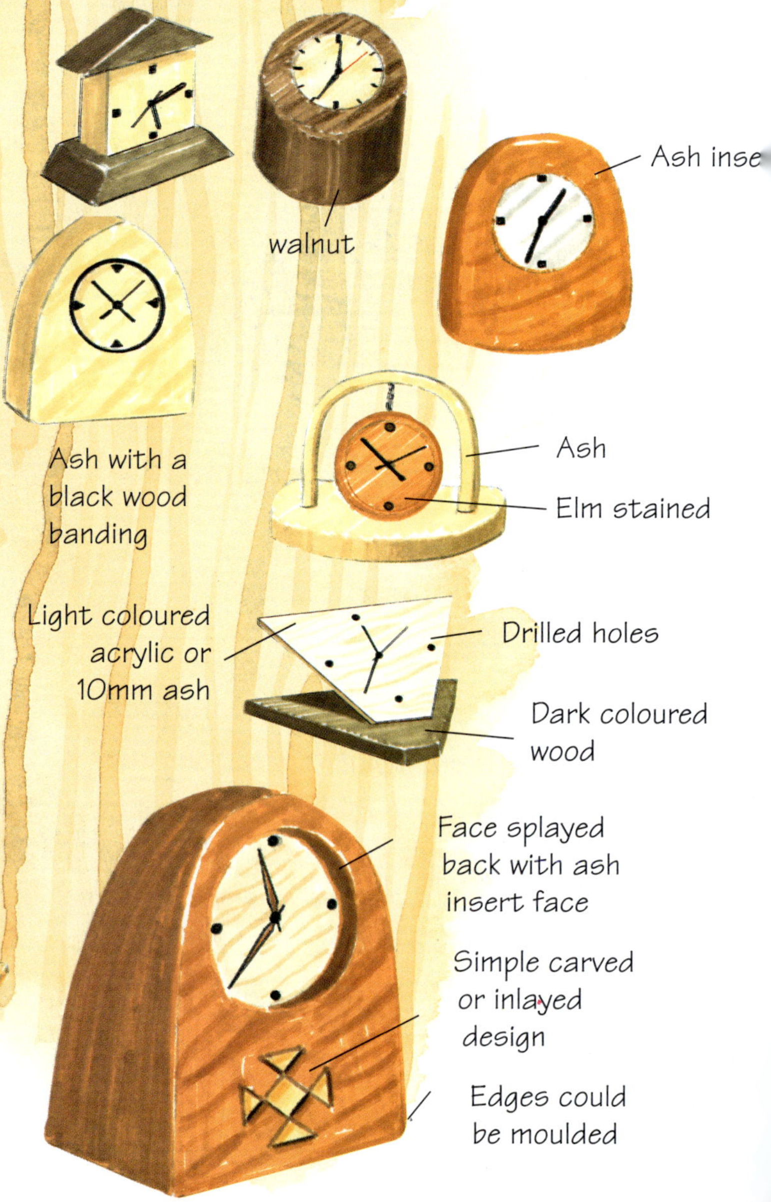

Working Drawing

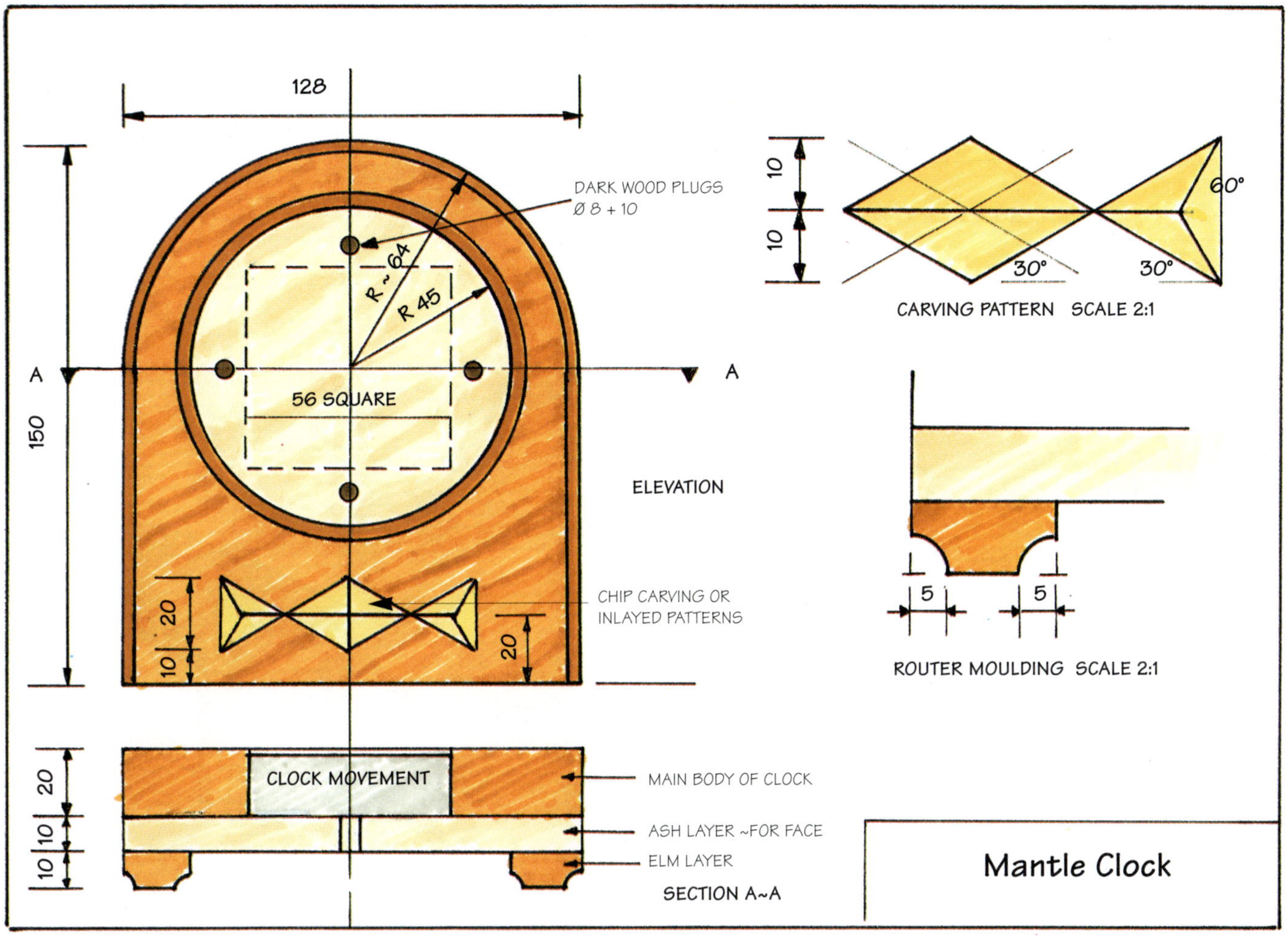

Evaluation:

Design:

I felt that the design is good and simple. The mouldings add to the appearance which would look dull without some decoration.

The design is of a traditional type and uses only wood. If I was making the piece again I would possibly try to make a more modern type of clock. Possibly using a theme such as that of nature.

Execution:

The pieces are marked out and the holes are cut. It is then that the three pieces are glued together. When dry the curve on the outside is worked and the mouldings are applied.

It is difficult to ensure a correct and smooth surface on the inside of the circular front face which must be sanded smooth before gluing up.

Final project:

The final piece was very nice, the mouldings improve its appearance.

- It will blend in well in the sittingroom of our house, but I feel a modern look might be better.
- The face is quite large but the hands had to be cut to length.
- It is heavy enough and the correct shape to be stabl[e] on the mantlepiece.

Project 8 Design and make a stool for use in a livingroom.

Analysis:

~ Should be able to hold the weight of an adult
~ Should be stable, and well made
~ Must be comfortable
~ Should be light and easily lifted
~ could be upholstered

Investigation:

Stool frames

Ideas & Solutions:

Sizes:

Working Drawing:

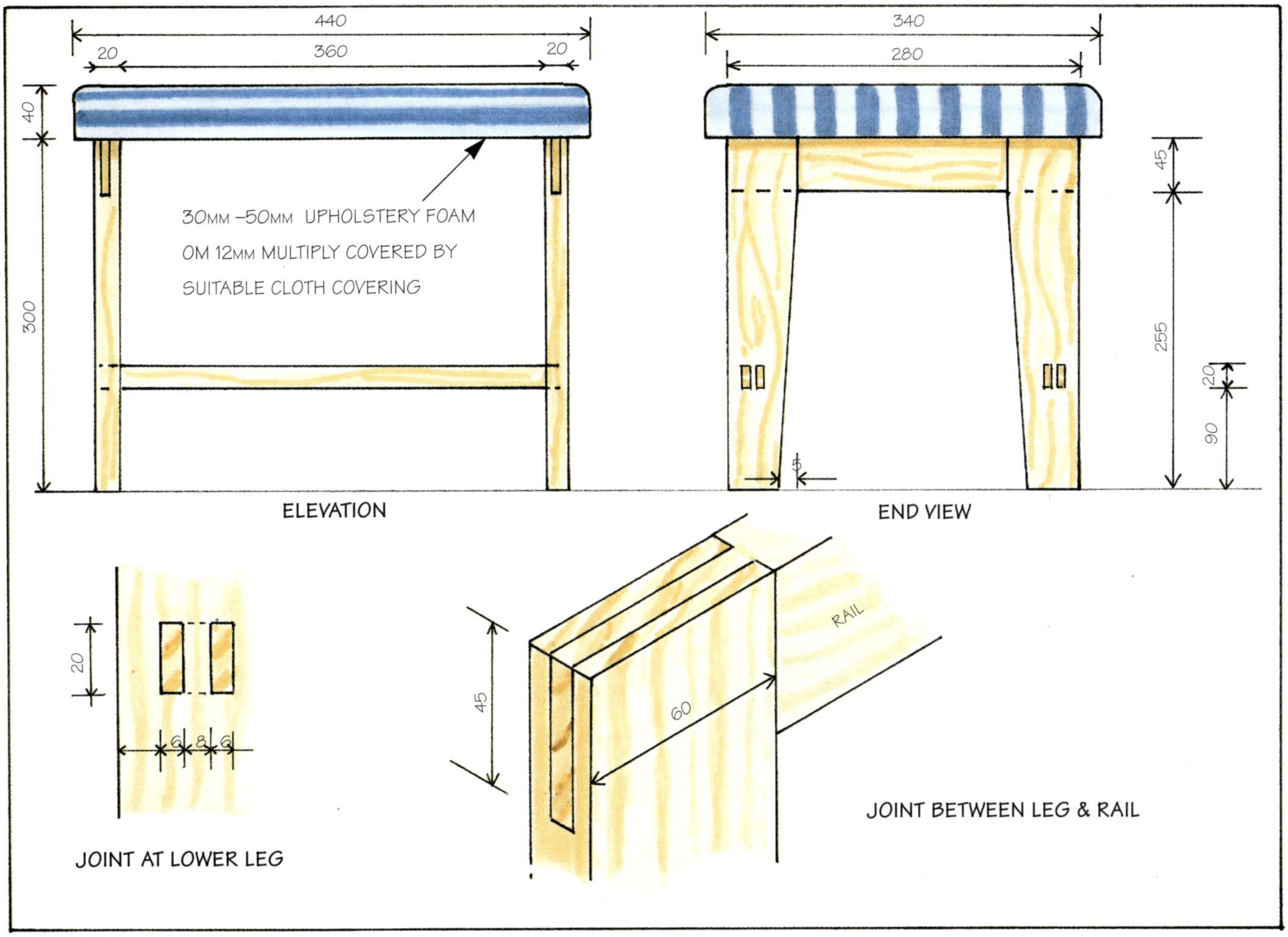

Evaluation:

Design:

The deign is quite stable, and is simply jointed. The sections of the legs are strong enough to hold the weight of an adult. The seat is made from 40mm foam which has to meet fire regulations and should be comfortable enough. A soft cloth covering seemed more suitable than leatherette as the stool is to be used in the livingroom.

Manufacture:

I found that the mortises for the rails on the bottom of the legs were small at 6mm and were not easy to complete accurately. The splay on the inside of the legs needed to be done carefully to ensure the legs are all the same and accurately done. The stool I made was done in Ash which is dense and difficult to work with at times.

Finished Item:

The stool is good and looks wel with a varnish finish which is durable and will keep well. The edge of the seat could be highlighted by some upholstery pins to decorate the edge.
I felt that although the piece looks well in Ash which is light in colour, I could have considered a darker native wood such as elm, which might have improved the appearance.

COMMUNICATION AND DESIGN

CHAPTER TWENTY

DESIGN

Design

Houses, clothes, factories, cars, etc. all have to be designed. Design can be used to improve things, how they look or how they function. Design can be used to arrive at ideas for new items from scratch.

Development of the car

Most items are designed by people who are specialised designers. However, we all use our sense of design when we choose clothes, furniture, cars or shoes that we like. Design is about much more than appearance – it involves ease of use and manufacture, strength, function, comfort, safety and much more. To make items which are well designed and meet these requirements, designers need to plan the process in detail. To ensure that nothing is left to chance, designers use a complex process to develop their designs. Here is a simplified version of this design process which we can use as a framework for our designs.

The design process

- Brief
- Analysis
- Investigation/research
- Design ideas
- Working drawings
- Manufacture
- Evaluation

As you go about designing you will keep a record of your progress. This record is called a folio or report.

Brief

The brief is a statement of what is to be made. The brief is usually given to the designer. Often the client gives the problem to be solved to the designer in the form of a brief. The brief outlines the problem and provides the starting point for the designer. As an example the client might ask the designer to design a note holder for keeping a record of items which need to be remembered or for phone messages. The client might also insist on some conditions, such as a maximum cost for example.

Analysis

The brief or problem must first be analysed before any further work is done. Analysis requires you to think about the brief and the problems that it poses. You should list all the requirements of the item to be designed. For the note pad example above:-

- It must accommodate a note pad or post-it pad
- It must look good
- It should be stable and strong (well made)
- It should have storage for at least one pen
- It should have storage for left messages

The analysis allows you to think about the item before you start forming ideas. In this way you can begin to make choices and form opinions about the way you should progress with the design. It is worthwhile to spend time on this stage, as it will make the designing process easier. Analysis lets you identify problems and helps you to plan solving them as you progress.

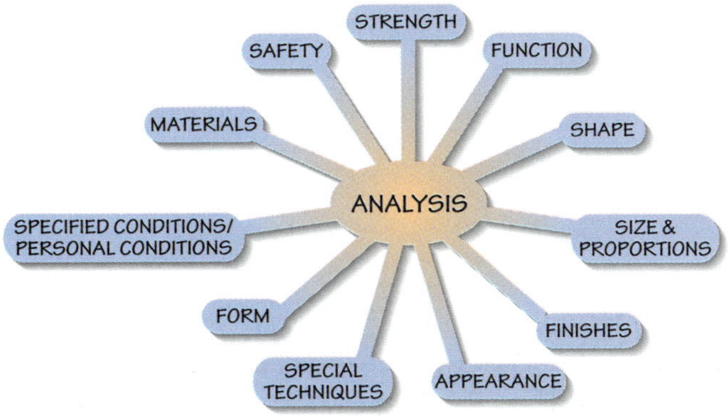

Investigation/research

When you have identified the many things which must be considered while designing the item you proceed to the next stage. The analysis will identify things which will have to be researched such as *"what type of adhesive should I use?; what type of finish would best suit the piece?; what kind of material would best suit the piece and where can these be obtained?"*

The size of the object will need to be determined. There are standard sizes for many things such as tables, chairs, desks, work surfaces, etc. These sizes and measurements have been developed through the study of human size and the relationship between the sizes of the body and the items we use. This study is called **ergonomics.** It is important that items which are designed for our use are comfortable to use. For example, if a couch or chair was too low to the ground it might be difficult to get out of. This would be poor design and would show that the investigation was not done very well.

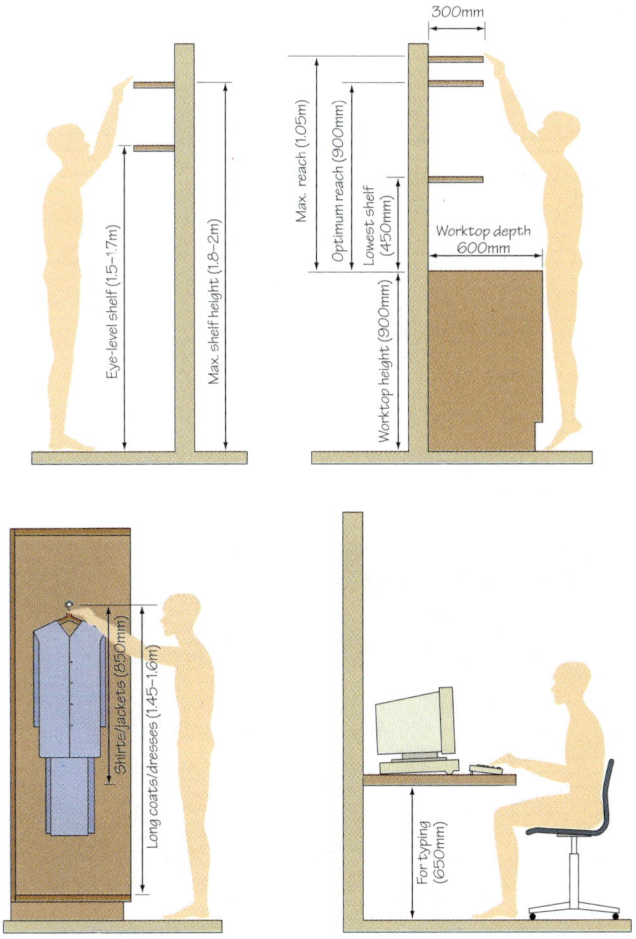

Some examples of standard sizes

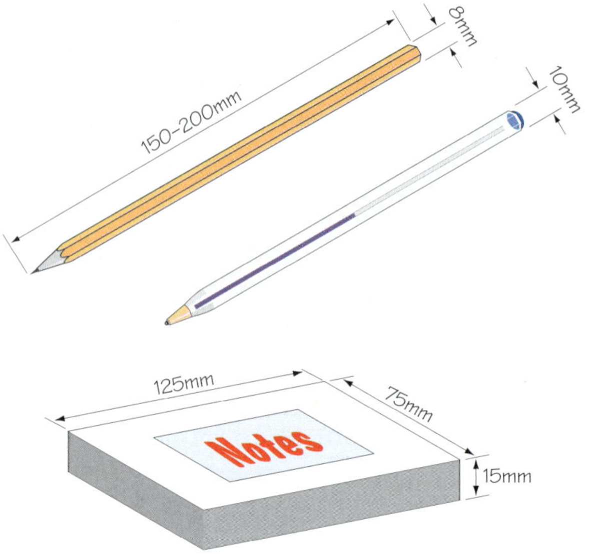

Investigation of sizes of some items for the note holder

You will also look for ideas which will help you to form your own design solutions (ideas). You will possibly visit shops to find similar items which you like. You should sketch these and include them in your folio/report. You might get ideas for shape, etc. from the style of a chair or some other object, which appeals to you, but might not be what you actually have to make. However, you will be able to use the style of the item and adapt it to suit your own needs.

Student pasting an idea into a report

Ideas can also be found in books magazines and catalogues. These can be photocopied, sketched or cut out and pasted into your report. It is important that you keep a record of all the investigation and items which help you to arrive at your final design.

There may be a great many things which need to be investigated during the design of the item, as this is a continuous process. Here are some areas of the design which would be included:

Design ideas

When you have thoroughly researched what is required for your design you can develop the ideas that have been forming inside your head. The process of designing is not easily defined and ideas can develop all through the process. These ideas should be sketched down as they occur and should be kept to be further developed later.

The ideas should be sketched neatly. They generally can be developed or improved. These improvements, decorations and changes should be sketched also. This improvement process is continued until you are happy with the final design. The ideas that you have may highlight areas needing more research, (which can be done before proceeding).

A small model of a piece of furniture

Often a simple model made from cardboard (old box or cereal packet) will give a good idea of the overall sizes and proportions. The model should be full size or to a definite scale. The model doesn't need to be very well made as it is only used to give a general impression as to sizes, proportions, appearance and stability. In industry a model or prototype is made to give the client a better and clearer view of the design.

The final design solution can then be carefully detailed before doing detailed drawings.

Working drawings

As the name suggests these drawings will be used to work from while making the item. Therefore, they should be complete with all the measurements that you will need to mark out and process the pieces. It is probably a good idea to do drawings or sketches of the joints that you will use to help you to avoid any mistakes. The drawings of the joints can include the detailed measurements for the joints. This avoids cluttering up the drawing of the whole piece.

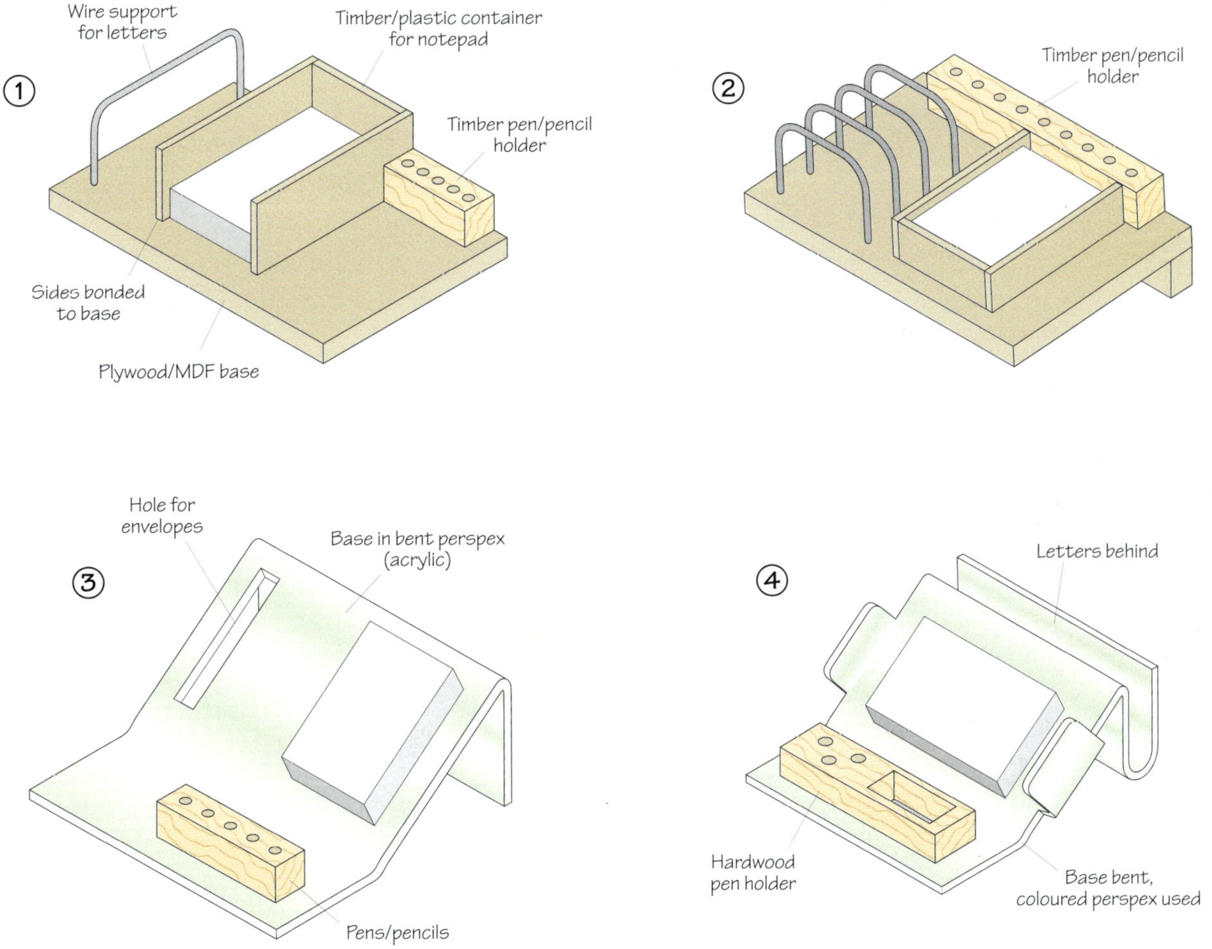

Development of ideas for the note pad

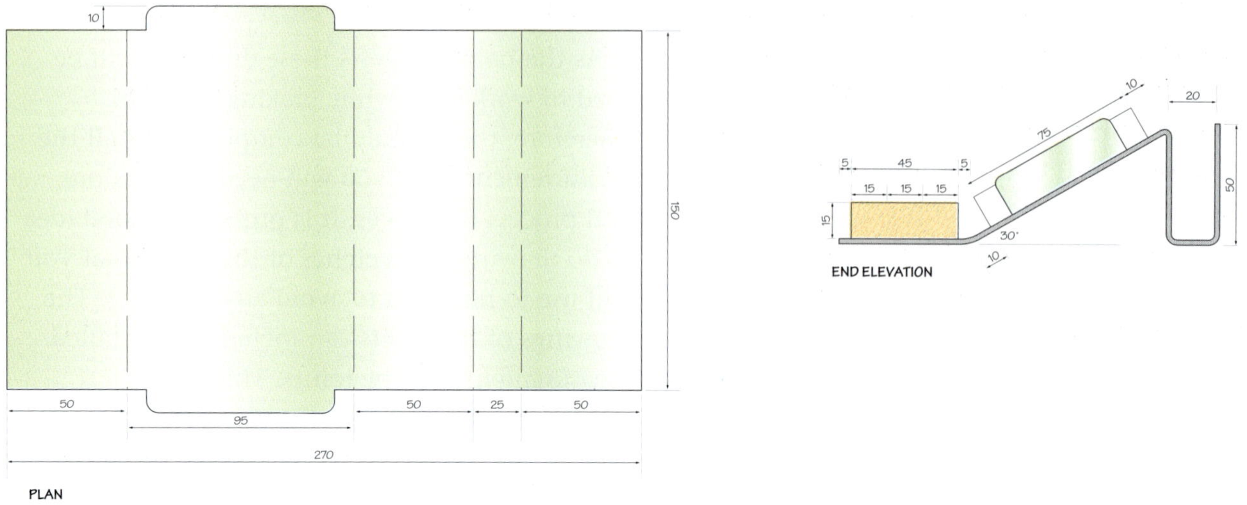

A view of working drawings of the note pad

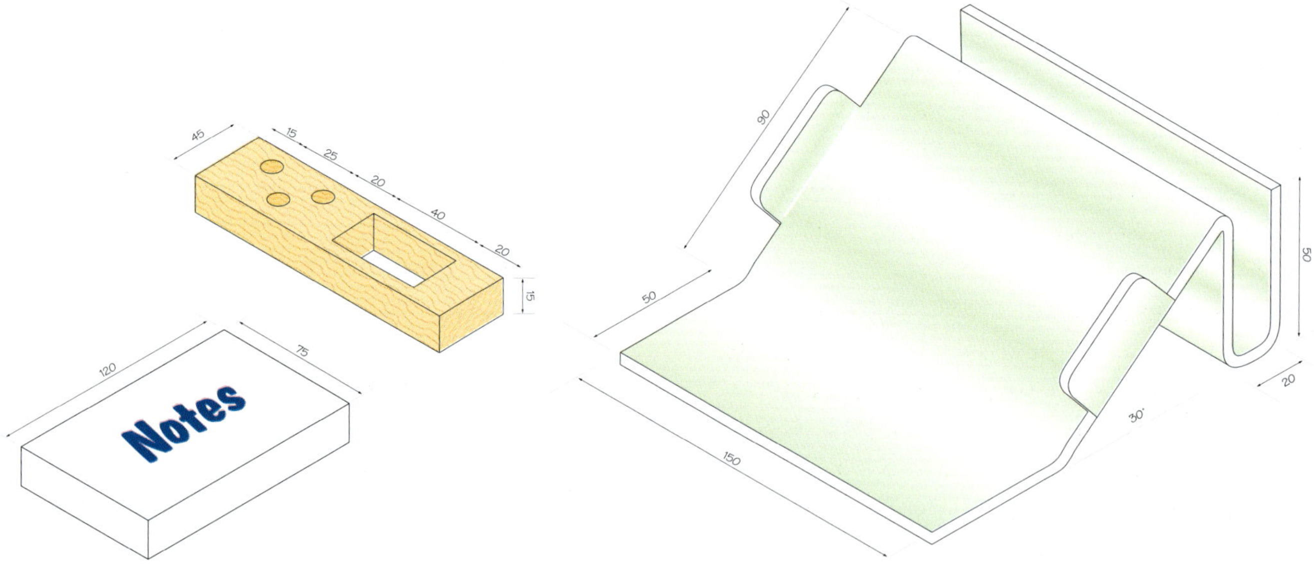

Project with joints and measurements

When the drawings have been done a list of all the sizes of the pieces must be made. This **cutting list** is used to prepare the necessary material for the project. You should be able to give this list to any wood machinist to prepare the material for you. The materials list should include hinges, handles, screws, cloth and other items which may need to be purchased in order to complete the project. This gives you time to find these items.

CUTTING LIST: NOTE HOLDER					
Item Name	Quantity	Length	Width	Thickness	Material
Base	1	265mm	170mm	3mm	Acrylic (blue)
Pen Holder	1	120mm	44mm	15mm	Ash

Cutting list for the notepad

The above format for producing the cutting list should be followed.

Making

When the drawings are complete work can begin. The making of the project, how it is to be marked out, joined, processed and assembled must be planned. The time that each stage will take should be considered so that you have a timetable to work to.

While making the item, minor changes may need to be made to the design. These should be checked before proceeding. It may be useful to record how unusual or complex processes were done, so that you can look back over these at a later stage to help you recall how they were accomplished or to apply the ideas to other projects you might take up later.

Evaluation

When the object is finished it is usually evaluated. This we always do even without thinking: we stand back to admire the work that we have done. In the evaluation we must look at the finished work in a critical way. Even the best craftspeople will find faults in their own work: things which might have been done differently to make the item better.

The evaluation can be done under at least three headings.

- **The design** – examining the chosen design for good and bad points.
- **The making** – detailing difficulties and how problems were solved, etc.
- **The finished article** – describing changes that you would make and your overall opinions of the finished project.

You might ask yourself questions like:

- Does it satisfy the requirements of the brief, and if so, how well?
- Does the project look well and explain why?
- Were the chosen materials, joints and finishes, etc. suitable and did they work well?
- Is the standard of work good – what steps could you have taken to make it better?
- Is the finish well done?
- What changes might you make if you were doing it again?
- Is it what you expected it to be like?

Designers use tests and evaluations of their designs to help them to make improvements to their designs.

Design is a mixture of problem solving and planning. It is important when designing that you cover all the possibilities in order to achieve the best results.

Before a climb the mountaineer plans to ensure that all possible difficulties can be overcome and that he/she has the necessary equipment to do the climb. Similarly, a designer must search for the answers to the possible problems posed by any design situation.

When faced with a design problem the process of planning is similar. All aspects of the problem must be examined, possible solutions are listed and then decisions are made which build up to a satisfactory solution.

Proportion

One of the main factors affecting the appearance of any design, is proportion. Proportion is the relationship of the size and shape of the parts of the object. No part of the item should be too large or too small.

Good & bad proportion

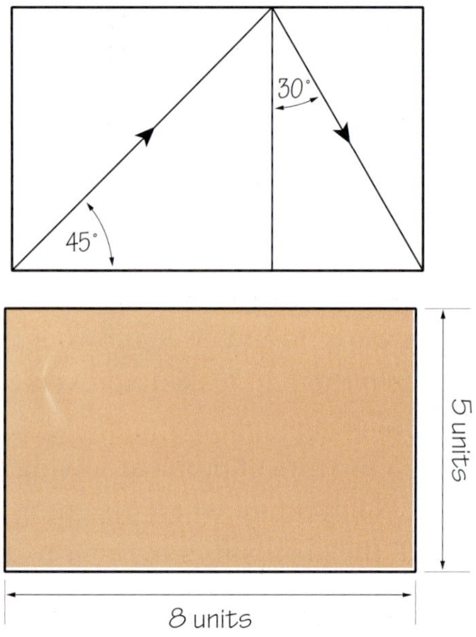

A quick way of getting the golden section

Ancient Greeks used a rule to make sure that the size and shape of their buildings were in good proportion. This rule is still used today and is known as the **golden section**. The golden section is a rectangle whose sides are in the ratio of **5:8**. They found that rectangles are more pleasing to the eye than squares and that the 5:8 rectangle was the most suitable.

The proportions of Trinity College, Dublin follow the golden section

Exercises

1. Some items are listed below which are to be designed – in each case give one major factor which would need to be considered in the design of each of these items.

Garden bench	Salad bowl
Window box	Child's rocking horse
Kitchen table	Pen/pencil box

2. Design a sign or nameplate for your house or room. Draw your ideas full size on graph paper.
3. You find it a problem keeping all of your pens, pencils and writing equipment together. They are easily broken in your school bag. Solve the problem.

4. Here is a selection of design briefs for you to work on.
   - **Situation:** The worktop in the kitchen is being marked by the bread knife.
   - **Brief:** Design and make a cutting board which will protect the worktop and can be easily stored away.

   - **Situation:** The nature club in your school want to put a number of bird nesting boxes around the school grounds.
   - **Brief:** Design and make a bird nesting box to suit small birds. You might add an electronic device to tell you when the box is occupied.

   - **Situation:** Your brother or sister would like their own money box.
   - **Brief:** Design and make a money box which will hold coins of different sizes.

   - **Situation:** Fruit is kept in the fridge at home but takes up too much space.
   - **Brief:** Design and make a container which will hold at least five apples and five oranges and will be a feature of the dining room table.

   - **Situation:** The fireplace in the sitting room is not used.
   - **Brief:** Design and make some decorative piece which will cover the fireplace.

   - **Situation:** You would like to brighten up a porch with some plants.
   - **Brief:** Design two types of planter, (i) to hand from the ceiling, (ii) to stand free on the floor.

   - **Situation:** The towel in the bathroom hangs over the radiator which looks untidy.
   - **Brief:** Design and make a towel hanger which can be mounted on the wall.

   - **Situation:** The coats in the house are always untidy.
   - **Brief:** Design and make a coat hanger to hold no more than five coats.

   - **Situation:** You have plenty of mugs in the kitchen but nowhere to put them.
   - **Brief:** Design and make a mug tree to hold six mugs.

   - **Situation:** The Materials Technology Room needs another first-aid cabinet.
   - **Brief:** Design and make a first aid cabinet which is neat and holds all the first-aid equipment.

6. The diagram shows an ash stool that is to be used in a child's play group.

   a. From the diagram identify one weak aspect of this design. Give reasons for your answer.

   b. Using notes and sketches to communicate your ideas, suggest an alternative design for a child's stool. The idea should suggest the idea of play or fun as well as work

7. a. Given in the following list are a number of the steps usually undertaken in a design process.

Place these in the order that they would be encountered and write a short note explaining any two of these.

Evaluation
Design brief
Investigation/research
Working drawings
Prototype
Analysis of brief
Ideas

b. The picture shows a Woodland Picnic Area for which a range of seating and table units is required. Using notes and sketches to communicate your ideas, suggest a possible solution to this problem.

c. Suggest suitable timber and applied finish that might be used for such items and give two reasons for each of your choices.

8 The diagram below shows a computer desk with some of the stationary, etc. that would be commonly associated with it.

a. With the aid of notes and sketches, design a suitable storage unit for these articles that could be located on the desk top. Identify the main requirements for such an artefact.

b. Select suitable materials for your design and give reasons for your choices.

9. Shown in the three diagrams below are examples of wooden projects. In each case prepare a cutting list of the materials needed to make these pieces.

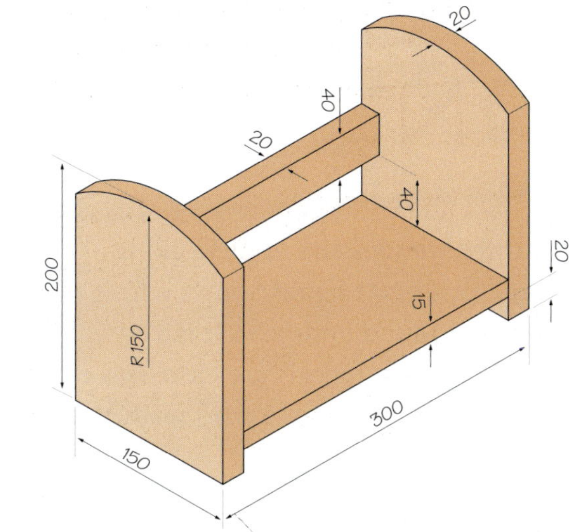

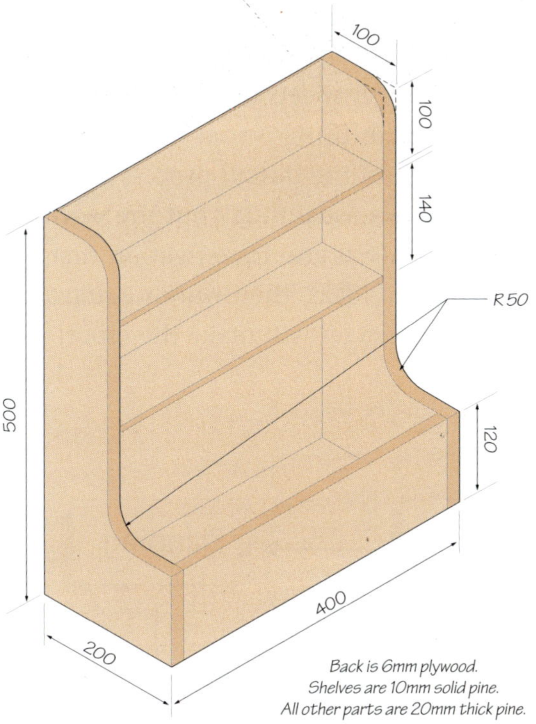

Back is 6mm plywood.
Shelves are 10mm solid pine.
All other parts are 20mm thick pine.

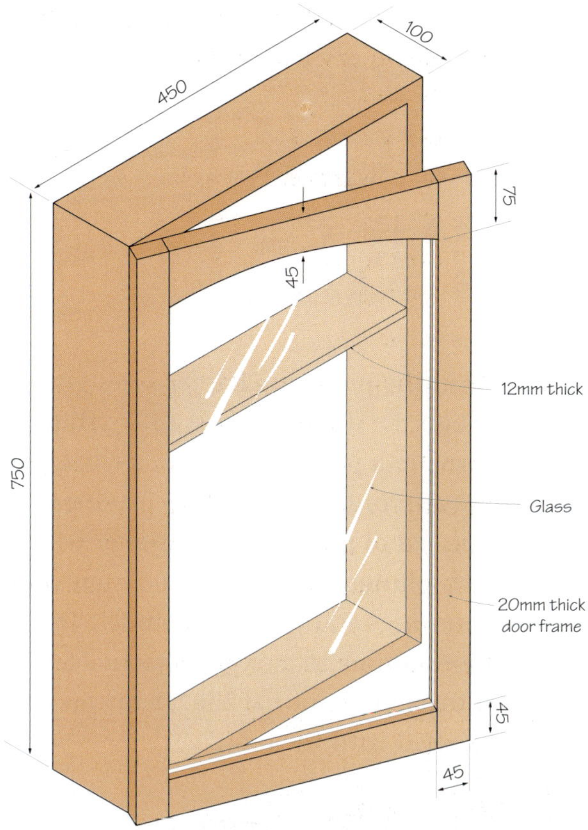

CHAPTER TWENTY-ONE

REPORT WRITING & PRESENTATION

As we saw in the previous chapter a designer will work through the design process of anything from a house to a postage stamp in a clear and definite way. In order to keep the customer or client informed of progress the designer will present the solutions and the final design with working drawings and perhaps a model. This presentation is done in a clear, attractive and understandable way, so that the client can decide how to proceed with the design.

Designer showing a client a drawing and model of a design

You will produce a similar report of the design process of each of the projects that you do. The report or folio will show all the aspects of your design. It will show how you researched and formed your ideas, how the ideas were developed into your final design and your working drawings, etc. A good report shows where the solutions were found and how. It is very important that your reports are clear and can be easily understood by anyone who reads them.

Layout

The report can be laid out in many ways depending on your personal preference. It may be done on larger A3 sheets or in book form on A4 sheets. The main thing is that it is set out neatly. Each stage of the design process should be covered and it is usual to lay out the work as it happened – analysis and investigation first, followed by design ideas, then working drawings, etc. These logical stages will make the report easier to follow.

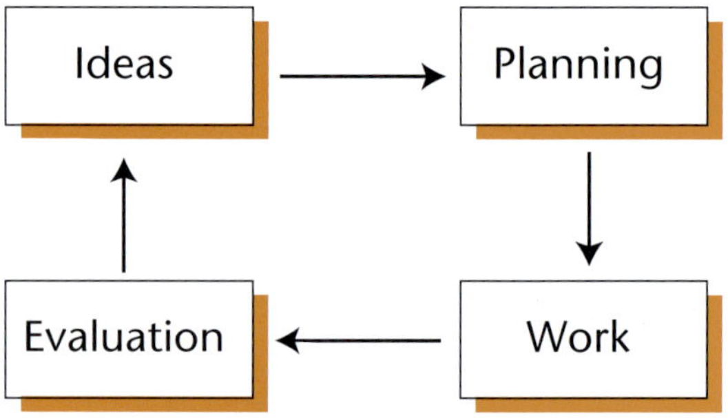

Stages in the layout of the report/folio

Written explanations are necessary and useful sketches and drawings will assist you to present your ideas clearly and in more detail. Photographs, drawings, etc. can be cut out from old newspapers, magazines and catalogues to show where ideas and inspiration came from.

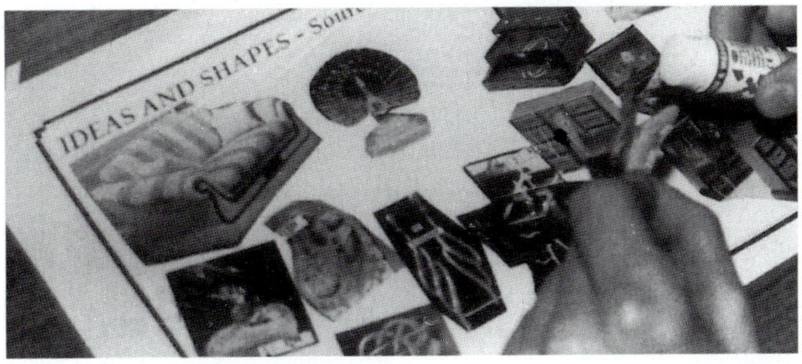

"A picture paints a thousand words"

Drawings can be done freehand or with instruments. They can also be produced on a computer using a number of CAD (Computer Aided Design) programmes which are available. When your drawings are complete they can be presented neatly in your report.

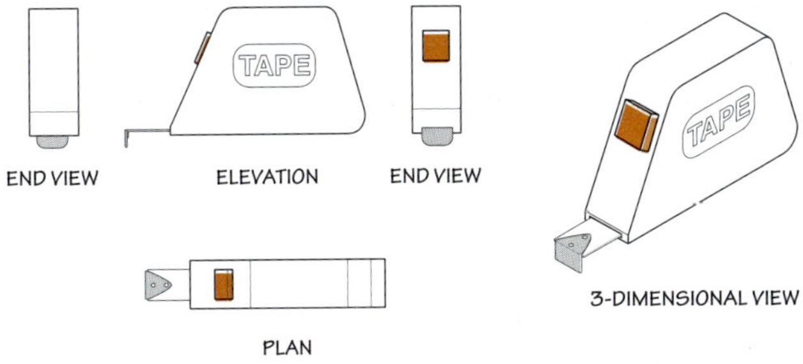

Drawings may be done freehand, using instruments or CAD

Drawings can be divided into two main types, two dimensional (2-D) and three dimensional (3-D) drawings. You can use both types in your report.

Paper and equipment

Paper is available in many sizes and qualities. White paper is usually used for drawing and computer printouts. The figure below shows some of the standard sizes of paper available.

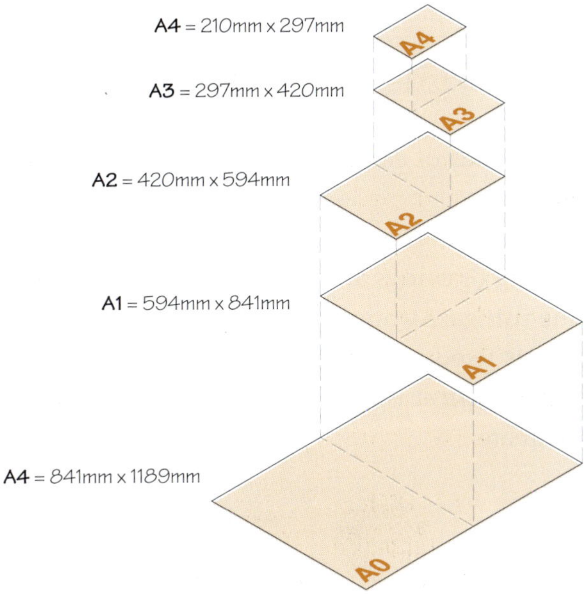

Standard paper sizes

Special ruled paper can be obtained which will help you to do freehand sketching. These papers have ruled grids pre-printed on them and are very useful.

Pencils

It is usual to do your sketches and drawings in pencil as it makes correcting mistakes easier. Pencils are obtained in different grades according to the hardness of their lead. You should use a 2H or 3H pencil for instrument drawing and a HB or B pencil for your freehand sketches. To keep your work tidy, it is important that you keep a sharp point on the pencil at all times.

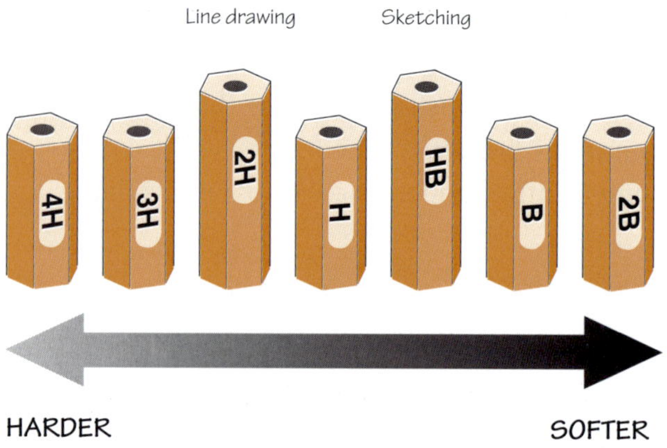

Grading of pencils

Instruments

Working drawings and joint details are usually done using instruments on a drawing board. The paper is fixed to the board with clips or masking tape. The sheet is kept level with the blade of the tee square

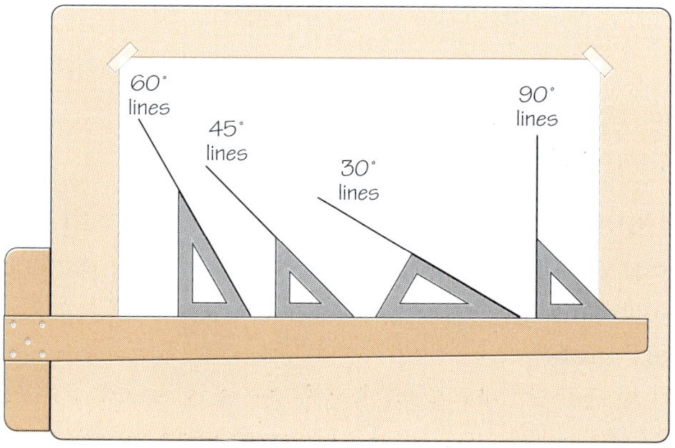

The set squares are used for drawing vertical lines and angles. They are used along the top of the tee square

Length is measured in millimetres, which are marked along the edge of the ruler or the set squares.

Standard metric ruler

Set squares 45° and 60°

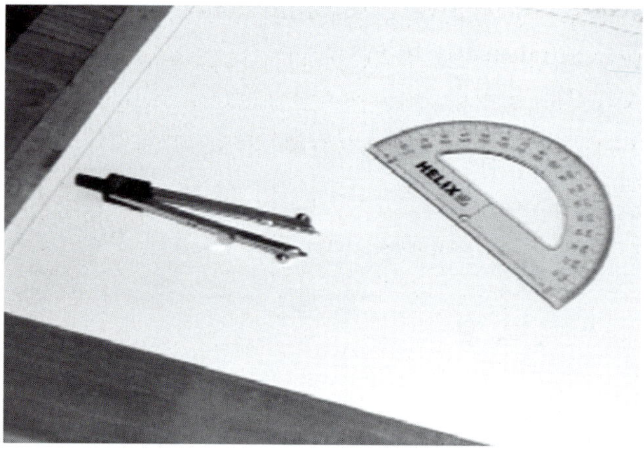

A protractor for measuring angles and a compass is used for drawing circles. The lead of the compass must also be kept sharp.

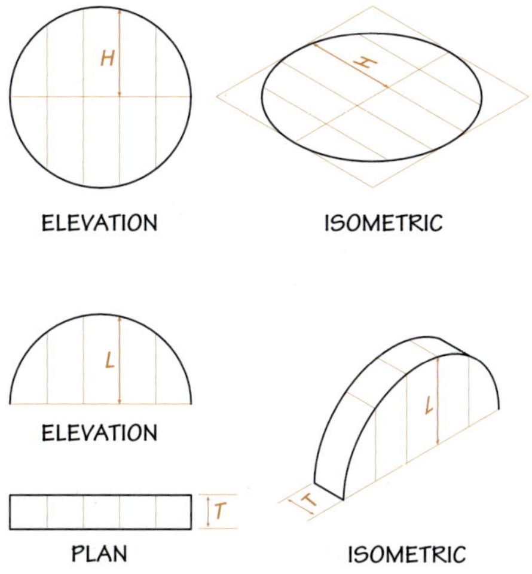

Using ordinates to construct a curve in isometric

Exploded pictorial drawing

Pictorial drawings can be 'exploded' to reveal a more detailed view of how the parts of an object are assembled. This type of view shows the parts of an object as if they have been taken apart.

Exploded isometric views and oblique views can be useful to show how joints go together. Freehand exploded views of parts of project work, including joints can be useful for understanding the work that needs to be done.

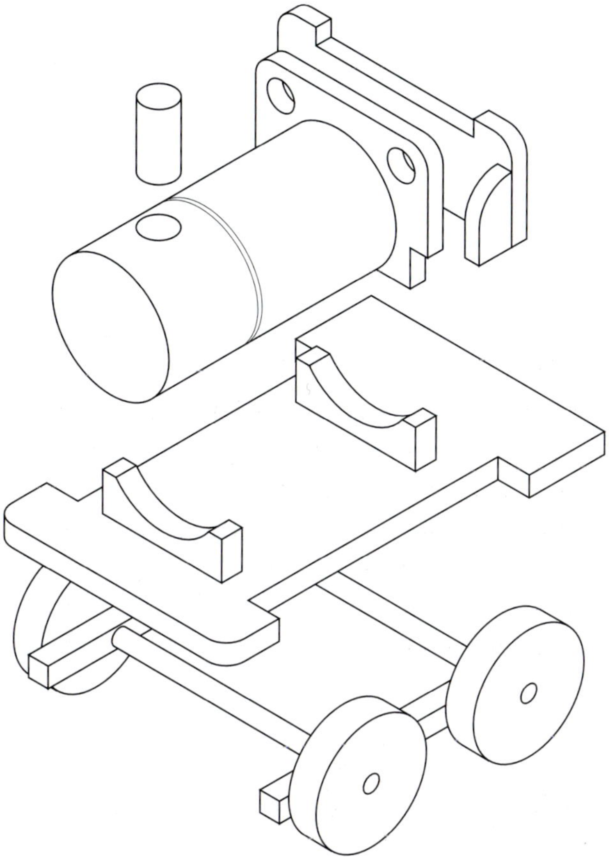

An exploded view of a toy train

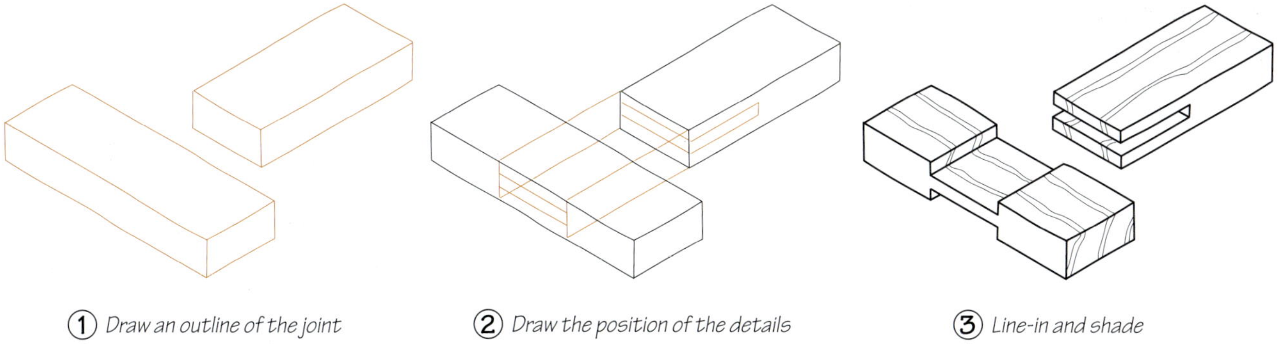

Stages in drawing an exploded isometric sketch of a bridle joint

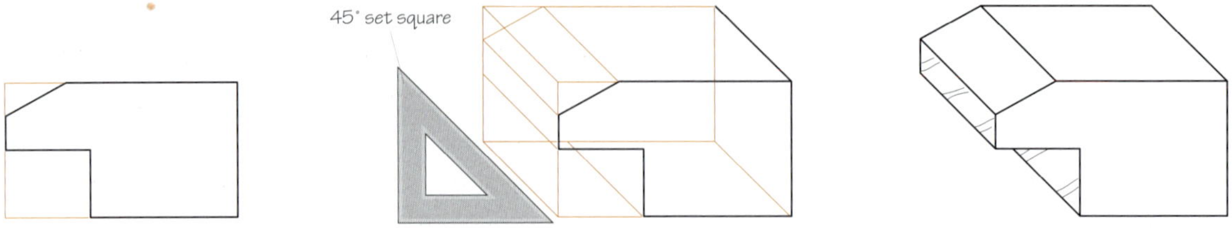

① *Draw the front face*

② *Project the corners back at 45° and mark off the thickness*

③ *Fill in the detail and line-in*

Steps for drawing a thumb gauge in oblique

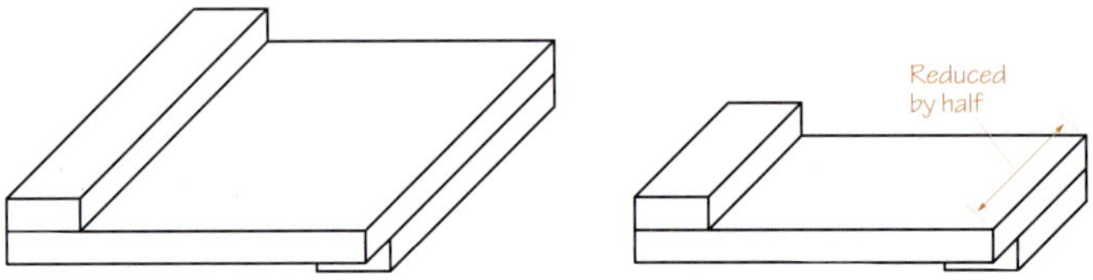

One of the major problems with this form of projection is that the finished drawing can look out of proportion. This is ***Cavalier Projection****.*

To overcome this problem the lines being projected back are halved giving a better proportioned drawing. This form of oblique is called ***Cabinet Oblique Projection****.*

Proportions can be improved in oblique drawings by using cabinet oblique projection

Oblique drawing

This simple method of drawing depends on lines being projected back at 45° from the front of the object being drawn.

One of the difficulties with this type of drawing is that the finished view can look out of proportion. This is called **cavalier oblique projection**. This effect can be overcome by halving the measurements of the 45° lines.

Curved surfaces and circles are specially treated. If a circle is in a vertical position it may be drawn with a compass. A second circle which is parallel to the first can be drawn with a compass after projecting back the centre point of the first to find the centre of the second.

A circle in a horizontal position must be found using ordinates in the same way as for isometric circles. When the points are located and a light curve is drawn, the final circle can be lined in.

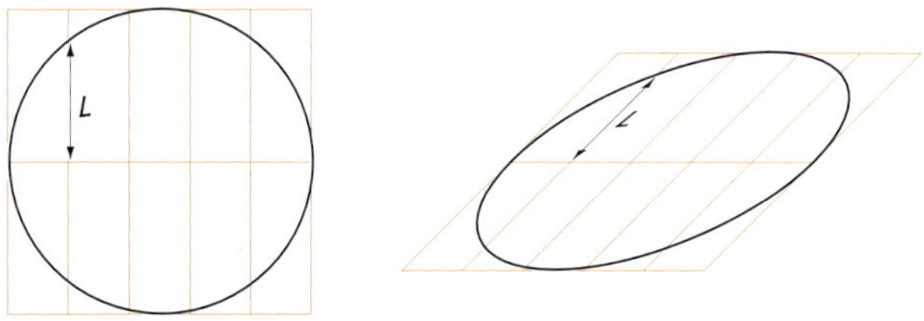

Construction for a horizontal circle in oblique

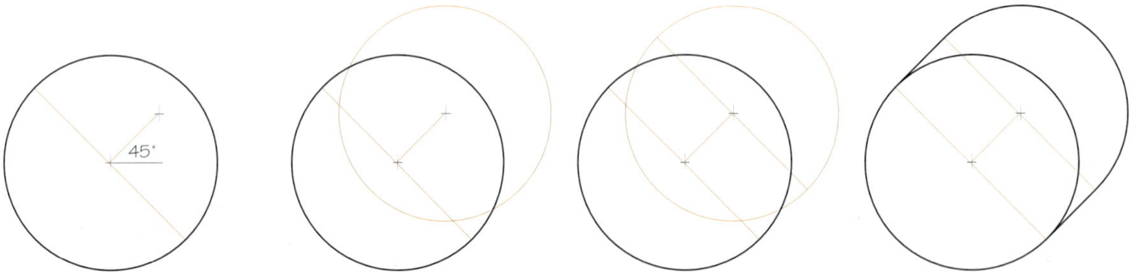

① ② ③ ④

Construction for a vertical circle in oblique

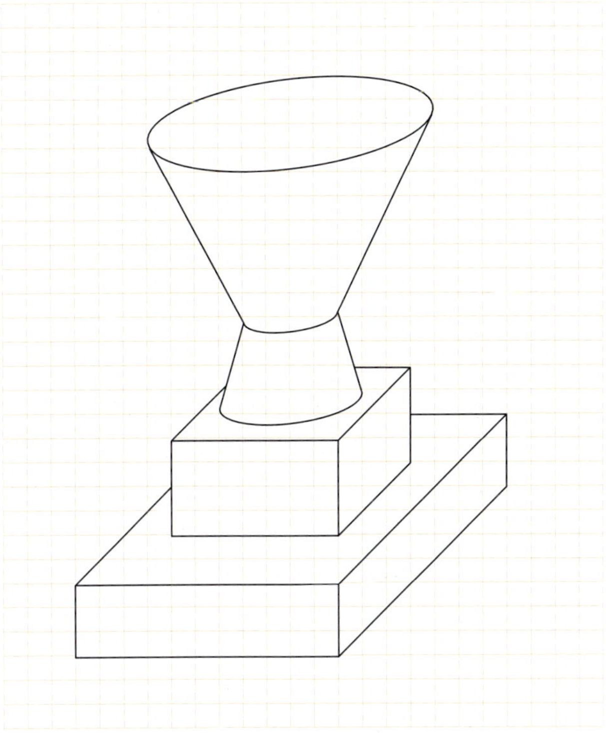

You can use squared grid paper to help you with your freehand oblique drawings

Planometric drawing

This type of drawing is very useful for looking down into something, for example a jewellery box or a room.

The main rule for forming the axis of this drawing is that the angles must always add up to 90°. Just as in oblique drawing the proportions of the items drawn in planometric can look poor. To rectify this the heights can be reduced to half their actual size.

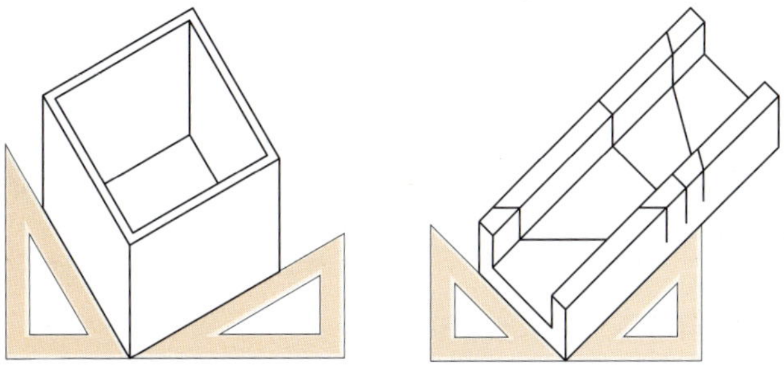

Planometric projection – any combination of angles may be used as long as they add up to 90°

Here is a sketch of a desk lamp with a *desktidy* which has been built up in stages. The stages are done in light pencil lines. When you are happy with your result you can line the drawing in heavily and add some rendering (shading/colouring).

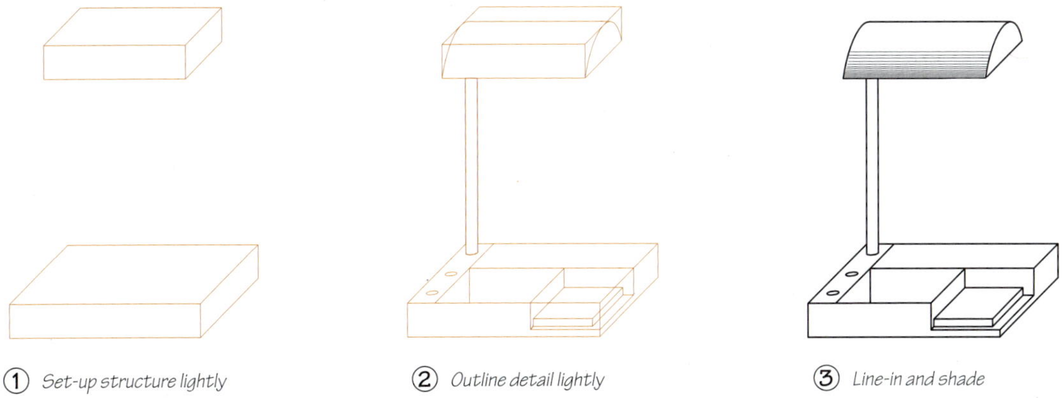

Drawing a desk lamp

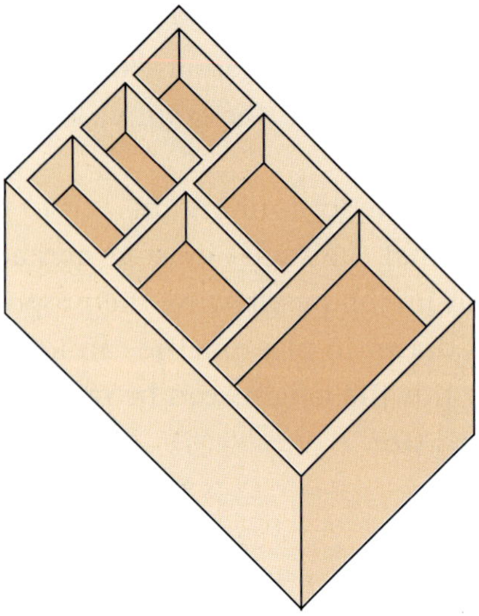

Planometric is ideal for showing the insides of things like jewellery boxes

Perspective drawing

Perspective drawing is the only pictorial drawing method which shows an object exactly as the human eye would see it. There are two basic types, **one point perspective** and **two point perspective**. Both types can be drawn with instruments or freehand.

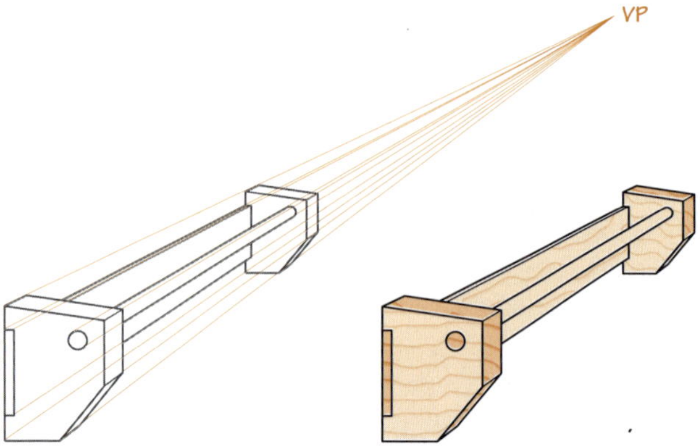

One point perspective gives a very impressive view of project, in this case a tie rack

One point perspective

This gives a very dramatic view of an object or project and is much used to show the interiors of rooms. The effect is clear with this view of a tie rack. It is clear that all the points vanish back to one single point which is called the **vanishing point.**

The front of the object is drawn first. The vanishing point is selected and light lines are drawn from the points on the front to the vanishing point. Distances are estimated in suitable proportion.

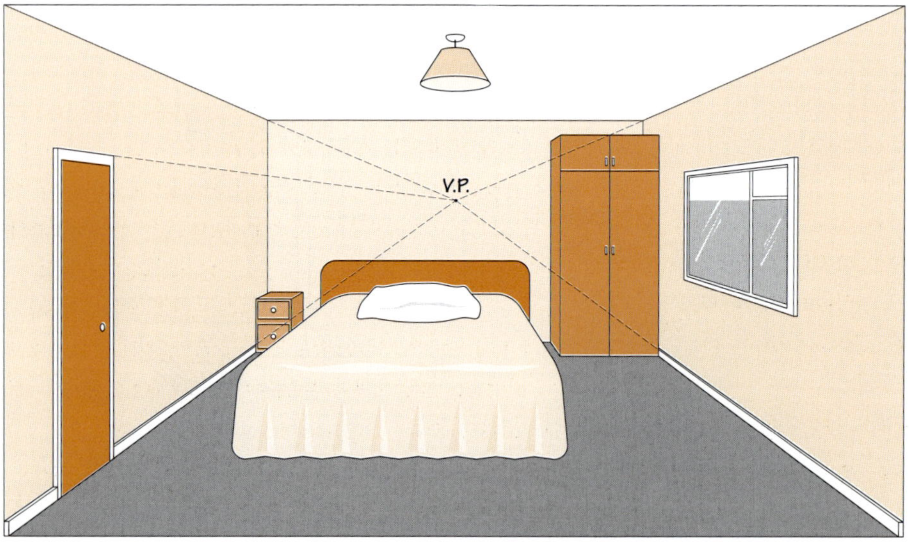

One point perspective is ideal for planning the interior of rooms

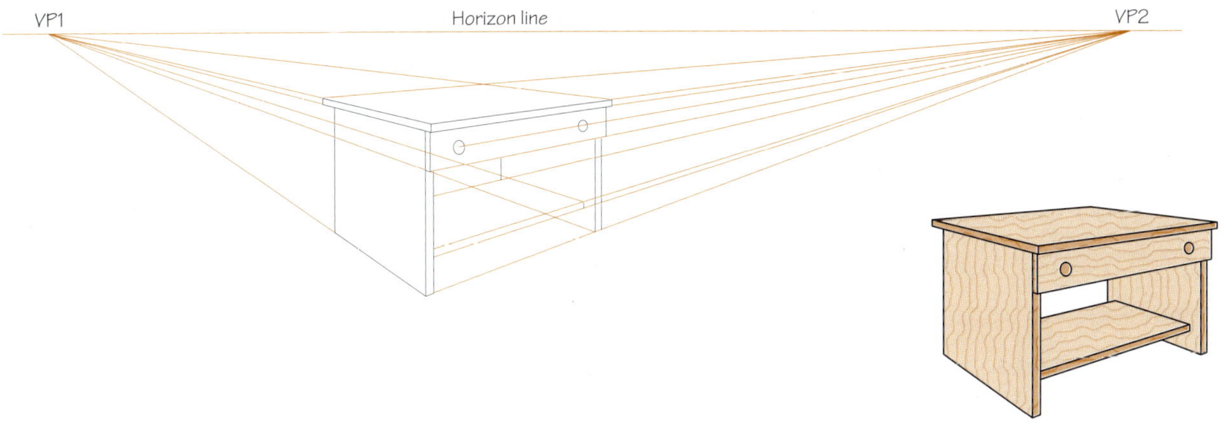

A simple two point perspective of a locker showing construction

Here is a two point perspective of a picnic table.
This type of drawing is good for interesting views of furniture or other projects

Two point perspective

This is sometimes called **architectural perspective** as it is used by architects to present building designs. It shows a view of an article as if the spectator were standing in front of it. The drawing is approached in a similar way to one point perspective but there are two vanishing points instead. The two vanishing points are situated on a horizontal line called the **horizon**. Again distances can be estimated in suitable proportion.

Drawing standards

Drawing standards have been developed so that everyone's drawings will read the same. It is important that drawings done in schools in Cork should be the same as those done in schools in Galway. In industry these standards are used so that there can be no question about what the designer, engineer or architect is trying to get across in the drawing. Here are some simple standards (rules) for you to learn and apply to your own drawings.

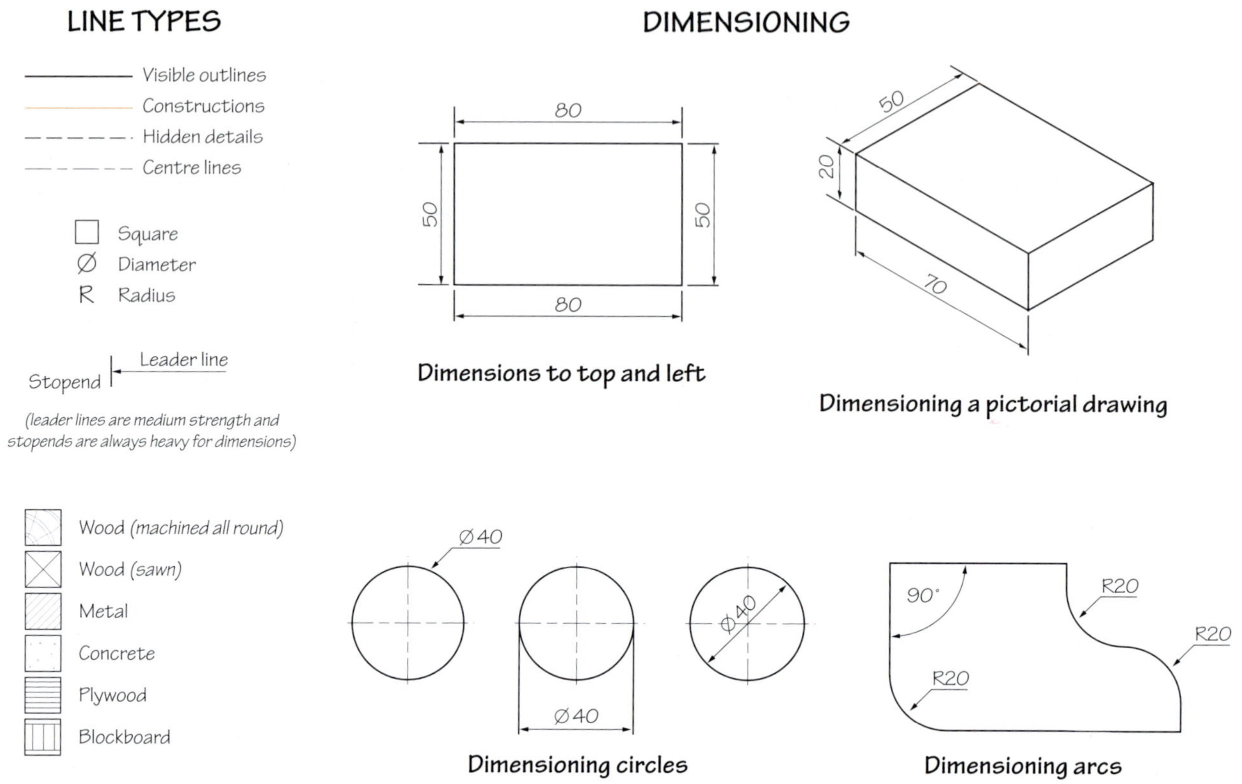

Drawing standards

Scales

It can often be difficult to fit drawings of large projects onto drawing sheets because they are too large. Scales allow drawings of large objects to be drawn onto smaller sheets of paper. Scales such as 1:2 (half full size) and 2:3 (two thirds full size) are commonly used. Scales can also be used to enlarge objects or parts of objects in order to make them clearer to see.

Scales are written as ratio on the drawing. This is so that the person who reads the drawing will know what scale the drawing is done to. The drawing is done to scale, but when you are putting measurements on the drawing, you fill in the full size measurements, so that you can just read them from the drawing.

Engineers and architects use scale rulers, which is a ruler that has a number of scales, premarked on it. This saves time dividing up measurements.

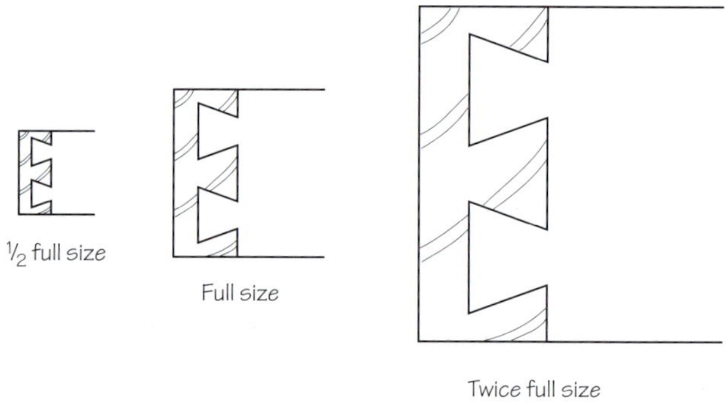

Drawings showing objects

Scale rulers

Colour and shading

Drawings, both instrument and freehand drawings can look good as simple line drawings. However, both can be enhanced greatly by the simple use of colour and shading.

There is a great variety of different ways of adding colour but possibly the best way is coloured pencils. These are easy to use, inexpensive and give a very pleasing effect.

A single pencil can also be used to give many tones on the one colour.

One colour – three tones

When using pencils one mistake which is often made is that too much pressure is applied on the pencil. The correct way to use the pencil for rendering (shading) is to hold it as shown below and apply the first shading very lightly, building up the colour step by step.

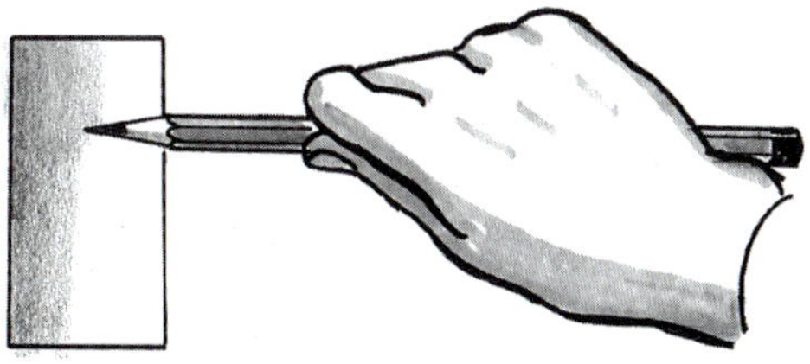

Holding the pencil

Using different densities of colour to give life to a drawing or sketch

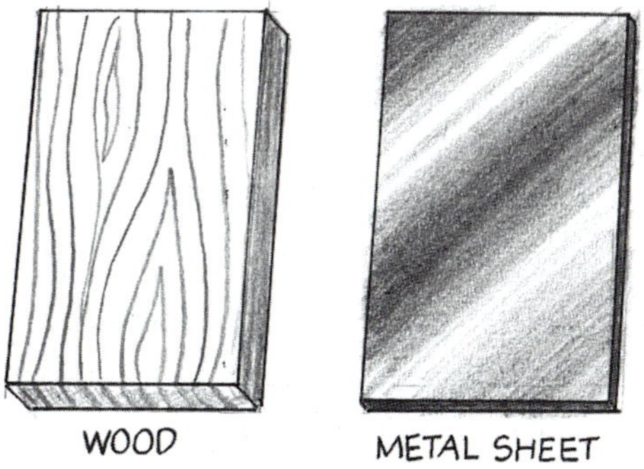

Adding texture to objects

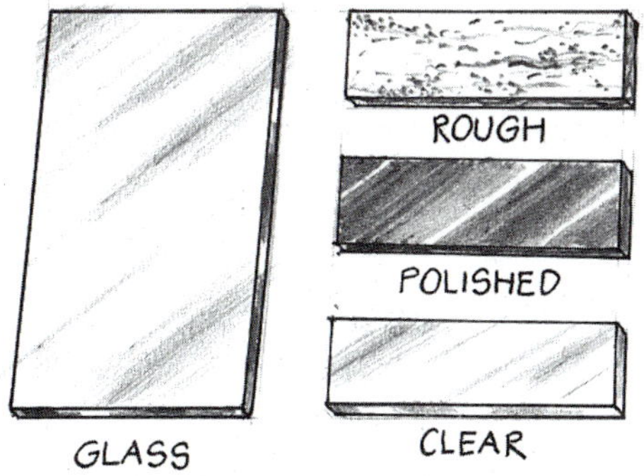

Adding texture to objects

Shading using only one colour can be used to show different materials. The sketches here have been rendered to show the various material surfaces. These techniques can be practised and used to improve the overall impression of your drawings, sketches and will enhance the presentation of your report.

Photographs

Your report can be enhanced by including photographs and cut out items from old magazines, papers and catalogues. It will form part of your investigation, but they should be presented as neatly and effectively as possible. You can also take pictures of things which relate to your project and include them. These items can be stuck into the page using a gum adhesive.

Flow charts

Flowcharts show a series of events in a diagram form.

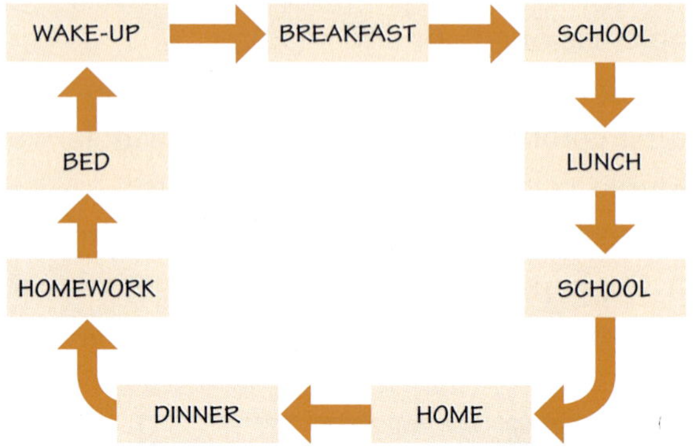

Flowcharts have many uses. They can show the stages of the design procedure, for example. Computer programmers use them to plan how a computer program should respond to different commands. We can use them in a similar way, here is one to show the design process.

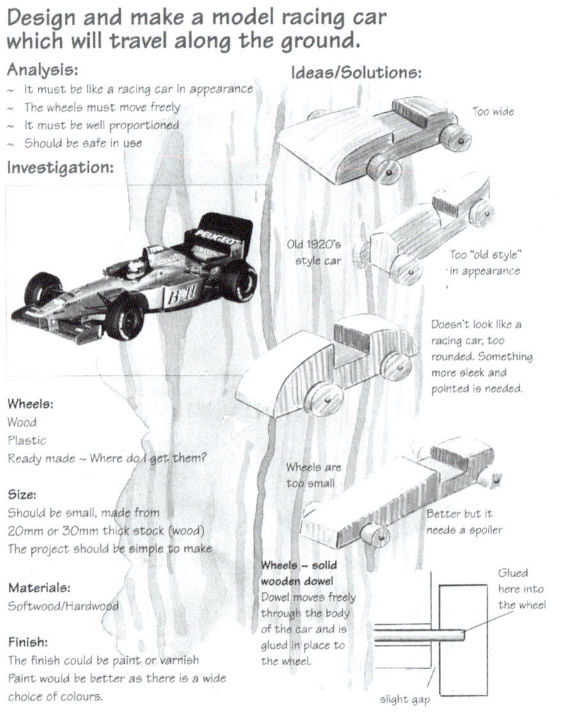

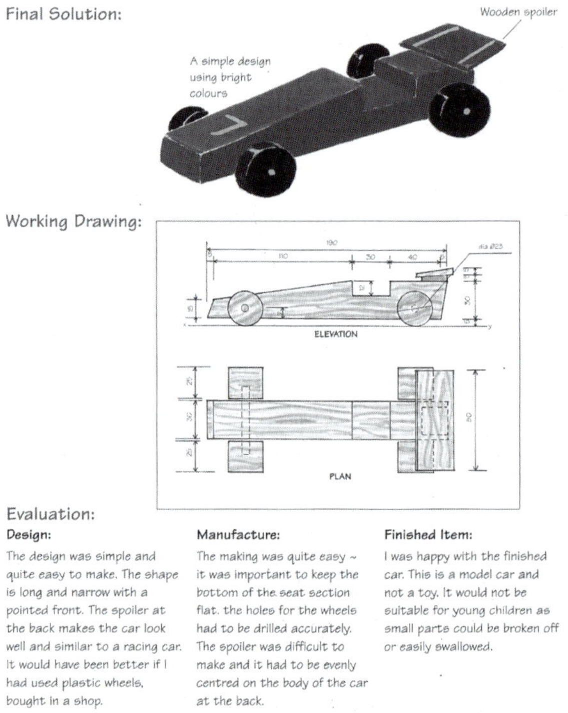

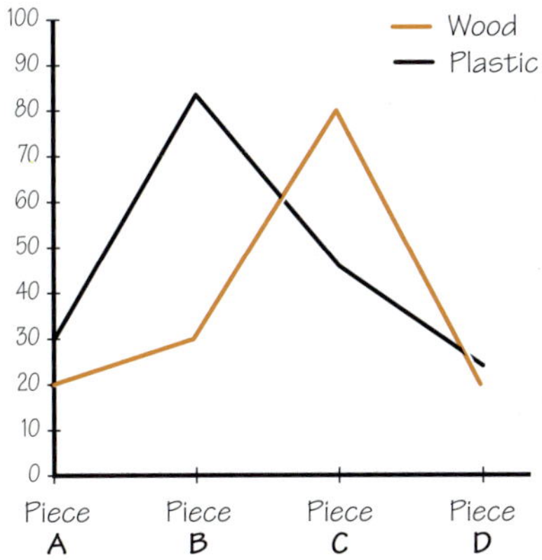

LINE GRAPH

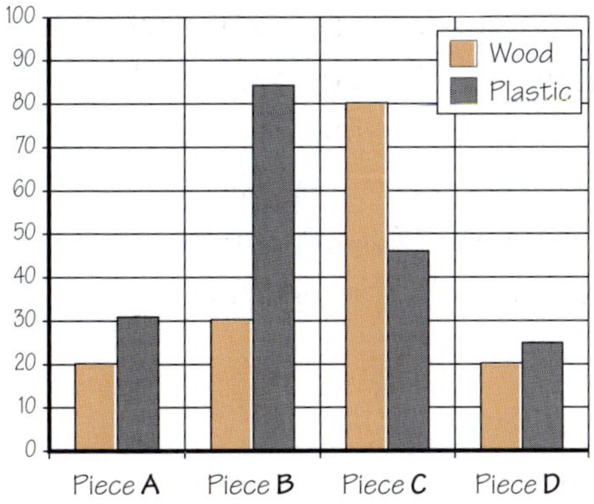

BAR GRAPH

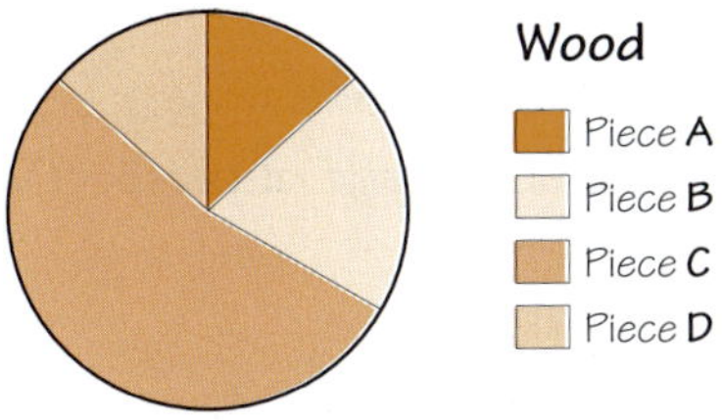

PIE CHART

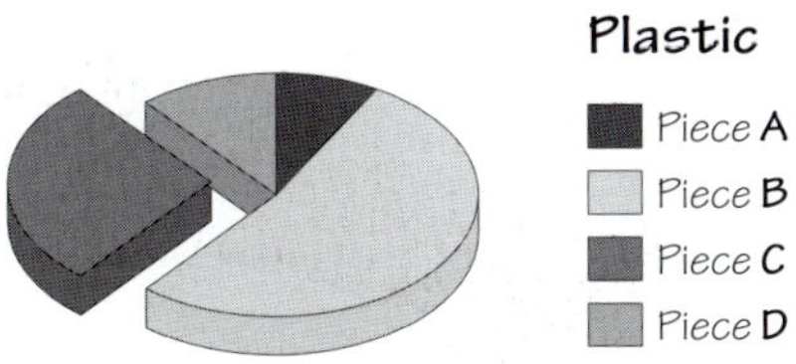

3D PIE CHART

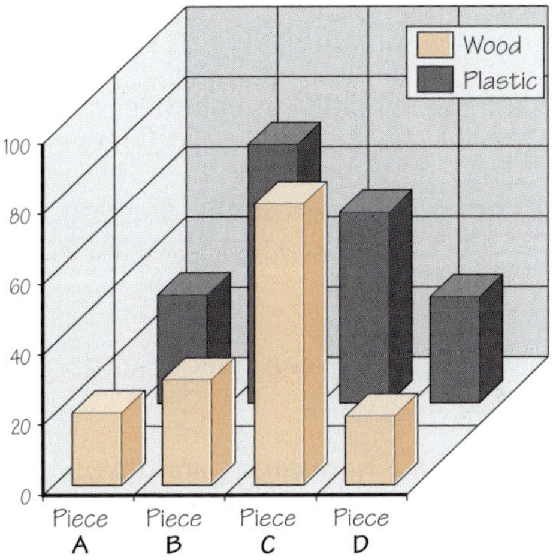

3D BAR CHART / BAR GRAPH

Types of graphs

Graphs

There are many types of graphs and they are used to show information in a picture format.

Experiments

It might be necessary to test a material or a finish to see if it is acceptable or to find out if it is strong enough for the purpose for which you intend it. The results of tests and experiments can be written up and should be included with the project.

Covers

The report which is written should be neatly and well presented. A nice folder or cover for the report may add to the presentation. The cover should keep the report clean, tidy and safe. There are many types available but each would be suitable as long as they protect the work and keep it neat.

Exercises

1. Why should your work be well presented?
2. What is the function of a report/folio?
3. What is a 2-dimensional drawing and what is a 3-dimensional drawing, give an example of each?
4. What is grid papers and how can they help you to sketch accurately?
5. Sketch the following items in either 2-D or 3-D:
   - clock/radio
   - phone
   - dovetail joint
   - television
   - mortise & tenon joint
   - corner bridle joint
   - toaster

   Use shading and some colour to enhance these sketches.
6. What are the common scales used in drawing and how do scales help us to produce working drawings?
7. State some differences between oblique and isometric drawing.
8. Using sketches, explain how circles are drawn in isometric drawing.
9. Make a flow chart to explain the stages in cutting a bridle joint.
10. Complete the table below and draw a bar graph to show the following information:

Tenon saw		teeth per inch
Panel saw		teeth per inch
Coping saw		teeth per inch
Pad saw		teeth per inch
Rip saw		teeth per inch

11. Design a flow chart to explain the stages in making a cup of tea.
12. Draw a perspective sketch of a coffee table and indicate the horizon line and vanishing points on the sketch.
13. Give one advantage of perspective drawing.

CHAPTER TWENTY-TWO

COMPUTER AIDED DESIGN (CAD)

Computers and microchip technology have been developing rapidly over the last number of years. This development is possibly most clearly seen in the area of computer graphics. You are probably familiar with the improving graphics in computer games. Computer generated graphics are being used increasingly more in advertising on the television and in the movie industry. Designers in industry also use computers to produce drawings and designs. Computer aided design (CAD) allows drawings to be produced, stored, altered and printed accurately and easily.

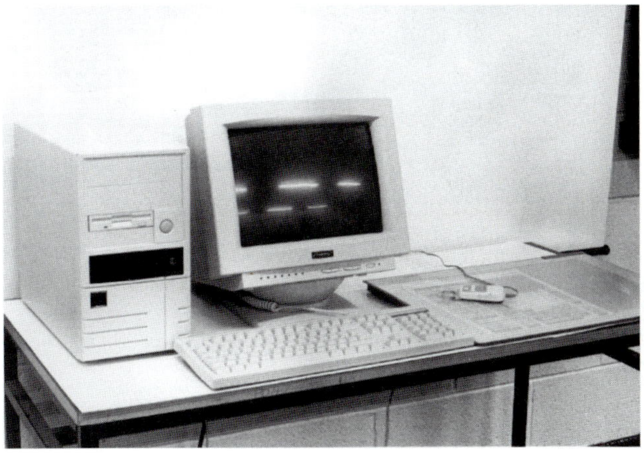

CAD system

Hardware and software

Computer systems can be divided into two parts, hardware and software.

Hardware all the parts which can be seen such as the hard drive, monitor, keyboard, mouse, printer, etc.

Software all the different programmes (applications) which make the computer work and which allow you to use the computer.

Hardware and software

Devices

Mouse An input device which is used to point to and select menus or items on the screen. It is used for most computer applications particularly drawing programmes.

Keyboard This input device is used to type text, numbers and symbols as well as other input functions.

Digitiser and drawing tablet

This board and special mouse is an input device which is used with some drawing programmes. It contains all the most widely used commands as small pictures, called icons. This allows all of the commands to be accessed easily on the drawing tablet.

Monitor The monitor or **VDU** (visual display unit) displays the document or drawing on its screen. Most modern monitors have a full colour display.

Printers Printers and plotters are output devices on which you can produce a copy of your drawing or document. The printed drawing is called a **hard copy.**

Scanner A scanner is an input device which reads information from a page like a photo copier and then sends this image to the computer electronically. The computer is then used to access the image. Text and graphical information can be inputted quickly in this way.

Floppy disk

Floppy disks are used for storing and retrieving information, such as drawings which are stored as files. They are both input and output devices.

CD-ROM A CD-ROM is like a CD player for your computer. Great quantities of information can be stored on CD and it can be read from the CD by means of a small laser in the CD drive. Most modern computers have a CD-ROM drive in their systems box, just as they have a floppy disk drive.

Floppy disks

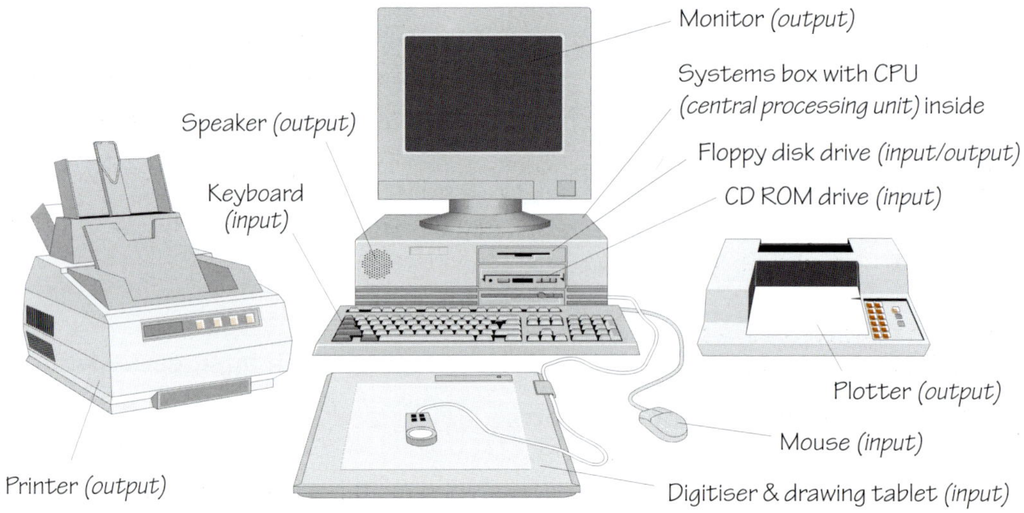

Computer system – parts

All of the information is processed in the central processing unit (CPU) which is located in the systems box. This box contains the floppy disk drive and CD-ROM as well as the computers **hard disk** and other electronics. The hard disk is a large memory storage disk which can store a large amount of files and programmes which can be used by the operator.

The drawing environment

When the CAD system is accessed, the work area is displayed on the screen. This screen is similar to the screens below although drawing programmes will differ. The menus containing the commands will be along the top or down the side of the screen. Work is carried out by pointing to the required command with the mouse and carrying out the command in the correct sequence.

Cross hairs on the screen will move to show the position of the cursor on the drawing area. This position is shown in relation to the X axis and Y axis.

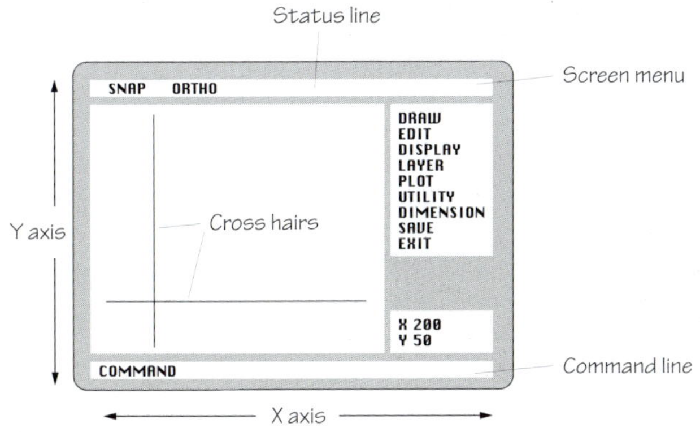

Computer screen with side menu

There are many added features to assist you in drawing. The command line is where the computer will communicate with you. For example, it will ask you the length of a line or the diameter of a circle.

Basic commands

Initially we must access the drawing package before we can begin drawing. A Windows based programme will be accessed through the relevant icon on the desktop or menu while a MS DOS based programme will need to be accessed through a series of typed commands. These commands will vary with the type of software package.

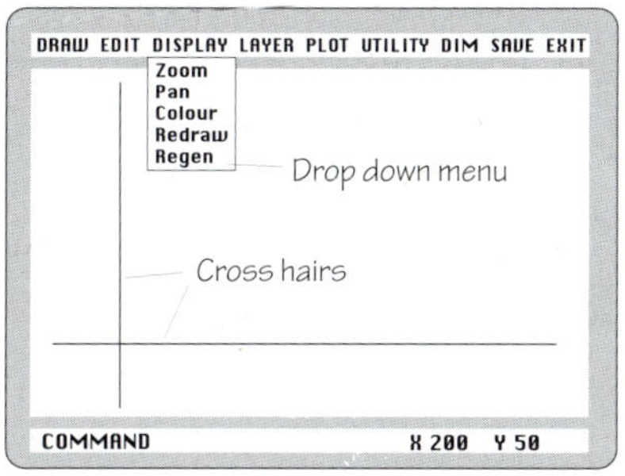

Computer screen with top drop down menu

Once the package is loaded, the screen will be visible and you can set up the screen working area. This is done automatically with most software packages, but the size of the area can be altered as you require.

Set up commands in CAD

Limits

This command allows the user to set up the size of the drawing area. This drawing area can then be displayed on the full screen. The limits are usually set to the size of a drawing sheet.

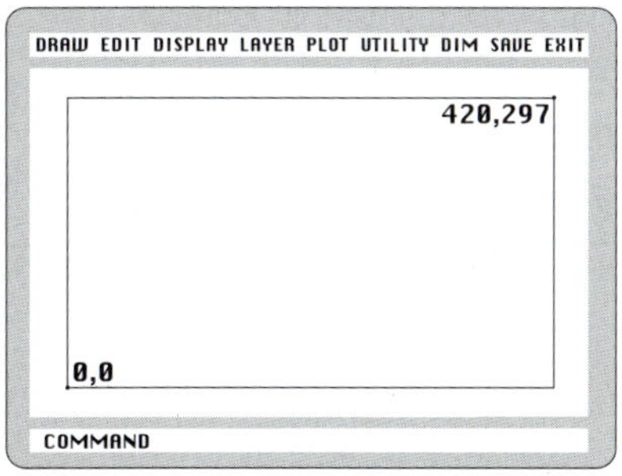

Limits set for an A3 drawing sheet – bottom left 0,0 and top right 420,297

Grid

The software package has a grid whose size can be set. The grid can be turned on or left off, as required. When the grid is on it will appear as a set of dots on the screen. The dots assist in the drawing of the object but will not appear on a print of the drawing.

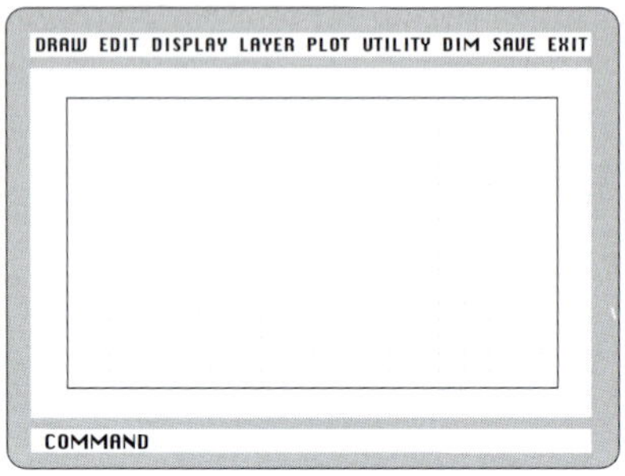

Screen with the grid on.

Snap

This setting will ensure that the cursor or cross hairs will only stop at regular intervals of snap which can be set. Often the snap is set at the same interval as the grid so the cross hairs jump between the dots of the grid.

Draw commands in CAD

Line

This allows lines of various length, thickness and angle to be drawn. Lines may be drawn between snap points or grid points. Accurate lengths and angles can also be drawn by entering these from the keyboard. The method for doing this will vary according to the software package being used.

Circle

Most systems allow you to draw a circle from one of the following pieces of information; radius, diameter, 3 points, or two tangents and a radius.

Arc

Arcs may be drawn from one of the following pieces of information; 3 points, start centre and end, start centre and included angle.

Draw commands (line, arc, circle)

Dimension

Allows the operator to add dimensions automatically. The start and end of the dimension are selected as is the position of the dimension and then the computer does the rest.

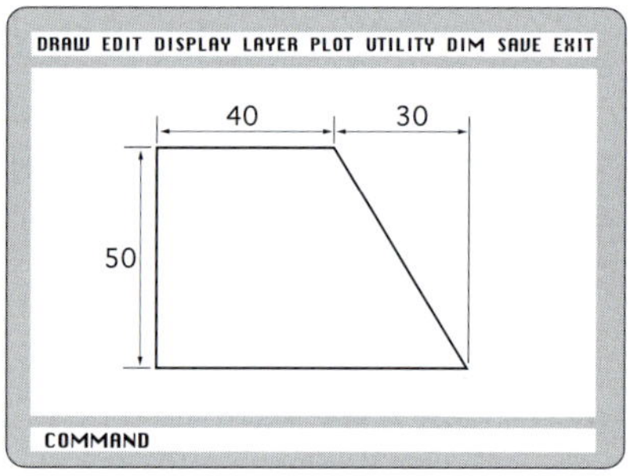

Dimension

Text

This command allows the operator add text such as titles and notes to drawings. Text can be entered in different styles and sizes.

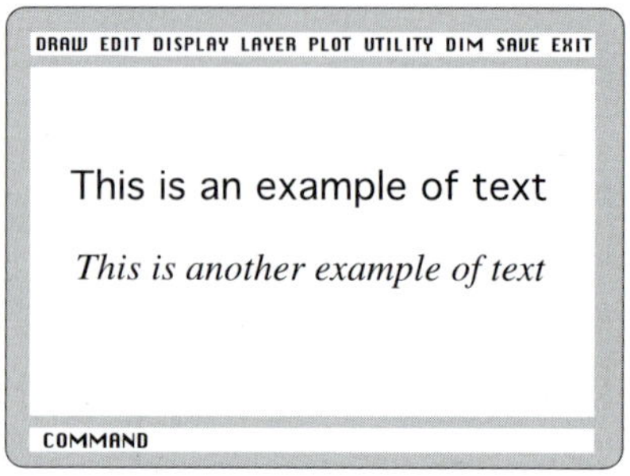

Text

Display commands

Zoom

Allows the user to magnify in a positive or negative way to get a close up or a wider view of the drawing. When doing a drawing it is a good idea to zoom close in to the object you are drawing to enlarge it to the size of the screen. When you are finished you can zoom out to give an overview. This will ensure that the drawing will be accurate.

Zoom command

Edit commands

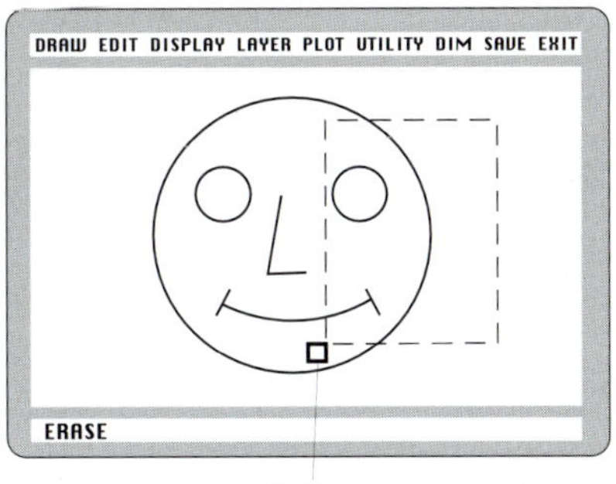

Pick box
(the pick box can be dragged to give a pick area)

Erase – the pick box can be dragged to give a pick area

Erase

This command allows you to remove or erase objects, lines, circles, etc. The command is selected and the object or objects to be erased are identified and the confirm button on the mouse is pressed to remove the objects. Alternatively, when the command is selected a box appears on the screen. This can be enlarged by dragging the cursor across the screen to enclose the objects to be erased. When confirmed they are removed. Most software packages have an undo command which will reverse the effect of the previous command. If an object has been erased in error the command can be reversed.

Break

This command will allow you to break a section out of a drawing.

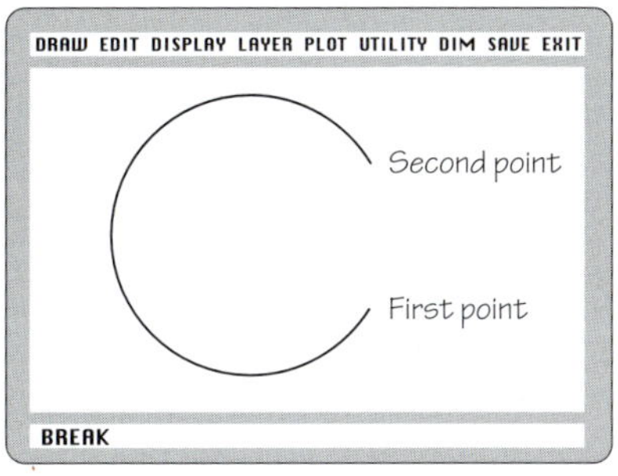

Break

Trim

Lines may be trimmed with the aid of another line which acts like a knife to cut the lines.

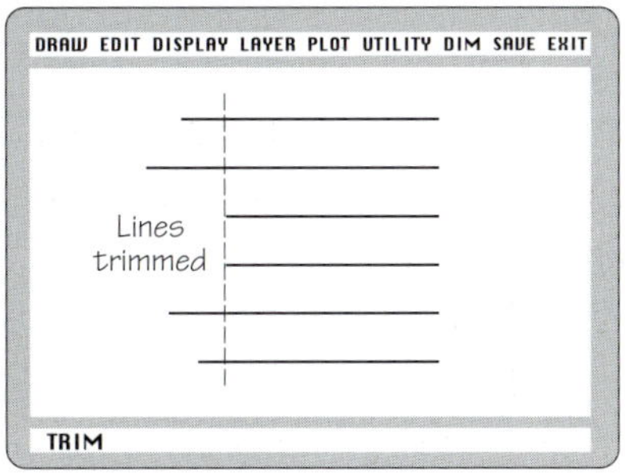

Trim

Fillet

Lines which meet at an angle may be rounded to a required radius. The desired radius must be set by the operator. If the fillet is set to zero, it is a useful command for cleaning up poorly drawn corners.

Chamfer

Lines which meet at angles may be chamfered to a required distance which can be set. As with the fillet, a chamfer set to zero will also clean up poorly drawn corners.

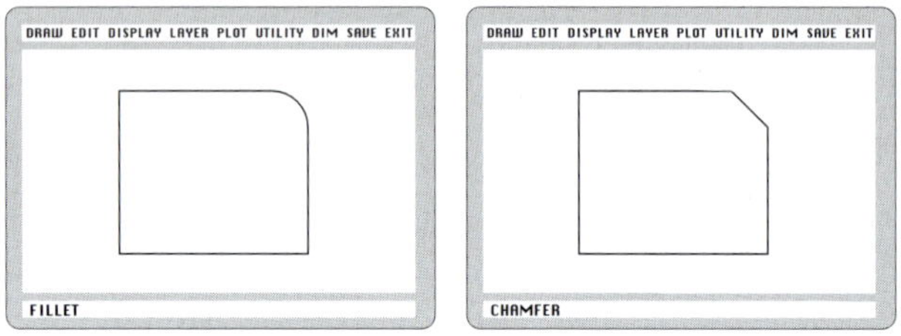

Fillet and chamfer

Move

This allows the operator to move parts of drawings around the screen. Select the item to be moved. Then select a point on the item (the anchor point). Select the destination point which is where the anchor point will finish up.

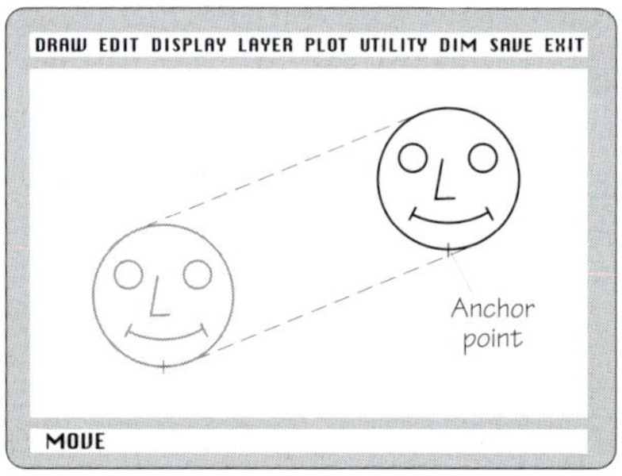

Move

Copy

This allows the operator to copy items such as lines, circles or parts of drawings and to place them in the drawing as required. The item to be copied is selected and confirmed. A point from which the copy is picked up is then selected. Then the point to copy to is picked and the copy is placed in this position there. Some software packages allows multiple copying which lets you produce a number of copies of the same object.

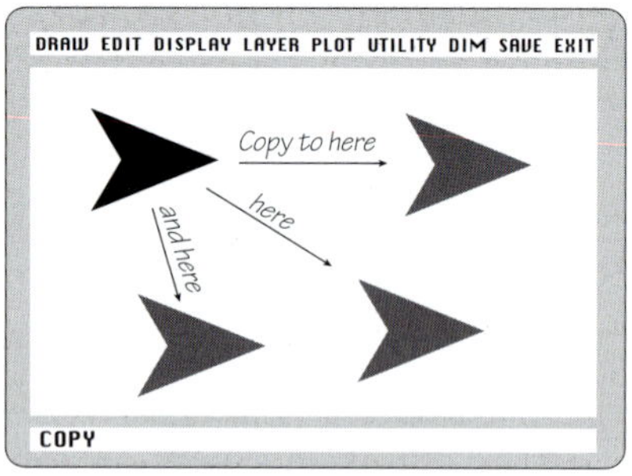

Copy and Multiple copy

Mirror

Items which are already drawn can be copied and reflected in an axis or line. This is ideal for complicated symmetrical drawings. The item to be mirrored is first selected. The ends of the line or axis are picked and the command is completed by selecting the side which the object is to be mirrored to.

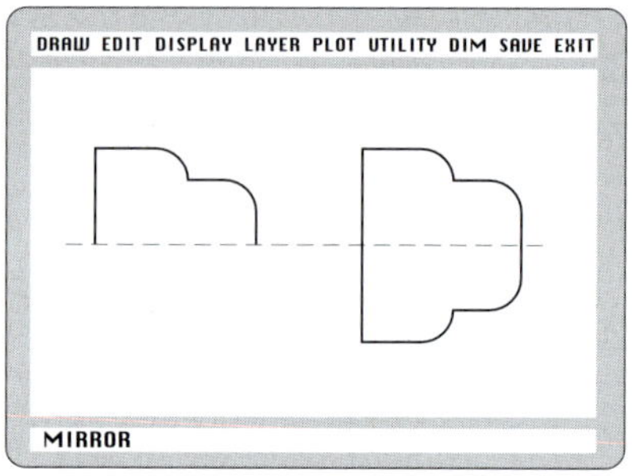

Mirror

Rotate

An item or group of items can be rotated through an arc or circle about a point. The object can be copied as it is rotated. The item to be rotated is selected along with the centre point of rotation. The command is completed by entering the angle of rotation.

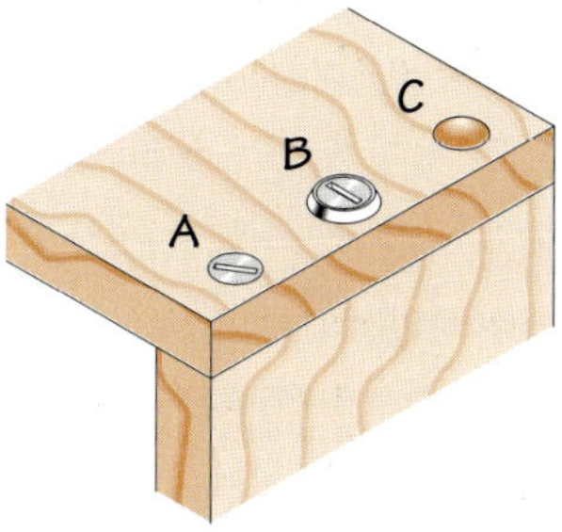

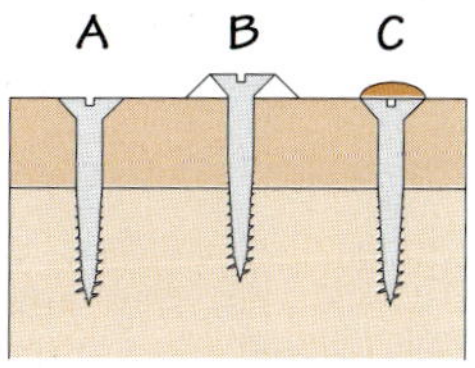

A: countersunk screw
B: brass screw and screw cap
C: plastic screw cover

Screw joint

The head of a screw can be unsightly, but it can be hidden if desired. The most effective way to hide the head of the screw is to bore a hole and sink the head of the screw down below the surface of the wood.

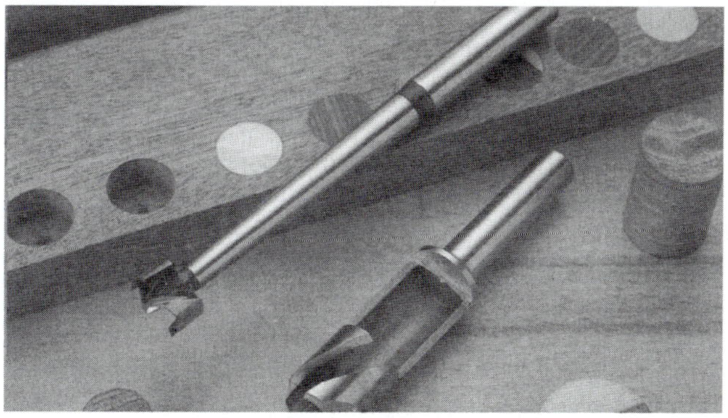

Wooden plug and cutters

A wooden plug can be cut from a waste piece of the same wood. This is done with a special plug cutting drill bit. The plug is then glued into the hole. To finish the process the plug is sanded flush with the surface of the wood.

Knock down fittings

Many pieces of modern furniture are held together with knock-down fittings. These fittings are designed, so that the piece of furniture can be dismantled.

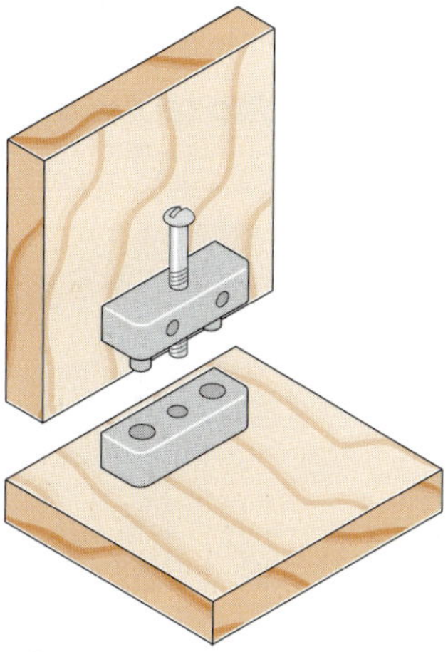

Knock-down fitting

Wooden blocks can also be used in a similar way to the knock-down fitting. The block can be used to hold up shelves or to attach the top of a table to the frame.

A metal bracket can also be used to secure a tabpe top to the frame. This bracket has slots to allow movement due to expansion and contraction of the wood.

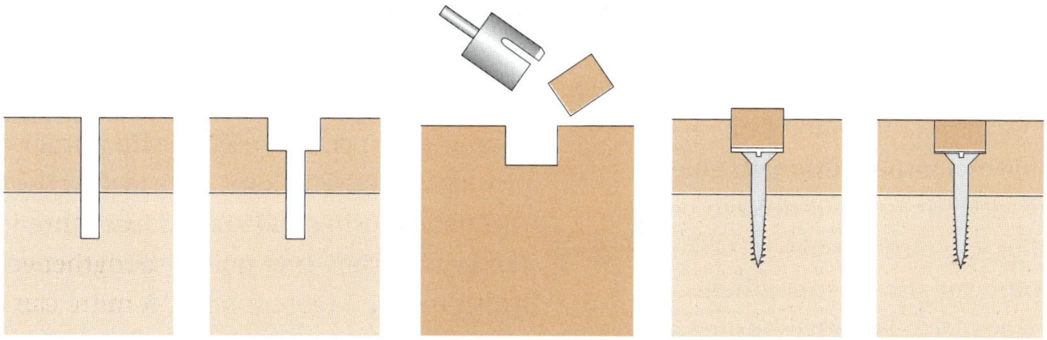

Method of plugging a hole

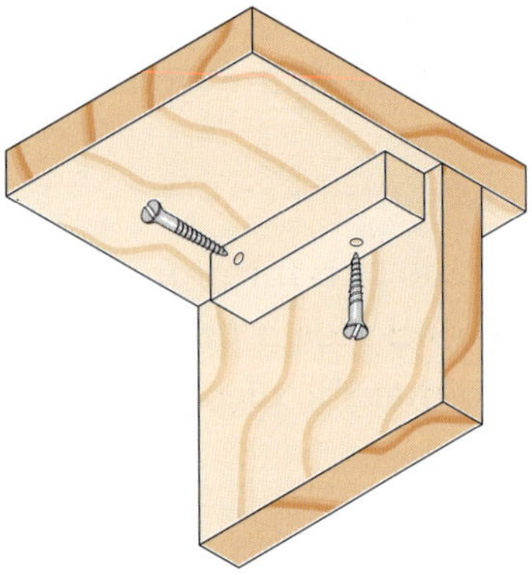

Wooden block used to secure a table top to the frame

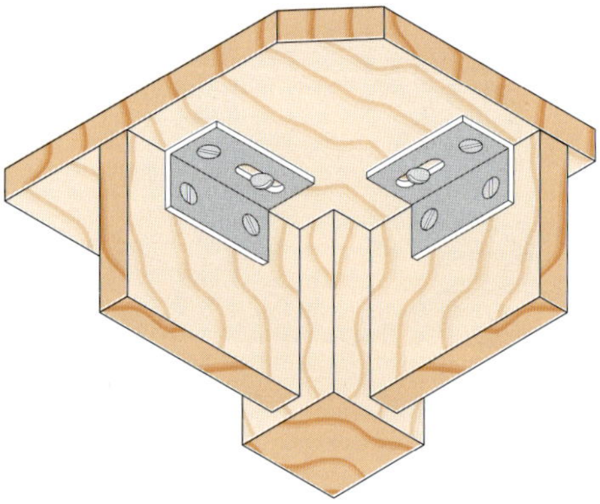

Slotted metal angle bracket

Wooden joints

Joints cut from a solid piece of wood are often the most effective method of joining two pieces of wood together. More simple joints may be strengthened with pins or screws but the best joints avoid this. A number of basic joints are described here but there are lots of variations of many of these joints.

Butt joint

This is made by butting the end of one piece against the side of another. Although glue is used, it is a weak joint and will need to be strengthened useing pins or screws.

The butt joint can also be strengthened by rebating the side piece. This gives more support to the joint and more surface area for gluing.

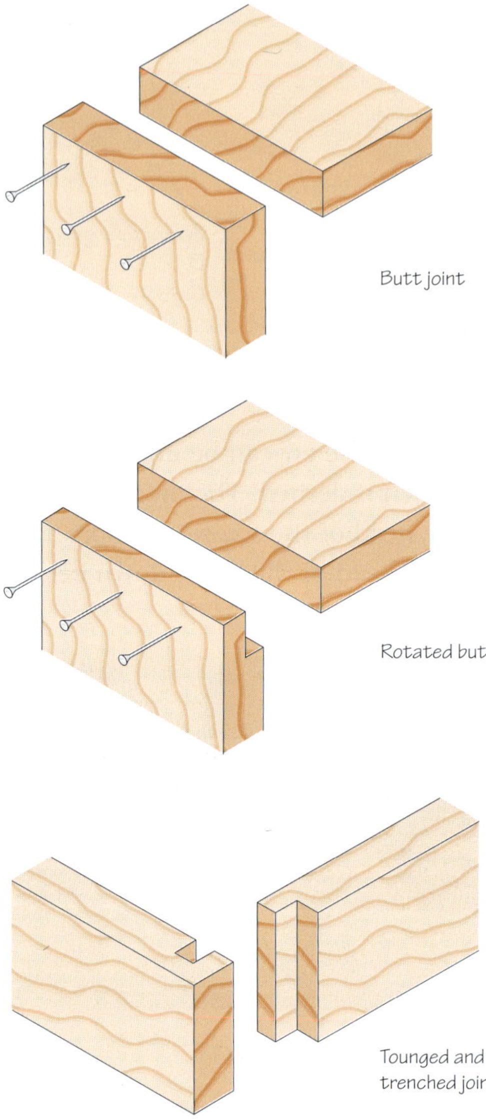

Butt joint & rebated butt joint & tounged & trenched joint

Mitre joint

The mitre joint is perhaps the simplest joint to have at a corner. It is used for the corner of picture frames. The joint is formed at the corner without exposing end grain. Plain mitre joints can be weak however unless strengthened by nails/pins, or a loose tongue. A mitre can also be incorporated into a bridle joint.

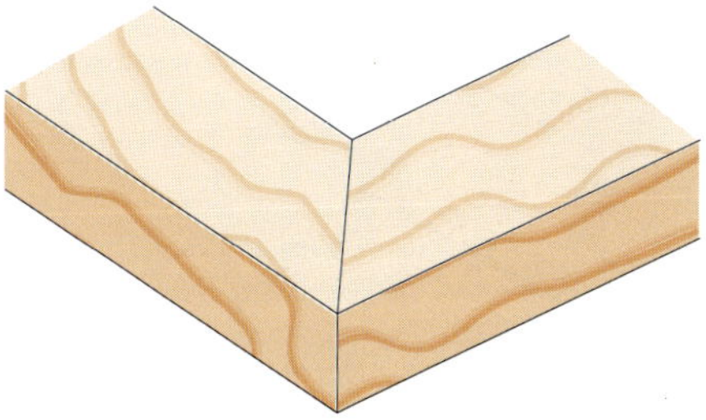

Mitre joint

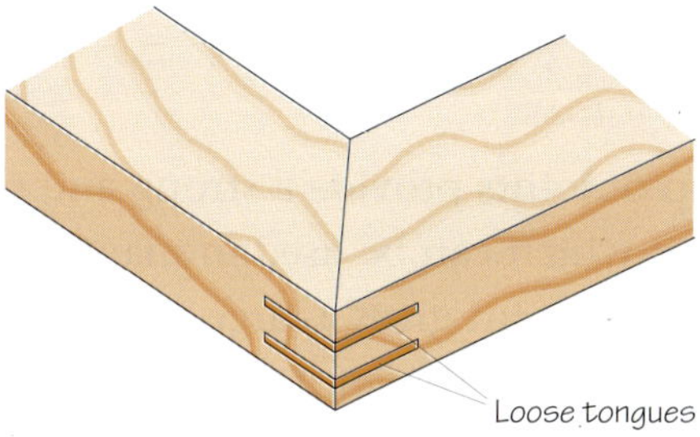

Mitre joint with loose tongues

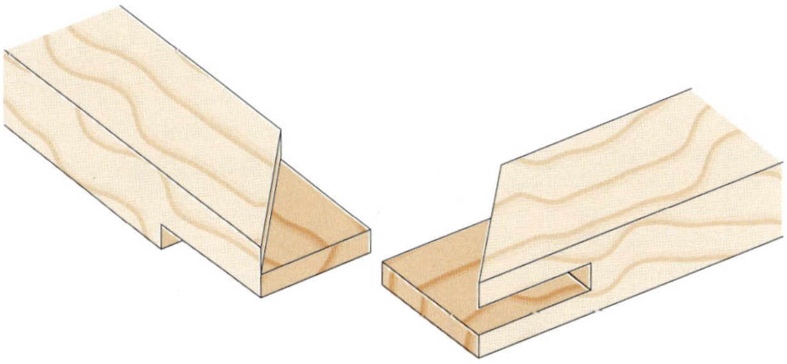

Mitre bridle joint

Halving joints

In a halving joint, half of the material is removed from each piece. There are a variety of halved joints and they are very widely used.

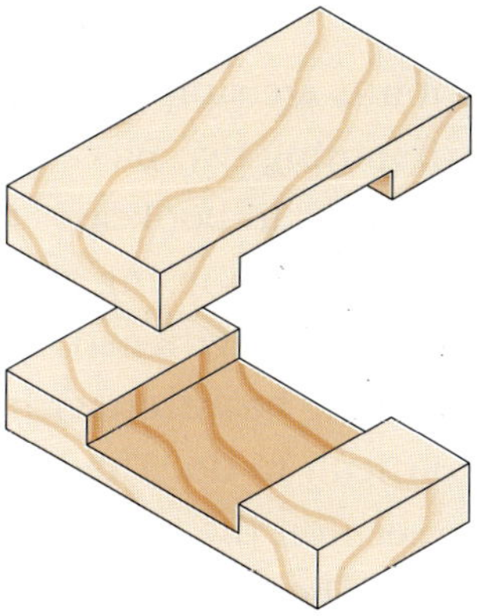

Cross halving joint

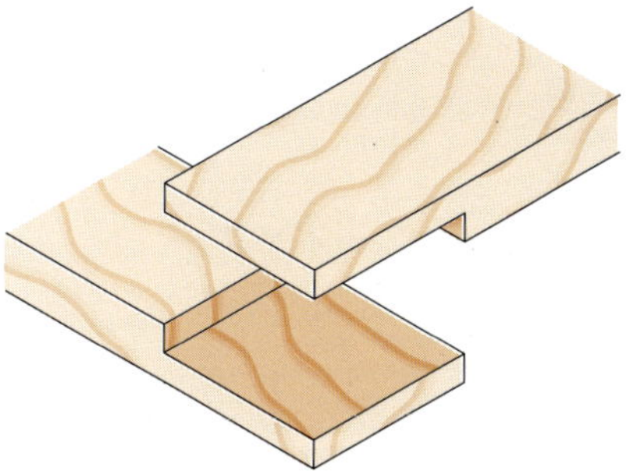

Corner halving

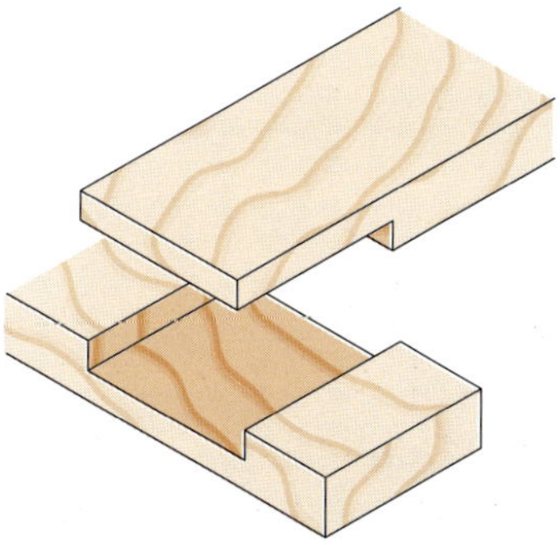

Tee halving

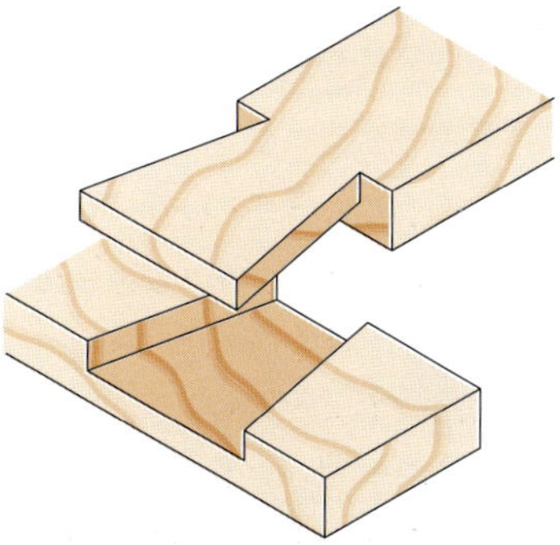

Dovetail halving

Housing joints

Housed or housing joints are simple, but effective methods, of joining two pieces of wood. It is used for fitting shelves in bookcases or divider pieces for boxes. The housing joint is glued and can be further strengthened by using pins. The dovetail housing has stronger holding power but is more difficult to do. The housing joint can usually be seen on the edge of the trenched piece. This can be hidden by using a stopped housing joint.

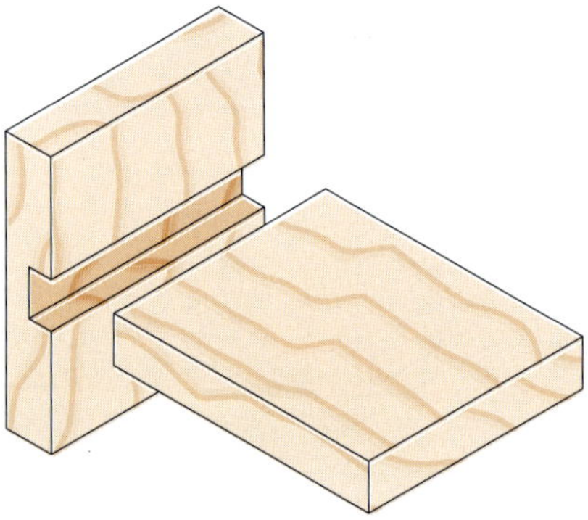

Plain housing

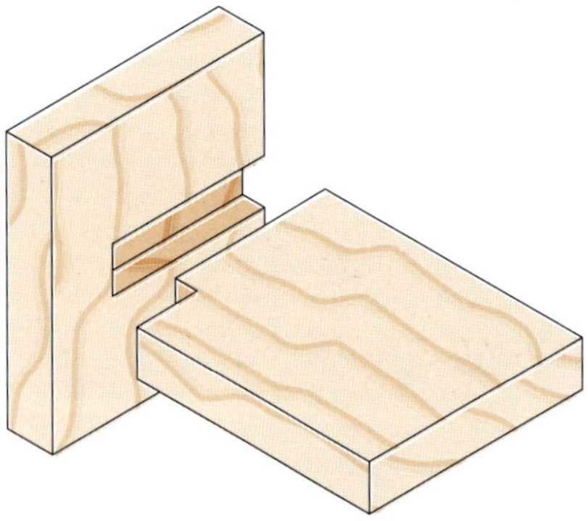

Stopped housing

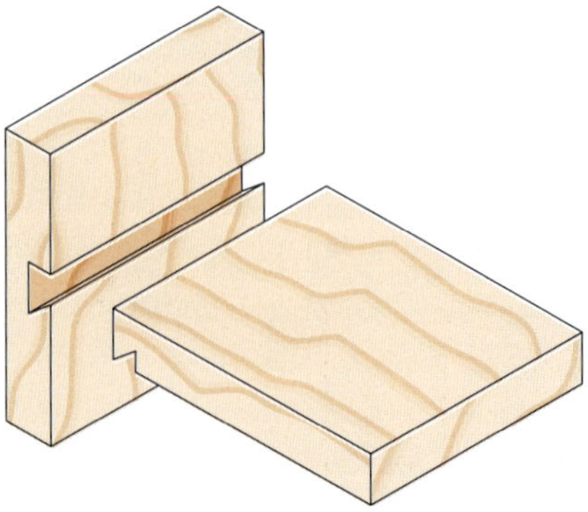

Dovetail housing

Bridle joints

This group of joints provide a strong and most useful joint which can be used in many different situations. The joint gives a large surface area for gluing, which gives the joint added strength. The bridle joint is used in constructing tables, chairs and other frame constructions. The bridle joint can be used as an alternative to the mortise and tenon joint.

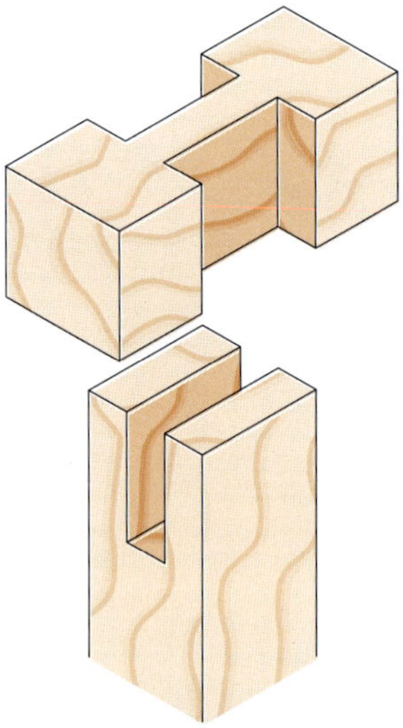

Tee bridle

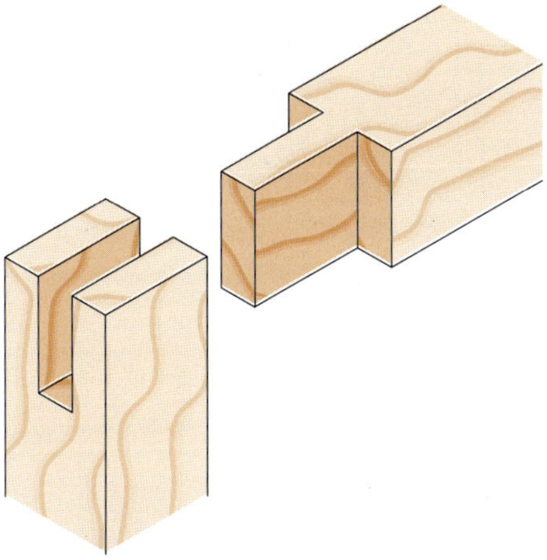

Corner bridle

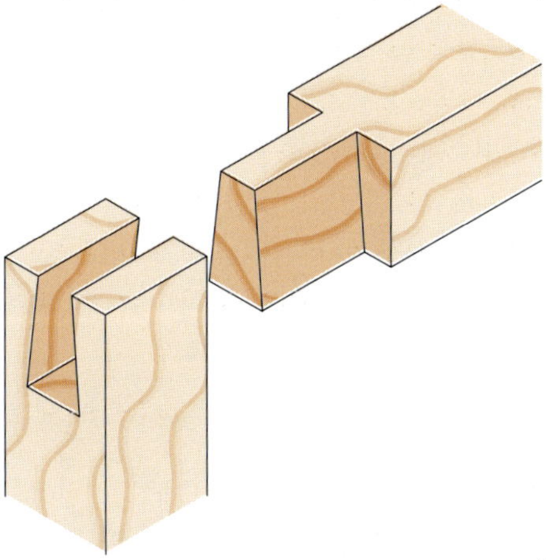

Dovetail bridle

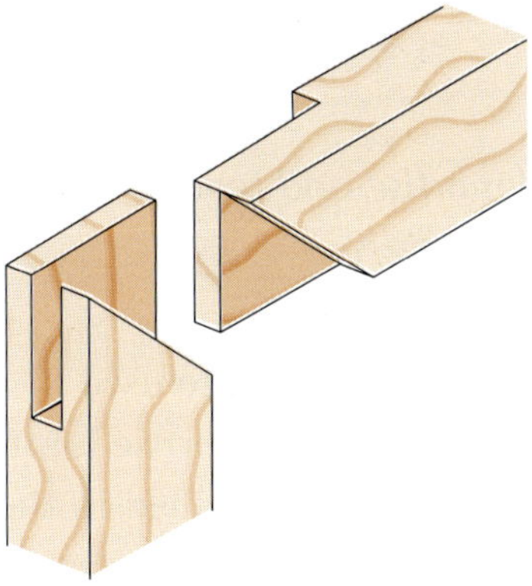

Mitre bridle

Mortise and tenon joints

This is the joint most widely used by woodworkers. The joint is formed by removing a hole from one piece into which a tenon, cut from the other piece, fits exactly. The joint is strongest if the thickness of the tenon is exactly $\frac{1}{3}$ the total thickness of the timber.

The joint can be made stronger by using wedges which are driven into the end of the tenon. The mortise is cut slightly larger than the tenon to accomodate the wedges which are glued and driven into position forming a sort of dovetail in the mortise.

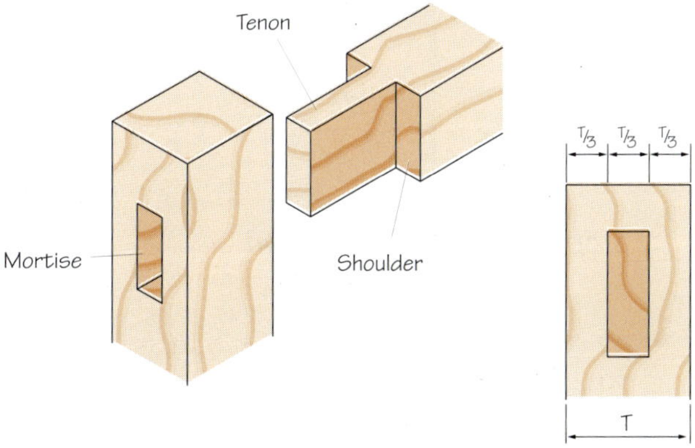

Mortise and tenon

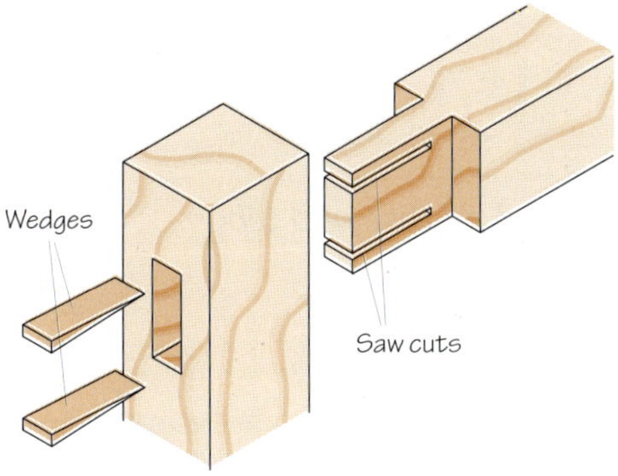

Wedged mortise and tenon

The stopped or **stub mortise** and tenon is used when you do not wish to see the tenon coming through to the other side of the piece.

When putting a mortise joint at the corner of

a frame it is usual to make a **haunched mortise** and tenon. The haunch of the joint prevents the two pieces twisting and increases the gluing area.

The mortise and tenon is used for joining the pieces of a door frame or the legs of a table to the rails. If two tenons are meeting on a corner of a leg of a table for example, the tenon can be mitred or halved. This allows the tenons to fit properly into the mortises.

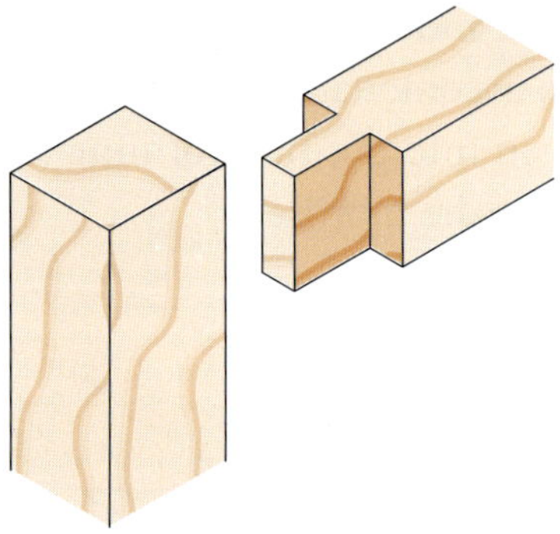

Stopped mortise and tenon

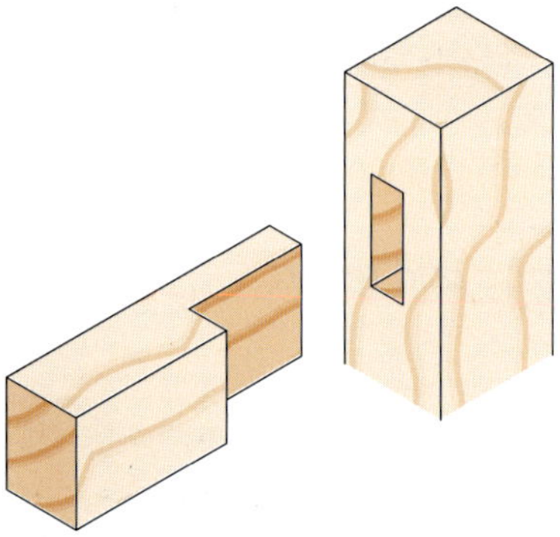

Barefaced mortise and tenon

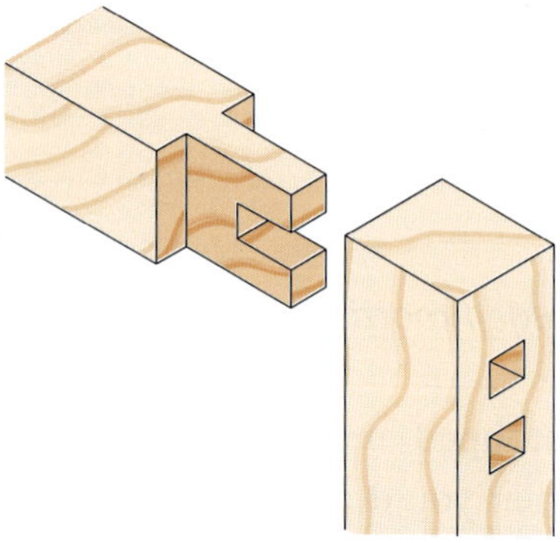

Double or twin mortise and tenon

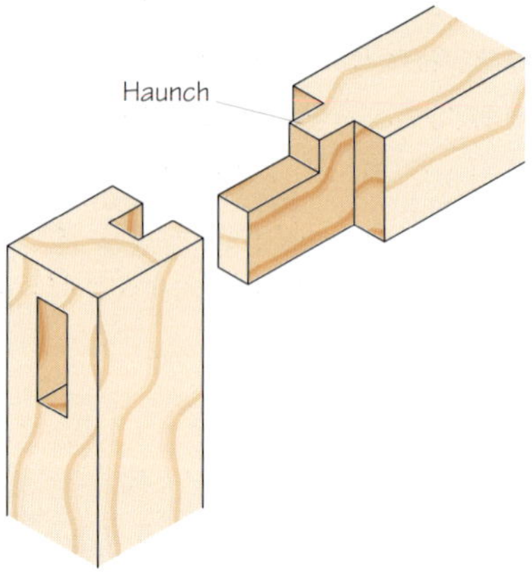

Haunched mortise and tenon

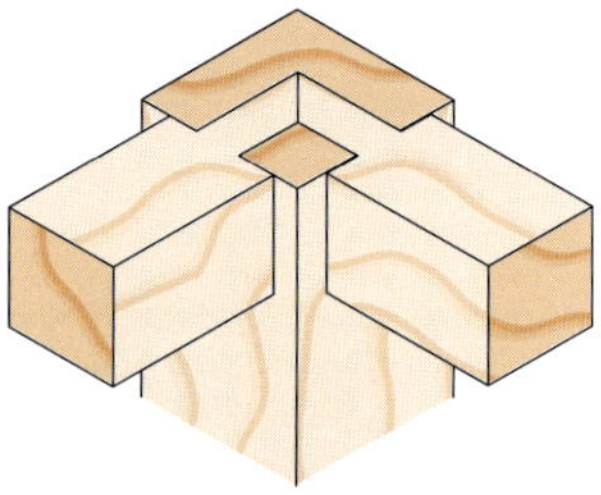

Mitred mortise and tenon

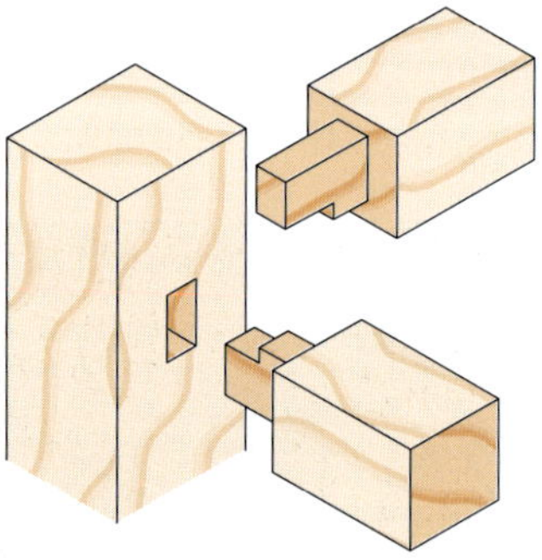

Halved mortise and tenon

Dowel joints

Dowels made from wood are used in joints which are similar to the mortise joint. Corresponding holes are drilled in the two pieces. Glue is applied to the holes and the dowels are inserted. The pieces are joined and cramped. The dowel joint is used for making frames and in stools and tables. It is important that the centres of the holes are accurately marked and drilled. Dowelling jigs are available to assist in ensuring the joint is accurately made. Ready made dowels are available with grooved sides to allow air and glue to escape from the holes. However, regular dowels can be grooved with a saw cut to give the same effect.

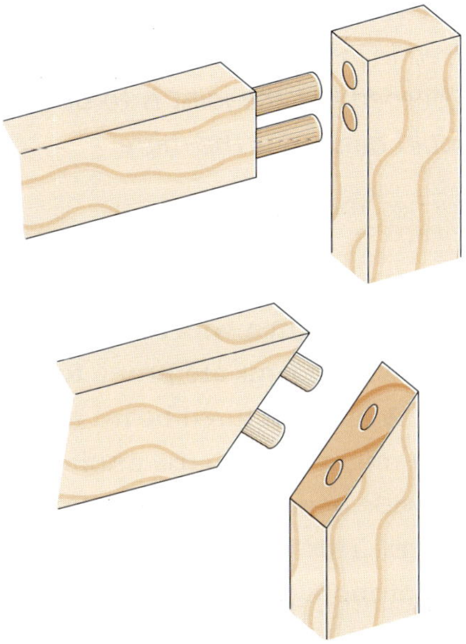

Dowel joints used in frames

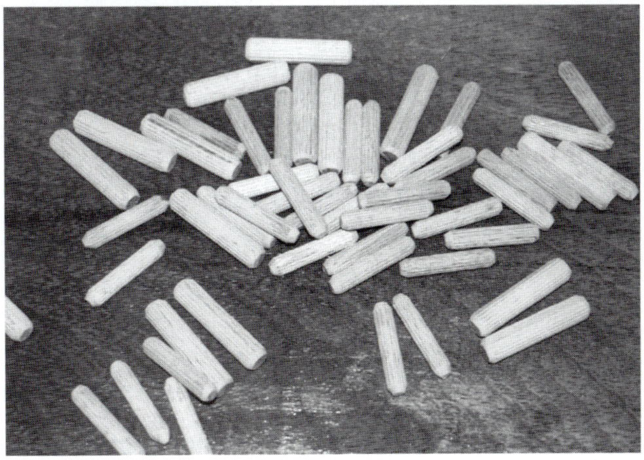

Dowels

Dovetail joints

Dovetail joints are widely used by cabinet makers for joining the corners of carcases, etc. The dovetail joint is strong and attractive joint if done well. The strength of the joint is greatest if the piece is in tension.

The dovetail is strong in tension

It is important that the maximum strength is obtained in the joint. This is achieved by ensuring that the taper on the tails is correct. The generally accepted taper for dovetails is:

Slope:	
Softwoods	1 in 6
Hardwoods	1 in 8

If too much slope is put on a dovetail the tips of the tail can splinter and the end of the tail can be too narrow and is weak. If the slope is small the joint can be pulled apart.

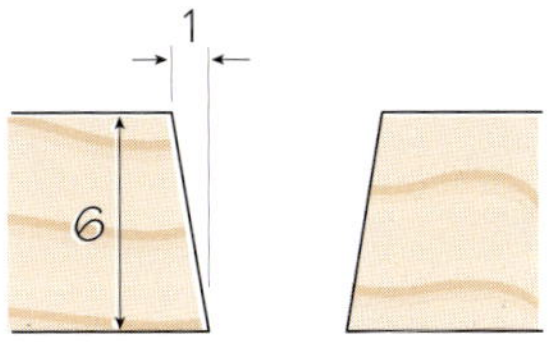

Softwood slope
1:6

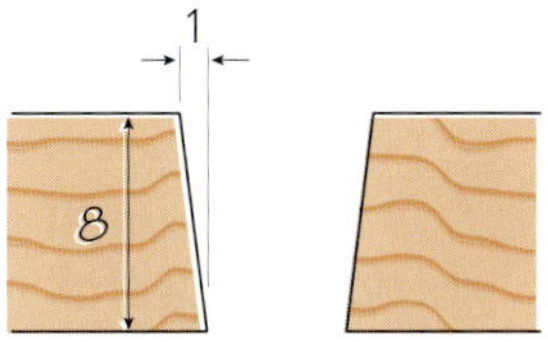

Hardwood slope
1:8

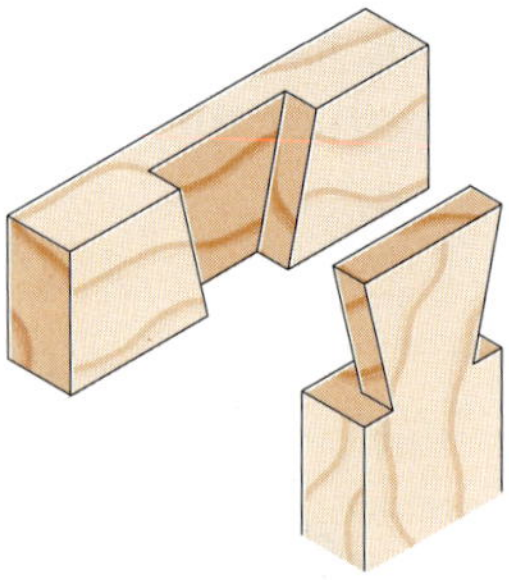

Tee dovetail halving joint

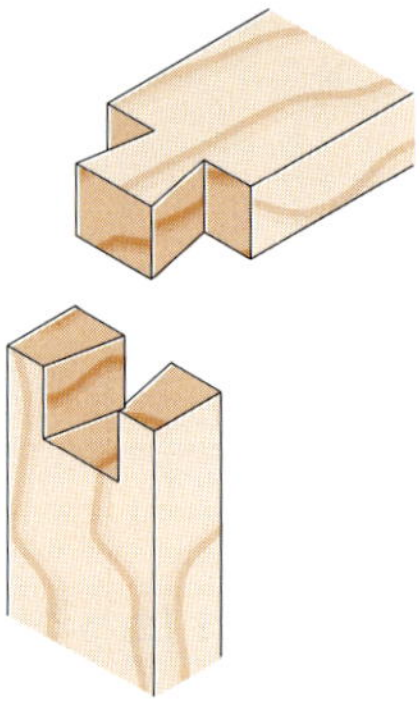

Single through dovetail joint – used for corners of boxes, where rails meet legs

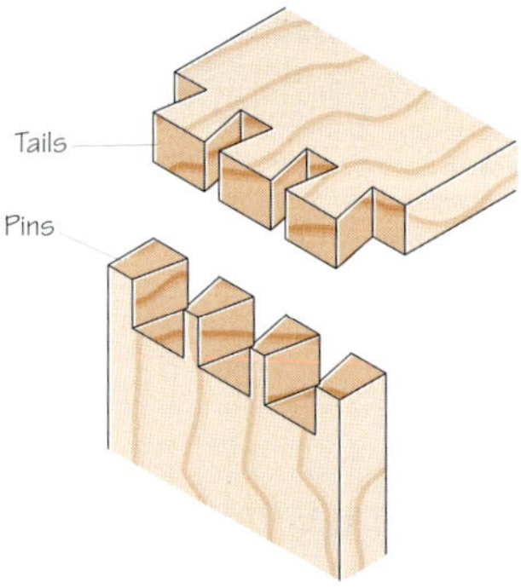

Through dovetail joint – used in box carcases, drawer carcases, etc. (boxed dovetail)

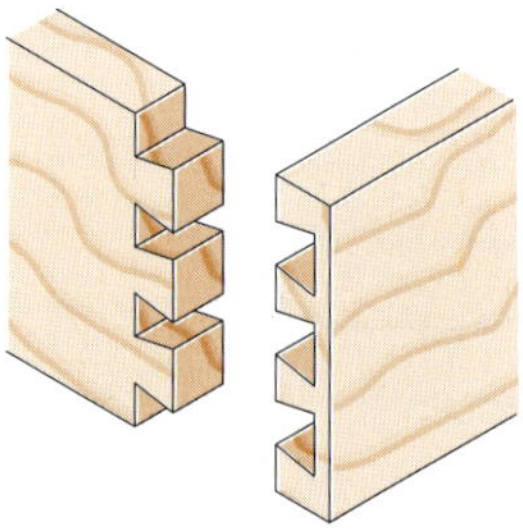

Lapped dovetail – used where strength is needed but the front end grain of the tails has to be hidden, such as in the fronts of drawers

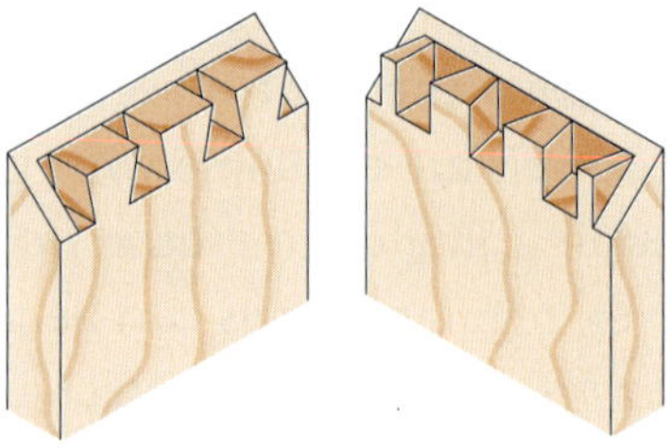

Secret mitred dovetails – the most specialised dovetail, used in very high class work where a dovetail is needed but the joint is to be hidden. All that should be seen is the mitre

Edge joints

You will sometimes need to join two or more boards together to form a wider board for your projects. Very wide boards are prone to warping and splitting. A manufactured board may be used, but you might wish to use a solid piece. Therefore, a wide board must be made from narrower pieces. This is done by joining the edges of two or more pieces to make a wider piece.

This can be done in a number of ways, but it is important that the edges are first planed perfectly flat. It is usual to allow the pieces to be a little thicker than necessary so that slight innaccuracies in the joint line on the surfaces can be planed flat after the adhesive has set.

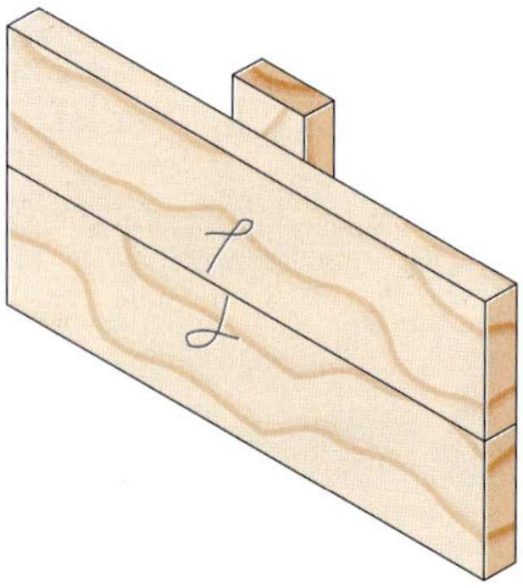

Rubbed glue joint

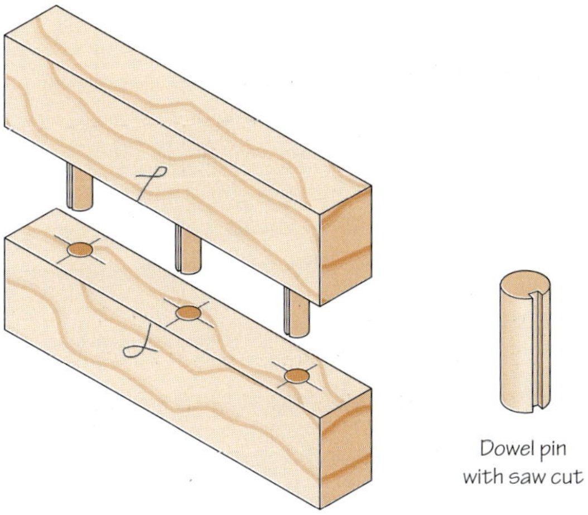

Dowelled joint

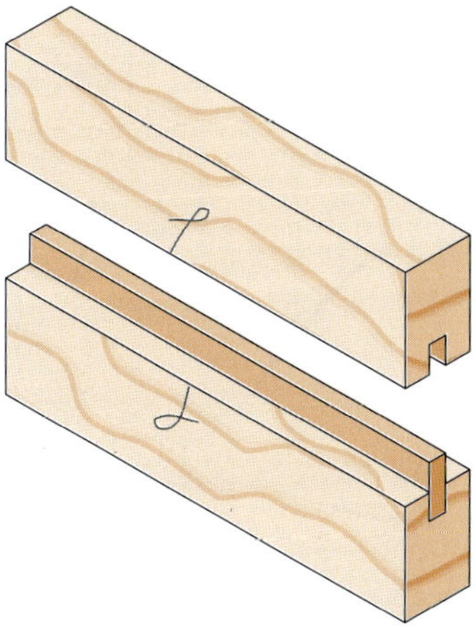

Tongued and grooved joint

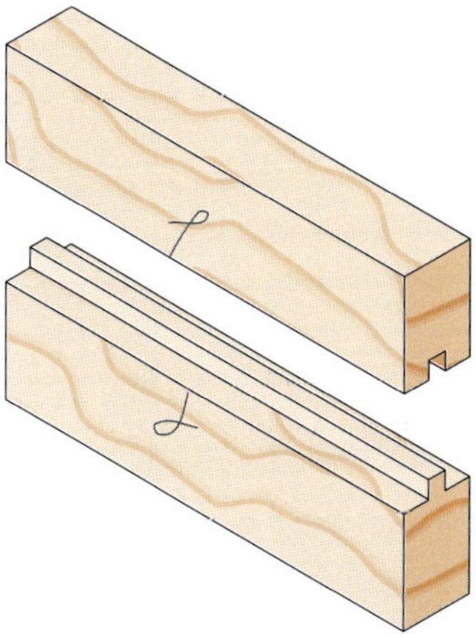

Loose tongue joint

Where joints are used

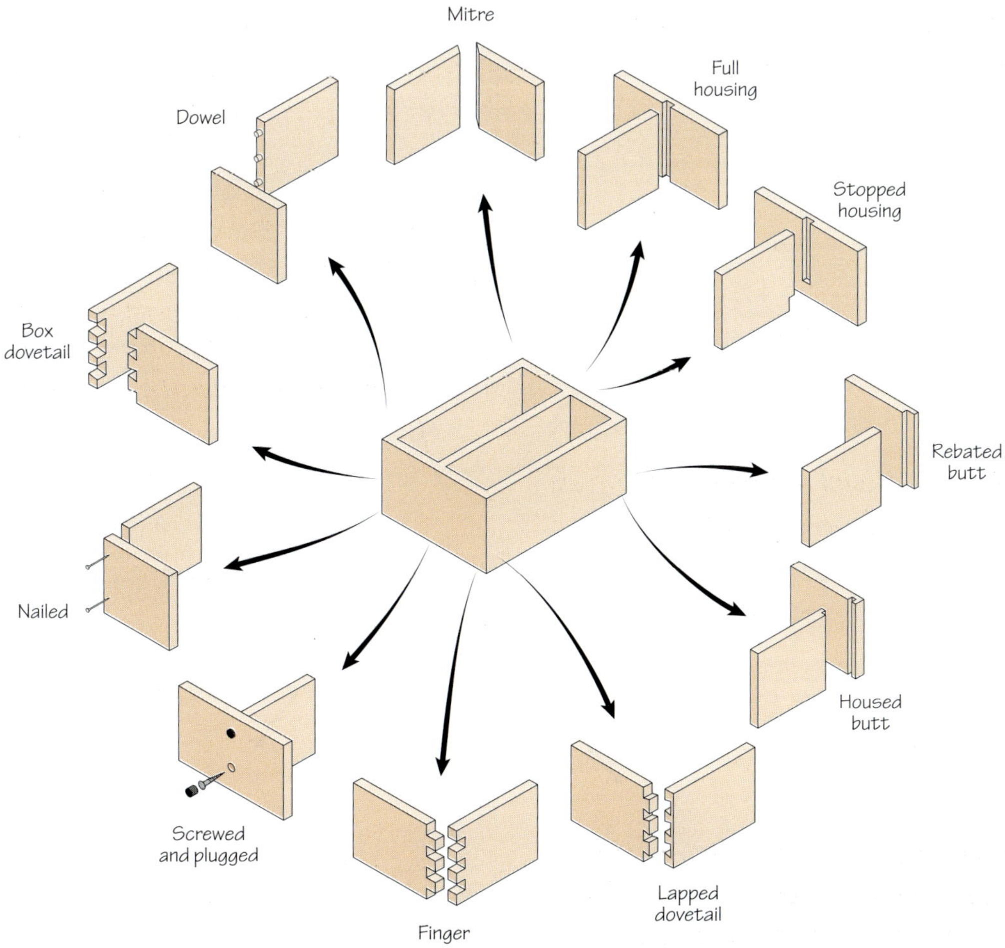

Carcase joints

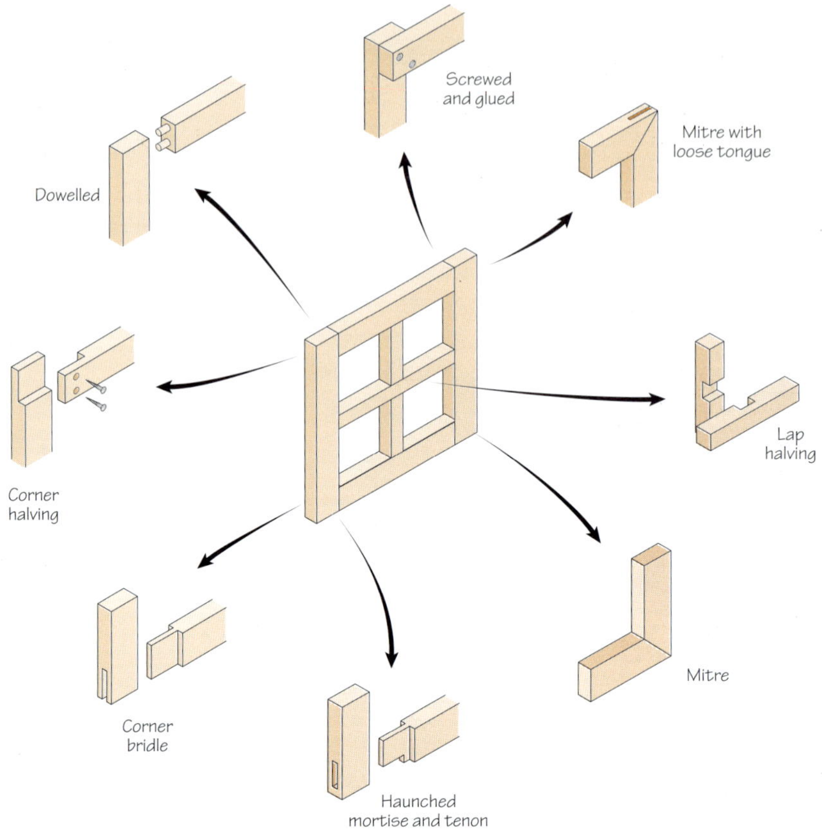

Frame joints

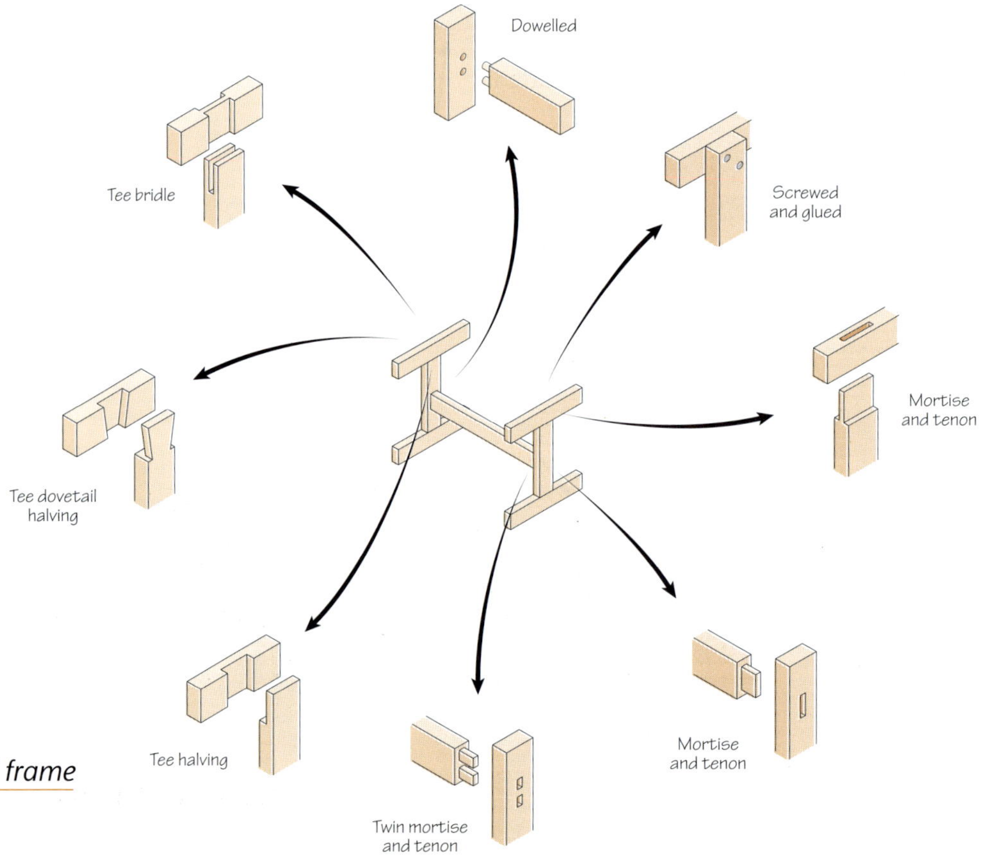

Table/stool frame

Example 1:

Shown is a sketch of a book stand made from 20mm thick solid ash. With the aid of sketches, suggest suitable ways of joining parts

a) A and B

b) C and D

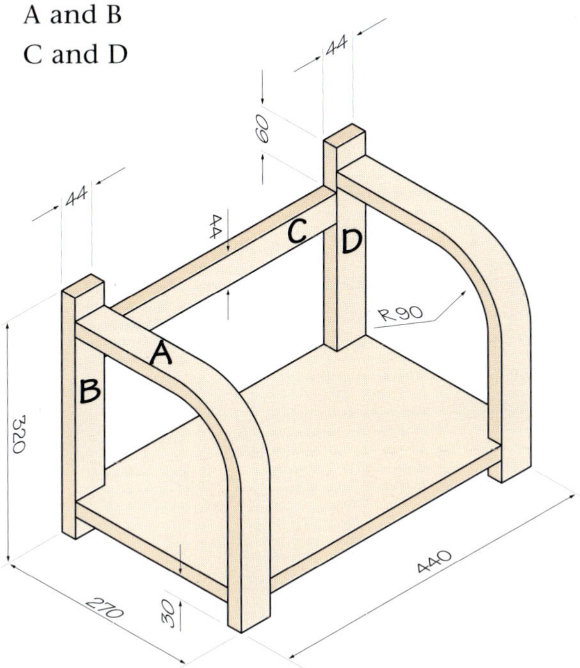

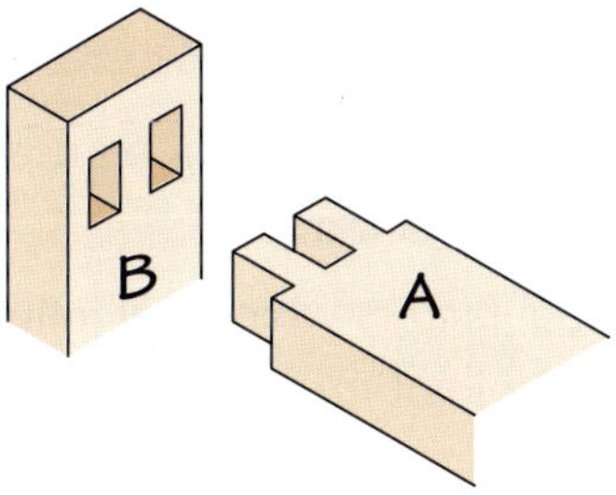

POSSIBLE SOLUTION (a)

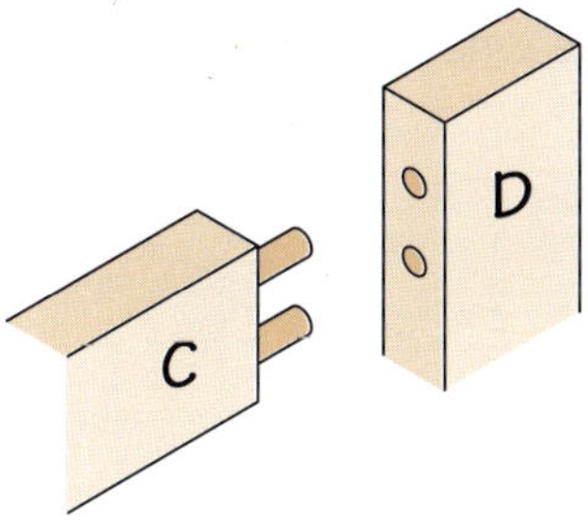

POSSIBLE SOLUTION (b)

Example 2:

Shown is a sketch of a small shelf unit made in solid wood. Show with the aid of notes and sketches how you would join side S to the shelf T.

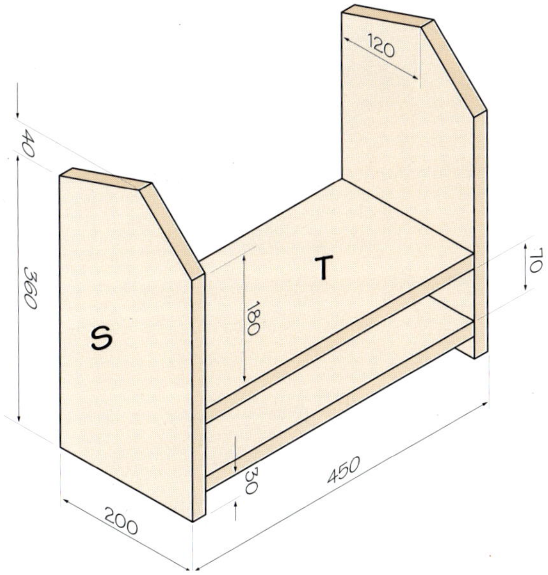

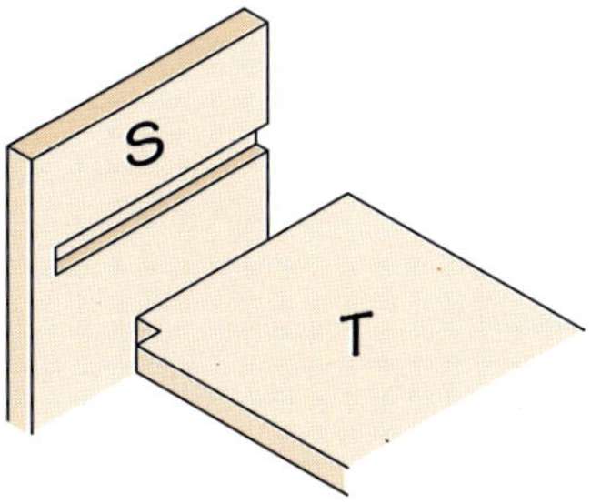

POSSIBLE SOLUTION

Exercises

1. List three joints which can be used in joining the corners of a frame.
2. Give three factors which will influence the choice of a joint for joining two pieces of material.
3. Using sketches show two ways of making a butt joint stronger.
4. Name the joints shown in the sketches below and state where each might be used.

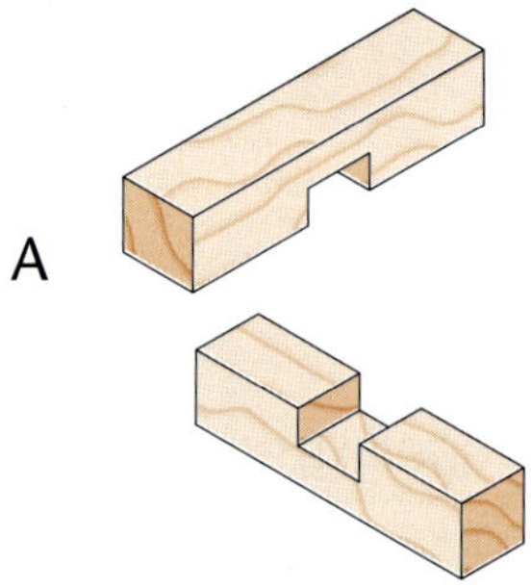

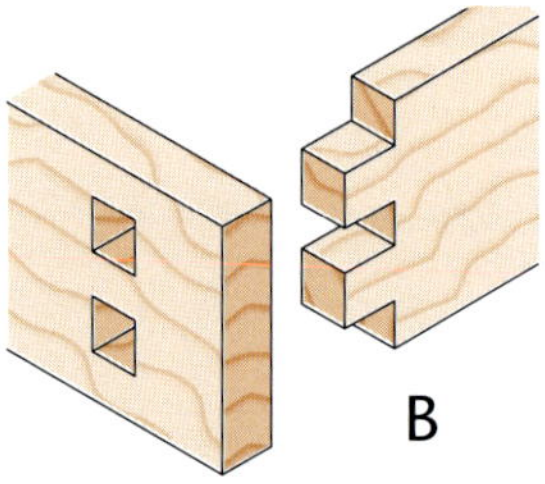

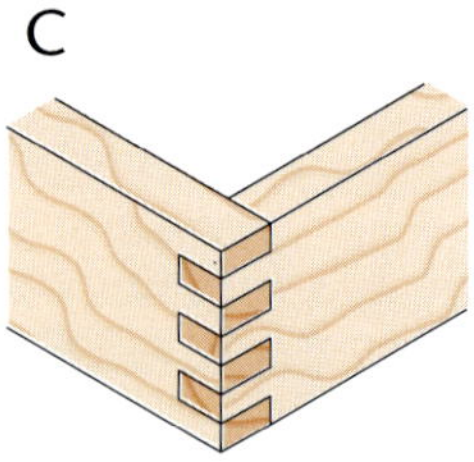

5.Name the parts of the following joints

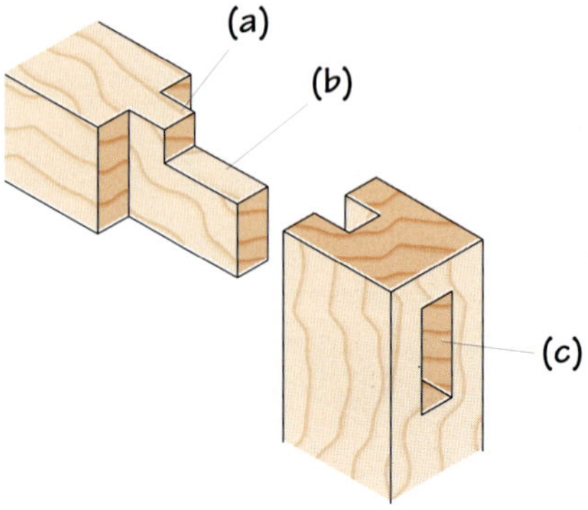

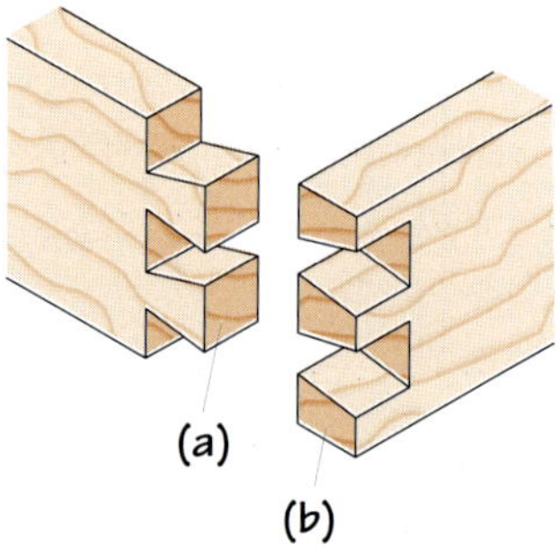

6. Sketch a joint, suitable for use at the front corner of a drawer

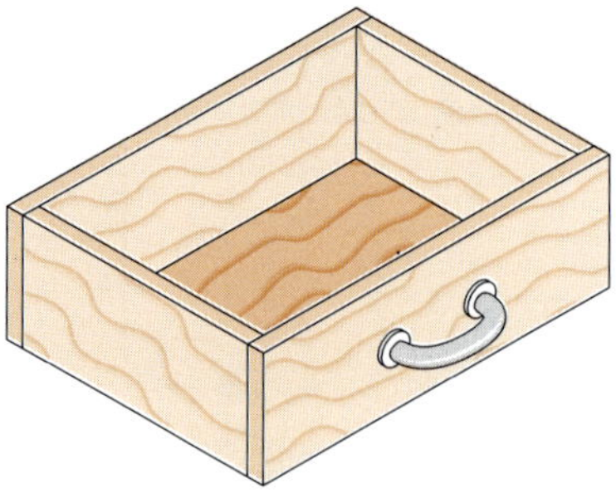

7. Shown are three items made from solid wood. Using sketches show in each case a suitable way of joining piece A to piece B.

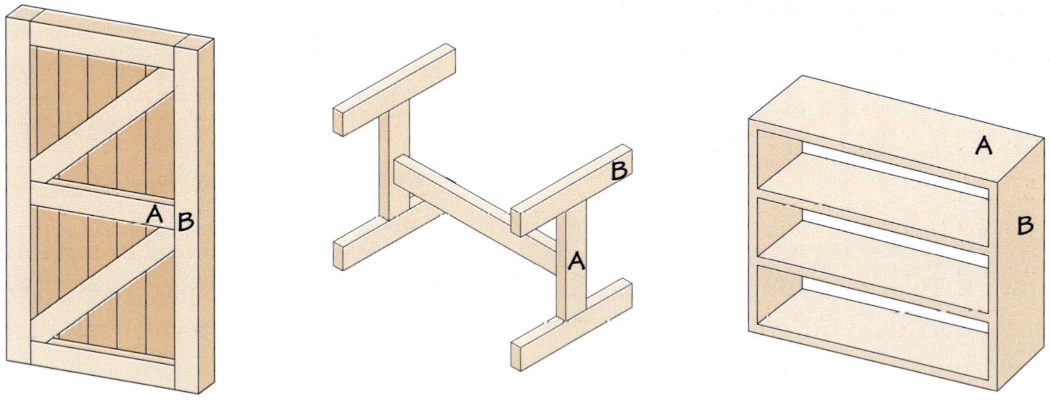

8. What are the common proportions for the parts of the haunched mortise and tenon joint? Name three tools which are used to make this joint.
9. Sketch and name two methods of edge jointing woods and give an example of where they might be used.
10. Using notes and sketches, explain where the following joints might be used:
    Corner bridle joint
    Twin mortise and tenon joint
    Lapped halving joint.
    Stopped housing joint

CHAPTER TWENTY-FOUR

SHAPING AND CARVING

Shaping and carving wood is probably the oldest form of woodwork. The first fishing spears were sharpened sticks. Carving is the cutting and shaping of wood and forming shapes and designs in the material. Craftspersons in different countries have different styles and forms of carving wood. In many countries carving is part of the culture of the people and is used to adorn houses, boats, furniture and other valuables.

In many countries carving is part of their culture

We can make use of carving in projectwork to enhance and decorate simple pieces. Even simple carved elements will add a great deal of interest to most objects.

Simple carving will enhance any project

Types of carving

There are a number of different methods of carving shapes into wood. Each is distinct and some are quite specialised.

Whittling

Whittling is a form of carving which uses special knives which can do intricate work. Whittling with a pen knife is probably familiar to us all. Very often whittling is done on branches and sticks of wood although it is done on other pieces also.

Example of whittling

Incised carving

This is when the outline of a design or shape is cut with a vee tool or a veiner. It is quite a simple form of carved work. The cuts should be even to give the best effect.

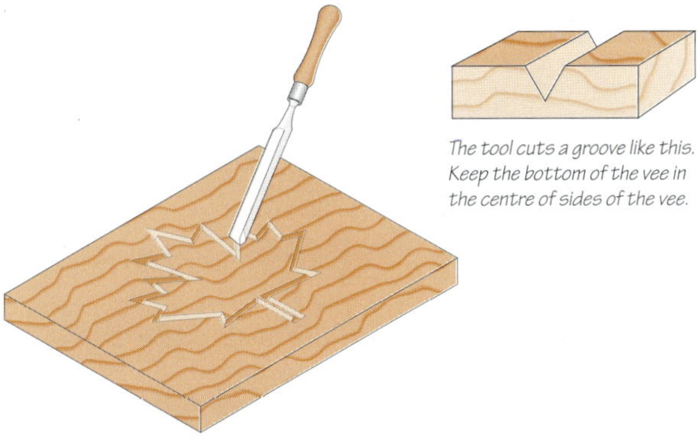

Incised carving

Chip carving

This is a simple form of wood decoration, using knives or chisels. The knife is used to make triangular cuts in the wood. The patterns look like inverted pyramids in the wood. Elaborate patterns can be made using these triangular patterns. Simple chip carving patterns are very decorative and can enhance a piece of work quite easily.

The patterns are first planned out on paper and then transferred to the surface of the wood, using carbon paper or by drawing the pattern straight onto the piece. Then the chiselling is carefully done to these lines.

You can start this method of carving by practising some simple designs or patterns or practice on waste pieces of timber. Then as you improve you can incorporate the method into your projects.

Chip carving – simple and complex patterns

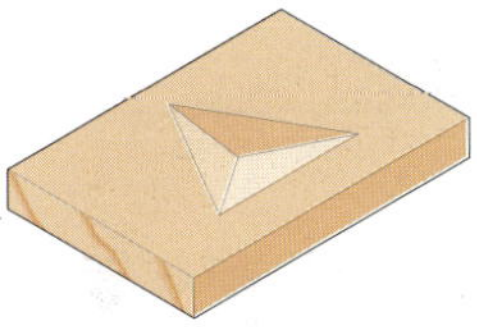

Basic six cut chip

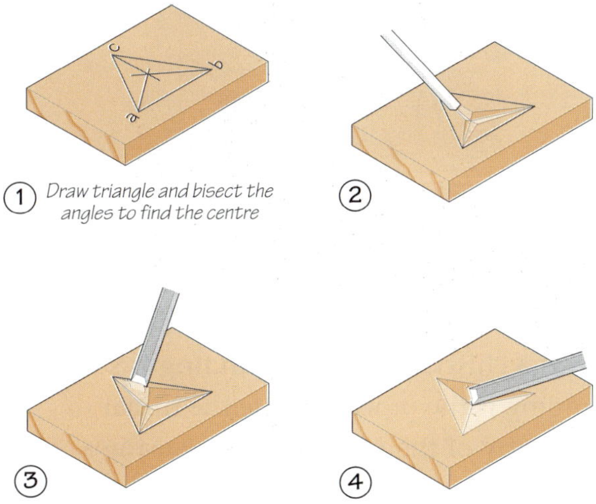

Chip carving method

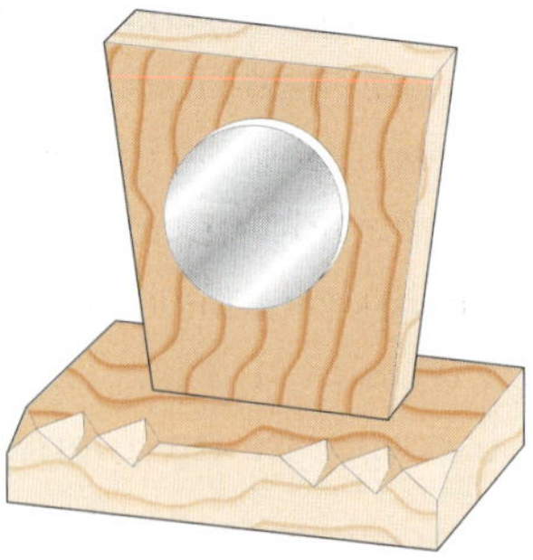

Decorative edges can be used to enhance projects. They can be made as elaborate as you like

Relief carving

In this method wood is removed around the shape being carved, which makes the shape stand out. The relief can be **low relief** (shallow) or it can be **high relief** (deeper) depending on the effect required. The high or deep relief carving gives a very 3-D effect to the carving.

Relief carving

The pattern of the carving is drawn onto the surface of the wood. The outline of the shape is cut with a chisel and then **grounding** is started. Grounding is the process where the initial cutting away of the material is done using a relatively flat gouge to lower the depth of the wood surrounding the shape itself. The work must be carefully planned so that the work is done successfully.

When the grounding is done, the finer details of the carving and the carved shape can be carved using various chisels and gouges. It is important to work accurately to lines, so that the carving is clear and the edges are well defined.

The cuts are taken in relatively small pieces to avoid mistakes. When cutting, using the chisels, care must be taken to work with the direction of the grain to avoid splitting or raising the grain.

Often the flat surface which is left low when the relief is done is textured with a special tool. This tool is a punch with serrated point and is used to produce an even finish to these surfaces.

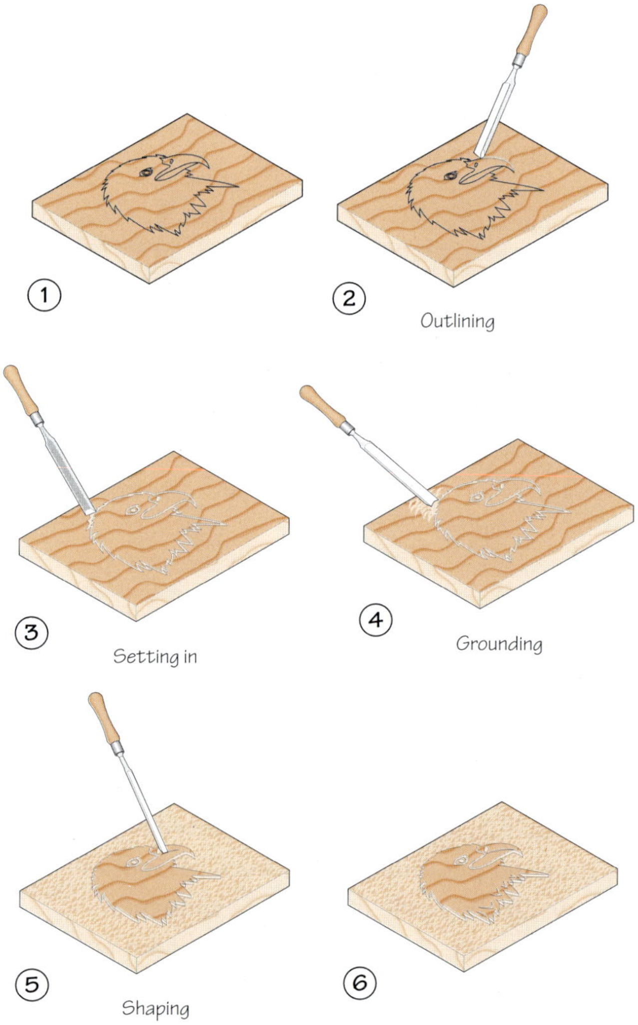

Relief carving method

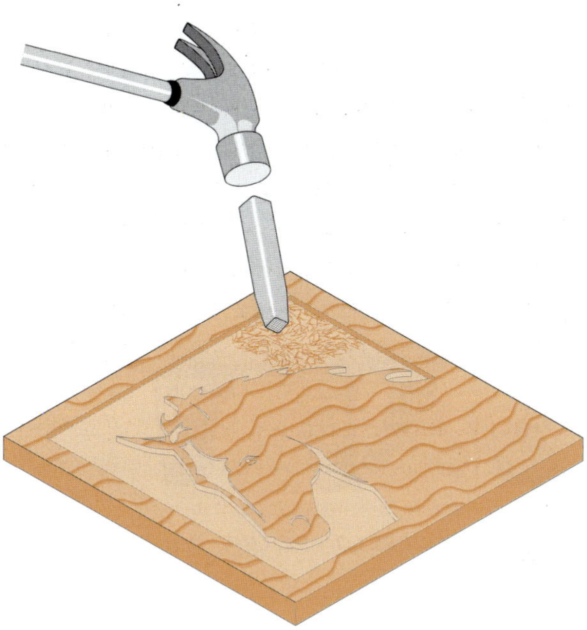

Texturing punch

Sculpture – 3D carving

Three dimensional carving is carried out using various chisels and gouges. It is sometimes known as *carving in the round*. Simple or complex shapes and forms can be made. Surform tools can also be quite effective for producing more simple shapes in wood. To produce the shape, the outlines or elevations must first be drawn onto the front, back and sides of the piece, often called a **blank**.

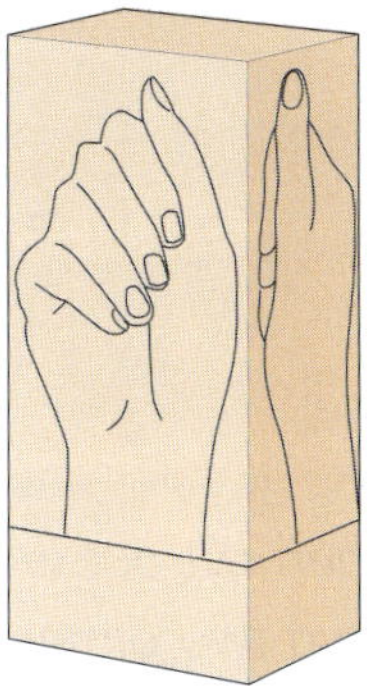

① Mark out shape on adjacent sides

Outline drawn onto the faces of the piece

The outline is cut out on the bandsaw giving a two dimensional shape. When this is completed, the details of the other views are transferred on to the cut surfaces. These lines can then be used as a guide while shaping the piece in three dimensions.

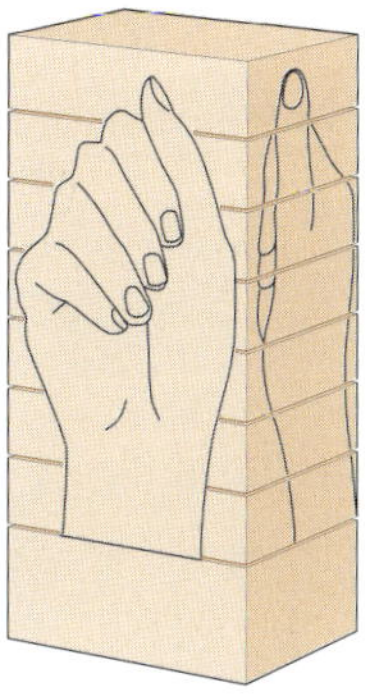

② Make a series of cuts with a handsaw or remove waste with a handsaw

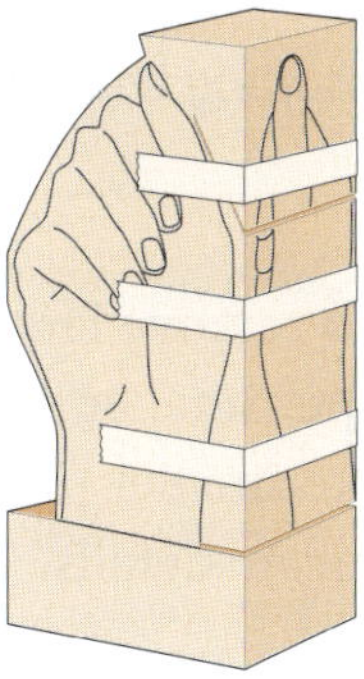

③ Replace the waste material to allow shaping in 3 dimensions

Further details of the outline are then transferred to the cut surfaces

When the overall shape has been established the final details are carefully carved.

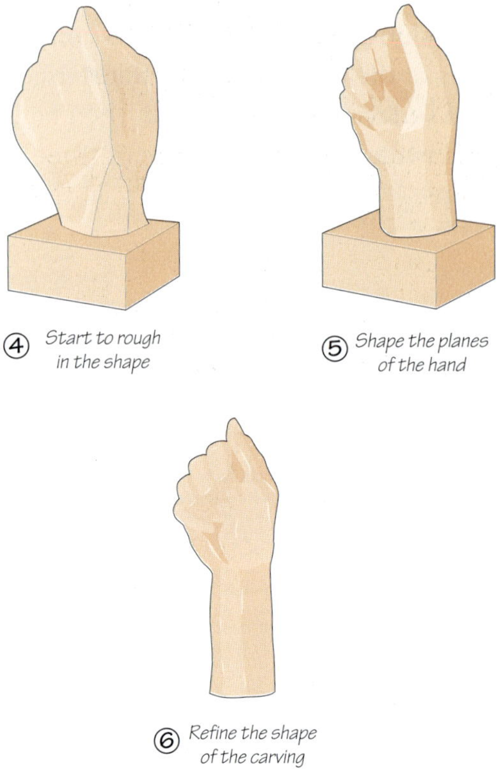

Following the shaping the final details are added

You use gouges to remove larger pieces and to get the general shape. Smaller gouges and chisels are then used to take smaller pieces off and to carve the more intricate details.

Shaping

Surform tools are fairly new to the area of woodwork. They allow wood to be easily shaped without a great deal of skill. These tools allow basic skills of sculpture work to be developed successfully. Surform tools can be used to shape material in both two and three dimensions. These tools are successful for simple shaping which can then be smoothed using sandpaper, either by hand or with a sanding attachment for the drill. The appearance of the finished piece is simple and smooth.

Simple shapes can be carved using surform tools

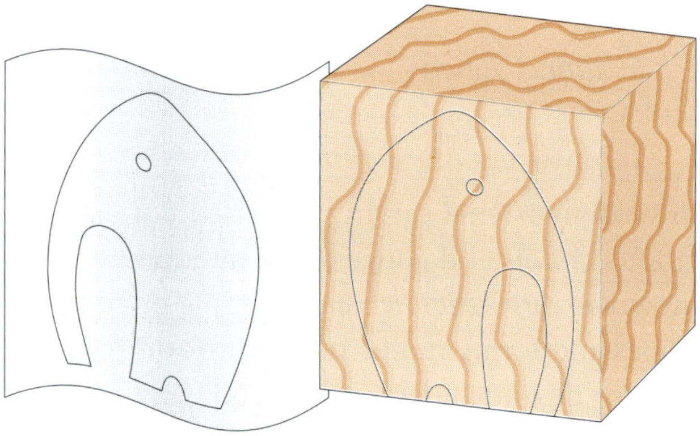

Draw the shape/design on the wooden block

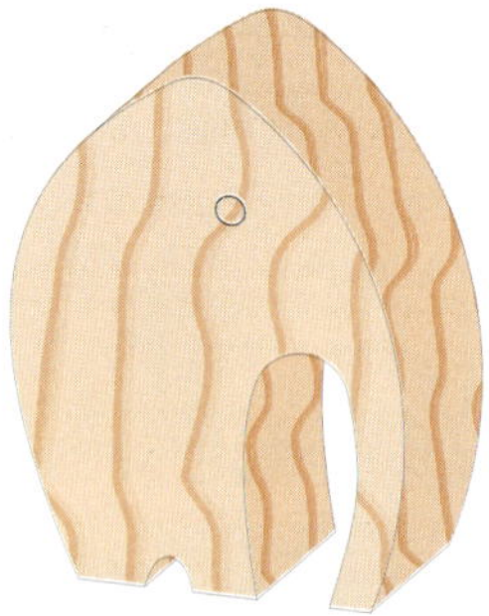

The shape is then cut out with a coping saw or bandsaw to give a two dimensional shape. This can be finished as a two dimensional piece or continued. A drilled hole will make the eye of the elephant. This can be filled with a dowel of darker timber before shaping continues

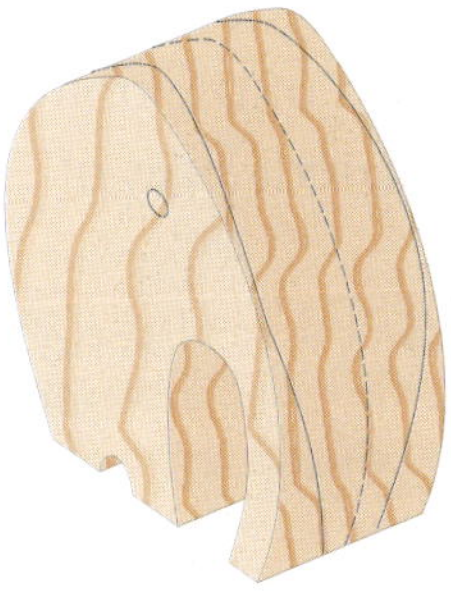

Draw the three dimensional shape on the cut surfaces. A centre line can be a useful guide when shaping symmetrical designs

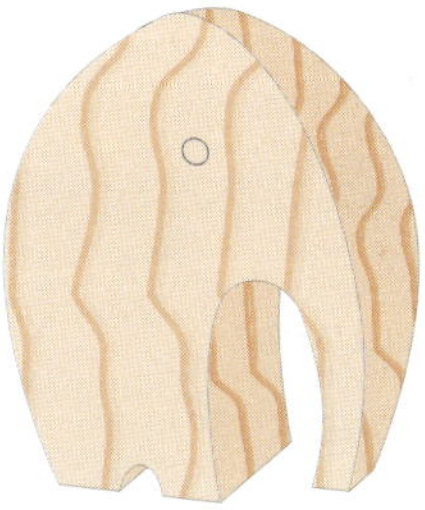

The waste is then removed using planer file and round file. The piece is smoothed down using abrasive paper

Carving tools

The tools used for carving are many and varied. They range from simple carving knives and surform tools to specialised chisels and gouges. The tools used to carve wood were developed from ordinary chisels and gouges (as these standard woodworking chisels and gouges are not very suitable for making the different cuts necessary).

Knives are used for chip carving and whittling. There are a number of knives with differently shaped blades, each designed to take various cuts.

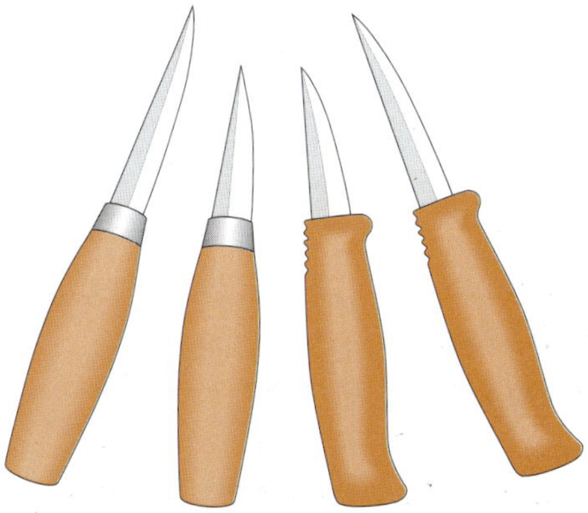

Some knives used for carving

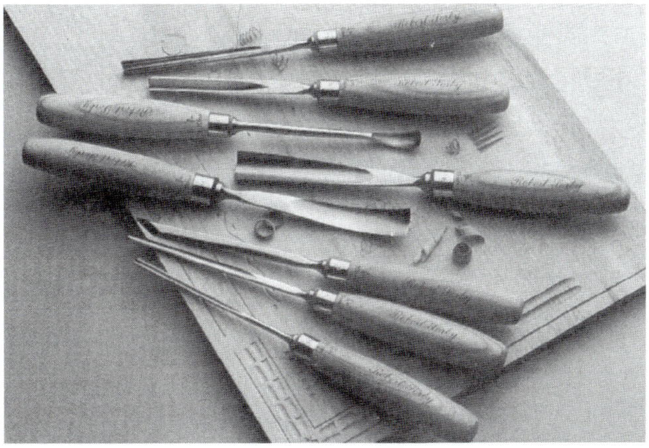

Gouges

There are two standard gouges which are used for making simple curved cuts in timber. These are the **firmer gouge** and the **paring gouge**.

The firmer gouge is a chisel-like tool with a hollowed blade and the edge is bevelled on the outside of its diameter. It is used to cut shallow hollows in the surface of wood.

Cutting a stopped groove with a firmer gouge

Firmer gouge

The paring gouge is similar to the firmer gouge, but the blade is ground on the inside. It is used for paring circular grooves.

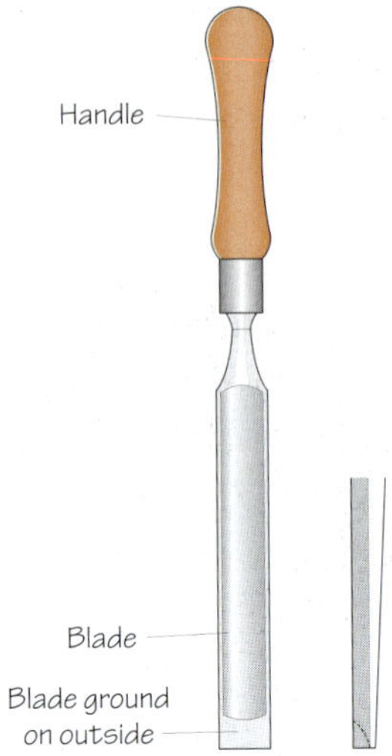

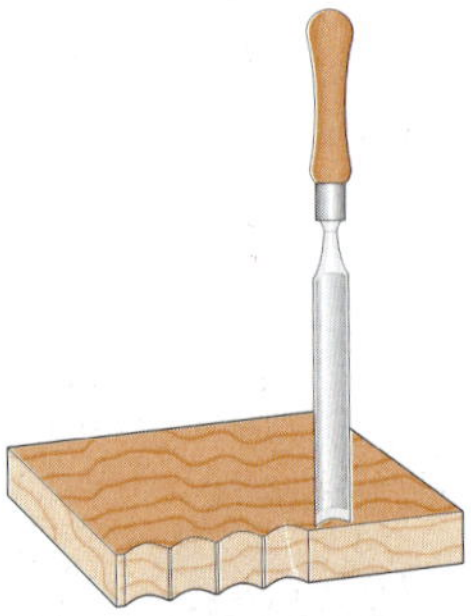

Fluting an edge with
a scribing gouge

Paring gouge

Carving gouges are similarly shaped with a hollow or curved blade. The blades are made from high quality steel and the handles are made from hardwood.

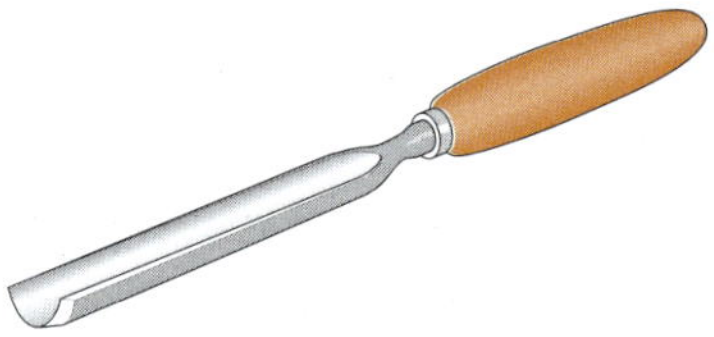

Carving gouge

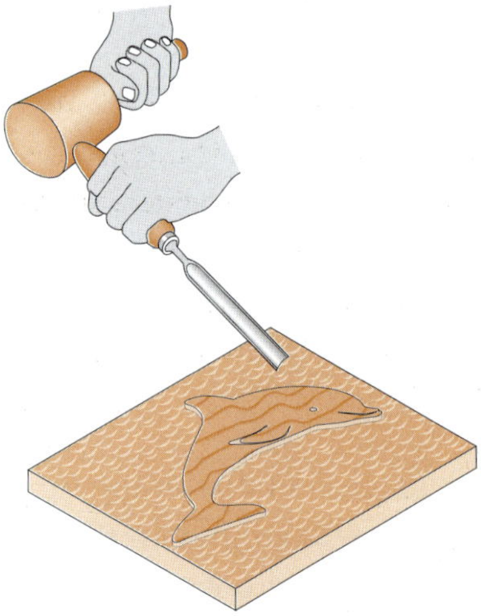

Gouge can be used with hand pressure or, with
difficult wood, using a beechwood carver's mallet

There are many types of carving gouge. The widths of the blade and the depth of the hollow of the blade vary, giving the different sizes of gouge.

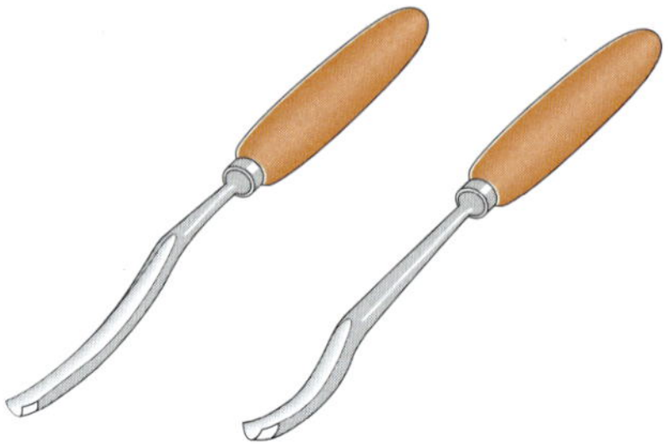

Curved and spoon-backed gouges are used
to take out concave cuts more easily

Curved and spoon backed gouge

Carving chisels

Carving chisels are different from ordinary chisels. Like the gouges, they have a high quality steel blade and hardwood handle. They are many different sizes of chisel to suit special cuts of different shapes and size. The blade is flat and rectangular in section. The edge can be either square or skew in shape. The edge of the chisel has the honing and grinding angles run into one another to give the cutting bevel.

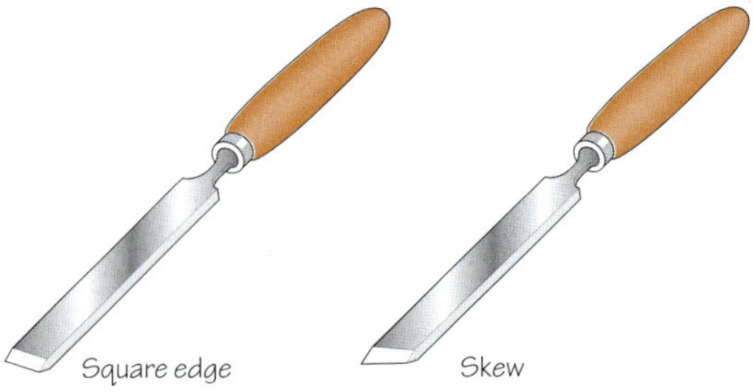

Carving chisels

The skew-edge carving chisel is used to get into cutting areas where the square edge will not fit.

The **veiner** is a gouge which has a very small size and has a deep narrow U shape to its blade. The blade is generally straight and is ground on the outside. It is used for detailed cuts and fine grooved cuts.

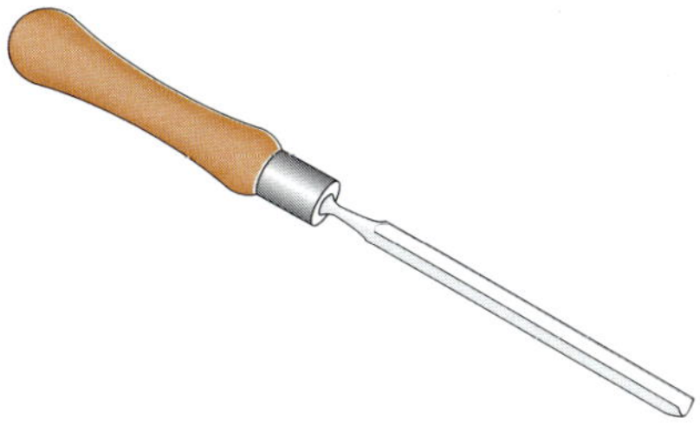

Veiner

The **vee tool** can be obtained in various blade sizes. It is used to cut grooves and channels in the wood. The blade is made from steel with a hardwood handle. The edge of the blade is in the shape of a V.

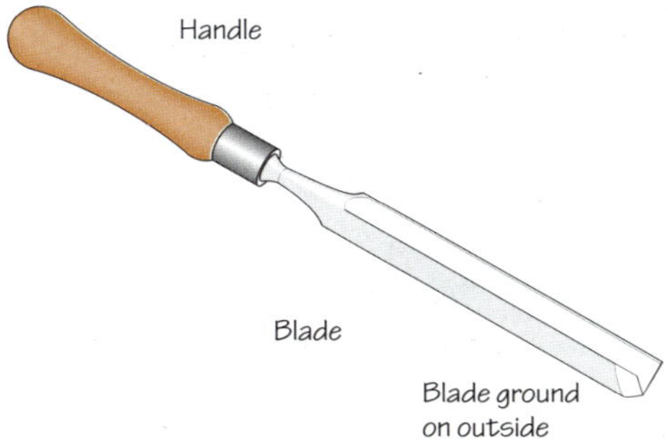

Vee tool

Surform tools

Surform tools are shaping tools in a variety of shapes and sizes. They consist of a handle of plastic, a blade held on to a frame made of steel or aluminium and a front rest. The front rest allows the tool to be held with both hands rather like a plane.

Surform tools

The tools are very light and easily managed by a beginner. The blades are set and sharpened when made and can easily be removed and replaced if they break and when they are worn. Surform tools can be used both across and with the grain. The tool is held diagonally across the piece and the cut is made on the forward stroke. When the blade gets blunt or broken it is simply replaced.

The blades of some surform tools are rounded or circular to allow various shapes to be formed. Because the tools are rather wide and large, the work done with the surform tends to be more rounded in appearance than work with other carving tools. When finished, the surface of the work is quite rough but it can be smoothed down using abrasive paper. Tight curves can be sanded by wrapping a piece of abrasive paper around a dowel.

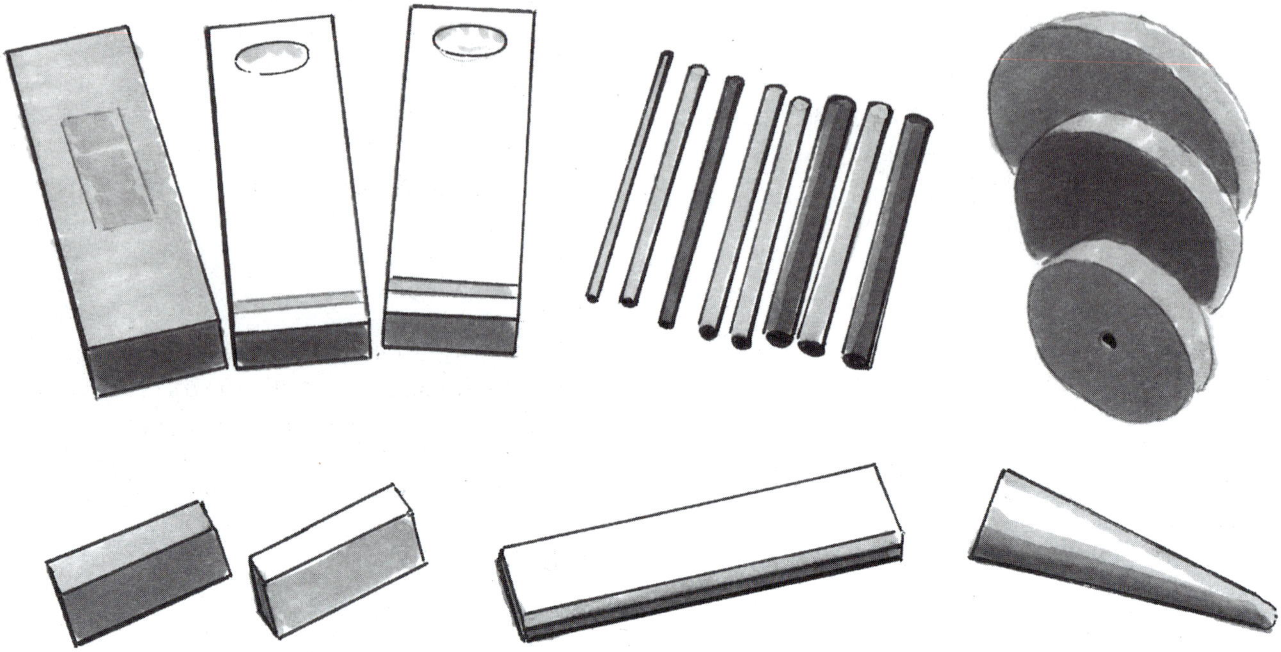

Slipstones and sharpening stones

Sharpening

Carving tools need to be kept very sharp. Carving chisels are sharpened using the oilstone. The burr is removed and the bevel is polished on a leather strop, leaving a sharp edge.

Gouges are sharpened by rubbing the outside bevel which forms the edge in a sweeping rolling motion along the oilstone. When the edge is formed the burr is removed using a slipstone.

The vee tool is sharpened differently. The two outside bevels are sharpened as a chisel, but this will form a hook at the bottom of the vee. This hook can be removed by rolling the tool as you sharpen on the stone.

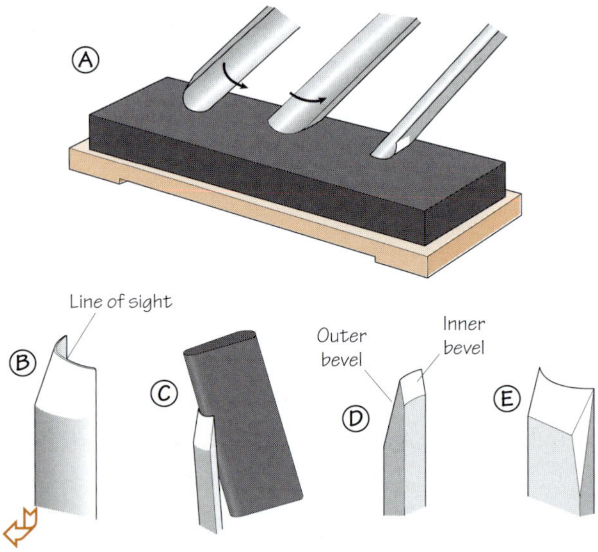

Sharpening the gouge

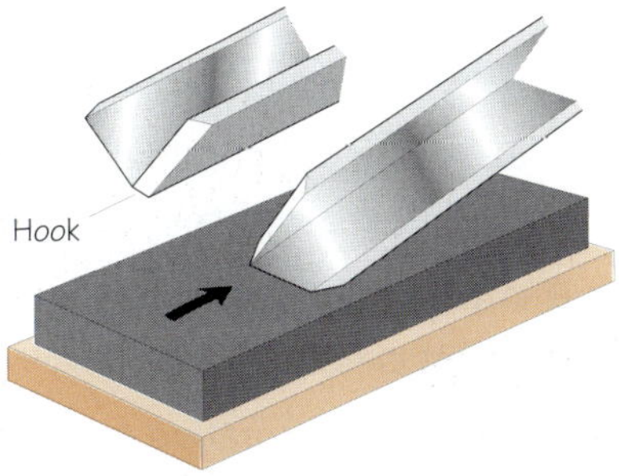

Sharpening the vee tool

Carving materials

What materials are best used for carving? Stone can be carved but it is a difficult process. In the Materials Technology Room you will most likely carve wood. Some woods are more suitable for carving than others. It may be very important to show certain colours, grain patterns and figure in the work piece.

The piece of wood chosen for carving should:

- Be free from large knots and other defects and be of straight uniform grain to allow ease of work. A skilled craftsperson can, however, use small defects to great effect in their work
- Be easy to work on
- Be properly seasoned.

Suitable woods

Sycamore, Lime, Pear and Holly

All four woods are light in colour and quite suitable for carving. They are especially good for delicate work due to their close grain.

Oak

This wood is very durable. It is difficult to carve as it is hard and coarse grained.

Walnut

There are several kinds of walnut, but they all have a close, even grain and very rich colour. All types are very suitable for carving – however, walnut is an expensive timber.

Mahogany

Good quality mahogany (e.g., Honduras) is ideal for all forms of carving. It has close and even grain pattern.

Ebony and Lignum Vitae

These are very tough durable hardwoods which are expensive and very difficult to carve. They are popular with expert wood carvers.

Pine

This is very suitable for carving particularly with surform tools. However, if other forms of carving are to be done with pine, the tools need to be very sharp as the wood will tear on blunt tools.

Carving finishes

Carving is usually decorative and it often includes very detailed work. For this reason it is important that the piece is well finished. Glossy finishes such as varnish may not be the most desirable on very decorative work, as it might clog up the smaller details and the gloss finish may take from the appearance of the work. In the case of carving which is part of a larger piece, such as a chair, the finish will generally be dictated by the piece.

Beeswax and oils such as Danish oil are particularly suitable for carved pieces as they protect the wood and give a nice matt or satin finish. Varnish, if applied, should have a satin or matt finish, although varnish is generally regarded as a poor finish on carved work.

Any staining which is used should highlight the deep lines and natural beauty of the piece rather than disguise its effect.

Exercises

1. Name the following tools used in carving:

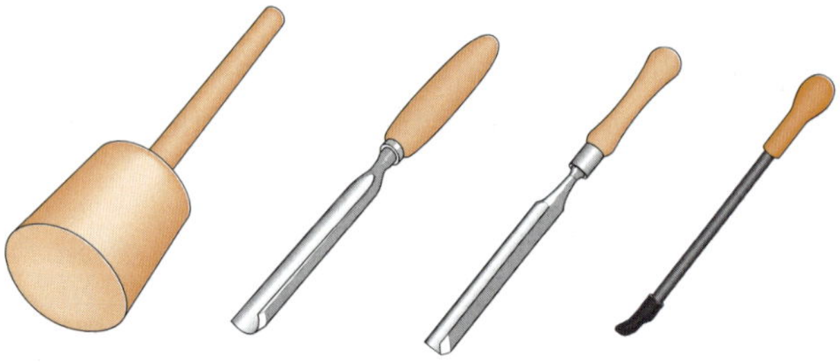

2. Name the three methods of carving shown below:

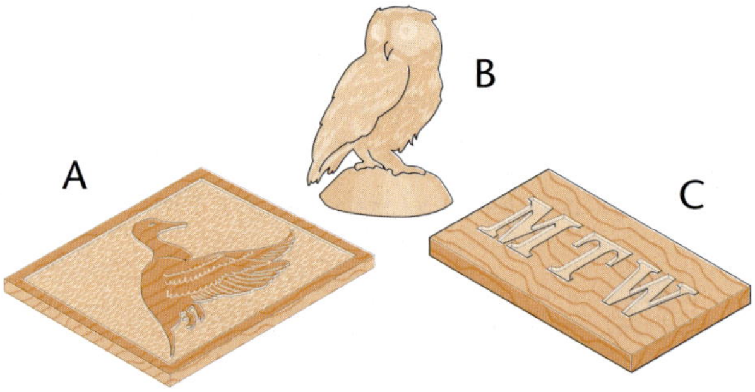

3. What is chip carving?

4. A design for a relief carving is shown:
   A. Show how how you would transfer the design to the wood.
   B. Sketch a tool suitable for finishing the area 'A' between the flower and the border.
   C. Name a wood suitable for making this carving and give two reasons for your choice.

5. Explain the term relief carving.
6. What is the veiner used for?
7. Name three woods which would be suitable for carving? Give reasons for your choice.
8. Why is it important to work in the direction of the grain when carving?
9. A book end with a decorative carved face is shown below.
   a. What is this type of carving called?
   b. Draw accurately the pattern which you would be required to draw on the wood before carving.
   c. Describe with notes and sketches, how you would cut the section of the carving labelled A on the diagram.

(Ord Level)

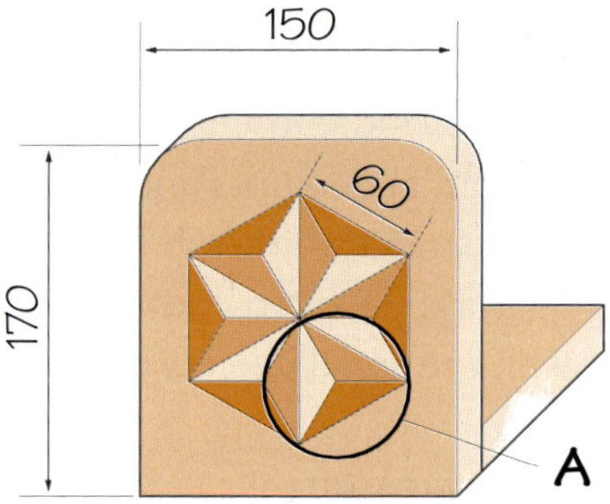

10. Recommend two finishes which are suitable for applying to carved pieces. Give reasons for your choice.

CHAPTER TWENTY-FIVE

VENEERING, INLAY AND MARQUETRY

Veneering, inlay and marquetry have been used for thousands of years. They provide a decorative surface to wood and they have become art forms in their own right.

Veneering is the bonding of thin layers of wood on to a stable base piece. The base can be solid wood but man-made boards such as plywood and MDF are more suitable. Veneers can be cut and bonded to wood in different ways. Various methods are used to make designs, patterns and pictures with the colours and grain patterns of different veneers. These patterns and pictures can be very attractive.

Example of veneered objects

Veneering was widely used during the golden age of furniture making (nineteenth century). It is still a popular way of decorating wooden articles. Veneering is an economical way of using rare and expensive solid woods also.

In past centuries tropical wood was difficult to get, due to transportation limitations. Veneering helped to make wise and economical use of the poor supply. Nowadays man-made panels, such as MDF, veneered with woods such as ash, oak, mahogany and teak are widely used in furniture and cabinet manufacture.

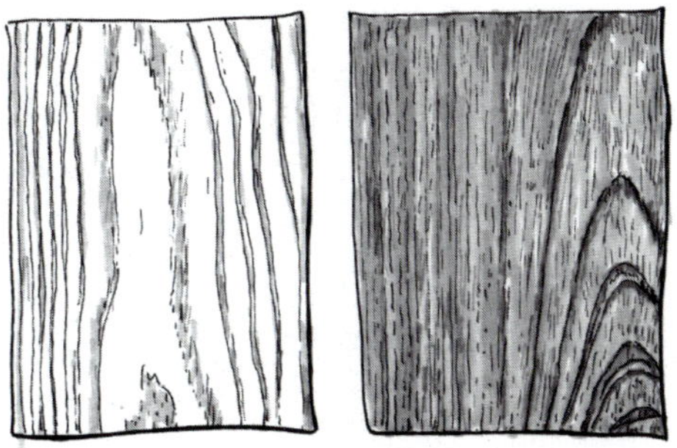

Samples of veneer patterns

Advantages of veneering

- Rare tropical woods are used economically
- Large flat surfaces can be covered without the risk of splitting
- Attractive patterns can be made with careful planning.

Veneers

Most of the world's beautiful timbers are very rare and very costly. The wood they produce is often unsuitable for furniture making, as it has irregular grain, etc. These timbers can be cut into veneers, thin sheets of wood, which can then be glued to the surface of a more stable and less costly wood such as chipboard, plywood and MDF.

When a log has been debarked and cut to length it is immersed in a bath of steam to soften the fibres of the wood. This may take a few hours or a couple of days, depending on the size and type of wood. Once soft, the veneers can be cut from the log in thin slices or in a continuous strip or peel. The thickness of the cut veneer varies but is usually between 0.6mm and 1mm.

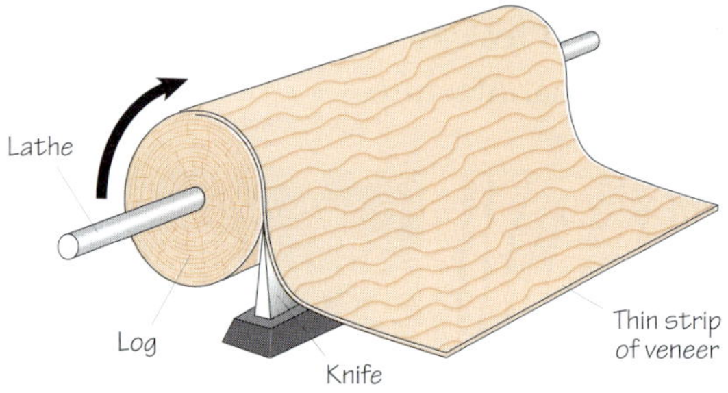

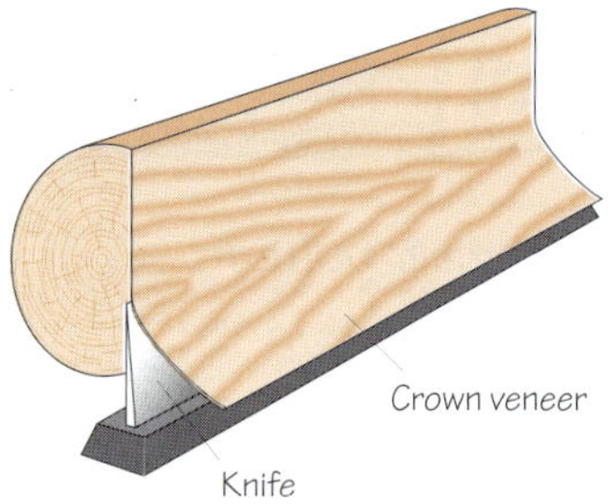

Cutting veneers from the log

Rotary cutting does not provide veneers with the best quality grain pattern, but is the quickest and least expensive method.

Veneers of many types are available, various colours and grain patterns can be got quite easily. Trees have some defects which are also valuable when cut to make a veneer.

Veneer is bonded to timber using a gluing process, but veneer is also available with a self adhesive backing. It can be obtained as a product called microwood. The paper backing is peeled off and the veneer is ready to apply.

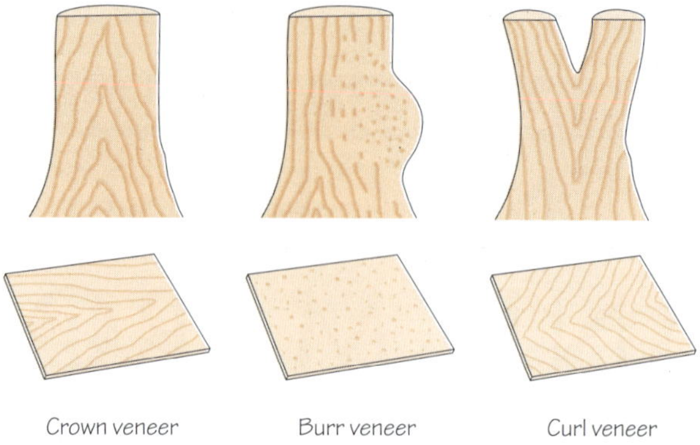

Other veneer products are available which would help to enhance the beauty of project work – motifs and bandings which are ready made but can be quite expensive.

Motifs are simple or elaborate pictures made from coloured and shaded veneer.

Bandings are strips of prepared veneered patterns. The patterns can be very complex and they are usually repetitive. Thin lines or strips in plain veneers are also available.

Motifs & bandings

Groundwork

When the veneer, veneered panel or picture is made, it is bonded to a piece of wood.

The piece of timber on which the veneer is fixed is known as a backing or **groundwork**. Solid wood is not as suitable as plywood or MDF for groundwork, because a single veneer on solid wood can cause warping. It is normal practice to counteract this warping effect with a backing or **balancing veneer** on the other side of the piece. This backing veneer is usually of the same type, but not usually as good in quality. This process is often called **counter veneering**.

The groundwork is veneered on both sides to keep the forces even

Veneering

When veneering the veneers must be flat to avoid bubbling. Buckled veneers must first be flattened with a damp cloth or sponge and then pressed between two flat surfaces which are weighted. They are left for a couple of days before use.

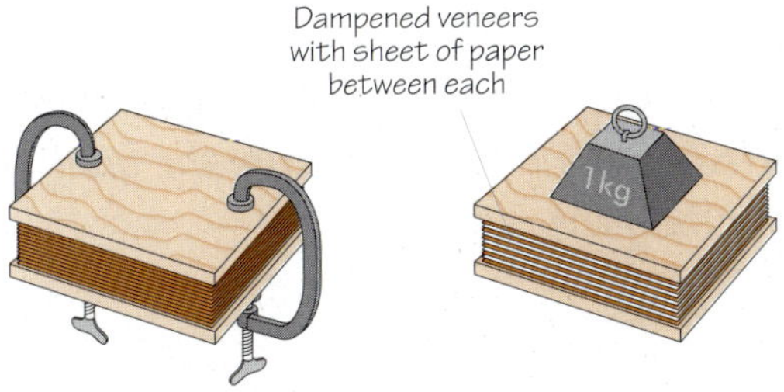

Flattening buckled veneers

The veneer is cut to make straight lines or to cut shapes in the veneer. The veneers can be cut using a very sharp craft knife or scalpel and a straight edge, such as a steel rule. Several passes may be necessary to complete the cut. Pressure is not applied to the knife when cutting, as this might tear the veneer.

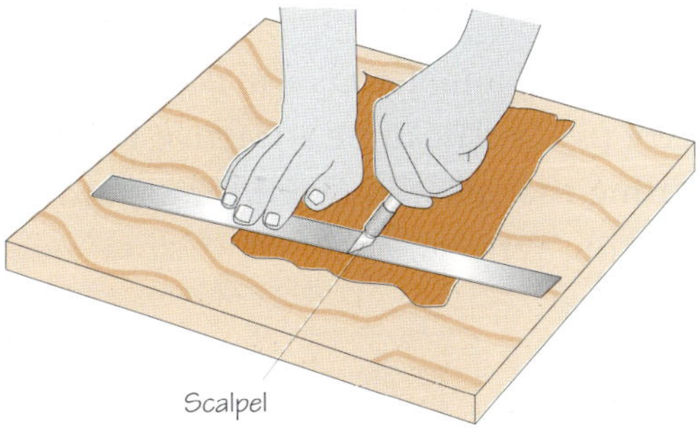

Cutting the veneer

Matching

Veneer can then be **matched** to form various symmetrical patterns, before being applied to the background piece. It is often necessary to join pieces of veneer to cover wider areas. Matching the veneers takes a keen eye and the pattern must be symmetrical. Simple grain patterns must also be applied so that the grain is lying the correct way.

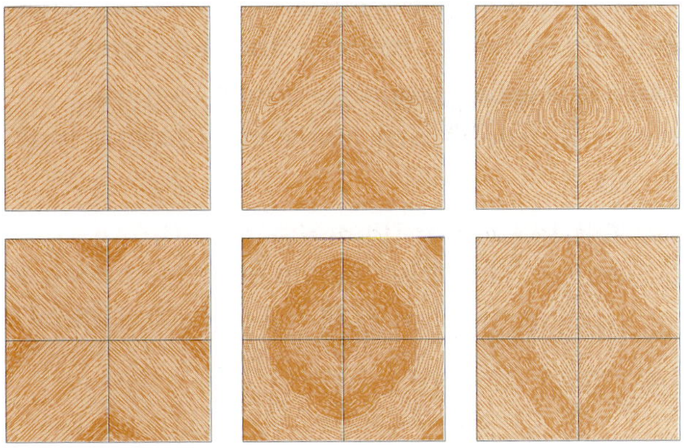

Matching veneers to form patterns

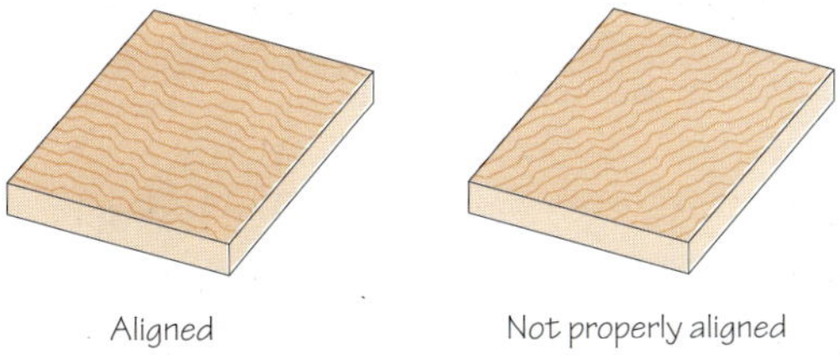

The grain of the veneer should be correctly aligned

Borders

When veneering a tabletop or making a marquetry picture it can be attractive to form a border using the veneers. Often these borders are of contrasting veneers.

(a) (b) (c)

Example of the use of veneers to create borders for veneered work

- *Plain mitred border (a)*
- *Crossbanding – using the direction of the grain to create the effect (b)*
- *Borders can be enhanced by using a contrasting strip of veneer (c).*

These borders are quite easily achieved, with some imagination, patience and the correct tools. It is usual to apply a border to most veneered panels, particularly small picture type panels.

- Cut and match the necessary strips of veneer. The strips should be long enough to overlap the corners of the piece and allow waste. When cross-banding the matching strips will be taped together. *All of the tape should be on the top side so that adhesive can be applied to the reverse side. Masking tape is the most suitable tape to use for this purpose*
- Tape the border to the veneered panel with care to ensure tight joint lines. When finished the border strips will overlap
- Carefully mark and cut the mitres at the corners of the border, remove the waste veneer and tape the joints at the mitres
- When you are happy with the panel it can be bonded to the groundwork.

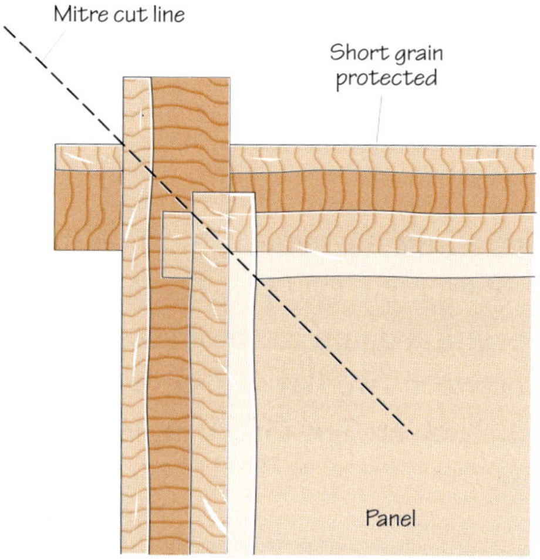

The short grain of crossbanding can be protected by using tape to secure the grain while cutting the mitres

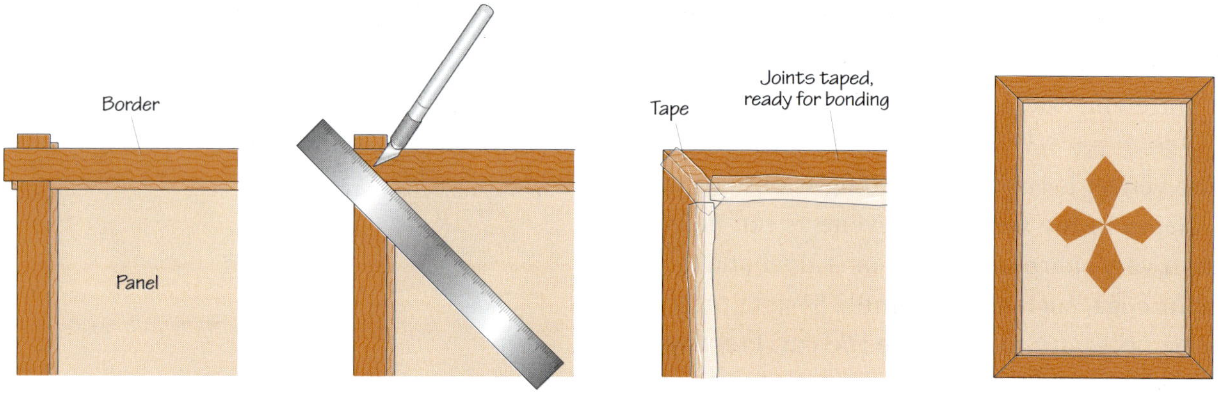

Applying a border to a veneer panel

Inlaying

Inlaying is another process of wood decoration which dates back to the 14th century. A small line or strip of a material is glued into a recess cut from solid wood surfaces to form a contrasting line or pattern.

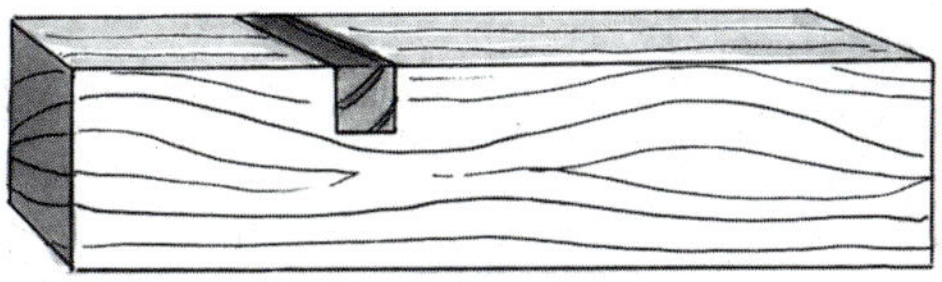

Materials used:

Ivory, tortoise shell, mother of pearl, bone, plastics, metals and motifs can be used. Wood is, however, the most popular material used and boxwood is widely used for inlaying. Boxwood is a yellow coloured wood.

Setting in a motif

Inlay strips and bandings can be inserted into grooves, which are cut or scratched out of the wood using a **scratch stock**. The groove for a piece of inlay is made with the aid of a piece of shaped steel (usually a piece of an old hacksaw blade), which is held in the scratch stock. This is shown in the diagram opposite.

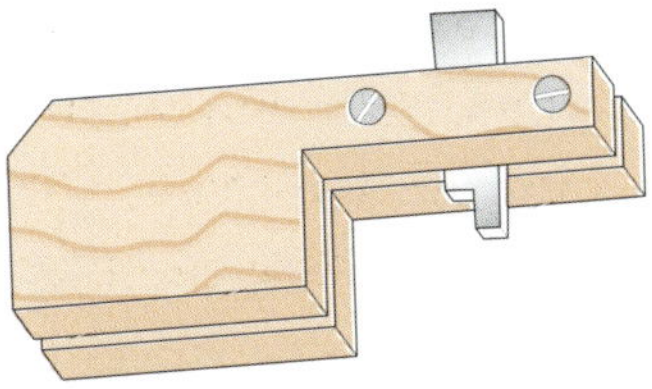

Scratch stock

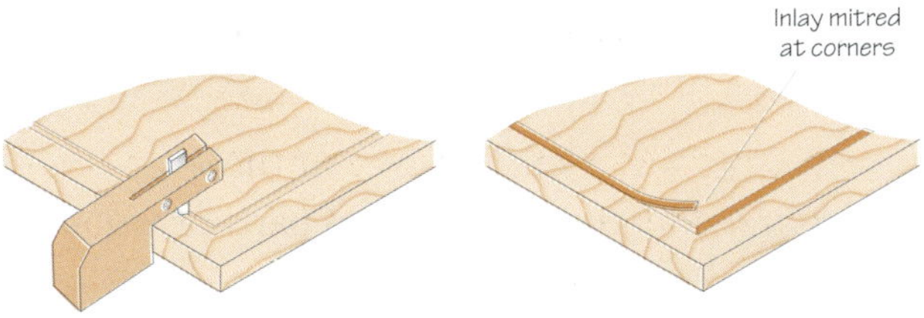

Using the scratch stock to apply inlay

Patterns and angled corners can be done by making a template, or jig, which a chisel can follow to cut the groove. The chisel is also used to cut mitres and joints in the inlay.

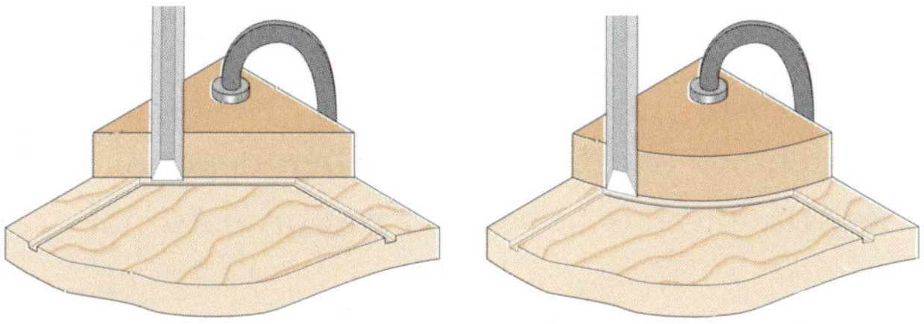

Making decorative corners with a template

Finishing

Inlayed or veneered work may leave slightly uneven surfaces on the timber as the thickness of the pieces may differ slightly. Finishing these surfaces requires a little patience and care.

After any tape has been removed from the veneered pieces the surfaces should be inspected and any small gaps in the veneer filled. Then the whole piece can be cleaned and smoothed with a cabinet scraper.

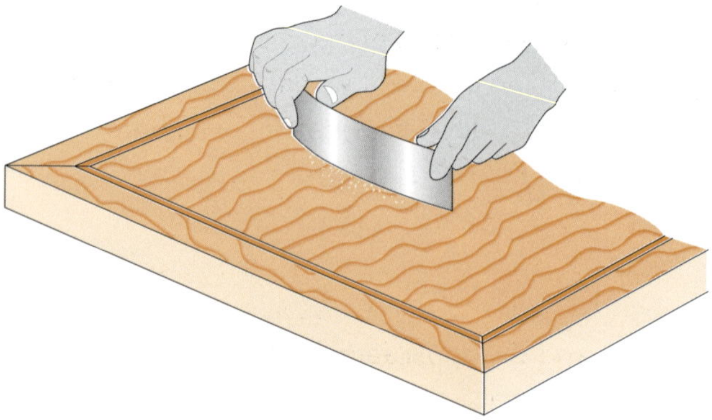

Use a cabinet scraper to clean down the surfaces of the veneer

When complete the surfaces can be sanded down with fine sand paper to get a good surface finish. Care must be taken when using sandpaper, particularly with powered sanders on veneered surfaces as veneers are thin and it is very easy to sand through the veneer to the groundwork.

The choice of applied finish then depends on where the piece is to be used and on personal taste.

Pyrography

Pyrography is the art of burning decorative designs in wood with a special heated tool. The pyrography tool looks similar to a soldering iron and the bit, which can be interchanged is heated electrically.

Note: The pyrography tool is very hot and you should be careful not to touch its heated parts.

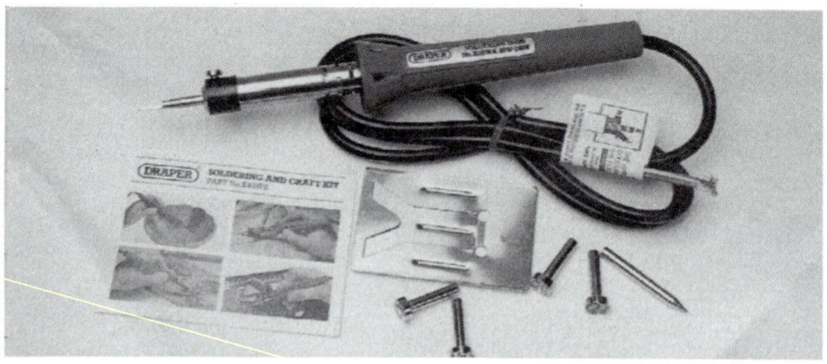

Pyrography tool

This type of wood decoration works best on light coloured woods such as lime, beech, sycamore, chestnut, etc. The wood should be sanded smooth before the pyrography is done as sanding would damage the design. Finally the piece is sealed and an applied finish is put on.

Exercises

1. List two materials which would be suitable as groundwork for veneering.
2. Name two light coloured veneers and two dark coloured veneers.
3. Name the tools shown below and state what each is used for:

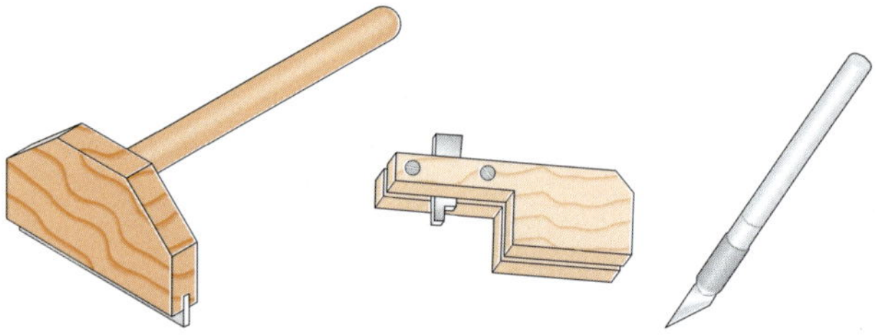

4. Describe what marquetry is.
5. What is parquetry and state the type of veneer that is most suitable for it.
6. What is the main advantage of the window method of producing marquetry?

7. Name two adhesives which are suitable for veneering projects.
8. Explain, using sketches, how veneers are cut.
9. What is counter veneering and state why it is important?
10. A small veneered box is shown below. A veneered design is to be applied to the lid:
    (a) Show by means of notes and sketches, how you would cut and fit the leaf motif into the veneer A, so that it would fit exactly.
    (b) Describe in detail, how you would apply the veneer A with the inset leaf, to the top of the box. Use notes and sketches to illustrate your answer.
    (c) Recommend a suitable adhesive for this veneering, and give one reason for your choice.

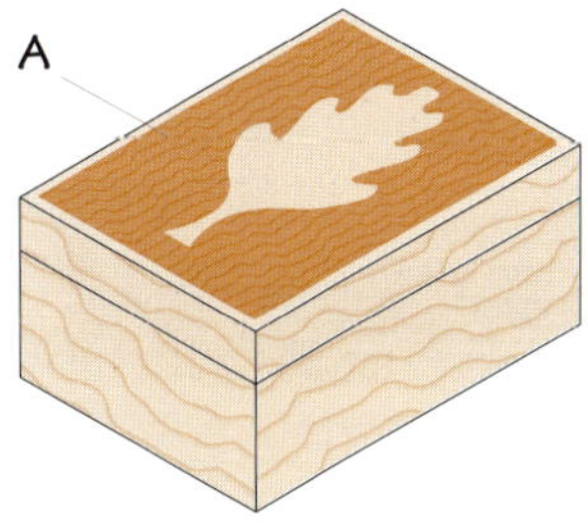

11. The diagram shows one corner of a chessboard. It is to be made from wood veneers on a manufactured board base.
    (a) Select materials suitable for the base and veneers (including the squares, border and the banding) and give reasons for your choice.
    (b) Select a suitable applied finish and describe the preparation of the board and the application of the finishing material.

12. Explain by means of notes and sketches how you would cut, fit and apply the veneered design to the lid of the box shown below.

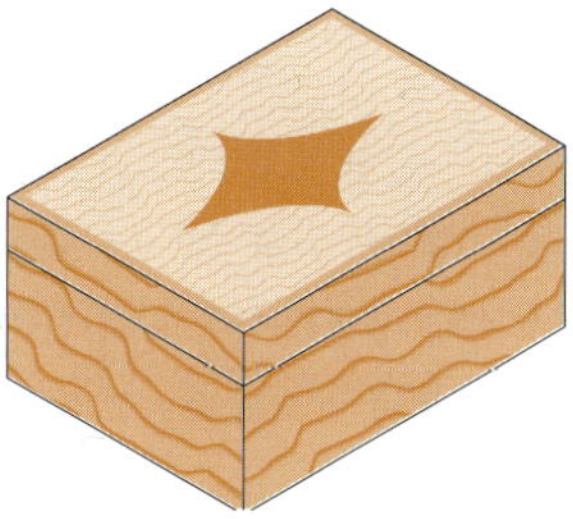

CHAPTER TWENTY-SIX

WORKING WITH WOOD

WOODTURNING

One of the oldest forms of wood machining is woodturning. In woodturning, a piece of wood, mounted on a lathe, is turned into various cylindrical shapes. Woodturning combines design, and skill in the use of tools, with machining skills to produce articles of beauty and function.

Examples of turning

Even before electrical power, a pole lathe was used to turn wood. The pole lathe is still used by some craftspeople today. The wooden pole acts as a spring and the chord which is attached to the workpiece is driven by a foot pedal. The pole lathe uses 'footpower' and the spring of the sapling turns the piece.

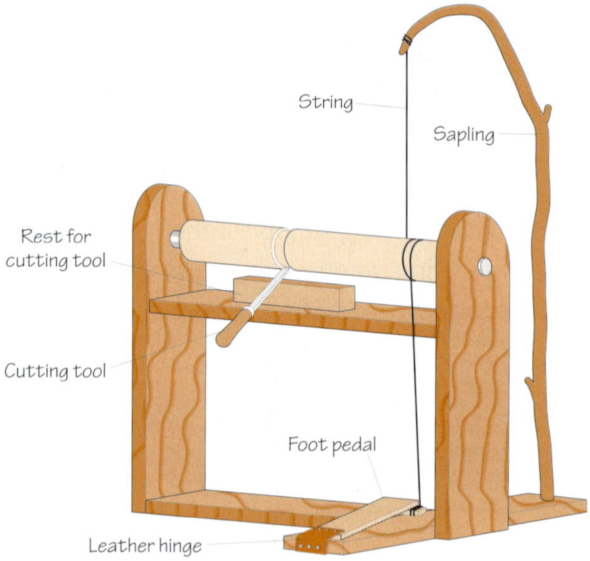

The pole lathe

The woodturning lathe

There are many makes of lathe – some are free-standing, some can be mounted on a bench. The parts of the lathe are the same on most machines. You must be familiar with the lathe before you use it.

The swing of the lathe governs the maximum diameter of material which can be turned. It is twice the distance between the centre of the threaded spindle and the bed of the lathe.

The length is the maximum distance between the two centres of the lathe.

The headstock is the main part of the lathe. It contains the motor and driving mechanism. The

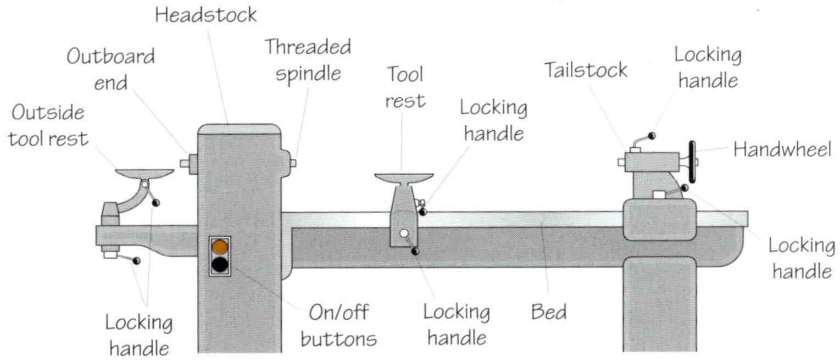

The woodturning lathe

drive centre is driven by pulleys and belts contained in the headstock. The drive speed of the lathe can be changed by changing the position of the belt. The spindle of the lathe accommodates the drive centre. The headstock also houses the on/off buttons.

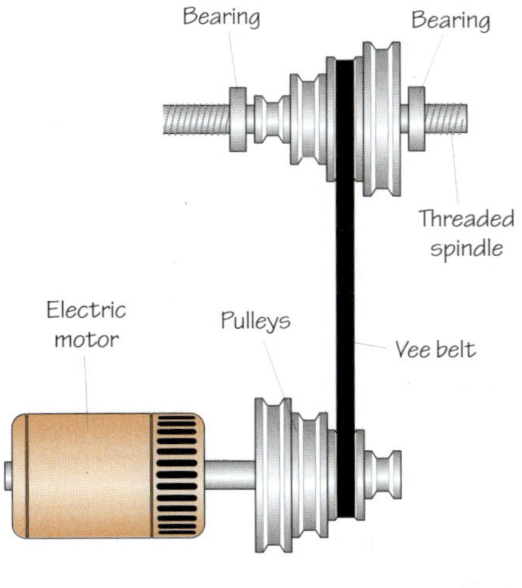

Diagram of the lathe driving mechanism

BEWARE!

The headstock which houses the driving mechanism is enclosed with a protective housing. Students should not adjust the speeds of the lathe or open this housing to get to the driving mechanism as an accident could easily result

The tailstock is a moveable block which can be fixed to the bed of the lathe by a locking handle. It contains the other centre which is often a live centre (turns with the workpiece). The tailstock holds the tail end of the workpiece, firmly holding it in place against the drive centre.

Sometimes a hollow centre is used when a hole needs to be drilled through the length of the workpiece. Holes are drilled with a special tool called a **long hole boring auger**.

The hole is drilled half way with the piece in the lathe and then it is reversed and the rest of the hole is drilled.

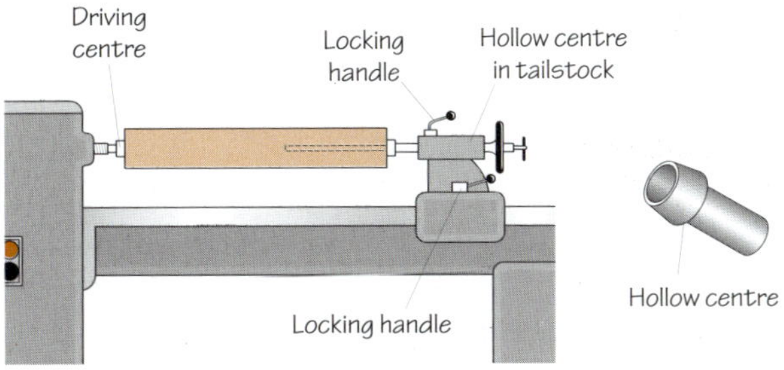

Drilling a lamp stand to take an electric flex, using a hole boring auger

The tool rest is used to rest the tool on while turning is being done. The rest has two parts, the rest and the banjo, which supports the rest on the bed of the lathe. Rests of different lengths can be interchanged as required.

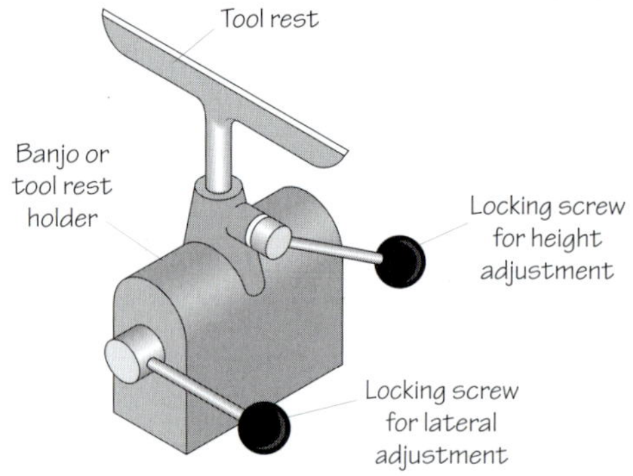

The banjo and tool rest

The height of the tool rest can be adjusted and it can also be turned about a vertical axis when faceplate turning. Many lathes have an outboard end for faceplate work and the rest can be moved to this position easily.

Centres are used to grip and drive the piece of wood when spindle turning. The centres can be changed also as required.

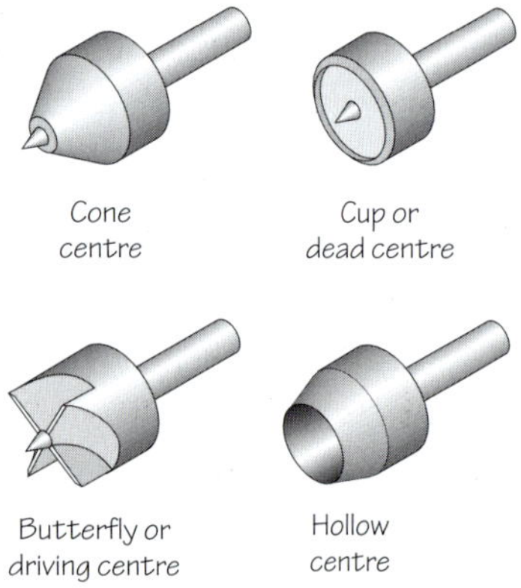

Lathe centres

The centre used in the tailstock can turn with the piece or it can be static (dead centre). The dead centre creates friction which will burn the wood. Oil is used on the wood to reduce this effect. The oil can, however, discolour the end of the piece so allowances must be made for this.

Faceplates are accurately machined metal disks which are used to hold a workpiece when turning a piece, such as a plate or bowl. They have a threaded hub which screws onto the headstock spindle. The workpiece is held onto the faceplate using screws inserted through special holes in it. Faceplates of different sizes can be used for various sizes of workpiece. When mounting a piece on the faceplate it is important that it is centred accurately. Concentric circles on the faceplate assist in this task.

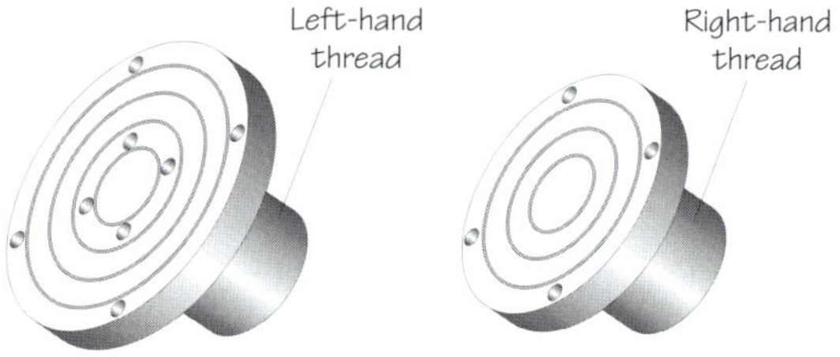

Faceplates

Chucks can also be used to hold pieces, large and small. They give a strong grip and great versatility when turning and are very popular. They are quite expensive and many variations are available. The chuck is screwed onto the spindle of the headstock. The piece is gripped tightly by jaws on the chuck and this allows unobstructed access around the piece.

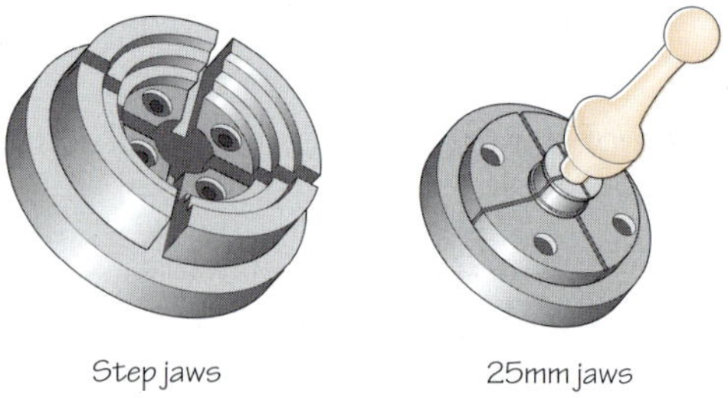

Woodturning chuck

Turning tools

The tools used for turning are made from **high speed steel** (HSS) blades which have hardwood handles. The blades are sturdy and the handles are quite long, so that they can be held firmly while turning. There are a great many different chisels, gouges and scrapers but a basic set is sufficient to begin with.

Turning tools are held against the moving piece to produce the cut.

Woodturning tools

Gouges are the most common tools used in turning. There are a number of different types and each is suited to a certain task. Gouges are used to rough down a blank (initial, unturned pipe) to a cylinder. They are also used to form coves and grooves and to hollow out bowls and plates.

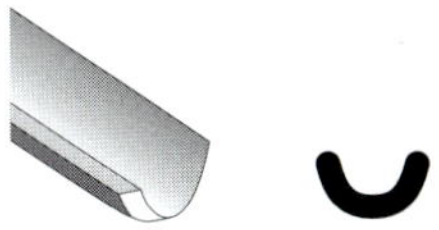

Roughing down gouge

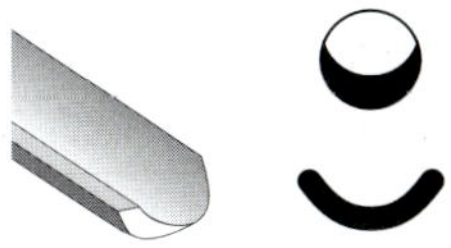

Shallow fluted gouge

Bowl gouge – deep fluted

Scrapers are used to turn spindle work although they leave a very rough finish. Commonly, they are used on the inside of deep bowls, etc. to achieve an even finish.

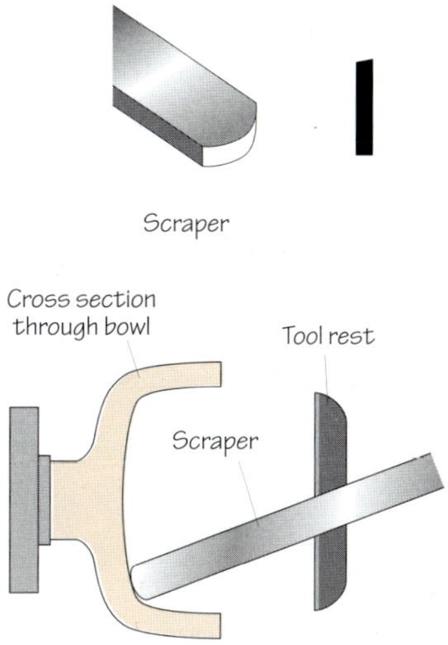

Scraper used to form the inside of a deep bowl

When using the scraper, the tool is held in the horizontal position and it scrapes the material from the work. Its use is easily learned, but the surface it leaves is rough and requires a lot of sanding to achieve a proper finish.

Parting tool is used to make thin grooves or recesses to a desired depth. These cuts have flat sides and a square bottom. The cut is the same thickness as the blade. The parting tool can be obtained in various sizes.

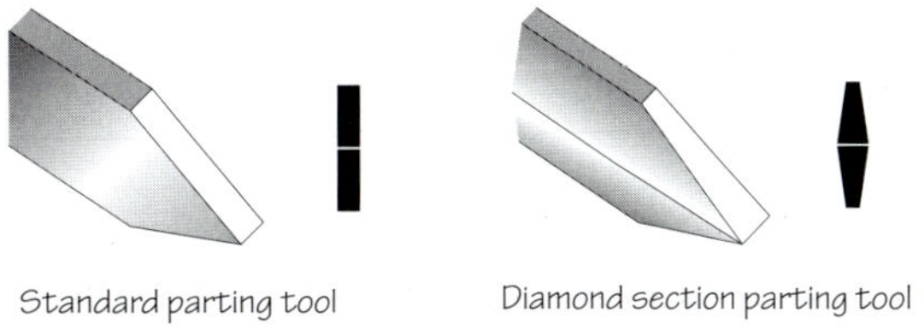

Parting tool removes material to required depth before making beads,etc

Skew chisels are named because their cutting edge, as well as having two cutting bevels, also has the edge swept back. The cutting edge, formed by the two bevels on the edge is approximately twice the thickness of the blade.

The skew chisel is used as a cutting tool and can be obtained in various sizes. The skew chisel is used to cut vee grooves and beads and they will give a smooth finish to pieces.

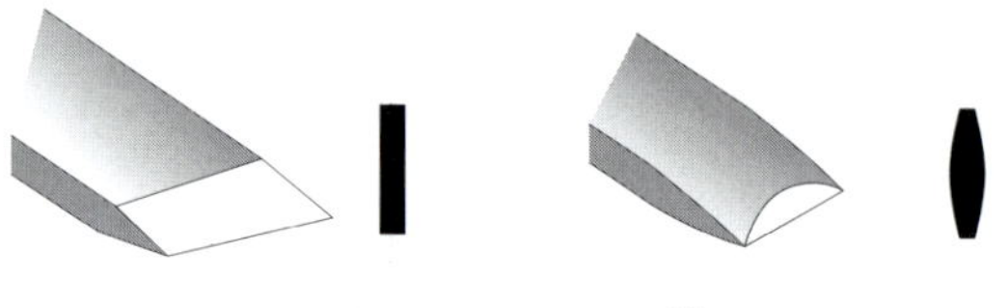

Skew chisel

Dividers are used for transferring measurements from a drawing to a piece. It also can scribe circles on faceplate work. It is similar to a compass but has two sharp steel points.

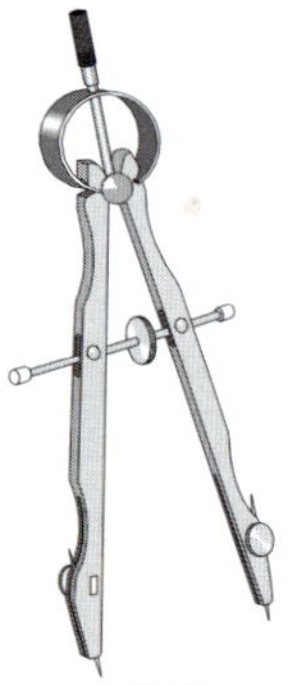

Dividers

Dividers

Callipers are used to accurately measure the thickness/diameter of pieces of turned work. The inside diameter of bowls, vases, goblets, holes, etc. also needs to be accurately measured, and is done using a vernier or other callipers. The **vernier callipers** is very accurate.

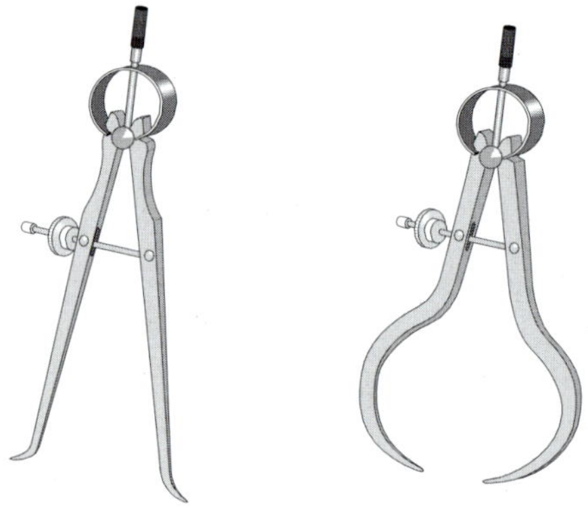

Inside calipers Outside calipers

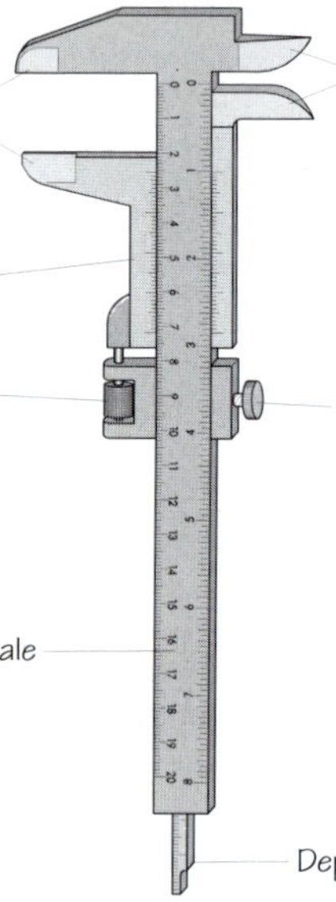

Vernier callipers

Types of turning

There are two types of turning commonly practised, faceplate turning and spindle turning. Spindle turning is perhaps the most widely used in schools.

Spindle turning

Spindle turning or between centre work is turning which is performed on a piece which is held between the centres in the headstock and tailstock.

Safety rules

- Know how to turn the lathe off, before turning it on
- Always wear full face protection
- Secure all loose clothing and hair. It is a good idea to roll up your sleeves
- Make sure all work has been properly prepared and is free from defects
- When using faceplates, ensure the work is properly secured
- Always use the lathe only as instructed and only under the supervision of the teacher
- Only set-up the pieces in the machine when the power is off
- Always rotate the piece of work by hand first to ensure it does not catch in the tool rest
- Ensure that the correct speed is selected for the type and size of the piece
- Always get the setting up of the machine checked before you begin working.

The workpiece called a blank is mounted on the lathe and the locking handles are tightened when the necessary adjustments are made.

When mounting the piece on the lathe, the drive centre is put into position and the tailstock is slid into position on the centre of the end of the workpiece. The tailstock centre is tightened, pressing the centre into the piece, until the work is secure and the locking screws are tightened.

The gouge is first used to turn down a rough cylinder. This is called 'roughing down'. The tool is held with the blade resting on the tool rest and the bevel on the end of the blade rubs against the rotating piece. Gradually, the cutting edge is raised until it begins to take a cut from the material. The gouge is moved along the piece to turn the cylinder. The cylinder can be further finished with a skew chisel.

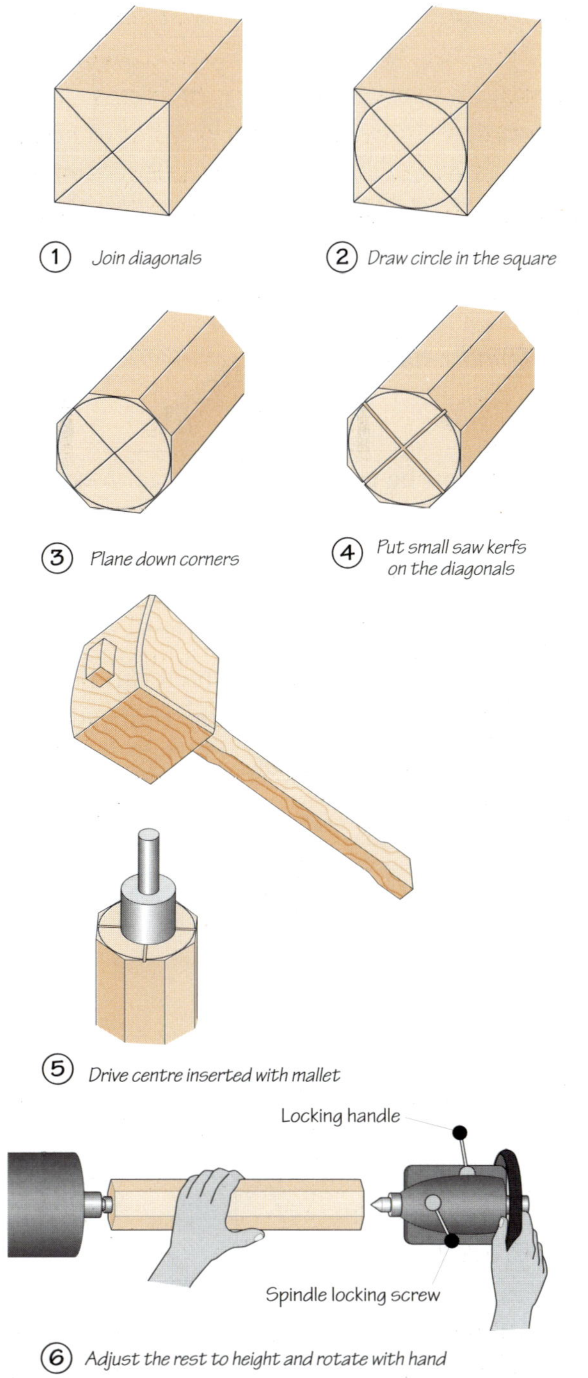

Preparing and mounting a piece for spindle turning

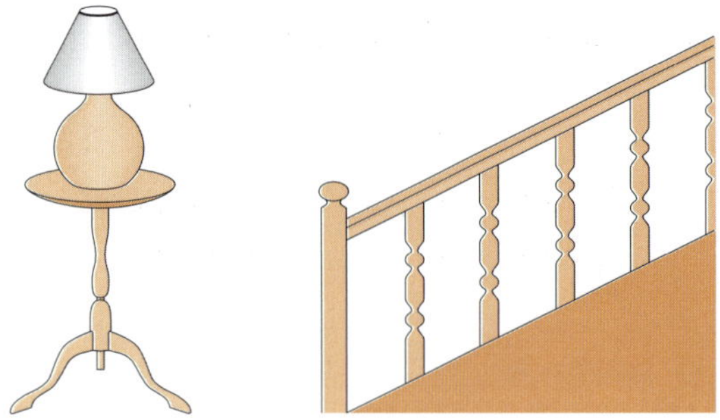

Spindle turning

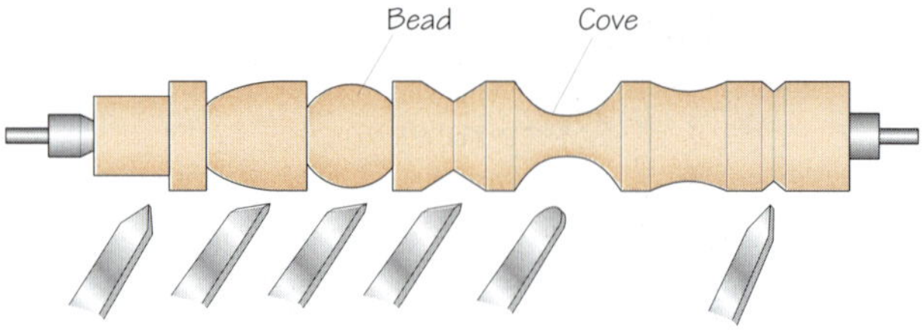

Different chisel and gouge cuts

Coves can be cut using the gouge. A cove is first marked and then the gouge is used from each side towards the centre, gradually increasing the depth until the correct profile is obtained.

Here are some other cuts which can be formed. You will learn the correct procedure for making these cuts in class.

Profiles

Before doing any work on the lathe a drawing of the piece to be done must be made. It is only necessary to draw an outline of the piece as the revolution of the piece will make this shape all around the piece. Often this profile is done on a grid, so that it can be reduced or enlarged easily.

A template can be made of this profile and it is used to check if the turned items are made to the correct measurements.

A profile especially important if you wish to make a number of identical pieces such as the legs of a stool or six goblets, etc.

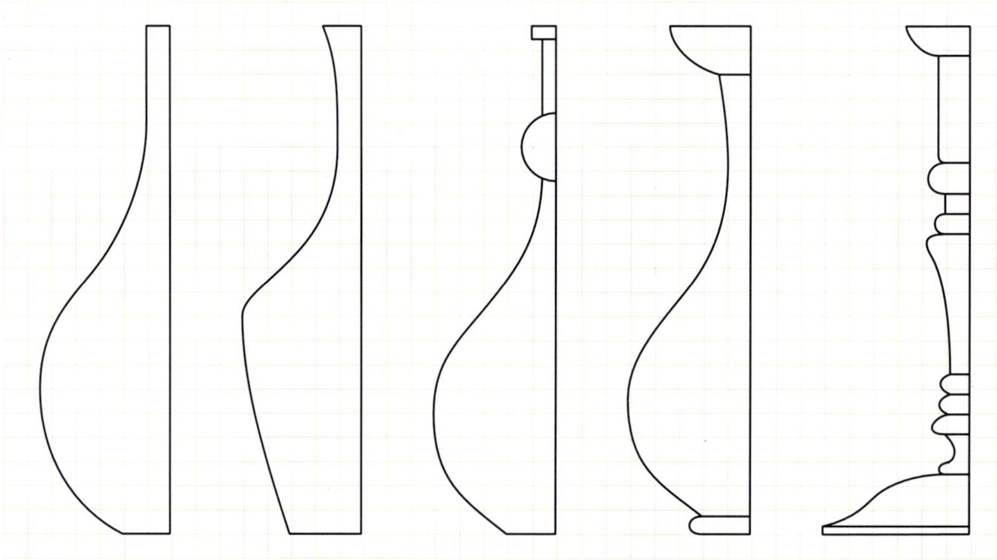

A drawing of the outline (profile) is used to plan the work

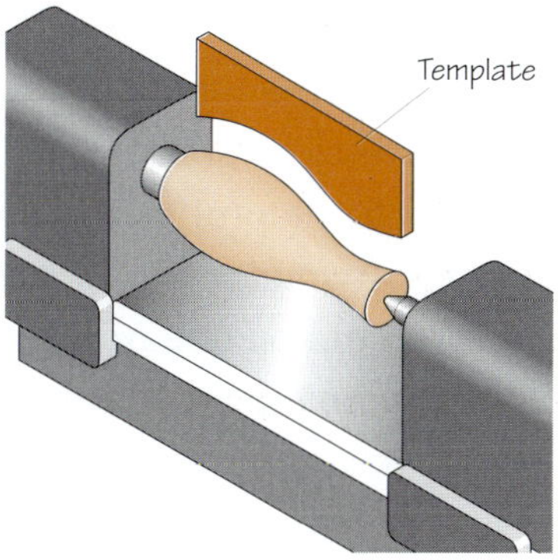

Using a profile template

Bowl/faceplate turning

Before the faceplate can be attached to the spindle, the workpiece or blank must be mounted onto the faceplate.

A circle is drawn on the piece which is approximately 3-4mm larger than the final dimensions of the finished piece. This circle can be cut on the bandsaw or the corners can be cut off using a tenon saw to make an octagon.

The piece is carefully centred and attached to the faceplate using screws. The screws used must be the correct size; if they are too short the piece could become loose on the faceplate, if they are too long they might come through the piece and pose a danger by getting caught on a tool during turning. The length and position of the screws must be carefully planned in advance.

In order to prevent too much damage being done to the piece by screws and auxiliary faceplate can be used to secure the piece.

In some cases a piece of work might be fixed to an auxiliary faceplate using adhesive. This is done when:

- Using a very thin piece
- Screw holes would spoil the appearance of the work
- Screws might catch in the lathe tools
- Some complex construction requires it.

When using an auxiliary faceplate the piece is planed flat. This is then glued to a prepared auxiliary faceplate made from wood and cut to a larger diameter than the faceplate.

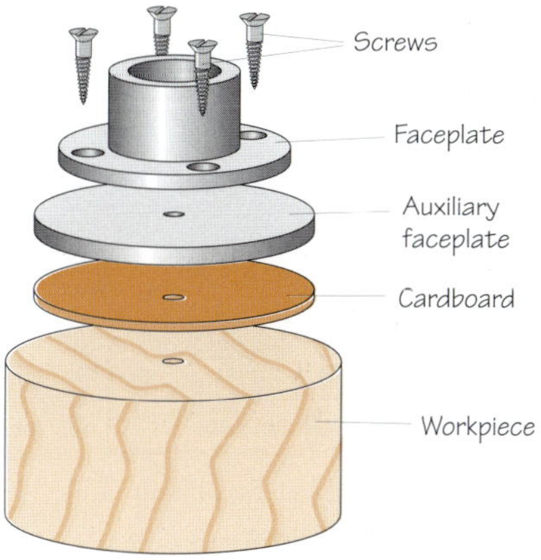

Attaching the work to an auxiliary faceplate

A piece of card is bonded to the pieces between the workpiece and the auxiliary faceplate – this allows the work to be easily separated from it later on. When the pieces have set they can be mounted on the lathes faceplate with the appropriate screws. The screws only penetrate the auxiliary faceplate, so do not mark the actual piece.

When the arrangement has been checked, it can be mounted on the lathe.

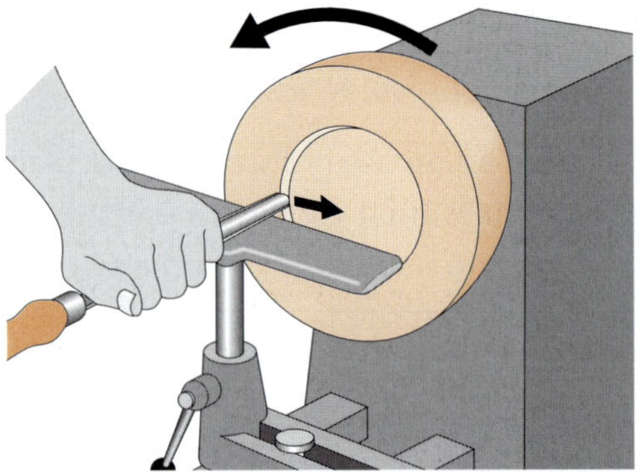

Faceplate turning.
Note the position of the tool rest

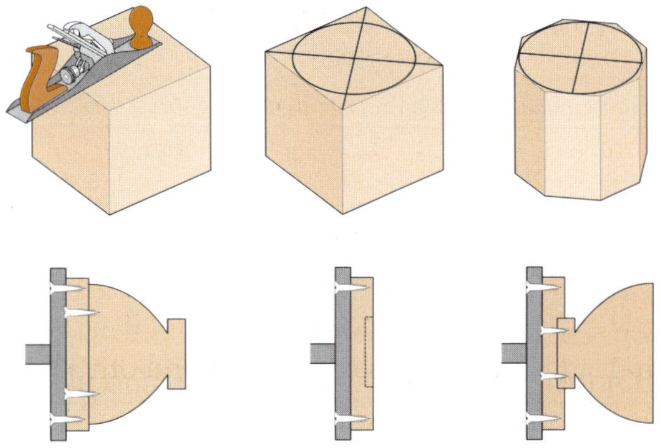

Stages in turning a bowl

Many people now use modern chucks as an alternative to using a faceplate. The chuck can grip the outside of a piece or it can also grip the inside of a recess which might be made in a bowl.

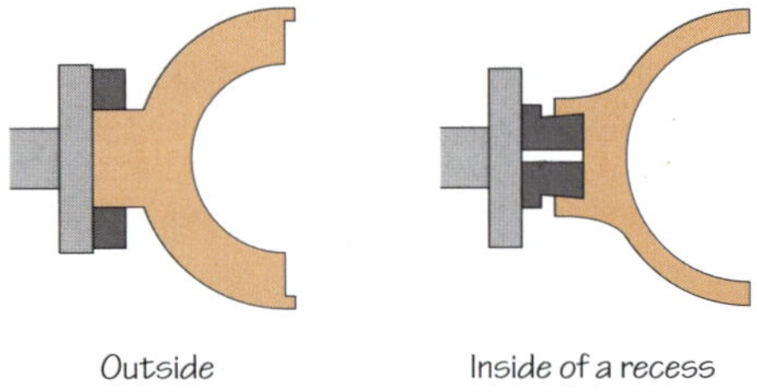

Chucks can grip a piece on the outside. It can also grip the inside of a recess

Suitable wood

Most woods can be turned, however the most suitable woods have close grain, usually hardwoods. It can be helpful to begin practising your turning on softwoods or even a freshly cut log. The timber should be free from defects. Suitable timbers are mahogany, beech, sycamore, elm, oak, cherry, yew and walnut. They all finish well on the lathe. Softwoods can be used, but they are usually less easily finished.

Finishing

When a piece is done it will require sanding before a finish can be applied. The sanding is usually done on the lathe, but care needs to be taken.

The tool rest should be removed before sanding begins.

Begin with a medium grit paper (such as an 80 grit) you can then progress on to finer and finer grits as the smoothness increases. Sandpaper grit will form tiny scratches on the surface of the turned piece. You should progress on to the next grade of paper when the scratches of the previous grade has been removed. The table on page 223 should give you a guide to the grit size to use.

Take care not to remove the crisp lines intended at shoulders, coves, etc. It is very easily done as is over sanding the piece.

When the piece is rotating on the spindle keep your hand in contact with the underside of the wood. This will ensure that your hand is not going against the force of the machine.

BEWARE! Always follow your teachers instructions in the use of the lathe

GRIT SIZE	PURPOSE	EXPLANATION
80-100	Rough sanding	Taking out blemishes
120-150	Fine sanding	General finishing
200-400	Very fine work	Very high quality finishing

Some surfaces will need to be sanded with the lathe stopped so that you can go with the grain to avoid scratches.

Steel wool can be used to smooth down the piece or to put on waxes. It is held in the same way as sandpaper but you must be careful that it doesn't become tangled in the work. As a result of the friction created both sandpaper and wire wool will become hot when used against the piece – take care you don't get burned.

Large areas require you to keep the sandpaper moving in order to get a uniformly smooth surface.

When you are satisfied that you have a smooth surface without scratches or blemishes you can apply a final finish. An applied finish will highlight all minor scratches and blemishes.

The pores of turned work may be sealed using a grain filler which is applied to the wood by cloth or brush and worked well into the grain. It is allowed to dry and then is burnished/polished with a clean cloth.

A wide variety of finishes can be used with turned work as with most wood. However, turners favour finishes such as Danish oil, waxes, tung oil and friction polish, which is similar to French polish but is suitable for lathe work.

Danish oil has the advantage that it soaks into the wood and hardens but it can be renewed regularly. This improves the appearance of the wood.

Where items are to come in contact with foodstuffs, they will need to be finished with a non-toxic finish. Cooking oil or salad oil are suitable for this purpose. Olive oils and other natural oils should not be used as they tend to go off and may cause an unpleasant odour or taste.

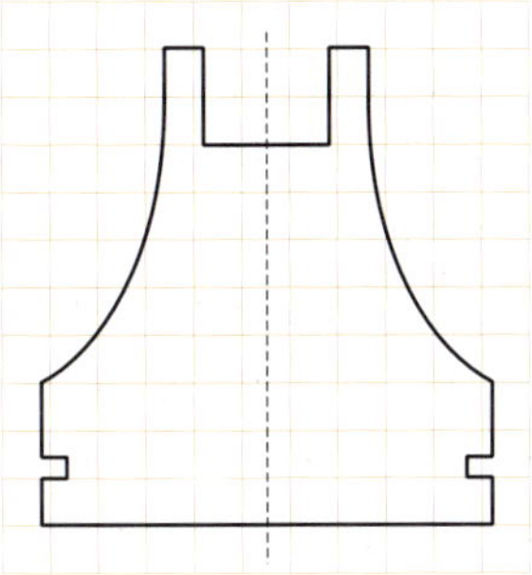

Profile

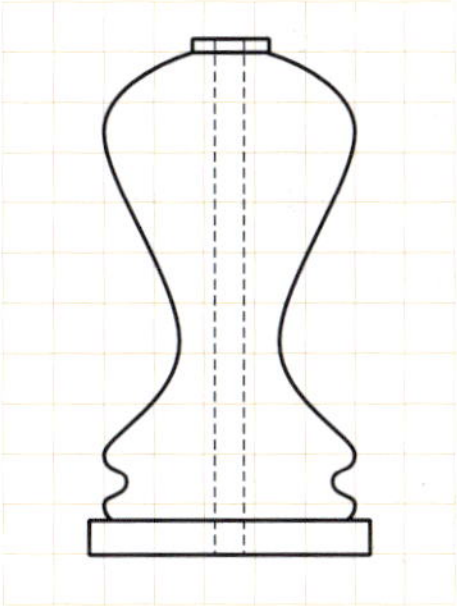

Profile

Some simple project ideas

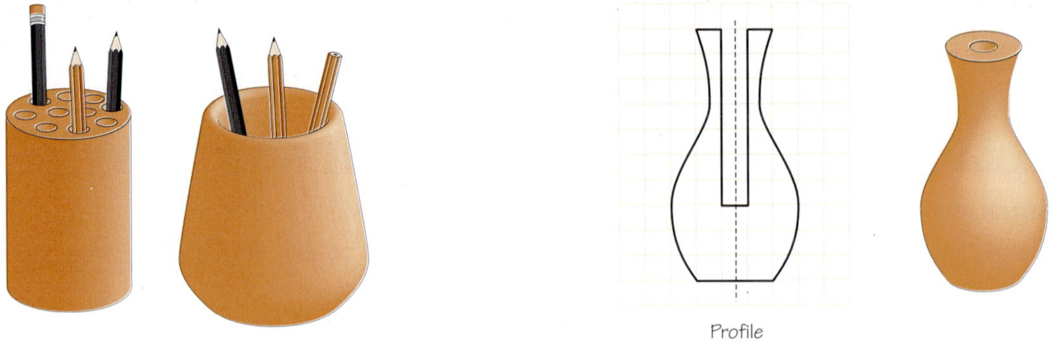

Some more simple project ideas

Exercises

1. Name the following items associated with woodturning and state the function of each one:

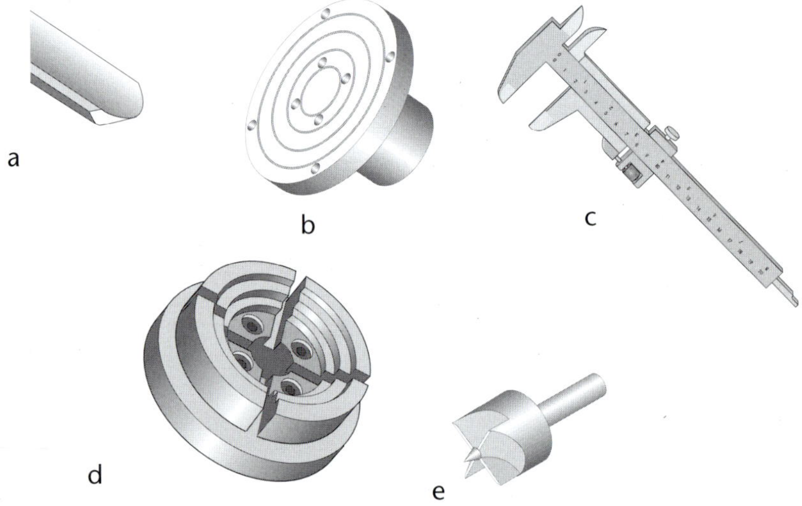

2. What is the function of these pulleys and belt in a lathe?

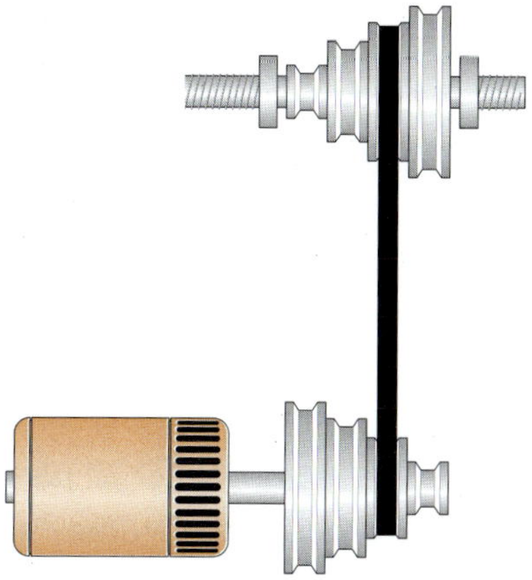

3. The diagram shows a stepped pulley arrangement for a lathe. Indicate on the diagram the position of the V belt, in order to obtain the highest rotational speed for the workpiece.

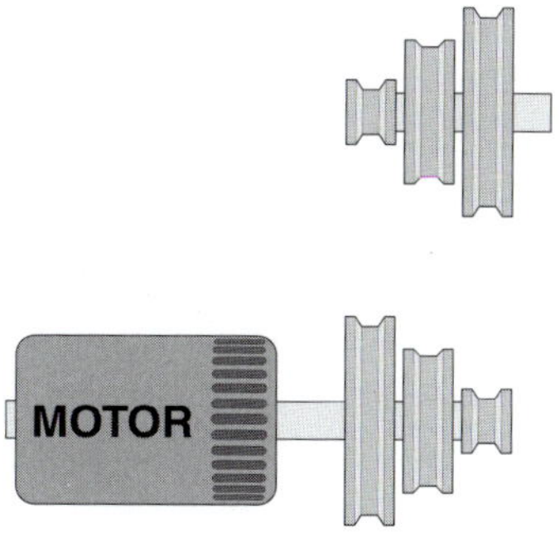

4. Using notes and sketches, describe how a workpiece is attached to the faceplate of the lathe.
5. List four safety considerations which must be observed when using the lathe.
6. List four woods suitable for woodturning.
7. Explain using notes and sketches how you would achieve a good finish on a decorative turned wooden bowl.
8. The sketch shows a spinning top which has been turned on the lathe. Also shown is a sketch of the piece of wood from which the spinning top has been turned.
   (a) You wish to make a number of these tops. Draw a sketch of the profile or template you would have to make in order to ensure that all the finished tops are the same.
   (b) Draw a neat sketch of one tool you would use to turn this top. Name the parts of this tool.

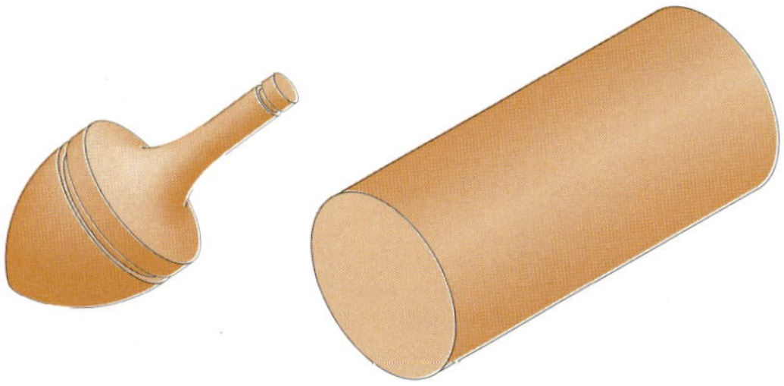

9. Here is a diagram of a lamp stand which is to be made from elm. The item is to be turned on the lathe. Show by means of notes and sketches how you would prepare the square section of wood A, for mounting on the lathe.

10. The diagram shows a salt cellar that is made from beech. The design is to be turned on a wood turning lathe.
    a. Show by means of notes and sketches, how you would prepare the square section of wood A, for mounting on the lathe.
    b. It is required to make a number of similar salt cellars. Show by means of notes and sketches, how the shape can be checked to make sure that they are all identical.
    c. State four safety precautions that must be observed when using a wood turning lathe.

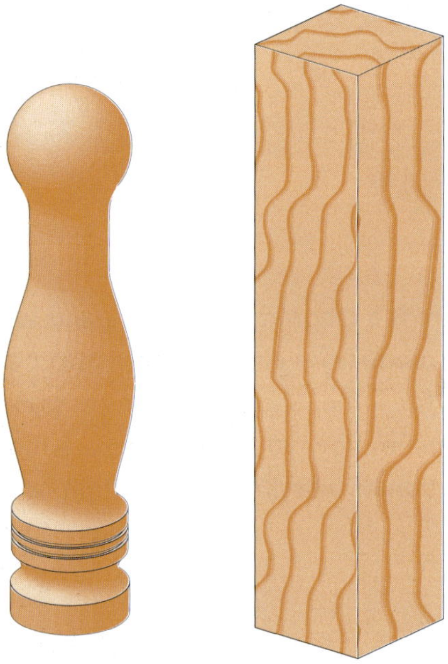

12. Shown in the diagram is a wood turning lathe.
    a. Name the parts of the lathe labelled A,B,C, and D, and state the function of each part.
    b. Shown also in the diagram is a candelabra of wood and mild steel.
        (1) Describe, with notes and sketches, how you would produce part P, and
        (2) How you would shape and form part Q.
    c. Select suitable finishes for all parts of the candelabre, and describe how they would be applied.

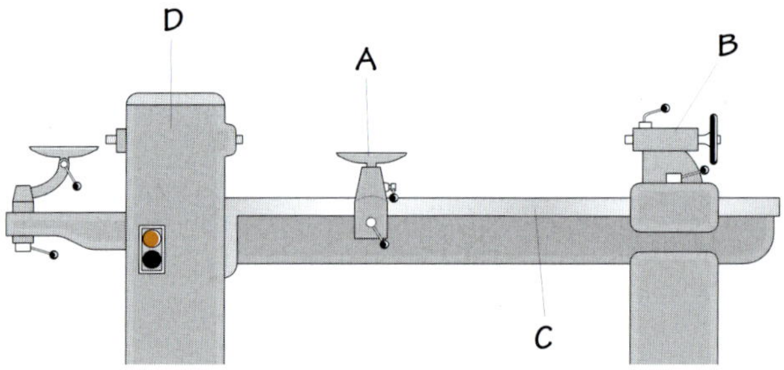

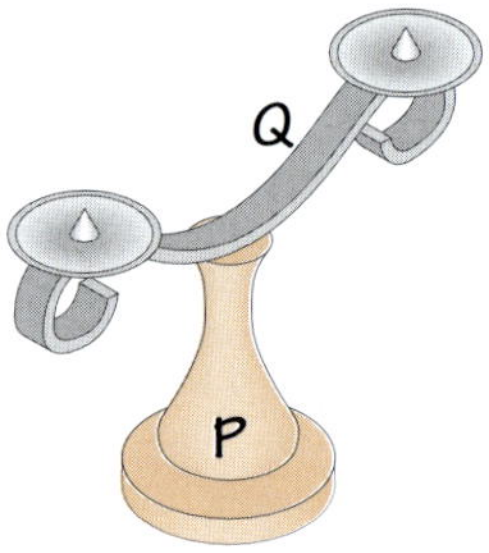

CHAPTER TWENTY-SEVEN
BENDING AND LAMINATING WOOD

We often need to use curved pieces of wood in our project work, for example, curved wooden pieces can be seen in the backs of chairs. If a curved piece is required it can be cut from a solid piece, although this is wasteful of timber. Wood can also be bent into shape.

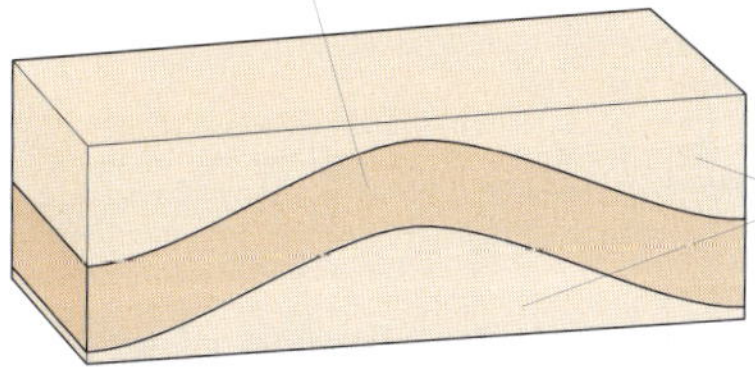

Cutting a curved piece from solid wood leaves a lot of waste

A solid piece is bent to form the chair back

There are two basic methods of bending wood to form a curve. The piece can be bent from solid wood or it can be formed using laminates, which are bent.

It has also been demonstrated that thin layers of wood bonded together can be stronger than solid wood of the same size. This has led to the possibility of different shaped pieces and new processes which have improved the way in which wood can be used. In the construction industry, laminated frames, beams and arches allow wide spans to be crossed. This is called glu-lamination.

Lamination of timber has allowed large spans of roof to be put up without supports in the middle

Sometimes it may be difficult to obtain material in the exact size that you require. Lamination makes it possible to join thinner strips of material together in order to make up the required thickness.

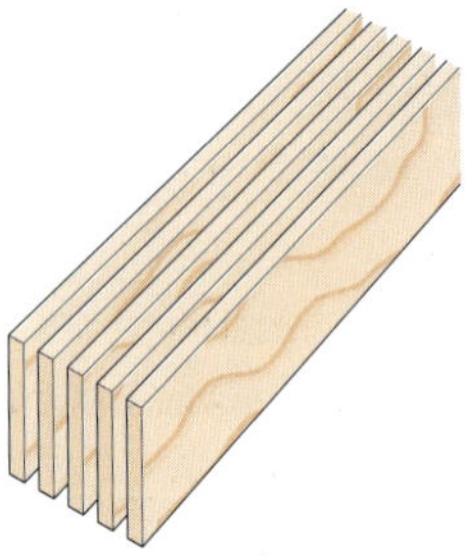

Laminates

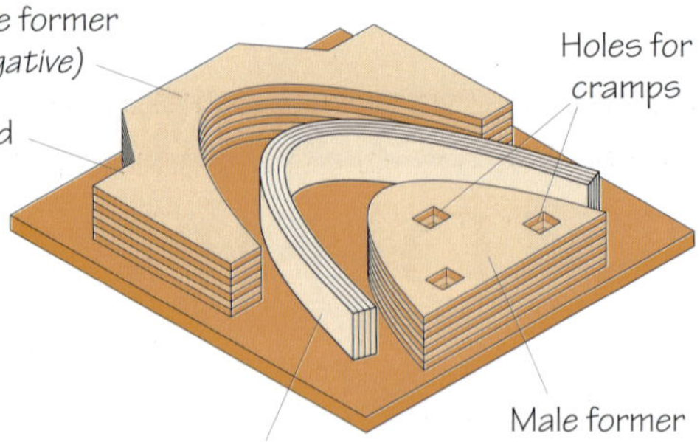

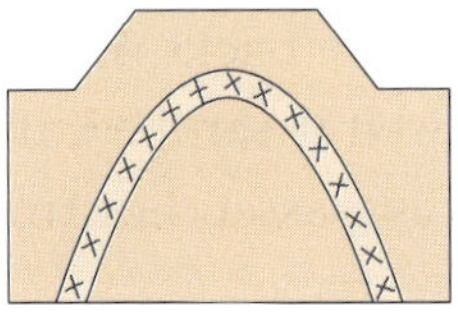

When making a former remove the thickness to be filled by the finished laminates

A former

Lamination – Advantages:

- The laminated piece is stronger than solid material of the same size
- It is also more stable and will not warp as easily
- Laminations can be easily bent into different curved shapes.

Laminated chair

Formers

Formers are usually blocks of wood which are made to form the positive and negative sides of a given shape.

It is important when designing and making formers, that you allow curves to be reasonably large, so that the laminates will bend easily to the curve. The curve on the former should be slightly less than the required curve as the laminates will spring slightly when the pressure is removed. The method of cramping must also be considered so that the former will go together easily.

When assembling laminated pieces, adhesive is applied to the surfaces of the laminates which are to be bonded. Then they are assembled and put loosely into the former. Cramps are used to gradually pull the former closed. It is important that the former be properly lined up so that it closes evenly.

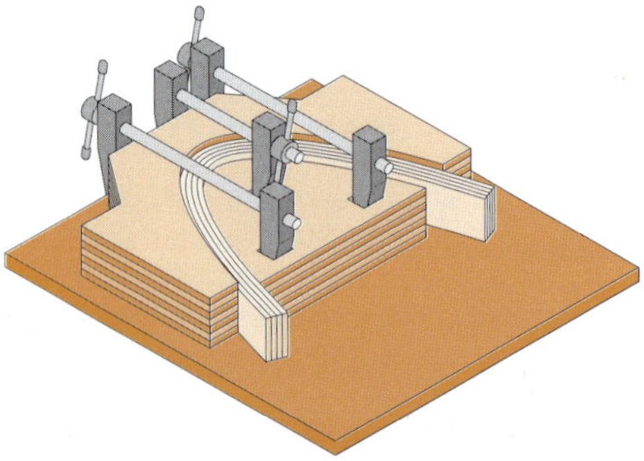

Cramps are used to gradually pull the former closed

Laminating

Laminates are first prepared and are usually relatively thin. When using them in project work they are generally 1mm-4mm thick depending on the thickness of the finished piece. Thinner laminates bend more easily and are less likely to split.

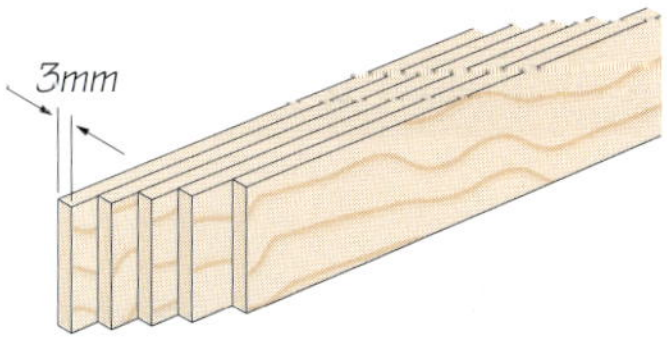

① *Prepare the former. Cut and plane the laminates to the correct thickness. Laminates can be softened with hot water before gluing up.*

These laminates are softened with hot water and then glued together and cramped into a former. This holds the laminates under pressure, until the adhesive has set.

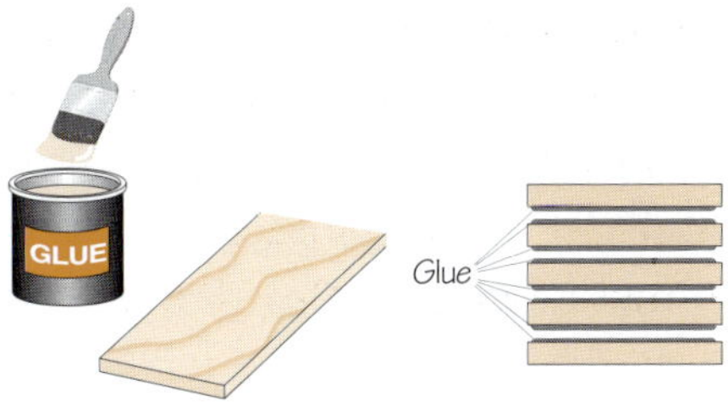

② *Apply glue to both surfaces of the pieces to be bonded.*

The adhesives used should be gap-filling, so that any small cracks between the edges of the laminates are filled. Synthetic resin adhesive or casein adhesive are best. Be sure to have plenty of adhesive ready for the laminates, as the process uses a lot of adhesive.

The grain of each laminate is positioned in the same direction as all the others. This is not the same as for making plywood. A piece of paper is usually placed between the former and the laminates to prevent the laminates being bonded to the former.

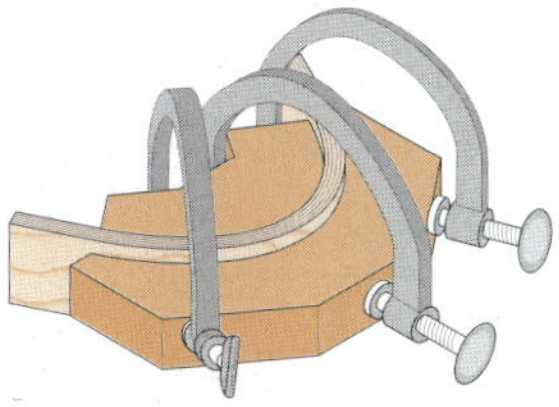

③ *Place the laminates in the former. Align the former and cramp up.*

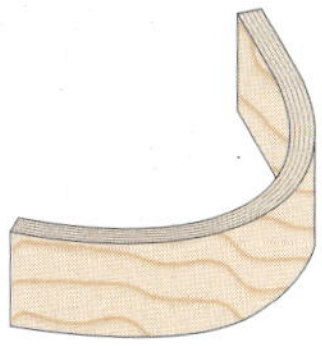

④ *Clean and plane the edges. Cut to length. Sand surfaces.*

Laminating is very successful. However, it is wasteful of timber as a lot of wood is lost in the making of the laminates. For smaller projects veneers can be used as laminates this will cut down the waste.

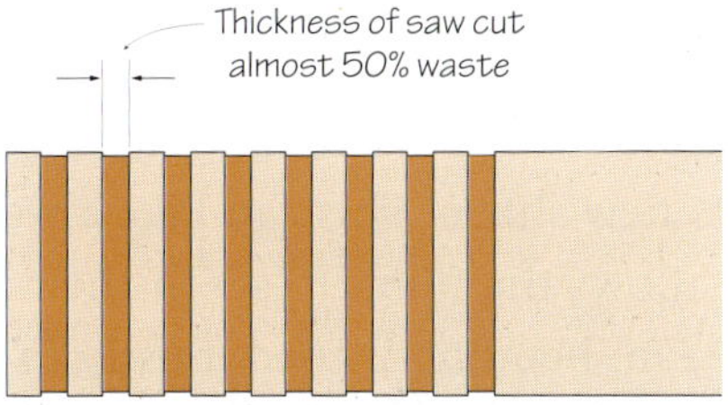

The waste in making the laminate

Steam bending

When bending solid wood it is necessary to soften the wood fibres by heating them with steam. When the fibres are softened the wood will bend more easily. The solid piece is heated in a special steaming box.

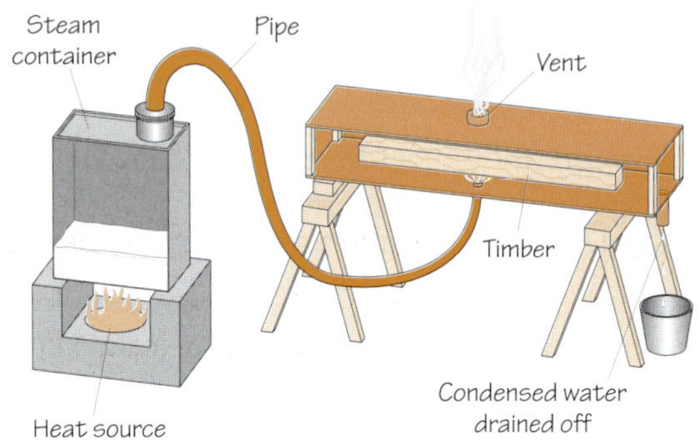

Simple steaming apparatus.
Water is heated in the container producing steam which keeps the inside of the box hot and wet.

The solid wood is heated until it is at a temperature of 100°C all the way through. Then it is left to steam for 45mins for every 25mm thickness. So a piece of 50mm thickness would be left for 90 minutes.

The sketch above shows a simple bending apparatus which would be suitable for small jobs. When the wood is hot it is taken out of the box it must be bent quickly around a former. The centre cramps are secured first and you work from the centre out to the ends. If a large bend is required, repeated heating of the wood and tightening of the cramps should give a good result.

The wood is kept under the pressure of the cramps until the wood is cool and dry and has taken on its new shape. This can take a week or two and it allows the fibres to set in their new position. Steam bending is used mostly in industry where larger, more suitable steaming units and powerful presses are available.

Suitable woods

All woods have some bending properties, but some are more suitable than others because of their durability and flexibility.

Woods suitable for bending	
Very flexible	Elm
Flexible	Ash, Beech, Birch, Oak, Sycamore, Walnut
Some flexibility	Mahogany, Spruce

Stacking

Often a large block of timber is needed such as for carved work. Smaller blocks of wood can be built up to make a larger block which is then turned, shaped or carved. A famous modern furniture maker, John Makepeace, uses this technique to make tables chairs, etc.

The blocks of wood are bonded with adhesive and are built up like brickwork with the joints staggered, which makes them strong.

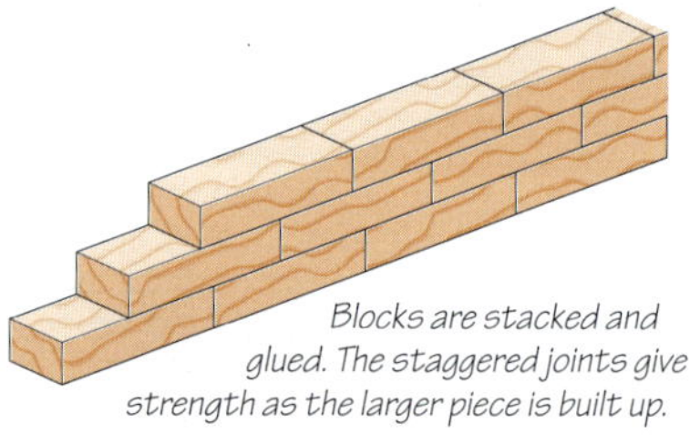

Stacking of blocks

Saw kerfing

This is a method of bending a piece of solid wood leaving the front face of the piece intact. A piece of wood will bend if it is thin enough so, by cutting grooves in a thicker piece it allows some bending to take place. When the piece is bent it is fixed into shape using screws and glue. The back of the piece must be hidden so this method has only limited use.

Saw kerfing

Exercises

1. List two ways in which wood can be bent.
2. Give the names of three woods which are suitable for bending.
3. Explain the term 'lamination'.
4. Give two examples of where laminating could be used in everyday furniture.
5. Why is lamination a costly method of construction?
6. Why is wood steamed before it is bent?
7. Give an example of where pieces of steam bent solid wood could be used in furniture.
8. The diagram shows a flower-pot stand/planter. With the aid of notes and sketches, describe a suitable method of forming the laminated leg A.

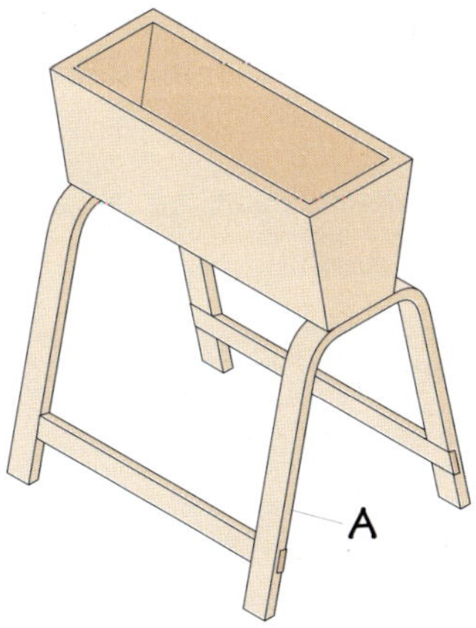

9. Shown in the diagram is a chair leg that is to be formed by laminating. What method is used to make the laminates more flexible when producing such a shape?

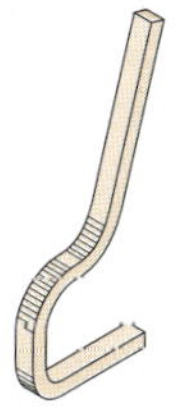

10. (a) Draw the elevation and one end view of the coffee table shown in the diagram. Insert four main dimensions scale 1:4.

10. (b) With the aid of sketches, suggest a suitable method of forming the laminated leg at A in the sketch of the coffee table.

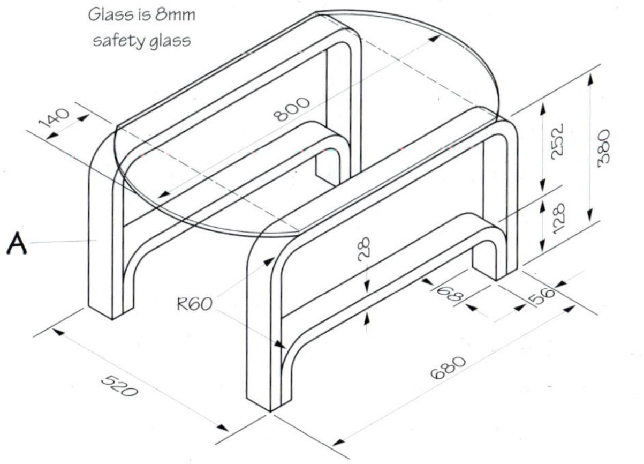

CHAPTER TWENTY-EIGHT

ADHESIVES

Adhesives or glues have been used for hundreds of years in woodwork. In recent times a huge number of new bonding products have been developed for use with wood and other materials. It is very important to choose the correct adhesive for the job so that you get the best results.

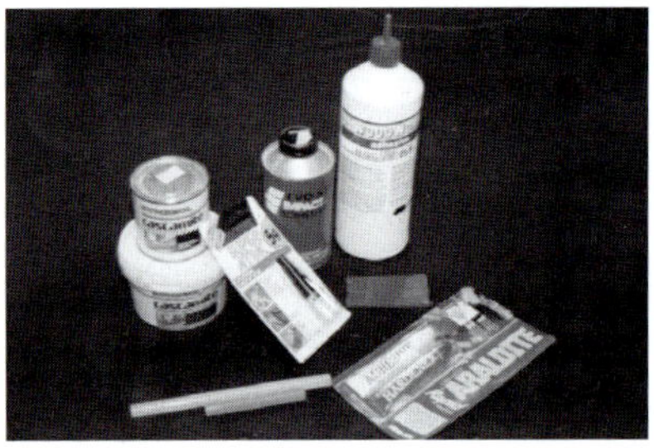

There are many adhesives available – each with different properties

Some of these adhesives are made with strong chemicals and it is important that great care is taken when preparing and using adhesives.

> **BEWARE!** Always read and follow all warnings and instructions on adhesive containers

Adhesives are used to bond materials together or to reinforce a joint in materials, to do this successfully the adhesive must be durable and strong. Adhesives may be required to set without the aid of cramps, or to be water resistant. These and other properties are being developed and improved all the time.

In many cases the adhesive joint can be stronger than the material itself. Under stress the material will often break before the bonded joint. You could try some tests to show this effect.

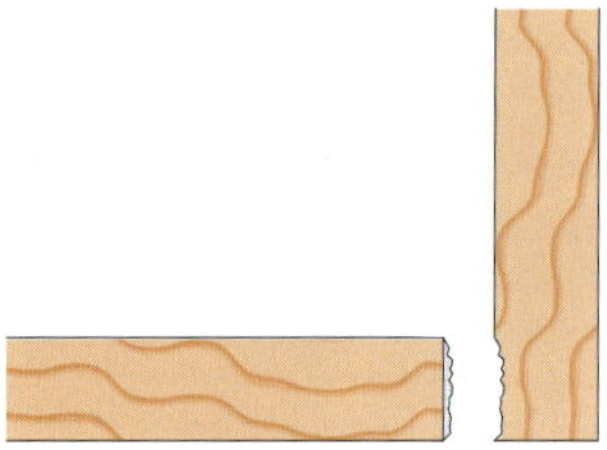

The bonded joint is often stronger than the material

How an adhesive works

An adhesive should be applied according to the manufacturer's instructions, usually covering the surfaces of the pieces to be joined. The adhesive should be thinly applied. When the pieces have been bonded together, the glue forms a layer of material which holds the surfaces together. When a joint is bonded this area of adhesive is large which makes the joint strong.

Adhesives set in a number of ways.

- Some set when a solvent evaporates
- Some need heat to allow the glue to set, these can be expensive

- Some need to be combined with a catalyst or hardener, which causes a chemical reaction allowing the glue to set.

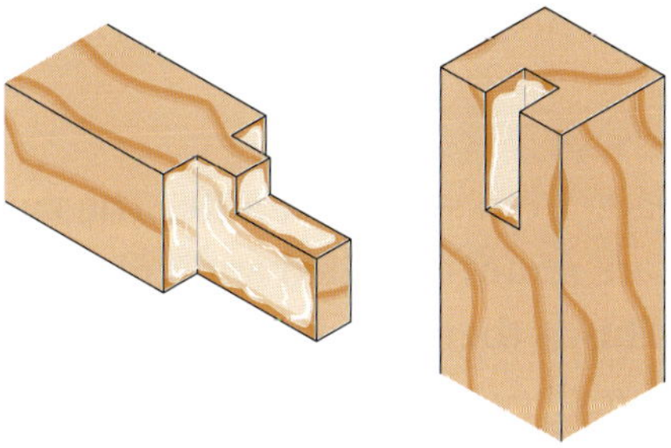

Sketch of adhesive correctly applied to a joint

The adhesive works in two ways to hold the joint together:

- **Specific adhesion** This is the bonding or holding power of the adhesive which holds the surfaces together.
- **Mechanical adhesion** The adhesive flows into cracks and cell cavities on the material and when it sets it gives increased grip to the adhesive joint.

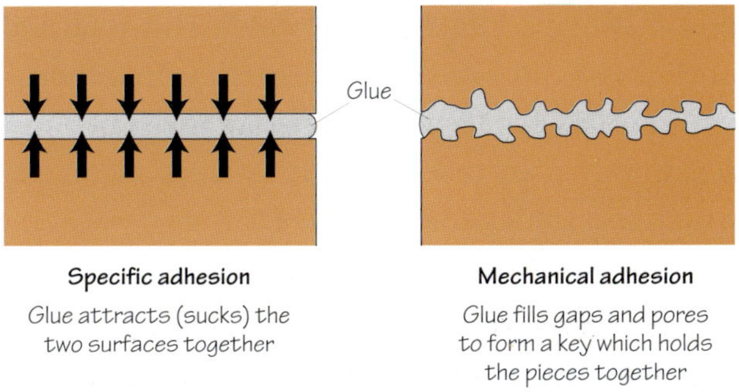

Specific adhesion – Mechanical adhesion

Adhesive terms

Shelf life

Adhesives can usually be stored before use. The shelf life of the adhesive is the time recommended by the manufacturer before which the adhesive should be used. Some adhesives will keep for a long time in their sealed containers. But this time reduces when the container is opened.

Pot life

Many adhesives must be mixed before use or a small amount is poured into a container to be used during assembly of a project. The pot life of an adhesive is the amount of time the adhesive or mixture will remain suitable for use. The adhesive must be used before this time has elapsed. Pot life is also known as **open assembly time**.

Closed assembly time

When the glue has been applied the pieces are assembled and they may require some adjustments. The closed assembly time is the amount of time which is available for adjustments before the final bond starts to form. With contact adhesives this time is very short.

Types of adhesive

Adhesives can be put into three broad groups:

- **Protein adhesives** – made from natural products
- **Synthetic adhesives** – made from synthetic products
- **Rubber based adhesives** – contact adhesives.

Protein adhesives

Scotch glue

This is often called **animal** or **pearl glue**. It is made from the bones and hides of animals. These are boiled and the liquid is drained off. This then cools to a jelly and eventually becomes hard. It is then cut into slabs these are broken into small pieces before they can be used.

Nowadays this adhesive is produced as small toffee coloured beads or 'pearls' which are ready to be processed into workable adhesive.

Scotch glue pearls

The adhesive is prepared by placing the pearls into water which is contained in the inner container of a glue-pot. This is allowed to soak overnight. After soaking the container is placed into the water filled glue-pot and heated. The water in the outer pot heats the contents of the inner pot without burning it (rather like melting chocolate in a bowl over a saucepan of hot water). The glue is stirred until it melts. If the mixture is too thick it can be watered down. Modern glue-pots are electrically heated.

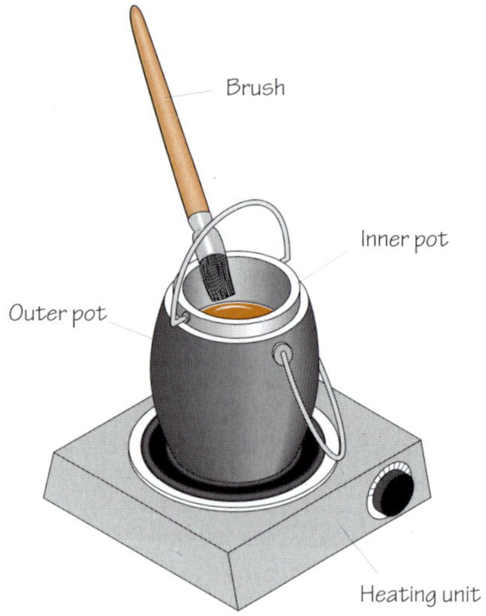

Glue- pot for preparing scotch glue

Scotch glue was very common at one time and is particularly suited for veneering. It has a number of advantages and disadvantages which are shown below.

Casein adhesive

This is made from skimmed milk. The curds of the milk are removed, dried and ground to a fine powder. This is then mixed with other chemicals to form the glue.

The glue which is a white powder must be mixed with water. The added chemical powders give the glue the following qualities:

Added Powders	
Chemical	**Quality**
Lime	Gives water resistance
Sodium salt & borax	Makes the glue powder soluble in water

To prepare the glue the powder is mixed in a non-metallic container with water. This is stirred until it is a thick creamy consistency. It is then left to stand for 15 minutes before use. The most commonly used casein glue is called 'Cascomite', which is a tradename.

Scotch Glue	
Advantages	**Disadvantages**
■ Soluble in water	■ The preparation of the glue takes a long time
■ Heat will break the bond (useful for rectifying mistakes)	■ Special equipment is needed.
■ Doesn't harden quickly so adjustments can be made before the glue sets	■ It has a strong smell
■ It has a long shelf life	■ It is not water or heat resistant
	■ The glue must be applied hot and the work must be done quickly before the glue cools
	■ Not as strong as synthetic glues

Casein glue	
Advantages	**Disadvantages**
■ It gives a strong bond	■ It can stain certain woods – e.g. oak and mahogany
■ It has a long shelf life	■ Pressure is required while the glue sets
■ It is heat resistant	■ It has a short pot life so only mix what is required
■ It is water resistant	■ It will not resist prolonged damp conditions
■ Quick and easy to mix	■ It can be attacked by moulds and bacteria
■ You only mix what you need so there is little waste	

Synthetic adhesives

There are a variety of synthetic adhesives and they have advantages over glues made from natural products. The most widely used modern adhesive is synthetic and is called **Polyvinyl acetate (PVA)**.

Polyvinyl acetate (PVA)

It is the most common wood adhesive. It is a thick white liquid which is soluble in water, but a water resistant type is available. It is used straight from the bottle or container and needs no preparation.

PVA is generally not as strong as the other types of synthetic resin adhesives, but it does not require a catalyst or accelerator to allow the bond to set.

Pieces being glued do need to be kept under pressure while the glue sets and this takes from 4 hours to 12 hours usually.

Urea formaldehyde

This is used for indoor work. It has adequate strength and water resistance. This adhesive is applied by putting the adhesive on one surface and the hardener on the other before putting them together. They are used in plywood manufacture.

BEWARE! Care must be taken with two part glues, like Urea formaldehyde, as the hardeners are sometimes damaging to the skin

Phenol formaldehyde

This glue is a very strong glue and is resistant to decay by moulds, acids and other solvents. These glues are durable and are used in the manufacture of plywood, including exterior quality plywood.

The glue line is dark and these glues are expensive. Heat is generally required for the glue to set.

Resorcinol formaldehyde

This is a very durable adhesive, even under extreme weather conditions. It is a **Weather and Boil Proof** Adhesive (WBP) and is used in the manufacture of WBP plywood. It is resistant to water and decay by micro-organisms, but it is an expensive glue.

Epoxy resins

Epoxy resin glues and hardeners come in the form of thick, stiff, creams. They have many applications and are specially suitable for bonding non-porous materials, such as metals, glass, wood and plastics. They are usually supplied as two part adhesives and they are very costly.

Super glues (cyanoacrylates)

Super glues are popular glues which have a wide variety of uses. The glue sets in seconds and forms a very strong bond. These glues are usually sold in small quantities and are expensive.

> **BEWARE** Be very careful when using super glues as they can be dangerous. Skin can be bonded together or to the piece of work quite quickly, and the bond is difficult to break

Rubber based (contact) adhesives

Contact adhesives are made from natural or synthetic forms of rubber. Contact adhesive is also called impact adhesive because the bond is formed very quickly when the two surfaces are brought into contact. There are many types available and they are used generally to bond thin pieces of materials together, such as veneers and laminates to wood, but they are not suitable for use on wood joints.

The glue is applied with a spreader or roller to both surfaces to be bonded. After being allowed to become 'touch dry' the surfaces are carefully brought into contact and the bond is immediately formed. Care must be taken to align the two surfaces and to avoid trapping air pockets under the material. Usually the piece being bonded is larger than needed and the excess is trimmed off when the glue has set.

Contact glue is used to bond veneers, metals, plastic laminates, leather, textiles and wood.

> **BEWARE** Rubber based adhesives usually contain solvents and chemicals which can be damaging to your health if they come in contact with skin or the fumes are inhaled.
> Read and follow all warnings and instructions on the labels

Synthetic resin glues	
Advantages	**Disadvantages**
■ Generally easy to work with	■ They can stain some woods
■ There are many types available for bonding many materials	■ They are generally expensive
■ Some types set rapidly	■ They may need heat to assist the setting of the glue
■ They have good strength	
■ They work well in low temperatures	
■ They are capable of bonding non-porous materials	

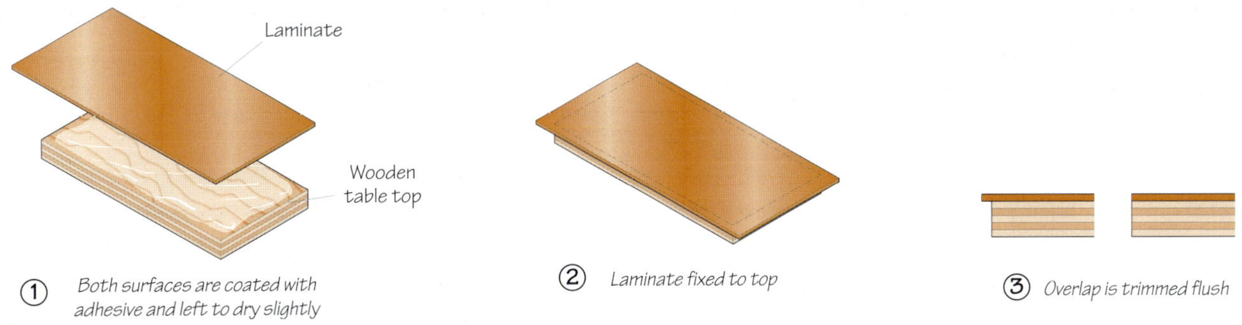

Bonding a laminate to a table top

Rubber based adhesives	
Advantages	**Disadvantages**
■ The bond is formed quickly	■ They are not suitable for woodwork joints
■ No need for cramps while glue sets	■ They can be dangerous if fumes are inhaled
■ They are easily applied	■ Care must be taken when bonding the pieces as the bond is immediate
■ There are a variety of different types for different purposes	■ They will bond a variety of materials
	■ They can be messy to work with

Applying adhesive

When working on a project, it is satisfying to finally see your work coming together. However, it is important to take care when applying adhesive because if not done correctly, joints may be weak or excess adhesive may cause staining if not properly cleaned off.

The correct adhesive should be selected for the particular materials being bonded. The table on the next page will act as a guide for you to select the correct glue for the job.

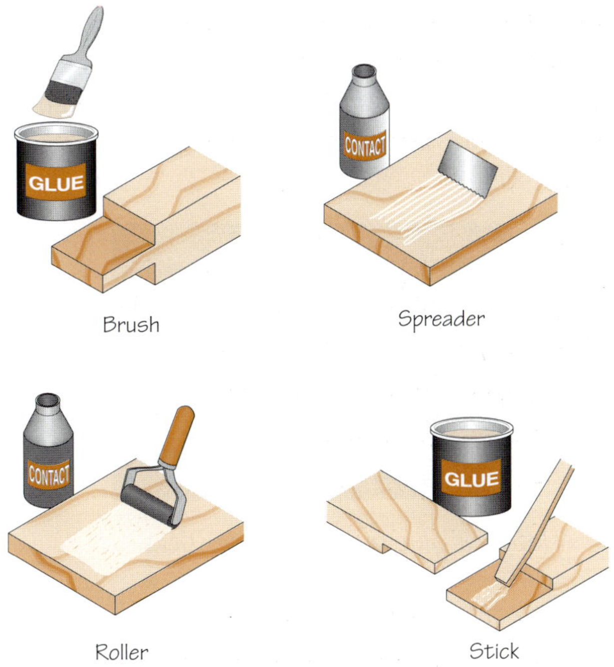

Methods of applying adhesive

Adhesive selection grid						
	Wood	**Metal**	**Acrylic**	**Plastic laminate**	**Rubber**	**Polystyrene**
Wood	PVA	Epoxy resin	Epoxy resin	Contact adhesive	Contact adhesive	PVA
Metal	Epoxy resin	Epoxy resin	Epoxy resin	Contact adhesive	Contact adhesive	PVA
Acrylic	Epoxy resin	Epoxy resin	Epoxy resin	Contact adhesive	Contact adhesive	PVA
Plastic Laminate	Contact	Contact	Contact	Contact	Contact	PVA
Rubber	Contact adhesive	Contact adhesive	Contact adhesive	Contact adhesive	Contact adhesive	PVA
Polystyrene	PVA	PVA	PVA	PVA	PVA	PVA

The method of applying the glue may depend on the type of adhesive. Usually PVA glue is applied using a small brush which will ensure that the surfaces are covered thinly and evenly. A spreader is often used with impact adhesive to get a film of even depth on the surfaces to be bonded.

Thermo-glues are made and these are heated electrically in a hot melt glue gun. The glue is supplied in the form of sticks of glue. Different glue sticks are available for various specialist jobs.

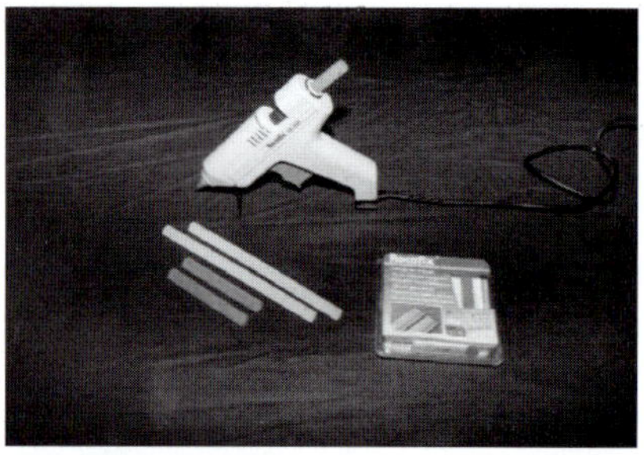

Hot melt glue gun with glue sticks

Joints should be glued soon after they have been worked as this gives a stronger bond. The natural oils contained in certain woods (e.g. teak) can be cleaned off using methylated spirit before bonding, as the oils may affect the strength of the bond.

Assembly

It is important to fit all joints dry, before applying glue to check the fit, etc. When the joints are glued they usually need to be held in place until the glue sets. This is generally done using cramps of some sort, although nails and screws can also be used to hold the pieces together. Different cramps are used according to the situation.

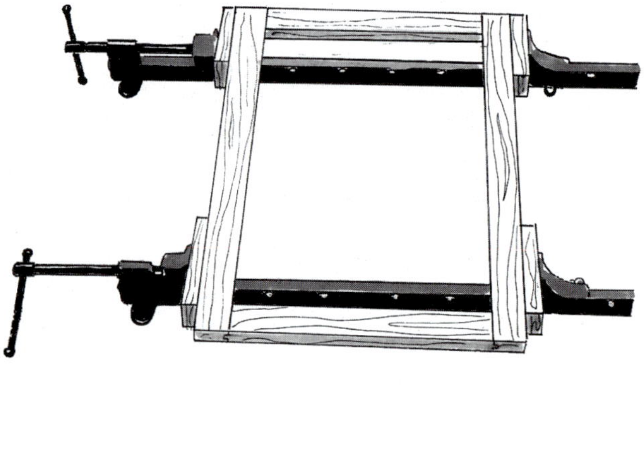

Assembling a frame using sash cramp

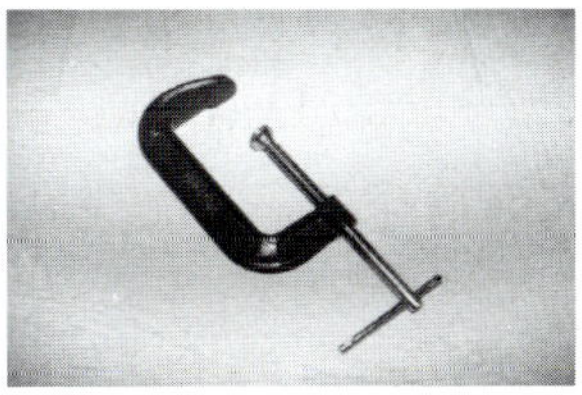

G-Cramp

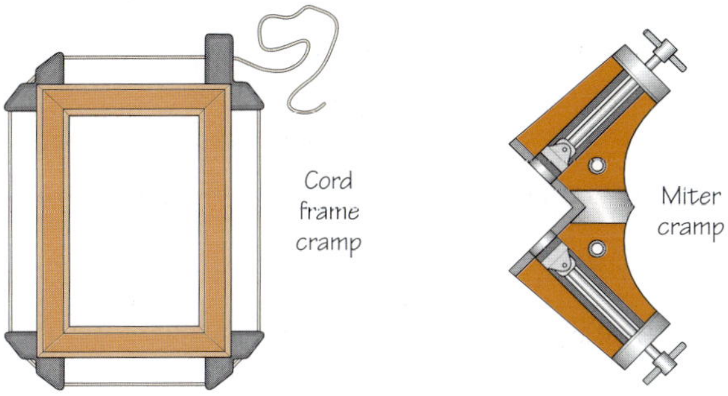

Mitre cramp & framing cramp

After assembly the joints are checked for squareness and all excess glue is wiped away (with a damp cloth). If the excess glue is left to set it will seal the wood surface and cause staining when a finish is applied.

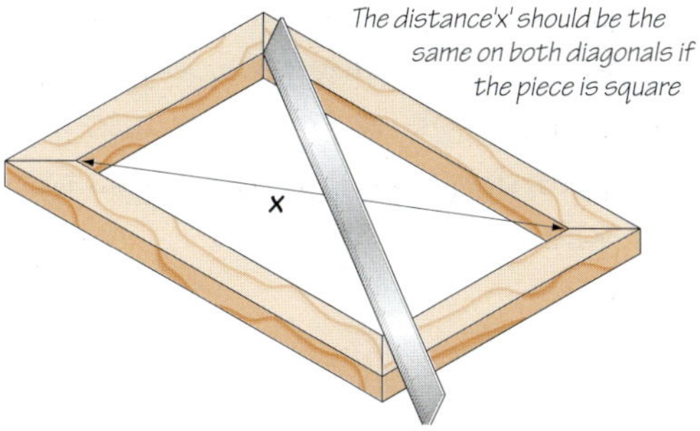

Checking a frame for square

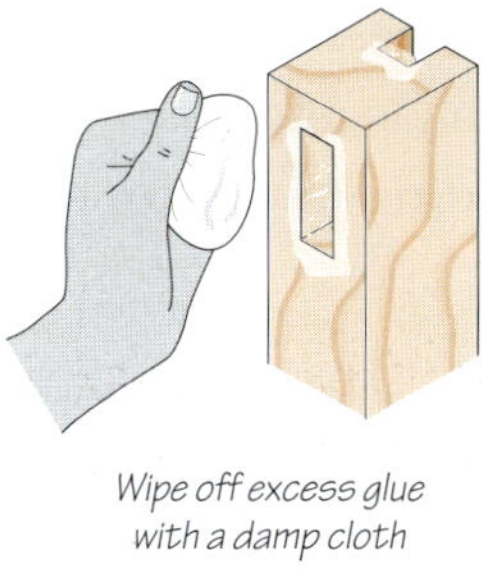

Wipe off excess glue with a damp cloth

Exercises

1. List three of the warnings on the labels on adhesive containers.
2. List two adhesives made from natural sources.
3. Explain the following terms associated with adhesives:
   Pot life — Glue spreader
   Shelf life — Glue gun.
4. Why is a joint that is glued normally much stronger than one which relies only on nails or screws?
5. Explain the terms 'specific adhesion' and 'mechanical adhesion'.
6. Give two ways in which adhesive can be applied.
7. What do the letters PVA stand for?
8. What do the letters WBP stand for?
9. Give three disadvantages of contact glue.
10. Suggest an adhesive for bonding .
    Fabric to wood — Acrylic to acrylic
    Wood to wood.
11. You wish to make a garden seat. Which type of glue would you recommend and why?
12. The diagram shows a decorative panel with a veneered design. Select the most suitable one for this panel, and give reasons for your choice.

CHAPTER TWENTY-NINE

FINISHES

Look at the furniture at home or any of the many items which we use every day. All of these items have surfaces which look well and are pleasant to touch. Can you imagine the handle of a hammer with a finish like rough sandpaper; or a road surface which is as smooth as glass? Surfaces must look well and they must also be practical and safe.

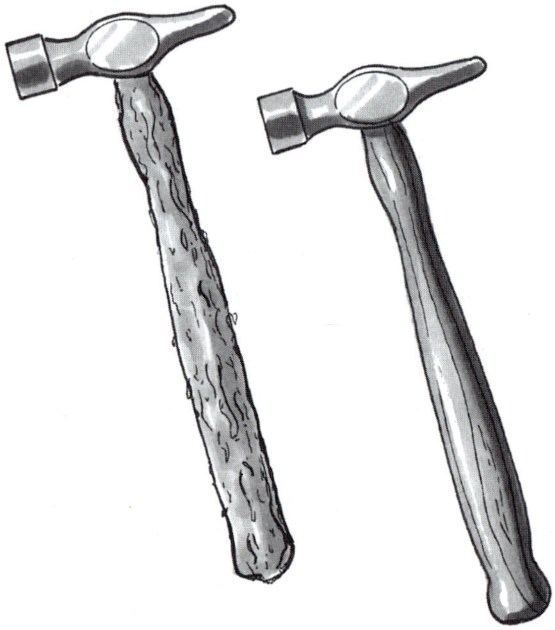

The reasons for finishing are as follows:

- To protect the surfaces and the material in an item
- To prolong the life of the item.
- To improve the appearance of the item.

Materials are damaged with general wear and tear, the weather, insects, fungi, chemicals, water, heat, etc. It is therefore important that items are properly finished.

Spending time and effort on finishing your work properly will give it a neat, well made appearance. It will be time very well spent.

The choice of finish will vary with the nature of the piece and also with the function of the item. Health and safety considerations for example will dictate that paints used on children's toys must be lead-free, as children will often put toys into their mouths. Food implements – bowls, plates, etc, must also be finished with finishes which will not affect the food in any way.

Abrasive paper

Most of the work you do in the preparation of a surface finish uses some sort of abrasive paper. Abrasive paper is often called sandpaper and in recent years there have been many developments in the way these are made and used. The widespread use of sanding machines has led to the need for abrasive papers of various shapes, sizes and quality.

Grit

There are many different types of grit which are bonded to the paper or backing to make the sandpaper that is familiar to us.

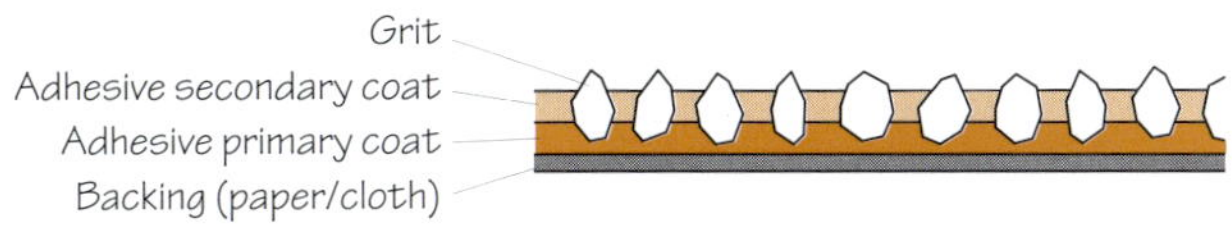

Composition of abrasive paper

The abrasive grit is crushed into pieces which are then passed through sieves to produce grits of different coarseness. The grit size graded according to the European Grading System for abrasive papers which uses the number of holes in $25mm^2$ of the sieve mesh.

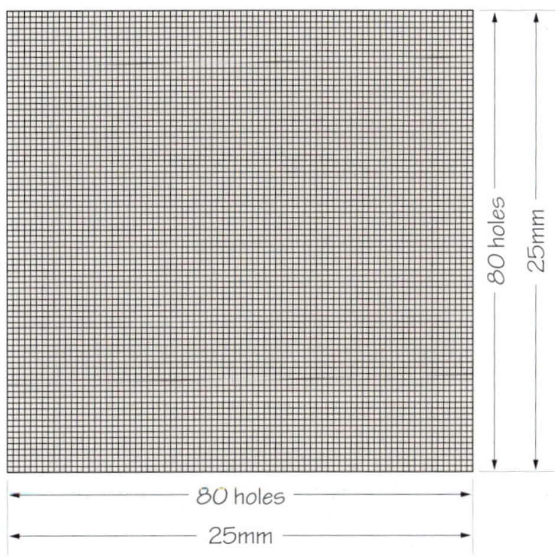

European grading system (80 grit)

The table below shows the British Standard and European Standard systems. The more common grades are shown, but individual manufacturers may vary slightly. The grades can normally be read on the back of the sheet.

	European System	British System
Coarse	36	3s
Medium	40, 60, 80	$2\frac{1}{2}$, M_2, F_2
Fine	100, 120, 150, 180	$1\frac{1}{2}$, 1, F
Very fine	220, 240, 360	0, 00, 000

Once the grit has been graded it is bonded to the backing with a suitable adhesive.

Glass

Bottle glass is used to make abrasive. It is perhaps the most widely used abrasive because it is freely available and inexpensive. Glass abrasive is soft compared with other modern abrasives. It is mostly used for sanding by hand and not for machine sanding.

Garnet

Garnets are semi-precious stones often found in the window displays of jewellery shops. The poorer quality and smaller sized ones are used for making abrasive paper. Garnet paper is made as described above and the abrasive is harder than glass and so wears better. Garnet paper is popular with cabinet makers, as it yields a very smooth finish to wood. It is bonded to cloth and paper backing and can be used for hand and machine sanding.

Aluminium oxide

This is an oxide of aluminium. It is a hard and tough abrasive and it can withstand the pressure of machine sanding. Its toughness makes it suitable for sanding hardwoods and for use on belt sanders. Softwoods will tend to clog the grains of the abrasive, however.

Silicone carbide

Silicone carbide is made by heating a mixture of coal and quartz in a furnace. This produces a substance called carborundum. This abrasive is the hardest of all abrasive grits, but it is expensive, due to the cost of processing the material. It is often referred to as wet and dry sandpaper as it can be used in a wet state as well as in a dry state. It is most suitable for sanding hard compact material surfaces such as glass, plastics, and metals such as brass and copper.

Backings

There are a number of different backing materials which can be used to make abrasive paper. The one used will depend on the type of use the abrasive will get. A strong, flexible backing is needed to make a sanding belt for a sander, for example.

Paper

Paper and light card is used with glass and other abrasives for producing papers to be used for hand finishing and light power tool work. They have good strength and durability for this kind of function.

Vulcanised cloth

This is cloth which has been treated with rubber to add strength and durability. It is used on belts for belt sanders and machine sanders.

Wire wool

As the name suggests this is similar to a kitchen pad but without the soap. Wire wool can be obtained in different grades of fineness from 0 grade (coarse) to 0000 grade (very fine). It is used for fine finishing particularly de-nibbing french polish and varnish between coats.

Wire wool

Finishing

There are two stages in achieving a good finish. The first is getting a smooth **surface finish** and the second is the **applied finish**. The applied finish is put on and gives the protection to the piece.

Surface finishing

Before an applied finish is put onto a piece of work the surfaces of the piece must be prepared properly.

The surfaces can be made smooth and flat with a smoothing plane. This removes any machining marks from the piece. The pencil lines, etc. can be rubbed out and cleaned off before sanding. Surfaces can be further smoothed down with a cabinet scraper.

Any nails or panel pins must be punched below the surface of timber and all holes and cracks filled with an appropriate wood filler. The excess filler is then wiped off with a damp cloth. There are many fillers available in different colours and you should choose the right one to match the wood.

The work is then sanded using an abrasive paper. This removes marks, scratches, or any other blemishes and also gives a smooth, clean surface. It is usual to use abrasives of varying fineness to gradually achieve the best result. You might begin with a 80 – 100 grit, then a 180 grit and finally a 300 grit to get the very best result with quality hardwoods.

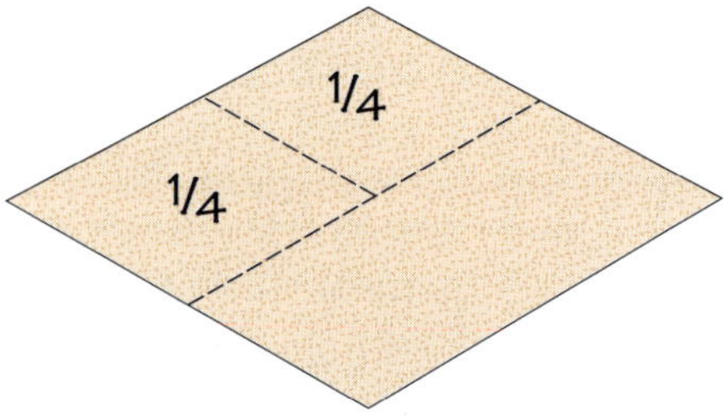

Quarter sheets of glasspaper easily fit around a sanding block

When sanding a piece by hand the sandpaper can be held around a cork sanding block for best results. **Cork** is a wooden material, which has elastic properties and is nearly waterproof. It is made from the thick bark of an evergreen oak tree, grown in Spain, Portugal and other Mediterranean countries. The elastic properties of cork allows the sandpaper to wear more evenly and the sand paper is less likely to clog.

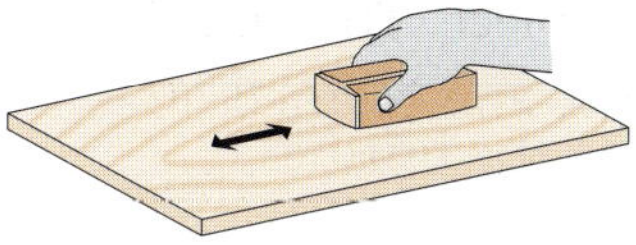

Sand in the direction of the grain

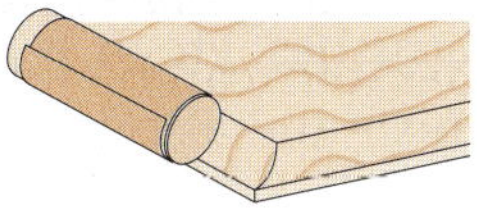

Wrap sandpaper around a dowel to sand a moulding

Direction of sanding

The sanding is done in the direction of the grain of the wood to avoid scratching the surface of the piece. When machine sanding this must also be observed on the surfaces of the piece, but the end grain of wood can be sanded in all directions. Any scratches caused or not removed by sanding will only be exaggerated by stains or other applied finishes. Softwoods should be sanded at an angle of 20° to the grain direction. This is because the wood is soft and if sanded straight along the grain the harder portions of the grain are left in ridges while the softer portions are cut away.

To leave your hands free to do the sanding, it is best to hold pieces being sanded in the vice or clamped to the bench by means of a G-clamp.

Sanding the surfaces of a piece will leave sharp edges where the surfaces meet. These need to be removed by making a couple of passes of the sandpaper over the edge.

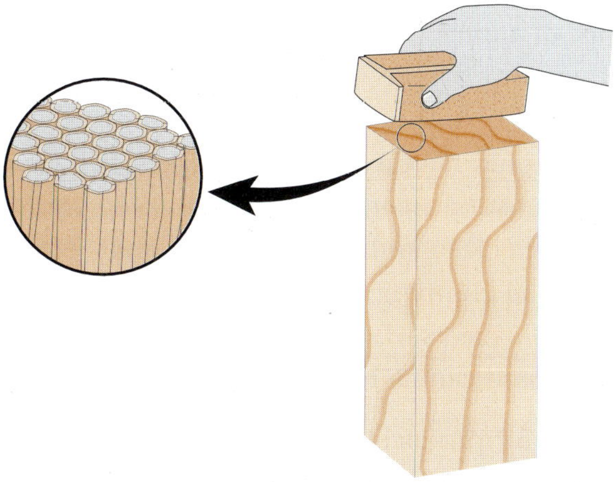

End grain can be sanded in almost any direction, because it is the ends of the cells which are being sanded and they have no particular direction.

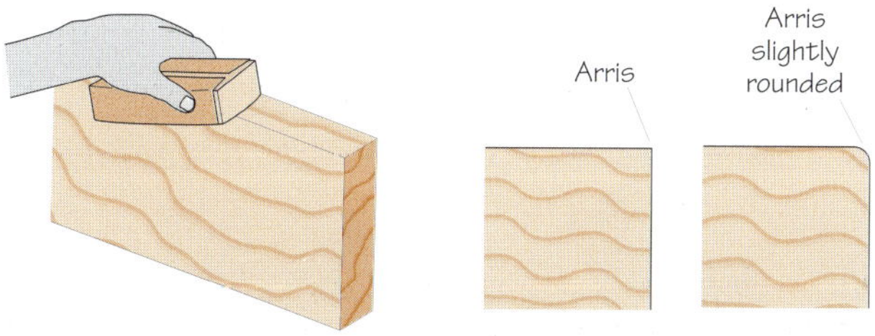

Sharp edges must be removed with a light pass of the sandpaper

Care should be taken when sanding joints before they are bonded, as too much sanding may loosen the fit when they are eventually bonded.

The insides of projects, for example, a jewellery box should be sanded before it goes together as it is difficult to sand into the corners afterwards.

When to stop?

You will be finished with the surface preparation when you are satisfied that you have achieved a smooth, clean, uniform finished surface on your piece. The degree of smoothness will depend on the type of wood, the type of project and the choice of applied finish which you will be putting onto the piece – for example, items which will be finished with danish oil or french polish should have a very well finished surface.

Care must be taken at all times to keep your bench area clean and free from chippings, etc, as bumps and chippings can easily damage a good quality finished surface. An old blanket or piece of cardboard can be used as a cushion to protect your work during surface finishing.

Scrapers

Metal cabinet scrapers can be used to help in the smoothing of the pieces. They can also be used to smooth out difficult rough pieces left after planing. Special scrapers are available to remove old finishes such as paint on old finished surfaces before refinishing.

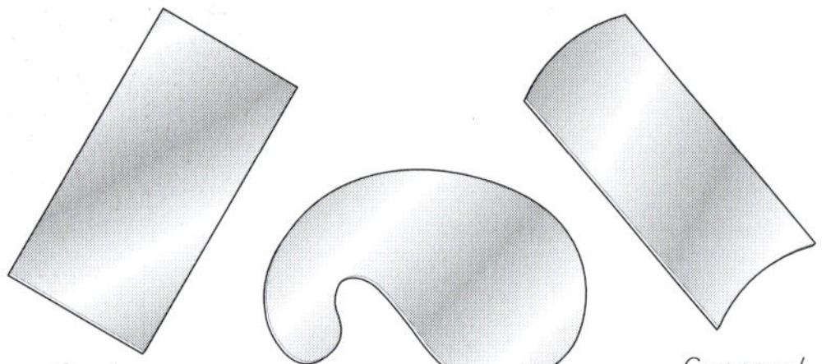

Cabinet scrapers

Applied finishes

Wood is rarely left unfinished or with just a smooth sanded surface, because this gives little protection to the wood. Usually there is a protective coating applied to it.

The choice of applied finish depends on the:

- Function of the item
- The type of wood – natural woods should be displayed in their natural beauty
- Where it is to be used – inside or outside
- Personal choice.

We have already covered wood preservatives and these too are wood finishes, which give protection against weathering, fungal and insect attack.

Usually finishes are suspended or dissolved in a liquid, usually a solvent such as white spirit or methylated spirits. The solvent helps penetration of the finish and allows it to dry more quickly.

White spirit

This solvent dilutes oil-based paints and varnishes, etc. It is used for thinning out the finish and also for cleaning the brushes afterwards.

Methylated spirit

This is an alcohol (methanol) spirit which is purple in colour due to a chemical additive. It is used for french polishing to make the polish and in the spiriting off process.

Bottles of methylated spirit and white spirit

Paint

Probably the most widely used (and possibly misused) wood finish in use at present. Paint is often used to cover naturally beautiful woods used in front doors, shop fronts and windows.

Paint is a finish which is particularly suitable for outdoor use because it is durable and tough. However, it is difficult to apply correctly.

Painting woodwork

Wood is first prepared with a good surface finish. The timber should be sanded to a 120 grit paper. All knots must be sealed with a **knotting** solution. The surfaces of the wood, especially the end grain, are then primed with a **wood primer**.

Do not overload the brush as the paint will run

Priming

This coat of special light paint acts as a base for the undercoat. It seals all holes and crevices of the wood, including end grain. The priming coat protects all of the surfaces and gives good protection against moisture. In external work it is good practice to give joints a coat of primer before assembly, to protect them from moisture should any cracks occur. It is important that all surfaces are covered well, making sure that all holes, cracks and end grain are covered with paint.

Two coats of primer can be applied for added protection. The next stage is to fill all nail holes, crevices and end grain with suitable filler such as *'polyfilla'*. The filler is generally applied using a spatula or filling knife. When dry it can be sanded smooth.

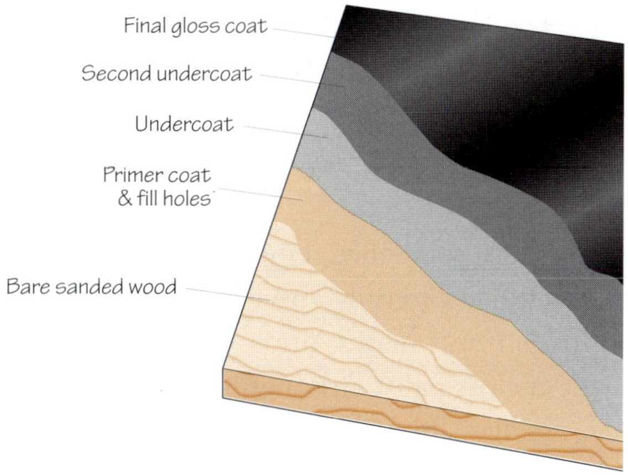

Stages in the painting process

Paint	
Advantages	**Disadvantages**
■ Comes in many colours	■ Hides the natural beauty of the wood
■ Durable and long lasting	■ Difficult to apply properly
■ Protects the wood/metal	■ Needs a lot of preparation
■ It covers many blemishes in the wood which have been filled – knots, cracks, etc.	■ Can blister and crack if not properly applied
■ Different surface finishes available – matt, satin, gloss.	

Once the filler has dried and been sanded smooth once more and dusted, the undercoat can be applied.

Undercoat

This is a separate coat of paint with a dull finish which further covers the wood and provides a base for the final gloss coat while also protecting the wood. It is usual to apply two coats of undercoat to give a uniform covering. The undercoat is applied without any sanding. The paint is applied in a thin even layer. No thin patches, runs or thick patches should be visible. Each coat of paint is allowed to dry, usually overnight, before applying the next coat. You should never use an undercoat which is darker than the final coat, the undercoat should compliment the final gloss coat so that the undercoat will not show through the final coat.

Final coat

This coat must be applied, when the undercoat is dry. It is applied carefully and evenly and must be free from brush marks, drips, dirt and runs. It is usually a gloss paint although satin and matt finishes are available. The final coat dries quite quickly and becomes 'tacky' so work must be done quick and steady, check after a short time for runs and drips and dust which must be removed.

Stains and staining

Stains and dyes are used to change the colour of wood for a number of reasons:

- To improve the appearance of the wooden piece
- To disguise flaws in the wood
- To make a cheaper wood look more like an expensive one (matching colours).

Staining can be a very effective way of enhancing the beauty of wood or even matching the colours and shades in a room. Some woods are stained to look like more expensive types, beech for example, is stained to appear like a rich mahogany. The trained eye will often be able to tell the different grain patterns. It is important that the stain should make an improvement to the piece.

Most stains used at present are spirit based. The spirit is the carrier for the staining chemical or dye. The stain is applied to the piece and is left behind in the wood surface when the spirit dries.

Water-based stains and dyes are also available. These are safer as there is no spirit but the water tends to raise the grain of the wood and it may take longer for the stain to dry.

Stains or dyes can be obtained in the form of a powder which can be dissolved in spirit or water, as required. This allows you to make stains of different shades easily. Coloured stains in many colours and natural shades are available. Colours available include blue, red, yellow, orange, green, etc. These are particularly suitable for children's furniture.

It should be remembered that stain is only a means to colour wood in some way and gives little protection to the wood itself. It is therefore important to further protect the wood using an applied finish after staining.

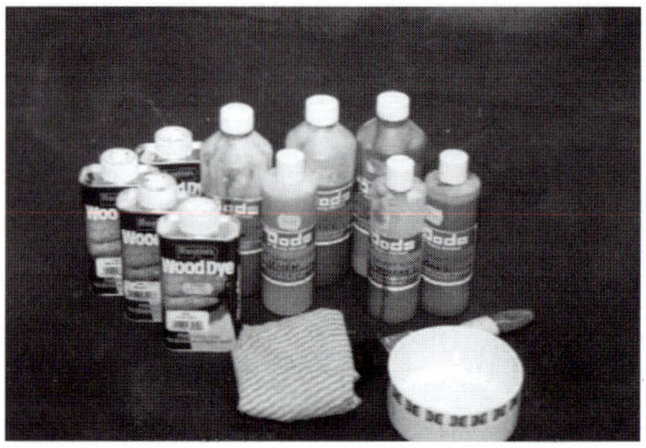

Selection of staining equipment

Staining can be a process of trial and error, but you can use a waste piece to test different stains before you decide on the one you want to use.

Stains are applied to the piece usually with a brush or a clean rag. Often the stain is applied with the brush to cover the whole piece evenly and quickly, to avoid blotches. The stain is allowed to soak briefly into the wood before the excess is wiped off, using a clean rag which has no loose fibres (cotton and linen are suitable). The stain can be applied again as extra coats will build up the depth of colour until the desired shade is achieved. It is a good idea to allow each coat of stain to dry before applying another one. If badly done, staining may look poor.

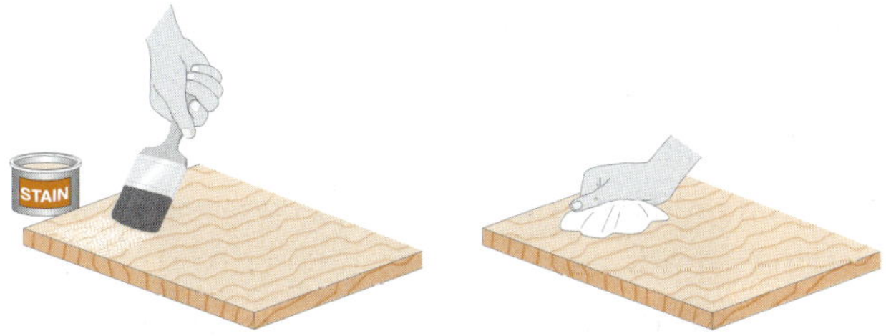

(1) Brush on the stain over the whole piece quickly and evenly

(2) Wipe excess off with a clean lint-free cloth

Stages in applying a stain

> **BEWARE!** When using stains wear protective gloves and work in a well ventilated room. Wash your hands after use

Varnish

Varnish is a protective coating for wood. It is the most commonly used wood finish, with different types being used on indoor furniture, doors, garden furniture, windows and boats.

There are very many kinds of varnish available (all made by different companies): some are clear, others contain a stain. Varnish can also be found with a matt, satin or gloss finish.

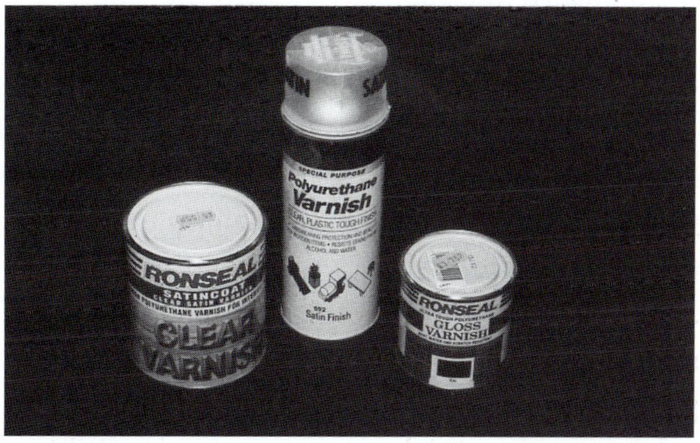

Varnishes

Varnish soaks into the wood initially, which causes the grain of the wood to swell. This also happens with water based stains. In order to minimise this effect the wood is first wiped with a damp cloth allowing the grain to a swell. When dry, the wood is smoothed down using a fine sandpaper before applying the varnish or stain.

Varnish is applied using a brush. The first coat which acts as a sealer can be thinned down with white spirit to improve penetration into the wood. When dry the surface will be slightly rough and should be cut down (de-nibbed) using fine sandpaper (180 grit) before applying a second coat. This process is repeated until you are satisfied with the result, generally three coats is sufficient.

Yacht varnish is a special varnish designed to give maximum protection to exterior woodwork and boats in particular. It contains tung oil and is very durable. Yacht varnish gives a high gloss finish.

Danish oil

This is made from tung oil, which is extracted from the nuts of trees which grow mainly in

China. The oil is blended with synthetic resins to produce the danish oil. It is generally applied with a cloth and rubbed well into the wood. When dry it becomes hard, sealing the wood and giving a dull shine. It can also be applied with a brush and the excess is wiped off with a cloth. A finish is built up with a number of coats. One advantage with danish oil is that you can apply more coats at any time in order to renew the finish. It is a finish that can be used indoors and outdoors.

> **BEWARE!**
> Cloths and rags used to apply danish oil may catch fire due to spontaneous combustion. They should be laid out flat to dry before disposal

Linseed oil

This is used for rubbing into wood to protect it and seal it. It darkens most woods and brings out a shine to the surface. Linseed oil is applied with a cloth and rubbed well into the grain. Its main disadvantage is that it remains moist and oily which attracts dirt to the timber. Linseed oil is a good filler before french polish is applied.

Teak oil

It is applied with a brush or cloth to oily woods like teak to renew the natural lustre in them. Any excess oil is wiped off with a clean cloth. Three or four coats are usually required. The oil soaks into the wood, drying to a shine. Brushes used to apply the oil can be cleaned with white spirit.

Waxes

There are a large number of waxes and ready to use wax preparations which can be used to finish wood. **Beeswax** forms the main ingredient for most preparations. There are two main groups of wax polish, one is intended for bare wood and the other is a polish for wood which already has a finish on it. Some waxes are coloured to add a staining effect to the timber.

Wax finishes

Penetrating oil finishes (danish oil, teake oil, linseed oil)	
Advantages	**Disadvantages**
■ Very easy to apply	■ Some cannot be used outdoors
■ They do not raise the grain	■ They can take some time to dry fully
■ They give a fine lustre to the wood	
■ They soak into the wood	
■ Can be re-oiled as required	
■ Some can be used outdoors	

Wax Finishes	
Advantages	**Disadvantages**
■ Very easy to apply	■ They cannot be used outdoors
■ They do not raise the grain	■ It takes time to build up a shine
■ They give a fine lustre to the wood	■ The finish is soft and easily damaged
■ They can easily be renewed if required	■ Wax is easily damaged by heat and moisture
■ They allow the polish to be built up gradually	
■ They do not require sanding between coats	

Wax finishes are very easily applied with a clean cloth and rubbing well into the grain of the wood. The wax must **not be put on too thickly** or it will just build up. After a coat of the wax has been applied it is left to dry for about 30 minutes before polishing with a clean, dry cloth. Many coats of wax will be needed to gradually build up a good shine. The process of waxing will be much quicker if you first seal the wood with thinned down varnish or a special non-toxic sanding sealer.

Lacquer

Lacquer is a hard, durable finish applied to wood using a spraying process. The wood is sealed using a non toxic sanding sealer and this is allowed to dry. The surfaces are slightly sanded again before the final coat of cellulose lacquer is sprayed on. It is a difficult finish to apply. This finish is much used for professional finishing. It is not in general use in school workshops because of the health risk associated with the solvents used in the spraying process.

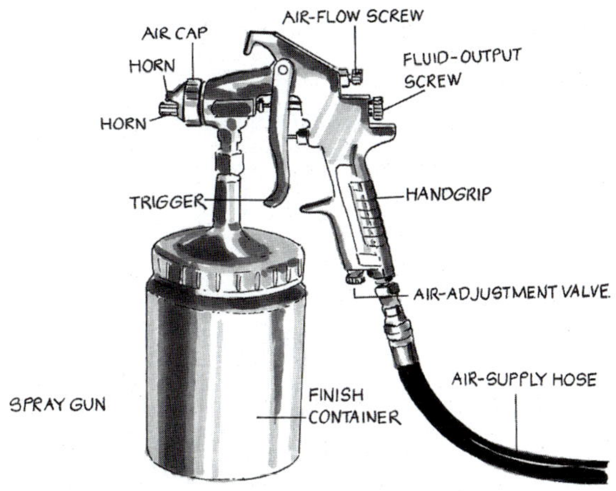

Spraying equipment

BEWARE! Suitable extraction and safety equipment are essential when spraying

French polish

French polish was first introduced into Europe in the sixteenth century. It is used as a quality finish for high class furniture. It wasn't until 1820 when the polishing process was improved by a french cabinet maker, that the term french polish was used.

The polish is made by dissolving shellac in alcohol. Shellac is a crust which surrounds an insect known as *Luciffer Lacca* which is found infesting trees in countries such as India.

The shellac is gathered by cutting away the infected branches and twigs and scraping the shellac from them. The shellac is then washed and dried. In this form it is known as 'seed lac'.

It is then wrapped in canvas and heated over a fire. The canvas is gradually wrung out, like a piece of wet clothing, squeezing the molten shellac out where it falls onto a cold stone. The shellac forms small disks on cooling, these are known as buttons, from which button polish is made. The shellac can be further processed and refined to form the different polishes available.

There are many types of french polish:

- **Button polish** – slightly orange in colour, used on darker hardwoods
- **Transparent polish** – gives a clear finish, used on darker hardwoods
- **White polish** – white/creamy colour used on lighter coloured woods.

These are some of the polishes available but most french polishers like to make their own polish, according to their own recipe.

Because it is such a very fine finish the timber is always well prepared before applying the polish. A silky smooth finish is required often sanding to a 400 grit paper. Preparation will include filling the grain with a grain filler to seal the wood and add shine. **Grain filler** is a creamy paste which has a linseed oil base and this gives the oily lustre to the wood, as well as filling the pores of the wood. The grain filler is rubbed well into the grain with a rough sack cloth. When dry, it can be polished (burnished) off with a clean cloth.

Stain can be applied before or after grain filling and once this is done the french polishing can take place.

French polish can be applied in a number of ways. A pad or rubber is most often used, but a fine brush can be used to apply polish which is thinned down with methylated spirit.

There are three stages in french polishing:

- Bodying in
- Building up
- Spiriting off.

All of these stages are done with the pad made by wrapping a piece of cotton wool or special cotton wool wadding, in a piece of cotton or linen cloth (old sheet or shirt). The size of the pad will vary according to the size of the area which is to be polished.

To charge the pad the wadding is placed in a dish or shallow bowl of polish. When it has soaked up the polish, the wadding is placed in the middle of the cloth.

Dish and the pad

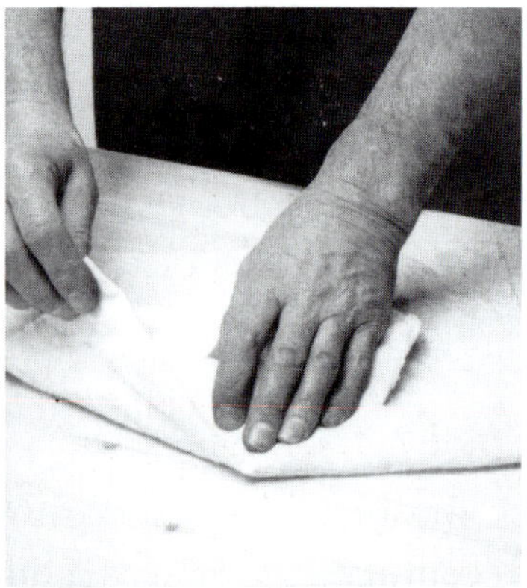

The loaded Pad of cotton wool is placed in the centre of the linen cloth

The cloth is folded over the pad

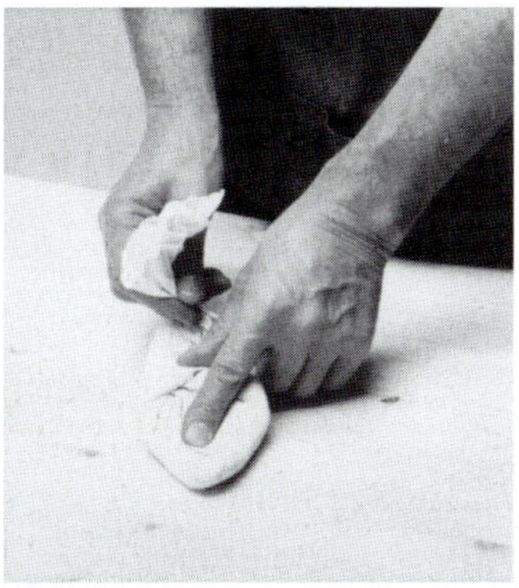

Fold over the corners to make a pointed pad

When the pad is made up and is tightly folded, the tail is twisted to squeeze out all of the excess polish back into the dish. This process can be repeated when the pad needs to be re-charged.

The damp pad is then rubbed in a circular motion, starting on the outside of the surface and working towards the centre. It is important that you cover the entire surface.

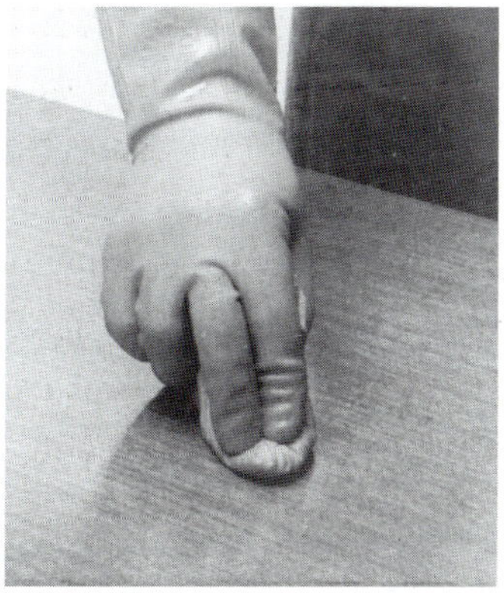

Holding the pad

A few coats can be applied in this manner. The pad will get 'tacky' and can be lubricated slightly using a small drop of linseed oil.

Pad & linseed oil

The pad is kept moist in a sealed jar with a little methylated spirit in the bottom of it. This prevents the pad drying and becoming hard.

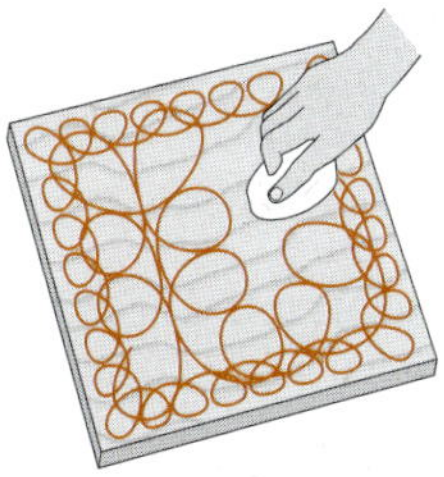

(1) Cover the panel with circular strokes

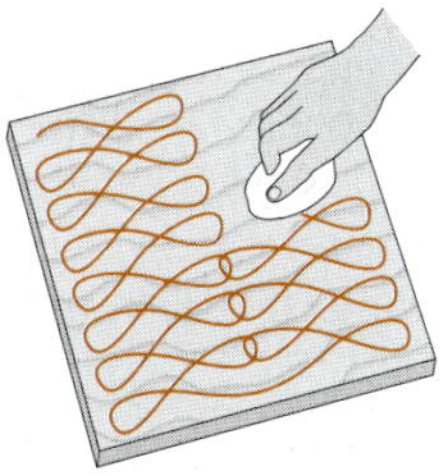

(2) Continue with figure-eight strokes

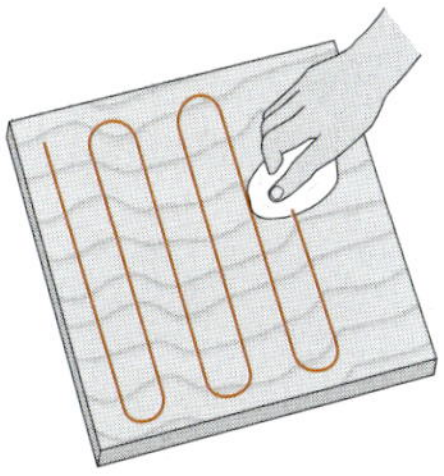

(3) Finish with straight parallel strokes

Work the charged pad in circular or figure eight motions to cover the surface

Polish & jar

About five coats should be applied at each sitting, then the polish is left to dry over night. The next day the surfaces should be lightly 'de-nibbed' with very fine wire wool (000 or 0000 grade). Then the polishing process is repeated to build up the layers of polish.

Spiriting off

As the polish builds up it can appear to have streaks. These are removed by rubbing the pad in long strokes in the direction of the grain.

Spiriting off is where a new pad is made and charged with methylated spirit. This is squeezed out completely and is rubbed lightly along the direction of the grain.

The methylated spirit forms a film on the surface of the polish which then dissolves. As the spirit evaporates it leaves behind a surface with a smooth shine.

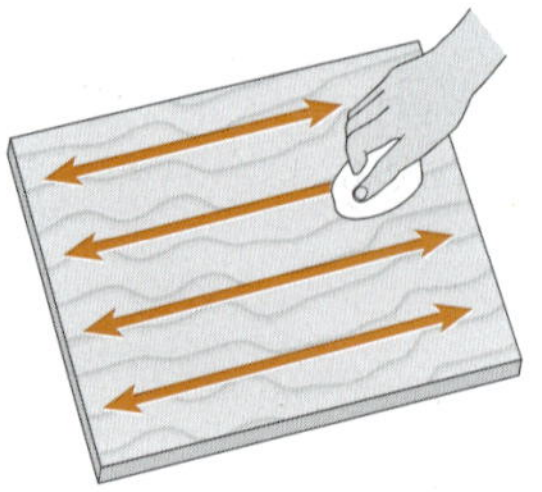

(3) Finish with straight parallel strokes

Spiriting off – rub the pad in the direction of the grain

Exercises

1. What is a surface finish?
2. How is abrasive paper made?
3. Give two reasons for putting an applied finish on timber.
4. List the stages necessary in producing a good surface finish on wood.
5. When should you wear a dust mask?
6. Why is it necessary to stain timber?
7. Describe the stages necessary in painting a new softwood front door.

French polish	
Advantages	**Disadvantages**
Gives a beautiful finish	It takes a lot of time to apply
Enhances the natural beauty of the wood and grain	It is difficult to do well
Gives a soft lustre	The finish is soft and easily damaged
It can be revived quite easily	It is damaged by heat
	It is damaged by moisture
	It is unsuitable for exterior use

8. Give three examples of where wood preservative would be used as the finish on timber.
9. Give two examples of where each of the following finishes might be used:
   (a) Danish oil
   (b) Beeswax
   (c) Polyurethane varnish
   (d) Gloss paint.
10. What is 'spiriting off' and how does it help in achieving a good finish in french polish?
11. How is stain applied to get the best results?
12. Give two advantages and two disadvantages of the following finishes:
   (a) Danish oil
   (b) Paint
   (c) Varnish
   (d) French polish.
13. Describe how you would prepare and finish a softwood birdhouse.
14. Select a suitable applied finish for the chess board shown and describe the preparation of the board and the application of the finishing material.

15. Recommend a suitable finish for the knife holder shown and give reasons for your choice. Also, name the carved effect shown in diagram 2.

Diagram 1

Diagram 2

16. An outside wall mounted wooden mailbox is to be fixed on two *mild steel brackets*. The box and the brackets are to have a paint finish:
   (a) describe the stages in painting the box.
   (b) describe the preparation and painting of the steel brackets.

CHAPTER THIRTY

FASTENINGS & FIXTURES

When working with materials we often need to use items of hardware such as handles, hinges, locks and fixtures. We also may need to use nails, screws and other fastenings to assist in holding simple joints and for other uses on our projects. These items put the finishing touches to our projectwork, but it is important that we choose them with care and that they are accurately applied.

Some of the most popular fastening methods will be discussed here but there are a multitude of different types available. It is a good idea to visit your local hardware store when planning a project to find out what is available. Magazines, trade shows and other exhibitions are also a useful guide to research, as is the internet.

Nails

Many different types of nail exist. Each type is suitable for different situations. Nails are used by the carpenter to fix two large sections of timber to each other, quickly. Smaller nails such as panel pins and tacks are used for lighter work. Nails are held in place by friction forces and they work best in a **shear force** situation. Shear force occurs when one piece of material tends to slide along another, if it were free to do so. A joint held together with nails is seldom very strong and should be strengthened with glue or a joint in the wood. Nails look poor when left on the timber surface, so the heads are usually punched below the surface and filled.

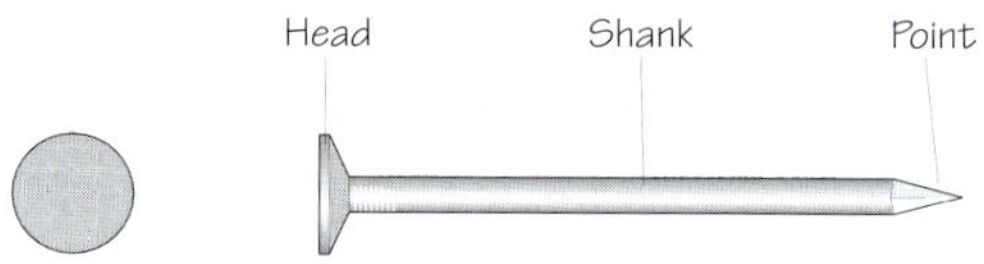

Parts of a nail

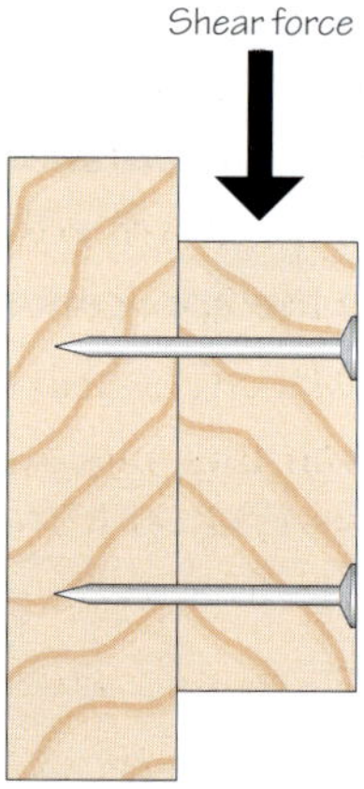

Nails work best in shear

Nails have been in existence for nearly 4,000 years. Until recently, nails were cut from pieces of rods or sheets of iron. Cut nails, as they are called, are still used today for nailing down floorboards.

Most nails are made from mild steel, although special nails for use in very damp conditions can be made from copper, which will not rust.

Panel pins

These are short narrow nails ranging in length from 12mm to 50mm. They are used mostly for fixing thin sheets, such as plywood, to larger sections. They are generally used with an adhesive. Panel pins are easily driven into timber. The heads are driven below the surface of the wood with a nail punch and the holes filled. This makes them very suitable for fixing mouldings onto timber. Panel pins can be obtained coated (galvanised) to make them resistant to dampness. If panel pins are not driven correctly with the hammer they will bend easily.

Panel pin

Oval wire nails

The oval wire nail is designed to be driven into the timber and below the surface. The hole is then filled. The nail has an oval shape which makes it easy for this to be done. It is suitable for nailing thin pieces of timber and for nailing close to the ends of timber pieces where splitting might occur. Oval nails should always be driven with the two points of the head in the direction of the grain as shown below. They can be obtained in sizes from 25mm – 150mm.

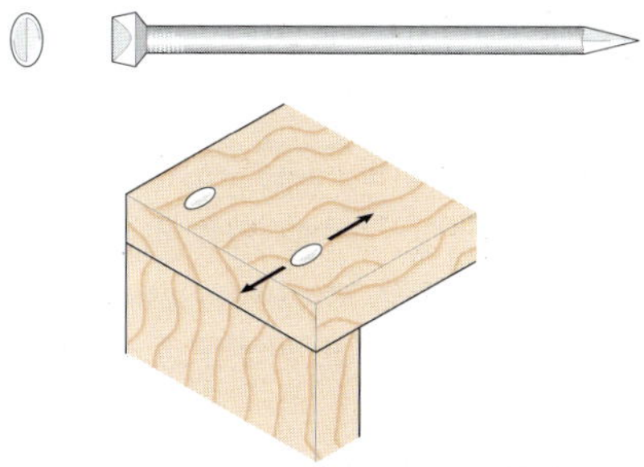

Oval wire nail. Nail should be driven with the oval shape of the head in line with the grain

Round wire nails

These are the largest type of nail. They are used by carpenters and joiners in roofing and in timber-framed walls (stud walls), where strength is required. In these uses, the nail isn't seen, e.g. in a wall or attic. The appearance is therefore not a major concern. These nails tend to split wood. The shank is circular in section with a flattened head. They are easily pulled using a pincers or claw hammer. Sizes range from 20mm – 160mm.

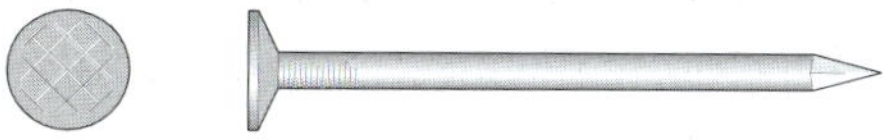

Round wire nail

Tacks

Tacks are used for fixing carpets to floorboards and fabrics to wood. They range in size from 6mm – 30mm. They have sharp points and flat heads which hold the fabric to the surface without tearing. They are sometimes called **cut tacks**.

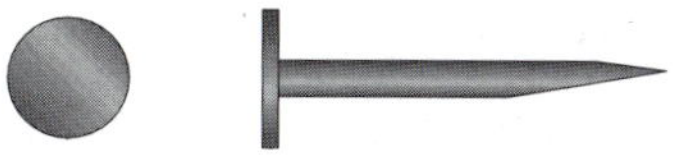

Tack

Upholstery nails (pins)

These are thin nails with dome shaped heads. The heads are often made of brass, copper, chrome, bronze or have an antique finish. The nails are used to finish off the edges of upholstery fixed to wood, in a decorative way.

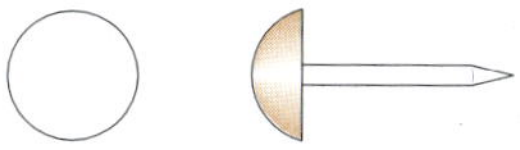

Upholstery nail

Long lengths of false headed nails can be bought and used to reduce the number of actual nails needed. Upholstery nails are used in every 4 – 5 spaces. This gives the appearance of a straight line of upholstery nails.

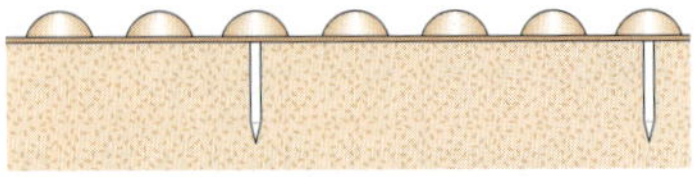

Line of false head nails

Lost head nails

These are used in carpentry and flooring. The small head can easily be punched under the surface of timber and the hole filled with a suitable filler. It can be obtained in a round section or an oval section. Sizes range from 25mm –150mm.

Lost head nail

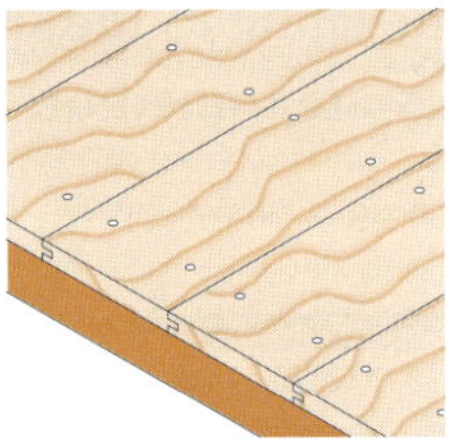

Lost head nails are used to fix flooring boards

Clout nails

These nails are galvanised for outdoor work and are used for fixing roofing felt to a timber flat roof, or fixing wire fencing, etc. Its large head exerts even pressure over the surface of the material it holds down.

Clout nail

Staples

This U-shaped nail has two shanks and no head. It is used to fix cables or wire to wood. Insulated staples should be used to fix electric cables to wood. Staples are generally galvanised.

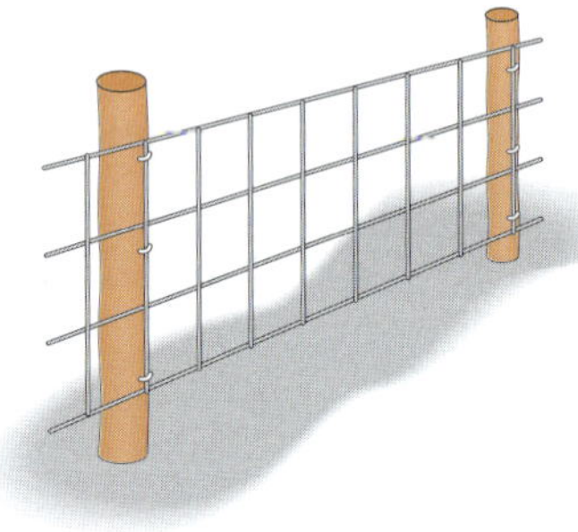

Staples used to fix fencing to posts

Special staples can be used in a staple gun for fixing fabrics to wood. The staples come in various sizes. Care must be taken when using a staple gun. If it is discharged into the air, a staple could easily go into a person's eye.

Corrugated fasteners

These are made from corrugated iron plate with one edge sharpened. They are used to aid the jointing of two boards (butt jointing) or mitre jointing at a corner. They are between 6mm and 22mm deep and 22mm – 30mm long. They are often called wiggle nails.

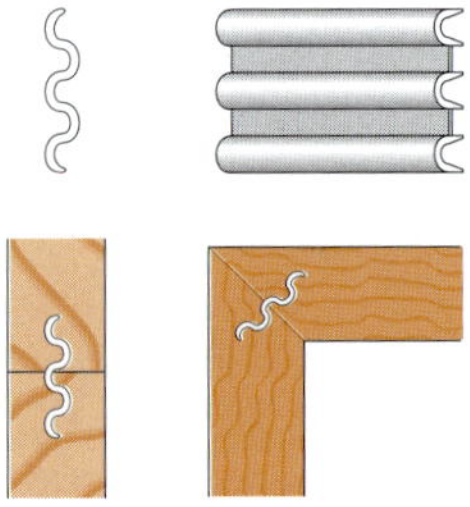

Corrugated fastener

Nailing

Driving a nail correctly is not an easy task. There are ways of driving a nail which adds strength to the joint.

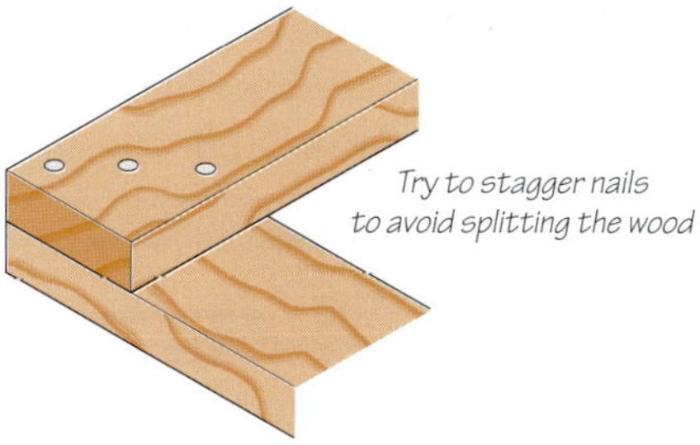

Try to stagger nails to avoid splitting the wood

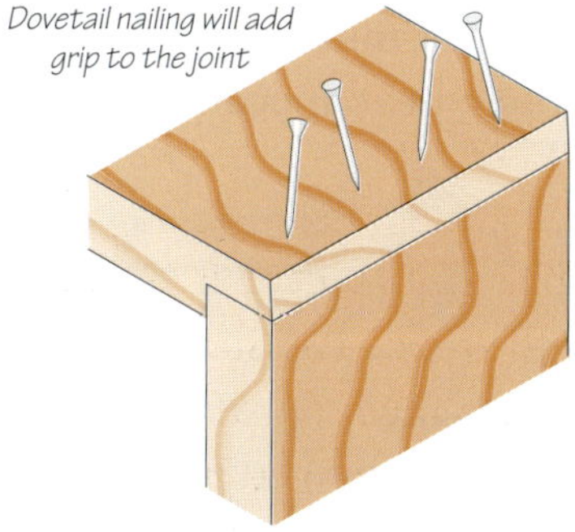

Dovetail nailing will add grip to the joint

Screws

Screws are a more sturdy and stronger method of fixing materials than nails. Their appearance enables them to be used as a functional decoration with their heads proud of the material surface or flush with it.

Screws are used for joining wood to wood and also for joining various other rigid materials together. They are also used for securing other fittings to wood and other materials, for example, hinges, locks handles, etc.

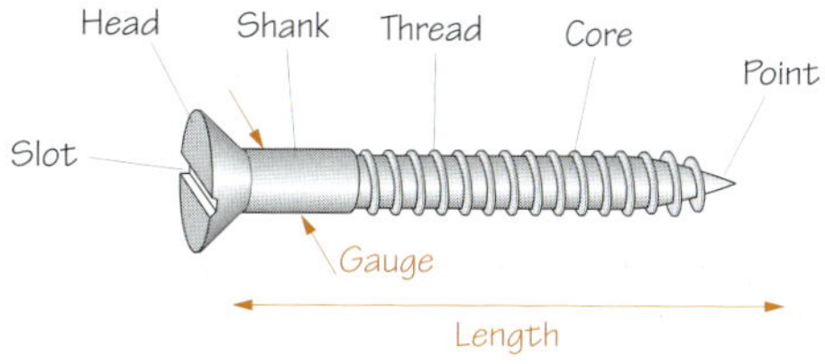

Parts of a screw

Screws have been in use since the sixteenth century but have only been widely used since the eighteenth century. There have been many developments in the size and shape of screws and their heads so that they suit modern materials and fixing methods, e.g., power screwdrivers.

Parts of a screw

Wood screws are made in mild steel, stainless steel, brass or aluminium. Screws can be finished or coated with particular finishes such as black japan, brass, zinc plate or chrome plate. Steel screws are the most widely used. They do, of course, rust easily in damp conditions. In these conditions it is best to use brass or chromium plated screws. Brass screws are very decorative, as well as being corrosion resistant. However, brass is soft and can break or be easily damaged while driving the screw into the materials.

Screw heads vary according to the type of slot or fixing head used. Here are some of the most common types.

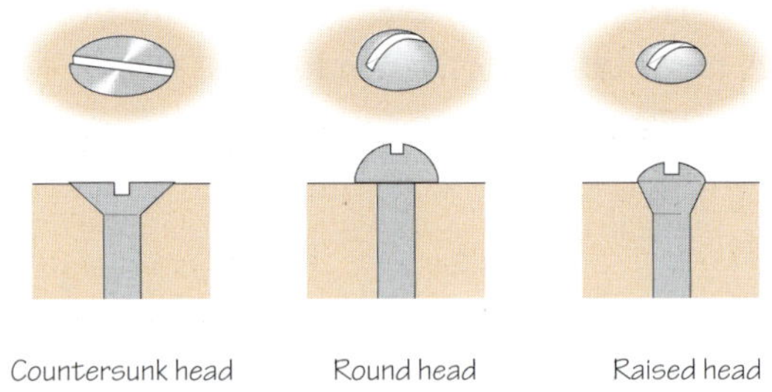

Heads of screws

Countersunk head – used with wood
Round head – used with plastic and metal
Raised head – used with metal fixings for decoration

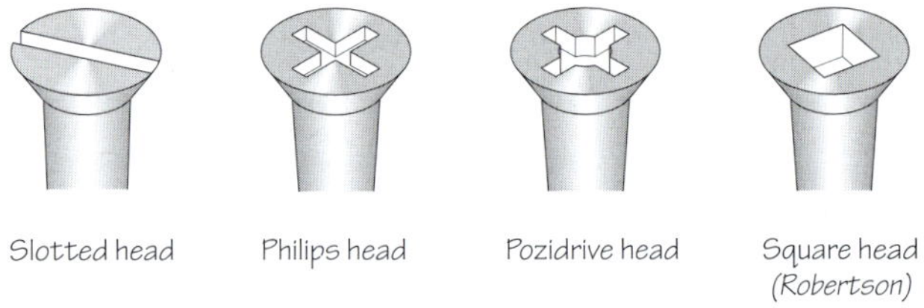

Heads of screws

The Phillips, posidrive and square heads were developed to reduce the risk of the screwdriver slipping out of the head, causing damage to the screw and the material's surface.

The size of a screw is measured in two ways:

- Length
- Diameter of its shank (gauge).

The gauge of the screw is given by a number. These range from the smallest O, to the largest being 20. Numbers 4,6,8 and 10 are the most common. Different lengths of each gauge can be obtained.

Ordering screws

When ordering screws you must give the exact details of the size, shape and type of screw that is required:

Example: 25 Brass, 50mm, No. 8, Csk.

This means that 25 brass screws, 50mm long with a number 8 gauge and a counter sink head are required.

Coach screw

This is a very large heavy screw. It has a hexagonal head which is driven with a spanner for leverage. It is used for heavy work such as fixings to large beams, gate posts or for siting heavy machinery.

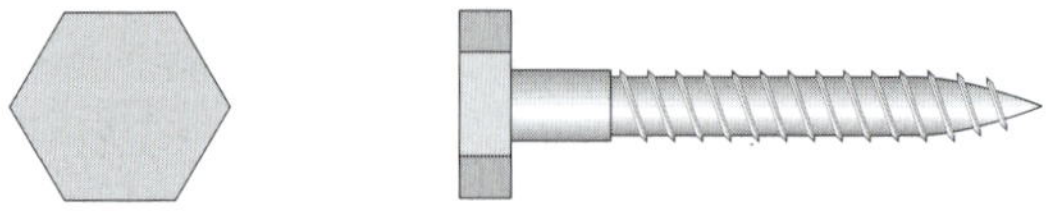

Coach screw

Dome head screws

These screws have round brass or chrome tops which screw into the heads of the special screws. They are used to fix mirrors to walls and in any other work where neat appearance is essential.

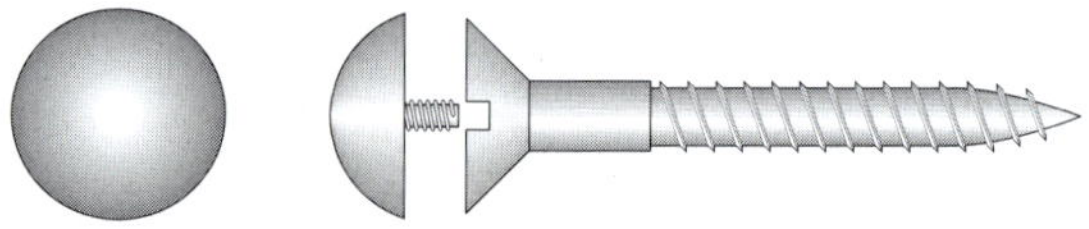

Dome head screw

Clutch head screw

This screw cannot easily be removed once it has been driven in. It is used in situations where you want to make it difficult to remove the screws, such as outside gate locks, notice boards, etc.

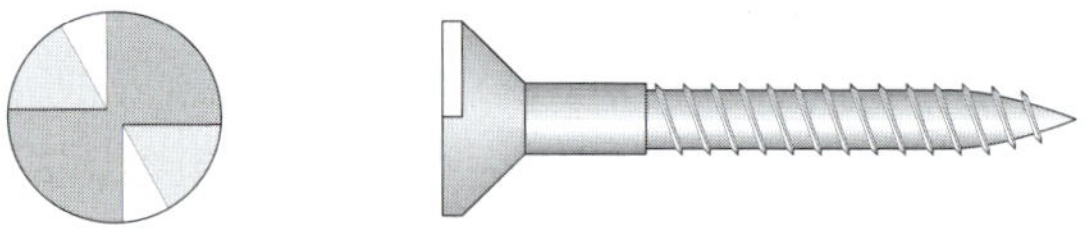

Clutch head screw

Chipboard screws

The threads of chipboard screws are deeper than normal and they extend to the head, giving better grip in chipboard. They can also be used on solid timber.

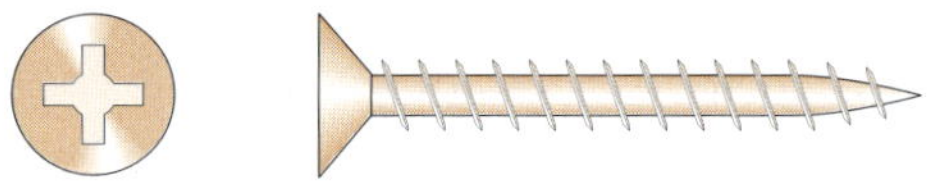

Chipboard screw

Self tapping screws

These screws are designed for use in metals. A pilot hole is drilled which is the same diameter as the screw's core. The screw then cuts its own threads into the metal.

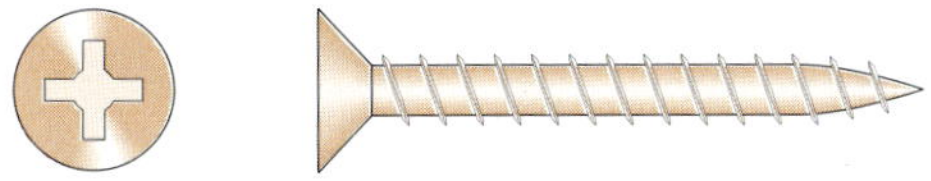

Self tapping screws

Screw cups and washers

These are used to spread the pressure of the screw over the surface of the material. The screw cup can be obtained in brass and will improve the appearance of the screw. A screw cup is useful when a screw needs to be occasionally removed.

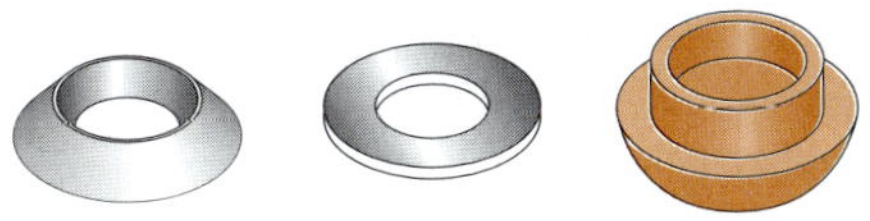

Screw cups

Cuphooks and screw eyes

These are pieces of hardware available in a variety of shapes, sizes and finishes. Some are coated in plastic of various colours. They are used for hanging things from walls, frames, doors, shelves, etc. They are small and not used to carry heavy loads. You may find that they are very useful when designing projects. Large storage hangers are available in various sizes materials and designs.

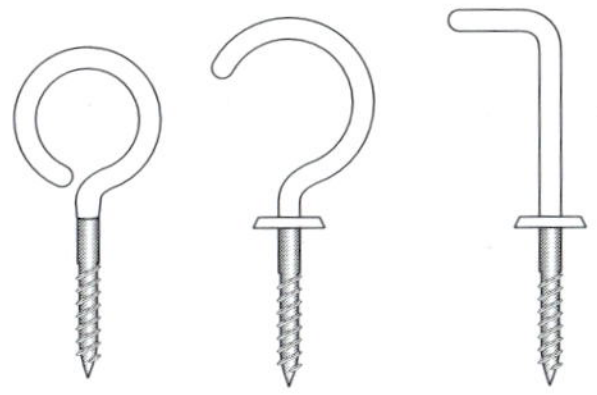

Cuphooks and screw eyes

Bolts

Bolts are used for fastening metals to each other and to wood and other material. They come in a range of various shapes, sizes and lengths. They are generally more unsightly than screws, but are much stronger and allow the piece to be taken apart. Different heads can be obtained for use with a spanner or screwdriver. The nuts used can be square, hexagonal, winged or locking. They are usually used with a washer to ensure the nut doesn't loosen and also to spread the loading to the surface of the material.

Driving screws

A screw should be 3 times as long as the piece it is securing. The piece should be marked and prepared and a pilot hole drilled and countersunk if required.

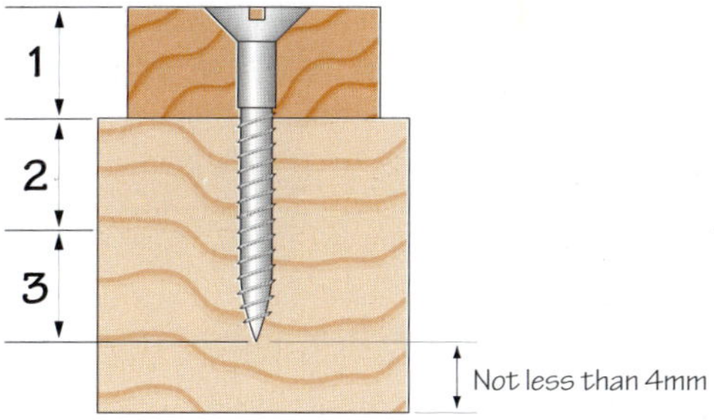

The length of the screw should be 3 times the thickness of the piece to be secured

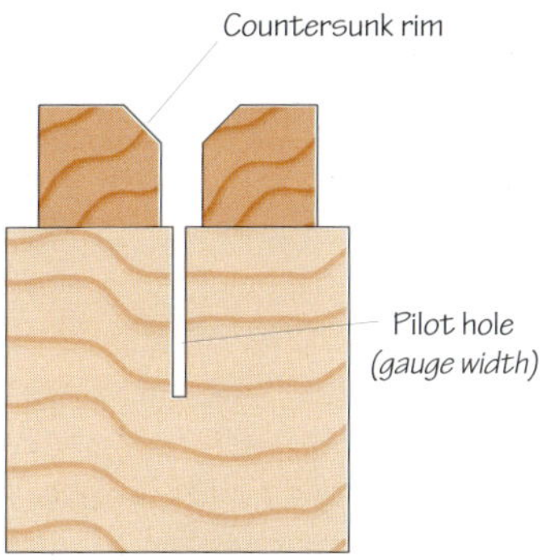

The piece should be prepared with a pilot hole and the hole should be countersunk for a countersink screw

Knock-down fittings

There are many different types of fittings designed to connect boards. They have been made popular also by the wide use of manufactured boards in carcase construction and the need for self or home assembly of modern furniture. Knock down fittings also allow the piece to be taken apart easily. The fittings are made from metal and plastic generally. They are usually two part joiners, with one part being attached or driven into one piece and the second part screws into the first part, to hold the two pieces firm. Knock down fittings are not as strong and durable as a traditional joint.

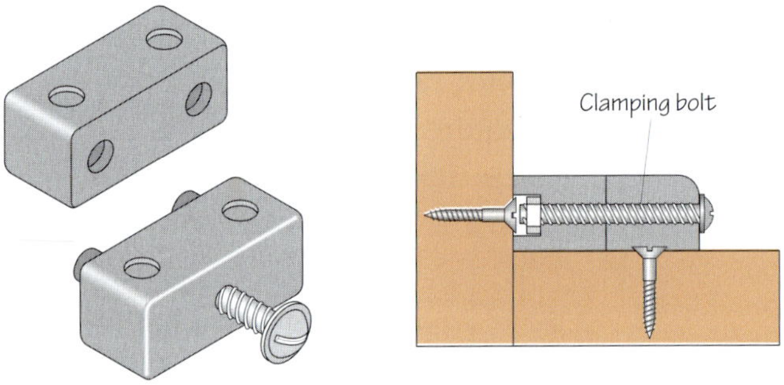

Plastic block joiner

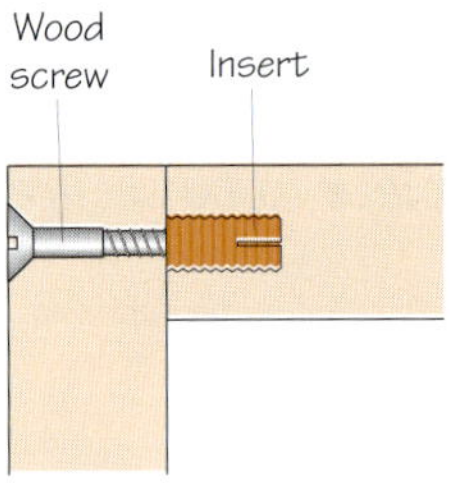

Unit connector

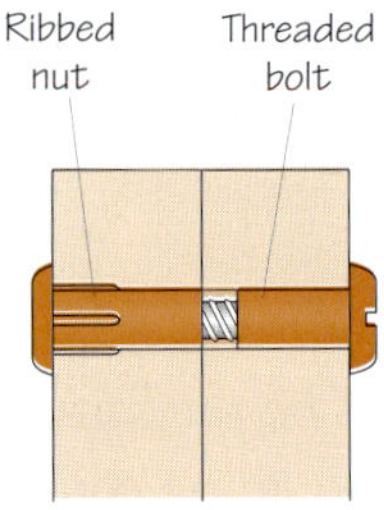

Bolt and barrel nut

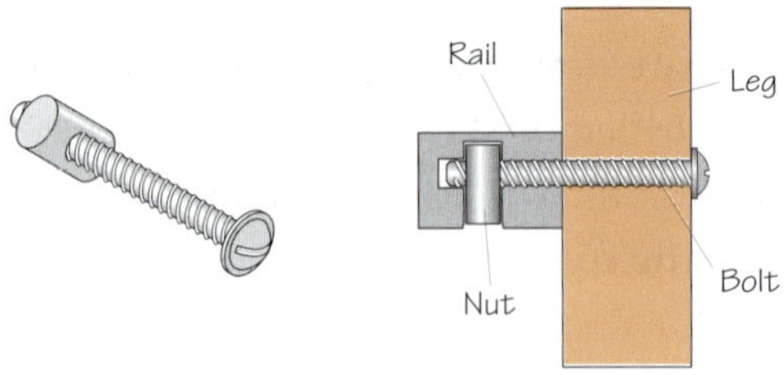

Chipboard insert

Timber battens are also used. This type of fitting is functional but may not look well.

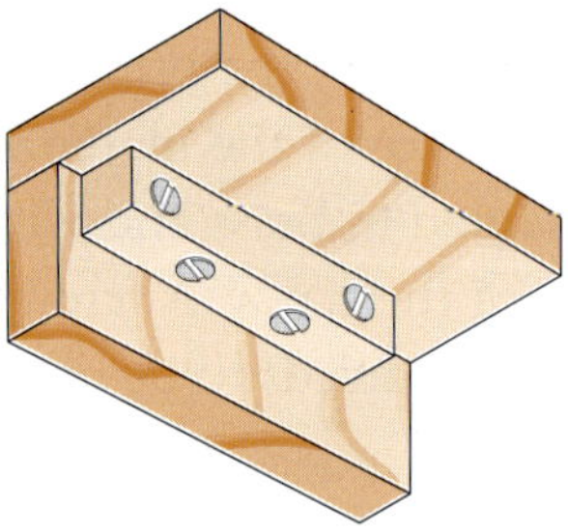

Timber batten

Angle brackets

These can be used to strengthen joints in wood or metal, particularly in frames. They are usually made from steel and are fixed into place with countersunk screws.

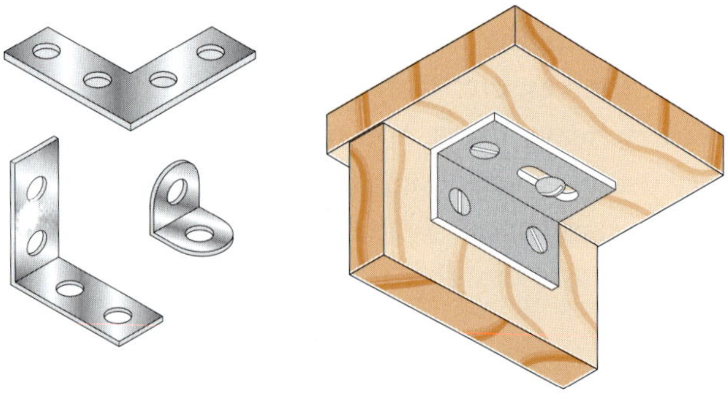

Angle brackets & plates

Hinges

There are many different hinges which suit most situations. Whether it is a front door, kitchen unit or jewellery box there is a hinge to suit each particular need. The most common types of hinge are detailed here. A hinge is made up of two leaves or plates with a central pivot, usually a steel pin. Some hinges are spring-loaded which can eliminate the need for catches and fasteners on small doors.

Butt hinge

This type of hinge is very common. It is used on all the doors in your house. It is also used in many windows, just look around and see where in the room you can find butt hinges. They vary in length between 12mm and 150mm. The door to your room is normally fitted with 100mm butt hinges.

The butt hinge is recessed into the door leaf and frame. Countersunk screws are used to fix the hinge to the material.

Butt hinges are made from brass, mild steel or cast iron. They can be difficult to fit if care is not taken, but they are strong. Brass hinges are more expensive than the other types and are used for decorative purposes, in damp conditions and outdoors.

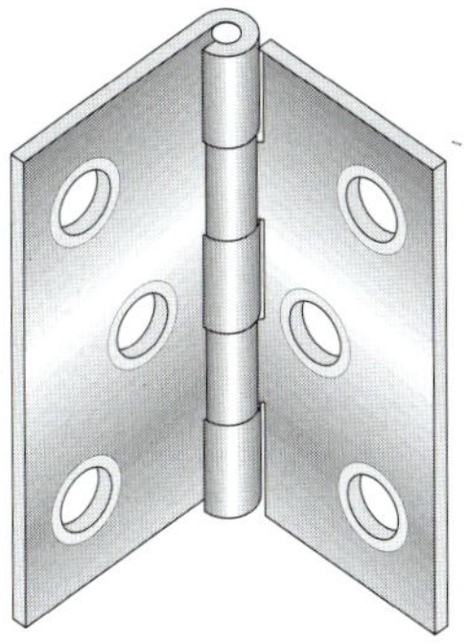

Butt hinge

The **piano hinge** is a type of butt hinge. It gets its name from its uses on piano lids. It is long and thin, usually made from brass or brass coated steel. It is used in cabinet lids, doors, etc. The **parliament hinge** is used to allow a door to swing clear of the surrounding frame and the projecting knuckles allow it to do this. The **rising butt hinge** allows the door to close by itself. The weight of the door tends to close it on the spiral in the knuckle. The door can also easily be lifted off its hinges. It is used where a self-closing door is needed or where a high pile carpet must be cleared as the door opens.

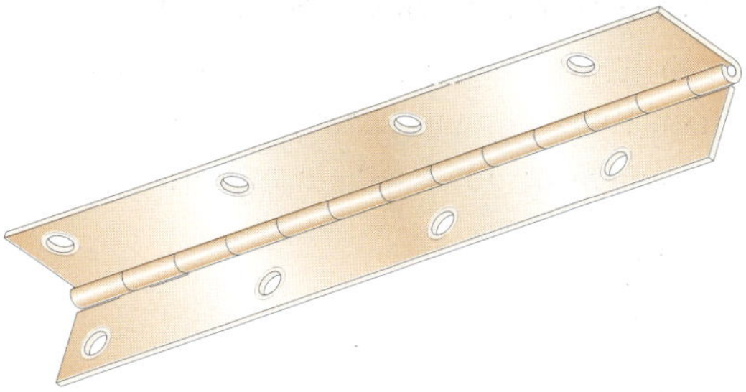

Piano hinge

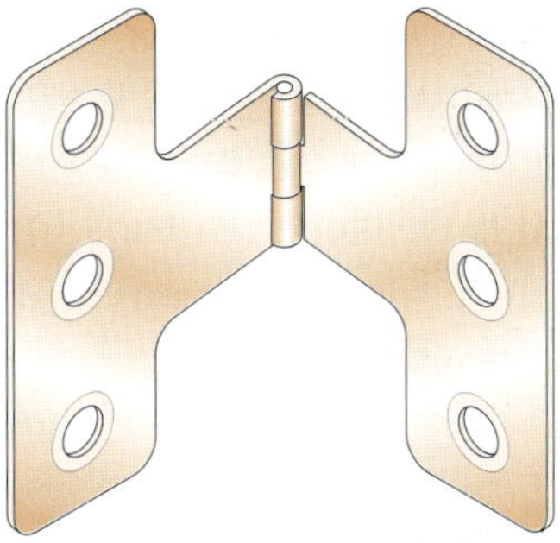

Parliament hinge

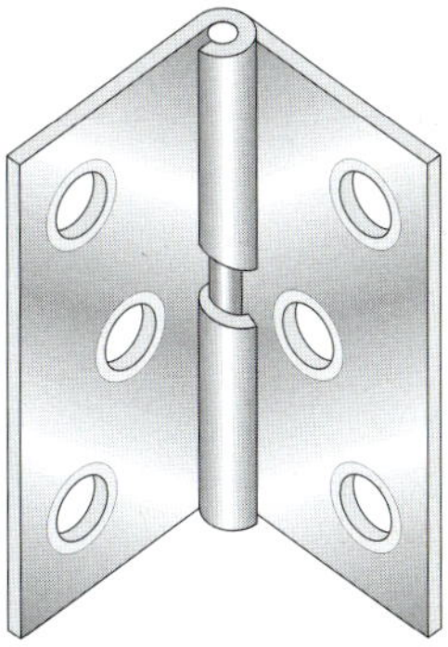

Rising butt hinge

Back flap hinge

The leaves of this hinge are wider than the butt hinge and its screw holes are positioned differently. Its wider leaves give more support and the hinge is used mostly on drop leafed tables, where more than normal support is needed.

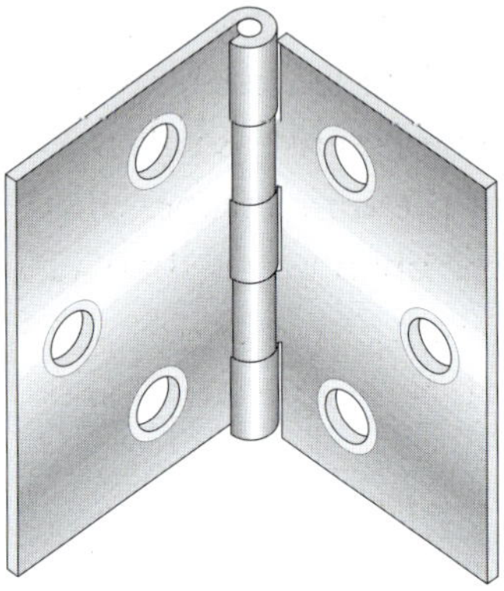

Back flap hinge

Flush hinge

This hinge is fixed straight to the timber so there is no chiselling necessary. It cannot be adjusted after fitting and is weaker than the butt hinge. It is quite satisfactory for small items and doors of cabinets. Sizes range from 38mm to 75mm.

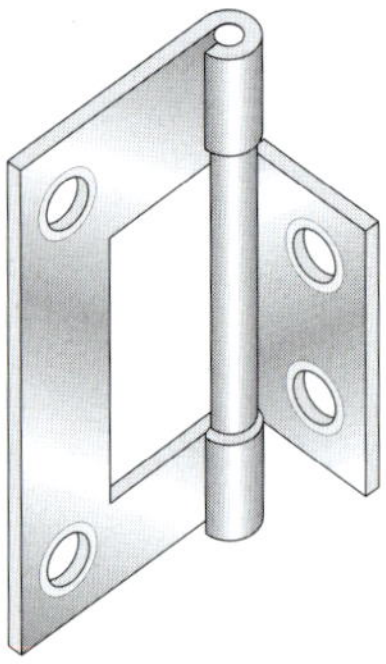

Flush hinge

Cranked hinge

This hinge is used on cabinet doors that are not flush with the frame. The door is allowed to open through 180˚. They are easy to fit as they overlap the frame. The angled leaf is secured to the frame. The hinge can have a chrome plated finish or brass finish. Sizes and designs vary, for face fixing and hidden fixing.

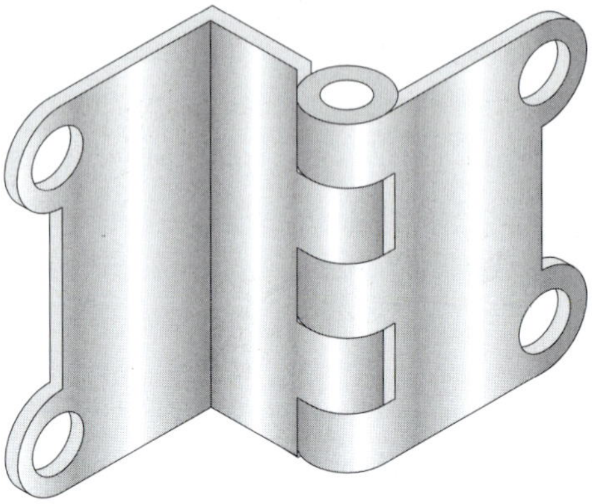

Cranked hinge

Blum adjustable hinge

This hinge is used widely in kitchen and bedroom units. It is partially recessed into the door using a special drill bit. The other leaf is attached to the carcase (frame of the unit). It can be adjusted after fitting to make the door fit to the frame. It is very suitable for chipboard or fibreboards. Correct drilling of the recess is essential. Two sizes are available, 25mm and 36mm.

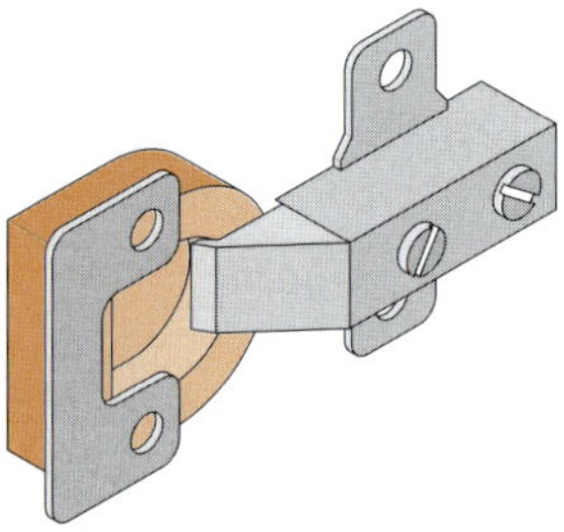

Concealed cabinet (blum) hinge

Heavy duty hinges

These hinges are used on wooden gates and large doors such as those in banks and churches. These hinges are often ornamental. The T hinge is named from its shape and is used in side gates and shed doors, or in wooden garage doors. They are available in various sizes.

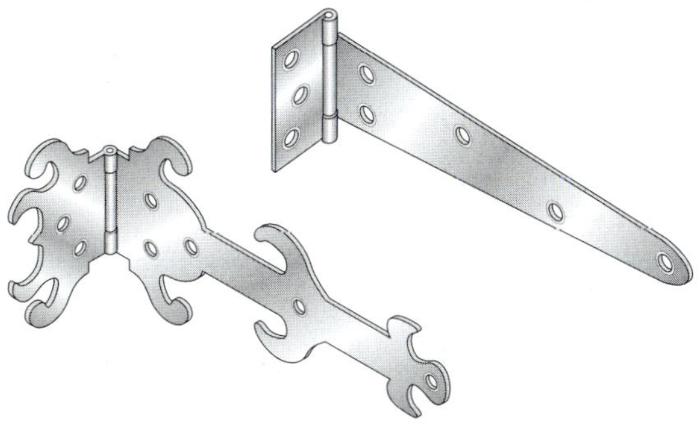

Heavy duty hinges

How to fit a butt hinge

Mark out the position and dimensions of the hinge on the frame. The dimensions are taken from the hinge with a marking gauge. The position is marked using rule and tri-square and the gauge is used to set the depth and thickness of the hinge.

The waste is marked (as shown below) and the waste is removed by first sawing down the sides and then chiselling out the remaining waste. The recess should be tapered as this prevents "pinching" of the hinge where the door or lid tends to spring open rather than stay comfortably shut.

The hinge is then fixed into place.

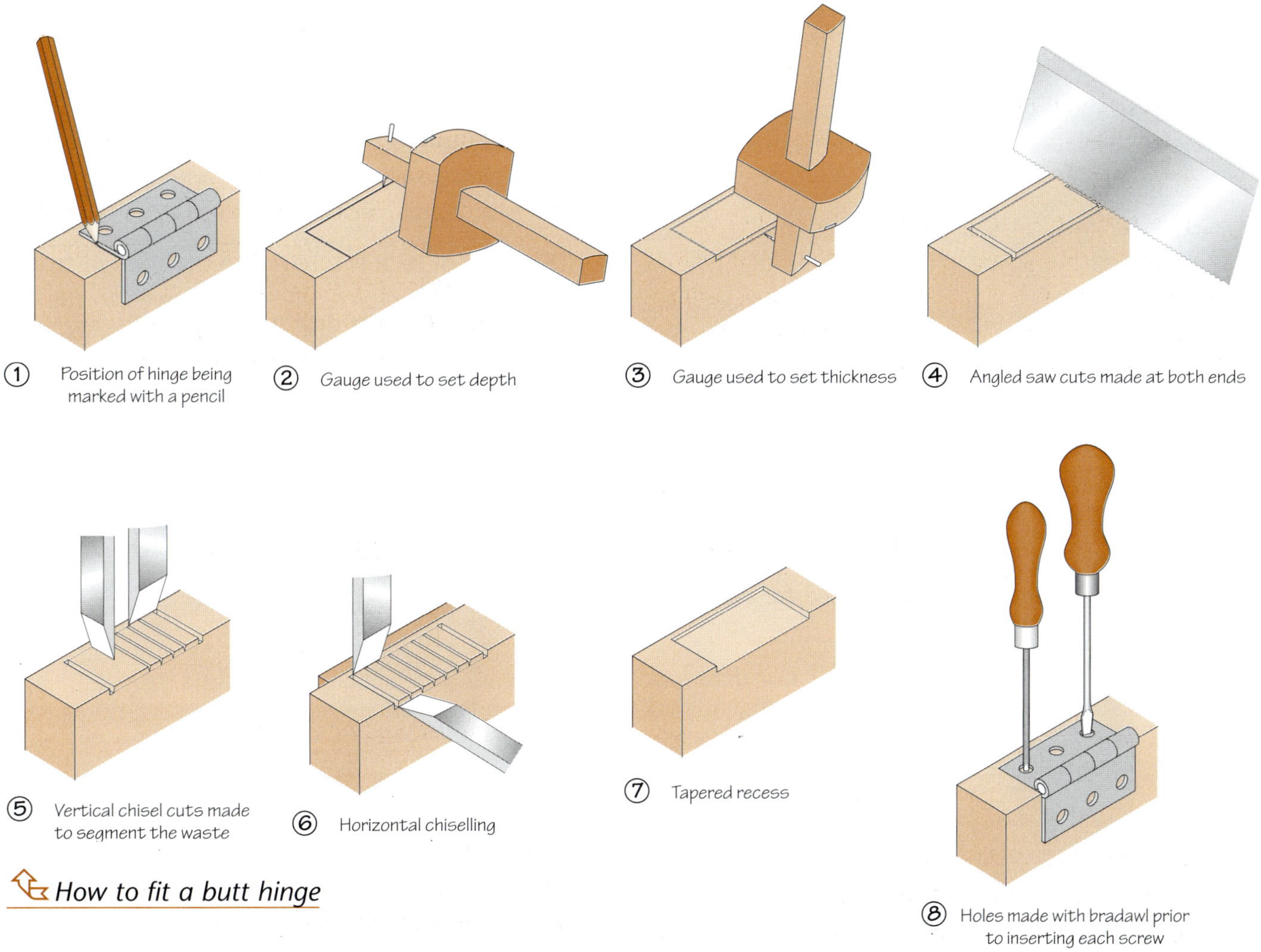

How to fit a butt hinge

Locks

Locks are used for security. Locks may be attached to the surface of doors, lids of boxes, and drawers. There are many sizes and types of lock to suit individual situations. Most locks have two main parts, the **ward** and the **receiver**. The ward moves into the receiver to close the lock.

Cupboard lock

This inexpensive lock fits directly onto the inside of the door of a cupboard or press. The ward bar will move left or right depending on how it is fitted. The ward fits into a recess or behind a steel plate which is attached to the door frame. These locks are available in brass and steel.

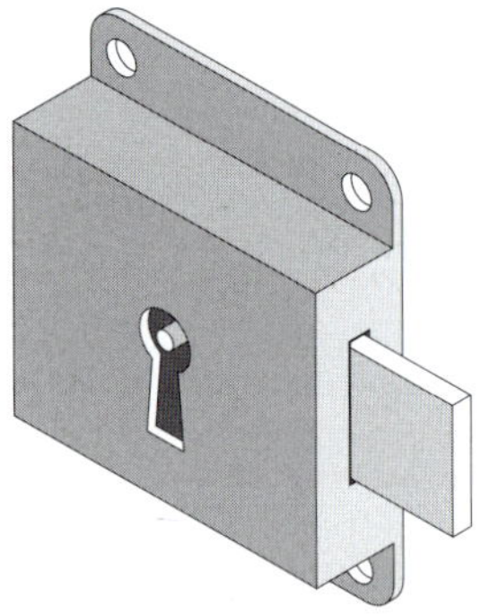

Cupboard lock

Cut door lock

This lock is fitted (recessed) into the timber. The single movement of the ward means that different locks must be chosen, depending on where the lock is used (right-handed or left-handed). This lock is widely used for drawers.

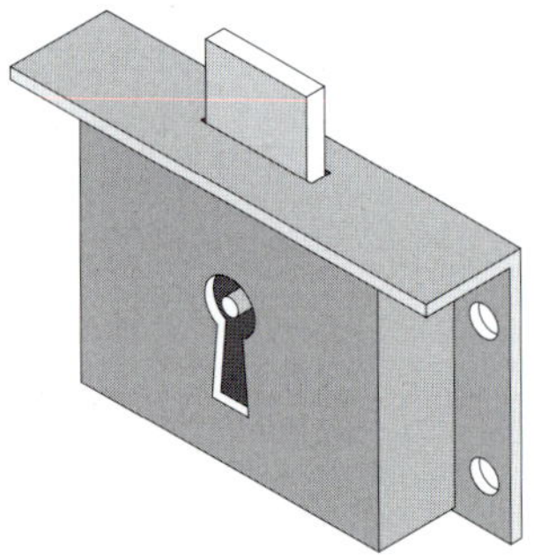

Cut door lock

Mortise lock

This is often called a dead mortise lock or dead lock and is mostly used on doors for added security. The ward moves across into a receiver in the frame of the door. The lock fits into the door stile. The mortise lock is frequently used in combination with a handle and catch on inside doors particularly. When this is the case it is not a dead lock, but just an ordinary mortise lock.

Mortise lock

Rim lock

This type of lock is screwed to the back of front doors. The keeper (receiver) is screwed to the frame. The rim lock often incorporates a catch which can be hand operated inside. A key is used to open the lock from the outside.

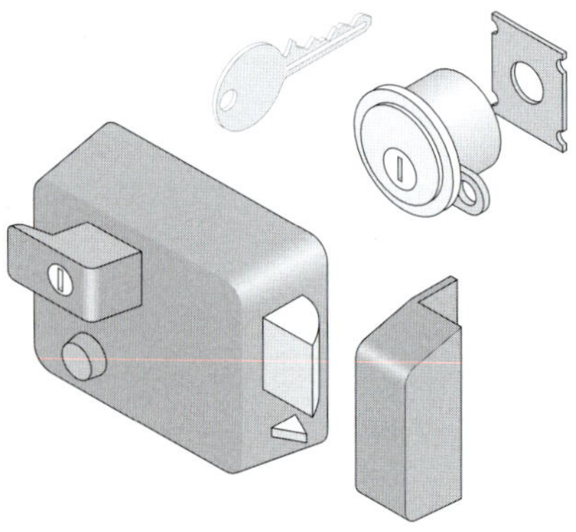

Rim lock

Box lock

The box lock is fitted (recessed) into the carcase of the boxes while the keeper, with two teeth, is recessed into the lid. The lid closes and the key turns a mechanism which holds the two teeth down, thus making the box secure. It is used on piano tops, jewellery boxes and cases. It can be a difficult lock to fit.

Box lock

① Mark the central position of the lock

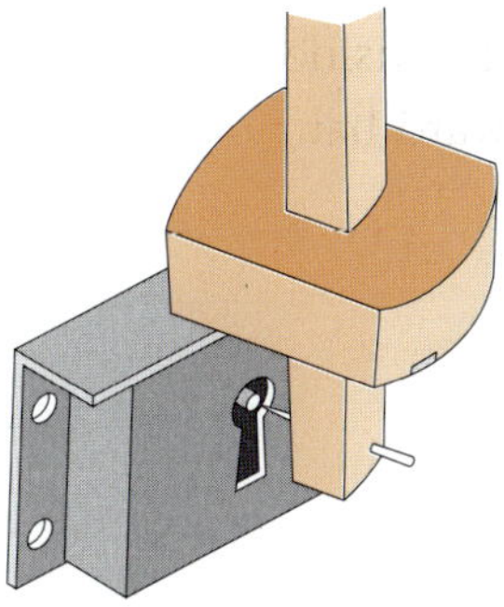

② Set the gauge to the centre of the keyhole

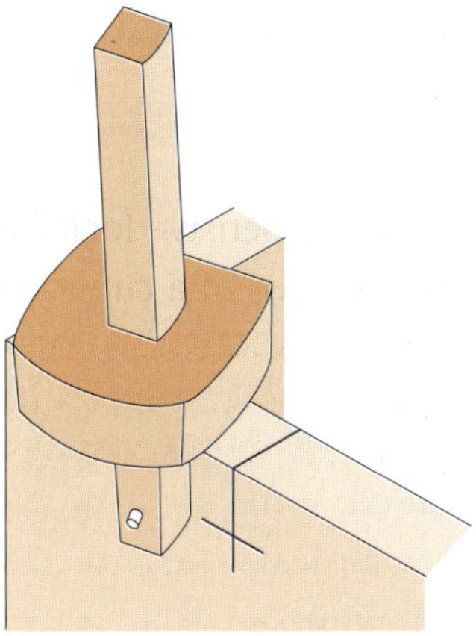

③ Mark this distance onto the face of the piece with the gauge. This gives the position to drill the keyhole.

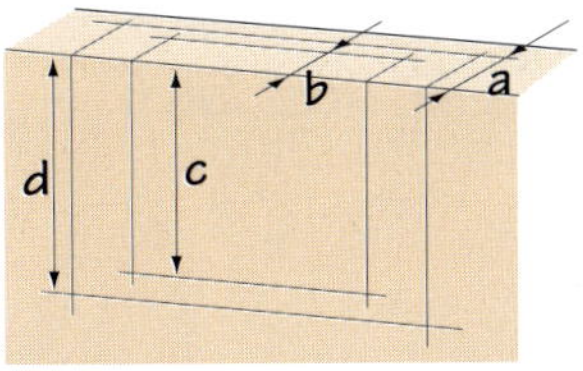

④ Mark out the inside recesses from th
These must then be removed.

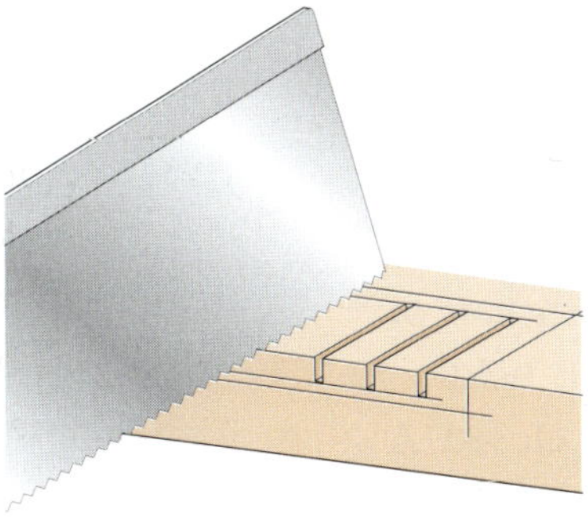

⑤ Saw to the waste side of the lines

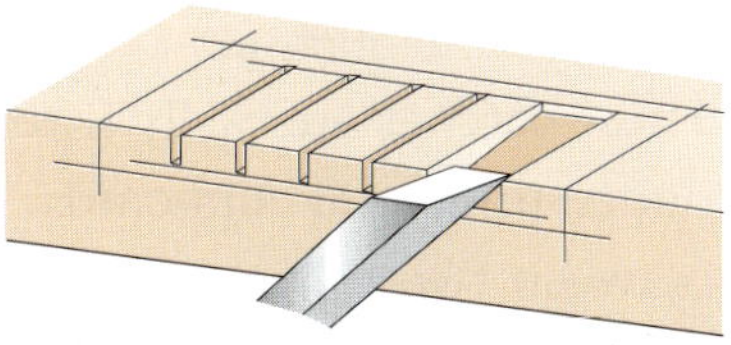

⑥ Chisel out the recesses very carefully

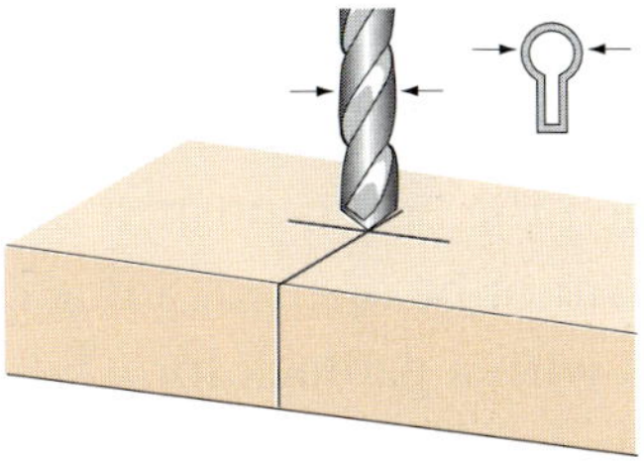

⑦ Drill, using the correct size bit, for the final escutcheon plate

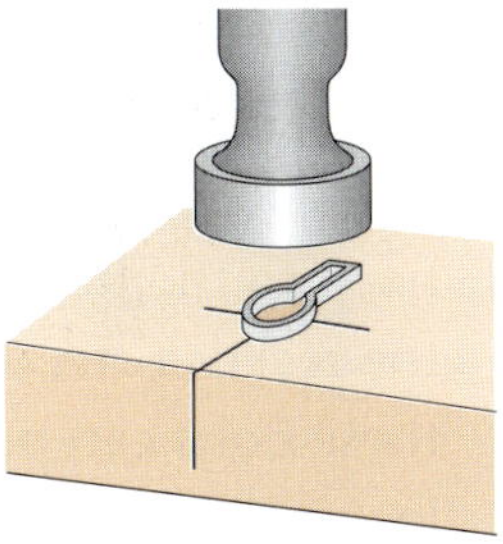

⑧ Mark the position of the escutcheon plate.

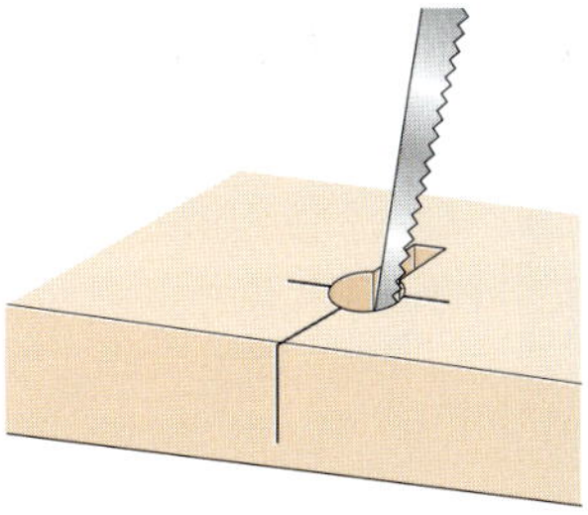

⑨ Cut out the rest of the keyhole.

⑩ Various escutcheon plates.

How to fit a box lock

Catches

Catches hold a door, lid or leaf of a table in one place to keep it firmly closed and to stop it swinging about on its hinges.

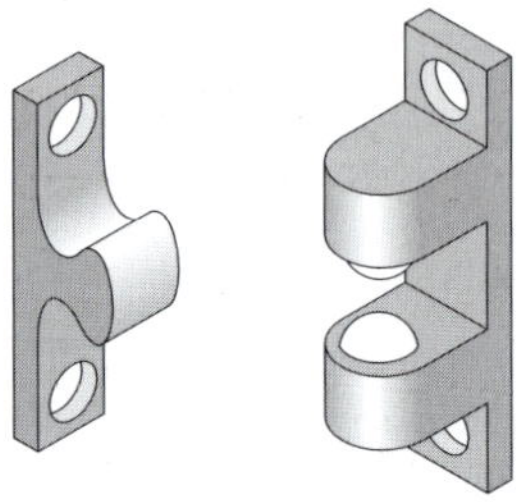

Double ball catch

There are many catches on the market, all using different methods to keep the doors and lids closed. Some use force, some are spring loaded, some are magnetic and some are mechanical. The choice of catch depends on the following:

- Size of door leaf
- Weight of door leaf – is the catch strong enough?
- Aesthetics, will the catch look good if seen? Will it suit the function of the door?

Roller catch

These catches are easily fitted on the insides of doors, units and cupboards. The clip is held between two rollers keeping the door closed. A slight pull forces the rollers to part and slide over the clip allowing the door to open. The rollers are spring loaded.

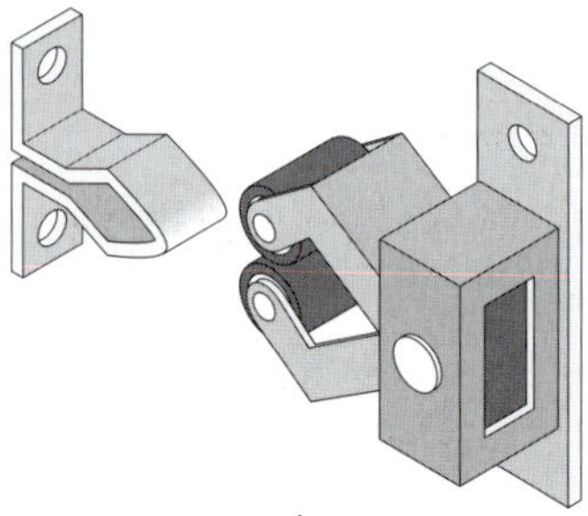

Roller catch

Magnetic catch

This catch is used frequently in cupboards. Usually it is a plastic catch, housing a magnet and a magnetic steel plate. The plate is fixed to the door and the magnet is fixed to the carcase. The catch is available in different colours. The catch can be adjusted to align with the door properly when closed. The attraction between the magnet and the steel plate keeps the door closed.

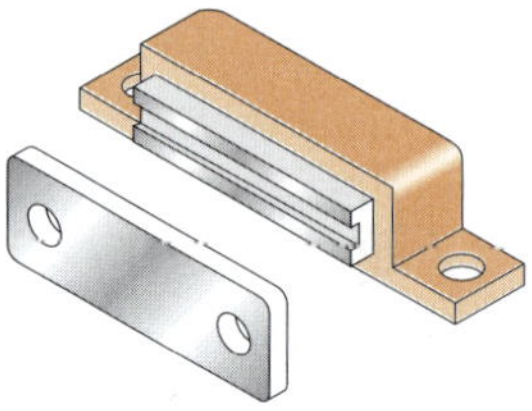

Magnetic catch

Door latch

This latch is usually used on side doors, outside doors and gates. The back plate of the latch rests in a frame plate holding the gate/door shut. The thumb presses a lever down, which raises the lever at the back, this in turn, lifts the back plate. When the back plate is raised the door can be opened. There are many variations of this latch.

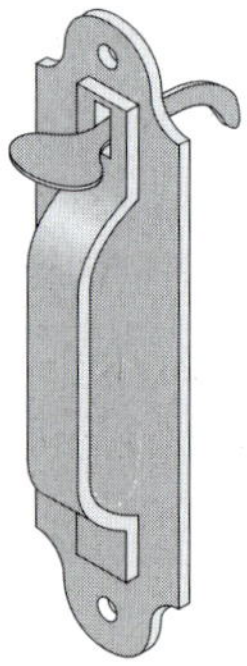

Door latch

Barrel bolt

This catch is fixed to the door. The receiver is fixed to the frame. When the bolt is pushed into the receiver the door cannot be opened. Some of these bolts can be used with a padlock for locking. They are widely used on double doors, sheds and garage doors and gates. They are galvanised for outdoor use. Smaller versions made of brass are used on cupboard doors.

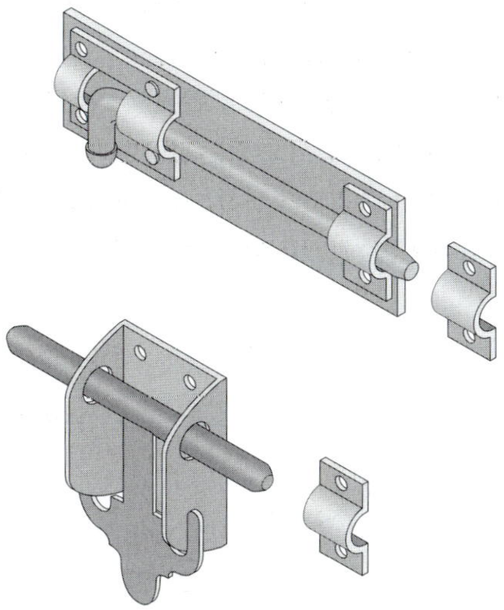

Barrel bolts

Handles

There are many different handles available to suit doors, lids, windows, boxes, containers and drawers. Handles on doors, for example, are usually used with a catch or a lock. Handles can be made from wood, metal, plastic, rope or chain. Handles can be attached by screws onto the surface from the front or back of the piece, bonded with adhesives or bolted on. Look around your local hardware shop to see how many types of handle are available. When choosing a handle for a project, make sure that the handle is the correct size for the piece – that it isn't too large or too small.

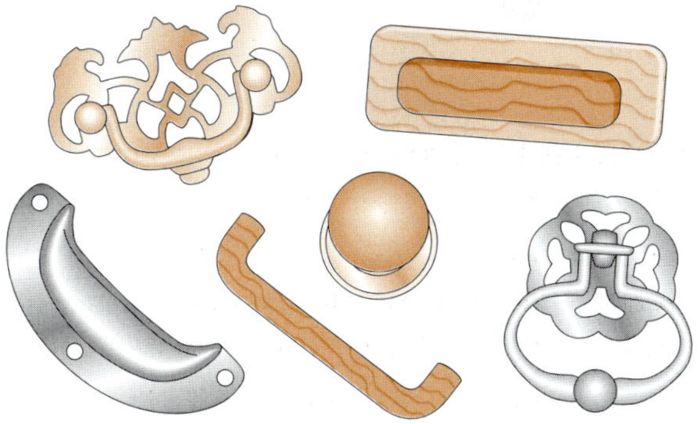

Types of handle

Exercises

1. Name each of the nails and indicate their parts.

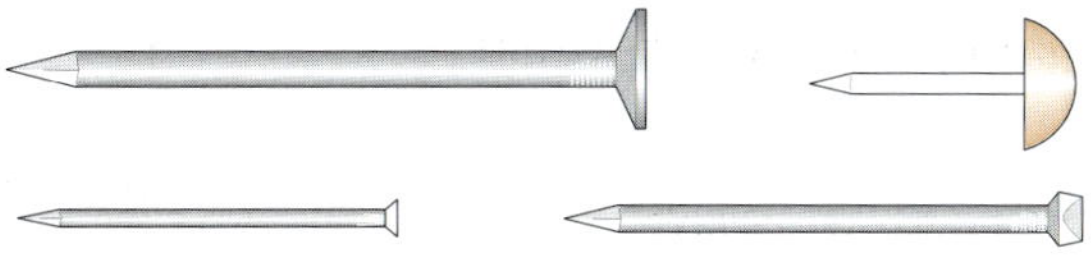

2. Name the fittings shown below and give one use for each

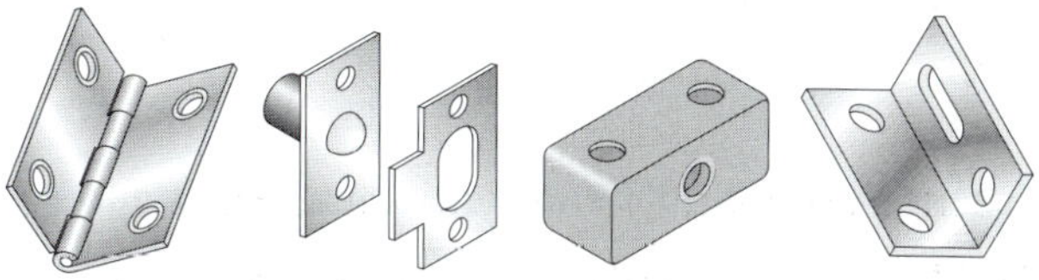

3. What are the differences between an oval wire nail and a panel pin?
4. Draw three types of screw. Label your diagrams and give uses for each type.
5. Describe two types of screw head and where each is used.
6. Explain using notes and sketches how you would fit a **butt hinge** to a door frame of a small cabinet.
7. Collect various screws and nails and make a display board to hold them.
8. Collect and display various types of small handle.
9. What would be the most suitable locks for the following situations:
   (a) Drawer
   (b) Jewellery box
   (c) Front door of a house?
10. What hinges would be most suitable for the following situations:
    (a) Piano (c) Bedroom door
    (b) Kitchen unit (d) Jewellery box?
11. What type of screw would you select for use in a piece of garden furniture. Give reasons for your choice.
12. What information should be given when ordering screws?

CHAPTER THIRTY-ONE

STRUCTURES, FORCES & MECHANISMS

Forces

Forces of different kinds act on everything we can see, including ourselves. Understanding some simple forces can help us to plan our projects and to use the equipment in the workshop. It will also help us to understand what makes joints work best.

Put simply – **A force is a PUSH or a PULL which causes change.**

Basic forces

There are a number of different forces.

Compression

This force is a pushing force which acts on an object (such as when a weight is applied to a glue roller when trying to squeeze out excess glue and air when veneering). Also a chisel works when a compression force is applied to push the blade down to pare the edge of a curve. A force of compression is applied by the vice to hold pieces firm and by cramps when gluing up a frame, etc.

Sketch showing a compression force

Compression is used to hold pieces firmly in the vice

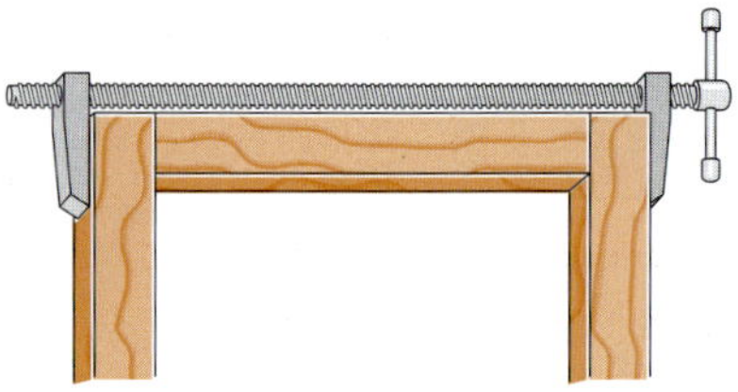

Cramps compressing joints together

Tension

Tension or tensile forces are pulling forces which try to lengthen or pull apart an item.

In a car being towed the tow rope is under a tensile force. A tensile force is put on the blade of a coping saw by the frame.

Tension force

A coping saw with blade in tension

Shear

Forces of shear will tend to move two objects in different directions over each other. A scissors or a metal snips applies a shear force to cut paper or metal sheet. This is why we use the term *to shear sheep* as the principle of the shear force is involved.

As we have already seen, nails are designed to work best under shear forces (stress).

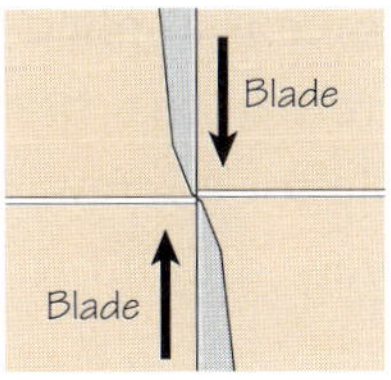

The shear force of a scissors cutting paper

Shear force

Bending

Bending forces are important in the design of projects as parts of a project which are too weak may bend if the weight (load) is too great. Also, we have already seen that a piece of solid wood or manufactured board will bend if it is not properly stacked.

Bending force

Torsion

Torsion forces are twisting forces or turning forces. A torsion force is applied to a screwdriver when driving a screw or to a bradawl when making a pilot hole for a screw. A torsion force is used also in the brace and bit to drill a hole.

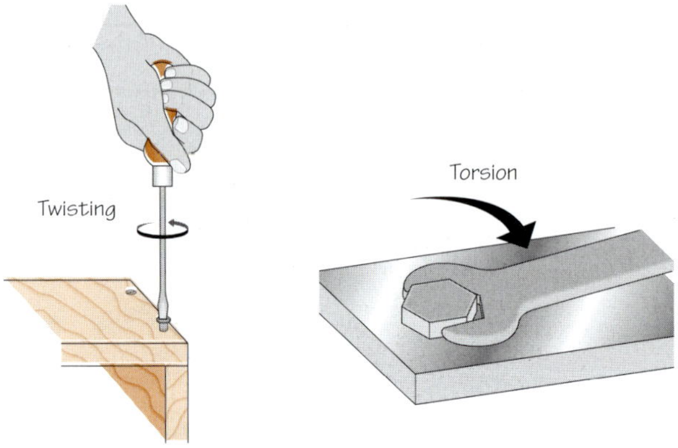

Examples of torsion forces

Mechanisms

We are all familiar with mechanisms as we use many of them each day.

Some mechanisms we use daily

We are perhaps too familiar with them to recognise that without mechanisms life would be very different and difficult. Mechanisms usually allow some task to be done more easily.

A mechanism is a simple mechanical device

A mechanism usually works by a force of some kind which results in the task being done, e.g. when you pull the brake lever of a bike the mechanism grips the rim of the wheel and this slows the bike down.

The most widely used mechanisms are:

- levers
- gears
- pulleys
- linkages.

Levers

The principle of the lever is important and many examples of levers can be found in the workshop. The simple lever is a rigid bar which pivots at a point called a fulcrum.

A screwdriver is used as a lever to remove the lid of a varnish tin. A pincers or claw hammer uses the lever to remove a nail from a piece of wood. Levers give us a **mechanical advantage** allowing us to lift weights more easily or to grip things more tightly, etc.

Simple lever

Gears

Gears are wheels of different sizes which have teeth that connect with the teeth of other gears to change the speed or direction of rotation of the other gears. A number of gears may be connected together into a **gear train.**

Gears are used in different sizes to speed up or slow down motion. If the driven gear is smaller than the drive gear motion will be speeded up. If it is larger than the drive gear motion will be slowed down.

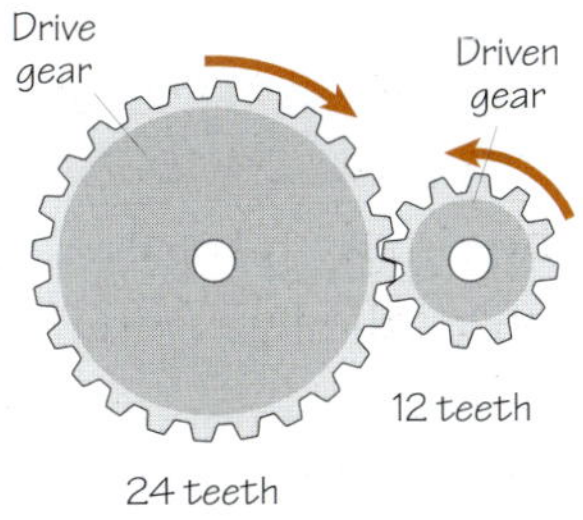

Speeded up motion

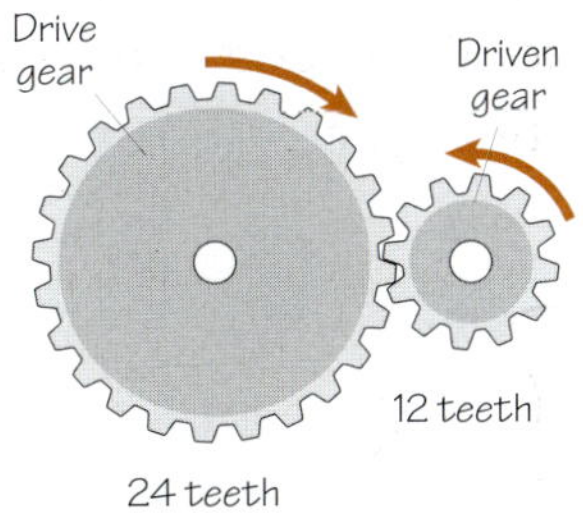

Speeded up motion

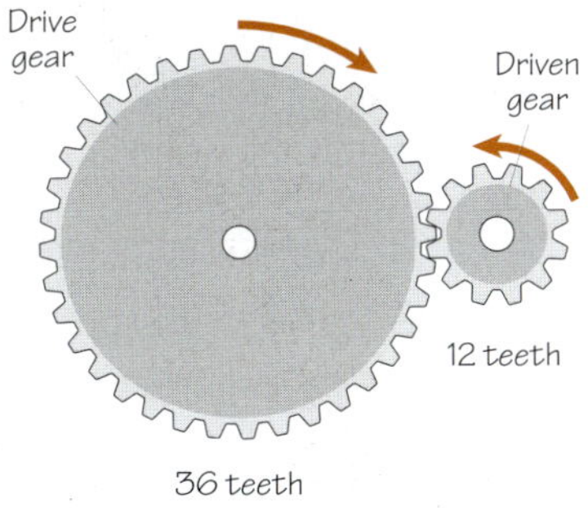

Simple spur gears

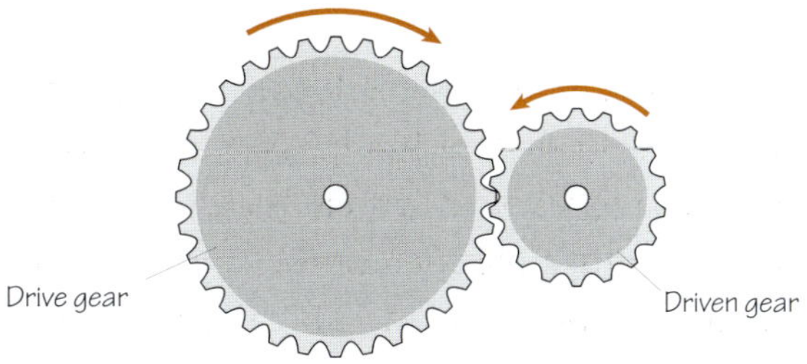

- The rotation in the drive gear will reverse the rotation in the driven gear

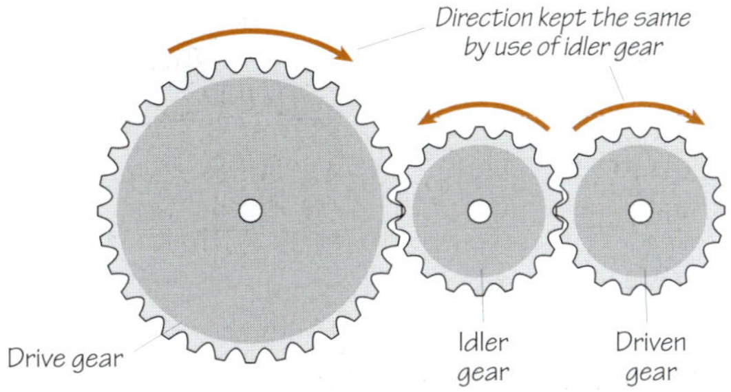

- If the direction in the driven gear is to be the same as in the drive gear an idler gear is used.

In the case of the gears just discussed the speed of rotation is called the **velocity ratio** and it can be calculated using this formula:

$$\text{Velocity Ratio} = \frac{12}{36}$$
$$= 1:3$$

A gear train can also be calculated using the formula:

$$\text{Velocity ratio} = \frac{\text{Number of teeth on driven gear}}{\text{Number of teeth on drive gear}}$$

$$VR\ (\text{total}) = VR_1 \times VR_2 \times VR_3$$

Worm gears have a single worm gear which drives a wheel at right angles to it. It has a very high velocity ratio.

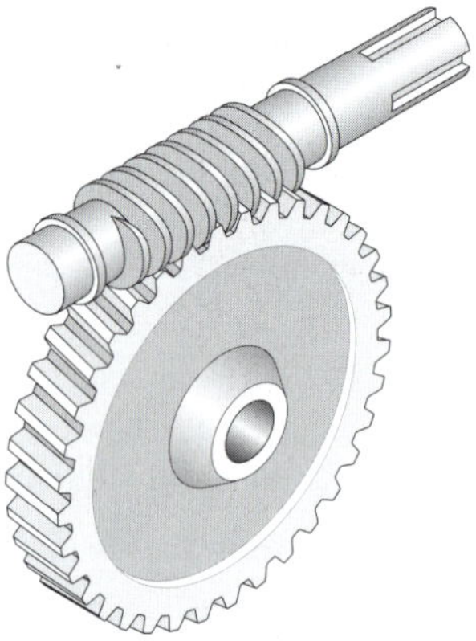

Worm gear

Helical gears have their teeth at an angle across the face and are used in car engines and gear boxes. They give good grip at high speed and they also run more quietly.

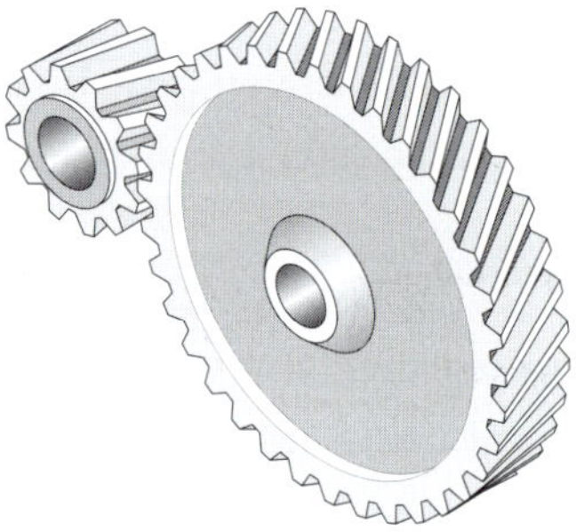

Helical gears

Bevelled gears are used in hand drills in the workshop.

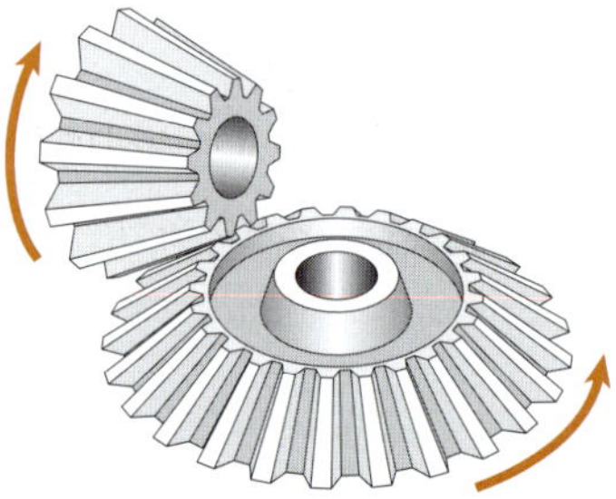

Bevelled gears are used in a hand drill

Rack and pinion gears transfer circular motion to a line motion (up/down) or vice versa. This can be seen on the mortising machine or on the small drill press.

Rack & pinion gears on mortiser & drill press

Pulleys

Pulleys are grooved wheels on which belts or ropes run. They are used to lift heavy weights or to change the drive speeds from motors.

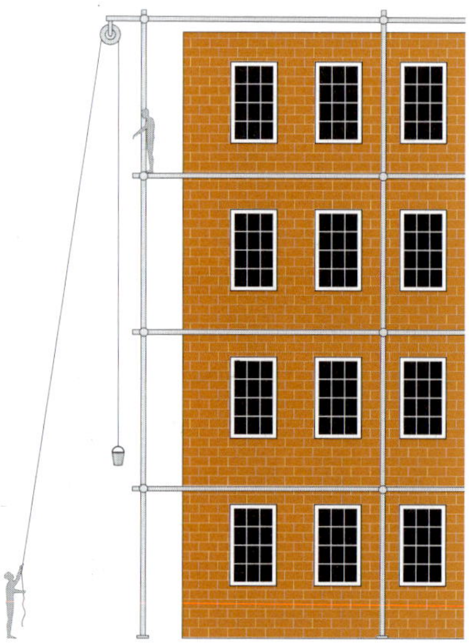

A block and tackle is used to lift heavy loads more easily

Pulleys driving parts of an engine

Pulleys used to drive and change the speed of the lathe

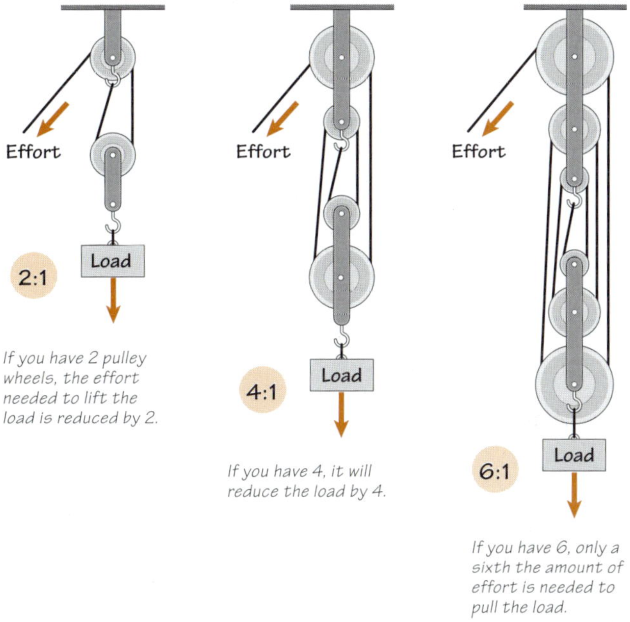

Pulleys

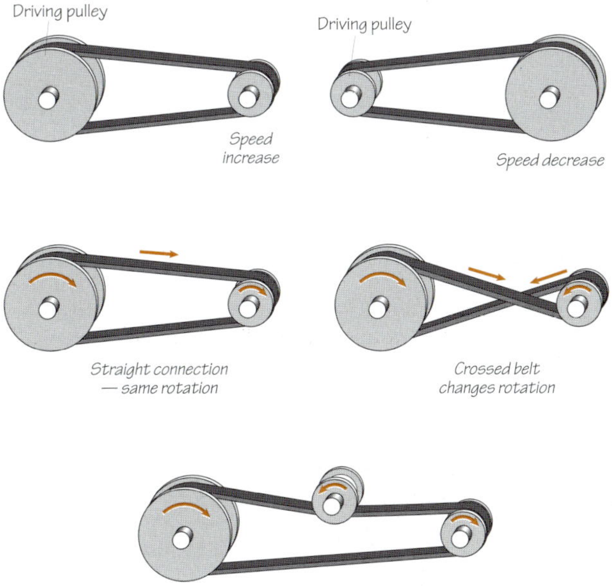

Pulleys are used to drive machinery. The lathe, for example, is driven using pulleys. Changes in speed can be achieved by using pulley wheels of different sizes. Pulleys generally drive in one direction only but if the belt is crossed it can be used to reverse the direction of rotation.

When lifting loads if two or more pulleys are used the force necessary to pull or lift the load will be reduced. It will be further reduced by adding a third or fourth wheel into the pulley system.

To calculate the **velocity ratio** for a pulley the following formula is used:

$$\textbf{VR} = \frac{\text{Diameter of driven wheel}}{\text{Diameter of driving wheel}}$$

The **output speed** can be calculated using:

$$\textbf{Output speed (OS)} = \frac{\text{Input speed}}{\text{VR}}$$

Example:

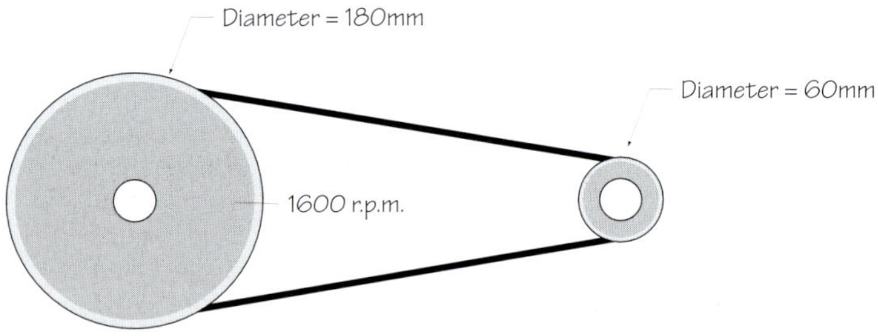

Calculate the r.p.m. (output speed) of the smaller pulley wheel

The drive wheel has a diameter of 180mm and the driven wheel has a diameter of 60mm, calculate the output speed of the driven wheel if the speed of the drive wheel is 1600 r.p.m.

$$\text{VR} = \frac{60}{180} = \frac{1}{3} = 1{:}3$$

$$\text{OS} = \frac{1600}{1{:}3} = 1600 \text{ X } \frac{3}{1} = 4800 \text{ r.p.m.}$$

Linkages

Linkages are levers connected together. Linkages allow us to change a force in magnitude, direction or both.

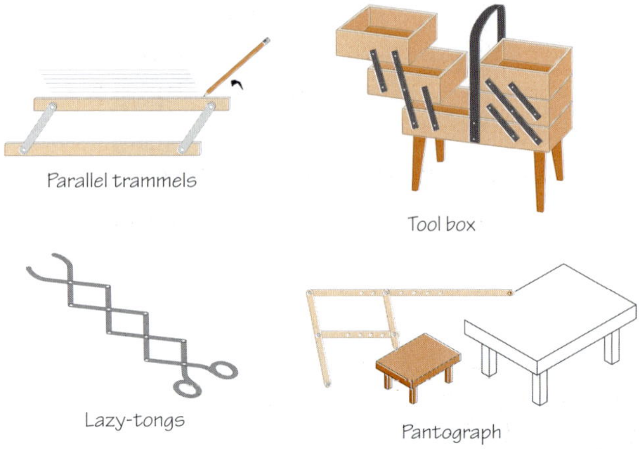

Some simple linkages

Structures

We are familiar with bridges, buildings, cranes, towers and so on as structures. The human body is also a structure and a table or a mirror frame is a structure. A structure is the method by which an object gets its strength and stability. If the joints in a bridge are not strong and well-made the bridge will collapse. In the same way the items or structures we make must be stable and strong, well-made and well-proportioned. When a box, chair or table is made, it must be a rigid structure capable of withstanding the forces which will be applied to it.

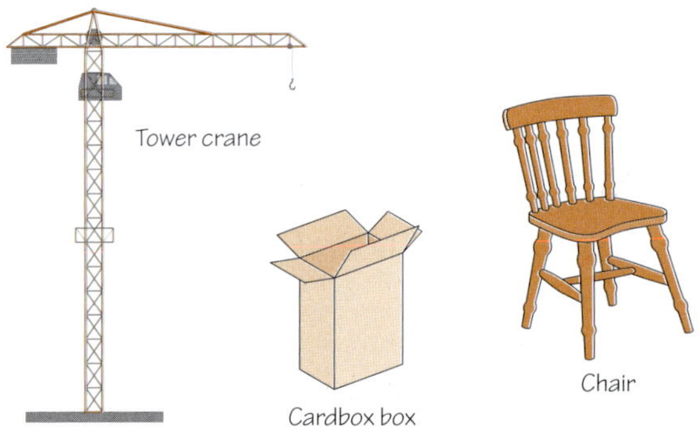

Examples of structures

A structure can be a frame and most good structures are made up of one or many frames. The frame gives strength and stability to the structure.

A triangle is the strongest structure. This is why roof trusses and electricity towers are built in structures based on triangles (**triangulation**).

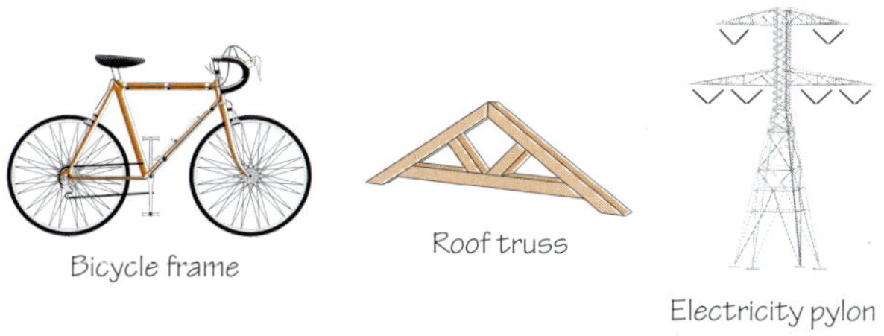

Triangulated structures

If we design a structure that is weak we may strengthen it by adding an extra piece.

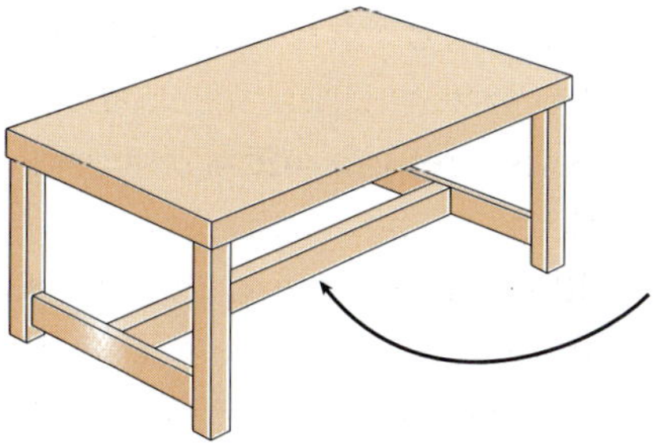

Structures strengthened by adding a member to make it rigid

Stability

Stability is also important when designing. An object should not topple over too easily. An object is made stable by keeping the weight of the object low and increasing the size of the base to keep the centre of gravity low.

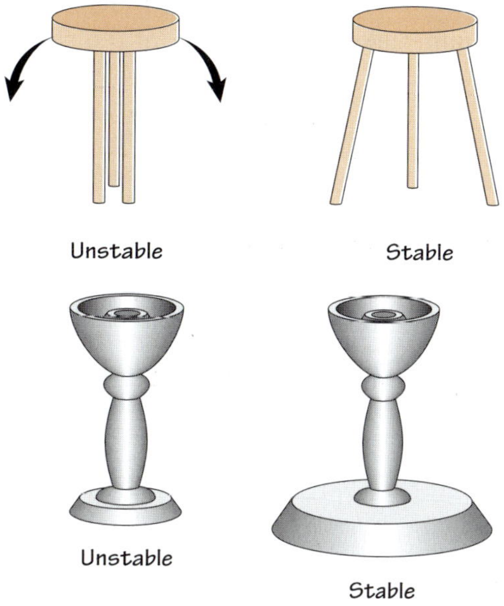

Exercises

1. What is a mechanism?
   What is a lever?
   Give three examples of each.
2. Name three types of forces.
3. Four forces are illustrated below. Name each type and give one example of each type.

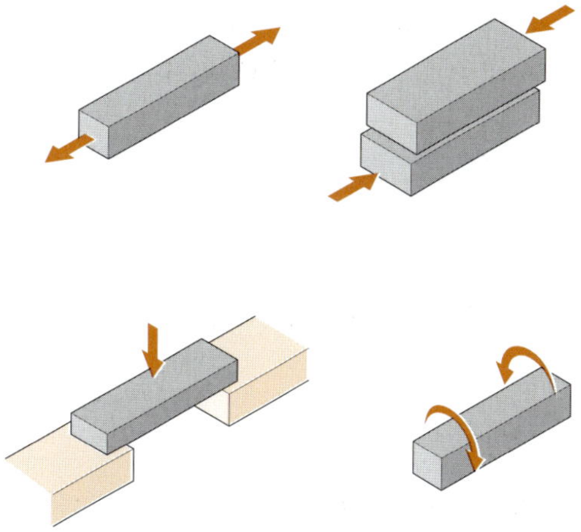

4. Describe what a force is?

5. A simple pulley system is shown in the diagram. Calculate the r.p.m. of the smaller pulley.

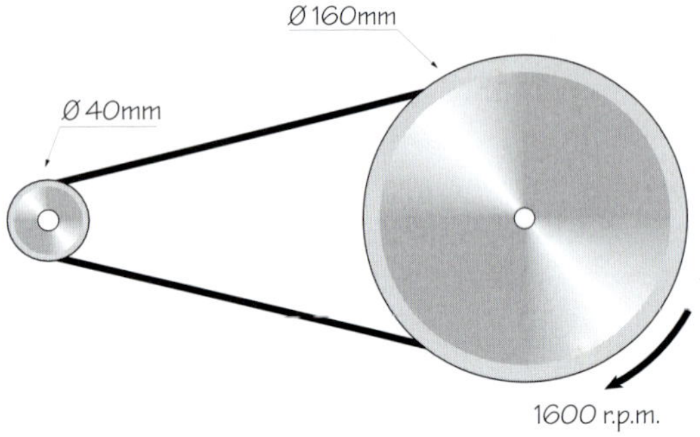

6. The diagram shows sections of gear trains in electric motors. If the gear wheel A rotates in the direction shown, indicate with an arrow the direction in which B will rotate in each case.

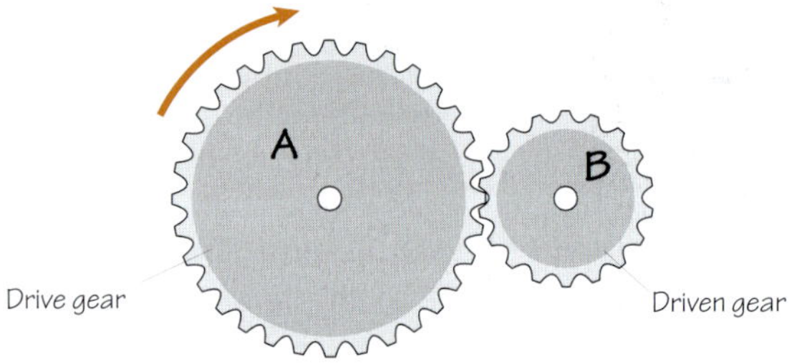

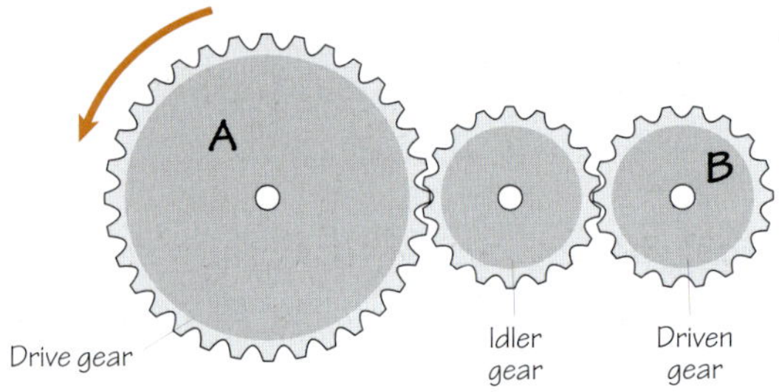

7. The diagram shows the gear and chuck mechanisms of a wheel brace. If the driving wheel is rotated at 20 revolutions per minute, what would the output speed of the drill be?

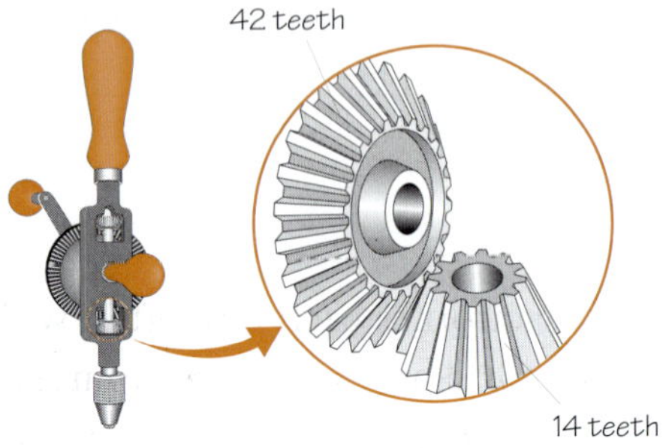

CHAPTER THIRTY-TWO

SIMPLE ELECTRONIC CIRCUITS

We all use electronics each day often without even realising it. Radios, TVs, computers, even very simple devices now incorporate electronics. Electronics help to provide us with heat, light and food.

In this chapter we will take a look at some simple electronic circuits which you can use in your projects. For example, here is a design for the electronic circuit of a portable bedside light.

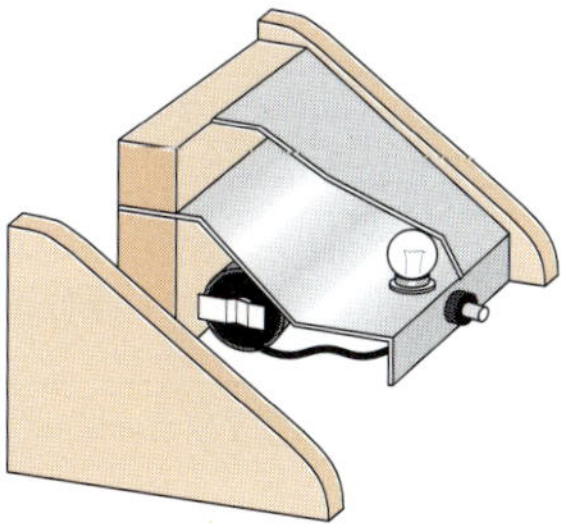

Electronics

Everything, including your own body, is made up of atoms. An atom has a nucleus of **protons** and **neutrons**. **Electrons** orbit the nucleus at very high speeds and they carry a negative charge. **Protons** carry a positive charge and neutrons carry no charge. Electronics, in its simplest form, is the movement of electrons along conductors. A conductor is a material which will allow electrons to move through it easily. Many materials will conduct electricity; however, some are better than others. The most popular conductor for use in electronics is copper.

Circuits

Do not interfere with electricity at home or school – electrical appliances are always dangerous. Remember electricity kills

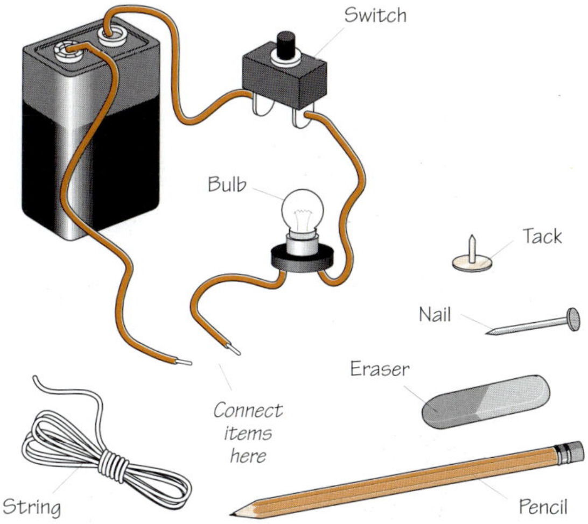

A light, battery and switch with some materials to connect items to test for conductors

Try the experiment shown in the diagram above and record which material will allow the bulb to light. Conductors complete a **circuit** which will allow the bulb to light. Bad conductors (insulators) will not allow the bulb to light. Electric cable or flex is covered with plastic as plastic is a good insulator.

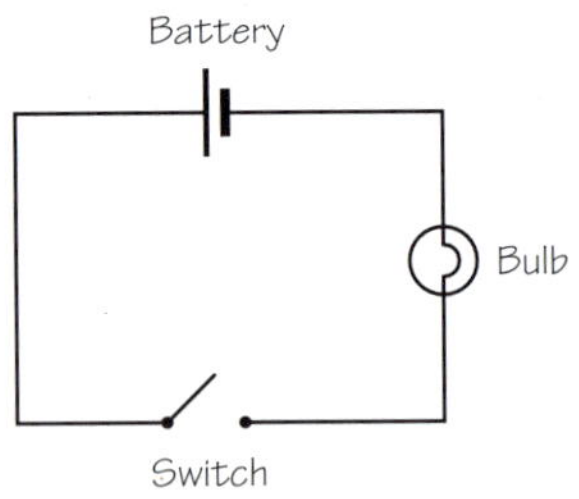

A switch is used to make and break a circuit

A circuit is formed when the terminals of the battery are connected to the bulb or any other set of components. To stop the circuit flowing a switch is used to prevent the current from flowing.

The battery has two terminals, one positive and one negative. When a conductor is attached to each terminal the electrons in the conductor are pushed by the negative terminal and attracted to the positive one. This causes the electrons to flow through the conductor. The flow of electric charge is called **current**. Current is measured in amperes (or amps). The **voltage** is the force which makes the electrons move and is measured in **volts**. A component (e.g. a bulb) must be included in a circuit or the battery may be damaged.

	COMPONENT	SYMBOL	DESCRIPTION
BATTERY		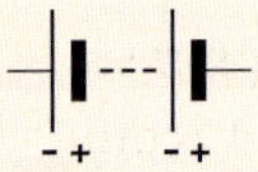	Provides the power or voltage in the circuit
BULB		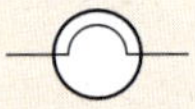	Small light bulb.
FUSE			Component with a resistance wire used to protect the circuit
MOTOR		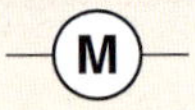	Driven by the current it provides movement
RESISTOR	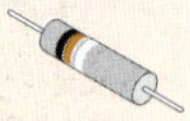		Controls current by resisting the flow of electrons
VARIABLE RESISTOR	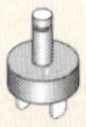	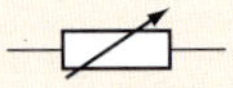	The resistance can be adjusted between resistance of a certain range
AMMETER		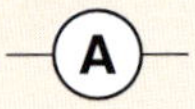	A device for measuring current
SWITCH			Allows the current to be turned on and off in the circuit
LDR Light dependent resistor		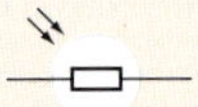	A resistor whose resistance varies with light intensity
LED		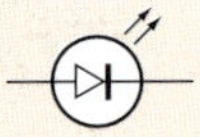	Light emitting diode
THERMISTOR		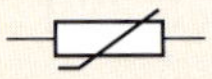	Resistor whose resistance varies with temperature
TRANSISTOR		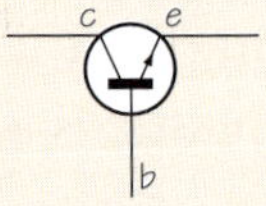	Acts as switch or amplifier

Symbols	
A	Amps
V	Volts

Circuits are drawn according to agreed standards and conventions similar to other working drawings. Components such as batteries, lights and measuring devices all have individual symbols so they can be easily recognised. The table below shows some of the more common ones.

The current between the terminals of a battery depends on the voltage. A small voltage generates a small current and a large voltage generates a large current. Voltage is also referred to as the **potential difference** or **PD**. This is the difference of electrical pressure between the terminals of a battery. For example, a 6V battery has a PD of 6V between its terminals. The best way to build a circuit is on a special board. There are three different types of board; printed circuit board, Veroboard and Matrix board.

Circuit boards

Printed circuit board (PCB)

A printed circuit board is a non-conducting board, usually fibre glass, which is covered with copper. The design for the circuit is drawn on the copper and the unwanted material removed by a chemical process. The various components are attached to these remaining copper tracks.

Veroboard

This is an non-conducting board with rows of copper strip. The copper strip has holes bored in it at regular intervals, so that the components may be inserted through the holes and soldered into place.

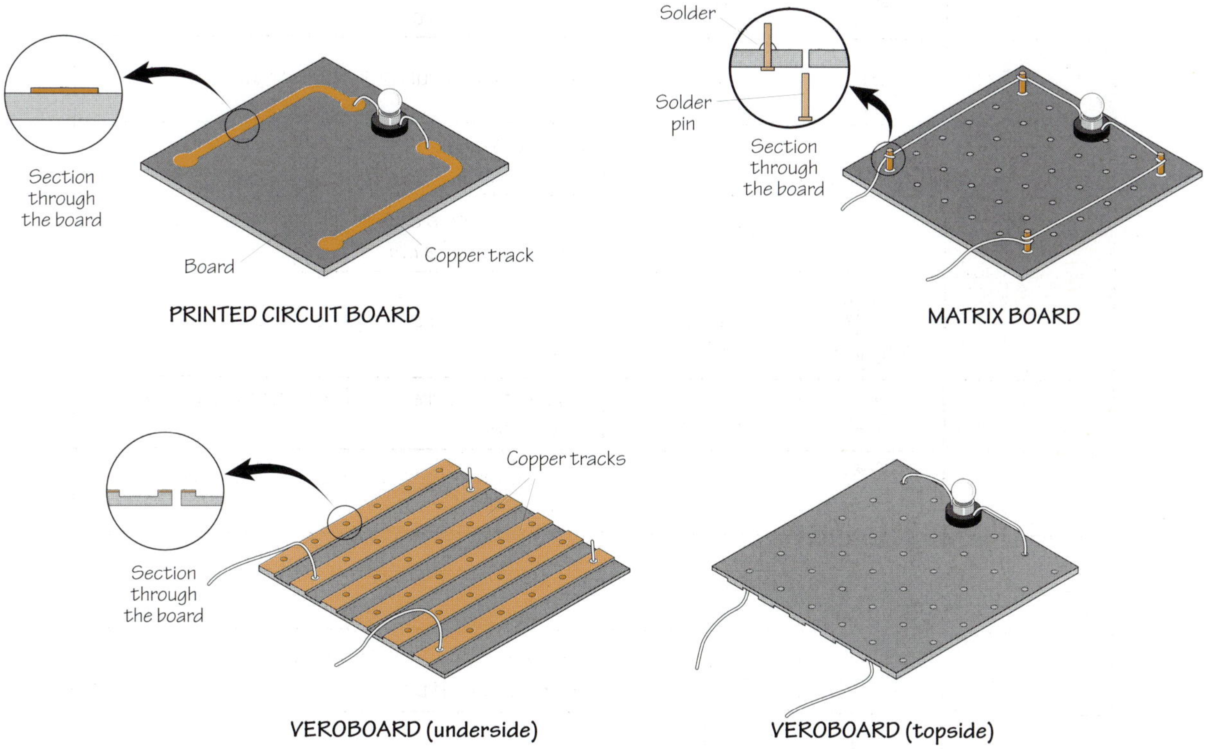

A printed circuit board, Veroboard & Matrix board

Matrix board

This is another non-conducting board with small holes drilled at regular intervals. Solder pins are pushed through the holes and the components are soldered to the pins.

Soldering

Soldering is a method of joining two metals with the aid of a third metal called **solder** (tin and lead). The solder is heated and melted onto the joint. When cool, it forms a bond between the pieces. The bit of a new soldering iron will need to be cleaned with a piece of very fine emery paper, and then coated with solder. This is called tinning the bit.

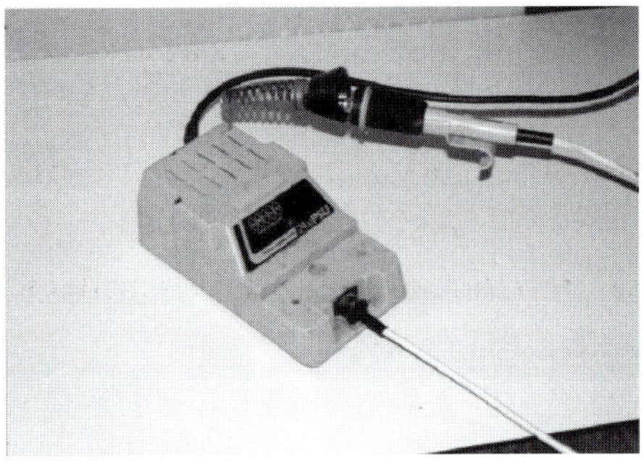

Soldering iron

> **BEWARE!** A soldering iron is hot. Be careful it does not burn your skin. Do not leave the hot iron near the electrical cable

Using the soldering iron

- Check that all surfaces are clean and free from grease, or other substances which will prevent the solder sticking. It is a good idea to give all surfaces a rub with wire wool or emery paper before starting work.
- Plug in the soldering iron and wait a few minutes for it to heat up
- Clean the tip of the iron on a damp sponge
- Touch the tip of the iron with the solder to "wet it"
- Position the solder pins in the required positions
- Holding the iron against a solder pin, heat the pin.While keeping the pin hot with the iron, apply some solder
- Position the leg of the component against the molten solder and remove the iron. Hold the component in place until the solder has set.

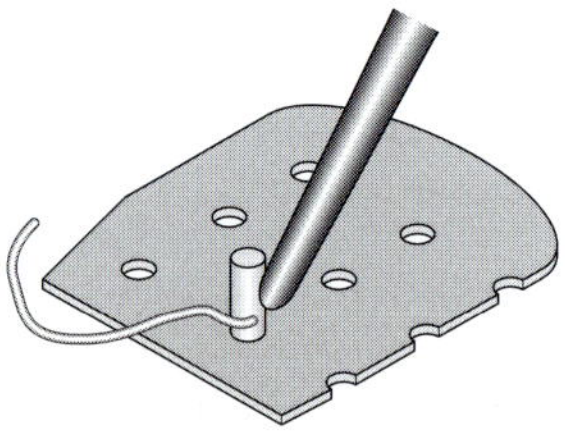

Heat solder pin then apply solder

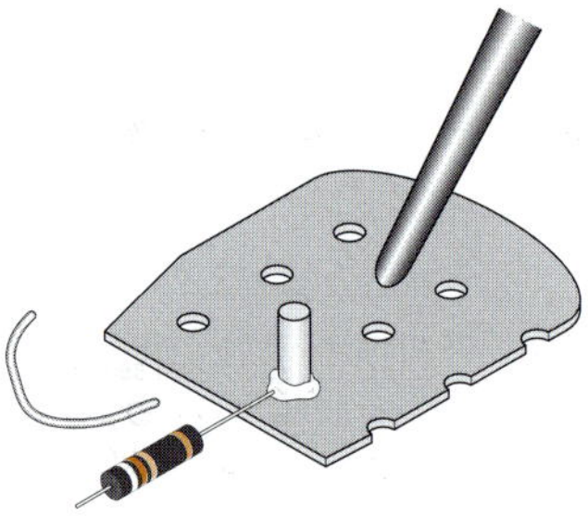

Hold the component in place while the solder sets

- Remember not to heat the solder with the iron. Heat the pin and allow it to melt the solder
- When the operation is complete, the excess component tails and waste wire may be removed with a wire snips.

Resistors

Components called **resistors** are specially made to restrict the flow of current. Resistance is measured in **ohms**. The size of a current depends on the resistance of the circuit. By varying the resistance in the circuit the current may be controlled.

Most resistors are made from carbon and they come in different strengths or values. This value can be calculated using the coloured bands which are found on each resistor. The following diagram shows how to calculate the value of a resistor.

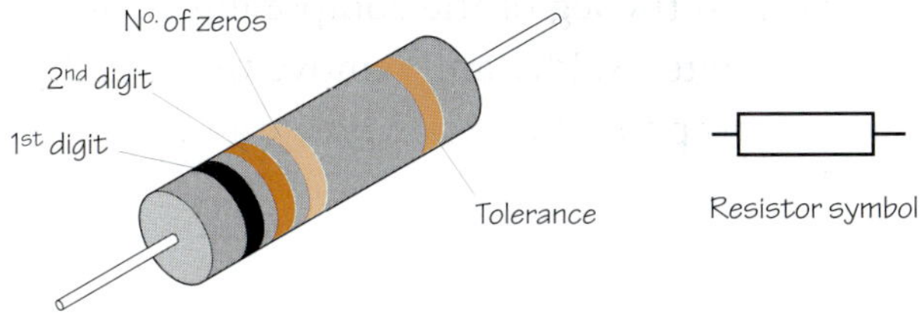

Resistors

Values			
Black 0	Brown – 1	Red – 2	Orange – 3
Yellow – 4	Green – 5	Blue – 6	Violet – 7
Grey – 8	White – 9		
Tolerance	Gold 5%	Silver 10%	

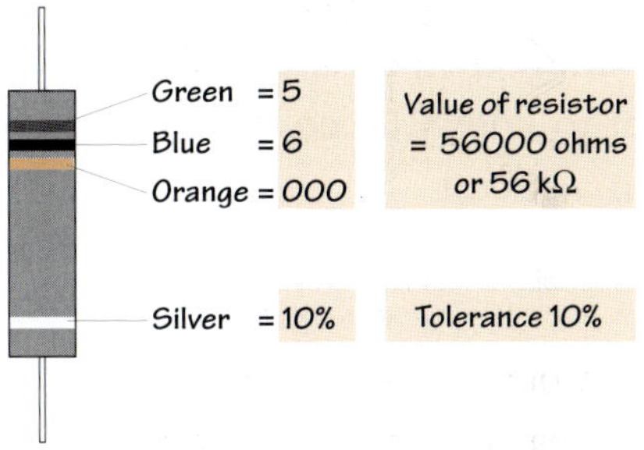

Calculating the value of a resistor

High resistances are measured in **kilohms**

1 K = 1000 ohms

There are also variable resistors available. By turning a dial the resistance in a circuit may be adjusted. The variable resistors come in different sizes and each can vary the resistance within a certain range.

Here are two resistors connected together in a circuit. These resistors are said to be in series, which means that the two resistances are added together. This will make the bulb light weak.

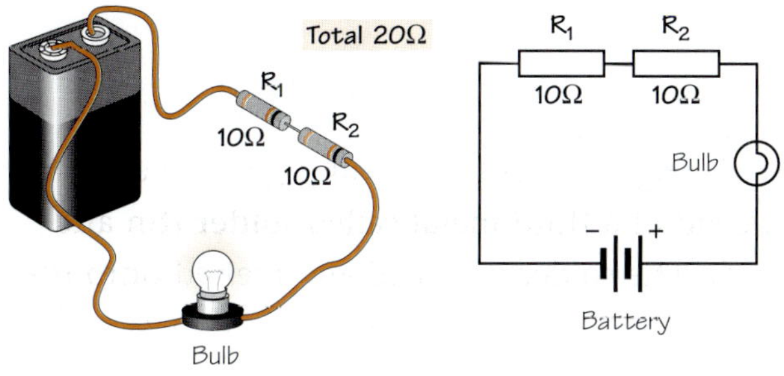

Resistors in series

$$R_{total} = R_1 + R_2 + R_3$$

Consider connecting the same two resistors side by side as shown. The bulb will be brighter. These resistors are said to be connected in parallel.

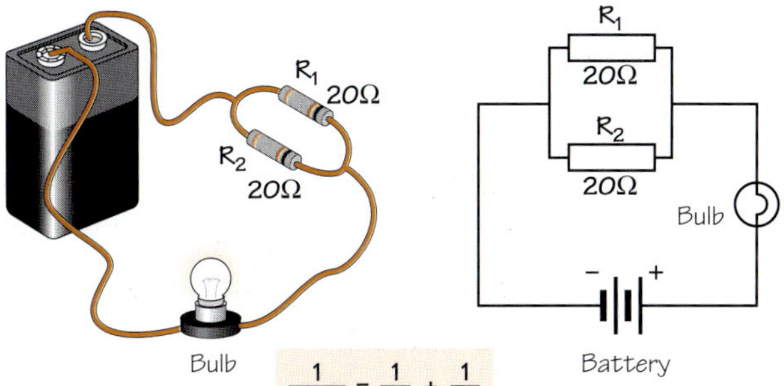

$$\frac{1}{R_{TOTAL}} = \frac{1}{R_1} + \frac{1}{R_1}$$

$$\frac{1}{R_{TOTAL}} = \frac{1}{20} + \frac{1}{20} = \frac{2}{20}$$

$$R_{TOTAL} = \frac{20}{2} = 10\Omega$$

Resistors in parallel

Here is the same experiment carried out with light bulbs. The bulbs in parallel will be brighter because the resistance of the two paths is shared giving a lower resistance overall.

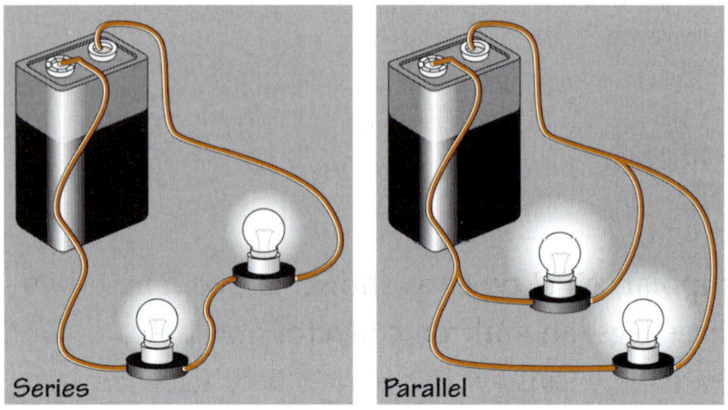

Ohm's Law

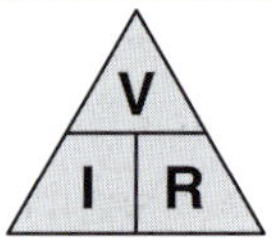

Voltage		Current		Resistance
Volts	=	Amps	x	Ohms

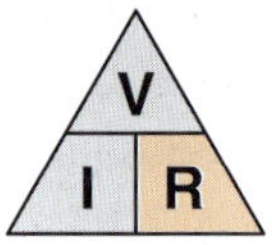

$$\text{Resistance} = \frac{\text{Voltage}}{\text{Current}}$$

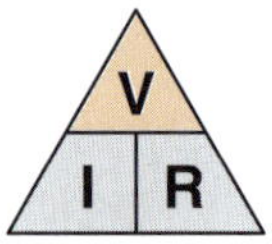

Voltage = Current x Resistance

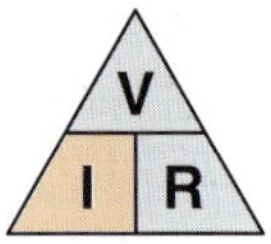

$$\text{Current} = \frac{\text{Voltage}}{\text{Resistance}}$$

Ohm's law

You can easily calculate the voltage, current or resistance in a circuit by using Ohm's Law. This rule or law is represented by the formula above.

When using this formula, it is possible to calculate the missing value when given any other two.

Light dependent resistor (LDR)

Light dependent resistors are components which can sense changes in light. Its resistance is high in brightness, but low in darkness. When added to a transistor /potential divider it can help to control the circuit. When it is covered, the bulb lights up and when uncovered, the bulb is switched off.

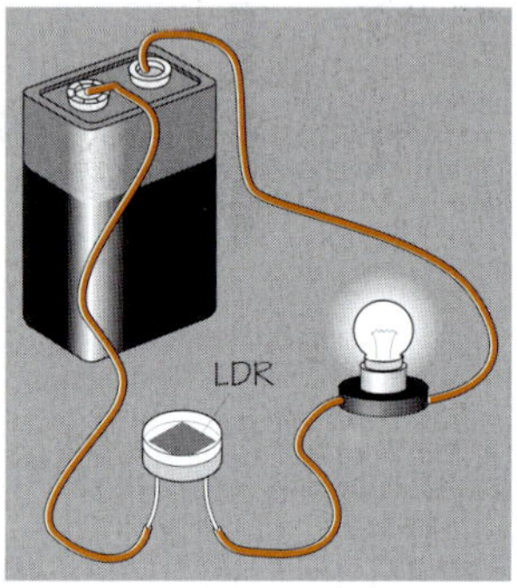

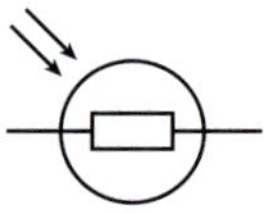

Symbol for light dependent resistor

LDR

Light emitting diodes (LED)

The light emitting diode, or LED, is like a small bulb. LEDs come in various colours, red, green, and yellow. A flashing LED is also available. When it is integrated into a circuit, however, it will only allow the current flow one way, so it is important to know the correct way to connect an LED in a circuit.

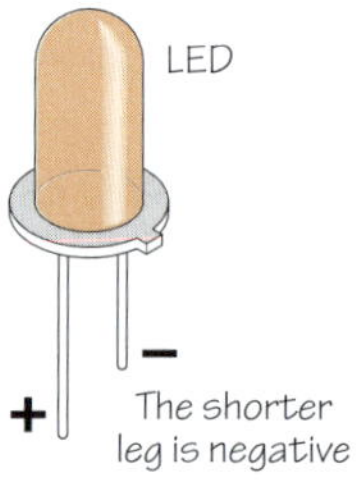

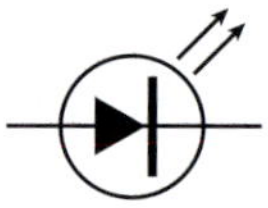

Symbol for light emitting diode

A LED

A resistor must be added to a circuit with an LED to prevent it from overloading. The circuit below may be useful for projects.

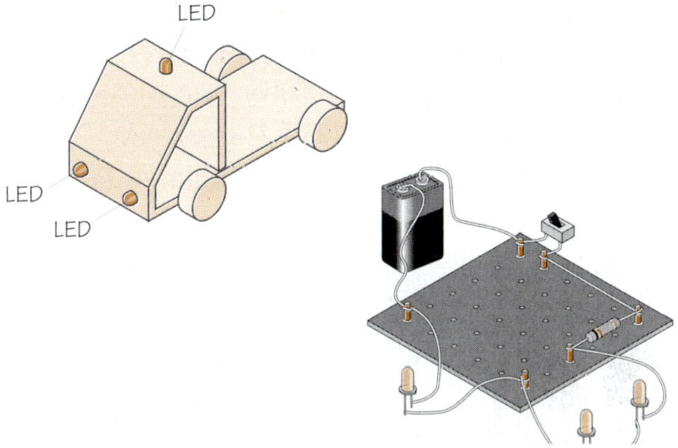

LEDs used in a lorry

Thermistors

The thermistor is a component that has a resistance which varies with temperature. There are two types. One whose resistance increases with a rise in temperature and the second whose resistance decreases with an increase in temperature.

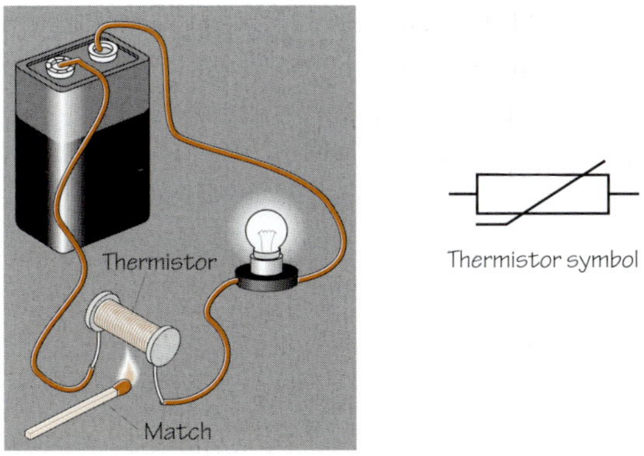

A thermistor

Transistors

Transistors are components which act like a switch. They are semi-conductor devices.

Transistors used in schools are generally

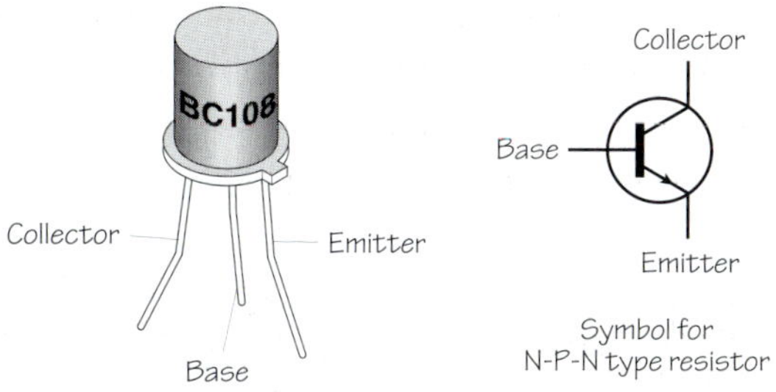

Transistor

(bipolar) NPN types as shown above. These have three legs, an emitter, collector and base. Transistors can act like a switch or they can also be used as an amplifying device.

All electronic manufacturers have catalogues that show which leg is which on their particular transistors. When a small current is applied to the base the transistor is ON and current flows from collector to emitter. When no current is present on the base the transistor is OFF and there will be no current flowing between the collector and emitter. In the same way as a push switch is controlled by your finger, the transistor is controlled by the small current on the base.

Capacitors

Capacitors are components which fill up with electrical charge when connected to a power supply and they store this charge until it is released. They are used in a television to build up and store the high voltages needed to make it work. They are also used in the flash units of cameras.

Have you ever noticed warnings on TV sets and other electrical equipment warning about the danger of removing the back or cover? The reason for this warning is that capacitors may remain charged when the equipment is turned off so you could still get an electric shock.

Capacitors come in all shapes and sizes but can be divided into two types; ordinary and electrolytic. The electrolytic type has a negative and a positive leg and must be connected the correct way round in a circuit. A stripe or other marking will indicate where the negative leg is on the capacitor.

The value of a capacitor is measured in **farads** which are large units. **Microfarads** are more often used.

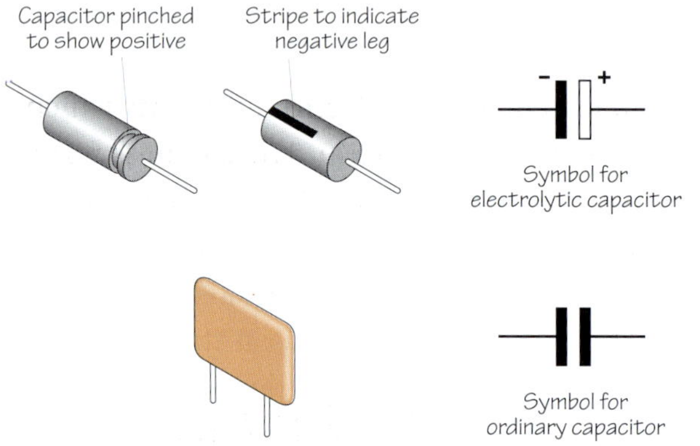

Capacitors

Circuits

Why not try making this circuit below, for an alarm buzzer? An alarm can be added to a jewellery box. This could be done with a switch which is activated when the lid is lifted. A push to break switch is used to activate the circuit.

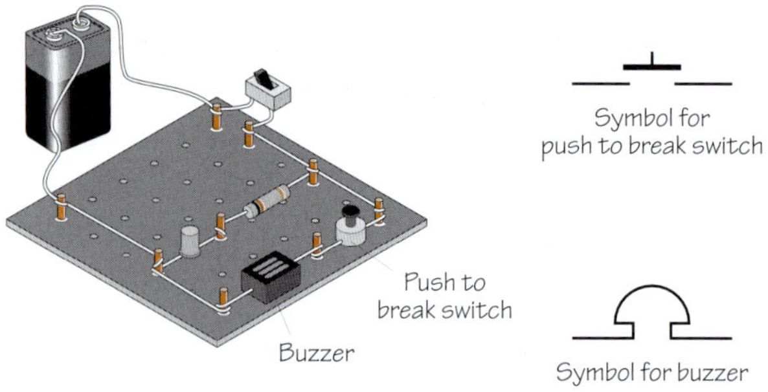

Alarm circuit

It is also possible to create a circuit which can detect water. When the water level in the beaker rises to the level of the probes, then the LED lights. This works because the water is a conductor and allows a current to flow between the probes thus sending a small current to the base of the transistor. This switches the circuit on by allowing current to flow through the collector the emitter. This is called making the transistor high. The base of the transistor becomes high when it receives a voltage of above 0.6V. There are different methods of providing a voltage to the base of the transistor, so that more than 0.6V is available to turn on the transistor. One of the most popular methods is achieved with a pair of resistors. This circuit is called a **potential divider.**

Total resistance = 25 ohms
Voltage = 5V
Current flowing
$I = {}^{V}/_{R}$
$I = {}^{5}/_{25}$
I = 0.2 amps

The diagram below shows two resistors and a 5V battery.

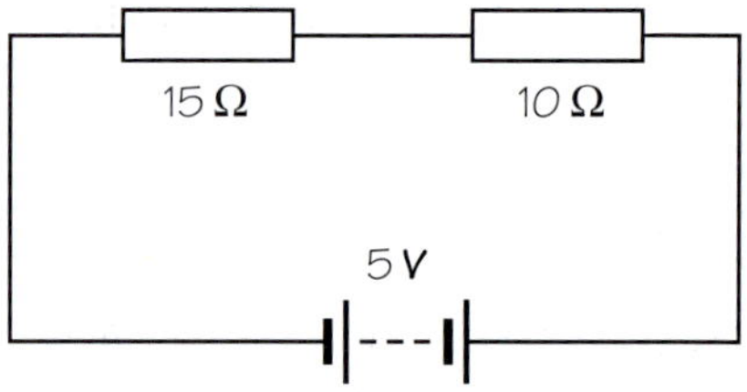

The potential divider

To calculate the voltage dropped across each resistor:

	V = IXR
Resistor 1	**0.2 x 10 = 2**
Resistor 2	**0.2 x 15 = 3**

Voltage drop across Resistor 1 = 2V
Voltage drop across Resistor 2 = 3V

You can calculate how much voltage is dropped by each component using Ohm's law. In this example the total resistance of A and B is 25 ohms and the battery voltage is 5 volts. The calculation shows the voltage drop across the resistors.

The circuit could be incorporated into a model car to make the lights go on in the dark. It uses a switch to activate the circuit and LEDs as lights.

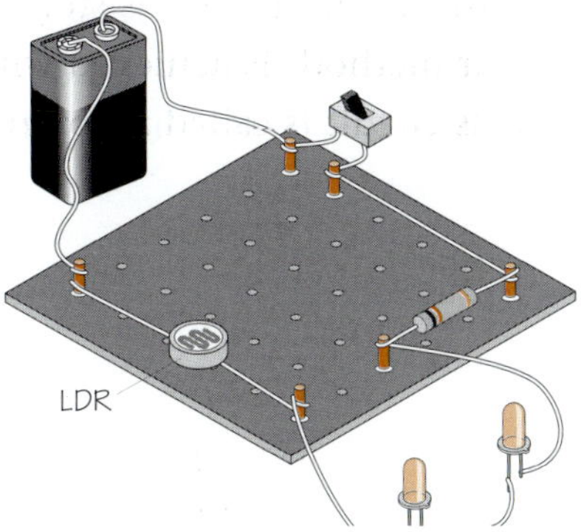

Car with lights

A thermistor can be used in a circuit to detect changes in temperature. This could be used in a device to warn of hot wax overflowing in a candle holder.

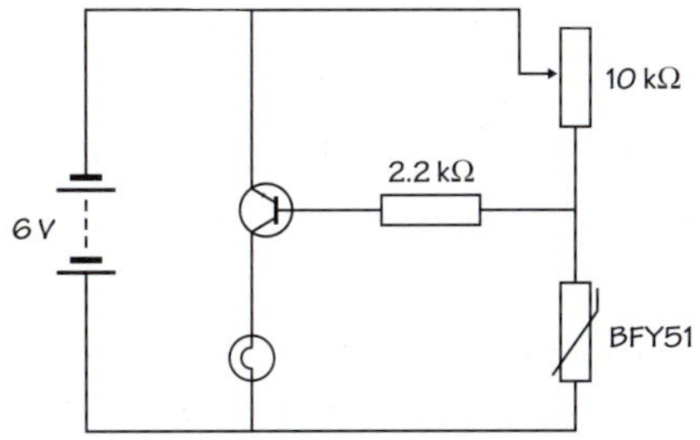

A circuit with a thermistor

Integrated circuits

Integrated circuits are electronic circuits which are incorporated on a chip. The circuit is formed on a silicon chip and this chip is mounted on a small plastic cover. The chip is connected to the circuit board through pins which come out of the side of the chip.

Integrated circuit (IC) chip

Exercises

1. Design a circuit which will activate a buzzer when a person stands on it.
2. Design a circuit which will switch a light on at your bedside when it gets dark.
3. Design a circuit which will detect heat.
4. Design and make a container for valuable personal items with an alarm fitted.
5. What is the total voltage of these sets of batteries.

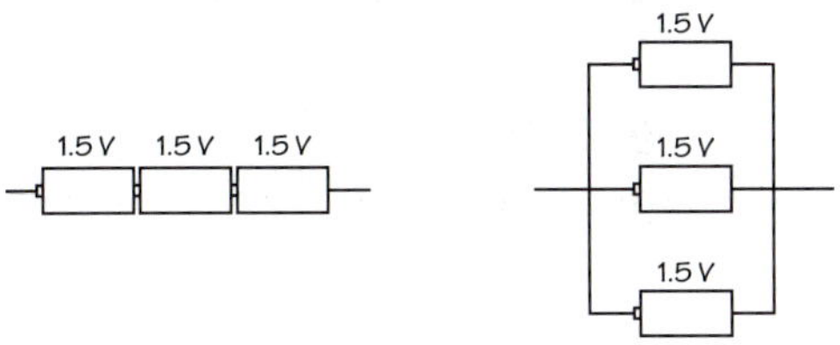

6. Sketch the following electronic components and their graphic symbols.
   (a) Switch
   (b) LED
   (c) Transistor
   (d) Variable resistor
   (e) Buzzer
   (f) Battery
7. What do the following terms mean:
   (a) Voltage
   (b) Resistance
   (c) Current?
8. State Ohm's Law.

Index

A

abrasive, grading, 251
abrasive paper, 251
acid rain, 34
acrylic, 79
adhesion, specific, 243
adhesion, mechanical, 243
adhesive, animal, 243
adhesive, contact, 246
adhesive casein, 244
adhesives, 242
adhesives, synthetic, 245
alloys (mixture of metals), 67
alumina, 69
aluminium oxide, 251
aluminium, 69
annealing, 71
annual rings, 30
arc (CAD), 182
applied finish, 254
array (CAD), 185
ash, 16
Auger bits, 105

B

baize, 88
balsa, 23
banding, 214
bandsaw 36, 131
bark (cortex), 30
basic oxygen furnace, 68
bast (phloem), 30
bauxite, 69
bead, 230
beech, 17
beeswax, 258
beetle, furniture, 51
beetle, powder post, 51
beetle, deathwatch, 51
bending, woods suitable for, 240
bending, seam, 240
bending, 279
bevel, sliding, 94
birch, 15
biscuit joiner, 125
blank, 205
blast furnace, 68
bolts, 277
boring a hole, 106
bowing, 48
boxwood, 24
bradawl, 106
brass, 70
break (CAD), 183
brushing and spraying, 55

C

cabinet scraper, use of, 222
cabinet scrapers, 254
CAD, 179
callipers, 228
callipers, Vernier, 94
callipers, inside and outside, 95
cambium layer, 30
capacitor, 293
carpenter's brace, 105
carving - suitable woods, 211
carving - suitable finishes, 211
carving, incised, 203
carving, chip, 203
carving, relief, 204
case hardening, 48
cast iron, 68
casting, 83
ceramics, 89
chamfer (CAD), 184
cherry, 17
chisel, mortise, 102
chisels, carving, 208
chisels, 101
chlorophyll, 29
circuit boards, 289
circuits, 287
closed assembly time, 243
coillte, 10
collapse, 49
colour, 66
colour and shading, 175
compass/dividers, 94
components, 288
compression, 278
computer aided design (CAD), 179
computer aided manufacture, 134
computer system, parts of, 180
computer devices, 180
computer screen menus, 181
conifers, 26
conversion, 36
copper, 70
copy (CAD), 184
cords, wools and rope, 88
cork, 253
cove, 230
creosote, 52
cupping, 48
currents, 288
cutting, rotary, 58
cutting list, 157

D

danish oil, 257
deciduous, 26
defects, natural 46
defects, artificial, 48
density, 65
design ideas, 154
dimension (CAD), 182
dipping, 74
discoloration, 49
dividers, 228
douglas fir, 20
drawing, oblique, 170
drawing, exploded, 169
drawing, isometric, 167
drawing instruments, 164
drawing standards, 173
drawing, perspective, 172
drawing, planometric, 171
drill, breast, 107
drill bits, 107
ductility, 65
durability, 65
dust extractors, 134
dust masks, 6
dutch elm disease, 14

E
ebony, 23
elastic limit, 65
elasticity, 65
electrolysis, 69
electrons, 287
electroplating, 75
elm, 14
enamelling, 75
end splitting, 48
epoxy resin glues, 245
erase (CAD), 183
ergonomics, 153
etching, 75
evaluation, 157

F
faceplates, 226
felling, 36
fibreboards, 62
fibres, 28
files and rasps, 111
files, 71
fillet (CAD), 183
flame figure, 39
flowcharts, 176
foam, 87
forces, 278
forestry in Ireland, 11
forests, natural and planted, 9
formaldehyde glues, 245
former, 83
formers, 238
forming, vacuum, 84
forming, press, 84
french polish, 259
french polishing, 260
fungal attack, 49

G
galvanising, 70, 74
garnet, 251
gauge, marking, 93
gauge, mortise, 93
gauge, thumb, 93
gauge, cutting, 94
gauge, setting the, 93
gear train, 281
gears, 281
gimlet, 106
glass, 89
glass reinforced plastic, (GRP), 85
glasspaper, 251
glue pot, 244
golden section, 158
gouge, carving, 208
gouge, firmer, 207
grain filler, 260
graphs, 177
greenhouse effect, 34
grindstone (electric), 115
grinding, 116
grounding, 204
groundwork, 214

H
hacksaws, 71
hammer, steel claw, 103
hammer, ball-pain, 103
hammer, veneer, 220
hammer, warrington, 103
hammer and mallet, 103
hammer, pin, 104
handles, 277
hard disk, 181
hardboard, 62
hardness, 65
hardware, 179
hardwood, 26
hardwoods, 13
heartwood, 30
hickory, 25
hinge, flush, 272
hinge, how to fit a, 273
hinge, rising butt, 271
hinge, piano, 271
hinge, butt, 271
hinge, cranked, 272
honeycomb checks, 48
horse chestnut, 17
humidity, relative, 40, 41
hygroscopic, 41
hyphae, 49

I
immersion, 55
inlaying, 221
insect attack, 50
insulation, 66
integrated circuit, 295
investigation, 153
iroko (teak), 24
iron, 123

J
joint, mitre, 190
joints, edge, 196
joints, dovetail, 195
joints, dowel, 194
joints, mortise and tenor, 193
joints, brindle, 192
joints, housing, 192
joints, halving, 191
joints, butt, 190
joints, carcase, 197
joints, frame, 198

K
kiln, compartment, 42
kiln, progressive, 43
knock down fittings, 189, 270
knots, 46
knotting, 255

L
lacquer, 259
lacquering, 74
laminates, 237
laminating process, 239
lamination, 238
larch, 21
lathe, parts of a, 225
lathe centres, 226
lathe, pole, 224
lathe, woodturning, 225
lathe chucks, 226
LDR, 292
lead, 70
leather, 88
LED, 292
levers, 280
lime, 18
limits (CAD), 181
line (CAD), 182
linkages, 284
linseed oil, 258
lock, fitting a box, 275
lock, box, 275
locks, 274
lodgepole pine, 22
loose tongues, 191

M
mahogany, 24
mallet, carver's, 208
mallet & carving mallet, 104

maple, 24
marine borers, 51
marking out tools, 91
marquetry, 218
materials technology room, 1
mechanisms, 280
merulius lacrymans, 50
metal coating, 74
metal, painting, 74
metal finishes, 73
metals, non-ferrous, 67, 68
metals, ferrous, 67, 68
metals, ferrous, 68
metalwork, beaten, 71
methylated spirit, 254
mirror (CAD), 184
moisture, bound, 40
moisture, free, 40
moisture content, 40, 43
mortiser, 131
motifs, 214
moulding, 84
mouse, 179
move (CAD), 184
multiply, 59
mycelium, 49

N
nail, round wire, 265
nail, upholstery, 265
nail, oval, 265
nailing, dovetail, 267
nails, 264
natural objects, 46
neutrons, 287
norway spruce (common spruce), 20
nylon, 79

O
oak, 13
Ohm's law, 292
oilstones, 116
open assembly time, 243
open (CAD), 185
ortho (CAD), 185
orthographic projection, 165
output speed, 284
overlay method, 218
oxidation, 73

P
paint, 254
painting woodwork, 255
panel pin, 265
paring a trench, 102
parquetry, 217
particle boards (chipboards), 61
patina, 73
pencil and marking knife, 92
pencils, 163
perspex, 79
photosynthesis, 29
pickling, 71
pig iron, 68
pincers, 104
pith (medulla), 30
pits, 27
plane, block, 110
plane, jack, 108
plane, smoothing, 108
plane parts, 108
plane, rebate, 109
plane, plough, 109
plane, try, 109
planer/thicknesses, 132
planer, electric, 125
planing end grain, 110
planishing, 72
plastic, natural, 78
plastic, filing, 81
plastic, bending, 82
plastic, thermosetting, 77
plastic coating, 74
plastic, types of, 77
plastic, drilling, 82
plasticity/malleability, 65
plastics, working with, 80
plumule, 29
plywood, marine, 59
plywood, 58
polymerisation, 80
polymers, 80
polystyrene, 79
polythene, 79
polyurethane, 79
pop rivets, 188
pores (vessels), 28
pot life, 243
power tools, advantages and disadvantages, 119
power tools, safety with, 6
power supply, 127
preservative, tar oil, 54
preservative, water-borne, 54
preservatives, organic solvent, 54
preservatives, types and properties of, 57
pressure treatment, 56
primer, 255
profile, 230
proportion, 158
protons, 287
punch, texturing, 205
punch, centre, 70
punch, dot, 70
PVA, 245
PVC, 79
pyrography, 222

R
radicle or root, 29
rainforests, destruction of the, 33
ratchet, 105
ray cells, 27, 30
receiver, 274
resin pockets, 47
resin, epoxy, 79
resin, polyester, 79
resisters, 290
respirator, 6
ripsaw, 95
rosewood, 24
rot, dry, 50
rot, wet, 50
rotary cutting, 214
rotate (CAD), 184
router, 126
router bits, 126
rubbers, synthetic, 79

S
safety rules in MTR, 4
safety equipment, 5
sanding endgrain, 253
sanding machines, 133
sapwood, 30
save (CAD), 185
saw, cross cut, 96
saw, circular, 124
saw, universal, 97
saw, panel, 97
saw, band, 101
saw, jig, 101

saw, pad, 100
saw, compass, 100
saw, tenon, 97
saw kerf, 97
saw, fret, 100
saw, dovetail, 98
saw, coping, 99
saw, bow, 100
saw, scroll, 101
saw, jig, 124
saw set, the, 118
saw, scroll, 130
saw, circular, 130
sawing, slash, 37
sawing, plain, 37
sawing, quarter, 38
sawing, tangential, 38
sawing, radial, 38
saws, 95
scotch glue, 244
scots pine (northern pine/scots fir), 19
scratch stock, 221
screw cups, 269
screwdriver, powered, 123
screwdrivers, 113
screws, heads of, 268
screws, ordering, 268
screws, parts of, 267
screws, 188
screws, self-tapping, 269
screws, driving, 269
screws, 267
scriber, 70
sculpture, 205
seasoning, kiln, 42
seasoning, natural, 41
seasoning, 40
sections, 167
shakes, radial, 47
shakes, tangential, 47
shakes, 47
shakes, cross (thunder), 47
shaping, 206
sharpening, 115
shear, 279
shear force, 264
shelf life, 243
silver grain 28, 38
sitka spruce, 21
slag, 68
slipstones, 116
snips, 71
software, 179
softwood, 26
softwoods, 19
soldering, 188, 290
soldering, 290
spindle turning, 228
spokeshaves, 111
spores, 49
sporophores, 49
spraying equipment, 259
stability, 285
stacking, 240
stains, chemical, 49
stains, 49
stains and staining, 256
steel, 68
steel, high carbon, 68
steel, high speed, 68
steel, stainless, 68
stoutheart, 59
strength, 64
structures, 284
superglue, 246
surface finish, 252
surform tools,112
sycamore, 19

T

tack, 265
teak oil, 258
teeth, 99
tension, 279
text (CAD), 182
textiles, 87
thermistor, 293
thermoplastics, 78
through and through, 37
timber and employment, 11
timber, green, 40
timber by-products, 12
tool, verner, 209
tool, vee, 209
tools, cutting, 95
tools, woodturning, 227
tools, surform, 209
tools, carving, 207
torsion, 280
toughness, 65
tracheids, 27
transistor, 293
transpiration, 29
trees, uses of, 8
triangulation, 285
trim (CAD), 183
try-square, 92
turning, faceplate, 231
turning – finishing, 232
turning – suitable woods, 232
twisting, 48

U

undercoat, 256
use of trees, 6
varnish, 257
velocity ration, 281
veneer, cutting a, 215
veneer, balancing, 215
veneering – borders, 216
veneering, adhesives for, 219
veneers, 213
veneers, matching, 215
veneers, applying, 220
voltage, 288
vulcanisation, 78

W

walnut, 24
ward, 274
warping, 48
wax, 258
WBP, 59
WBP, 245
welding, 188
whellbrace, 107
white spirit, 254
whittling, 202
window method, 218
wooden plug and cutter, 189
woodworm, 51
working drawings, 155

Y

yacht varnish, 257
yew, 25

Z

zoom (CAD), 183